CHRISTIANITY AND FAMILY LAW

The Western tradition has always cherished the family as an essential foundation of a just and orderly society, and thus accorded it special legal and religious protection. Christianity embraced this teaching from the start, and many of the basics of Western family law were shaped by Christian theologies of nature, sacrament, and covenant. This volume introduces readers to the enduring and evolving Christian teachings on betrothals and weddings; marriage and divorce; women's and children's rights; marital property and inheritance; and human sexuality and intimate relationships. The chapters are authoritatively written but accessible to college and graduate students and scholars, as well as clergy and laity. While alert to the hot-button issues of sexual liberty today, the contributing authors let the historical figures speak for themselves about what Christianity has contributed and continues to offer to the protection and guidance of our most intimate association.

John Witte, Jr. is Robert W. Woodruff Professor, McDonald Distinguished Professor, and director of the Center for the Study of Law and Religion at Emory University. He has published numerous articles and thirty books, including *Law and Protestantism: The Legal Teachings of the Lutheran Reformation* (Cambridge 2002), *The Reformation of Rights* (Cambridge 2007), *Christianity and Law* (Cambridge 2008), *The Sins of the Fathers* (Cambridge 2009), *Christianity and Human Rights* (Cambridge 2010), and *The Western Case for Monogamy over Polygamy* (Cambridge 2015).

Gary S. Hauk is university historian and senior adviser to the president of Emory University. He is the author of *A Legacy of Heart and Mind: Emory since 1836* and editor of *Where Courageous Inquiry Leads: The Emerging Life of Emory University*, and has published numerous essays. He serves as senior editorial consultant to the Center for the Study of Law and Religion at Emory University.

Law and Christianity

Series Editor

The Law and Christianity series publishes cutting-edge work on Catholic, Protestant, and Orthodox Christian contributions to public, private, penal, and procedural law and legal theory. The series aims to promote deep Christian reflection by leading scholars on the fundamentals of law and politics, to build further ecumenical legal understanding across Christian denominations, and to link and amplify the diverse and sometimes isolated Christian legal voices and visions at work in the academy. Works collected by the series include groundbreaking monographs, historical and thematic anthologies, and translations by leading scholars around the globe.

Books in the Series

Christianity and Natural Law
Norman Doe
Agape, Justice, and Law
Robert F. Cochran and Zachary R. Calo
Great Christian Jurists In English History
Mark Hill QC and R.H. Helmholz
Calvin's Political Theology and the Public Engagement of the Church
Matthew J. Tuininga
God and the Secular Legal System
Rafael Domingo
How Marriage Became One of the Sacraments
Philip L. Reynolds
Christianity and Freedom
edited by Timothy Samuel Shah and Allen D. Hertzke Vols. 1 & 2
The Distinctiveness of Religion in American Law
Kathleen A. Brady
Pope Benedict XVI's Legal Thought
edited by Marta Cartabia and Andrea Simoncini
The Western Case for Monogamy over Polygamy
John Witte, Jr.
God and the Illegal Alien
Robert W. Heimburger

Christianity and Family Law

AN INTRODUCTION

Edited by

JOHN WITTE, JR.

Emory University, Atlanta

GARY S. HAUK

Emory University, Atlanta

CAMBRIDGE
UNIVERSITY PRESS

CAMBRIDGE
UNIVERSITY PRESS

University Printing House, Cambridge CB2 8BS, United Kingdom

One Liberty Plaza, 20th Floor, New York, NY 10006, USA

477 Williamstown Road, Port Melbourne, VIC 3207, Australia

314-321, 3rd Floor, Plot 3, Splendor Forum, Jasola District Centre, New Delhi - 110025, India

79 Anson Road, #06-04/06, Singapore 079906

Cambridge University Press is part of the University of Cambridge.

It furthers the University's mission by disseminating knowledge in the pursuit of education, learning and research at the highest international levels of excellence.

www.cambridge.org
Information on this title: www.cambridge.org/9781108415347
DOI: 10.1017/9781108233255

First published 2017

A catalogue record for this publication is available from the British Library

ISBN 978-1-108-41534-7 Hardback
ISBN 978-1-108-40119-7 Paperback

For Eliza Ellison and Sara Haigh Hauk

Contents

Illustrations

Contributors

Eileen Hunt Botting (PhD, Yale) is Professor of Political Science at the University of Notre Dame.

Gerald V. Bradley (JD, Cornell) is Professor of Law at the University of Notre Dame.

James D. Bratt (PhD, Yale) is Professor of History, Emeritus, at Calvin College.

Don S. Browning† (PhD, Chicago) was the Alexander Campbell Professor of Ethics and the Social Sciences at the University of Chicago Divinity School and Robert W. Woodruff Senior Fellow at the Center for the Study of Law and Religion at Emory University.

Rafael Domingo (PhD, Navarra) is Professor of Law and ICS Research Professor at the University of Navarra, and Francisco de Vitoria Senior Fellow at the Center for the Study of Law and Religion, Emory University.

Charles Donahue, Jr. (LLB, Yale) is Paul A. Freund Professor of Law at Harvard University.

Elliot N. Dorff (Rabbi, Jewish Theological Seminary; PhD, Columbia) is Rector and Distinguished Service Professor of Philosophy at American Jewish University and Visiting Professor at UCLA School of Law.

Robert P. George (PhD, Oxford) is McCormick Chair in Jurisprudence and Founding Director of the James Madison Program in American Ideals and Institutions at Princeton University.

M. Christian Green (JD, Emory; PhD, Chicago) is Senior Fellow at the Center for the Study of Law and Religion, Emory University.

Judith Evans Grubbs (PhD, Stanford) is Betty Gage Holland Professor of Roman History at Emory University.

Vigen Guroian (PhD, Drew) is Professor of Religious Studies in Orthodox Christianity at the University of Virginia.

Gary S. Hauk (PhD, Emory; MDiv, Methodist Theological School in Ohio) is university historian and senior adviser to the president of Emory University.

Russell Hittinger (PhD, St. Louis) is Warren Professor of Catholic Studies at the University of Tulsa.

David G. Hunter (PhD, Notre Dame) is Cottrill-Rolfes Chair of Catholic Studies at the University of Kentucky.

Mark D. Jordan (PhD, Texas-Austin) is Andrew W. Mellon Professor of Christian Thought and Professor of Studies of Women, Gender, and Sexuality at Harvard University.

Henry Ansgar Kelly (PhD, Harvard) is Distinguished Research Professor at the University of California, Los Angeles.

John Anthony McGuckin (PhD, Durham; DLitt, Sibiu) is Nielsen Professor of Ancient Church History at Union Theological Seminary, Professor of Byzantine Christian Studies at Columbia University, and Arch-Priest of the Romanian Orthodox Church.

Steven Ozment (PhD, Harvard) is McLean Professor of Ancient and Modern History at Harvard University.

Barbara Pitkin (PhD, Chicago) is Senior Lecturer in Religious Studies at Stanford University.

Michael Plekon (PhD, Rutgers) is Professor of Sociology and Religion and Culture at Baruch College of the City University of New York and Arch-Priest in the Orthodox Church in America.

Stephen J. Pope (PhD, Chicago) is Professor of Theology at Boston College.

Philip L. Reynolds (PhD, Toronto) is Charles Howard Candler Professor of Medieval Christianity, Aquinas Professor of Historical Theology, and Senior Fellow at the Center for the Study of Law and Religion, Emory University.

Jason P. Rosenblatt (PhD, Brown) is Professor of English, Emeritus, at Georgetown University.

Peter Sarris (DPhil, Oxford) is Reader in Late Roman, Early Medieval, and Byzantine History at the University of Cambridge.

Giulio Silano (PhD, Toronto) is Professor of History at the University of Toronto.

Anders Winroth (PhD, Columbia) is Forst Family Professor of History at Yale University.

John Witte, Jr. (JD, Harvard) is Robert W. Woodruff Professor, McDonald Distinguished Professor, and director of the Center for the Study of Law and Religion at Emory University.

Preface

This volume is one of several fresh introductions commissioned for the Cambridge Law and Christianity Series. Before this book series was established, Cambridge University Press published two similar anthologies, coedited by John Witte, Jr. and Frank S. Alexander: *Christianity and Law: An Introduction* (2008) and *Christianity and Human Rights: An Introduction* (2010). Soon, Cambridge will publish Norman Doe's *Christianity and Natural Law: An Introduction*, and the press has commissioned additional introductory volumes on "Christianity and Constitutional Law," "Christianity and Criminal Law," "Christianity and Private Law," and "Christianity and Economic Law." Others titles will soon follow.

Each of these introductions offers fresh scholarship into historical, doctrinal, and comparative perspectives on Christian sources and dimensions of familiar legal topics. Although the chapters are written by leading experts, they are intended for nonspecialists in colleges and in graduate and professional schools, as well as for clergy, interested laity, and scholars from other fields. The aim is to illuminate what Christianity has contributed and continues to offer to the world of law, particularly in the West.

The volume in hand analyzes Christian influences on Western family law. The main legal topics include the formation, maintenance, and dissolution of marriage; relations between husbands and wives, parents and children, and siblings and kinsmen within and beyond the household; and important dimensions of human sexuality and intimacy. This volume also touches more lightly on related legal topics of marital property and inheritance; the structure of the household and its role in public and private life; and household order, including women's rights, children's rights, and master–servant relations. Christian theology and the church's canon law had a decisive influence on these topics of Western family law for nearly two millennia.

From the fourth to the nineteenth centuries, church and state cooperated in the governance of the marital family, and an established Christian culture shaped sexual ethics. Today the modern secular state has assumed jurisdiction over most family law questions, and Western culture has disestablished Christianity and liberalized sex, marriage, and family norms. Nonetheless, many churches in and beyond the West continue to maintain internal laws and procedures to govern the family lives of their members, and Christian leaders continue to influence family law policies and advocate for their reform.

To tell this complex story in a single volume, we focus on twenty-eight titans who helped to shape the theory and law of sex, marriage, and family life in the West from biblical times until today. We have selected illustrative figures whose contributions to this tradition were both distinct and enduring. We have sought to balance Catholics, Protestants, and a few Orthodox figures who had influence in the West, and have placed leading popes, emperors, and kings alongside influential jurists, theologians, and philosophers. What emerges is a running set of portraits chronologically arranged – Moses, Jesus, St. Paul, Emperor Constantine, St. Augustine of Hippo, St. John Chrysostom, Emperor Justinian, Theodore Balsamon, Gratian, Peter Lombard, Pope Alexander III, Pope Innocent III, Thomas Aquinas, Martin Luther, John Calvin, King Henry VIII, Thomas Sanchez, John Selden, Mary Wollstonecraft, Abraham Kuyper, Emil Brunner, Pope Leo XIII, Pope Pius XI, Pope Paul VI, Pope John Paul II, Paul Evdokimov, D. S. Bailey, and Jean Bethke Elshtain. Scores, if not hundreds, of others deserve a place in this gallery of leading Christian thinkers on the family, but this set of portraits provides a cursory yet thorough introduction and illustration of what Christianity has offered to the theory and law of Western family life.

Each chapter follows a common structure to facilitate its use as a classroom text and research guide. Beginning with a short biographical introduction to its subject, each chapter explains why that person is important to the development of Western family law, concisely analyzes the person's main contributions, and ends with a list of recommended readings. The editorial introduction sets these twenty-eight figures in context, distills the key family law teachings of the Western tradition, and identifies their main points of convergence and contestation.

This volume eschews strong normative and confessional claims, seeking to edify, rather than enflame, popular debates today about sex, marriage, and family life. The contributing authors have let the historical figures speak for themselves about a wide range of Christian teachings on sex, marriage, and family life. This volume also avoids strong methodological or disciplinary biases. Instead, it incorporates law, theology, ethics, politics, history, women's studies, and LGBTQ studies to assess central topics of Christianity and family law.

We would be remiss if we did not express our deep appreciation to a number of people who have supported the production of this volume. We give special thanks to Mr. Cary Maguire, president of the Maguire Oil Company, who so kindly underwrote the costs of this volume and encouraged its preparation. It has been a joy to get to know Mr. Maguire in recent years, and for John Witte, Jr. to have the privilege of sitting in the Cary and Ann Maguire Chair in Ethics and American History at the Kluge Center in the Library of Congress to plan this and other volumes in the Cambridge Law and Christianity Series. We are indebted to John Berger, senior commissioning editor in law at Cambridge University Press, for masterminding the production and publication of the series. Amy Wheeler, in the Center for the Study of Law and Religion at Emory University, has earned our great gratitude for her skilled administrative support of all aspects of this volume. Finally, we express profound thanks to each of the authors of these chapters for distilling their immense learning into pithy and accessible essays that provide sharply etched portraits of a few of the great men and women who have shaped Western family law.

We two editors have enjoyed many years of friendship, both with each other and with our wonderful wives, Eliza Ellison and Sara Haigh Hauk, to whom we dedicate this volume.

Introduction

John Witte, Jr. and Gary S. Hauk

Christianity has had a decisive influence on Western family law for two millennia, though it drew heavily on classical and Jewish prototypes and has gradually given way to modern liberalism and post-Christian teachings. In the centuries before Christ, ancient Jewish and Greco-Roman cultures viewed the marital family as a spiritual and temporal institution that was subject to both religious and political authorities and norms. Early Christians adapted this dialectic of religion and law in the church's efforts to govern family life, and eventually integrated ancient norms and practices into natural, covenantal, and sacramental frameworks. Particularly after the Christianization of Rome in the fourth and fifth centuries, church and state authorities came to enforce parallel norms of sexual etiquette, courtship, and betrothal; marital formation, maintenance, and dissolution; conjugal duties, debts, and desires; and parental roles, rights, and responsibilities. Church and state authorities issued parallel prohibitions on fornication, adultery, sodomy, incest, polygamy, prostitution, contraception, abortion, and other matters of sexuality and reproduction. And they operated interlocking tribunals to enforce these norms: the church governed the spiritual aspects of family life through its canons and courts, its consecration and registration of weddings, its baptism and catechesis of children, and its blessing and burial of the dead. The state governed the temporal aspects of family life by policing and punishing sexual crimes, controlling marital property and inheritance, and regulating household relations. Church and state officials separately and together also prosecuted sexual and marital crimes of fornication, adultery, incest, bestiality, clandestine marriage, bigamy, marital violence, and abuse.

While church and state officials often cooperated in creating and enforcing Western family laws, they also clashed over the scope of their respective jurisdiction and authority over family life – especially in the fifth, twelfth, sixteenth, and nineteenth centuries, when momentous shifts redefined church–state relations in Western societies. In particular, the nineteenth-century reforms, born of Enlightenment liberalism, permanently broke Christianity's dominant influence over the theory, law, and culture of the family, though many early Enlightenment figures retained traditional teachings about sexual ethics and family law, albeit with new arguments from nature, reason, utility, and common sense. The liberalization of traditional family norms has accelerated in the past half century. While today the secular state dominates Western family law, key aspects of this state law still reflect the teachings and practices of earlier Christian, classical, and Jewish cultures. Moreover, Christian clergy, scholars, and advocates still remain deeply involved in family-law policy and reform movements in the West and well beyond. And numerous churches today – Catholic, Protestant, and Orthodox alike – still operate internal legal and disciplinary systems to help govern the family lives of their voluntary members.

To tell this complex story in a single volume, we focus on twenty-eight titans who helped to shape the theory and law of sex, marriage, and family life in the West from biblical times until today. We have selected illustrative figures whose contributions to this tradition were both distinct and enduring. We have sought to balance Catholics, Protestants, and a few Orthodox figures who had influence in the West, and we have placed leading popes, emperors, and kings alongside influential jurists, theologians, and philosophers. What emerges is a running set of twenty-eight portraits chronologically arranged over some twenty-eight hundred years.

In Chapter 1, Elliot N. Dorff surveys the intricate Mosaic laws on sex, marriage, and family life set out in the Hebrew Bible and their elaboration by the rabbis of the Mishnah and Talmud. The Jewish tradition established many of the basic Western rules of betrothal and marriage, marital gifts and property, weddings and celebrations, endogamy and exogamy, marital sex and spousal duties, procreation and education of children, adultery and incest, divorce and remarriage, death and inheritance. Early Christianity inherited this complex Jewish legal system and absorbed many of its teachings, even while rejecting Jewish rules of polygamy, levirate marriage, concubinage, and unilateral male divorce. Christian theologians and jurists returned often to these Mosaic rules and the biblical narratives and prophetic elaborations surrounding them. Some Christian jurists also engaged the rabbinic expositions of particular rules, none more fully than English jurist John Selden in the seventeenth century (Chapter 16).

In Chapter 2, on Jesus and St. Paul, Gary S. Hauk shows that Jesus called Christians to live by the letter and spirit of many of the Jewish laws of marital fidelity, sexual purity, and love of children. Yet Jesus also redefined the family to include all who serve the reign of God, and he transformed weddings and marriages into metaphors for the relationship between God and the faithful. Jesus's most famous statement on marriage was set out in Matthew 19, where he refers to the verses in Genesis in which God "made them male and female" and said, "For this reason a man will leave his father and mother and be united to his wife, and the two will become one flesh." Thus, Jesus proclaims, "they are no longer two, but one flesh. Therefore, what God has joined together, let no one separate." St. Paul, a Jew who converted to Christianity, elaborated Jesus's teaching by calling Christian marriage a *mysterion*, or *sacramentum*, modeled on Christ's sacrificial love for the church. Paul further urged Christian spouses to love, nurture, and care for each other and their children, to respect the conjugal rights and needs of the other spouse, and to avoid fornication and sexual vice, even sexual activities permitted by the Jewish and Roman law of his day. Like Jesus, Paul also severely limited divorce and remarriage among Christians and called believers to lifelong devotion to their parents, spouses, and children. These New Testament teachings have remained a perennial touchstone for Western family law to our own day.

In Chapter 3, on Emperor Constantine (r. 306–37 CE), Judith Evans Grubbs makes clear that Christian teachings on the marital family were shaped not only by Jewish law, but also by prevailing Greco-Roman family law and culture. For nearly half a millennium before the time of Jesus, Rome had worked out a complex system of law regarding marriage and family, marital property, and inheritance. In the fourth century, the first Christian emperor, Constantine, began to blend Roman and Christian traditions in his new legislation on the family. Constantine's laws strengthened engagement contracts that protected young women from exploitation; restricted marriages and inheritances across class lines; put new limits on the exposure or enslavement of unwanted children; directed that public aid be given to poor parents with young children; eased testamentary restrictions on the celibate and childless; and prohibited married men from having both a wife and a concubine. Some of these family reforms were not (necessarily) Christian in inspiration, Evans Grubbs insists, but they became an important part of later Christian family laws. Moreover, Constantine's legislative efforts set the stage for the more overtly Christian family legislation of later Christian emperors, most notably Justinian (Chapter 6).

In Chapter 4, on St. Augustine of Hippo (354–430), David G. Hunter shows how this leading Western church father offered the most comprehensive theology of sex, marriage, and family life in the first millennium of the Western church. Augustine steered a course between the sexual renunciation of some church fathers and the sexual liberties still allowed by Roman law and culture in his day. Calling marriage and family life good, even if celibacy and chastity might be better, Augustine identified three main goods or goals of marriage: the procreation and nurture of children (*proles*); the fidelity and troth of husband and wife (*fides*); and its permanence or indissolubility, which enables the marital union to function as a sacred symbol (*sacramentum*). Augustine also emphasized the need for sexual purity and restraint, even in the marital bed, and reduced divorce to mere separation of a couple in cases of serious fault, with a right to remarry only after the death of one's spouse. He also confirmed traditional Aristotelian teachings that the marital family was the foundation of the republic. Catholics and Protestants alike would return often to Augustine's insights, and his account of the three marital goods of children, fidelity, and sacrament remains part of the backbone of modern Catholic canon laws and theologies of marriage to this day.

In Chapter 5, Vigen Guroian outlines the thought of the leading Eastern church father St. John Chrysostom (347–407), who offered the most comprehensive teachings on sex, marriage, and family life for the Orthodox Christian tradition. Describing the marital family as a "little church," Chrysostom encouraged marital couples to practice mutually sacrificial love and respect for each other and their children. Unlike Augustine and other church fathers, Chrysostom emphasized the importance of marital sex, insisted on equal conjugal rights for husbands and wives, and encouraged clergy to marry. He also encouraged both fathers and mothers to invest deeply and sacrificially in the care, nurture, education, and spiritual formation of their children. Although he prescribed marital fidelity and stability in accordance with the Bible, he allowed for divorce and remarriage in serious cases of family breakdown, especially when a wife or children were seriously imperiled. Following St. Paul's teachings, however, he discouraged widows and widowers from remarriage, instead calling on the church to embrace and support them as members of the broader Christian family. Chrysostom's teachings about the family had a monumental influence on Eastern Orthodox and Western Christianity alike, and they have been key parts of the neopatristic renaissance in Orthodox circles today (see Chapter 23).

In Chapter 6, on Emperor Justinian (r. 527–65), Peter Sarris presents Justinian's massive *Corpus Iuris Civilis* and Novel Constitutions as the most important synthesis of Roman and Christian laws on sex, marriage, and family life to survive from the first millennium. While privileging chastity and celibacy, Justinian's laws established clearly that marriage is a consensual, heterosexual, monogamous union, presumptively for life, designed for the mutual protection and support of husband and wife, their shared procreation and nurture of children, and the legitimate transmission of family property to the next generation of relatives. Justinian's laws strengthened marital formation requirements, sharply restricted divorce and remarriage (albeit temporarily), streamlined inheritance rules among family members, and provided new protections for children and slaves within the marital household. These laws also called for severe punishment of adultery, incest, polygamy, and prostitution, and took strong steps to stamp out sodomy and homosexual practices. Justinian's collation and synthesis of Christianized Roman laws, though largely lost to the West after the sixth century, were rediscovered in the eleventh century. They provided a strong legal foundation for the laws of Western churches and states throughout much of the second millennium and inspired hundreds of legal commentaries by leading Western jurists.

In Chapter 7, on Theodore Balsamon (ca. 1130–99), John Anthony McGuckin shows that Justinian's family laws continued to govern the Eastern Byzantine Empire and were periodically supplemented by fresh imperial and canonical laws and commentaries. In the twelfth century, Theodore Balsamon, a great monastic jurist and later Orthodox patriarch, brought all these first-millennium laws together in a massive legal synthesis that remained at the heart of Orthodox canon law until modern times and spilled over into Western canon law. Balsamon largely retained Justinian's family laws, but he placed new emphasis on elaborate church liturgies for valid marital formation, elevated marriage into a sublime expression of a hypostatic divine union, and emphasized the need for sexual purity within and beyond the marital bed, especially around the many holy days of the church. Balsamon also, however, severely limited the status and rights of women in society, churches, and homes, and issued several misogynist and patriarchal directives. Although these ran contrary to the more egalitarian teachings of earlier Greek fathers, they became commonplaces in some later Orthodox and Western Christian communities.

In Chapter 8, Anders Winroth shows how the rediscovery of many Roman law and patristic texts in the later eleventh century helped create the medieval church's law and theology of marriage and family life. The anchor legal text of medieval canon law was Gratian's twelfth-century *Decretum*, which, in two iterations, assembled many of the legal, theological, and canonical sources of the first millennium and synthesized them authoritatively. Gratian drew a clear distinction between betrothals, which could be broken for a number of causes, and valid marriages, which were indissoluble once properly contracted. A valid marriage, Gratian insisted, required both consent and sexual consummation between a man and a woman, each of whom could thereafter claim conjugal rights against the other. The parties had to have the fitness and capacity to marry each other, however, and various blood, family, and spiritual ties between the couple were absolute impediments of incest that would lead to annulment. Gratian regarded divorce as separation only, permitting no right to remarry until one's spouse died. He insisted that clergy and monastics be celibate and chaste, echoing conciliar decrees of mandatory celibacy, which became an absolute requirement for ordained Catholic clergy after 1123. Gratian's *Decretum* inspired hundreds of glosses and commentaries over the next centuries and comprised the first part of the *Corpus Iuris Canonici* (1582).

In Chapter 9, Giulio Silano demonstrates that while Gratian collected many first-millennium canons, Peter Lombard (d. 1160) added many first-millennium theological sources on the family and drew them together in an impressive synthesis in his four-volume *Book of Sentences*. Lombard repeated the three Augustinian goods of marriage, but he emphasized that marriage was itself the first sacrament, reserved only to baptized members of the church in good standing. He repeated Gratian's rules of marital formation and impediments, but he stressed that mutual consent alone could make a marriage, even without wedding ceremonies and other formalities or, for that matter, sexual intercourse. Lombard had a positive view of marital sex as an expression of love, fidelity, and conjugal rights, but he stressed that children were an essential part and product of the institution of marriage. He also stressed that the nuclear family of husband, wife, and child was the Christian family ideal, modeled on the holy family of Mary, Joseph, and Jesus. Peter Lombard's collection and syntheses of texts shaped Christian theologies of marriage and the family for the next half millennium and, like Gratian's *Decretum*, were subject to hundreds of commentaries.

In Chapter 10, Charles Donahue, Jr. shows how two powerful popes, Alexander III (r. 1159–81) and Innocent III (r. 1198–1216), put into legal form many of the family-law teachings of Gratian and Lombard and their commentators. These popes' many encyclicals and canons, collected in the *Liber Extra* of 1234 (the second core text of the *Corpus Iuris Canonici*), confirmed that marriage was both a heterosexual, monogamous union and an indissoluble sacrament of the church. A valid marriage was formed either by a betrothal promise followed by intercourse, or by mutual consent of marriage stated in the present tense with or without consummation. Couples were urged to marry with parental consent, witnesses, liturgies, and priestly blessings, but none of this was required. Parties could separate for serious causes like adultery, but they could not remarry until their spouse had died. Marriages could be annulled if the parties discovered various defects of consent (like, fear, error, insanity, or frigidity), religious impediments (like differences in religion or one party's prior solemn vow of chastity), or incest born of blood, family, or spiritual ties between the man and woman. These intricate canon-law rules were assiduously enforced by the church courts and comprised the principal family law of the West until the sixteenth-century Reformation. Thereafter, many of these laws penetrated deeply into the state laws of Catholic and Protestant lands, and they remain at the core of the Catholic Church's canon law to this day.

In Chapter 11, Philip L. Reynolds probes the sophisticated and influential natural-law theories of the marital family developed by Dominican friar Thomas Aquinas (1225–74). Aquinas advocated enduring and exclusive pair-bonding unions as the best means for humans to achieve the principal goals of procreation of healthy children and protection from sexual sin. He also wrote with great insight into the ways fornication, adultery, prostitution, concubinage, polygamy, and unilateral divorce all unjustly and disproportionately harm wives and children. Humans thus have natural inclinations toward enduring and exclusive monogamous marital families, said Aquinas, which both natural reason and sacramental theology serve to affirm and strengthen – especially against men, who are by nature more prone to wander sexually. Aquinas's refined natural-law arguments about the marital family remained axiomatic for the Western legal tradition. They were given special new impetus first by the Spanish neoscholastics of the sixteenth century (Chapter 15), and later by the architects of modern Catholic social teachings on the family, notably Popes Leo XIII (Chapter 20) and John Paul II (Chapter 22).

In Chapter 12, Steven Ozment and John Witte, Jr. explore the Protestant reform of marriage and family law engineered by former Augustinian monk Martin Luther (1483–1546). Luther rejected the canon-law rules of clerical and monastic celibacy as a dangerous denial of God's soothing gift of marriage to remedy lust. He rejected the church's sacramental theology of marriage as a self-serving biblical fiction, and instead called marriage a social estate of earthly life, open to Christians and non-Christians alike. Moreover, he rejected the church's legal control over the family and called instead for the state to govern family law, leaving the church to offer marital counseling to couples, pastoral care to families, and catechesis to children. The resulting new state family laws that emerged in Lutheran lands incorporated many traditional canon-law and Roman-law rules. But they also now called for mandatory parental consent, two witnesses, civil registration, and church consecration for valid marriages; strongly encouraged clerical marriage; greatly reduced the impediments to betrothal and marriage; permitted inter-religious marriages; created new structures for the catechesis and education of children; and allowed for divorce in cases of serious fault, and remarriage for the innocent party. Luther's views remained foundational for later Protestants and were given progressive new expression in the early twentieth century by Emil Brunner (Chapter 19).

In Chapter 13, Barbara Pitkin shows how French jurist and theologian John Calvin (1509–64) engineered a top-to-bottom reformation of sex, marriage, and family life and law for sixteenth-century Protestant Geneva. Calvin's reforms radiated widely in European and North American Protestant lands for the next three centuries. Like Luther, Calvin preserved many traditional ideas about the nature and purpose of marriage, the place of children in church and society, and the regulation of sexual morality and behaviour, and he also adopted many of the same theological and family-law reforms that Luther had introduced. However, he integrated them into a covenantal framework that provided a Protestant interpretation of the spiritual dimensions of faithful marital and family life. In addition, he created a new model for the cooperation between church and state in family affairs that underscored the essential role that the clergy and consistories must play in family governance. Even more than Luther, Calvin insisted that engagements were serious contracts that could not be easily broken, and he emphasized the essential publicity requirements for valid marital formation, especially mandatory public church weddings. He stressed the role of parents, godparents, and the church community in baptizing, nurturing, educating, and catechizing children. At the same time, he underscored children's spiritual equality within the community and advanced a new rationale for infant baptism that emphasized the infant's right to the sacrament as members of God's covenant. Both as preacher and consistory leader, Calvin sought to root out sexual immorality – not only traditional offenses of fornication, adultery, prostitution, polygamy, and incest, but also more attenuated offenses like lewd art and literature, bawdy songs, sexy dancing and dress, and inappropriate courtship.

In Chapter 14, Henry Ansgar Kelly focuses on the Reformation in England, which was catalyzed by the famous dispute between King Henry VIII (r. 1509–47) and the papacy over his desire to end his marriage with Catherine of Aragon in order to marry Anne Boleyn. This high-stakes conflict, which reverberated throughout Western Christendom, involved intricate disputes over the canon-law rules and procedures surrounding marital impediments and annulment. Henry resolved the dispute locally when Thomas Cranmer, Archbishop of Canterbury, annulled the marriage in 1533. In the following year, Henry withdrew from all papal jurisdiction by having Parliament recognize him as supreme head of the Church in England, with final authority over marriage and family law. Henry followed Protestant criticisms of monasticism and ordered a massive dissolution of English monasteries, but he did not release the clergy from their obligation of celibacy. He also reduced a number of the traditional canon-law impediments to marriage, yielding a distinct common law of incest that allowed cousin marriages, among others, in emulation of Mosaic law (Chapter 1). But Henry and his Tudor successors ultimately rejected most of the other Protestant reforms of marriage and family law, as well as the later Catholic family-law reforms of the Council of Trent. England thus lived largely under medieval canon-law rules of the family, but now subject to parliamentary legislation that introduced incremental reforms, which are traced into the twenty-first century.

In Chapter 15, Rafael Domingo explores how the most important early modern reforms of Catholic family-law teachings came out of the Council of Trent (1545–63), which was in part the Church's final formal response to the Protestant Reformation. It was Spanish Jesuit Thomas Sanchez (1550–1610) who most thoroughly systematized Catholic teachings on the family thereafter. Echoing Trent as well as the learned Salamanca neoscholastics, Sanchez defined heterosexual monogamous marriage among baptized Catholics as a natural institution formed by a consensual contract, but elevated into a sacrament of the Church. Valid marriage required witnesses and priestly blessing and could not be dissolved except by the death of one spouse. The essence of marriage, Sanchez argued, lies in the unique and permanent conjugal bond by which spouses are formally united as a consequence of mutual self-giving. The principal end of marriage is the procreation and Christian nurture of legitimate children, which cannot be obstructed by any form of contraception or abortion. Procreative sex within marriage was thus important, making impotence and frigidity serious impediments that could lead to annulment. Sanchez dwelt at great length on the strict sexual morality that married couples needed to follow to avoid the mortal sin of lust, and he emphasized the intense pastoral care that the church owed to the Christian family, even if the state now administered secular family law. Sanchez's family-law treatise remained a foundational text for Spain and its many Latin American colonies until well into the twentieth century.

In Chapter 16, Jason P. Rosenblatt unveils the unique synthesis of Jewish laws and traditional Western laws of the family offered by English jurist John Selden (1584–1654). Taking the Hebrew Bible, the Talmud, and Maimonides as valuable but neglected sources of natural-law teachings, Selden argued that the rabbinic Noachide laws were divinely promulgated universal laws of perpetual obligation, which he compared closely with the laws of ancient Greece, Rome, Christianity, and Islam. Regarding the degrees of incest according to natural law, he accepted as authoritative the rabbinic minimalist four modes of differentiation: between the species, which prohibits bestiality; between the sexes, which prohibits male homosexual relations; between what is one's own and what belongs to another, which prohibits adultery; and between oneself and one's close relations, which prohibits sex with one's mother, stepmother, and birth sister. Selden went farther than any early modern Christian Hebraist to demonstrate that far from corrupting the Bible, the rabbis offer humane interpretations of its harshest laws. For example, he interpreted the conjugal debt expansively to require a husband to provide his wife with sex, food, clothing, dowry, medicine, protection, and ransom if she were abducted. He also interpreted the right to divorce and remarry expansively, arguing that Jesus's allowance for divorce on grounds of adultery (*porneia*) involved all manner of uncleanness, not just extramarital sex, thereby implying that England should no longer be under the thrall of canon-law prohibitions on divorce and remarriage. Selden's neo-Hebraist account of the natural law of sex, marriage, and family life was controversial in his day, but he anticipated many of the reforms of Anglo-American family law in succeeding centuries.

In Chapter 17, Eileen Hunt Botting writes about Mary Wollstonecraft (1759–97), an English pioneer of women's rights. Drawing on liberal Christian and classical teachings, Wollstonecraft proffered a new argument that marriage should be structured by law and culture as a "dyadic perfectionist friendship" between a man and a woman who are vested with rights and duties toward each other and their children. Rejecting traditional Christian arguments of male headship, she argued that God created men and women as equals and gave them equal rights to education, property, and opportunities to flourish in private and public life. This God-given gender equality does not and should not change with marriage, even if husbands and wives by nature need to play different parental roles, especially in their children's early years. Wollstonecraft called for the abolition of traditional common-law rules of coverture, primogeniture, and entail, all of which subsumed a woman's identity and subordinated her property and inheritance claims. She also called for the robust protection of children's rights to nurture and support from their parents, to custody and care from the most suitable parent in the event of separation or divorce, and to education for boys and girls alike. Wollstonecraft's arguments blended a number of progressive Protestant and new liberal teachings about marriage and family life, and they resonate strongly with contemporary views of what the structure and function of the family ought to be.

In Chapter 18, James D. Bratt shows how Dutch theologian, journalist, and statesman Abraham Kuyper (1837–1920) helped to revitalize European Protestantism in the aftermath of the French Revolution, much as his contemporary Pope Leo XIII revitalized Catholicism (Chapter 20). Kuyper called the marital family both a covenantal order of creation and redemption and a pillar of society equal in status and importance to the church and state. Drawing on classic Protestant teachings, Kuyper developed a theory of social pluralism that protected the integrity and "sovereignty" of the family sphere from the intrusions of both the totalitarian state and the authoritarian church. The nuclear Christian family was for him the first incubator of morality and piety, the first school of welfare and education, and a vital seedbed of virtue for society and the state. He thus resisted the erosion of the family by intrusive secular education laws, corrosive labor laws, and sexual permissiveness outside the marital bed. While generally respecting the rights of women and children to be educated and to participate in the life of the church, state, and society, Kuyper insisted that children thrived best in an intact family, where mothers were at hand to care for them in their tender years, and fathers worked hard to support their families but had Sabbath days and other time to enjoy life with them. Kuyper's writings, which have been widely translated, have had a shaping influence on Protestant and Evangelical communities throughout the West and well beyond.

In Chapter 19, on Emil Brunner (1899–1966), Don S. Browning and John Witte, Jr. show how this leading Swiss theologian combined Leo XIII's social teachings on the family with Kuyper's theory of sphere sovereignty to develop a liberal Protestant family ethic, contrary to the more traditional biblical views of his compatriot Karl Barth. Brunner treated the family as a natural order of creation, alongside the state and economy. The family has a natural monogamous structure and a built-in set of spousal and parental rights and duties that cannot be invaded by other social spheres or reconstructed by family members or liberal reformers. The state has to protect and enforce these family rights and duties as a matter of justice, but Christians should honor them spontaneously in expression of agapic love. Brunner prized children and their rights. For him, the bond of husband, wife, and child was a "Trinitarian union" built on mutual natural attraction and it reflected the triune Godhead. He insisted, moreover, that marital sex was a unique expression of love, not just a means to a procreative end, and he firmly rejected as unrealistic the procreative perfectionism of some parts of the Catholic tradition. A marital couple without children was a complete family, he believed, just as a widowed or divorced person with children remained a complete family.

In Chapter 20, Russell Hittinger shows how Popes Leo XIII (r. 1878–1903) and Pius XI (r. 1922–58) led a neo-Thomist renaissance of the Catholic Church, and created the Catholic social teachings movement to counter the devastating liberal attacks on Christian institutions during the French Revolution and Napoleon's legal reforms. Against new strains of liberal naturalism, subjectivism, and contractarianism that reduced marriage to a simple, transient, and malleable contract, these popes affirmed strongly that marriage is by its nature an indissoluble sacrament created by God for the procreation of children, the mutual assistance of husbands and wives, and the quieting of sexual desire. Against both liberal and totalitarian state policies that aimed to control children, they asserted that the family is more sacred than the state, and that Christian parents have the right and duty to raise their children in their own homes – and to educate them in their own churches and Catholic schools, which were being built with great alacrity in the later nineteenth and twentieth centuries. And against the new practices of both contraception and sexual liberation, they affirmed traditional teachings that sex was to be confined to the marital bed and directed first and foremost to procreation. These early statements of family autonomy and social subsidiarity, created during the "Leonine era," have been centerpieces of Catholic family life and law over the past century.

In Chapter 21, Stephen J. Pope tells the story of Pope Paul VI (r. 1963–78), who guided the monumental Second Vatican Council of 1962–5 that transformed the Catholic Church into a champion of modern democracy, religious freedom, and human rights, and offered a promising fresh approach to marriage and family questions. The Council's signature document, *Gaudium et Spes*, issued by Paul VI in 1965, portrayed marriage as a divinely established "intimate partnership of married life and love rooted in a covenant of irrevocable personal consent," and as a "school of deeper humanity." In succeeding documents, Paul VI encouraged clergy and laity alike to promote social justice, orderly development, and relief of the poor around the world, with the family serving as "the domestic church" to help achieve these ends. In 1968, however, Paul issued the encyclical *Humanae Vitae*, which was the Catholic Church's strongest prohibition to date on contraception. It called the faithful to practice self-restraint and chastity to avoid pregnancy or sexually transmitted diseases. While celebrated in some quarters and defended with new arguments from natural law and moral theology, this encyclical was and remains deeply controversial among Catholic laity and other Christians.

In Chapter 22, Robert P. George and Gerard V. Bradley show how the powerful Pope John Paul II (r. 1978–2005) confirmed modern Catholic teachings that marriage is both a natural and a sacramental institution, subject both to state laws that govern all citizens and to canon laws that govern only Catholic communicants. Children are the "crowning piece" of the marital family, he believed, and are thus an essential end and good of conjugal union, which must not be obstructed by contraception or abortion. Contrary to modern individualism and sexual libertinism, John Paul offered a robust philosophy of personalism that featured enduring covenantal commitments to the marital family, the holy church, and other non-state associations. Responding to the antireligious strains of some forms of modern feminism, he offered a powerful Christian defense of the fundamental dignity and essential equality of women and the compelling need to remove gender discrimination in many areas of life. Responding to the growing fragility of the marital family, the growing acceptance of nonmarital sex and cohabitation, and the growing movements for gay, lesbian, and transsexual rights, John Paul urged the faithful to return to the biblical essentials that God created humans as "male and female" and called them to join "two in one flesh" for life and "to be fruitful and multiply" for the flourishing of themselves, the church, and the world.

In Chapter 23, Michael Plekon introduces Paul Evdokimov (1900–69), a leading Orthodox theologian, whose intellectual orbit in Paris and devotion to ecumenical dialogue formed the basis of a poignant meditation on marriage as at once a sacrament, covenant, and vocation of Christian life. Marriage for Evdokimov is a sacrament of mutually sacrificial love modeled on Christ's relation to the church. It is a covenant of vulnerability, fidelity, and trust that reflects God's enduring bond with the elect. And marriage is a vocation to holiness, even sometimes an "image of heaven." Evdokimov had a very positive view of human sexuality, encouraged marital sex as a sublime expression of love, countenanced contraception when couples were not ready for children, embraced children and parentage as profound gifts of God, and allowed for divorce and remarriage if these marital ideals could not be realized. While he did not dwell on the nuances of sexual ethics or the intricacies of canon law, his strong pro-family teachings, based on scripture and patristic tradition (most notably the writings of John Chrysostom, Chapter 5), have proved welcome additions to modern Western Christian understandings of the family.

In Chapter 24, Mark D. Jordan shows how few issues in family law have divided modern Western Christians more than the battle over same-sex unions and marriages. Anglican theologian and church historian Derrick Sherwin Bailey (1910–84) was one of the pioneers in preparing church, state, and culture to address these issues in and on theological and legal terms. Bailey strongly affirmed the traditional idea of marriage as a loving, exclusive, and consensual "one flesh" union analogous to the relations within the Trinity, the union of divine and human in the Incarnation, and the relation of Christ to the church. This metaphysical, even mystical view celebrated the sexual body and made sexual intimacy an essential practice of marriage, independent of procreation or contract. Marital sex need not be restricted to vaginal intercourse, Bailey insisted. Other sexual acts, including those between persons of the same sex, can be expressions of enduring love, and their criminalization is a product of faulty biblical interpretation, false history, and misguided psychology. These arguments slowly opened the door to the reform of British laws prohibiting same-sex acts and some other sex crimes. They also opened the door to reimagining marriage to include same-sex parties who naturally desire mystical dyadic union and are morally committed to the same exclusive and enduring love for each other. Bailey did not step through this door of reform, but later Western scholars and church leaders have done so with ever greater alacrity.

In Chapter 25, M. Christian Green presents Jean Bethke Elshtain (1941–2013), a leading Christian feminist and political theorist, who inveighed against the patriarchal family and the false public–private divisions between men and women. She advocated instead egalitarian marriages and enduring family structures, which she drew out of sundry insights from classical and Christian sources alike. Elshtain was concerned to carve out a safe space for the nuclear family, given its immense values and virtues for men, women, and children as well as for states, churches, and communities. Much like Kuyper (Chapter 18) and Leo XIII (Chapter 20), she castigated state policies that threatened the autonomy and self-determination of families and that separated sex, procreation, marriage, and childcare from each other. While recognizing divorce as a release valve in cases of real marital breakdown, she rebelled against unilateral no-fault divorce laws and cultures that disproportionately harmed women and children. While promoting women's rights at home and abroad, she challenged androgynous expressions of feminism that deprecated childbearing or glorified the plasticity of the sexual body. While a committed capitalist, she criticized economic and labor policies that left too little time for spouses and children and led to the harmful warehousing of children in public schools and day-care centers. Elshtain, along with her University of Chicago colleague Don Browning, was a leader of the modern marriage movement that urged religious institutions, states, media, and corporations alike to promote, protect, and privilege what she viewed as the most essential institution of the nuclear family.

RECOMMENDED READING

Browning, Don S. et al., *Marriage and Modernization: How Globalization Threatens Marriage and What to Do About It*. Grand Rapids, MI: Wm. B. Eerdmans, 2003.

Brundage, James A. *Law, Sex, and Christian Society in Medieval Europe*. Chicago: University of Chicago Press, 1987.

Donahue, Charles, Jr. *Law, Marriage, and Society in the Later Middle Ages*. Cambridge: Cambridge University Press, 2007.
Epstein, Louis M. *Marriage Laws in the Bible and the Talmud*. Cambridge, MA: Harvard University Press, 1942.
Glendon, Mary Ann. *The Transformation of Family Law: State, Law, and Family in the United States and Western Europe*. Chicago: University of Chicago Press, 1989.
Howard, George Elliott. *A History of Matrimonial Institutions*, 3 vols. Chicago: University of Chicago Press, 1904–7.
Hunter, David G., ed. *Marriage in the Early Church*. Minneapolis, MN: Fortress Press, 1992.
Joyce, G. H. *Christian Marriage: An Historical and Doctrinal Study*, 2nd ed. London: Sheed and Ward, 1948.
Kertzer, David I. and Marzio Bargagli, eds. *The History of the European Family*, 3 vols. New Haven, CT: Yale University Press, 2001–3.
Noonan, John T., Jr. *The Power to Dissolve: Lawyers and Marriages in the Courts of the Roman Curia*. Cambridge, MA: Belknap Press, 1972.
Ozment, Steven E. *Ancestors: The Loving Family in Old Europe*. Cambridge, MA: Harvard University Press, 2001.
Phillips, Roderick. *Putting Asunder: A History of Divorce in Western Society*. Cambridge: Cambridge University Press, 1988.
Reynolds, Philip L. *How Marriage Became One of the Sacraments: The Sacramental Theology of Marriage from Its Medieval Origins to the Council of Trent*. Cambridge: Cambridge University Press, 2016.
Searle, Mark and Kenneth W. Stevenson. *Documents of the Marriage Liturgy*. Collegeville, MN: The Liturgical Press, 1992.
Stone, Lawrence. *The Family, Sex, and Marriage in England, 1500–1800*. New York: Harper & Row, 1979.
Waters, Brent. *The Family in Christian Social and Political Thought*. Oxford: Oxford University Press, 2007.
Witte, John, Jr. *From Sacrament to Contract: Marriage, Religion, and Law in the Western Tradition*, 2nd ed. Louisville, KY: Westminster John Knox Press, 2012.

1

Moses, the Prophets, and the Rabbis

Elliot N. Dorff

Christianity is rooted in Judaism. That rootedness includes not only the Hebrew Bible (the "Old Testament"), but also the oral traditions that accompanied it and that continued after the chronologically last book of the Hebrew Bible, the book of Daniel, was completed by 170 BCE. Jesus and the writers of the Gospels and the other books of the New Testament knew both the Hebrew Bible and these oral traditions, as a number of passages of the New Testament attest.[1] Jesus, in fact, is called "Rabbi," meaning master and teacher of the Jewish traditions, in a number of places in the Gospels.[2] So to understand Christian ideas and practices about families, one must first know something about the texts and traditions that New Testament writers knew and, at least in part, probably practiced. The goal of this chapter is to describe the Jewish origins of Christian ideas and practices regarding the family.

JEWISH SOURCES

Biblical scholars maintain that the vast majority of the written materials that comprise the Hebrew Bible began as traditions communicated from generation to generation by word of mouth and by the example of how people lived daily. Only gradually were these stories, ideas, and practices committed to writing in what we know as the Hebrew Bible. The Hebrew Bible consists of three parts: (1) the Torah (the Five Books of Moses); (2) the Prophets,

[1] For a thorough treatment of the Jewish background of Jesus and the writers of the books of Christian scriptures, see *The Jewish Annotated New Testament*. Levine and Brettler, eds.

[2] Matthew 22:16; 22:23–4; 23:36; 26:25, 49; Mark 9:5; 10:51; 11:21; 14:45; Luke 7:40; 12:13; 18:18; 19:39; 20:27; John 1:38, 49; 3:2; 4:31; 6:25; 9:2; 11:8. Matthew 23:7–8 refers generically to those who are called "rabbi," indicating the pervasive recognition of experts in the Jewish traditions that Jesus and Paul, among others, knew.

FIGURE 1.1. *Moses Smashing the Tablets of the Law*, 1659 (oil on canvas), Rembrandt Harmensz. van Rijn (1606–69) / Gemaldegalerie, Staatliche Museen zu Berlin, Germany / Bridgeman Images

including the historical books of Former Prophets (Joshua, Judges, 1 and 2 Samuel, and 1 and 2 Kings) and the books of literary prophecies (e.g., Isaiah, Jeremiah, Ezekiel, Amos, and Micah); and (3) the Writings, including Psalms, Proverbs, Job, Song of Songs, Ruth, Lamentations, Ecclesiastes (Kohelet), Esther, Daniel, Ezra, Nehemiah, and 1 and 2 Chronicles.

For Jews, the Torah holds the most authority, much as the U.S. Constitution has the most authority in the American legal canon. Although Orthodox Jews believe that the whole Torah was revealed by God to Moses at Mount Sinai, Conservative and Reform Jews accept the conclusions of biblical scholarship that the Torah consists of documents originating in oral traditions and committed to writing between the eleventh and sixth centuries BCE, and edited together by the time of Ezra (mid-fifth century BCE). Some later strands of the Torah interpret earlier strands,[3] and this process of creating new interpretations and applications of earlier materials and new traditions altogether in the latter centuries of the biblical period and after the close of the biblical canon constitutes what we know as Rabbinic literature.

The origins of Rabbinic literature go at least as far back as the second century BCE. Some of the books of Rabbinic interpretations of the Bible, or *midrash*, although based on materials dating earlier than the sixth century CE, were not committed to writing and edited together until the eleventh or twelfth century CE. The scholars of the Bible from the time of Ezra on are first called "scribes," because their first job was to make copies of the Torah. They are then called "sages" (*ḫakhamim*), because in copying the Torah they came to know it and to interpret and apply it. The title "rabbi," meaning master and teacher of the tradition, appears in the first century CE. The title persists to this day, but it is the classical Rabbis of the second century BCE through the sixth century CE to whose words we refer when we speak of Rabbinic literature.

For purposes of this chapter, the most important collections of Rabbinic literature are the Mishnah, which consists of oral traditions dating back to circa 200 BCE and extending to circa 220 CE, when it was edited; and the Talmud, consisting of interpretations and expansions of the Mishnah over the next three centuries or so, when those traditions were edited together circa 550 CE. There are two Talmuds, the Jerusalem (or Palestinian) Talmud (J or PT), consisting of the interpretations and expansions of the Mishnah that occurred in Israel between 220 and 400 CE, when it was edited together; and the Babylonian Talmud (BT), consisting of the interpretations and expansions of the Mishnah that took place among the Jews of Babylonia (modern-day

[3] Fishbane, *Biblical Interpretation in Ancient Israel*.

Iraq) between 220 and 550 CE. Because the Babylonian Jewish community happened to be at the center of Muslim rule in the centuries following the editing of the Talmud, the Babylonian Talmud spread widely during the time of the Muslim rule of the Middle East and the later Christian rule over Europe, so it is much better known than the Jerusalem Talmud. Later codes of Jewish law include Maimonides's *Mishneh Torah* (MT), completed in 1177 CE, and Joseph Caro's *Shulhan Arukh*, completed circa 1565, with glosses added by Moses Isserles to indicate where practices of the Northern European (Ashkenazi) Jewish communities differed from those of the Mediterranean (Sephardi) Jewish communities that Caro described.

Another genre of Rabbinic literature is interpretations of biblical verses, or *midrash*. One collection of such interpretations is the *Rabbah* series on the books of the Torah and several other books read in the synagogue at various seasons. *Rabbah* means "great" or "expanded," and hence *Genesis Rabbah*, for example, consists of many Rabbinic interpretations and expansions of the text of Genesis, arranged according to the order of Genesis.

MARRIAGE AND DIVORCE

The Status and Formation of Marriage. Marriage is the ideal in Judaism. In fact, contrary to the expectation of celibacy for Roman Catholic priests and nuns, the Talmud tells of a young rabbi who was praised to an older rabbi. When the older rabbi met the younger rabbi, it was clear from the latter's dress that he was single. The older rabbi turned his back on the younger rabbi and told him to return when he was married.[4] This view of the human being as ideally married derives from the first chapter of Genesis, in which God tells the first human beings, "Be fruitful and multiply" (Genesis 1:28), the very first commandment in the Torah.

The Rabbis recognized, however, that finding a suitable mate was not easy. They tell the story of a Roman matron who asked a rabbi what God does with his days. The rabbi responded that God spends a third of each day bringing together couples for marriage. The Roman matron scoffed and said, "I can do that myself," and she took her male slaves and matched them off to her female slaves. The next morning there were a lot of angry people among her newly married slaves. Seeing this, she told the rabbi, "Now I understand why God has to spend a third of each day bringing together men and women for marriage."[5]

4 B. *Kiddushin* 29b.

5 *Genesis Rabbah* 68:4; *Leviticus Rabbah* 8:1; *Numbers Rabbah* 3:6; 22:8.

Whatever God's role is in bringing together a couple – and God's activity toward this end continues to be a strong belief among some religious Jews – in the ancient world and until the twentieth century, marriages were arranged by young people's parents. The Talmud asserts that it is a father's duty to find mates for his children, and if the father has died or is otherwise unable to fulfill this duty, it falls to the community to find mates for orphans and otherwise-unattached young people. This responsibility included the community's duty to pay the dowry that normally would be paid by the bride's father, and the bride price that the groom is required to pay, if they could not afford to do so on their own and had no family to help them.[6] The musical *Fiddler on the Roof* is historically accurate in illustrating this practice of arranged marriages into the early twentieth century, when Enlightenment ideas of people finding their own mates based on romantic love gradually became the norm in the Jewish communities of the West. (Some groups of Orthodox Jews still have parent-arranged marriages.)

The Mishnah asserts that a man should marry by age eighteen,[7] usually to a woman a few years younger, but a girl could be married from age twelve and a half on. If a man is not married by twenty, according to the Rabbis, God says, "Blasted be his bones!"[8] This, however, reflects the reality before the twentieth century that girls received little or no formal education and boys did not do much better. Again, *Fiddler* is historically accurate in having the sons sing, in the opening number, "At three I started Hebrew school; at ten I learned a trade." With the vast majority of Jews now going to college and many to graduate school, they commonly marry in their twenties or later.

Endogamy. A number of stories in the Torah depict negotiations for marriage. What is clear from the stories of the patriarchs and matriarchs is that endogamy was the norm – that is, one had to marry within the extended clan. So, for example, Abraham sends his servant, Eliezer, back to Haran, from which Abraham's family had migrated to Canaan, to find a wife for Isaac among Abraham's relatives.[9] Conversely, Isaac and Rebekah are distressed when Esau marries one of the Hittite women instead of someone within the clan, so, in an effort to please his parents, Esau takes another wife from the related family of Ishmael.[10] Later, Dinah, daughter of Jacob, wants to marry Shekhem, one of the Canaanite men. Jacob convinces the men of

6 Father's duty to marry off his children: B. *Kiddushin* 29a, 30b. Father's duty to pay for daughter's dowry: B. *Ketubbot* 52b; B. *Kiddushin* 30b. Community's duty to marry off orphans: B. *Ketubbot* 67b.

7 M. *Avot* 5:24.

8 B. *Kiddushin* 29b. Other opinions on that page and the following one give the man to age twenty-two or even twenty-four.

9 Genesis 24.

10 Genesis 26:34; 28:6–9.

Shekhem's tribe that they can marry within the Israelite clan only if they are circumcised, and they agree to be circumcised. While they are still hurting from their wounds, two of Dinah's brothers kill Shekhem, his father, and all the men of his clan – such a nasty way of enforcing the rule of endogamy that Jacob complains that it will make it hard for Jacob and his clan to live among the Canaanites.[11] Deuteronomy 23:3–8 later prohibits Ammonites and Moabites from joining the Israelites (presumably by marriage) for ten generations, and Edomites for three.

There are, however, biblical figures who defy this ban against marriage outside the clan. King Ahab, for example, marries the Canaanite woman Jezebel, who brings many Canaanite gods to the court and thus indicates the problems of marrying out. King Solomon, likewise, marries many women, both Israelite and non-Israelite, including the Queen of Sheba.[12]

Rabbinic law preserves the requirement of endogamy, but it establishes procedures for conversion of Gentiles to Judaism. Thus one can become Jewish and marry a Jew not only by being born to a Jewish mother, the way most Jews become Jewish, but also by being reborn through the rites of conversion into the Jewish people. In modern times, as Jews have become more accepted socially in Western nations, especially the United States, many "Jews by choice" (in contrast to Jews by birth) convert to Judaism precisely to marry a Jew (even though Jewish law requires rabbis to make sure that the person converting to Judaism loves Judaism and not just a particular Jew!).

The Mishnah has two conflicting rulings about children of mixed-faith marriages. One says that the child of a Jewish woman and a non-Jewish man is illegitimate and therefore may not join the Jewish people for ten generations, in accordance with Deuteronomy 23:3. The other asserts that the child of a Jewish woman and a non-Jewish man is a Jew.[13] Later Jewish law follows the latter ruling. According to both, however, the child of a Jewish man and a non-Jewish woman is not Jewish, thereby discouraging men, who until recently would be the more likely to marry outside the Jewish people, from doing so, for if they did that, their children would not be Jewish.

Forbidden Sexual Relationships. Leviticus 18 and 20 contain long lists defining which blood and familial relationships are incestuous and therefore forbidden, and prescribing the death penalty for engaging in such relationships. Unlike many state laws in the United States, Jewish law allows the marriage of first

11 Genesis 34.

12 Solomon marries many non-Israelites: 1 Kings 3:1; 11:1–6. Ahab marries a non-Israelite: 1 Kings 16:31.

13 The child is illegitimate: M. *Yevamot* 7:5; B. *Yevamot* 45a, 70a. The child is Jewish: M. *Kiddushin* 3:12; B. *Kiddushin* 68b.

cousins, and such marriages were quite common in the early modern period in the villages of Eastern Europe, where the list of potential mates was limited.[14] The Rabbis effectively eliminated the death penalty, however, through narrowing the cases in which it could apply and through making the required evidentiary procedures to produce a capital conviction impossible to fulfill. Still, couples who did engage in incest were historically punished in other ways, including excommunication.

Those same two chapters in Leviticus also prohibit adultery, bestiality, and homosexual relations between males, and they prescribe the death penalty for these forms of sexual activity. As part of the Rabbis' effort to limit capital punishment, they defined adultery as occurring only between a married woman and a man not her husband, or between a man (married or not) with a woman married to someone else. A married man having sex with a single woman is not adultery before the law; such activity is either licentiousness or an act of marriage to another woman, essentially an act of polygyny.

Again, to limit the death penalty, the Rabbis interpret the verses prohibiting same-sex male intercourse in these chapters in Leviticus to forbid only anal sex between men.[15] On their own authority, however, and therefore with lesser penalties, they prohibit other homosexual activities. They also prohibited lesbians from "rubbing up against each other,"[16] but viewed such activity as banned by Rabbinic decree, not by the Torah itself.[17] Only in recent years have the non-Orthodox movements in Judaism, including the Conservative movement in the middle of the spectrum, approved rabbis officiating at same-sex marriages and the legitimacy of sexual activity within a same-sex marriage. Along with this approval has come recognition that same-sex couples bear the same responsibilities toward each other and their children as do heterosexual couples.[18]

14 See Chapter 14 in this volume by Henry Ansgar Kelly, who shows that early modern English common law allowed for first-cousin marriages on the strength of these Hebrew Bible precedents.

15 B. *Sanhedrin* 55a. For a detailed discussion of this, see the rabbinic ruling by Dorff, Nevins, and Reisner cited in note 18.

16 *Sifra*, Aharei Mot 9:8. See B. *Yevamot* 76a, where lesbian sex is characterized as *pritzut d'alma*, general licentiousness, in contrast to a biblically prohibited act.

17 See Chapter 24 by Mark D. Jordan in this volume, discussing homosexual relations and activities in the modern Christian thought of D. S. Bailey.

18 In the Conservative movement, see the rabbinic ruling by Dorff, Nevins, and Reisner, approved by the Committee on Jewish Law and Standards on 6 December 2006, which permits rabbis to officiate at same-sex weddings and, with that, also permits same-sex carnal relations within a married, same-sex couple, with the exception of male-male anal sex; and the ruling by Roth approved on the same day that prohibits officiating at same-sex unions and prohibits same-sex carnal relations: www.rabbinicalassembly.org/sites/default/files/public/halakhah/teshuvot/20052010/dorff_nevins_reisner_dignity.pdf for Dorff, Nevins, Reisner;

Sex within Marriage. In contrast to the prohibitions of sexual relations between relatives and with people married to someone else, the Torah and later Rabbinic tradition are very positive about sex within marriage. In fact, sex is commanded in two different places in the Torah, indicating two different goals of sex within marriage: "Be fruitful and multiply," God says to the very first couple, and so procreation is one of the goals of sex within marriage. In addition, Exodus 21:9–10 says that when a man marries a maidservant (and, all the more so, a free woman), "her food, her clothing, and her rights to sex he may not diminish."[19]

The Mishnah then proceeds to define exactly what the couple must do to fulfill these commandments. With regard to procreation, the Mishnah says this:

> A man may not stop propagating unless he [already] has children. The School of Shammai say: two males. The School of Hillel say: a male and a female, as the Torah says, "Male and female God created them" (Genesis 5:2) . . . The man is commanded to propagate, but not the woman. Rabbi Yohanan ben Beroka says: God says to both of them, "And God blessed them and said to them . . . Be fruitful and multiply."
>
> (Genesis 1:28)[20]

The Rabbis clearly knew that producing children requires both a man and a woman, and they also knew what Rabbi Yohanan ben Beroka points out – that God is speaking to both the first man and the first woman in saying, "Be fruitful and multiply." The majority, however, limited the commandment to procreate to the man, for an exegetical reason as well as for some practical reasons. The exegetical reason is that the verse in Genesis 1:27 continues in this way: "Be fruitful and multiply, and fill the Earth and conquer it." The Rabbis then reasoned thus: Whose mode is it to conquer? It is the man's, and because the last part of the verse applies only to men, the first part of the verse, the commandment to procreate, applies only to men as well.

There are two practical reasons why the Rabbis chose to interpret the verse in this unusual way (unusual because God, after all, is addressing both the

www.rabbinicalassembly.org/sites/default/files/public/halakhah/teshuvot/20052010/roth_revised.pdf for Roth.

19 Some biblical scholars think that the Hebrew word used here for the third item on the list originally meant "ointments," based on Hosea 2:7, Ecclesiastes 9:7–9, and ancient Middle Eastern texts; see *The JPS Commentary: Exodus*, 121. The Rabbis, however, following all the early translations of the Torah (the Septuagint, Peshitta, and Targums), interpreted that word to mean her rights to sex.

20 M. *Yevamot* 6:6.

man and the woman, and both are needed for procreation). First, men are not endangered in carrying out their role in procreation, but women are, as evidenced by the fact that Rachel dies in giving birth to Benjamin,[21] and the Rabbis did not want to command women to take the risks of pregnancy and delivery. Another possible reason is that men would be required to support whatever children they had, so men had to be commanded to have children, despite the economic burden that children impose.

As the Mishnah records, the Rabbis of the House of Hillel and later Jewish law interpreted Genesis 1:28 to require a minimum of two children – specifically a boy and a girl, so that human creation would mirror divine creation. Couples who were able to have more children, however, were supposed to have as many as they could, based on the verse, "Sow your seed in the morning, and do not refrain from doing so in the evening," interpreted to mean the beginning and later stages of life (Ecclesiastes 11:6).[22] This undoubtedly reflected the reality of a time when fewer children survived to adulthood.

In our own time, the Jewish people are facing a demographic crisis. With a third of the Jewish people killed during the Holocaust, and with the birth rate among Jews considerably lower than replacement level, the world population of Jews is declining. Moreover, only a small minority of the many Jews who marry people of other faiths are raising their children in accordance with Jewish tradition. As a result of this demographic crisis, Rabbi Kassel Abelson and I wrote a rabbinic ruling, approved by the Conservative movement's Committee on Jewish Law and Standards, urging Jewish couples to have one more child than they were planning on having, for the sake of the continuity of the Jewish people and Judaism.[23]

The commandment to procreate does not apply to couples who cannot have children, for a commandment makes logical and legal sense only if the commanded parties can fulfill it. With some restrictions,[24] couples may use modern techniques to overcome infertility, but they are not required to do so; the commandment is understood to apply only to couples who can procreate without medical assistance. Infertile couples, however, may and should consider adoption, for adoption has an honored place in Judaism. The Talmud

[21] Genesis 35:16–20. [22] B. *Yevamot* 62b interprets the verse from Ecclesiastes to mean this.

[23] Kassel Abelson and Elliot N. Dorff, "Mitzvah Children," www.rabbinicalassembly.org/sites/default/files/public/halakhah/teshuvot/20052010/mitzvah_children.pdf (accessed 14 October 2015).

[24] Rabbis differ on the legitimacy of some of the methods used, in particular the use of donor sperm or eggs. For my own view, adopted by the Conservative movement's Committee on Jewish Law and Standards, see Dorff, *Matters of Life and Death*, chapters 3 and 4.

maintains that someone who adopts and raises an orphan "follows God each and every moment of his life."[25]

Regarding Exodus 21:9–10, the commandment that a man not diminish his wife's sexual satisfaction, the Mishnah asserts that the number of times a man has to offer to have sex with his wife depends on his profession and, therefore, the number of nights that he would likely be home:

> The time[s] for marital duties enjoined in the Law are: for men of independent means every day; for workmen twice weekly; for ass-drivers, once a week; for camel-drivers once every thirty days; for sailors once every six months. This is the opinion of Rabbi Eliezer.[26]

Of course, nobody would know whether the man was following this calendar unless his wife complained to the court that he was not sexually satisfying her. Couples getting along well would set the schedule of their sexual activity for themselves; the real goal was to satisfy the woman's sexual needs, not to follow a particular regimen. Furthermore, in ancient times, as in modern times, the hormones stimulating sexual desire diminished over time, so older couples almost definitely did not follow this schedule.

The man also has rights to sex within marriage. British common law and the law in all American states until 1976 held that a license to marry gave the husband the right to have sex with his wife whenever and however he wanted, making marital rape legally impossible. In 1976, Nebraska legislated the first law in the United States prohibiting marital rape, and by 1993 all fifty states had such a law. In many states, however, the burden of proof is higher in cases of marital rape than in cases of rape by a stranger, because the couple's marriage establishes a presumption that all sex between them is consensual.[27] In sharp contrast to this Anglo-American common law, the Talmud recognized more than fifteen hundred years ago that a man could rape his wife, and the Talmud prohibits that.[28]

If a man may not force his wife to have sex with him, though, how are his rights to sex within marriage preserved? The answer, according to the Mishnah, is that he may diminish the amount of money he would have to pay his wife in a divorce settlement – a specified (and disputed) amount for each week that she refuses to have sexual relations with him, until he ultimately can divorce her without paying her anything.[29]

[25] B. *Ketubbot* 50a, interpreting Psalms 106:3. [26] M. *Ketubbot* 5:6.

[27] Deborah C. England, "The History of Marital Rape Laws," www.criminaldefenselawyer.com/resources/criminal-defense/crime-penalties/marital-rape.htm (accessed 15 October 2015).

[28] B. *Eruvin* 100b; M. T. Laws of Marriage 14:15. [29] M. *Ketubbot* 5:7.

The Talmud was not at all prudish about how the couple had sex. Modesty had to be preserved in the sense that sexual relations, while very good and even commanded, must be private. When most people had only one-room houses, the couple had to have a partition between where they were having sex and where the children were sleeping. Within those bounds of modesty, however, the couple were allowed to have sex in any way they wanted. Rabbi Moses Isserles, drawing on passages in the Talmud, says this in his gloss on Rabbi Joseph Caro's code, the *Shulhan Arukh*. It is addressed to the man, but, as the code says, the man had to procure the woman's agreement to the way they were having sex as well as to having sexual relations in the first place:

> A man may do whatever he pleases with his wife [during intercourse]. He may have sexual relations with her at any time that he pleases, he may kiss her in any part of her body, and he may have intercourse with her whether in the usual way [vaginally] or not in the usual way [anally] or orally ... He may not have sexual relations with her except with her consent, so if she does not want to have sex, he should entice her until she wants to. He should be very modest in sexual relations, such that he does not engage in sexual relations in front of any person, even a child, except for a baby who does not know what is going on.[30]

Sex Outside of Marriage. Marriage is the required context for sexual relations. Deuteronomy 22:23–9 prescribes the death penalty for a man who rapes a woman. If a man has consensual sex with a single woman to whom he is not married, he must pay her father fifty shekels of silver as the bride price; if the father consents, the man must also marry the woman and may never divorce her. Adultery is punished by death for both the man and the woman involved.[31] But in a concerted effort to limit culpability for the death penalty, the Rabbis limited adultery to the case of a married woman having sex with a man who is not her husband, or a man having sex with a woman married to another man. If a man, married or not, has sex with a single woman, that is not classified as adultery but rather as a way for the man to take a wife – even another wife, for until the decree of Rabbenu Gershom in the tenth century, polygamy was allowed. Thus Abraham and Jacob both have two wives as well as concubines.[32] The Rabbis also permitted polygyny,[33] but they

30 S.A. *Even Ha-Ezer* 25:2, gloss, to the three dots, followed by Caro's code itself. The permission for a man to have sex in any way with his wife is based on B. *Nedarim* 20b.

31 Leviticus 20:10; Deuteronomy 22:22.

32 Abraham's wives: Sarai, later Sarah, Keturah(Genesis 11:29, 25:1). Abraham's concubine, Hagar (Genesis 16:1ff). Jacob's wives: Leah and Rachel (Genesis 29:16ff). Jacob's concubines: Bilhah (Genesis 30:3–8), Zilpah (Genesis 30:9–13).

33 B. *Yevamot* 65a; *Piskei Ha-Rosh*, *ibid.*, 17; M.T. Laws of Marriage (*Ishut*) 14:3. S.A. *Even Ha-Ezer* 1:9; 76:7.

discouraged it by requiring that the man satisfy each of his wives sexually and then only if, according to some Talmudic rulings, he either divorces his first wife and pays her the amounts owing her upon divorce or gains her consent.[34]

Rabbenu Gershom's decree prohibiting polygamy, however, applied only to Ashkenazi Jews – that is, Jews living in Northern Europe, where Christians had the same rule. Sephardi Jewish men – that is, those living in the Mediterranean basin or the Middle East – were, and still are, officially allowed by religious authorities to have more than one wife simultaneously, as were the Muslim men among whom they lived. The State of Israel allows Sephardi men who immigrate to Israel with more than one wife to keep all their wives, but once there, such men may not add to the number of women to whom they are married simultaneously. Single Sephardi men may marry only one woman at a time; that is, monogamy is the law in Israel for everyone with the exception of those who immigrated to Israel married to more than one. Sephardi Jews who have immigrated to other countries – e.g., Moroccan and Tunisian Jews who immigrated to France – are usually required to divorce all but one of their wives, although this depends on the country to which they immigrate.

Divorce. Divorce, though almost always sad, is permitted in Judaism, as Deuteronomy 24:1–3 makes clear. Divorce is not considered a sin. Still, unless there is abuse, abandonment, or some other reason that makes divorce the right thing to do, rabbis seek to reconcile the couple to each other, especially if the couple have dependent children. In the end, though, because Deuteronomy 24 establishes that marriage in Jewish law is not only a social and sacred act but a contractual one as well, the couple can mutually decide to dissolve their contract of marriage.[35] In such cases, divorce is accepted without having to provide any justification; what American law calls irreconcilable differences are enough.[36]

The only mention of divorce in the Torah is in Deuteronomy 24, where a man is permitted to divorce a woman. For that textual reason, and probably because the Bible and Rabbinic literature were written in the context of patriarchal communities, the Rabbis determine that Deuteronomy 24 is normative, so that a man may initiate a divorce, but a woman may not. Neither may a court, whether Jewish or governmental, initiate a divorce. This means that, although Jewish law has its own way for a couple to marry but will retroactively recognize a civil marriage as valid, the same is not true for

34 B. ibid. *Piskei Ha-Rosh*, ibid., S.A., ibid., 76:8.

35 On the contractual, social, and sacred elements of Jewish marriage, see Dorff and Rosett, *A Living Tree*, 442–511.

36 M. *Gittin* 9:10.

divorce. Only the husband may initiate the divorce, and no court, civil or Jewish, may do that. Therefore a Jewish couple who want to divorce must do so both in civil law and in Jewish law in separate procedures.

To divorce a woman, according to Deuteronomy 24, a man must give his wife a writ of divorce, later called a *get*. This provides the woman with proof that she is divorced and therefore eligible to marry another man. In other ancient cultures, and in Islam to this day, the man need only proclaim that she is divorced in front of witnesses to effect a divorce, but then the woman depends on the memory, integrity, and availability of the witnesses to affirm that she is eligible to marry someone else.

In the vast majority of cases, these arrangements to effect a divorce are not a problem, for if there has been a civil divorce, the man is usually willing and able to follow through with a Jewish divorce, so that he and his former wife can both remarry in Jewish law as well as in civil law. Sometimes, however, the man refuses to initiate a Jewish divorce and may even seek to extort money or other consideration as the price for doing so. In some cases, the man has become insane and cannot execute any Jewish legal act, while in other cases, the man's whereabouts are unknown. In all these cases, the woman is an *agunah*, a woman chained to her first husband and therefore ineligible to marry someone else, for if she did so, she would be committing adultery.

This legal result is clearly unjust, so the Rabbis of the Mishnah say that if the husband is recalcitrant, rabbis should first try to convince him to grant the divorce (to give her a *get*) by appealing to his better self. If that does not work, rabbis apply social pressure by telling his employer and his friends about his recalcitrance, in the hopes that those important people in his life will convince him to give his former wife a *get*. If that does not work, in the State of Israel, rabbinic courts can fine the man or even imprison him until he grants the divorce. Despite these pressures, there still are unfortunately a number of *agunot* (the plural of *agunah*) in the Orthodox community in both Israel and the Diaspora.

Already in the 1950s, the Conservative movement – the middle movement in Judaism, with Orthodoxy on its right and Reform on its left – resolved this issue in several ways. It gave rabbis the option to use a form of the marriage document (the *ketubbah*) with a clause that says that in the event of divorce in the civil courts, the couple (really, the man) agrees to appear before a rabbinic court and do what it requires, which, of course, will be that the man give a *get* to his wife.

Unresolved, though, is what happens if, despite such a clause, the husband refuses to appear before the rabbinic court or to do what it requires of him. Several such cases went to trial in the state courts of New York in the 1970s and 1980s, with varying results. Some courts saw the *ketubbah* as a religious document and therefore unenforceable on First Amendment grounds. Other courts saw the *ketubbah* as a prenuptial agreement between the couple and therefore enforceable in American law. Ultimately, in 1983, the highest court in New York ruled that such clauses were enforceable.[37]

The New York ruling has no bearing on other states, of course, and, in any case, for many years Conservative rabbis felt uncomfortable turning to the civil courts to resolve a problem in Jewish law. In 1969, the Conservative movement's Committee on Jewish Law and Standards approved a prenuptial agreement, whereby the couple (really, the husband) agrees that if they are later divorced in civil law, and he does not grant her a *get* within six months after the divorce decree of the civil court, the marriage is null and void from its beginning. This agreement has the advantage of requiring no action by any court, civil or Jewish, to free the woman to remarry, and it thus makes the *agunah* problem disappear. Dissolving the marriage in this way does not make the children of the marriage illegitimate in Jewish law, for that status is limited to children of adultery or incest. But this arrangement does transform the status of the couple's marital sex to that of licentiousness rather than holy matrimony. That, however, has no legal consequences.

If, though, the couple did not sign such an agreement before their marriage, and the husband refuses to grant a *get* or cannot do so, then the Conservative movement will use the power of contemporary rabbis, as granted several times in the Talmud, to annul the marriage (*hafqa'at kiddushin*) so that she can remarry. The Orthodox hesitate to use this power to annul marriages granted to rabbis by the Talmud, because it was not used during the Middle Ages to resolve the problem of *agunot*. Some Orthodox rabbis instead now require a prenuptial agreement that would impose a fine on the man for each day that he refuses to grant a *get* to his wife after the divorce decree in the civil courts. This requires the civil courts to impose such fines, and it is not at all clear that they will be willing to do so, as this amounts to the state forcing a man to do a religious act.

The Reform movement has resolved the problem of *agunot* by recognizing civil divorce as sufficient to effect a Jewish divorce as well. That is an elegant solution, completely circumventing the problem of *agunot* by enabling a woman to divorce her husband as well as a husband to divorce his wife. But this method to dissolve the marriage violates classical Jewish law, according

[37] *Avitzur v. Avitzur*, New York Court of Appeals, 58 NY 2d 108, 459 S.2d 572 [1983].

to which only the husband has the power to divorce, not any court, civil or Jewish. As a result, people seen as divorced and eligible to remarry by the Reform movement would still be seen by the more traditional Jewish movements as married to their first spouse and therefore committing adultery if they remarry. This view has detrimental implications not only for the couple, but also for their children, who would be considered illegitimate (*mamzerim*) by classical Jewish law and thus ineligible to marry other Jews; this resolution of the status of *agunot* thus creates a problem for the Jewish community as a whole.

CHILDREN

The Bible sees children as a great blessing. Thus, when God blesses Abraham, the blessing is for the land of Israel and children, and that blessing is repeated to Isaac and Jacob.[38] Infertility, on the other hand, is portrayed as a curse that affects all of the patriarchs and matriarchs, at least for a time.[39] It is the source of both anxiety and tension for a couple, as articulated perhaps most graphically in the testy exchange between Jacob and Rachel, when Jacob has had children with Leah but not with Rachel: "Rachel said to Jacob, 'Give me children or I shall die.' Jacob was incensed at Rachel and said, 'Can I take the place of God, who has denied you fruit of the womb?'"[40]

Having children not only obeys the Torah's first command to "be fruitful and multiply and fill the earth," but also increases adults' maturity. The Rabbis recognized this in a very interesting ruling, according to which only people with children of their own were eligible to serve as judges in capital cases.[41] Only such people, the Rabbis seem to be saying, can know the true value of life – both the life of the alleged perpetrator and the life of the victim.

Children, however, are not always sources of joy and maturation. Exodus 21 prescribes the death penalty, no less, for children who strike or even curse their parents, and Deuteronomy 21 likewise prescribes the death penalty, with the parents throwing the first stones, for "a stubborn and rebellious son." The Rabbis' effective elimination of the death penalty applies to these cases as well, but these commands underscore the reality that raising children can be very trying.

[38] Abraham: Genesis 15:5; 17:3–8. Isaac: 26:4. Jacob: Genesis 35:9–12.

[39] Abraham and Sarah: 15:2–3; 16:1–2; 17:17. Isaac and Rebekah: Genesis 25:20–1. Jacob and Leah: Genesis 29:35; 30:9–13. Jacob and Rachel: Genesis 30:1–8, 22; 35:16–19.

[40] Genesis 30:1–2.

[41] T. *Sanhedrin* 7:3; B. *Sanhedrin* 36b.

The Talmud stipulates that fathers have the following duties toward their sons:

> Our Rabbis taught: A man is responsible to circumcise his son, to redeem him [from Temple service if he is a couple's firstborn child and a son, *pidyon ha-ben*], to teach him Torah, to marry him off to a woman, and to teach him a trade, and there are those who say that he must also teach him to swim. Rabbi Judah says: Anyone who fails to teach his son a trade teaches him to steal.[42]

The duties to circumcise one's sons and to redeem a firstborn son from service in the ancient Temple clearly do not apply to daughters, and in the patriarchal world of the past, the duty to teach sons a trade did not apply to daughters either, who would presumably be supported by their fathers and then later by their husbands. That said, we have ample historical evidence that women helped their husbands earn a living, especially after their children were grown.

Whether the duty to educate one's sons in Torah also applies to one's daughters was the subject of a dispute among the Talmudic Rabbis,[43] but in contemporary times even the ultra-Orthodox provide a formal Jewish education for their daughters as well as their sons, although in gender-specific classes and with different curricula. In the more liberal movements of Judaism, boys and girls – and later men and women – learn the same curriculum in coeducational classes from preschool through rabbinical school.

The father's duty to marry off his sons and daughters reflects the custom of patriarchal societies in which marriages were arranged by fathers. We see evidence of this as early as Abraham, who sends Eliezer to Haran, where his extended family lives, to find a wife for Isaac,[44] and it extends to the early twentieth century. Both sons and daughters had to agree to the marriage their fathers arranged for them, but in most times and places, such consent was taken for granted.

That said, we also have early evidence of men and women finding their own spouses, sometimes to the consternation of their parents. As noted earlier, on his own initiative Esau marries one of the Hittite women instead of someone within the clan. Afterward, in an effort to please his parents, he takes another wife from the family of Ishmael, also on his own initiative.[45] Later Dinah, daughter of Jacob, wants to marry Shekhem, one of the Canaanite men.[46]

[42] B. *Kiddushin* 29a. [43] M. *Sotah* 3:4; B. *Kiddushin* 29b, 30a; J. *Sotah* 19a; B. *Yoma* 66b.
[44] Genesis 24. [45] Genesis 26:34; 28:6–9. [46] Genesis 34.

Fathers were responsible for supporting their children. Because boys could go out and beg with less danger to themselves than girls, if a father could not support both his sons and his daughters, his first obligation was to his wife and then to his daughters:

> If he did not stipulate in writing for her, "Your female children by me shall stay in my house and be maintained from my possessions until they are wed to husbands," he is nevertheless liable, as this is a condition instituted by the Court.[47]
>
> Rabbi Abba said in the name of Rabbi Yose: They [the Rabbis of the Mishnah] made the widow vis-à-vis her daughter like the daughter vis-à-vis her brothers in situations of few resources: Just as with regard to the situation of a daughter vis-à-vis her brothers, the daughter would be sustained [by the father's meager resources] and the brothers would go begging, so too with regard to the situation of a widow vis-à-vis her daughter: the widow is sustained from her late husband's [meager] property, and the daughter goes begging.[48]

Conversely, the Torah imposes two duties on children – to honor their parents (Exodus 20:2; Deuteronomy 5:16 – *kavod*) and to revere (or fear) them (Leviticus 19:3 – *yir'ah*). The Rabbis, in their usual style, then define exactly what each of these commandments entails:

> Our Rabbis taught: What is "fear" and what is "honor"? "Fear" means that he (the son) must neither stand in his (the father's) place nor sit in his place, nor contradict his words [in public], nor tip the scales against him [in public]. "Honor" means that he must give him food and drink, clothe and cover him, lead him in and out. The Scholars propounded: At whose expense? Rab Judah said: The son's. R. Nahman b. Oshaia said: The father's. The Rabbis gave a ruling to R. Jeremiah – others state to R. Jeremiah's son – in accordance with the view that it must be at the father's expense. An objection is raised: The Bible says, "Honor your father and your mother," and it also says, "Honor the Lord with your substance": just as the latter means at personal cost, so the former too. But if you say [that the son provides goods and services to his father] at the father's (expense), how does it affect him? – Through loss of time.[49]

Although here, as usual, the Rabbis interpreted biblical commandments that refer to emotions (respect, fear, love) in terms of the actions required to demonstrate those emotions, they were keenly aware that the same acts can be done in ways that either honor or demean one's parents:

[47] M. *Ketubbot* 4:11. [48] B. *Ketubbot* 43a. [49] B. *Kiddushin* 31b–32a.

> A man may feed his father on fattened chickens and inherit Hell as his reward, and another may put his father to work in a mill and inherit Paradise.
>
> How is it possible that a man might feed his father fattened chickens and inherit Hell? It once happened that a man used to feed his father fattened chickens. Once his father said to him: "My son, where did you get these?" He answered: "Old man, old man, eat and be silent, just as dogs eat and are silent." In such an instance, he feeds his father fattened chickens, but he inherits Hell.
>
> How is it possible that a man might put his father to work in a mill and inherit Paradise? It once happened that a man was working in a mill. The king decreed millers should be brought to work for him. The son said to his father: "Father, go and work in the mill in my place, (and I will go to work for the king). For it may be (that the king's workers will be) ill treated, in which case let me be ill treated instead of you. And it may be (that the king's workers will be) beaten, in which case let me be beaten instead of you." In such an instance, he puts his father to work in a mill, but he inherits Paradise.[50]

Even though fathers had considerable duties with regard to their children, and children had significant duties with regard to their parents as well, there were limits to what parents could expect of their children. Parents were not allowed to have sexual relations with their children or grandchildren.[51] Some biblical sources allow and even encourage parents to strike their children when they misbehave, as part of the parents' duties to educate their children,[52] while others urge parents to "Educate the child according to his ways."[53] The debate in Jewish sources about parents hitting children has continued through the Middle Ages to our own time.[54] The Talmud, though, says this: "If you must strike a child, strike him/her with the string of a shoe,"[55] and the bulk of the Jewish tradition was against hitting children to discipline them.

CONCLUSION

Biblical and Rabbinic sources understand marriage as the ideal state for human beings and encourage sexual relations between spouses for the companionship and intimacy that sex expresses and for the sake of procreation.

50 B. *Kiddushin* 31a–31b. 51 Leviticus 18:6, 10.
52 Proverbs 23:13–14; 29:15; see also Proverbs 3:11–12, 13:24, 19:18, 20:30, 29:17.
53 Proverbs 22:6.
54 Dorff, "Family Violence," in *Love Your Neighbor and Yourself*, chapter 5.
55 B. *Bava Batra* 21a.

Parents and children have significant obligations toward each other, but in the end, children are seen as one of God's most important blessings:

> Blessed are all who revere the Lord,
> Who follow in His ways.
> You shall enjoy the fruit of your labors,
> You shall be happy, you shall prosper.
> Your wife will be like a fruitful vine within your house,
> Your children like olive shoots round about your table.
> This is the blessing of one who reveres the Lord.
> May the Lord bless you from Zion,
> May you see Jerusalem prosper all the days of your life.
> May you live to see children's children.
> May there be peace for the people Israel.
>
> *(Psalm 128)*

RECOMMENDED READING

Biale, David. *Eros and the Jews: From Biblical Israel to Contemporary America*. New York: Basic Books, 1992.

Biale, Rachel. *Women and Jewish Law: An Exploration of Women's Issues in Halkhic Sources*. New York: Schocken, 1984.

Cohen, Abraham. *Everyman's Talmud*. New York: E. P. Dutton and Company, 1949, esp. chapter 5, "Domestic Life."

Cohen, Martin S., ed. *The Observant Life: The Wisdom of Conservative Judaism for Contemporary Jews*. New York: Rabbinical Assembly, 2012, esp. the following chapters (not numbered in the book): Carl N. Astor, "The Jewish Life Cycle," 239–304; David J. Fine, "Marriage," 611–31; Jeremy Kalmanofsky, "Sex, Relationships, and Single Jews," 632–56; Elliot N. Dorff, "Same-Sex Relationships," 657–72; Daniel S. Nevins, "Between Parents and Children," 673–92; David M. Greenstein, "Between Siblings," 693–708; Gerald C. Skolnik, "Between Grandparents and Grandchildren," 709–12.

Dorff, Elliot N. *Love Your Neighbor and Yourself: A Jewish Approach to Modern Personal Ethics*. Philadelphia, PA: Jewish Publication Society, 2003, esp. chapters 3–5 on sex, parents and children, and family violence.

The Way into Tikkun Olam (Repairing the World). Woodstock, VT: Jewish Lights, 2005, esp. chapters 8–10 on duties of spouses to each other, filial duties, and parental duties.

Haut, Irwin H. *Divorce in Jewish Law and Life*. New York: Sepher-Hermon Press, 1983.

Kraemer, David, ed. *The Jewish Family: Metaphor and Memory*. New York: Oxford University Press, 1989.

Labovitz, Gail. *Marriage and Metaphor: Constructions of Gender in Rabbinic Literature*. Lanham, MD: Lexington Books, 2009.

Rosenberg, Shelley Kapnek. *Adoption and the Jewish Family: Contemporary Perspectives*. Philadelphia, PA: Jewish Publication Society, 1998.

Ruttenberg, Danya, ed. *The Passionate Torah: Sex and Judaism*. New York: New York University Press, 2009.

2

Jesus and St. Paul

Gary S. Hauk

Christian thought has its foundation in the life and teachings of Jesus. This unconventional life and these sometimes confounding teachings, however, make it difficult to draw out a clear and coherent understanding of the "law" governing the family. Jesus's life in many ways defied the familial conventions of the day, even as he often relied on metaphors of family as a means for discerning God's ultimate purpose for humanity. His teachings often undermined traditional norms of relationship but sometimes offered a more radical interpretation of those norms. Adding to the difficulty is the conviction, in Jesus's own words and in the witness of the church, that his Resurrection marks the culmination of history and the anticipation of a divine reign of peace and justice. Life as usual is no more; yet clearly life goes on, with all of its natural impulses, its need for order, and its inescapable relationships. How, then, can the Christian community regulate sexual relations, family responsibilities, and the occasional failure of marriage, while awaiting the Eschaton?[1]

The answer to this question for Jesus – and later for the earliest canonical New Testament writings, the letters of the Apostle Paul – lay partially in the Jewish law, or Torah. Comprising the first five books of the Hebrew Bible, the Torah was elaborated and expounded upon in the books of the prophets, the wisdom literature, and poetry. All of these texts – together often called "the Law" by early Christians – constituted a far-ranging system of rules governing everything from diet to family arrangements to clothing to the rituals of the Temple. Moreover, as the eastern Mediterranean region

[1] The key foundational texts are the Gospels of Matthew, Mark, Luke, and John and the letters of Paul. All of these texts were set down between 50 and 100 CE in a society whose cultural, intellectual, and political contours were shaped by both the Jewish heritage of Hellenistic Palestine and the Roman law that governed the Mediterranean basin during that time.

FIGURE 2.1. *The Conversion of St. Paul* (oil on canvas), Crozat, Ambroise (eighteenth century) / Musee des Augustins, Toulouse, France / Bridgeman Images

experienced a succession of empires, new laws, and cultural influences, Jewish communities looked to their rabbis to interpret the Torah in previously unimagined situations. This large body of texts and commentary in first-century Judaism formed the background for the "Good News" proclaimed by Jesus and for the ministry carried out by Paul. While Jesus and Paul are informed to a large extent by Jewish law, however, their own teachings often contradict or depart from it.

Beyond the complications of how Jesus interprets the Law and, subsequently, how Paul interprets Jesus, the lives of both Jesus and Paul provide confusing examples for persons trying to obey a divine word while wrestling with the human stuff of sex and family life. The Gospels of Matthew and Luke portray positive images of Jesus's family (Joseph the angel-obeying, protective husband and father; Mary the young and mystery-pondering mother). The Gospels of Mark and John, on the other hand, show Jesus rejecting his own family and calling on his disciples to leave father, mother, sister, brother, wives, and children to follow him. Jesus appears never to have married, and Paul states proudly that he himself lives a disciplined celibacy, even while he advises church members about sex, marriage, and family life.

JESUS: THE PARADOX OF HARD COMMANDS AND COMPASSIONATE EXCEPTIONS

Before turning to specific matters of sex, marriage, and family in the teachings of Jesus, it may be helpful to look briefly at his general attitude toward the Law.

In several passages in the Gospels Jesus subordinates specific strictures of the Law to the overarching rubric of love. For instance, regarding Sabbath observance, Jesus shows no compunction when others are offended that his disciples pluck grain on the Sabbath (Mark 2:23), or when he heals the sick on the Sabbath (Mark 3:1–6). His attitude is summed up in his statement that the Sabbath was made as a blessing for humanity rather than humanity being made subservient to the Sabbath (Mark 2:27). For Jesus, the Law appears to be an instrument for reminding individuals of the virtue of loving-kindness and for encouraging members of the community to treat each other humanely. This seems to be the point of his exchange in Luke with the expert in the Law, who sums up the teachings of the Law and the prophets with only two commandments – to love God with all one's heart, soul, strength, and mind, and to love one's neighbor as oneself (Luke 10:25–37).

On the other hand, in the Sermon on the Mount, Matthew 5–7, Jesus demonstrates not a relaxation of the Law but an intensification of it, especially of the Ten Commandments. Jesus teaches that even to express anger is equivalent to murder (5:21–2); even to experience lust is equivalent to committing adultery (5:27–8); to divorce one's wife, even according to permissible rules (Deuteronomy 24:1), is to risk forcing her to commit adultery (5:31–2).

How can one make sense of this apparently contradictory approach to the Law – the loopholes, on the one hand, and the hard sayings, on the other? Critical to answering this question is the repeated assertion of the Gospels that in Jesus, the word of God has become incarnate – that is, the Law in all of its meaning has been made visibly present in the form of this single human being. All that God has intended to say to humanity about how to live can be known in the life, teachings, death, and Resurrection of Jesus. Speaking in the synagogue in Nazareth, Jesus quotes Isaiah and claims to fulfill the scripture by his own proclamation of good news to the poor, freedom to the oppressed, and sight to the blind (Luke 4:14–30). He announces (Matthew 5:17) that he has come not to abolish the Law or the prophets, but to "fulfill" or complete them – to be the final word about them. The Gospel of John makes explicit this sense of Jesus as the incarnate word with the pronouncement that the "Word," which "was God," became flesh and dwelled among us (John 1:1–14). As Incarnate Word, Jesus presents anew the Law as God intended it and manifests God's continuing communication to humanity.

"I and the Father are one," Jesus says (John 10:30).[2] The authority of God thus resides in Jesus, who constantly refers to the Father as the source of his own authority. He interprets the Law with the freedom that comes from being the Son of God, while he also uses the Law to remind his hearers of God's ultimate command of love. By word and action Jesus undermines merely human traditions in favor of God's ultimate command to love God and one another. Thus, overturning the tables of the money changers in the Temple, he challenges human custom and renews the purpose of God's house as a place of worship and prayer, as a source of mercy and kindness. Whenever the Law gives greater emphasis to human traditions than to the power of divine love to heal, free, and nourish, Jesus

[2] All biblical quotations are from The Holy Bible, New International Version (Grand Rapids, MI: Zondervan Press, 1978). Copyright ©1973, 1978, 1984, 2011 by Biblica, Inc. Used by permission of Zondervan. All rights reserved worldwide. www.zondervan.com. "NIV" and "New International Version" are trademarks registered in the United States Patent and Trademark Office by Biblica, Inc.

turns away from tradition and reminds the people of the generous grace of God; whenever the Law points to the power of divine love and justice to overcome lust, anger, and oppressive human rules, Jesus ratifies and intensifies the Law.

JESUS AND FAMILY

The Gospels depict Jesus as a wandering rabbi with apparently no home of his own, although occasional passages refer to "his house." Nowhere do the Gospels mention that he had a wife or children. Frequently, however, he is portrayed as valuing family life in various ways. In his first miracle, at a wedding in Cana, the blessing of matrimony serves as an illustration of God's abundance, as Jesus turns gallons upon gallons of water into wine. Here the liquid necessity of daily sustenance becomes the means for toasting the divinely ordained relationship of marriage (Genesis 2:24; Matthew 19:3–9). Jesus, the prophesied Immanuel or "God with us," points to the stuff of daily life – wine, marriage, family – as the bearers of divine mystery. He shows that quotidian rituals – preparing meals, serving guests, living together – are means of grace, the places where God is encountered "with us."

That Jesus values the communal and personal benefits of family is also found in his relationship with the siblings in Bethany – sisters Mary and Martha and their brother, Lazarus. Jesus enjoys meals in the company of this family (John 12), and he weeps in grief when he finds that Lazarus has died (John 11:35). It is in their home that he pauses, as if to gain strength and renewed purpose, before entering Jerusalem for his final ministry, trial, death, and Resurrection.

In each of the stories that occur in the home in Bethany, however, it is not family per se that is the focus of Jesus's teaching. Rather he uses every experience in this home – the raising of Lazarus, the conversation with Mary and Martha, a woman's pouring oil on his head to anoint him – to reveal insights about who he is, about his relationship with the Father, and about what that relationship tells us about God. Marriage and family thus constitute a medium for pointing to the ultimate authority and power of God over all of human existence, as well as God's loving care for humanity.

This insistent habit of Jesus to remind his listeners of humanity's relationship to God becomes still more evident in the way in which Jesus diminishes the importance of his bonds to his own natural family and warns against those who place too great a value on the natural order of family. Told that his mother and brothers have come to see him, he replies that his true family is those who hear and obey God's word (Luke 8:19–21). Shockingly, he tells would-be disciples to ignore their filial duties if they wish to follow him (Luke 9:57–62). He excludes from discipleship anyone who clings to brothers, sisters, mothers, fathers, wives, and children (Mark 10:29; Luke 14:26). Disturbingly, he pronounces woe to women who are expectant or are nursing infants (Matthew 24:19) when the time of tribulation comes. The lesson is clear: as important and valuable as family is, hearing and obeying God's word is more so.

That call to obey God's word resounds elsewhere in the Gospels when the Law regarding family comes to the fore. The Law required the people of Israel to look after widows and orphans, those who had been cut off from the protection afforded by customary family structures. The Hebrew scriptures recognized the vulnerability of widows within a tightly structured society based on endogamy and organized around the patriarchal family, and the Law established ways to provide security for these vulnerable women.[3] Similarly, the prophets warned over and over against mistreatment of widows (Isaiah 1:17, 23, 10:2; Jeremiah 7:6, 22:3; Ezekiel 22:7; Zechariah 7:10). In some ways the community's faithfulness (or unfaithfulness) in caring for widows stands in the prophetic literature as a metaphor for Israel's faithfulness (or unfaithfulness) toward Yahweh.

Echoing this prophetic strain, Jesus turns to widows and orphans in his parables as illustrations of those who not only exhibit the freedom of life under divine grace but also serve as exemplars of faithfulness. The widow who gives all that she has (Mark 12:38–44, Luke 21:1–4) stands in contrast to the proud rich men who give a pittance of their wealth; despite her vulnerability to mistreatment by society, she is free under the reign of God, while the rich are imprisoned by pride and miserliness. The widow who insistently demands justice from an indifferent judge exemplifies the faithful praying to God, whose loving care stands in contrast to the judge (Luke 18:1–8). Jesus thus reaffirms the value the Law accords to the widow, but he does this in a way that signals God's final authority over all things.

The Law also recognized the financial and social vulnerability of orphans and warned against mistreating them (Exodus 22:21). Jesus uses the word "orphan" only once, in John 14:18, where he promises his followers that he will not leave them as orphans after his death but will come to them. Here his

[3] Some widows were protected by means of the Jewish law of levirate marriage, in which the brother of a man who has died without children was obligated to marry the man's widow. This obligation seems to have been intended to ensure the continuation of the dead man's name through his heirs, as much as to ensure the well-being of the widow.

close identification of himself with the Father and the disciples – "I am in my father, and you are in me, and I am in you" (verse 20) – emphasizes that God cares so greatly for the "orphans" as to adopt them as children of the Divine. In the same vein, Jesus rebukes his disciples when they try to keep children from pressing around him: "Let the children come to me," he tells them (Luke 18:16), because children exhibit the qualities of those who receive the reign of God (Luke 18:17).

The reign of God brought to reality by Jesus inflects his response to the sort of question that might have been posed commonly to rabbis helping the people understand the demands of the Law in unusual circumstances. In Luke 20:27–38, the Sadducees, who are doubtful about resurrection, pose a question about levirate marriage. Suppose, they say, that a man dies childless, and the eldest of his six brothers marries his widow, but he, too, dies childless, and each of the other brothers in turns marries the widow, and all die childless, and she herself finally dies: whose wife will she be after the resurrection? In his response, Jesus distinguishes between those of "this age," who marry and are given in marriage, and those who are thought to be worthy of the age to come, when men and women will neither marry nor be given in marriage. No reason is given why those worthy of resurrection do not (or should not?) marry, but the implication is clear: for the person prepared for the reign of God, marriage may be a disqualifier, or at least a complication. At any rate, one's ultimate devotion is owed not to marriage or family, but to God.

JESUS AND DIVORCE

While Jesus often rejects tradition to offer a more compassionate interpretation of God's intention in the Law, the one subject on which he does the opposite is divorce. Here he overturns a more lax set of regulations and puts in their place the most rigorous commands about marriage found anywhere in the Bible or, for that matter, in the codes of first-century Judaism or Greco-Roman society.

Jewish law made divorce a one-way option; husbands could divorce their wives by giving them a certificate of divorce, but wives had no such prerogative. Roman law allowed either women or men to initiate divorce. Against these common practices, Jesus calls his listeners to a stricter code: "I tell you that anyone who divorces his wife, except for sexual immorality, makes her the victim of adultery, and anyone who marries a divorced woman commits adultery" (Matthew 5:31–2). No further explanation or narrative context for this saying is given. It is simply set in the midst of a series of statements in which Jesus ratchets up the demands of the Law, making anger equivalent to murder, lust equivalent to adultery, the swearing of oaths anathema, and traditional retributive justice ("an eye for an eye") an indulgence that must give way to love of enemies.

Parallel accounts are told in Matthew 19:1–12, where divorce is permitted in case of the wife's immorality, and in Mark 10:2–12, where not even that exception is permitted. Luke 16:18 similarly offers a one-sentence command against divorce, with no exceptions.

In Matthew 5, Jesus alludes to Deuteronomy 24:1, which says that a man may write a certificate of divorce if his wife "becomes displeasing to him because he finds something indecent about her." Two different schools of thought had developed in first-century Judaism about what "displeasing" and "indecent" meant. One school, following Rabbi Shammai, held that only adultery qualified; another school, following Rabbi Hillel, held more broadly that anything the husband found displeasing in the wife was sufficient grounds for divorce.[4] Jesus appears to hold the more restrictive view.

In Matthew 19:3, the Pharisees ask Jesus whether it is lawful for a man to divorce his wife for any reason, as if to see which school he follows. In his response, Jesus makes clear that divorce was a concession to the brokenness of human nature and the propensity to sin: Moses permitted divorce "because your hearts were hard. But it was not this way from the beginning" (19:8).

Here Jesus comes to the crux of the issue. Referring to Genesis 2:24, Jesus recalls that in the beginning, the Creator "made them male and female" and said, "For this reason a man will leave his father and mother and be united to his wife, and the two will become one flesh." Harking back to the created foundation of the human family, Jesus points to what will become the basis for a sacramental view of marriage and the use of that view as a metaphor for Christ's relationship with the church. This mysterious union of two in one, bound indissolubly through the creative grace of God, makes marriage once again the signpost for God's relationship to humanity. Jesus proclaims that it is as impossible to divorce a man from his wife as it is to divorce humanity from God. Even the attempt has grave consequences.

To sum up, in many ways Jesus redefines the family to mean those who serve the reign of God, and he warns against the entanglements of the natural family as a distraction from that service. Similarly, he redefines the customary view of marriage in his day, transforming marriage from a contract involving property

[4] Johnson, "Divorce," 201. See further Chapter 1 herein by Elliot Dorff.

rights and mutual obligations, and lifting marriage instead into the realm of mystery, as a metaphor for divine–human relationship. He thus poses a difficulty for anyone intent on fulfilling the commands of the Law. On the one hand, he deepens the sense of accountability the Law imposes on the individual conscience (Have I looked with lust? Have I spoken in anger?). On the other hand, he shatters the sense of family that served as a clearly identifiable means of accountability in Judaism.

In Jesus's teaching, adherence to the commands of God remains objectively measurable: old-fashioned adultery remains just that, abuse of orphans and widows is still abuse, and immoral behaviour still matters in the eyes of God. But Jesus has opened the pathway toward a much stricter law – one by which the individual soul is governed by her knowledge of her own inward desires and failings and, in turn, is known as well by God. That is a law not easily codified.

PAUL: DRAWING GENERAL GUIDANCE FROM SPECIFIC CASES

Scholars agree that Paul's letters were the earliest writings now found in the New Testament, composed before the Gospels and the other epistles. The letters indisputably attributed to him are Romans, 1 and 2 Corinthians, Galatians, Philippians, 1 Thessalonians, and Philemon. The deutero-Pauline letters of Colossians, Ephesians, and 2 Thessalonians are widely regarded as written by someone else assuming the mantle of Paul's authority. Paul put his faith to pen sometime between 50 and 66 CE, decades after the phenomenon experienced by the early church as the Resurrection of Jesus from the dead, which occurred during the prefecture of Pontius Pilate, who served from 26 to 37 CE.

Paul thus represents the earliest "witness" to the risen Christ, in the sense that his is the first recorded experience of Christ and the first written instructions on how the faithful are to live in the new age ushered in by the Resurrection. At the same time, his writings appear to draw on teachings and traditions already circulating among the communities that formed the first-century church. For instance, admonishing the church in Corinth on how to observe the Sabbath meal (1 Corinthians 11:23–6), Paul uses language identical or similar to the words of Jesus at the Last Supper recounted in Matthew 26:26 (cf. Mark 14:22 and Luke 22:17). Thus, just as Jesus preached and ministered within a context of Jewish traditions, so Paul – himself a Jew who had been a faithful adherent of those traditions – preached and taught within a Christian tradition that was established before his own conversion into it.

More significantly, the teachings of Jesus and Paul – as well as the early church – are marked and shaped by the felt immediacy of the end of time and the beginning of God's reign. The reign of God is at hand, proclaims Jesus, as he sends out the disciples and tells them what to preach (Luke 10:9). Likewise, Paul, in 1 Thessalonians 4–5, makes the eschatological present an urgent foundation for faithfulness to new life in Christ – as if to say, God has taken charge in a new and real way, so behave accordingly.

For Jesus, the sign of the nearness of God's reign is himself. For Paul, the proof of the imminent end of history is the death and Resurrection of Jesus Christ, an event that has ushered in a new age that demands a new form of obedience. Faithfulness now can neither simply adhere to the old law and tradition nor give way to lawlessness. Instead, the faithful are called to discern – to "test and prove" – God's will (Romans 12) for life in an age that is already but not yet fully the reign of God's righteousness. For Paul, discernment depends on the Holy Spirit (Romans 8:1–27) and a new law revealed in Christ. This is the law not of Torah, but of love. Like Jesus, Paul finds all of the Law summed up in a single commandment to love God and one's neighbor (Romans 13:8–10; Galatians 5:13–14). Faith active in love is the defining power of the new age and is borne to (and born within) the believer through the Holy Spirit. The Christian life must imitate the active love of God revealed in the death and Resurrection of Jesus Christ. Whatever law governs marriage, family life, and sexuality must be discerned by the help of the Holy Spirit within the contours of that unparalleled divine love.

Paul's letters thus comprise a remarkable set of examples of spiritual discernment. His writings are not a systematic unfolding of his theology. They are, rather, responses to specific questions or controversies that arose within particular Christian communities. His views on sex, marriage, and family are thus developed episodically as he seeks to hear the Word of God speaking to the faithful.

MARRIAGE AND SEXUAL MORALITY

The clearest outline of Paul's understanding of marriage is found in 1 Corinthians 5–7. Here, as in other epistles, Paul draws on both contemporary philosophical currents and Jewish tradition.[5] At the same time, just as Paul

[5] Horrell, "I Corinthians," 58.

calls upon Christians not to conform to the teachings of the world, but to be transformed by the renewal of their thinking (Romans 12:2), he himself transforms the conventions of the day by his attention to Christ.

As in all of Paul's writings, one needs to understand the context he is addressing. In the case of the Corinthian church, an apparent division had grown up in view of the expected imminent return of Christ. Some Corinthian Christians believed that the call to holiness meant that they should abstain from sex, even in marriage. Separating the spiritual from the physical, they renounced the desires of this world. Other Corinthian Christians apparently believed that they had been guaranteed salvation and therefore could indulge every desire and could practice any licentiousness; their place in the reign of God was secure. Paul advises a middle way, which opens the door to a revolutionary way of thinking about sexuality, marriage, and family.

In 1 Corinthians 7:2–4, Paul echoes the Jewish understanding of marital duty: it is the husband's obligation to satisfy his wife sexually, just as it is the wife's obligation to satisfy her husband. Paul thus affirms the goodness of sex. But he also reminds the community that sex is good only within the covenant of marriage: "each man . . . with his own wife, and each woman . . . with her own husband." In the previous chapter, he has noted that sex with a prostitute is immoral for the very same reason that sex with one's marriage partner is good: because, as Genesis 2:24 affirms, the sexual union of man and woman makes them "one flesh."

Here the Incarnation becomes of paramount importance, as in the Gospels. None of Paul's views on sex, marriage, or divorce can be separated from his Christology. For just as Christ was raised from the dead, so believers will be raised: "Do you not know that your bodies are members of Christ himself?" (1 Corinthians 6:15). One must take care, then, to respect one's body, a "temple of the Holy Spirit" (6:19) and to "honor God" with one's body (6:20). In a covenantal relationship of marriage, one honors God by honoring one's marriage partner with one's body – and one dishonors God by sexual activity outside of the covenant relationship. Paul says something similar in 1 Thessalonians, advising that the faithful should control their bodies "in a way that is holy and honorable," avoiding the lust of pagans (1 Thessalonians 4:4–5). Paul emphasizes, importantly, the quality of marriage, which should be marked by faithfulness, holiness, and mutual care.

Paul goes on: although the husband and wife might decide to abstain from sex for a time, they should do so only by mutual consent, and only for the purpose of fasting and prayer, then they should "come together again" (1 Corinthians 7:5). Sex, in other words, is a constituent part of a good marriage. Addressing those

Corinthians who would extirpate sexuality from life altogether, he says that to do so would be wrong.

Jewish law emphasized that one reason for marriage was procreation. Paul does not mention this, owing perhaps to his view of the imminent end of time. (Why have more children, when they are likely to distract you from service to the Lord and also likely to be drawn into Christ's new kingdom before they reach maturity?)

The Law's other reason for marriage, however, was that it was a means to avoid sexual immorality. Paul agrees. This is not an ascetic view of sex, however. Paul does not say that believers should stay away from sex or should get married only if their sexual impulses are too strong. Rather, Paul recognizes that different Christians have different gifts – a view he reiterates in 1 Corinthians 12, the famous passage about the various parts of the body of Christ. He wishes that others would have his gift of celibacy, but he also grants the giftedness of those called to a different way of being in community. This, too, is freedom in Christ, who calls and strengthens married persons to submit themselves in love and mutual care to each other's needs. Importantly, the emphasis throughout 1 Corinthians 7 rests on the interdependence of the marriage partners – an interdependence echoed in 1 Corinthians 11:11: "in the Lord, woman is not independent of man, nor is man independent of woman."[6]

Paul's personal view ("not from the Lord") is that it is best to stay unmarried, because history is coming to a close, and because marriage can distract from service to God (1 Corinthians 7:8–9). But again, his understanding of the Christian community as the "body of Christ" leads him to affirm the different gifts of the different parts of the body. That he himself views marriage as a good appears evident in his admonition that believers married to nonbelievers should not separate themselves from their mates: "For the unbelieving husband has been sanctified through his [believing] wife, and the unbelieving wife has been sanctified through her believing husband. Otherwise your children would be unclean, but as it is, they are holy" (1 Corinthians 7:14). Much as Jesus conveys a sense of marriage as a means of understanding the grace of God, so Paul suggests that marriage can actually be the path to sanctification. Paul thus ratifies and expands Jesus's meaning: marriage in the Christian community goes from being a covenant of faithfulness to becoming a sacrament of union and growth in holiness.

[6] Furnish, *The Moral Teaching of Paul*, 34.

The concept of covenant appears in many varieties in the Hebrew Bible. Covenant creates a relationship bound by certain behaviour on both sides, with consequences for failure to fulfill the oaths that confirm the relationship. As the basis of Yahweh's relationship with Israel, traced to Genesis and Deuteronomy, the covenant between God and the people came to be seen as God's promise of everlasting protection and preference in exchange for Israel's faithful obedience to the Law. In Malachi 2:14 and Proverbs 2:17, marriage itself is described as a covenantal relationship.[7] Perhaps the most striking use of the notion of covenant in the Hebrew Bible appears in Hosea, where God tells the prophet to marry and have children with a promiscuous woman; she will serve as God's metaphor for the adulterous behaviour of Israel, the people who have been unfaithful to the covenant between them and Yahweh.

The deutero-Pauline letters convey some sense of the covenantal nature of marriage through their "household instructions," which outline responsibilities and obligations of husbands and wives toward each other. These passages are often criticized or outright rejected for their apparent perpetuation of a hierarchical family structure (Ephesians 5:22–33; Colossians 3:18–4:1, Titus 2:1–10; see also 1 Peter 2:13–3:7). Wives, for instance, are exhorted to "submit" to their husbands, as the husband is "the head of the wife." The writers of these letters may be repeating conventional codes of etiquette for their time and place.

What distinguishes these instructions from conventions of the day, however, is the foundation of the marital relationship on "reverence for Christ." Wives should submit to their husbands as the church submits to Christ (Ephesians 5:24); husbands should love their wives as Christ loves the church (5:25) and as husbands love their own bodies (5:28). The quotation of Genesis 2:24 in verse 31 – "the two will become one flesh" – points to the union of male and female not only with each other, but also with Christ: "for we are members of his body" (5:30). "This is a profound mystery [*mysterion; sacramentum*] – but I am talking about Christ and the church" (5:32). Thus, as in 1 Corinthians, mutual care, respect, and love move beyond a purely covenantal relationship of mutual obligations. Rather, the sacramental relationship, participating in the mystery of the Resurrection, nurtures the married pair in holiness.

Such holiness has no room for sexual impurity, which impedes the Christian's growth and freedom in new life in Christ. Letters by Paul and

7 For a thorough overview of the many nuances of the Hebrew and Greek words in the Bible translated as "covenant," see Viviano, "Covenant," 130–8. See Chapter 13 herein by Barbara Pitkin on John Calvin's views of the marital covenant.

the deutero-Pauline writers comment about sexual impurity, whose manifestations include incest (1 Corinthians 6:9), sex with a prostitute (1 Corinthians 6:15–17), lust and idolatry (Colossians 3:5–6), adultery (Hebrews 13:4), and homosexuality (Romans 1:24–7; 1 Corinthians 6:9; 1 Timothy 1:10).[8] As 1 Thessalonians 4:3–8 makes clear, sexual immorality opposes God's will that the Christian should be sanctified, should live a holy life. This passage also underscores the principal reason for avoiding sexual immorality: it is not the sexual act itself that constitutes sin, but the wrong of another, the taking advantage of a brother or sister in the community. This activity tears at the fabric of the community – or, to use Paul's own metaphor of the church, it wounds the body, which also is the body of Christ.

The same lesson appears more fully in Galatians 5, where life in the spirit is contrasted with life in the flesh. The context is one in which Paul advises the community to fulfill the law of love for one another and to avoid destroying one another (and the community) by provocation, envy, and arrogance. The "fruit of the spirit" – "love, joy, peace, forbearance, kindness, goodness, faithfulness, gentleness, and self-control" (Galatians 5:22–3) – is contrasted to the "acts of the flesh" – "sexual immorality, impurity and debauchery, idolatry and witchcraft, hatred, discord, jealousy, fits of rage, selfish ambition, dissensions, factions and envy, drunkenness, orgies, and the like" (5:19–21). It is worth noting that these acts of the flesh include violent emotions as well as sexual activity per se. Those freed by the Spirit for life in Christ must seek to live fully into that freedom, which leads to love, rather than continuing to be enslaved by the passions that lead to death.

In addressing the question of divorce, Paul echoes the teaching of Jesus and confirms the commitment of the young church to what it has heard from its Lord. "To the married I give this command (not I, but the Lord): A wife must not separate from her husband. But if she does, she must remain unmarried or else be reconciled to her husband. And a husband must not divorce his wife" (1 Corinthians 7:10–11).

In summary, then, Paul's teaching on marriage emphasizes the mutual obligation and care of marriage partners for each other; recognizes that Christians have (and should celebrate) a variety of gifts when it comes to their needs and capacities for sex; admonishes married couples not to abstain from sex in marriage, while remaining sexually faithful to that one

[8] Strikingly, in view of continuing debates in the twenty-first-century church about homosexuality, the Gospels nowhere record that Jesus himself ever said anything about men having sexual relations with men, or women with women, nor about the Mosaic laws on this point (Leviticus 18:22, 20:13). Paul includes terms referring to homosexuality in two of his lists of immoral acts, specifically at Romans 1:24–7 and 1 Corinthians 6:9.

relationship; reiterates the command of the Lord regarding the impermissibility of divorce; makes room for flexibility in allowing believers to remain married to unbelieving spouses, unless their spouses choose to leave; and holds forth a sacramental notion of marriage as a means of grace and sanctification.

FAMILY

Taking its cue from its Lord, the early church in many ways redefined the family. Just as Jesus replaced the importance of kinship ties with an imperative of obedience to the Gospel (Luke 14:26), so the early church came to understand that traditional family norms could not bind the faithful community. This is clear in Paul's advice that believers need not separate from their unbelieving spouses: the family of faith may or may not include others in one's legal family; what matters is one's relationship to Christ.

The new birth in Christ indeed creates a whole new order of siblings, because those led to new life in Christ "are the children of God," (Romans 8:14), "adopted" as sons and daughters of God (Romans 8:23; Galatians 4:5), and "heirs" of what God has granted to Christ in glory (Romans 8:17). This inheritance obtains regardless of convention or social distinction. Since, in Christ, all are "children of God through faith … there is neither Jew nor Greek, neither slave nor free, nor is there male and female; for you all are one in Christ Jesus" (Galatians 3:26, 28).

One consequence of this new understanding of family is the beginning of a new social structure. Like Judaism, early Christianity defined itself in many ways as existing over against the surrounding culture – as "called out" (*ecclesia*) from the world. Unlike Judaism, however, the distinction of the faithful community from its surroundings depended on the vision of the church as a new family undefined by blood relationship, national identity, or even ritual practice. This vision undermined the traditions of patriarchy and hierarchy, the authority of law courts, and household relationships like those between slaves and masters.

The new family has its most poignant expression in Paul's letter to Philemon, whom he addresses as "friend and fellow worker" and, later, "brother." The crux of the letter is Paul's urging Philemon to receive back his slave Onesimus. No reason is given why Onesimus has been absent from Philemon and present with Paul, but during Paul's current imprisonment Onesimus has become his "son" – a reference to his conversion. This new existence for Onesimus now brings him, in Paul's view, into a different relationship with Philemon as well: "He is very dear to me but even dearer to you, both as a fellow man and as a brother in the Lord (1:16)." As Paul has said in Galatians, there is neither free nor slave, but all are brothers and sisters in Christ and therefore are bound to each other through love in Christ. Love, then, active through faith under the guidance of the Holy Spirit, becomes the primary law that claims obedience of the individual Christian, whether married or celibately unmarried, in the family of the church.

RECOMMENDED READING

Furnish, Victor Paul. *The Moral Teaching of Paul: Selected Issues*. 2nd ed., revised. Nashville, TN: Abingdon Press, 1985.

Johnson, Luke Timothy. "The Complex Witness of the New Testament Concerning Marriage, Family, and Sexuality." In *Contested Issues in Christian Origins and the New Testament*, 659–78. Leiden and Boston: Brill, 2013.

Johnson, Luke Timothy and Mark D. Jordan. "Christianity." In *Sex, Marriage, and Family in World Religions*, edited by Don S. Browning, M. Christian Green, and John Witte, Jr., 77–97. New York: Columbia University Press, 2006.

Ruden, Sarah. *Paul among the People: The Apostle Reinterpreted and Reimagined in His Own Time*. New York: Pantheon Books, 2010.

Schnackenburg, Rudolf. *The Moral Teaching of the New Testament*. New York: Herder and Herder, 1971.

Strawn, Brent A., ed. *The Oxford Encyclopedia of the Bible and Law*. New York: Oxford University Press, 2015.

3

Emperor Constantine

Judith Evans Grubbs

BIOGRAPHICAL INTRODUCTION

Constantine was born in the mid-270s CE in the Roman city of Naissus (modern Nis in Serbia). His father, Constantius, was later elevated to the rank of Caesar, or junior emperor, as a member of the four-man Tetrarchy established by the emperor Diocletian (r. 284–305). Upon Constantius' death in York in 306, Constantine was acclaimed emperor by the army there; this was contrary to the line of succession established by the Tetrarchy and led to conflict with several other claimants to the western empire. In October 312, Constantine defeated Maxentius (son of Diocletian's former co-emperor, Maximian) at the Milvian Bridge outside of Rome; he attributed this victory to the Christian God and to encouragement from a divine vision he had had sometime before the battle. From 313 to 324, Constantine ruled the western half of the Roman Empire in tandem with the eastern emperor, Licinius (who had married Constantine's sister). Together they ended all persecution of Christians and gave Christianity legal standing in 313. However, theirs was a troubled alliance and ended in late 324, when Constantine conquered Licinius and took over his territories. From then until his death in 337, Constantine was sole ruler throughout the empire and even established a new imperial capital, Constantinople (modern Istanbul), on the Bosporus. He had adopted Christianity as his personal religion after the battle of the Milvian Bridge, and throughout his reign he fostered the growth of Christianity among his subjects and made large benefactions to Christian churches. However, he did not make Christianity the official faith of the empire or outlaw paganism; those acts were left to his successor, Theodosius I, in the late fourth century. Constantine died on 22 May 337, in Nicomedia on the Black Sea, having been baptized on his deathbed.

FIGURE 3.1. Emperor Constantine I the Great (ca. 274–337) (mosaic), Byzantine / San Marco, Venice, Italy / Bridgeman Images

Constantine was neither a great theologian nor a great jurist. He finds a place in this collection not for his intellectual achievements, but as a powerful ruler and lawgiver who used his authority to benefit (and benefit from) the rapidly growing religion of Christianity. In addition to ending the persecution of Christians and granting legal status to their religion, Constantine intervened actively in theological matters (most notably at the first ecumenical Council of Nicaea in 325) and erected several major church complexes in Rome and in the Holy Land. Few of his laws on marriage and family matters show signs of Christian motivation or influence, but as a Christian ruler who actively legislated on the family, he provided an example to later emperors, most notably Justinian in the sixth century.[1]

CONSTANTINE'S LEGISLATION ON MARRIAGE AND FAMILY

As the longest-reigning emperor since Augustus, Constantine was in a better position to influence Roman law than most other emperors. The remains of about 350 constitutions attributed to him survive in the legal sources, most of them found in some form in the Theodosian Code. Approximately 25 percent of these laws in some way concern the family or sexual relationships.[2]

There is the question of how much of this legislation really can be called Constantine's and how much is in fact the work of imperial secretaries or members of Constantine's consistory. The amount of an emperor's responsibility in making the laws of his reign would depend on the individual ruler. By all accounts Constantine was very much a hands-on emperor, and I assume that he had control over what his legislation said and approved its wording, whether or not he had a hand in its composition. This does not mean that Constantine was responsible for initiating all his laws; on the contrary, the emperor was often reacting to reports or requests from magistrates to resolve disputes arising from private cases.[3]

Constantine's legislation on the family can be divided into five general categories. This is not to imply that Constantine himself employed such a classification: this legislation is spread over twenty-five years and is only part of

[1] What follows is an abridged version of my 1993 article, "Constantine and Imperial Legislation on the Family," originally published in *The Theodosian Code*, edited by Jill Harries and Ian Wood (Duckworth 1993; reprinted with a new preface by Bristol Classical Press, 2010). In addition to abbreviating the text, I have deleted some footnotes and updated others. I thank Bloomsbury Publishing and Professors Harries and Wood for permission to reprint this chapter.

[2] Evans Grubbs, *Law and Family in Late Antiquity*, 51; ibid., 342–9, gives a list of all Constantine's laws relevant to the family. Laws are cited from the Mommsen-Meyer edition of 1905.

[3] See further Harries, *Law and Empire in Late Antiquity*.

a large body of laws enacted on many different matters. This chapter briefly surveys the legislation on marriage and the family as a whole, focusing on some of the more interesting and innovative laws.

INHERITANCE AND THE TRANSMISSION OF PROPERTY

The financial aspects of matrimony, especially questions of inheritance, dowry, and gift-giving, had always been of great interest to classical jurists and to the upper-class elite for whom they wrote.[4] This was still the case in the Late Empire, and Constantine was responsible for several reforms of the Roman laws of succession making the transfer of property easier and less encumbered by legal constraints. Of the twenty-six extant Constantinian laws on the transmission of family property, more than three-quarters date from the first decade of his reign, among them the famous constitution of 320 repealing the Augustan penalties for celibacy and childlessness (CTh 8.16.1).[5]

To encourage marriage and childbearing among upper-class Romans, the first emperor, Augustus, had deprived unmarried men between the ages of twenty-five and sixty and unmarried women between twenty and fifty of the ability to receive inheritances or legacies from those beyond the sixth degree of kinship. Those who were married but childless could take only half of what had been left them, and only a tenth of their spouse's property (unless they had been granted the *ius liberorum*, giving them the same privileges as those who had children). When the recipient of a legacy could not take it, it could be claimed by eligible relatives of the deceased; failing that, it went to the public treasury. After the Edict of Caracalla in 212, these restrictions would have applied to all imperial subjects, and by the time of Caracalla unclaimed legacies were going directly to the imperial fisc.[6]

The effects and extent of application of Augustus's laws have often been exaggerated. In fact, these restrictions did not apply to most inheritances within families. They were originally aimed at those Romans whose moral and social behaviour was of the greatest importance to Augustus – the Roman senatorial aristocracy and the wealthier and more distinguished classes in general. The Augustan laws on marriage and adultery were long a source of irritation to the upper classes. Nor were they ever particularly effective in increasing the population and improving the morality of well-born citizens

4 For pre-Constantinian marriage legislation, see Treggiari, *Roman Marriage*.

5 The repeal of the Augustan legislation is discussed more fully in Evans Grubbs, *Law and Family in Late Antiquity*, 103–39.

6 On the Augustan legislation, see Astolfi, *La lex Julia et Papia*. The Edict of Caracalla granted Roman citizenship to all free inhabitants of the empire.

On 31 January 320, an edict addressed "to the people" was issued from Serdica (modern Sofia); on 1 April, it was posted at Rome. Seven excerpts from this edict survive. Three of these, preserved only in the Code of Justinian, relax the very strict rules regarding the proper wording and witnessing of wills (CJ 6.9.9.; 6.23.15; 6.37.21). Two excerpts, found in the Theodosian Code, mitigate what had been very harsh treatment of delinquent debtors (CTh 3.2.1; 11.7.3).[7] But the most famous decision of this edict was the repeal of the Augustan inheritance restrictions (CTh 8.16.1). Constantine proclaimed that the unmarried and childless were no longer at a disadvantage in regard to inheritance and were freed from the "imminent terror of the laws." But Constantine did not relax the restrictions on inheritance between childless spouses. This disapproval of legacies between spouses is in keeping with earlier Roman law, and restrictions remained on inheritance between childless spouses for almost another century.[8]

Discussions of Constantine's repeal of the Augustan penalties usually ignore the original context and imply that it was a separate law in and of itself, whose sole purpose was the lifting of the financial penalties on celibates. But it was in fact part of a wide-ranging law designed to facilitate inheritance procedures in general and to prevent the mistreatment of debtors. The surviving extracts indicate that in enacting it Constantine claimed to be liberating his subjects from a number of arcane and oppressive regulations that had inhibited their property rights. By abolishing what had always been an unpopular law, whose effectiveness must have seriously deteriorated by the fourth century, Constantine was conferring a favor on the wealthier classes, who were the only ones really affected by the Augustan laws. Foremost among these beneficiaries was the senatorial aristocracy of Rome. Much of Constantine's legislation in the first decade of his reign was aimed specifically at Rome, to demonstrate his good will and his desire to eradicate the abuses of Maxentius. It is in this context that we should see the law of 320.

The usual explanation for Constantine's repeal of the penalties for celibacy and childlessness attributes its enactment to Christian motives. Proponents of this interpretation point to a passage in Eusebius's *Life of Constantine* (VC 4.26). The implication is that Constantine was showing his support for Christian asceticism by repealing the unfair penalties such practices entailed. Certainly, Constantine's repeal of the Augustan penalties would have

7 There are problems in dating some of these extracts, but most scholars agree in joining them.

8 Rescinded in 410 (CTh 8.17.2 and 3) in the eastern half of the empire, but evidently not in the west until the reception of the Theodosian Code there in 439. Gifts between living spouses were forbidden under Roman law.

benefited those Christian celibates who were wealthy enough to be affected by the law. But how many wealthy ascetics were there in the Roman west in 320? At that time most Christians, wealthy or not, lived in the eastern half of the empire, still ruled by Licinius, and Constantine's laws would not have applied to them until after Licinius' defeat in 324. This law was directed at Rome, especially the senatorial aristocracy of Rome, where Christians were still very much a minority. The well-known enthusiasm for Christian asceticism among some senatorial families is a post-Constantinian phenomenon, no doubt encouraged by his removal of the old inheritance restrictions.

Constantine's edict of 320 was a masterstroke of political strategy, a law pagans and Christians alike could applaud. At the expense of some loss to the imperial treasury, easily made up by other measures, Constantine removed a thorn from the side of the wealthier classes, particularly the senatorial aristocracy. At the same time, he could be seen as promoting Christian ascetic ideals, and his action could be interpreted by contemporary and future Christians as a fundamentally "Christian" law.

BETROTHAL AND DIVORCE

The exchange of gifts by betrothed couples was an old Roman tradition. In classical Roman law, a distinction had been made between gifts given by the prospective husband specifically for the purpose of cementing the marriage alliance, and gifts made by either fiancé(e) simply out of affection. The latter type, usually of less value, could not be reclaimed by the giver if the marriage did not take place, but gifts given "for the sake of contracting an alliance" could be (unless the giver had been responsible for breaking the betrothal). Though logical, such a distinction could lead to confusion in practice, and many third-century imperial rescripts respond to requests for advice on broken betrothals and the status of prenuptial gifts.

Constantine did away with the distinction between the two types of gifts. In a law of 319 (CTh 3.5.2), he declared that henceforth, if a betrothal were broken off unilaterally, the partner responsible for the break-off must forfeit to the other any gifts given or received. The law also regulated the return of gifts in the event that one fiancé(e) died before the marriage took place. It was later modified by a law of 336 (CTh 3.5.6), giving special status to betrothals in which a kiss had been exchanged between the betrothed. In those cases, if either partner died, half of any prenuptial gifts given by the man were to be returned and half kept by his fiancée or, if she had died, by her heirs. This legislation has been seen as the first appearance in Roman law of the concept of *arrhae sponsaliciae*, the contractual exchange of betrothal gifts, although the term *arrhae sponsaliciae* is not found in extant Roman law until 380, by which time a penalty had been added: the party breaking the betrothal without justification had to return four times the value of the gifts that he or she had received (CTh 3.5.10–11, 3.6.1, 3.11.1).[9]

In 332, another law set a statute of limitations of two years on betrothals (CTh 3.5.4 and 5). If a man had made a betrothal agreement with a girl but had not married her after two years or more, she could marry someone else. But if she had been engaged to a soldier and married someone else before the two years elapsed, her father or guardian was to be relegated to an island.

Constantine's legislation indicates that he considered betrothal a serious undertaking not to be entered into lightly. His laws diverge significantly from classical Roman law in making a betrothal a binding legal contract and enacting sanctions against those who break it. The role of possible Christian or Near Eastern influences on these laws is debatable: betrothal pacts were always considered serious matters by upper-class Romans before and after Constantine, and in very early Roman law they had been legally actionable. Most of the evidence for the importance of betrothal among Christians is post-Constantinian.[10]

There is more evidence for Christian motives behind the divorce law, enacted in 331 and addressed to the praetorian prefect Ablabius, in which Constantine drastically restricted the legal possibilities for initiating a unilateral divorce (CTh 3.16.1). In classical law, either partner could end a marriage by notifying the other of his or her intentions. A husband who repudiated his wife would have to return her dowry, though he might retain part of it if there were any children or if her behaviour had been open to question. Under Augustus' law on adultery, husbands were required to divorce adulterous wives; if they did not, they were themselves liable to charges of *lenocinium* (pimping).[11]

Under the new law of Constantine, a woman could repudiate her husband for only three reasons: if he was a murderer, an employer of magic, or a destroyer of tombs. In those cases, she would receive praise and recover her entire dowry. But if she repudiated him for any other reason, she would be deported to an island, and her husband would get everything she owned, "down to a hairpin." A husband could legally divorce his wife only if she was an adulteress, a poisoner, or a procuress. Otherwise, he had to return her entire

[9] Anné, *Les rites des fiançailles et la donation pour cause de mariage sous le Bas-Empire*; Evans Grubbs, *Law and Family in Late Antiquity*, 156–71.

[10] Evans Grubbs, *Law and Family in Late Antiquity*, 172–82.

[11] McGinn, *Prostitution, Sexuality, and the Law in Ancient Rome*, 140–247.

dowry – as he would probably have had to do anyway under earlier law. He was also not supposed to remarry, but if he did, his former wife had the right to enter his home and seize the second wife's dowry.

In effect, a spouse could initiate a unilateral divorce with impunity only if the other partner had been guilty of a serious crime. Murder, magic, destruction of tombs, and adultery by or with a married woman were all capital crimes in the Late Empire, for which there could be neither appeal nor pardon, and which would probably have resulted in the guilty person's execution. Furthermore, unlike earlier imperial legislation, Constantine's law was much harder on a woman who wanted divorce than on a man. However, it applied only to cases where one partner wanted a divorce and the other refused. Divorce by mutual consent, which was probably more common than unilateral repudiation, was still not penalized. In any case, the law of 331 was repealed less than thirty-five years later by the emperor Julian. And although restrictions on unilateral divorce were reintroduced by fifth-century emperors, divorce by mutual consent remained legal until Justinian prohibited it in 542 – and his law was soon repealed by his successor, Justin.[12]

Constantine's divorce law is notable for its unusual vocabulary: eight words in it appear nowhere else in the Theodosian Code. The odd vocabulary and the distinctly nonclassical idea that an unjustly divorced wife could invade her ex-husband's home and seize his new wife's dowry led Edoardo Volterra to suggest that this law was written by someone outside the imperial chancellery, someone unfamiliar with classical law – in fact, a Christian cleric.[13] This is unlikely, but Volterra was not alone in attributing it to Christian influence. Until about thirty years ago, scholars generally agreed in seeing Christian inspiration behind CTh 3.16.1, since condemnation of divorce goes back to the New Testament and was echoed by many ante-Nicene writers. More recent work has questioned this interpretation, however.[14] The law as we have it gives no indication of Christian motivation, and in fact it conflicts with Christian teachings in several respects. Constantine allowed divorce for reasons other than adultery, whereas Christian writers stressed that adultery by the wife was the only possible justification. Moreover, while Christian writers believed that both men and women should be held to the same standard of sexual conduct,

12 Julian's law is known from Ambrosiaster, *Liber quaestionum veteris et novi testamenti* 115.12. Justinian's law: *Novel* 117.10 (dated 542), repealed by Justin, *Novel* 140 in 566.

13 Volterra, "Intorno ad alcune costituzioni di Costantino," 61–89; idem, "Quelques remarques sur le style des constitutions de Constantin," 325–34.

14 Castello, "Assenza d'ispirazione cristiana in CTh 3.16.1," 203–12; Bagnall, "Church, State and Divorce in Late Roman Egypt," 41–61.

Constantine upheld a double standard. And although Christians felt that a marriage could not be dissolved even if both partners wished it, Constantine's law does not ban divorce by mutual consent.

Yet Christian doctrine in the early fourth century was not a monolithic body of beliefs agreed upon by Christians throughout the empire. In fact, the majority of ante-Nicene writers (following Matthew 19:9) believed that divorce was justified, indeed necessary, if the wife had committed adultery (one of the few causes for divorce allowed by Constantine). Most Christians probably would not have thought that Constantine's law differed significantly from their own beliefs.

Nor, as Antti Arjava suggested, would most pagans.[15] Contrary to the once-popular view of pagan Roman society as a hotbed of immorality where multiple marriages were common, divorce seems to have been rare outside the senatorial aristocracy, and not very common even there.[16] Most Romans and Greeks did not approve of divorce, and they especially disliked the idea of the wife initiating a divorce. Thus, although Christians were certainly the most outspoken opponents of divorce, they may have been expressing in extreme form what many others felt.

As with the repeal of the inheritance penalties for celibacy, then, CTh 3.16.1 responded to concerns that were not exclusively Christian. Still, we have to ask why this constitution, so harsh and so opposed to classical law, was enacted in 331. It is possible that there had been an increase in the number of unilateral divorces, especially those initiated by women. From 329 to 337 Ablabius, a Christian, was praetorian prefect, and thus the emperor's proxy in the court of appeal for divorce cases. In 331, he was also consul; the divorce law is addressed to him. Perhaps Ablabius had suggested to Constantine that it was time to put a stop to the freedom of one partner to break up a marriage, particularly in view of the emperor's professed Christian beliefs.[17]

This is all hypothetical. But we may recall that in 320 Constantine had repealed the Augustan legislation penalizing the unmarried and childless (CTh 8.16.1). Whatever Constantine's reasons for repealing the Augustan laws, he surely did not intend to encourage the dissolution of already existing unions.

[15] Antti Arjava, "Divorce in Later Roman Law," *Arctos* 22 (1988): 5–21.

[16] Kajanto, "On Divorce among the Common People of Rome," 99–113; Raepset-Charlier, "Ordre sénatorial et divorce sous le Haut Empire," 161–73; Treggiari, "Divorce Roman Style," 31–46.

[17] Sargenti, "Il diritto privato nella legislazione di Costantino," 280–1. See further Evans Grubbs, *Law and Family*, 253–60.

PROHIBITED UNIONS

In contrast to the divorce law, which sought to prevent the dissolution of marriages, other laws forbade and penalized unions between those of different social status, particularly between freeborn people and slaves.

Roman law had never recognized as legal marriages the sexual relationships of slaves, nor those of free people with slaves. Before Constantine, however, unions of free men and slave women, though deprived of the privileges of legitimate marriage, were not prohibited or punished. A free woman who cohabited with someone else's slave fell under the provisions of the *senatus consultum Claudianum* of 52 CE. If the owner of the woman's partner condoned the union, she was reduced to the status of his freedwoman; if not, she became his slave, and children of the union were also slaves. Under the marriage legislation of Augustus, senators and their descendants could not contract legal marriage with former slaves or with actors, and freeborn people could not marry prostitutes, pimps, or others branded with legal infamy. If a man of senatorial rank had wanted to live in a monogamous relationship with his freedwoman, she could have been his concubine – a perfectly acceptable relationship, though not accorded the privileges of legitimate marriage. Their children would be illegitimate, but could still have received legacies from their father if he included them in his will.[18]

Constantine extended the Augustan prohibition on marriage between senators and freedwomen to apply also to the marriages of local and provincial dignitaries with former slaves or the daughters of slaves or other women of low birth or occupation. Children born from such unions would be illegitimate. Furthermore, he threatened with severe sanctions men who attempted to give financial benefits, either during their lifetime or in their wills, to any children they had by such women or to the women themselves (CTh 4.6.2 and 3).[19]

Even harsher was the punishment ordained for a *decurion* (town councilor) who forsook his municipal responsibilities to take refuge on another landholder's estate and cohabited with one of the landholder's slaves. The *decurion* was to be deported, his property was to be handed over to his town council, and the slave woman was to be sent to the mines (CTh 12.1.6). Four laws modifying the provisions of the first-century law on the unions of free women with someone else's slave were promulgated under Constantine (CTh 4.12.1–4).

[18] *Sc. Claudianum* (Claudian decree of the Senate): Tacitus, *Annales* 12.53; Gaius, *Inst.* 1.84; *Sententiae Pauli* II.xxi[a] (in *FIRA* II, 346–50); trans. Evans Grubbs, *Women and the Law*, 145–6. Augustan law: *Dig.* 23.2.44 pr (Paul); Evans Grubbs, ibid., 149–50.

[19] McGinn, "The Social Policy of Emperor Constantine," 57–71; Evans Grubbs, "Illegitimacy and Inheritance Disputes in the Late Roman Empire," 25–49.

And if a free woman was cohabiting with her own slave, they were both to be exiled and their children deprived of all inheritance rights. If any such unions were discovered in the future, the woman would be executed and the slave burned alive (CTh 9.9.1).[20]

The unions Constantine sought to suppress were not promiscuous or extra-marital affairs symptomatic of some sort of general moral decline, as has sometimes been supposed, nor is there any reason to see Christian influence in these laws. It is clear from the wording of this legislation that it is aimed at long-term quasi-marital relationships, and virtually every one of these laws mentions children whom the parents had wished to make legitimate heirs. What Constantine seems to have found so alarming, in fact, was the possibility that children of slaves or others of low social status would inherit the rights and property of freeborn and socially respectable people. He was particularly anxious to preserve the distinction between slave and free birth. Another law of Constantine, known only from its revival by the fifth-century emperor Zeno, decreed that if a man married his freeborn concubine, children she had previously borne to him would be legitimated, provided he had no legitimate children from a previous marriage (CJust 5.27.5). The law did not apply to concubines of slave origin, even if their children had been born after the concubines had been freed. On the other hand, Constantine's attitude was quite different when it was a question of unions between slaves rather than between slave and free, as we see in his law forbidding the break-up of slave families on imperially owned estates when the estates were leased out to new proprietors (CTh 2.25.1).

The explanation for these laws lies in the social and economic confusion of the third century. The social and legal distinctions between slaves and the lower-class free were becoming increasingly blurred. And, although after 212 Roman law was supposed to replace the local legal systems of the various provinces, many people, particularly among the lower, less-educated classes, remained ignorant of Roman law. Third-century legal sources provide abundant evidence for this confusion about status boundaries. Slaves or former slaves could live for years "as if freeborn." Free people might contract what they believed to be valid marriages with slaves, unaware either of their partner's true status or that unions with slaves were not recognized under Roman law. Questions would then arise about the status of children of such unions or validity of dowry.[21] Constantine's legislation sought to arrest this

[20] Evans Grubbs, "Marriage more Shameful than Adultery," 125–54; Harper, "The SC *Claudianum* in the *Codex Theodosianus*," 610–38.

[21] Slaves or freedmen living "as if freeborn": CJust 7.20.1, 7.21.6 and 7. Free woman inadvertently marries slave: CJust 5.18.3; *Dig.* 24.3.22.13. Confusion about status of children: CJust 7.16.7; cf. 4.19.10; 4.19.17; 7.16.28.

intermingling of social classes, and to reestablish traditional status distinctions. Later legislation on such unions by his successors indicates that, not surprisingly, he failed to do so.[22]

THE SALE AND ABANDONMENT OF CHILDREN

In classical Roman law, the sale or pledging of freeborn children was illegal, and the children's claim to free birth was not impaired by the sale. However, some parents did sell or pledge their own children, usually because of poverty or food shortage. As for infants who had been exposed (abandoned) at birth, pre-Constantinian Roman law maintained that they also retained their original status. Thus, if a freeborn child who had been exposed was brought up by someone else as a slave, the child was still legally free and could be reclaimed later by the parents. Clearly this could result in conflicts between a child's natural parents, who had exposed it at birth, and the legally invalid but often compelling claims of those who had rescued the infant and perhaps even brought it up as their own child.[23]

Before the Edict of Caracalla, the legal status of exposed children varied from province to province. After 212, the Roman rule that freeborn children kept their right of free birth and that fathers who exposed their children retained legal power over them would in theory have held for the whole empire. But in all probability local customs still prevailed, and confusion about the status of *expositi* prompted several third-century rescripts.[24]

A law dated 18 August 329 is found in both the Theodosian Code and the Code of Justinian, although the addressees and texts are different (CTh 5.101; CJust 4.43.2). Both contain essentially the same ruling: parents, under the pressure of extreme poverty, may sell their children, and the buyer of a newborn infant has the right to use the child as a slave and can even sell it to pay debts. If those who sold the child later wish to reclaim it, they must pay the market price or provide another slave in its place.[25] It has been suggested that this was not a real sale into slavery, but more of a long-term "hiring out" of the

22 E.g., CTh 4.12.5 (dated 362); 4.12.6 (366); 4.6.4 (371); 5 (397); 6 (405); 7 (426–7); 8 (428); Theodosius II, *Novel.* 22.1 (442); Valentinian III, *Novel.* 31 (451); Marcian, *Novel.* 4 (454); Majorian, *Novel.* 7 (458); Anthemius, *Novel.* 1 (468).

23 Parents selling or pledging children: CJust 7.16.1, 8.16.1, 8.16.6, 2.4.26, 4.43.1, 7.16.37; cf. *Dig.* 20.3.5, 21.2.39.3. Infant exposure: *Dig.* 40.2.29; CJust 5.4.16; cf. 8.51.1.

24 Evans Grubbs, "Hidden in Plain Sight," 293–310.

25 Much the same ruling appears in an earlier private rescript of Constantine (*Fragmenta Vaticana* 34) to a woman who had bought a newborn from parents who later wanted to reclaim it. Unlike the rescript, the law of 329 applied to all such cases.

child's services, perhaps to pay off a parent's debt.[26] Clearly such a distinction was rather vague and was probably frequently ignored: no doubt children often fell into permanent servitude, especially if their parents died before redeeming them.

Constantine went even further in a law of 331 on the status of children who had been abandoned by their parents or masters and rescued and brought up by someone else (CTh 5.9.1). In this law, addressed to the praetorian prefect Ablabius, the emperor declares that the child's rescuer has all rights over it and can bring it up as a slave or as his own child, and any attempt by the natural parent or original owner to reclaim the child is forbidden. Once a father has rejected a child, his legal power over it ceases. This law is indeed innovative, because although earlier emperors had felt that those who brought up abandoned children ought to be compensated for their trouble, they had always respected the claims of paternal power.[27]

Two other laws should be considered along with these rulings. In 322, Constantine learned that impoverished parents were selling or pledging their children and ordered that officials all over Africa immediately provide such families with assistance from imperial grain storehouses (CTh 11.27.2). Another constitution, again addressed to Ablabius, ordered that parents too poor to raise their children be provided with food and clothing at once "since the raising of a newborn infant cannot suffer delays" (CTh 11.27.1).

These were temporary reactions to emergency situations, perhaps regional food shortages. Constantine's rulings that those who bought a newborn baby or rescued an exposed infant had full power over the child were probably also responses to contemporary social conditions. There had always been confusion about the status of such children, and Constantine's laws, though out of line with earlier imperial policy, attempted to settle the question.

There is reason to see Christian influence behind the alimentary laws and the law of 331 on *expositi* (CTh 5.9.1). Christian writers had long denounced the abandonment of infants, and one of the most impassioned condemnations of exposure was made by Lactantius in his *Divine Institutes*. Lactantius, who served as tutor to Constantine's son Crispus, dedicated his *Divine Institutes* to Constantine, and we may reasonably assume that the emperor was familiar with the work.[28] Both CTh 5.9.1 and 11.27.1 (the law directing that aid be given to impoverished families in Italy) were addressed to Ablabius, a known

[26] Humbert, "Enfants à louer ou vendre," 189–203.

[27] Evans Grubbs, "Church, State, and Children," 119–31.

[28] Lactantius, *Div. Inst.* 6.20; cf. 5.9. See Barnes, "Lactantius and Constantine."

Christian. But, like Constantine's ruling on divorce (also enacted in 331 and addressed to Ablabius), the ruling on exposed infants is not entirely in line with Christian thought. A completely "Christian" law would have banned the exposure of infants altogether (which was not done until 374: CJust 8.51.2) and would not have allowed the person who picked up an exposed child to use it as a slave. For what most distressed the Christian writers who spoke out against the exposure of infants was precisely the possibility of their enslavement and their use as prostitutes. Constantine's law probably discouraged parents from exposing their newborn children and encouraged others to rescue abandoned infants, but it did not by any means guarantee that *expositi* would have a decent life.

CONCLUSION

What conclusions can be drawn about Constantine's legislation on the family? Although the emperor was usually not the instigator of imperial legislation, which might evolve from the suggestion of a particular official or as a solution to a legal dispute between private citizens, we can still see some pattern in his decisions. For instance, the preservation of status distinctions was clearly important to Constantine: a distinct dichotomy between the freeborn, privileged classes and those of slave or "base" birth appears in many of his laws, not just those on marriage. Of course concern with status distinctions in Roman law was hardly new with Constantine. But the number of laws attacking marriages between those of different statuses tells us two things: Constantine himself, unlike his Christian God, was very much a respecter of persons; and imperial attempts to keep social boundaries fixed were simply not working.

In much of his legislation, Constantine was simply giving a solution to problems that individuals had been bringing to the emperor for at least two centuries. After the decline in the use of the rescript system in Diocletian's reign, there would have been a need for general rulings on such issues.[29] Constantine was replacing the individual responses (rescripts) given by earlier emperors with edicts that applied equally to everyone. Unfortunately, the result of instituting general policies to cover situations previously dealt with case by case is that instead of the generally straightforward replies of the rescripts, we get heavy-handed and sometimes clumsily worded decrees imposing a uniform policy.

[29] On the rescript system see Honoré, *Emperors and Lawyers*; Corcoran, *The Empire of the Tetrarchs*.

It has been said that Christian influence on Constantine's legislation is most apparent in his laws on the family. But this raises an often-ignored question: was there, in the early fourth century, a recognizably "Christian" ethos of marriage and family relationships to which Constantine could look if he had wanted to incorporate Christian teachings in his legislation? In fact, it is anachronistic to attribute a developed set of ideas on the marital bond to ante-Nicene writers; not until Augustine was any real attempt made to define marriage in Christian terms, and even then Augustine did not speak for all Christians. Indeed, as Constantine discovered to his dismay, fourth-century Christians were not inclined to agree about many issues of doctrine and discipline.[30]

Ante-Nicene writers who do discuss Christian marriage and family life mention only those aspects in which they claim Christians differ significantly from pagans (or in which mainstream Christians differ from the radical fringe who rejected marriage and sexuality altogether). Briefly summarized, these are: rejection of divorce and of the practice of infant exposure, and preference for celibacy over marriage, particularly chaste widowhood over remarriage. None of these attitudes was alien to the non-Christian Roman world, but Christians claimed to put into practice ideals to which pagans gave only lip service.

In only a handful of cases can an argument really be made for Christian influence on Constantine's legislation on marriage and the family – perhaps half a dozen out of the more than eighty extant laws relevant to the family. Even in those cases, Constantine offers a solution only partly in keeping with contemporary Christian principles, or responds to concerns held by non-Christians as well as Christians. I am inclined to see only four laws as primarily "Christian" in intent: the divorce law (CTh 3.16.1), the law concerning infants exposed by their parents (CTh 5.9.1), and the laws directing that aid be given to parents whose poverty may drive them to sell or kill their children (CTh 11.27.1 and 2).

Three of these laws have the same addressee, Ablabius, Constantine's right-hand man during the last eight years of his reign, and they are the only extant laws concerning the family that are addressed to Ablabius. It is worth considering the possibility that Ablabius himself was responsible for the enactment of these laws. As praetorian prefect from at least 329 to 337, he was the second most powerful man in the empire. It is clear that Ablabius was a

[30] For Christian attitudes on marriage before and after Constantine, see Reynolds, *Marriage in the Western Church*.

Christian, but his understanding of both Roman law and Christian theology may have been quite tenuous.

In general, Constantine, rather than applying Christian principles to imperial law, preferred to grant to Christians powers and privileges that enabled the church to take over new functions and to amass more wealth and influence. Granting bishops judicial authority in civil cases was simpler and more efficient than trying to make secular officials employ Christian doctrine in their decisions (CTh 1.27.1, Sirm. Const. 1 to Ablabius). Constantine also lavishly endowed church buildings and provided local churches with funds for supporting the needy. According to another law to Ablabius, the emperor felt that "the rich ought to take upon themselves the needs of the *saeculum* (present age), and the poor ought to be sustained by the wealth of the churches" (CTh 16.2.6).

Much of Constantine's family legislation pursues policies quite different from what we know of the law of his predecessors. But our knowledge of pre-Constantinian law is very incomplete, being for the most part dependent on the Justinianic corpus. Constantinian policies that appear innovative may have had precedents in earlier imperial decisions that were not preserved because they were not in line with the law of Justinian's day.[31] Interestingly, several of Constantine's laws, while imposing policies that differ markedly from classical Roman law, appear to hark back to a much earlier period. In the early Republic, betrothals were considered contractual agreements and a broken betrothal was legally actionable. Divorce on insubstantial or unfair grounds was subject to penalties, and wives did not initiate divorces. Fathers could sell their children, but their right of recovery was restricted.[32]

In fact, the attitudes found in both Constantine's legislation and in early Roman law had probably always existed, but were usually not expressed in classical legal writings because classical law was aimed primarily at the urban, wealthier, more sophisticated classes. Unlike the classical jurists, Constantine also addressed issues of concern to those outside the urban upper classes, like abduction marriage or infant exposure.[33] Thus Constantine's legislation may provide some clues to the private lives of ordinary people, who are otherwise so invisible in the ancient sources.

31 Unlike Theodosius II, Justinian instructed the compilers of his Code to include only legislation relevant to his own day.

32 For early Roman law, see Watson, *The Law of Persons in the Later Roman Republic* and idem, *Roman Private Law around 200 BC*.

33 See Evans Grubbs, "Abduction Marriage in Antiquity."

RECOMMENDED READING

Arjava, A. *Women and Law in Late Antiquity*. Oxford: Clarendon Press, 1996.

Barnes, T. D. *Constantine and Eusebius*. Cambridge, MA: Harvard University Press, 1981.

Constantine: Dynasty, Religion, and Power in the Later Roman Empire. Chichester, UK: Wiley-Blackwell, 2011.

Dillon, J. N. *The Justice of Constantine: Law, Communication, and Control*. Ann Arbor: University of Michigan Press, 2012.

Evans Grubbs, J. *Law and Family in Late Antiquity: The Emperor Constantine's Marriage Legislation*. Oxford: Clarendon Press, 1995.

Women and the Law in the Roman Empire: A Sourcebook on Marriage, Divorce, and Widowhood. London and New York: Routledge, 2002.

Harper, K. *Slavery in the Late Roman World AD 275–425*. Cambridge: Cambridge University Press, 2011.

Harries, J. "Constantine the Lawgiver." In *From the Tetrarchs to the Theodosians: Later Roman History and Culture, 284–450 CE*, edited by S. McGill, C. Sogno, and E. Watts, 73–92. Cambridge: Cambridge University Press, 2010.

Harries, J. and I. Wood, eds. *The Theodosian Code*. London: Duckworth, 1993; reprinted with a new introduction as *The Theodosian Code: Studies in the Imperial Law of Late Antiquity*. London: Duckworth, 2010.

Humfress, C. "Civil Law and Social Life." In *The Cambridge Companion to the Age of Constantine*, edited by N. Lenski, 205–25. Cambridge: Cambridge University Press, 2006.

Lenski, N., ed. *The Cambridge Companion to the Age of Constantine*. Cambridge/New York: Cambridge University Press, 2006.

Matthews, J. *Laying Down the Law: A Study of the Theodosian Code*. New Haven, CT: Yale University Press, 2000.

Mommsen, Th. and P. Meyer, eds. *Theodosiani Libri XVI cum Constitutionibus Sirmondianis et Leges Novellae ad Theodosianum Pertinentes*. Berlin, 1905.

Pharr, C., trans. *The Theodosian Code and Novels and the Sirmondian Constitutions: A Translation with Commentary, Glossary, and Bibliography*. Princeton, NJ: Princeton University Press, 1952.

4

St. Augustine of Hippo

David G. Hunter

BIOGRAPHICAL INTRODUCTION

Probably no Christian writer has influenced the course of Western thought on marriage and sexuality as strongly as St. Augustine. His contributions include numerous sermons and letters on pastoral problems, doctrinal treatises on original sin and sexual desire (*concupiscentia*), and his famous *Confessions*, in which he explored the connection between his own experience of lust and the bondage of the human will. But Augustine's writings are also significant because they addressed topics that were of pressing concern to his Christian contemporaries: in early treatises against the Manichaeans he argued against his former coreligionists for the goodness of marriage; in response to debates about marriage and celibacy, he offered a balanced account of the good features of marriage, while insisting on the superior status of celibacy; in his later writings against the Pelagians, he noted in the vagaries of sexual desire a privileged symptom of the "original sin." All of these contexts shaped the development of the distinctive ideas that have come to be known as "Augustinian."

The course of Augustine's early life is well known because of his own narrative in the *Confessions*, but some salient features should be mentioned here. Born in 354 in the backwater town of Thagaste in North Africa (now Souk Ahras in modern Algeria), he pursued his studies and career as a teacher of rhetoric in Carthage, Rome, and eventually Milan, which was then the residence of the Roman emperor. Although he was enrolled as a catechumen from a young age and was the son of a devout Christian mother, Monica, Augustine did not fully embrace the Christian faith and receive baptism until Easter of 387, at the hands of Bishop Ambrose of Milan. At that point he renounced his secular career, returned to North Africa, and resolved to live in a monastic community. In 391, however, he was recruited

FIGURE 4.1. Algeria: *Saint Augustine of Hippo Regius (Annaba)*, painted by Antonello da Messina (ca. 1430–79) / Pictures from History / Bridgeman Images

into the clergy of the seaport city of Hippo Regius, where he became bishop in 395. From that point until his death, in 430, he served the church in North Africa as preacher, pastor, and polemicist, engaging in vigorous debate with Donatists, Manichaeans, pagans, and ultimately the monk Pelagius and his followers as well.

For purposes of a volume on marriage and family, perhaps the most relevant aspect of Augustine's biography is his own experience of sex and family life. As Augustine tells it, when he was about nineteen, he entered into a relationship with a young woman who eventually became the mother of his son, Adeodatus. While not a full marriage by Roman standards (i.e., *matrimonium iustum*), their union was monogamous and would have fallen under the rubric of concubinage, that is, a sexual relationship usually between partners of unequal social status without the intention of marriage.[1] In the *Confessions*, Augustine underscored the distinction between concubinage and legitimate marriage: "This experience taught me at firsthand what a difference there is between a marriage contracted for the purpose of founding a family, and a relationship of love charged with carnal desire in which children may be born even against the parents' wishes – though once they are born one cannot help loving them."[2] While he stressed here the difference between concubinage and marriage, slightly later, when he composed *The Good of Marriage*, Augustine suggested that a union of concubinage could be considered a marriage, if both partners remained faithful for life and did not prevent the birth of children.[3] For Augustine, as for Roman law in general, intentionality and consent were the key factors in the making of marriage, and it was contracted primarily for procreation.

MAJOR THEMES AND CONTRIBUTIONS

Creation and Fall. The theological foundation of Augustine's reflections on marriage and sexuality was his reading of the creation and fall of the first human beings, as described in the book of Genesis. Here, as in so many aspects of Augustine's thought, it is possible to discern significant development. In his earlier writings, up to and including his *Confessions*, Augustine

[1] Cf. Treggiari, *Roman Marriage*, 52: "Upper-class men are attested by literary and juristic sources as having concubines of lower social status either when they were relatively young and unready for marriage, like Augustine, or after the death of a wife who had given them enough children, like Vespasian."

[2] *Conf.* 4.2.2; Boulding, *The Confessions*, 93. In *Conf.* 6.15.25, Augustine makes clear how deeply affected he was by their separation thirteen years later.

[3] *De bono coniugali* 5.5; *St. Augustine: Treatises on Marriage and Other Subjects*, 9–54.

was drawn to an allegorical interpretation of the biblical text. This was especially the case with the creation stories in the book of Genesis. Jewish and Christian commentators had long puzzled over the two conflicting accounts of creation in Genesis 1 and 2. Do they represent two phases in a creative process? Did chapter 1 describe the creation of a spiritual and androgynous creature made in the image of God (Genesis 1:27, "male and female he created them"), while chapter 2 depicted their later physical and sexual differentiation? Or, were material bodies given to Adam and Eve only after their act of disobedience in Genesis 3 (the "garments of skins" in Genesis 3:21)? In the last case, physicality itself, as well as sexual reproduction, was understood to be a consequence of sin.

In his earliest writings on Genesis, written under the influence of the allegorical reading of scripture he had learned from Bishop Ambrose of Milan, Augustine favored a nonliteral interpretation of certain critical verses of Genesis, such as "increase and multiply" (Genesis 1:28). For example, in an early commentary, *On Genesis against the Manichaeans*, composed in 389, Augustine argued that this verse could not refer to sexual intercourse, but could have only a spiritual meaning: prior to the Fall, "there was a chaste coupling of male and female, accommodated to his directing and her complying; and a spiritual brood of intellectual and immortal joys filling the earth." The divine blessing came to have a "fleshly" meaning (i.e., to refer to sexual intercourse and procreation) only after Adam and Eve sinned.[4] As late as the *Confessions* (circa 400) Augustine remained reluctant to take the text in its literal sense, preferring to multiply allegorical readings of the words "increase and multiply."[5]

By the early 400s, however, Augustine seems to have realized that he could no longer escape confronting the literal meaning of the Genesis creation narrative, which placed the command to increase and multiply two chapters before the story of the Fall. He broached the topic in the opening paragraphs of his treatise *The Good of Marriage*, begun shortly after the *Confessions*, where he asked how the offspring of the first humans would have come into being, if they had not sinned. Augustine offered a variety of interpretations and declined to provide any definitive resolution, although he acknowledged that it was possible that God had intended Adam and Eve to procreate

[4] *De Genesi contra Manichaeos* 1.19.30. In his comment on this work in his *Retractationes* 1.10.2, Augustine explicitly repudiated an allegorical reading of Genesis 1:28 that restricted sexual procreation to the postlapsarian world. See also *De Genesi ad litteram* 8.2.5.

[5] *Confessiones* 13.24.37. For a fuller discussion of Augustine's developing interpretation of Genesis, see the studies of Elizabeth A. Clark cited in the bibliography.

sexually, even if they had not sinned and become liable to death.[6] But Augustine eventually overcame his reluctance to give the text a literal meaning, and in book 9 of his *Literal Commentary on Genesis* he finally determined that God had indeed intended the first human beings to have a full bodily life, including procreation.

Augustine's new reading of Genesis was to have a significant impact on his thought about human sexuality and marriage. On the one hand, his new approach to the text served to ground the good of marriage ever more firmly in the positive will of the Creator. Unlike many of his contemporaries, both among the Greek fathers and among Latin Christian writers, Augustine no longer regarded sex and procreation merely as concessions granted to human beings to compensate for the penalty of death. Augustine could now argue that it was precisely because Adam and Eve were expected to live forever that they were enjoined to produce "companions" to fill up the world.[7] He now insisted that Adam and Eve originally had a social duty to populate the earth, one that was present even before sin and death came into the world. And, more importantly, Augustine could now contend that the original purpose of sexual union and the original blessing to increase and multiply remained in effect in human life and history, despite the presence of sin and death.[8]

There was, however, a negative dimension to Augustine's development. Once he had begun to think of the first human beings as genuinely physical persons, he could also begin to think of their sin as having an impact on their bodies and on the originally harmonious relation of their bodies and souls. In his *Literal Commentary on Genesis* Augustine explicitly rejected any notion that the original sin might have involved sexual relations. The root of sin, he insisted, was the first human beings' disobedience, which was motivated by their "perverse imitation of God and noxious liberty," that is, by human pride.[9] However, in his later reading of Genesis Augustine also began to teach that the first sin had disrupted the natural union of body and soul that had formerly been in place: "their bodies contracted, as it were, the deadly disease of death, and this changed the gift by which they had ruled the body so perfectly."[10] The first human beings now began to experience "a movement of concupiscence which they had not known previously."[11] This was the cause of the shame they felt when they realized they were naked (cf. Genesis 3:7). After

6 *De bono coniugali* 2.2. 7 *De Genesi ad litteram* 9.9.14. 8 *De Genesi ad litteram* 9.3.5.
9 *De Genesi ad litteram* 8.14.31.
10 *De Genesi ad litteram* 9.10.17; J. H. Taylor, *St. Augustine*, 81.
11 *De Genesi ad litteram* 9.31.41.

their sin, Adam and Eve became "subject to the same drive by which there is in animals a desire to copulate and thus provide for offspring to take the place of those that die."[12] What was originally supposed to be the product of a free and rational choice to obey God's will (i.e., sex for the purpose of procreation) now became an act performed under the impulse of an "animal instinct." Augustine's new physicalist reading of Genesis, therefore, was double-edged: on the one hand, he asserted the original goodness of sexual relations and their place in the divine plan, but, on the other hand, he insisted that after the Fall sexual acts are necessarily performed under the influence of bodily desires that can (and often do) run counter to the distinctively human traits of rationality and free choice. His new emphasis on the physical effects of original sin on bodily desire was to have permanent influence on his view of sex and marriage.

The "Goods" of Marriage. Despite the pessimistic features of Augustine's developing notion of original sin and its influence on human sexual functioning, he remained committed to the belief that marriage and procreation were good in themselves. In fact, one of the most influential aspects of Augustine's teaching is his doctrine of the "three goods" of marriage. He first developed this set of ideas in his treatise *The Good of Marriage* (*De bono coniugali*), composed in the opening years of the fifth century, along with a companion treatise *On Holy Virginity* (*De sancta virginitate*). It is important to note the context in which these two books were written, because it shows Augustine entering into a controversy that had previously engaged some of the leading lights of Latin Christianity, such as Ambrose and Jerome. In the year 393, the monk Jovinian had been condemned by synods at Rome and Milan for teaching that all baptized Christians (married and celibate) were equally meritorious before God and that all would receive an equal reward in heaven.[13] Among the opponents of Jovinian, such as Siricius of Rome and Ambrose of Milan, the presbyter Jerome stood out for his intemperate response to Jovinian, *Adversus Jovinianum*.

Although Augustine did not mention either Jovinian or Jerome by name in *De bono coniugali* or *De sancta virginitate*, in his *Retractationes* (the review of his own writings that he composed toward the end of his life), he noted that these books were written as an attempt to respond to the controversy around Jovinian. Specifically, Augustine observed that supporters of Jovinian continued to boast, "the only way to refute Jovinian is to condemn marriage, not to

12 *De Genesi ad litteram* 9.32.42.

13 For a detailed study of Jovinian and the controversy generated by his teaching, see Hunter, *Marriage, Celibacy, and Heresy in Ancient Christianity*.

praise it."[14] Most contemporary scholars rightly interpret Augustine's remark as an indirect allusion to the *Adversus Jovinianum* of Jerome, which had attracted a great deal of opposition in its day because of its extremely hostile treatment of marriage. In his own two treatises, therefore, Augustine had set himself the task of demonstrating the superior status of virginity over marriage (against Jovinian), while at the same time defending marriage as something truly good (against Jerome). He accomplished this by arguing that there were, in fact, three distinct goods proper to the marital relationship: procreation (*proles*), fidelity (*fides*), and the presence of a sacred symbolism (*sacramentum*). *The Good of Marriage* is dedicated primarily to articulating the nature of these three goods.

Procreation. There is a sense in which, for Augustine, the original and primary good of marriage is procreation. As we saw earlier, Augustine's ongoing reflections on Genesis were leading him to recognize the place of procreation in God's plan for humanity even before the entry of sin and death. In the opening paragraph of *The Good of Marriage* Augustine argued that sexual union was instituted as the means of establishing a bond of kinship or blood relationship that would strengthen social ties among human beings and make possible the great good of friendship:

> And so the first natural union of human society is the union of husband and wife ... The result is the bonding of society in children, who are the one honorable fruit, not of the union of male and female, but of their sexual intercourse.[15]

Augustine's point is that God chose sexual union as the preferred method of multiplying human beings (rather than, for example, a spontaneous creation of each human being or a virginal conception of everyone) because it establishes ties of blood that are stronger than a simple similarity of nature. It is important to note that Augustine does not reduce marriage merely to its procreative dimension. Indeed, he explicitly affirms that a true marriage can exist on the basis of a "natural fellowship between the two sexes" apart from sexual intercourse or procreation.[16] Such would have been the case, Augustine believed, with the marriage of Mary and Joseph, with the elderly, or with those for whom sexual intercourse had become impossible or

[14] *Retractationes* II.22 (48).

[15] *De bono coniugali* 1.1. Augustine went on to note that even without sexual intercourse there could have been a "friendly and brotherly union" between male and female, based on the submission of one sex to the other. All translations from *De bono coniugali* are my own.

[16] *De bono coniugali* 3.3.

undesirable. In such cases, an "order of charity" could persist, despite the cessation of sexual relations. Nonetheless, it is clear that Augustine, in conformity with traditional Roman and Jewish perspectives, regarded marriage as an institution whose purpose was primarily to provide for the legitimate production of children.[17]

One important qualification, however, must be made to any suggestion that procreation has such primacy in Augustine's understanding of marriage. Augustine also viewed marriage, and specifically the activity of procreation, not only in the light of its origins in Genesis, but also from the perspective of the history of salvation. For Augustine, procreation served not only to build up the human race from its origin in Adam and Eve, but also to generate the line of descendants from Abraham to Jesus Christ. Because the generation of the people of Israel was a prerequisite to the coming of Christ, the ancient patriarchs and matriarchs had a positive duty to increase and multiply in order to fulfill the divine purpose. This role of procreation in the history of salvation even provided Augustine with a justification for the practice of polygamy in the Old Testament: one man with several wives could produce more children and thus fulfill the biblical mandate more readily. Augustine could even argue that there was a special "sacrament" or sacred symbolism in the polygamous marriages in the old dispensation: "the several wives of the ancient fathers were a sign that our churches would be drawn from all nations and subject to the one man Christ."[18]

But now that Christ has come, according to Augustine, a new era of history has begun, and procreation has lost the important role it once played in the history of salvation. Now there is no longer a positive duty for Christians to produce children:

> In the earliest times of the human race, in order to propagate the people of God, through which the prince and savior of all peoples might both be prophesied and be born, the saints were obliged to make use of this good of marriage ... But now, since the opportunity for spiritual relationship abounds on all sides and for all peoples for entering into a holy and pure association, even those who wish to contract marriage only to have children are to be urged to practice the greater good of continence.[19]

[17] Cf. *De bono coniugali* 17.19: "Marriage exists among all nations for the same purpose: the procreation of children; no matter how the children turn out later, marriage was instituted so that they would be born in a regulated and honorable way."

[18] *De bono coniugali* 18.21. [19] *De bono coniugali* 9.9.

Because the last days are near and because the world is already full of people who might become Christian, Augustine argued, there is no longer any need to produce children. Echoing 1 Corinthians 7:9 ("If they are unable to be continent, let them marry"), he held that, in the present age, marriage and procreation are intended only for people who lack self-control. Even if someone should choose to marry only to have children and not out of lust (a possibility Augustine considered unlikely), even such a person was not equal to the saints of old: "For in such persons [i.e., in the present] even the desire for children is something carnal, whereas in those people [i.e., in the past] the desire was spiritual because it was in accord with the sacred symbolism of that past time."[20] While sexual relations and procreation remain good in themselves, they no longer play any essential role in the history of salvation.

Fidelity. The problem of self-control (or the lack of it) brings us to the second of Augustine's goods of marriage, fidelity (*fides*). Augustine's discussion of the good of marital fidelity has two distinct dimensions. On the one hand, fidelity refers to the requirement that marriages be monogamous, that is, that both of the spouses abstain from adultery or sex with another person. In this regard, note that Augustine, like most of the Christian tradition before him, expanded the notion of adultery beyond the legal parameters it had in Roman law. For the Romans *adulteria* involved either a married woman having sex with someone other than her husband, or a man having sex with a married woman who was not his wife. For a married man to have sex with a woman who was not married, especially a slave or woman of the lower classes, was not considered adultery from a legal point of view. One of the innovations of Christian morality that Augustine reflects is a stricter definition of adultery to encompass all acts of extramarital intercourse by married persons. As we will see, Augustine, like most Christian preachers, encountered resistance to this novel moral standard from the men in his congregation, who were accustomed to laxer customs.

But this is only one dimension of fidelity according to Augustine. For him, *fides* also involved the positive duty that all married persons have to engage in sexual relations with each other in order to avoid illicit sexual activity. Because human beings are beset with intense sexual desires, one function of marriage, as Augustine saw it, was to channel these desires in a positive way:

> For this is why such spouses were married, so that concupiscence might be directed toward a legitimate bond and not flow in a disordered or haphazard way. While in itself concupiscence bears the uncontrollable weakness of the

[20] *De bono coniugali* 17.19.

> flesh, from marriage it has the indissoluble fellowship of fidelity; in itself concupiscence leads to immoderate intercourse, but from marriage it receives the limit of chaste procreation.[21]

Fidelity to the conjugal bond, for Augustine, involved both abstention from adultery and what he called "a kind of mutual servitude," in which each spouse supported the other's weakness by engaging in sex when the needs of the other required it.[22]

Sacrament. The third good specific to marriage, according to Augustine, is what he calls its *sacramentum*, that is, the sacred significance or symbolism found in the marriage bond. As noted previously, Augustine could speak of the *sacramentum* found in the polygamy of the Old Testament patriarchs: the plurality of their marriages prophetically signified the multiplicity of Christians that would someday be drawn from all the nations of the earth. After Christ, however, a new *sacramentum* is found in marriage, at least in the marriages of Christians. According to Augustine's interpretation of the sayings of Jesus found in the Synoptic Gospels (Matthew 5:31–2, 19:19; Mark 10:11–12; Luke 16:18) and in Paul (1 Corinthians 7:10–12), Jesus forbade remarriage after divorce or separation. From this, Augustine concluded that the indissolubility of marriage must be the basis of a new sacrament in marriage. Unlike the marriages of the patriarchs, which could be polygamous and could be dissolved by divorce, the marriages of Christians were to be monogamous and could not be dissolved by divorce, but only by the death of one of the spouses. Drawing on the teaching of Ephesians 5:31–2, which referred to the union of husband and wife as a mystery or symbol (the Latin word was *sacramentum*) of the union of Christ and the church, Augustine concluded that it was the indissolubility of the human marriage that provided its new *sacramentum* or sacred meaning. While the plurality of marriages in the Old Testament symbolized the future gathering of the Church from many nations, the singleness of Christian marriages symbolizes the eschatological union of Christ and the church.

It is important to distinguish Augustine's notion of the sacramentality of marriage from later Christian formulations of the concept, particularly the medieval enumeration of the seven sacraments. While Augustine's teaching became the source of much later Christian theory and practice, especially in the West, the notion of *sacramentum* in his day was much more fluid than it later became. When applied to marriage, the concept was more a matter of

[21] *De bono coniugali* 5.5.

[22] *De bono coniugali* 6.6. As we will see, in pastoral practice Augustine saw the duty of marital fidelity overriding any desire for ascetic sexual abstinence.

symbolism than of ritual. This is evident in his application of the term *sacramentum* both to the polygamy of the patriarchs and to the monogamy of Christians. It is also clear in his argument in *The Good of Marriage* that the prohibition of remarriage is interpreted even more strictly in the case of the clergy: no one who has married more than once (even if his first wife has died) is allowed to be ordained. The reason, Augustine argued, was "the sanctity of the sacrament." Even though remarriage is permitted to lay Christians, it is not allowed to the clergy: "It is a matter of the sacrament, not of sin."[23]

PRACTICAL QUESTIONS: DIVORCE AND REMARRIAGE

Augustine's most extended discussion of divorce and remarriage is found in his two books *On Adulterous Marriages*, composed in late 418 or early 419. This treatise, which is the only text from the first five centuries after Christ devoted solely to this topic, was a response to questions posed to him by a certain Pollentius, whose identity is otherwise unknown. Pollentius had read Augustine's earlier book, *On the Lord's Sermon on the Mount*, and was troubled by his strict interpretation of Jesus's teaching in Matthew 5:31–2 and Matthew 19:9, as well as his reading of 1 Corinthians 7:10–11. Pollentius had proposed to read the Pauline text ("[T]he wife should not separate from her husband; but if she does separate, let her remain unmarried or else be reconciled to her husband") in the light of Matthew 19:9 ("Whoever divorces his wife, except because of fornication, and marries another commits adultery"). Pollentius argued that a distinction should be made between divorce that takes place because of fornication and divorce that occurs on other grounds. In both cases, divorce is allowed; when adultery has occurred, remarriage is allowed as well, because of Matthew's exception. Paul's prohibition of remarriage, Pollentius argued, applied only in cases in which spouses separated for reasons other than adultery.[24]

Augustine strongly rejected Pollentius' interpretation of the biblical evidence. He argued that Matthew 19:9 implied that the only legitimate reason

[23] *De bono coniugali* 18.21: "De sacramento enim agitur, non de peccato." Augustine applied the same language and logic to the "sacrament" of consecrated virginity: "On account of the sacredness of the sacrament, a woman who has been violated, even if she was a catechumen at the time, cannot be consecrated among the virgins of the church after her baptism."

[24] Pollentius' view may have been widespread in Augustine's day. His contemporary, the anonymous biblical commentator now called "Ambrosiaster," had previously argued that a man who divorced his wife because of her adultery was allowed to remarry. See his *Commentary on 1 Corinthians* 7:11.

for separation was adultery. Even in these cases, according to Augustine, the marriage remained intact and remarriage was forbidden. In response to Pollentius' objection that Matthew 19:9 made a clear exception for divorce in the case of adultery, Augustine suggested that this exception meant that remarriage after adultery is less culpable than remarriage in other cases, although it is still prohibited. Augustine appealed to the fact that the Gospels of Mark and Luke contain the prohibition of divorce in an unqualified form and that the Matthean exception must be read in the light of these other texts.

In the first book of *On Adulterous Marriages*, Augustine also discussed 1 Corinthians 7:12–16, the so-called Pauline privilege, where Paul suggested that a Christian was not bound to remain in marriages with a non-Christian, if the non-Christian wished to separate. In this case, Augustine acknowledged, the apostle has made an allowance for separation between a Christian and a non-Christian, when the faith of the Christian is endangered. He emphasized, however, that a separation that is lawful may not always be expedient. When the non-Christian spouse presents no obstacle to the faith of the Christian, charity dictates that the spouses should remain together, so that the non-Christian might be converted.

In book 2, Augustine turned to additional questions Pollentius had raised. He began with 1 Corinthians 7:39, where Paul had written, "A wife is bound as long as her husband lives. But if the husband dies, she is free to marry anyone she wishes, but only in the Lord." Pollentius had suggested that the "death" to which Paul referred was the spiritual death caused by adultery. Pollentius had thus taken Paul to agree with Matthew 19:9, the passage in which (as he interpreted it) Jesus had allowed an exception to the rule against divorce and remarriage in cases where one spouse was guilty of adultery. Here, too, Augustine rejected Pollentius' reading of the text, arguing that even when a spouse has been legitimately divorced because of adultery, the "bond of chastity" remained until the death of one of the spouses (2.4.4). Like the sacrament of baptism, which remains valid even after serious sin and excommunication, Augustine argued, the bond of marriage remained intact even when a divorce occurred because of adultery (2.5.4).

While Augustine's arguments against Pollentius might seem uncompromising, it is worth noting that Augustine himself expressed some uncertainty about them. In his *Retractationes*, composed near the end of his life, when he came to discuss *On Adulterous Marriages*, Augustine indicated that he had not adequately solved all of the questions in the interpretation of the New Testament evidence:

> I wrote two books on adulterous marriages with the desire of solving, according to the scriptures, to the best of my ability, a very difficult question. I do not know whether I have done this very clearly. On the contrary, I think that I did not reach a perfect solution of this question, although I have clarified many of its obscurities, as anyone who reads intelligently will be able to judge.[25]

Augustine's hesitation about the cogency of his arguments is revealing. It indicates that he was probably aware of the weaknesses in his biblical exegesis, especially his interpretation of the exception clause in Matthew 19:9. Pollentius' interpretation was unacceptable to Augustine because it seemed to contradict Mark 10:11–12 and Luke 16:18. Because he was unable to admit that the New Testament writers might contradict each other, Augustine was unable to interpret Matthew 19:9 other than by maintaining that it could not mean what it appeared to mean.[26]

AUGUSTINE AS PASTOR AND PREACHER

In addition to the specialized treatises on marriage and divorce that we have examined thus far, Augustine also authored numerous letters and sermons that dealt directly with pastoral issues in the lives of his congregation. What is striking about Augustine's discussion of marriage in these texts is his moderation and his insistence on preserving the bond of fidelity, especially in cases where one of the partners desired to embrace sexual abstinence. In his famous Letter 262 to Ecdicia, Augustine rebuked the matron for adopting sexual continence without the agreement of her husband. In addition to this breach of conjugal morality, Ecdicia had decided to give away all or most of the family possessions to two itinerant monks, again without her husband's permission. This last infraction was the final straw, because it caused her husband, who had embraced continence only very reluctantly, to put aside his vow and engage in extramarital sex.

Augustine harshly rebuked Ecdicia for her decision to withdraw from her conjugal obligations without the permission of her husband. Although her husband eventually agreed to adopt sexual continence, Augustine assured Ecdicia that if her husband had not done so, her vow of continence would have been invalid. As Augustine saw it, married persons who were capable of

25 *Retractationes* 2.57 (83). Augustine expressed the same hesitation about his own views in *On Adulterous Marriages* 1.25.32.

26 See the excellent analysis of Augustine's argument by Philip Lyndon Reynolds, *Marriage in the Western Church*, 207–12.

sexual continence were still responsible for the spiritual well-being of their spouses. If there was any chance that one of the partners might lapse into extramarital relations, Augustine argued, then it was the duty of the stronger spouse to engage in sex in order to assist the weaker spouse. God would credit the stronger with the virtue of continence, since their actions were motivated by charity and mercy, not by lust.

It is also worth noting that Augustine's advice was not given only to women as part of their duty to submit to their husbands. He gave the same prescriptions to men. In fact, in Letter 220 to Boniface, Augustine told the imperial official that he could not impose his own earlier resolution about sexual continence upon his new wife. She had entered into the marriage in good faith, and Boniface had to respect her conjugal rights and live with her in marital purity, if he could not persuade her to adopt continence.[27] Augustine exhorted Boniface to continue to love God and not the world and to fulfill both his civic and his marital duties:

> to keep the faith and seek peace, even in the midst of wars, if it should be necessary to engage in them; to do good works with the goods of the world and not to do bad works on account of the goods of the world – in none of these matters is a wife an obstacle; at least she ought not to be.[28]

It is clear from his letters to Ecdicia and Boniface that Augustine saw the conjugal bond as the source of moral responsibilities that were incumbent on both sexes and that superseded any desire for sexual continence.

Augustine took a similar approach in the sermons that he delivered publicly to his congregation. In the sermons, however, Augustine addressed people who generally had less ascetic ambitions than those harbored by Ecdicia and Boniface, and who desired to engage in sexual intercourse apart from any intention to procreate. Augustine's response to them was characteristically humane. He based his view on 1 Corinthians 7:5–6, where Paul instructed the married couple to abstain from sex only for brief periods for prayer and then to "come together again, lest Satan tempt you through lack of self-control. I say this by way of concession, not of command." In his sermons, Augustine emphasized that the concession Paul granted was not to sex for the purpose of procreation, which was sinless, but rather to acts of intercourse that occurred purely out of excessive desire. For example, in one sermon devoted entirely to the topic of marriage, Augustine wrote:

> The fact that married people, when overcome by desire, make use of one another beyond what is necessary for producing children, is something that

[27] *Ep.* 220.12. [28] *Ep.* 220.12.

> should be placed among those things for which we say each day, "Forgive us our debts, as we forgive our debtors."[29]

Augustine considered sensual indulgence one of the daily sins that all human beings commit almost without thinking. In another sermon, he noted that daily almsgiving would expiate sins of this sort, which included speaking an unkind word or giving way to excessive laughter: "When you wish to make use of your wife more than is necessary to produce children, this is a sin. And it is sins such as these that daily almsgiving cleanses."[30] As Augustine had argued in *The Good of Marriage*, it was the good of marital fidelity that served to excuse the evil of marital incontinence.

CONCLUSION

Augustine's thinking on marriage, like so much of his thought, is rich, complex, and often misunderstood. Writing in a time of ascetic enthusiasm, he struggled to make a place for the ordinary married Christian in a church that increasingly valued sexual renunciation. Though shaped by high philosophical concerns, Augustine developed insights into the human psyche and sensitivity to human foibles that were unmatched in the ancient Christian world. At the same time, he strived, not always successfully, to be faithful to the texts of scripture, in their own complexity and historical context. While his assessment of human nature in its postlapsarian condition was decidedly pessimistic (some would say realistic), paradoxically this led him to develop an attitude toward human sinfulness that stressed reliance on God's mercy and forgiveness. Augustine's writings on marriage reflect all of the strengths and weaknesses of his broader view of human nature.

RECOMMENDED READING

Brown, P. *The Body and Society. Men, Women, and Sexual Renunciation in Early Christianity*. New York: Columbia University Press, 1988.

Burns, J. Patout. "Marital Fidelity as *remedium concupiscentiae*: An Augustinian Proposal." *Augustinian Studies* 44 (2013): 1–35.

Cavadini, John C. "Feeling Right: Augustine on the Passions and Sexual Desire." *Augustinian Studies* 36 (2005): 195–217.

Clark, Elizabeth A. "'Adam's Only Companion': Augustine and the Early Christian Debate on Marriage." *Recherches Augustiniennes* 21 (1986): 139–62.

29 Ser. 354A.12. 30 Ser. 9.18.

"Heresy, Asceticism, Adam and Eve: Interpretations of Gen 1–3 in the Later Latin Fathers." In her *Ascetic Piety and Women's Faith*, 353–85. Lewiston, NY: Edwin Mellen Press, 1986.

"Vitiated Seeds and Holy Vessels: Augustine's Manichaean Past." In her *Ascetic Piety and Women's Faith*, 291–349.

St. Augustine on Marriage and Sexuality. Washington, DC: The Catholic University of America Press, 1996.

Hunter, David G. "Augustinian Pessimism? A New Look at Augustine's Teaching on Sex, Marriage and Celibacy." *Augustinian Studies* 25 (1994): 153–77.

"Augustine, Sermon 354A: Its Place in His Thought on Marriage and Sexuality." *Augustinian Studies* 33/1 (2002): 39–60.

"Augustine and the Making of Marriage in Roman North Africa." *Journal of Early Christian Studies* 11 (2003): 63–85.

Lamberigts, Mathijs. "A Critical Evaluation of Critiques of Augustine's View of Sexuality." In *Augustine and His Critics: Essays in Honour of Gerald Bonner*, edited by Robert J. Dodaro and George P. Lawless, 176–97. London: Routledge, 2000.

"Augustine on Marriage: A Comparison of *De bono coniugali* and *De nuptiis et concupiscentia*." *Louvain Studies* 35 (2011): 32–52.

Reynolds, P. L. *Marriage in the Western Church. The Christianization of Marriage during the Patristic and Early Medieval Periods*. Leiden: Brill, 1994. See chapters XI–XIII on Augustine's theology of marriage.

Schreiner, Susan E. "Eve, the Mother of History: Reaching for the Reality of History in Augustine's Later Exegesis of Genesis." In *Genesis 1–3 in the History of Exegesis: Intrigue in the Garden*, edited by Gregory A. Robins, 135–86. Lewiston, NY: Edwin Mellen Press. 1988.

Shaw, Brent. "The Family in Late Antiquity: The Experience of Augustine." *Past and Present* 115 (1987): 3–51.

5

St. John Chrysostom

Vigen Guroian

BIOGRAPHICAL INTRODUCTION

St. John Chrysostom (347–407 CE) arguably is the most celebrated Eastern church father. This is not to suggest that he was the most talented theologian of the fourth century, but rather that his fame as a bishop, pastor, and preacher is second to none among the Greek fathers – testified to by his name, Chrysostom, which means "golden-mouthed."

St. John Chrysostom also is beyond question that patristic figure, East or West, Greek or Latin, who most consistently addresses the subjects of marriage and family. His reflections on the meaning of marriage and the role of the family in the church's life and mission are found principally in his homilies. While he was conversant with the great doctrinal issues of the day, his profound concern was for the moral dimensions of everyday life – not only sex, marriage, and family life, but also the role of wealth in church and society and the presence of poverty and attitudes toward popular entertainments. His observations and ethical exhortations are steeped in the Bible yet also are shaped by a training in rhetoric.

Chrysostom was the son of a distinguished military official who died when John was an infant. John remained very close to his mother, whose decision not to remarry was owed to her profound Christian convictions about the permanence of marriage and gifting of oneself to Christ and his church. She not only brought John up in this faith, but also saw to it that he received a superior classical education under the tutelage of the renowned neopagan sophistic rhetorician Libanius.

John's education was to prepare him for civil service and thus follow in his father's footsteps. At eighteen, however, he abandoned this path and joined the monks in the mountain caves outside of Antioch. His severe asceticism nearly

FIGURE 5.1. St. John Chrysostom (fresco), Italian School (twelfth century) / Chiesa della Panaghia, Rossano, Calabria, Italy / Bridgeman Images

ruined his health, and in 377, he returned to the city. Almost immediately, John entered the service of the church under Melitius, bishop of Antioch. He became a reader, was made a deacon, and in 386, was ordained a priest.

In Antioch, Chrysostom's talent as a rhetorician and preacher was quickly recognized. His homilies drew large crowds, and he is best known for these commentaries on scripture. When Nectarius, bishop of Constantinople, died in 397, Chrysostom was summoned to the imperial capital, whisked off under-cover lest the local Antiochian populace stand in the way. In Constantinople, Chrysostom's skills as an orator shone but also drew out enemies, as he relentlessly chastised the Christian populace for its moral laxity and abandon to the entertainments, indulgences, and allures of the popular culture. He ran into trouble with the empress Eudoxia, who may well have interpreted some of these criticisms personally. Chrysostom's efforts to reform the church, strengthen the see of Constantinople, and extend its authority angered Theophilus, the powerful bishop of Alexandria, and other Asiatic bishops. Theophilus succeeded in convening a regional synod in 403 that called for Chrysostom's deposition. Chrysostom was banished, recalled, and in 404 banished again. He died in Comana Pontica on 14 September 407.

MARRIAGE AND THE CHRISTIAN HOUSEHOLD

Chrysostom's early enthusiastic defense of monasticism in such tracts as *On Virginity* and *Against the Opponents of Monasticism* give little indication of his later strong and sometimes passionate defense of marriage. Yet as a pastor, Chrysostom became acquainted with married couples and their problems. From the pulpit and presumably in his pastoral activities, Chrysostom gave thought to the meaning of marriage and the role of the Christian household in the life of the church. The positive views on marital sex that show up in his writings contrast strikingly with those of other patristic authors, most notably St. Augustine, who regarded sex as not much better than a necessary evil.[1] On various occasions, Chrysostom also addressed the office of parenthood and the proper upbringing and education of children. This interest is admirably represented in his inventive and rhetorically brilliant tract *An Address on Vainglory and the Right Way for Parents to Bring Up Their Children*, composed toward the end of his years in Antioch or early in his tenure at Constantinople.

Chrysostom lived at a time when pagan antiquity was in decline. Christianity was exerting an increasingly strong influence on society that had not been felt even a generation before. Indeed, during Chrysostom's life, the church initially

[1] See Chapter 4 herein on St. Augustine.

endured its final full-scale "persecution" under Julian the Apostate (r. 361–3), but not long afterward Theodosius I (r. 379–95) made Christianity the official religion of the empire.

A Christian culture was rising up; Christendom was being born. Chrysostom was, however, among a significant group of leaders at the close of the fourth century, including St. Basil of Caesarea (ca. 330–79), who were uneasy about the new world that was coming into being. He had serious misgivings about the shape of the emerging triumphant church in its relationship to the state and the greater society. He wanted Christians to retain their distinct identity as followers of Christ, even as they entered into secular occupations. He decried an assimilation that robbed the Christian community of its "saltiness."

Also like Basil, Chrysostom was of a mind to reform *both* church and society. This was not a reflex to return to the past, but neither was Chrysostom sanguine about the future. He would not countenance a dual Christian ethic, one for monks and another for laypeople. He applied the monastic spirit and rigor to his critique of society, expounding a radical Christian ethos consistent with Christ's teaching in the Beatitudes. By the late fourth century, to be a Christian was no longer a social liability. Indeed, it was becoming not just a preferred means to social status, wealth, and power, but also a prerequisite to these ends. Many were entering the church without the religious and moral discipline Chrysostom expected of persons baptized in the faith.

Chrysostom sought to reform society from within the church,[2] as he identified the proleptic presence of the kingdom of God with neither empire nor cloistered monastery, but with the near and familiar Christian household. This was a revolutionary notion. In his full vision of Christ and culture, Chrysostom distinguished Christian marriage from secular and pagan marriage. To be married "in the Lord" (1 Corinthians 7:39), as St. Paul put it, is a calling, a vocation, to follow Christ and his teachings and to build up the church as his body in the world. Throughout the whole of his life, Chrysostom favored celibacy above marriage; nonetheless, he argued that the Gospels and the letters of St. Paul give Christians a choice between two legitimate courses of life, celibacy and marriage. When entered into and lived in a holy manner, both are acceptable to Christ and serve his kingdom.

Even in his youthful tract *On Virginity*, which he wrote during his first years in Antioch, when the monastic life was still fresh in his mind, Chrysostom warns rigid proponents of celibacy that the "detractor of marriage reduces the glory of virginity . . . For what appears good in comparison

[2] Ladner, *The Idea of Reform*, 129.

with something inferior would not be very good."[3] He insists that marriage and virginity "both lead to heaven."[4] When husbands and wives practice sacrificial love, chastity, charity, and hospitality, Chrysostom explains, they are a great aid to the church and serve the kingdom of God no less than monastics.

On occasion, Chrysostom emphasizes the importance of the family for the health and strength of society. Yet the secular function of the family is rarely at the top of his mind. Rather, his vision of marriage and family is emphatically ecclesial. In his homily on Ephesians 5:22–33, for instance, he likens the household to "a little Church," and also argues that "by becoming good husbands and wives" Christian spouses also become "fit to oversee the Church."[5] The godly family is the family in which all of its members rehearse the redeemed and sanctified life in their daily relations and affairs in a manner resembling the church's continual offer of sacrifice and service to God. Such a family is an image of the church.

Repeatedly in his writing, Chrysostom strikes the note that although married people live their lives amid myriad distractions and obstacles to holiness, Christ expects no less of them than of the monks in constant spiritual and moral struggle to be holy. Much like Clement of Alexandria (ca. 150–ca. 215) before him, Chrysostom unhesitatingly states that marriage is, in fact, a more difficult calling than celibacy. But he warns married persons against using the adversities and trials of their station in life to excuse themselves from the commandments of Christ "If ... [the] beatitudes were spoken to solitaries only, and the secular person cannot fulfill them, yet He [Christ] permitted marriage," he exhorts, "then He has destroyed all men. For if it be not possible, within marriage to perform the duties of solitaries, all things have perished and are destroyed, and the functions of virtue are shut up in a strait." Rather, "if any persons have been hindered by their marriage state, ... marriage is not the hindrance, but their purpose which made ill use of marriage."[6]

In his homilies on the book of Acts, Chrysostom employs a typological reading of the Old Testament stories of the Abrahamic household to enjoin married people to make their household a "little church." He explains that the Abrahamic household practiced the virtues of the kingdom of God in an exemplary manner prophetic of the future church.

3 Chrysostom, *On Virginity and Against Remarriage*, 13 (*On Virginity* X).

4 Chrysostom, "Homilies on Philippians," in *A Select Library of Nicene and Post-Nicene Fathers of the Christian Church*, vol. 13, 240 (homily 13).

5 Chrysostom, *On Marriage and Family Life*, 57 ("Homily 20: On Ephesians 5:22–33").

6 Chrysostom, "Homilies on Hebrews," in *A Select Library of Nicene and Post-Nicene Fathers of the Christian Church*, vol. 14, 402 (homily 7).

> Abraham received the strangers in the place where he abode himself; his wife [Sarah] stood in the place of a servant, the guests in the place of masters. He [Abraham] knew not that he was receiving Christ; knew not that he was receiving Angels; so that had he known, he would have lavished his whole substance. But we, who know that we receive Christ, show not even so much zeal ... Let our house be Christ's general receptacle.[7]

Here Chrysostom draws attention to something even more concrete than the network of persons and relations, which is the heart that pumps life-giving blood through the household. He speaks of the dwelling place itself that must become a physical vessel of the mystical body of Christ. Abraham's tent is the Old Testament type of the Christian dwelling that is a house of God. "Let the house be a Church consisting of men and women," Chrysostom declares. "'For where two,' He [Christ] says, 'are gathered together in My Name there am I in the midst of them' [Matthew 28:20]."[8] When he looks to the New Testament, Chrysostom applauds Aquila and Priscilla in the book of Acts (Acts 18:1–3, 18, 26), friends of St. Paul (Romans 16:3; 1 Corinthians 16, 19; 2 Timothy 4:19), who opened their home to the disciples. This couple, he says, is exemplary of a Christian marriage whose home became a temple of God. It was "no small excellency that they made their very house a Church."[9]

THE NATURE OF MARRIAGE: ITS BEGINNINGS AND PURPOSES

Before his return to Antioch and for several years afterward, Chrysostom, like other patristic writers, regarded marriage as much the inferior to celibacy. In his early writings, he describes marriage as a concession to human weakness and sinfulness and as a guard against debauchery and fornication. Moreover, he does not seem to have believed that in Eden Adam and Eve were married, or that they had coitus. God had other means by which to multiply humankind. Sin and death had not yet entered human existence, so there was no need to reproduce in the way human beings have done since the Fall into sin.

The opinion that in Eden Adam and Eve were not married is unrelated, however, with a belief as to whether there was sexual intercourse before the Fall. Differing from the dominant trends of interpretation in Western church fathers, Chrysostom does not regard coitus as the act that consummates a

7 Chrysostom, "Homilies on Acts of the Apostles," in *A Select Library of the Nicene and Post-Nicene Fathers of the Christian Church*, vol. 11, 277 (homily 45).

8 Ibid., 172 (homily 27).

9 Chrysostom, "Homilies on First Epistle of St. Paul the Apostle to the Corinthians," in *The Homilies of S. John Chrysostom*, part 2, 620.

marriage. In his early tract *Against Remarriage*, likely composed during his first years as a deacon in Antioch, he emphatically states, "Marriage is not called marriage because of coitus … but because the married woman is content with one man."[10]

Even in his later writing, when Chrysostom consistently speaks of Adam and Eve as married in Eden, he does not change his mind about sexual intercourse. It is his settled view that sexual intercourse began after the Fall in order for the race to procreate,[11] but not just for that purpose. The pleasure of coitus, he declares, is "a genuine pleasure … according to nature."[12] When God created Adam and Eve, "God linked them together by their natural needs, linked them as if by an unbroken bond when he encircled them with the chain of desire (*epthymias*)."[13] He expands on this theme in his homily on Ephesians 5:22–33:

> The power of this love [of man and woman] is truly stronger than any passion. This love [*eros*] is deeply planted within our inmost being. Unnoticed by us, it attracts the bodies of men and women to each other because in the beginning woman came forth from man, and from man and woman other men and women proceed. Can you see now how close this union is, and how God providentially created it to form a single nature?[14]

Thus, while Chrysostom believes that sexual intercourse is an aftermath of the Fall, he does not conclude that it is a corrupted byproduct of original sin. Rather sexual intercourse is in its essence a positive thing; and it can be a healthy expression of the marital bond. In a homily on the New Testament letter to Titus, Chrysostom explains: "The fornicator is not unclean on account of the intercourse, but on account of the manner of it."[15] Whereas in a chaste marriage, it is "as if she [the wife] were gold receiving the purest gold. [T]he woman receives the man's seed with rich pleasure … It is mingled with her own substance, and she returns it as a child." Even when "there is no child, … their intercourse effects the joining of their bodies, and they are

10 Chrysostom, *On Virginity and Against Remarriage*, 132 (*Against Remarriage*, 2).

11 He appears to base this conclusion on a literal reading of the Genesis account that following their expulsion from Eden (Genesis 3:24), "Adam knew Eve his wife, and she conceived and bore Cain" (Genesis 4:1 [RSV]).

12 Chrysostom, "Homilies on the Epistle to the Romans," in *A Select Library of the Nicene and Post-Nicene Fathers of the Christian Church*, vol. 11, 356 (homily 4).

13 I am using Elizabeth A. Clark's translation of this passage from Chrysostom's fourth sermon on Genesis. See *Women in the Early Church*, 43. The full text in English may be found in *St. John Chrysostom: Eight Sermons on the Book of Genesis*.

14 Chrysostom, *On Marriage and Family Life*, 43–4 ("Homily 20: On Ephesians 5:22–33").

15 Chrysostom, "Homilies on Titus," in *A Select Library of the Nicene and Post-Nicene Fathers of the Christian Church*, vol. 13, 531 (homily 3).

made one, just as when perfume is mixed with ointment."[16] For Chrysostom, "sexual attraction . . . is an integral part of our human nature, which is basically good after the Fall."[17]

Chrysostom does not believe, as Augustine did, that human sexuality is inherently tainted by lust and concupiscence, but he is not sanguine about the goodness or health of human sexuality either. He emphasizes that Satan has perversely turned our sexuality against its original purpose, its "course thereof into another fashion."[18] The lust and concupiscence that darken so much of human sexual expression and do such harm to the integrity of relations between the sexes are the devil's tools to prevent sexual intercourse from genuinely uniting male and female so that they become "two in one flesh," as God had intended for Adam and Eve. This harmful turning can be combatted, however. It is possible for marriage to be an environment in which the original harmony and unity between the sexes are restored. Through discipline, sexual passion can be contained and directed toward positive ends, including the bearing of children.

Chrysostom offered the elements of a sacramental vision of marriage. Marriage is the "location" of a transforming and sanctifying grace. The Adam-Eve humanity "of one flesh" that God wishes to bring about by marriage (Genesis 2:25 NKJV) is not "an image of anything on earth, but of God himself,"[19] he declares. Indeed, the chaste union of husband and wife is an emblem of the communion of life that God in Christ has secured for humankind through the union of his divinity with humanity and by his taking the church as a bride. As Eve came from the side of Adam, so "the church was made from the side of Christ, and he united Himself to her in a spiritual intercourse."[20] This is how Chrysostom understands St. Paul's pronouncement that the "one flesh" union of man and woman reveals a "great mystery . . . concerning Christ and the church" (Ephesians 5:31–2). In a fallen world, marriage's first purpose is to unite the sexes, or, to be more accurate, to reunite the sexes in a bond of love for which God intended them from the beginning.

All of this is to say that for Chrysostom, "the primary reason for marriage" is neither procreation nor the good of society, but rather, as Catherine Roth remarks, "the unity of love and holiness of the couple themselves."[21] In other terms, the principal good of marriage is the love bond that unites husband and

[16] Chrysostom, *On Marriage and Family Life*, 76 ("Homily 12: On Colossians 4:18").

[17] Ford, *Women and Men in the Early Church*, 47. I draw heavily on Ford's analysis of Chrysostom's views on sexuality.

[18] Chrysostom, "Homilies on Romans," 356 (homily 4).

[19] Chrysostom, *On Marriage and Family Life*, 75 ("Homily 12: On Colossians 4:18").

[20] Ibid., 77. [21] Chrysostom, *On Marriage and Family Life*, Introduction, 22.

wife. Not only does the unitive energy of postlapsarian marriage have the capacity to remedy the alienation of male and female from each other, which the ancestral sin has brought about, but the conjugal union itself also symbolizes the oneness and interdependency of the human race, of which the family is a microcosm.

In his homily on Ephesians 5: 22–33, Chrysostom states with palpable feeling:

> Can you see how close this union is, and how God providentially created it from a single nature? He permitted Adam to marry Eve, who was more than sister or daughter; she was his own flesh [taken from his side (Genesis 2:21–4)]. God caused the entire human race to proceed from this one point of origin. He did not, on the one hand, fashion woman independently from man; otherwise man would think of her as essentially different from himself. Nor did He enable woman to bear children without man; if this were the case she would be self-sufficient. Instead, just as the branches of a tree proceed from a single trunk, he made one man Adam to be the origin of all mankind, both male and female, and made it impossible for men and women to be self-sufficient.[22]

Chrysostom's symbology of marriage is theanthropic. It follows from his understandings of the image of God in man, the union of divinity and humanity through the Incarnation, and the Trinitarian existence of God. It indicates that the human telos is communion with God. He implores: "A man should love his spouse as much as himself, not merely because they share the same nature; no, the obligation is far greater, because there are no longer two bodies but one ... Husband and wife are one body in the same way as Christ and the Father are one."[23]

Here is the ground on which Chrysostom's objection to divorce rests, even though he makes limited allowance for both divorce and remarriage. He is aware, certainly, of the contractual entailments of marriage, but his objection to divorce is not premised on a presumed indissolubility of the marriage contract. Rather, his opposition to easy or frequent divorce among Christians derives from his strong view of the integrity of the conjugal union of husband and wife, that the union is enjoined by none other than God in Christ and is an image of God, who himself is an absolute and eternal unity of persons.

Marriage, therefore, is a holy union; it is next to inviolate. And yet the church will accept that in certain instances the two who were joined as one are in reality twain. He comments: "Certain marriages simply are not ordained by God, even though the institution of marriage as a whole is consecrated."[24] In one of his homilies on Romans, he states:

[22] *On Marriage and Family Life*, 44 ("Homily 20: On Ephesians 5:22–33"). [23] Ibid., 52.

[24] Quoted by Ford, *Women and Men in the Early Church*, 183.

> Thus when a certain wise man says, "It is by the Lord that man is matched with a woman" [Proverbs 19:14], he means that God made marriage, and not that it is he who joins together every man who comes to be with a woman. For we see many who come to be with one another for evil, even by the law of marriage, and this we should not ascribe to Christ.[25]

Chrysostom also counseled strongly against remarriage, though he was acutely aware of the plight of widows. He seems to have wanted to affirm to those who sought his counsel that the love of a husband or wife for his or her spouse should extend through the whole of life, even if the spouse is deceased, and that fidelity to a deceased spouse by remaining single is an expression of belief in resurrection. "As much as virginity is superior to marriage, so much is a single marriage preferable to a second marriage," he states. Importantly, however, he adds: "I repeat that I do not say these things wishing to condemn those women who refuse to remain widows."[26]

With St. Paul, Chrysostom affirms the equality of husband and wife in matters of sexual relations. He also follows the apostle's teaching (and the cultural norm of the time among Christians, Jews, and pagans alike) of male headship. His views on marriage and family are not democratic or egalitarian, but Chrysostom was not a misogynist. Chrysostom reads Genesis with an understanding that God created Adam and Eve as ontologically equal. Since the Fall into sin, however, this equality, though the ideal, no longer exists functionally. After the original sin, the Bible says, Eve's "desire shall be for [her] husband and he [Adam] shall rule over you" (Genesis 3:16 RSV). Chrysostom recognized that this debased postlapsarian condition of marital relations was the norm in the culture of his day. His religious vision, specifically his Christological and protosacramental vision, of marriage opens on to a restoration of the original equality and reciprocity of the sexes. That restoration begins in this life, but is completed only in the kingdom of God.

In spite of a sobriety or realism about the degree to which marriage "in the Lord" can be perfected in this life, Chrysostom yet believes that marriages in the Lord must rise above the often brutal relations of men and women in his day. For he understands St. Paul to be saying that by virtue of their baptisms, a man and a woman joined in holy matrimony enter into the new eschatological humanity of the Second Adam and become one nuptial being. Marriage in the Lord transcends nature's hierarchies based in strength or power. It brings man and woman into a life in which the corrupted forms of dominance that human beings have exercised over one another throughout

[25] Chrysostom, "Homilies on Romans," 511 (homily 23).

[26] Chrysostom, *On Single Marriage* 6, quoted by Ford, *Women and Men in the Early Church*, 71.

recorded history may be overcome and left behind. Though sin is a hindrance to humankind, God has sought to set marriage once again on a more loving footing. Christ beckons married couples to conform themselves to the standards of the kingdom of God, in love aspiring to a full and genuine communion of being.

In the fourth of a series of eight Lenten homilies on Genesis, Chrysostom discusses in depth the unfortunate consequences of the Fall for the sexes. He interprets the yearning of Eve for Adam after the Fall as inordinate, servile, and demeaning, and Adam's subsequent mastery over Eve as unnatural and bound to corrupt the male. He counsels that God seeks to overcome the distorted relations between man and woman through Christ like, self-sacrificing, and donative love (*agape*). He believes that the husband who is in a position of dominance must initiate this love of Christ. He cites St. Paul's instruction to husbands in 1 Corinthians to "love your wives" (1 Corinthians 5) and comments: "Do you see how trouble-free the lordship when the lord is an ardent lover of the subject . . . In this way, in fact, the burdensome element of subjection is removed."[27]

It is clear that Chrysostom does not seek a revolution in the prevailing cultural norms, but rather believes these norms may be transcended in new relationships that are established in Christ-like love. While he accepts Paul's language about the headship of the husband in the marital union (1 Corinthians 11:3; Ephesians 5:23), he interprets Paul's speech about headship of the husband Christologically. Christ is the pioneer of our salvation. He "heads it up." And as "the husband is the head of the wife, so also Christ is the head of the church, and he is the Savior of the body" (Ephesians 5:23 NKJV). The headship of Christ over the church is a work of salvific love; the headship of the husband within a Christian marriage will be the same. "Husbands love your wives just as Christ loved the church and gave Himself for her," St. Paul writes (Ephesians 5:25 NKJV). Chrysostom interprets this to mean that the wife's subordination within a Christian marriage is recognition of the authority of the husband as a bearer toward her of the same love with which Christ loves the church. This subordination is no more a sign of inferior or servile status than is the church's submission to Christ.

Chrysostom does speak of the wife as "lesser" (*elasson*) than the husband. The Greek word *elasson* is often translated "inferior," but this translation risks a confusion of meaning, as if the wife is "worse than," or ontologically and morally inferior, to the husband. Chrysostom's use of the word is more restrictive, truer to its primary meaning in the Greek. The wife is a "lesser" or "second authority" within the household. Chrysostom is identifying roles

[27] Chrysostom, *Eight Sermons on the Book of Genesis*, 67.

and a hierarchy that he thinks are necessary to the proper ordering of any household, roles and a hierarchy that many today reject. He is in this sense a person of his own time. Yet he is not uncritically accepting of the cultural roles of his day. As David Ford writes, "St John Chrysostom fills the pattern of male headship/superiority with profoundly Christian content, enriching it to a far greater degree than it was understood and practiced at the time by his surrounding non-Christian society."[28]

A stunning illustration of this occurs at the start of Chrysostom's homily on Ephesians 5:22–33, where he brilliantly juxtaposes Genesis 1:27 and Galatians 32:28, so that there can be little doubt about his high, even sacramental understanding of being married "in the Lord." This homily excludes a servile subordination of the wife to her husband, but indicates, rather, a unity of two human beings as a single nuptial and ecclesial "body," which transcends the artificial gender differences and ideologies that human beings, not God, have invented. He states:

> A certain wise man, when enumerating which blessings are most important, included "a wife and husband who live in harmony" (Sir. 25:1) . . . From the beginning God in his providence has planned this union of man and woman, and has spoken of the two as one: "male and female He created them" (Gen. 1:27) and "there is neither male nor female, for you all are one *in Jesus Christ*.[29]

All the forms of sinful divisions that St. Paul catalogues in Galatians 3:28 – "There is neither Jew nor Greek, there is neither slave nor free, there is neither male nor female; for you are all one in Christ Jesus" – Christian baptism puts to death, perhaps most especially the division and alienation of male and female. As the church is the arena of the elimination of these divisions, so also, in microcosm, is marriage "in the Lord."

CHILD AND PARENT IN CHRYSOSTOM'S VISION OF THE FAMILY

The child lies at the heart of Chrysostom's vision of family, community, and ultimately the kingdom of God. He does not hold to a doctrine of original sin, which teaches that all human beings have inherited Adam's sin as well as his guilt. Thus, again, unlike St. Augustine, who believes that even the smallest infant is under the condemnation of original sin, Chrysostom regards infants and small children as innocents, although they soon and

[28] Ford, *Women and Men in the Early Church*, 143.

[29] *On Marriage and Family Life*, 43 ("Homily 20: On Ephesians 5:22–33").

inevitably become habituated to the sin that has been pervasive in human society since the Fall. The image of God in human beings is degraded: the luster of the image of God is lost. But a right relationship of parents and children can remedy this loss.

God has instilled in human beings a natural bond between parents and their offspring that can help children grow in a likeness to God rather than diminish further from it. Parents are in a position to exercise a "divine" pedagogy that restores in their children some of the original luster of the image of God. Parenting is not primarily about preparing children to be autonomous selves or to be successful in a trade or profession, but rather about bringing children into the communion of saints. The high duty and obligation of the office of parent, which God has ordained and effects through consanguinity, is salvific in character. Parenting is a solemn responsibility to prepare children for the kingdom of heaven and not let them slip into the hands of Satan.

In *An Address on Vainglory and the Right Way for Parents to Bring Up Their Children*, Chrysostom offers advice to parents on how to build up godliness in their children. This concerns character, the stamping again or refashioning of the image of God in them. He returns repeatedly to one of his favorite metaphors, the child as a statue of God.

> To each of you fathers and mothers, I say, just as we see artists fashioning their paintings and statues with great precision, so we must care for these wondrous statues of ours. Painters when they have set the canvas on the easel paint on it day by day to accomplish their purpose. Sculptors, too, working in marble, proceed in a similar manner: they remove what is superfluous and add what is lacking. Even so must you proceed. Like the creators of statues do you give all your leisure to fashioning these wondrous statues for God.[30]

Because he is confident in the child's potential to increase in God-likeness, Chrysostom expects parents to commit themselves to restoring and refining the image of God in their children. He maintains that the office of parent is imitative of Christ's divine pedagogy. Parents are not the saviors of their children, but they are their natural teachers. When parents apply themselves to this pedagogical vocation, they themselves also grow in godliness by doing so. "Don't think that only monks need to learn the Bible;

[30] Chrysostom, *An Address on Vainglory and the Right Way for Parents to Bring Up Their Children*, 96.

children about to go out into the world stand in greater need of Scriptural knowledge,"[31] Chrysostom argues. And he continues:

> When we teach our children to be good, to be gentle, to be forgiving (all of these are attributes of God), to be generous, to love their fellow men, to regard this present age as nothing, we instill virtue in their souls, and reveal the image of God within them. This, then, is our task: *to educate both our children and ourselves in godliness* [my emphasis].[32]

There is a weighty implication in all of this. Though a parent may lead an otherwise virtuous life, if he or she neglects the needs of the child, especially the child's growth into godliness, then the parent's personal virtue counts for little or nothing in God's eyes. "When parents are concerned only with their own affairs and do not wish to give priority to their children's, they necessarily neglect their children, as well as their own souls."[33] Chrysostom exhorts, "Not only does God punish children who behave badly toward parents, not only does he receive favorably those who are good, but he also does the same thing to the parents, severely punishing those who neglect their children, but honoring and praising those who care for them."[34]

In Chrysostom's view, love of God is correlative to fear of God, the respect and honor due to God because God is perfect and holy. He says that something analogous should obtain in the child–parent relationship. Trust, humility, and obedience belong to the office of child, whereas presence, authority, and loving care belong to the office of parent.

In sum, Chrysostom's ecclesial vision of marriage carries over into his views on raising children. Those "wondrous statues" of God cannot stand alone. Rather, children belong to a great and ever-increasing company that love binds. That which is private within the family should not remain so. It must expand into diaconal activity, in other words, service in community with others. Chrysostom regards parenthood as a heroic vocation of unselfish contribution to a divine peoplehood. Family includes children, so both parents and children alike have responsibility for the community.

Thus, while a comparison of children to statues is helpful for certain purposes, we must not take the analogy too far. Children are not inert material merely to be molded by adults. Rather, Chrysostom insists, children should be raised as responsible moral agents. Indeed, the question at the heart of human

31 Chrysostom, *On Marriage and Family Life*, 69 ("Homily 21: On Ephesians 6:14").

32 Ibid., 71.

33 Chrysostom, *A Comparison between a King and Monk/Against the Opponents of the Monastic Life*, 133.

34 Ibid., 132.

community is not whether it takes a family *or* a village to raise a child, but rather that for the family and village to flourish, we must raise children who fill responsibly their office of child. He teaches us that only if we recognize the child in his or her office of child, son or daughter, and prepare the child to occupy and fulfill the responsibilities of that office – only then – will we clearly apprehend what a family is.

RECOMMENDED READING

Brown, Peter. *The Body and Society*. New York: Columbia University Press, 1988.

Chrysostom, St. John. *On Virginity and Against Remarriage*. Translated by Sally Rieger Shore. Introduction by Elizabeth Clark. Lewiston, NY: Edwin Mellen Press, 1983.

St. John Chrysostom: On Marriage and Family Life. Translated by Catherine P. Roth and David Anderson. Introduction by Catherine P. Roth. Crestwood, NY: St. Vladimir's Seminary Press, 1986.

A Comparison Between a King and a Monk/Against the Opponents of the Monastic Life: Two Treatises by John Chrysostom. Translated and with an introduction by David G. Hunter. Lewiston, NY: Edwin Mellen Press, 1988.

Clark, Elizabeth A. *Jerome, Chrysostom, and Friends*. New York: Edwin Mellen Press, 1979.

Ford, David C. *Women and Men in the Church: The Full View of St. John Chrysostom*. South Canaan, PA: St. Tikhon's Seminary Press, 1996.

Frost, Carrie Frederick. "A Theology of Motherhood." PhD diss., University of Virginia, 2015.

Guroian, Vigen. *Ethics after Christendom: Toward an Ecclesial Ethic*. Grand Rapids, MI: Wm. B. Eerdmans Publishing Company, 1994.

"The Ecclesial Family: John Chrysostom on Parenthood and Children." In *The Child in Christian Thought*, edited by Marcia J. Bunge, 61–77. Grand Rapids, MI: Wm. B. Eerdmans Publishing Company, 2001.

Ladner, Gerhart B. *The Idea of Reform: Its Impact on Christian Thought and Action in the Age of the Fathers*. New York: Harper and Row, 1967.

Laistner, M. L. W. *Christianity and Pagan Culture in the Later Roman Empire*. Ithaca, NY: Cornell University Press, 1951 (Appendix includes a translation of John Chrysostom's *Address on Vainglory and the Right Way for Parents to Bring Up Their Children*).

Zion, William Basil. *Eros and Transformation: Sexuality and Marriage: An Eastern Orthodox Perspective*. Lanham, MD: University Press of America, 1992.

6

Emperor Justinian

Peter Sarris

BIOGRAPHICAL INTRODUCTION

Between the fourth and sixth centuries CE, the lands bordering the Mediterranean Sea underwent profound social, economic, political, and cultural change.[1] This change is most readily discernible in terms of political history, as the unifying, trans-Mediterranean Roman hegemony progressively broke down. In much of the West (i.e., Italy, North Africa, Gaul, Britain, and Spain), the Roman Empire gradually faded as a militarily and governmentally effective power structure during the fifth century, giving way to a series of "sub-Roman" or "Romano-Germanic" successor kingdoms.

To the east, however, the Roman Empire survived, ruled from Constantinople, which had been accorded the title of "New Rome" by the emperor Constantine upon his formal inauguration of the city in 330. From this new capital, emperors scanned a political horizon that included Greece, much of the Balkan peninsula, and the provinces of Asia Minor, Syria, Palestine, and Egypt. Importantly, these territories had long-standing and deeply rooted Christian communities whose leaders had been drawn into an increasingly close relationship with the imperial government by virtue of Constantine's adoption of Christianity as his favored cult around the year 312 and the subsequent elevation of the Christian faith as the official religion of the empire by the end of the fourth century.

The eastern Roman Empire experienced a major wave of economic growth from the fifth to early sixth centuries. Populations increased, the economy became increasingly monetized, and even settlements in marginal zones were expanding and being drawn into networks of commercial exchange.[2] Thus, although

1 See discussion in Sarris, *Empires of Faith*.

2 See Banaji, *Agrarian Change in Late Antiquity*.

FIGURE 6.1. Emperor Justinian I (483–565) ca. 547 CE (mosaic) (detail of 83451), Byzantine School, (sixth century) / San Vitale, Ravenna, Italy / Bridgeman Images

the Roman Empire of the early sixth century was geographically diminished, the provinces under Roman control were more prosperous, and the leadership of the Christian church within them was coming to wield greater authority and influence.[3]

From the perspective of the imperial government, however, the outlook in the early sixth century was more ominous, bringing a sense of political crisis.[4] To the east, warfare with the Sasanian Empire of Persia led to heightened insecurity. To the west, ancient heartlands of the Roman Empire (such as Italy) were ruled by "barbarian" kings who, although Christian, typically held theological stances the imperial church regarded as heretical.

Within the empire, rulers found the day-to-day exercise of power increasingly problematic. Although the economy was expanding, tax revenues were being embezzled by state officials and powerful landowners; although the empire possessed a deeply rooted legal culture, the proliferation of imperial legislative enactments and the social clout of powerful plaintiffs made it difficult for judges to ascertain the current state of the law or for emperors to effect it. Moreover, although much of the Christian leadership remained committed to the ideology of empire, the imperial church was increasingly riven by theological disputes about the relationship between the human and divine in the person of Christ.

Every one of these challenges to imperial unity would elicit a concerted response in the reign of the emperor Justinian, who ascended the throne as sole emperor in April 527, succeeding his elderly uncle Justin I, with whom he had briefly shared power. Justinian was a military man of relatively humble background, whose advance to the acme of power had been carefully choreographed by his uncle and Justinian's indomitable wife, the empress Theodora. The new imperial couple rapidly set about to isolate and eradicate their opponents. In 532, they took advantage of civil disturbance in the capital to arrest their senatorial foes, accusing them of launching an attempted coup. In 533, Justinian took advantage of a succession dispute within the Vandal kingdom of Africa to initiate a successful campaign of reconquest in that former Roman territory. In 535, he initiated the reconquest of Italy, and by the end of the 550s, the Italian peninsula had been restored to imperial control. At the same time, Justinian sought to contain the Persian threat to the east. He and his advisers also attempted a theological resolution to the Christological

3 These processes are discussed in Rapp, *Holy Bishops in Late Antiquity*.

4 For this and what follows, see Sarris, *Empires of Faith*, 125–68.

dispute in a genuine effort to address doctrinal issues while removing bishops deemed insufficiently cooperative.

CHRISTIANIZING THE LAW AND CHRISTIANIZING THE STATE

Justinian's military endeavors did much to restore the political and military dominance of the Roman Empire in the central Mediterranean. Likewise, the Christological formula that his court theologians pieced together and expounded at the church council that he summoned, the Second Council of Constantinople (553), gave clarity and cohesion to the imperial church at a moment when it was in danger of splitting. In other respects, however, these policies were less productive. After Justinian's death in 565, his successors had great difficulty holding on to the reconquered territories, and Justinian's repackaging of imperial Christology ultimately failed to persuade the eastern dissidents at whom it had been aimed. Certain administrative and tax reforms produced equally mixed results.

With respect to legal reform, however, the emperor had much greater success; between 528 and 534, his law commissioners produced a fifty-book collation and homogenization of the writings of the classical legal scholars, or jurisconsults, establishing which of their writings could be cited in court (the *Digest*, promulgated in 533); a condensed legal textbook designed for those beginning the study of law with a view to government service (the *Institutes*, also promulgated in 533); and a collection, homogenization, and codification of laws issued by Roman emperors (the *Codex Iustinianus*, the second recension of which was published in 534). Justinian would continue to legislate thereafter, issuing an important series of laws known as the *Novels*, which contain his most important legislation on marriage, the family, and sexual morality. But through his program of legal codification, the emperor managed to impose order on the Roman law tradition, deciding in what form the writings of legal scholars and the laws of his imperial predecessors would be transmitted to posterity and cited in legal proceedings. It is a sign of the emperor's success that Roman law as we know it remains largely as it emerged from the hands of Justinian's law commissioners.[5]

Justinian represented his program of legal codification and the laws he issued as restoring Roman law to its pristine glory. In practice, however, many of his laws fundamentally recast important Roman social and other

[5] For the workings of the commissioners, see Honoré, *Justinian's Digest*.

institutions. Justinian justified such reform by redefining the concept of natural law (*lex naturalis* or *ius naturae*) that had long been important in Roman philosophical and legal discourse. The natural world (as a result of divinely ordained creation) had traditionally been believed to embody immutable moral principles, which it was the duty of the philosopher to distill and of the legislator to express through civil law, which in turn, therefore, was meant to aspire to immutability. Justinian, by contrast, argued that only God and the divine will were immutable, whereas the natural world existed in constant flux, reflected in the inconsistency of human behaviour (see the prefaces to *J.Nov.* 18, 73, and 107). Such inconsistency on the part of humanity required moral correction through legal reform to make human behaviour conform with the divinely ordained moral truths set out in scripture and expressed by the church.[6]

Thus, for example, Justinian reshaped the Roman institution of marriage by inflecting the Roman law tradition in a direction more aligned with the increasingly strident moral teachings of the church. As a result, a secular tradition that had accepted non-marital sexual unions became increasingly defined by Christian concepts of sexual continence and monogamy; a relatively liberal attitude to the dissolution of marriage by mutual consent was replaced by growing emphasis on the indissolubility of the marital tie save for in the most extreme circumstances; and the church for the first time was given an important role in recording and placing under sacrament the union between husband and wife. Long-standing traditions of marriage within the kin group (especially to first cousins) of which the church disapproved were also the subject of imperial prohibition. The medieval Christian conception of marriage, in short, first found legal expression in the laws of Justinian. This was the result of a broader legal program of Christianization to which the emperor was personally committed.

The emperor made his intention publicly manifest in 533, when he confirmed the promulgation of the *Digest* "In the Name of Our Lord God Jesus Christ," thereby symbolically baptizing (and exorcizing) the intellectual inheritance of the non-Christian classical jurists.[7] Likewise, the opening volume of the *Codex Iustinianus* gave pride of place to laws concerned with "the most exalted Trinity and the Catholic Faith."[8] Only once the rights

[6] See discussion in Bjornlie, *Politics and Tradition between Rome, Ravenna and Constantinople*, 254–82.

[7] See discussion in Humfress, "Law and Legal Practice in the Age of Justinian," 168.

[8] *Codex Iustinianus* 1.1.

and concerns of the church had been addressed did the *Codex* proceed to detail those of the state.

What Justinian's legal reforms enshrined, in brief, and what the emperor's agenda sought to advance was the final transformation of the Roman Empire into a confessional state: one that was officially orthodox and Christian, not only in its ideology, but also in its interactions with its subjects, progressively advancing the rights of those who upheld the imperially sanctioned definition of the Christian faith, while curtailing the rights of religious and other minorities regarded as outsiders in what Justinian described in a law of 536 (*J.Nov.* 45) as the "orthodox republic" (*orthodoxos politeia*).

The positive construction of this confessional state to a certain extent continued a line of imperial policy that had been initiated in the Constantinian era: growing legal authority, including the right to hear legal proceedings, for example, was accorded to Christian bishops (e.g., *J.Nov.* 79, 86, and 123). Bishops were effectively to act as imperial agents.[9] The interests of the church as a landowner were advanced, and efforts were made to build up and protect the church's property portfolio (e.g., *J.Nov.* 7 and *J.Nov.* 9).

At the same time, a number of Justinian's laws record measures the state took to make life for non-Christians and heretics increasingly difficult. Among the emperor's first acts, for example, was a purge aimed at removing pagans from government service.[10] Deliberate efforts were made to marginalize and treat religious outsiders – heretics, Jews, Samaritans, for instance – as second-class citizens and to make it increasingly difficult for them to maintain familial cohesion and religious identity by transmitting property from one generation to the next.

SEXUAL MORALITY

Justinian's Christianizing agenda carried major implications for those whose religious stance he rejected. To some extent, however, the emperor was willing to respond pragmatically to the interests of religious outsiders when political or other circumstances demanded. In 551, for example, Justinian restored to the Samaritans of Palestine their right to make wills and leave property to non-Christians, signaling that the prohibition was being lifted in recognition of improved relations between the Samaritans and the local representatives of

9 Sarris, *Economy and Society in the Age of Justinian*, 210.

10 See discussion in Honoré, *Tribonian*, 14–15.

the imperial government (*J.Nov.* 129). Likewise, in another law (*J.Nov.* 139) the economically highly productive Jews of Tyre were exempted from Justinian's legislation against endogamous marriage (*J.Nov.* 12), which infringed upon Jewish tradition.

The reign of Justinian also served to focus legal attention, however, on those whose sexual conduct the leaders of the church deemed injurious to the public good or a potential source of divine displeasure. Foremost among these were men accused of homosexual acts (referred to in the sources as pederasts).[11] Constantinople in the age of Justinian fell victim to both the first known outbreak of bubonic plague (in 542) and a series of earthquakes, with an especially major one striking the capital in 557, when it destroyed the dome of Justinian's great cathedral church, Hagia Sophia. In each of these instances (and on the model of the biblical narrative of Sodom and Gomorrah), those accused of homosexual acts were expressly blamed for inciting divine wrath. The 557 earthquake, for example, was explained as divine punishment for "debauchery between males, by which some males godlessly dare to inflict their obscenity on others" (*J.Nov.* 141). Likewise, in another law the emperor warned of those "who are in the grip of the working of the devil, and have plunged into acts of very grave licentiousness, and behaviour contrary to nature itself." Justinian continued, "We exhort these, too, to take to heart the fear of God and the coming judgment . . . in order that their cities as well, along with their inhabitants, may not be found being destroyed under God's righteous anger" (*J.Nov.* 77).

Contemporary historian Procopius of Caesarea records that the prohibition on pederasty was effected with considerable savagery: "those who were thus convicted had their private parts removed and were paraded through the streets." He goes on to claim, however, that Justinian regarded the new legislation as providing an opportunity to publicly shame individuals against whom he was already minded to act, using the allegation of homosexual acts as a pretext.[12] It is perhaps significant "that the only persons known by name to have been punished for homosexual acts were prominent bishops," whose generally unmarried status perhaps left them especially vulnerable to such accusations.[13]

Justinian's concern to crack down on sexual immorality and licentiousness also led him to legislate against other groups. Constantinople in the early sixth century was home to a thriving flesh trade, with pimps traversing the countryside

[11] See discussion in Boswell, *Christianity, Social Tolerance, and Homosexuality*, 172–3.
[12] Procopius, *Anecdota* XI.34–6.
[13] Boswell, *Christianity, Social Tolerance, and Homosexuality*, 172–3.

to lure girls into prostitution by promising them clothes and food and binding them by means of what appeared to be legitimate contracts of employment. These contracts Justinian declared thoroughly illegal, and in a major imperial intervention brothels were completely banned (*J.Nov.* 14). In another (highly revealing) measure, he legislated against actors and prostitutes who dressed up as nuns and monks for the titillation of their clients, and he sought to ensure that the conduct of priests and religious women placed them beyond reproach (*J.Nov.* 123). Justinian's moral vision was carefully focused on encouraging chastity and continence, to the extent that he actively discouraged the remarriage of widows. While such remarriage was, to him, understandable, chastity was regarded as a higher state to which it was reasonable to encourage widows to aspire by rewarding them with legal privileges (*J.Nov.* 22). Moreover, in the same law, he declared that any husband or wife who wished to enter the religious life was permitted to dissolve his or her marriage without incurring any legal penalty.

THE CHRISTIAN FAMILY

As his attitude toward widows makes clear, Justinian's moral vision carried especially major implications for the institutions of marriage and the family. According to the *Digest*, marriage was "a union between a man and a woman, an association for the whole life, a community of human and divine law" (*Digest* 23.2.1). Traditionally, all that was required to contract a marriage was that the parties concerned wished to be married (what was known as the *affectio maritalis* or intention to be husband and wife), chose to live together as husband and wife, and had the consent of the head of their household (the paterfamilias) or guardian, if they were not legally independent. Marriage had long been prohibited between parent and child, brother and sister, or uncle and niece (or aunt and nephew), and the offspring of any such union were deemed illegitimate and could not inherit (see *Codex Iustinianus* 5.5).

The Roman institution of marriage was comparatively informal, and Roman legislators had traditionally adopted a relaxed attitude toward the dissolution of marriage, permitting both unilateral divorce and divorce by mutual consent. Moreover, compared to many other legal systems, the Roman law of marriage traditionally had limited implications for property relations between the contracting parties and preserved a strict regime of separation of the spouses' property. The two exceptions to this were the *dos* or dowry (see *Digest* 23.3) and *donatio propter nuptias* or prenuptial gift (on which, see *Codex* 5.3). The former consisted of property or some other contribution given to the husband by the wife or her family, which effectively comprised "the wife's contribution to the matrimonial home."[14] The latter comprised a gift from the husband to the wife before their marriage "to ensure provision for the wife in the event of the husband predeceasing her."[15] All other major gifts within marriage were traditionally prohibited to prevent "large capital settlements being made from one side of the family to the other."[16] Roman law was thus primarily concerned with preventing marriage from destabilizing the patrimonies of families joined through the marriage of their members. In particular (and in accordance with the patriarchal assumptions on which Roman social institutions rested), the law sought to protect property interests of the so-called agnatic kin (those on the husband's side) against interests or claims by the cognatic kin (those on the wife's side).

Much the same was true with respect to Roman inheritance law. The transmission of property by will was one of the great preoccupations of Roman legislators. Roman law established three types of testamentary heir, whose responsibility was to execute a will if one were left. First, there were the *sui heredes*, or members of the deceased's family who had hitherto been under his authority and now had become independent upon the testator's death (by definition, only the male head of a household, or paterfamilias, could possess such heirs, who primarily consisted of children and grandchildren born in wedlock or, if born out of wedlock, subsequently legitimized). Such individuals had originally not been permitted to refuse the status of heir and the obligation to execute the will (although a right to abstain had later been granted). Second were *necessarii heredes*. These were slaves manumitted by will of the testator and appointed as heir. Manumitted slaves were obliged to accept the role and responsibilities of heir if so appointed (it was this that made them "necessary"). Slaves were generally nominated as heirs to insolvent estates so as to spare the testator's kin or free household the moral taint associated with financial embarrassment. Roman law also permitted the testator to appoint an heir from outside the household. Such heirs, however, could not be forced to accept the appointment, and Roman law thus developed means of inducing them to do so. Foremost among these was the *Lex Falcidia* of 40 BC, which directed that the heir (or heirs) was entitled to 25 percent of the estate, meaning that not more than 75 percent of an estate could be assigned to legacies or trusts.

In event of intestacy, those with the first claim on an estate were the *sui heredes*, among whom it had to be divided in equal shares. If no such heirs

[14] Plessis, *Borkowski's Textbook on Roman Law*, 128. [15] Ibid., 131.
[16] Johnston, *Roman Law in Context*, 34. See also *Digest* 24.1.

existed (either because of childlessness or because the testator was a woman), the claim passed to the deceased's agnatic relatives (those in the male line of the deceased). If no agnatic relatives survived, the claim passed to the extended family. The logic of the law suggested that the main reason for making a will in the first place was to avoid a widespread dispersal or distribution of property.[17]

Justinian's legislation with respect to marriage is characterized first by its much greater emphasis on formality, partly to prevent couples from simply drifting into sexual unions that they then presented as marriage. In *J.Nov.* 74, for example (dating from 538), the emperor declared that dowries and pre-nuptial gifts were to be obligatory for those of senatorial status, with the written instrument detailing the dowry effectively becoming an obligatory contract of marriage. In the same law, the emperor decreed that other members of respectable society (above the level of the peasantry and the military rank and file, but beneath those of senatorial status) were to have their marriages sworn, witnessed, and registered at a church. The last provision would subsequently be modified by *J.Nov.* 117, but the emperor's desire to establish greater documentary and ceremonial proof of marriage foreshadowed later sacramental developments.

Moreover, as already noted, Justinian was a strong advocate of the permanence of the monogamous marital tie and (rather more unusually) the equality of husband and wife within marriage. The tendency to emphasize monogamy has most commonly been ascribed to the influence of the emperor's Christianity, while the emphasis on equality has sometimes been explained as owing to the influence of his wife. Justinian's commitment to the permanence of marriage to the exclusion of other relationships is perhaps most evident from the fact that, when compiling the *Codex Iustinianus*, his law commissioners emended the text of a law dating from the fourth century to permit judges to levy the death penalty for adultery (*Codex Iustinianus* 9.9.29.4).[18] Although this penalty does not appear to have been much handed down in practice, its presence on the statute books sent a stark message.

As well as discouraging remarriage by the widowed, Justinian's legislation rendered it increasingly difficult for married couples to divorce. In his extensive *Novel* 22 of 536 (which effectively codified the Roman law of marriage according to Christian principles), the emperor imposed additional penalties on those who divorced without just cause (while providing

17 Johnston, *Roman Law in Context*, 49–52.
18 See Evans Grubbs, *Law and Family in Late Antiquity*, 216–8.

clearer and narrower guidance about what "just cause" meant). In 542, an additional measure was introduced (*J.Nov.* 117), in which the grounds for legitimate unilateral divorce were further constrained, severe penalties were introduced for those who chose to dissolve a marriage through mutual consent (effectively making it illegal), and military wives whose husbands were missing in action were presented with additional legal hurdles before being allowed to remarry.

In contrast to some of his other laws on marriage (which were highly solicitous of the concerns of women), Justinian's measure of 542 adopted an especially harsh tone toward wives: it ordained that a wife who attempted to obtain a divorce from her husband without just cause as defined by the law was subject to life imprisonment in a monastery or nunnery (this penalty would eventually be extended to similarly unenthusiastic husbands in *J.Nov* 127). On the other hand, in an attempt to bolster the institution of marriage, the same law also made it considerably easier for men to marry their concubines (typically lower-class women whose social status had rendered them ineligible for marriage in the eyes of a socially superior partner) and to legitimize the offspring of such extramarital unions. In typical Justinianic fashion, therefore, the law of 542 was both liberal and restrictive and combined philanthropy with severity.

So long as a wife did not wish to dissolve her marriage for any reason other than to join a nunnery, Justinian's reforms of the inherited Roman law significantly advanced the rights of the wife, both within marriage and upon the death of her husband. The wife acquired greatly enhanced claims to the property of her deceased husband against any claims made by his agnatic kin (see *J.Nov.* 22) and an absolute right to reclaim her dowry (or an equivalent sum), with her claim taking precedence over those of other creditors or claimants (*J.Nov.* 91). Husbands and wives were permitted to derive the same material benefit from any dowry or prenuptial gift brought into the marriage (*J.Nov.* 68), and the wife was permitted to receive such a gift from the husband (to support her in the event of his death) even after they had actually married (*J.Nov.* 22). This latter provision stood in sharp contrast to the traditional Roman law of marriage and its concern with upholding the agnatic principle that prioritized the inheritance rights of male kin. This principle, too, Justinian's relatively liberal treatment of the interests of the wife increasingly eroded.[19]

This tendency to undermine the claims of the husband's kin would culminate in *Novel* 118 (issued in 543), which abolished the distinction between male and female kin in the event of intestate succession (i.e., succession to an

[19] See Arjava, *Women and Law in Late Antiquity*, 107.

estate not explicitly ordered by a will). Instead, relatives were to succeed in order of proximity, emphasizing a concept of blood relationship and putting male and female on an equal footing.[20] Both these tendencies were already evident in earlier legislation, but the pace of change may have been expedited by circumstances, for it is striking that so fundamental a change in the law on intestate succession occurred at the very moment when the empire found itself struck by the bubonic plague, which had a devastating demographic impact.[21]

If Justinianic law with respect to marriage significantly advanced the interests of wives, legislation concerning the family also revealed greater concern for the interests of children. This was particularly so with respect to children born out of wedlock. Justinian enhanced their ability to inherit from their father and (as already noted with respect to the offspring of concubines) made it considerably easier to legitimize them, allowing them to inherit fully (*J.Nov.* 38, *J.Nov.* 74). The law under Justinian also reveals a striking interest in issues of child neglect. Justinian protected the rights of children whose parents remarried and produced further issue, or who simply separated and abandoned their offspring, obliging them to beg (*J.Nov.* 98).

The Roman concept of the family was not, of course, a purely biological one; family also encompassed individuals who were members of the household not by blood, but by the legal authority of the male head of the family (the paterfamilias). In late antiquity, such individuals included slaves and, if the family owned land, *coloni adscripticii*. These were agricultural workers who worked on a landed estate on which they also were expected to reside by way of hereditary obligation, and who had been placed under the authority of the landowner by imperial law.[22] The family was also understood to include freedmen: these were former slaves who had been emancipated but still owed a social obligation of obedience and respect to their former owner.

The institution of slavery was left largely untouched by Justinian's legal reforms, but the legal interests of both freedmen and *coloni adscripticii* were advanced. First, Justinian confirmed with respect to *coloni* that estate workers who provided their masters with thirty years' continuous service entered into a new legal category of free *coloni* (*coloni liberi*). They thus acquired ownership of their working capital (such as a plot of land or cattle), known in Latin as the *peculium*, which had hitherto been under the control of their master, and which they could now bequeath to their heirs, who were likewise free, although they remained obliged to work on the estate (*Codex Iustinianus*

[20] Ibid., 96. [21] Sarris, "The Justinianic Plague: Origin and Effects," 169–82.
[22] Sirks, "The Colonate in Justinian's Reign," 120–43.

11.48.19). Moreover, any child born to a father who was a *colonus adscripticius*, but whose mother was fully free, was to be regarded as free and could not henceforth be claimed as a *colonus adscripticius* by the estate owner (*Codex Iustinianus* 11.48.24). Estate workers greeted this law with such alacrity that the emperor had to intervene to make clear that it did not apply retrospectively, and that adult *coloni* whose mothers had been free could not simply abandon their masters (*J.Nov.* 54).

With respect to freedmen, Justinian decreed that the act of emancipation was absolute: there was henceforth no distinction between "free" and "freed," and, in particular, women who had been slaves but were formally emancipated were henceforth to be regarded as cleansed of any social stain associated with their servile past and could thus marry whomever they wished (*J.Nov.* 78). The liberal tendency of certain of Justinian's legal reforms thus, yet again, served to undermine an institution that had long been central to Roman social perceptions, despite the emperor's much-vaunted propagandistic claims to be restoring both the Roman Empire and Roman law to pristine glory.

THE CORPORATE FAMILY

Justinian's legislation with respect to marriage and the family clearly reflected shifting social attitudes informed to a great extent (as we see in the case of divorce) by the growth and institutionalization of Christianity. But other, broader patterns of social evolution informed the emperor's laws or necessitated an imperial response. One of the key economic and social characteristics of the fourth to sixth centuries was the extent to which the period witnessed the emergence across the eastern empire of a new imperial aristocracy of service, whose members forged careers in the imperial government and bureaucracy while also carving out and acquiring ever larger landed estates.[23]

The families of members of this aristocracy appear to have possessed a strongly "corporate" character, and in particular, attempts were made by members of this new elite to secure the dynastic survival of their families by prohibiting their heirs from alienating property outside the family or bequeathing it to nonrelatives. Thus Justinian's novels record members of the aristocracy seeking to take advantage of the legal instrument known as the *fideicommissum* (akin to the English common-law "trust"), to oblige their heirs

23 See discussion in Banaji, *Agrarian Change in Late Antiquity*.

to keep property within the family, deploying the *fideicommissum* in order to try to make familial landholdings inalienable, similar in intent to the entail aristocratic families employed in early modern Europe.[24]

Roman law did not traditionally approve of the concept of leaving property to "unknown persons" and thus baulked at the concept of testators instructing their heirs to leave property only to their descendants before such descendants were even born. Broader patterns of social change, however (combined, no doubt, with lobbying on the part of wealthy interests), obliged Justinian to be more pragmatic, and in 555, the emperor issued a law permitting such fideicommissary settlements so long as they did not extend beyond four generations, thus attempting to reconcile the new wishes of testators with the traditions of the law.

At the same time, Justinian's own legislation pushed Roman family law still further down the "corporatist" path: as already noted, the emperor's laws reveal changing attitudes to the idea of the family, with the agnatic principle increasingly supplanted by the concept of the blood relationship (*J.Nov.* 118). Likewise, in 538 (*J.Nov.* 98), the emperor declared that upon the death of a parent, ownership of the dowry or prenuptial gift that the parent had brought into the marriage should pass to the children, with the surviving parent enjoying merely a right of use. If sixth-century testators did not wish their heirs to dissipate the family's property, neither did sixth-century heirs wish to see their parents do the same; testators were obliged to leave an increasingly large proportion of their estate to those entitled to inherit (known as the "heirs in intestacy"). In a law of 536, for example, the share of the reserved estate was increased from one quarter to a third (*J.Nov.* 18). Indeed, it is in Justinian's laws that we find the clearest expression of the increasingly corporatist view of the propertied family emerging, with the emperor declaring in a law of 537 that the heir and the testator should be viewed as a single person (*J.Nov.* 48). This was the first time in the history of Roman law that this position had ever been expressed.

CONCLUSION: CONFLICTING TRADITIONS

Justinian's laws reveal a dialectic between Roman legal tradition and shifting social attitudes, informed to a great extent by processes of Christianization, but also by broader and largely unrelated patterns of social and economic change. In certain areas of legislation, such as with respect to *fideicommissa*

24 See Sarris, *Economy and Society*, 194–5; and Johnston, *The Roman Law of Trusts*.

or trusts, Justinian attempted to triangulate between the spirit of the civil law and the evolving and changing ambitions of Roman testators. In other cases, such as with respect to divorce, on the subject of which Roman law had traditionally been relatively permissive, it was the emperor who spearheaded change.

Indeed, for some, Justinian's reform of divorce law went too far, and in 566, his successor, Justin II, reversed Justinian's effective prohibition on divorce by mutual consent.[25] In a carefully crafted constitution, the new emperor attempted to justify his abandonment of Justinian's reform on the grounds that it had failed to take into account the frailty of the human condition. Justin declared:

> Mankind has nothing more admirable than marriage: from it stem children and successive generations, the peopling of villages and cities, and society's best bond. Hence, it is our prayer that marriage should be so successful for those contracting it as never to be the work of an unlucky daemon, and that married couples should not split up without just cause for their marriage to be dissolved. But as it is difficult for this to be maintained for all mankind – in such a large population, it is outside the realms of possibility that some unreasonable enmities should not supervene – we have thought it appropriate to devise some remedy for this, in particular where the consequences of pettiness have escalated so far as to engender real, irreconcilable hatred between the partners.
>
> (*J.Nov.* 140)

To the modern reader, Justin II's admission of human weakness perhaps resonates more loudly than it did with some of his more morally strident contemporaries, and we can appreciate why he was minded to pull back from the austerity of some of Justinian's more extreme forays into the domestic sphere. But it should be noted that, thereafter, the writings of legal commentators would suggest that Byzantine judges and rulers were primarily inclined to apply the stricter legislation of Justinian rather than Justin II's more liberal measures. For Justinian's more Christianizing family law, with its focus on the family as an institution bound by blood, united by corporate identity, and galvanized by dynastic ambition, was one that increasingly appealed to contemporary social as well as religious sensibilities in Byzantium and beyond, as is clear from the way in which it would ultimately lay the bedrock of medieval canon law on marriage and related topics to both East and West in the centuries ahead.

25 See Clark, *Women in Late Antiquity*, 26–7.

RECOMMENDED READING

Arjava, A. *Women and Law in Late Antiquity*. Oxford: Clarendon Press; New York: Oxford University Press, 1996.

Banaji, J. *Agrarian Change in Late Antiquity*. 2nd edition. Oxford; New York: Oxford University Press, 2007.

Boswell, J. *Christianity, Social Tolerance, and Homosexuality: Gay People in Western Europe from the Beginning of the Christian Era to the Fourteenth Century*. Chicago: University of Chicago Press, 1980.

Clark, E. *Women in Late Antiquity*. Oxford: Clarendon Press; New York: Oxford University Press, 1993.

Evans Grubbs, J. *Law and Family in Late Antiquity: The Emperor Constantine's Marriage Legislation*. Oxford: Clarendon Press; New York: Oxford University Press, 1995.

Harper, K. *From Shame to Sin: The Christian Transformation of Sexual Morality in Late Antiquity*. Cambridge, MA: Harvard University Press, 2013.

Honoré, A. M. *Tribonian*. London: Duckworth, 1978.

Justinian's Digest: Character and Compilation. Oxford; New York: Oxford University Press, 2010.

Humfress, C. "Law and Legal Practice in the Age of Justinian." In *The Cambridge Companion to the Age of Justinian*, edited by M. Maas, 161–84. Cambridge, UK; New York: Cambridge University Press, 2005.

Johnston, D. *The Roman Law of Trusts*. Oxford: Clarendon Press, 1988.

Roman Law in Context. Cambridge, UK; New York: Cambridge University Press, 1999.

Maas, M. ed. *The Cambridge Companion to the Age of Justinian*. New York: Cambridge University Press, 2005.

Rapp, C. *Holy Bishops in Late Antiquity*. Berkeley: University of California Press, 2005.

Sarris, P. "The Justinianic Plague: Origin and Effects." *Continuity and Change* 17 (2002): 169–82.

Economy and Society in the Age of Justinian. Cambridge, UK; New York: Cambridge University Press, 2006.

Empires of Faith: The Fall of Rome to the Rise of Islam, 500–700. Oxford: Oxford University Press, 2011.

Sirks, B. "The Colonate in Justinian's Reign." *Journal of Roman Studies* 98 (2008): 120–43.

7

Theodore Balsamon

John Anthony McGuckin

BIOGRAPHICAL INTRODUCTION

Theodoros Balsamon flourished near the end of the twelfth century CE, during the reign of Emperor Manuel Komnenos and the incumbency of Balsamon's patron, Constantinopolitan Patriarch Michael Anchialos. Balsamon was born between 1130 and 1140 and died around 1199. Although he was one of the most important minds of his age in both civil and ecclesiastical law, his biography is little known, except for flashes of light shining on it largely from his own preludes to his works. There is a dearth of critical study of the man or the significance of his work.

Balsamon began his ecclesiastical career as a deacon of the Great Church (Hagia Sophia) in the imperial city, while he simultaneously held the positions of *nomophylax* (senior legal advisor to the imperial administration) and ecclesiastical *chartophylax* (chief archivist of the patriarchal library). As nomophylax (literally "custodian of the law"), he had the right to impeach anyone in political office and dismiss them from the emperor's service; he thus had membership in the Senate, though for a monk this was not technically permissible. In addition, Balsamon headed the law school of Constantinople as its most eminent professor and executive administrator. Throughout his life, he enjoyed the favor of the court (with one period of disgrace), though he was often its critic. Eventually he was given preferment as abbot of the important imperial monastery of Vlachernae, adjacent to the palace of the same name in the north of the city.

In 1193, Balsamon was ordained bishop and then elevated as Patriarch Theodoros IV of Antioch. His nomination to that great patriarchal see was largely symbolic. He was never able to take up residence in the Syrian city, because the Latin occupation had already installed a Latin-rite patriarch there. The crusader military occupation (to be followed throughout the

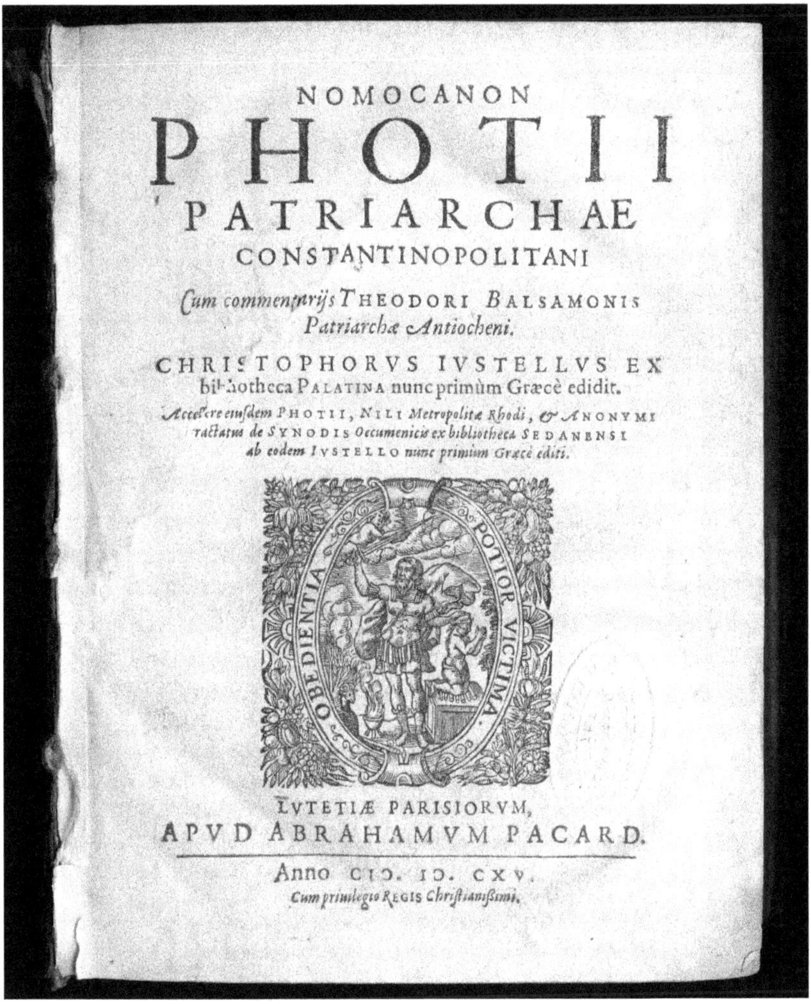

NOMOCANON
PHOTII
PATRIARCHAE
CONSTANTINOPOLITANI
Cum commentariis THEODORI BALSAMONIS
Patriarchæ Antiocheni.
CHRISTOPHORVS IVSTELLVS EX
bibliotheca PALATINA nunc primùm Græcè edidit.
Accessere eiusdem PHOTII, NILI *Metropolitæ Rhodi, &* ANONYMI
tractatus de SYNODIS *Oecumenicis ex bibliotheca* SEDANENSI
ab eodem IVSTELLO *nunc primùm Græcè editi.*

LVTETIÆ PARISIORVM,
APVD ABRAHAMVM PACARD.
Anno CIↃ. IↃ. CXV.
Cum priuilegio REGIS *Christianissimi.*

FIGURE 7.1. Theodore Balsamon, Nomocanon Photii Patriarchae Constantinopolitani.
Courtesy of the Pitts Theology Library, Candler School of Theology, Emory University

thirteenth century by the ousting of Orthodox clergy by Latins after the Fourth Crusade), sharpened Balsamon's hostility to Western Christianity, which he saw as predatory and careless in relation to both civil and ecclesiastical law of long-standing tradition. After his consecration as patriarch, he insisted on standardizing liturgical practice in the Orthodox Antiochene and Alexandrian churches, making the contemporary Constantinopolitan rite predominate over local practices. Much of his thought was taken up with issues related to the growing divorce between the Greek and Latin churches, which had never healed since the schism of 1054 and would be deepened after the crusader devastation of Constantinople in 1204.

BALSAMON'S CONTRIBUTIONS TO THE ORTHODOX CANON LAW OF THE FAMILY

While serving as nomophylax, around the year 1170, Balsamon was asked by Patriarch Michael to publish a significant review of church law attributed to the ninth-century Patriarch Photios, called the *Exegesis of the Nomokanon in 14 Titles.*[1] This was an authoritative listing of the key church canons and parallel civil norms. Balsamon made this major revision,[2] earning his greatest fame. He was instructed by both church and court authorities to harmonize the contradictions between imperial and ecclesiastical law in the *Nomokanon*'s prescripts, especially those cases where the tenth-century legal collation *Basilika* either ignored or contradicted laws of Emperor Justinian's sixth-century *Codex* reproduced in the ninth-century *Nomokanon* collation.[3] In general, Balsamon gave preference to the *Basilika* over Justinian, and since the *Nomokanon* is more

[1] Abbé Migne, *Patrologia Graeca*, 104. cols 441–2.

[2] His *Scholia* were first published in the West in a Latin edition by Hervet at Paris in 1561, reissued at Basel in 1562. At Paris in 1615, a bilingual Greek and Latin edition was brought out, and the English canonical scholar Beveridge published them in his *Pandecta Canonum* at Oxford in 1672. It was this edition that the nineteenth-century Abbé Migne republished in his monumental library, *Patrologia Graeca*, vols. 137–8. They were issued in the critical collection of Greek canons by Rhalles and Potles at Athens between 1852 and 1859 (G. A. Rhalles & M. Potles, *Syntagma ton Theion kai Ieron Kanonon*, Gk. txt., vols. 1–6, reprint 1966), and from there entered the very influential collection of Eastern Christian canon law made on Mount Athos by Nikodemos the Hagiorite in the later nineteenth century, known as the *Pedalion* ("Rudder of the Church"), which in both Greek and English editions is often the collection of canon law found on most presbytery shelves to this day. Cummings, *Pedalion*. Nikodemos regards Balsamon as one of the most eminent Greek scholiasts.

[3] The Byzantine *Nomokanon* was the Eastern church's medieval synopsis of both civil (*nomos*) and church (*kanon*) law that tried to harmonize both sets of regulations, which were theoretically meant to work in harmony and were given equal validity in the Byzantine state. By the ninth century, Justinian's *Codex* and the complete collection of conciliar canon laws had grown too large to be understood easily as harmonic voices.

faithful to Justinian, Balsamon thus tended to prefer the *Basilika* to the *Nomokanon* too. This preference for more current imperial legislation does not generally lead him to raise imperial civil legislation higher than ecclesiastical (canon) law, which Balsamon thinks always has a higher character; in several cases, however, he does prefer a clearer civil adjudication to a more antiquated conciliar one.[4] His legal editing work is most original when he adds personal notes or annotations, known as *scholia*.

Balsamon intended, in this very demanding editorial task, to comment on all the synodical canons and patristic rules, first presenting the annotations of his predecessor, legal expert John Zonaras (active circa 1118), on the import of the *Nomokanon*'s legislation, then adding his own clarifications as scholia, especially with regard to more recent imperial and patriarchal decrees. He tended to argue that where tension existed between similar civil and ecclesiastical laws with divergent instructions, precedence should be given to the canonical legislation. The immediate cause of his revisionary work was a conflict between his patron, Patriarch Michael, and the metropolitan bishop of Amaseia over Michael's decision to appoint an episcopal candidate to a vacant see who had not been nominated by the metropolitan's own local synod. The emperor had sided with the bishop, who had appealed to him directly after the patriarch's intervention. In this ruffle of feathers over limits of jurisdiction in matters of patronage and patrimony, Balsamon was asked to clarify the relative weight of civil and ecclesiastical legal judgment: where did one end and the other begin in disputed matters? Balsamon was respected and trusted in both the court and the church.

Balsamon took as his main civil text the *Basilika*, the list of extant state laws published in the early tenth century. If civil laws affirmed in the earlier *Nomokanon* were not repeated and validated in the *Basilika*, Balsamon followed civil precedent and considered those laws to have been superseded and rendered defunct in canon law too.[5] When he discovered contradictory elements in the ancient collections, Balsamon made critical interventions and

4 Meyendorff, *Byzantine Theology*, 85–6.

5 The emperor argued that the ancient canons did not give the patriarch the right to intervene, because the secular laws involved had not been confirmed in the *Basilika*, an abbreviated edition of the Roman laws. Balsamon, accordingly, elevates this principle. But while confirming the right of the emperor, as regnant Christian ruler, to determine what laws will hold sway over the church as well as the state, Balsamon and the patriarch tell the ruler that this power must be exercised with great discretion and only rarely. The power to interfere in doctrinal matters, on the other hand, is stated to lie wholly outside the emperor's power.

suggestions for resolution.[6] He took care to note which canons had been superseded by later canons, and which were no longer to be considered as having any practical force. His work would assume a great authority and wide dissemination in the Christian East, but several later Byzantine canonists, particularly Neilos Cabasilas,[7] drew attention to a certain level of "inattentiveness" in aspects, especially where he seemed to contradict himself. In 1195, Balsamon addressed a treatise to Patriarch Mark of Alexandria in the form of canonical *Questions and Answers*. He also compiled a collection of ecclesiastical constitutions known as the *Syntagma*, as well as letters on the subject of fasting and admission of monastic novices, which gained status as authoritative works.

The earlier canonical tradition, of course, had much to say on marriage and family. Part of the Byzantine reforms and new collations of law were meant to give a more systematic treatment: resolving issues where legal intents seemed to conflict, but also bringing together "titles," or sections, of law where similar matters were discussed under one heading, instead of being scattered chronologically over the history of lawmaking. The canonical references to marriage and family life might appear strange to the modern reader. Rather than speaking to the social order or spelling out theological definitions, the canons generally were developed to protect the sanctity of the altar: that is, they governed access to holy communion in the course of the divine liturgy. Some of the canons do deal with the legal definition of marriage, but by far the greater number concern purity laws regulating sexual expression, with the general intent of keeping sexuality far from the worshipping community at prayer.

In the first category, defining marriage, are canons that clarify its meaning; even then, the concept of marriage is approached tangentially. This can be seen, for example, in the Thirty Canons issued at the Council of Chalcedon in 451. Canon 14[8] addresses the issue of marriages contracted between men and women "of different faiths." It explains that this means marriages between an Orthodox party and a Jew, a pagan Hellene, or a heretic. Marriage with a heretic, left unspecified, is tolerated if the form of baptism of the respective dissident group is recognized by the Catholic Church. If not (as also in marriages with pagans and Jews), the marriage must be solemnized in the church or not be recognized at all. Children of the marriage are to be baptized in the Orthodox faith as a condition of permissibility. This canon was inspired by the realization of bishops at the Great Council that the practice of several

[6] The first edition of Balsamon's commentaries was completed before September 1180; the second edition, dedicated to Patriarch George II Xiphilinos, before February 1195. His canonical predecessor, John Zonaras, served as a model of clarity in method, which attempted to get the sense of legislation and see how it remained relevant for a contemporary context.

[7] See Faillier, *Revue des Études Byzantines*, 211–23.

[8] *Pedalion*, 259.

churches varied as to the strictness with which marriage regulation was enforced on the minor clergy (readers and cantors). Marriages of those who had anything to do with celebration of worship were to be strictly regulated. It is not stated explicitly, but this canon reflects a time, after the late fourth century, when Christian canonists were closely reading Old Testament laws regarding the cultic purity of the temple priesthood.

A similar trend can be seen in Canons 12 and 13 of the seventh-century Quinisext Council.[9] Canon 12, demanding that all candidates for episcopacy not be married, arose from reports that some African bishops of the seventh century were still married. Canon 13 allows Orthodox presbyters to marry, despite pressures from the Latin church to conform to their custom of celibacy for all bishops, priests, and deacons. Canon 12 needed some casuistry to explain why the practice (since the late fourth century) requiring bishops to be monastics must now be preferred, even though the New Testament explicitly allows married bishops. The following regulation (13) defends itself against Latin criticism by insisting that this permission for presbyters to marry is so that marriage may not be dishonored in the church: "When a man is elevated to ordination he must not be required to refrain from lawful intercourse with his wife, in case we are forced to be downright scornful of marriage, which was instituted by God and blessed by his presence [at Cana] as is attested by the clear declaration of the Gospel sayings" (citing Matthew 19:6; Hebrews 13:4; 1 Corinthians 7:27). The vision of marriage is here entirely circumscribed by priestly conceptions. They emerge out of the anxiety that ministers serving at the altar ought to have irreproachable marriage status.

The Eastern canons generally distinguish, for civil society, between legal marriages, on the one hand, and the threefold category of illicit, "irregular," and "damnable" unions, on the other. These distinctions relate to the legal severity of the reason that causes defect in the marriage contract (such as contracting marriage with a heretic or with a relative in a prohibited degree, or a union that breaks a nun's consecration). In the Apostolic Canons,[10] irregular unions are considered a debarment for the male partner to seek ordination later. Later Byzantine regulation of these early canons became increasingly punitive for those who contracted marriage within close consanguineous degrees,[11] ordering that such illicit marriages be dissolved immediately upon discovery and adding potential civil penalties (for marrying a niece) of having one's nose cut

[9] Ibid., 303–7. [10] Canons 17–19 of the eighty-five Apostolic Canons, *Pedalion*, 28–31.

[11] The degrees of prohibition are defined in Canons 53–4 of the 102 Canons of the Sixth Council of Constantinople. *Pedalion*, 351–2; Nicodemos offers a short treatise in a synopsis on the subject in *Pedalion*, 977–99.

off "after a severe cudgeling."[12] A few other canons concern the possibility of divorce for a range of other causes allowed by the church, although the Gospels allow, at most, only adultery as a reasonable cause.[13]

So much for the canons dealing with the abstract issue of marriage. The rules never really address the subject head-on, but almost always as a subfield of cultic purity issues. In terms of lay sexual matters, however, there is abundant detailed instruction. In each case, it seems, the bishops in council who issue these canonical rules are governed by the idea of cultic purity. For example, a range of sexual practices is prohibited, and in each case the penalty is a debarment (for varying lengths of time) from communion. This excommunication not only was a liturgical penalty, but also had strong social implications.[14] The celebration of marriage is not permitted in Lent, the canons insist. The reason for this was that a festive marriage banquet could not be held in a period designated as an extended fast. By the Byzantine era, and reinforced by Nicodemos in the nineteenth century, this ancient regulation, originally designed to enhance the celebratory aspect of a wedding, was being interpreted analogically to say that married couples must not engage in sexual intercourse during the Wednesdays and Fridays of Lent. Since these were especially strict fasting days, it was felt that the concept of fasting must, by extension, include abstention from sex.[15] A penitential character seeped into the larger perspective of marriage. The overwhelming "monasticization" of the Eastern canonical tradition is clear in the affirmation, already present in Athanasius's fourth-century *Letter to Amun*, that marriage is permissible and honorable but significantly less perfect as a way of life than virginity.[16] Moreover, in those canons that demand that married couples abstain from sexual relations prior and subsequent to communion,[17] the implication is that such practice defiles the sacrament. The canonical commentary relates the growth of this practice of distancing sexual relations from communicating at the Eucharistic altar to the Old Testament cultic rules cited in 1 Samuel 21:5, where David and his warriors swear off sexual relations for cultic reasons. It is for such a reason (that the wedding couple could not consummate the marriage sexually if they had communicated that morning) that the Eastern

[12] Byzantine Civil Code, Book 6, Title 37, *Pedalion*, 31. [13] *Pedalion*, 68–76.

[14] Marrying a woman promised to another is treated as adultery: *Pedalion*, 405–6; regulations against bestiality, *Pedalion*, 497–8; against incestuous relations, *Pedalion*, 503–4; against marital anal intercourse, *Pedalion*, 941–52; against sexual relations in times of a wife's menstrual cycle, *Pedalion*, 718–20; though all other women may marry more than once, a priest's wife is not allowed a second marriage, *Pedalion*, 348–9.

[15] *Pedalion*, 125–6. [16] *Pedalion*, 760.

[17] Canon 13 of the 102 Canons of the Quinisext Council, *Pedalion*, 306.

church eventually stopped the ancient practice of celebrating marriage in the context of Eucharist.

Balsamon's reputation as a master canonist lasted long after his death. To this day he is regarded as a major and authoritative voice in the Orthodox tradition. For historians, he is an important preserver of Byzantine legal sources that are otherwise unknown apart from his archival work. In the nineteenth century, canonist and theologian Nikodemos of the Holy Mountain (Athos) made a very popular collation of the canons of the Eastern church called the *Pedalion* and placed Balsamon's opinions at the end of a list of other classical-era commentators, following the original text of the ancient conciliar decrees. Because of this, Balsamon's opinions are still regularly consulted by Orthodox clergy as "the last word" for issues governing even the minutiae of parish life as well as matters of larger moral questions. His prominence is in many ways lamentable, given the more limited philosophical perspectives he brings to bear, especially his readiness to abandon many of the equitability issues the fourth-century fathers wished to introduce into the framework of the pre-Christian Roman law governing marriage. To prefer Balsamon's medieval "realism" to what he sees as their quixotic saintly, idealistic attempt to raise society to a higher standard of equitability under law, seems a rather gloomy turn the Eastern canons took in the high Middle Ages, and one that was certainly reinforced by the editors of the *Pedalion* in modern times. In many instances, Nicodemos's own comments, as he edited and presented the laws in the *Pedalion*, demonstrate an equally narrow, anxious, and prejudiced view of women – something perhaps not surprising from an Athonite monastic in a very low period of intellectual culture in the monastic republic to which he belonged.

BALSAMON'S LEGISLATIVE ATTITUDES TOWARD WOMEN

Women in ancient Greek society were largely invisible in the public forum. From the third to the fifth centuries CE, Christian theologians reformed Greek social conventions (short of allowing women to hold executive positions in church orders) to enlarge the social space where women could express themselves and move from invisibility to a certain "opacity." In high medieval times in Byzantium, however, as Balsamon witnesses, women once more were sequestered from mixed-gender contexts, a return to pre-Christian classical Greek mores.

Byzantine Christian attitudes followed many of the social customs and presuppositions of the ancient Greek world. In that intellectual universe, women occupied the "private" domain and men the "public" domain. The home and domestic interiority were seen as female, and the open space of the agora and intellectual discourse (logos, or word) were seen as male. Textuality was thus seen as an inalienable part of the male domain. And textuality, of course, became the primary historical record, thus keeping women historically invisible for much of the ancient and medieval periods. It is clear enough that wealthy women, both in antiquity and in medieval Byzantium, were often educated and textual, even to the point of being powerful princesses and empresses. But it was never common for women to be highly educated and literate. This explains the relative textual invisibility of women in the records of Greco-Roman society, and especially in the annals of early Christianity. Women are spoken of extensively, but always from the male perspective. Ancient Greek stage dramas summarize the problem exactly: the characters who present the views of women are using words entirely supplied to them by male authors, for the exclusive benefit of male viewers, and are themselves (as the law required) male actors impersonating females.

In the early church, women were disadvantaged by this Greek tradition. Generally, ill-educated women were married young, in their mid-teens, to considerably older men, who enjoyed extensive social and financial authority over them. Families made the decision of marriage for their daughters, and with a life of childbirth and domestic labor ahead, without sophisticated medicines, the female death rate was high and long life relatively rare. Women played no great part in the formation of the patristic textual tradition (being closed out of the major leadership offices of bishop and priest in antiquity). And in monastic life, their houses were much more confined, less opened by travel and political bond making than a comparable male monastery. Balsamon's legislative remarks show him at several instances considering the revision of legislation affecting women.

BALSAMON ON WOMEN'S POSITION IN MARRIAGE

One legal case referred to Balsamon concerned whether it was permissible for a man to marry a second cousin of a deceased wife. He took the opportunity, in a recorded adjudication (*Diakrisis*) in the form of a short treatise,[18] to set the issue in a wider consideration of gender in civil and ecclesiastical perspectives. He here defines marriage as two distinct "personal" realities, or *hypostases*, sharing the same nature of embodied soul, making one humanity

[18] *A Decision Regarding the Question Discussed in Synod, as to Whether It Is Possible for the Same Man to Be Joined to Second Cousins.* Text discussed more fully in Viscuso, "Marital Relations in the Theology of the Byzantine Canonist Theodore Balsamon," 281–8.

philosophically undifferentiated under the eyes of God. Gender thus did not alter human nature as such, but simply presented it as a different mode of existence (*tropos tes hyparxeos*) of the same nature. In so elevating the key terms *hypostasis* and *tropos tes hyparxeos*, Balsamon makes it obvious to his readers that he is quoting from St. Basil the Great's fourth-century doctrine of the Trinity. In Trinitarian theology one *ousia* (being or nature), that of the Father, is given as the common gift to Son and Spirit. They have the same nature, for they have only one nature among them and are thus one God. They are differentiated in the manner they exist within that singularity of being, namely, by the mode of their subsistence as distinctly named persons; the Father as cause; the Son by being engendered; the Spirit as being "processioned."[19]

For Balsamon, the marital relation is, therefore, a reflection of the Trinitarian mystery: a spiritual correlation of two human hypostases bonded by "almost sameness" of nature. Both the Trinitarian relations of the three divine hypostases and the two married hypostases represent an achievement of spiritual communion. The Trinity is the ideal form of spiritual communion: a mystery of perfect unity in differentiation, and distinctness in identity. In marriage, the spiritual relation devolves from the use of the two bodies to serve as a soul instrument of particular closeness and spiritual fecundity, where physical intimacy reflects the deeper aspect of finding a spiritual communion rising from erotic proximity as well as shared enterprise. For Balsamon, the exclusive sexual sharing of complementarily balanced flesh, male and female, clearly subjects the couple to civil and ecclesiastical law regulating marriage. In other words, it is not just a private affair, but a matter that models society, indeed the deeper cosmic order.

One might think, then, that such an elevated approach to marriage, one that views the contractual part as secondary to the profound theological mystery, might be liberative. Indeed, one of the most important deductions the classical Trinitarian fathers (Basil, Gregory Nazianzen, and Gregory of Nyssa) derive from their original hypostatic theory is the key point of the equality of the divine hypostases. One might have thought that a theologian who locates marriage in a base of such ontological primacy as Trinitarian language, rather than legal transaction, might be led to thoughts of the inalienable rights of (all) persons (hypostases). Not Balsamon. The two genders may be hypostatically equal before God, but women are certainly not equal, in Balsamon's view, in any socially contracted marriage. The wife is subordinated to the power of her husband by entering into a contract of submission. Balsamon gives no ground

19 See John 15:26.

for this deduction, no philosophical reflection on it. It seems to emerge, therefore, from his reading of the civil law, not from the ideas of the earlier Christian fathers trying to correct the Roman law with the refinement of the Gospel.

This posing of marriage in a Trinitarian context shows Balsamon's reading of Basil the Great and indicates some reliance on the work of Basil's contemporary and colleague, fourth-century theologian Gregory Nazianzen. Gregory had been acting archbishop of Constantinople in 381 and author of the church's definitive Trinitarian theology[20] when Emperor Theodosius I asked him to write an explanation why divorce and remarriage were forbidden in the Latin church but permitted in the Greek church.[21] Gregory defended the pastoral compassion of the Eastern canon law toleration of divorce by arguing that the mind of the lawgiver was the key issue that had to be sought in interpreting a law's intent.[22] Since Christ, Gregory said, was above all else a compassionate and merciful Savior, he would not wish to impose on his followers, "who were like fishes swimming in the turbulent and sorrowful sea of this life,"[23] the harsher legislation of the Latin church. It would be out of character with the Divine Lawgiver. Accordingly, Gregory resisted the pressure of Theodosius to bring Byzantine law into line with the Latin church's blanket proscription of divorce under any circumstances.

Knowing he would initiate controversy, Gregory adds other remarks on how Roman law can be wrong on matters concerning the relations of the sexes. The fourth-century Roman civil law, Gregory writes, obviously has a defective bias in other places when it comes to marriage. It ought not to be followed blindly, but refined and changed by the higher standard of Christian sentiment. As examples, he lists a series of objections he has heard raised against his opinion, such as the argument that Eve sinned first, so women now should be always kept under subjugation to men who will govern them more "rationally" than they can live themselves. He answers this by saying that Christ has redeemed both Eve and Adam and reconfigured their fallen natures. Moreover, he adds, only a woman gave bodily form to the Lord incarnate and thus rose as "our nature's solitary boast," something no man can claim. Even the male disciples ran away from the cross, Gregory says, while the women stood fast and ministered. He turns all objections on their head in a way that is unusual for an elderly

[20] In the form of his *Five Theological Orations* (Orats. 27–31). J. P. Migne, *Patrologia Graeca*, vol. 36.

[21] Cf. Crouzel, *L'Église primitive face au divorce di Iière auVième siècle.*

[22] Greg Nazianzen, *Oration* 37. Text discussed more fully in McGuckin, *St. Gregory of Nazianzus*, 332–6.

[23] Oration 37.1. Migne, *Patrologia Graeca*, vol. 36, 284.

celibate hierarch. Laws that do not treat women with equitableness compared to men, he concludes, cannot possibly reflect the mercy of God, who is always equitable to all.[24] "I do not accept such law," Gregory says; "I do not approve of such customs" that cannot demonstrate equitability. "God does not behave like this." But when he considers the exact legislative point (whether divorce can be tolerated), he is very decisive. A marriage is ideally meant to be once for all. Such a position is "according to law." A second marriage after divorce is "according to indulgence." It is an economy of mercy offered by the church in the name of the compassionate Christ. Such a canon law offering an economy of leniency allows for mistakes to be made and rectified.

This concept of economy is why Gregory thinks Eastern canon law must stand against any attempt to make it conform to the Western church. Moreover, he considers it unjust when Roman law decrees that a married man having sexual relations with a woman commits fornication and bears a lesser penalty, while a married woman having sexual relations with another man commits adultery, with concomitant severe ecclesiastical and social penalties. Gregory concludes: "Who made this law? Men surely." He holds this double standard up as a blatant example of male self-interest that casts aside equitableness in favor of vested self-interest. It is for Gregory, then, not only civilly disgraceful and unjust as a law, but ecclesiastically disgraceful as a departure from Christian charity and communion. It is paganism ripe for change.

Gregory Nazianzen's liberative treatment is also mirrored in the work of his protégé, St. Gregory of Nyssa. The younger Gregory was the brother of Basil the Great and was Gregory Nazianzen's student. He was appointed after 381 as a highly respected court theologian and orator. His patristic canonical decisions were collated later and had an enduring application.[25] Gregory of Nyssa regarded the liberative force of law as a mark of the proper application of the evangelical spirit. He is the only church father, for instance, who completely denounces the institution of slavery as an indefensible evil.[26]

In the fourth of his patristic canons, Gregory of Nyssa returns to the relative status of women in marriages that Gregory Nazianzen had discussed. He comes to the same conclusion: that women are equal in the sight of God, although Roman law holds married men and married women to different standards and proffers different penalties for men and women engaged in extramarital sex. All three of the greatest patristic voices – Basil and the two

[24] Gregory Nazianzen, *Oration* 37, 6; Migne, *Patrologia Graeca*, vol. 36, 289.

[25] As the Patristic Canons of St. Gregory of Nyssa.

[26] Gregory of Nyssa, *Homily* 4 (*On Ecclesiastes*).

Gregorys – had strongly leaned toward the principle of equitability to refine Roman law in their canon law judgments on marriage.

All of these promising patristic attitudes toward women and wives get snuffed out in the hands of Balsamon. When Balsamon comments on this patristic legacy,[27] he cites patristic language, but actually sustains the pre-Christian sense that the imbalance of power in marriage is suitable and acceptable. He will not equalize the canonical penalty attached to male as distinct from female infidelity, because the husband's authority within marriage has greater weight. By the marital contract, a woman is subordinated to the man. A husband's illicit relations with a woman not his wife is a sin of fornication yet "injures no one," Balsamon (naively) says. If a man has an affair with a married woman, he severely injures another man's legal rights. But his own wronged wife is held to have no legal claim. What, then, of the earlier patristic sense that there was a substantial issue of equitability, and the implication that the early church fathers wanted to see a Christian revision of law code recognizing it? Balsamon dismisses the patristic aspirations as idealism with no relevance in his (medieval) age. Eight hundred years after the patristic age, he thinks that such "unattainable standards" of equal valence for men and women were appropriate as ideals for such "exceptionally holy men," but not advisable or realistic for Byzantine society. Clearly, medieval Greek attitudes moved away from new potentialities raised at the dawn of Christian legislation and adopted a more feudal mentality that saw nothing wrong in the uneven marital legislation that worried the Cappadocian fathers.

A related issue shows Balsamon in a similar modality. In the canons of the ancient Council of Ancyra (314),[28] the earlier fathers insisted that Christian women who had been promised to men (the rite of betrothal) but were then abducted in time of war and later released were to be restored to their fiancés without any impugning of honor. Basil[29] commands that any woman abducted in war must be restored to the man to whom she was promised in marriage. The woman's rights have to take priority over any subsequent attachment. If the woman was not affianced, she has to be restored to her family, who may, if agreements can be made, restore her so as to be the acknowledged wife of her abductor. Canon 11 of the Council of Ancyra states that the restoration of the woman to her fiancé must take place even if she is no

27 Rhalles and Potles, *Syntagma* IV. 312–14; see Viscuso, "Theodore Balsamon's Canonical Images of Women," 318–19.

28 Canon 11: "It is decreed that virgins who have been betrothed, and who have afterwards been carried off by others, shall be restored to those to whom they had formerly been betrothed, even though they may have suffered violence from the ravisher."

29 Canon 22 of the ninety-two Basilian Canons. See *Pedalion*, 809–10.

longer a virgin, having been raped by her abductors. The force of this legislation is that the fiancé must take her back, even if he is now unwilling to do so because she is despoiled and would reflect poorly on his own and his family's honor. The church, knowing well that this was a regular outcome of such events, and prevalent in border regions where the realities of conflict were common, decreed that damage to the man's honor because of the rape of his fiancée was not an acceptable ground for dissolution of a betrothal. The canons seemed predominantly concerned to defend the honor of the woman, refusing to require her to pay a double penalty of rape as well as dismissal by her own fiancé.

Balsamon thought this canon too socially inapplicable in the medieval period. For Balsamon, it is scandalous that a Greek Christian man should be expected to take back a deflowered fiancée. It would be too great an affront to his honor. So Balsamon adds an element ostensibly taken from Basil's Canon 22 and says, "If the fiancé is willing to accept her back, of course." This completely voids the sense of both the Council of Ancyra and Basil. For what Basil had said was that the abducted woman ought not to be kept as the wife of an abductor, but should be restored to her first fiancé, if the fiancé still wanted to go ahead with the union. Basil's implication was that if the fiancé demurred from the relation, then the abductor would be allowed ecclesiastically to retain her as his wife. But Balsamon's interpretation removes all protection from the abducted woman, and all defense of her honor. Yet again, for him, there is no comparison between the loss of honor a woman might suffer (one suspects he is thinking she has already lost it in any case), compared to the loss of honor a man would suffer by having to take her back as "damaged goods." Once again this is a medieval reversion to a lower standard of compassion and a poorer sense of equitability than was represented in the classical patristic age.

A similar trend is evident in Balsamon's treatment of Canon 70 of the Council of Trullo[30] that prohibited women from talking during the liturgy. In Constantinople (where this council was held), women occupied the large upper gallery, not the main floor, of the church. The council defends its prohibition of talking by repeating biblical injunctions for women to be silent in worship (1 Corinthians 14:34–5). When Balsamon comments on this canon, however, he says it extends to women's positions in all religious services: they must never preach or teach publicly. What is more, Balsamon argues, this religious injunction justifies civil disabilities imposed on women by Roman law: they may not represent anyone in court, may not serve as witnesses in a trial, and may not act as legal guardians for a minor.[31] Balsamon adds a further justification by connecting the argument to the text of Genesis 3:16: "Your

[30] *Pedalion*, 373–5. [31] Rhalles and Potles, *Syntagma* 4, 312–14.

submission will be to your husband, and he shall rule over you." For Balsamon, female submission to the male is part of the divine order, bolstered by divine command in scripture, and this justifies civil proscriptions against women taking over men's traditional functions. In this instance, the archaic Greek idea that logos and agora are male domains, and silent domesticity is the female domain, is given a Christian dressing – though one that seems to be drawn from his contemporary prejudices about gender roles rather than from deep engagement with scriptural or patristic theology.[32]

BALSAMON ON FEMALE SEXUALITY

Balsamon was a high aristocrat, pushed, perhaps, into monastic life in middle age when he fell from grace under Emperor Constantine IX Monomachos. His reading, nevertheless, remained aristocratic rather than particularly ascetic, and his writing shows access to some rare Byzantine erotica that gave him vivid opinions on female sexuality. In interpreting the fourth-century *70th Canon of Saint Basil* censuring clergy indulging in erotic kisses, he opines whether the lips being kissed were not necessarily those on the face. He gains this opinion from his reading of the classical text of Julius Pollux's *Onomasticon* and Aristotle's *On the Parts of Animals*, where he notes the term *lips* also refers to female genitalia. Balsamon concludes that the Basilian canon ordains that clergy indulging in penetrative illicit intercourse should be deposed from office permanently, but those engaging merely in cunnilingus can be confessed and communicate without any public disability. Once again the context he imposes is not that of the antique legislator but one that draws from contemporary attitudes that give latitude to male clerical misbehaviour while casting the female as defiled, abominable, and shameful. The cleric who performs cunnilingus and desists from full intercourse, Balsamon says, has "been saved by grace" from a terrible crime and a drastic punishment. When Balsamon's near predecessor, canonist John Zonaras, treats the same Basilian canon, he shows no sense whatsoever that it can be taken as a reference to cunnilingus. And although Balsamon says, "there are some who say," as authority for his own approach, no such references can be found in prior ecclesiastical sources.

When it comes to women's biology more generally and its theological implications, however, Balsamon sustains a definite monastic view, highly conservative and restrictive: women are sources of pollution and must be kept

[32] One thinks also of Paul's equally dramatic utterance: "There is no longer male nor female, for you are all one in Christ" (Galatians 3:28).

from the altar at all costs. Abbesses in convents may exercise teaching authority in the church, he argues, because of the discipline they undertake and the obedience they require from their subordinates. Their teaching role is authentic and honored. "But on the other hand," he says, "the thought of a woman teaching in a parish church, where a number of men and weak women with conflicting views are gathered together, would be most unbecoming and destructive."[33] He thinks that, if stabilized by the male seed and thus rooted, the "wandering of the womb" will cease, and women will be less "hysterical."[34] In this he follows the biology of the pagan sages Aretaeus[35] and Galen. If not rooted by pregnancy, the "plague of the monthly distress," as he calls it, will afflict the woman, who also suffers the "readily wandering nature of female thought in general."[36] Balsamon argues strongly to Patriarch Mark of Alexandria that the diaconal ministry of women in the church is unfitting because of menstruation, which would pollute the sacred spaces near the altar. His opinion (for which he offers no evidence) is that the menarche was exactly why this ancient ordained office fell out of usage in the church.[37] He pays no attention to the fact that it might have been because all the ordainers by the seventh century were male monastics like himself, though even in the sixth century, there were more than sixty ordained female deacons on the staff of Hagia Sophia cathedral alone.

This is one more instance where the commentator of the thirteenth century is less progressive by far than the commentators of the ancient period. Bodily flux, menses, or seminal expulsion had long worried clerical canonists. Was the correct approach to such matters the one in Jewish law – a period of seclusion marking the sense of a ritual defilement, followed by a ritual cleansing and restoration to the prayers of the community?[38] Balsamon gives a strong nod to a canonical tradition that says yes to this, and thus effectively re-Judaizes the approach to female menses. He requires that menstruating women stay away from communion absolutely and implies that they should even have a separate place to stand in the church. They can pray to God, but it might be better if they did not come to the public buildings during their period.

33 Rhalles and Potles, *Syntagma*, 3. 181; Viscuso, "Theodore Balsamon's Canonical Images of Women," 320.

34 *Hystera* (womb) is the Greek etymological root of the theory of hysteria as the constant tendency of female nature.

35 Medical writer of the time of Nero. *On Diseases*. 2.11.1–3, 6.10.1–4.

36 Comment on Canon 46 of the Synod in Troullo; cf. Rhalles and Potles, *Syntagma* 2. 415; Viscuso, "Theodore Balsamon's Canonical Images of Women," 320.

37 Viscuso, "Menstruation: A Problem in Late Byzantine Canon Law," 116–25.

38 See, for example, Leviticus 15:16–17, 19–30.

How different is the approach to the matter in the patristic canons. The third-century *Didascalia Apostolorum*, one of the earliest books of church order, insisted that making bodily secretions a matter of taboo elevated the Levitical law, which the church had already declared obsolete. The natural flows of the body were instituted by God and should not be regarded as defiling. The same approach was affirmed by the *Apostolic Constitutions*, a fourth-century church order, and the same opinion on menses was confirmed by Pope Gregory the Great, who insisted that it did not prohibit women from taking communion or appearing in public. Sadly, the antique Greco-Roman taboo mentality, well reflected in the Roman Pliny's *Natural History*,[39] had a comeback in later Byzantium.

Here, in his relation to a significant part of female experience and the ways in which women are regarded in the church, Balsamon again reverses the liberalizing trend of the classical fathers in preference for an affirmation of contemporary (medieval) Greek social and moral attitudes, which in some cases are little more than archaic Greek prejudices sustained by men protecting a sense of entitlement. Balsamon's ecclesial society is more restrictive than that of the earlier fathers. His legislative imagination is less bent on equity and innovation than theirs. He is less ready to change the law if it is perceived as inequitable. Medieval Byzantine society had adopted gender roles much more restrictive than those of the classical Christian past, and Balsamon is often the spokesman for that conservative and delimiting role in his legislative judgments.

His enduring reputation as a canonist in the Eastern Christian tradition is unfortunate, in that it affords a higher premium to law as social control than the pastoral process of several of the Christian fathers who saw legislation as more about liberating potentialities and overcoming the hard-heartedness of pagan society. Balsamon is a startling case of the inadvisability of having ecclesiastical legislators speak about women, sex, and family life who have never had a remote experience of these things and cannot rise beyond contemporary prejudices. The enduring (often unreflective) preference given to his opinions in contemporary Orthodox collections of canons is perhaps something that has allowed gender prejudices to endure longer in Orthodox ecclesiastical circles than elsewhere in modern Christianity.

39 Pliny, *Natural History* 28.23 and 7.65. "Contact with the female monthly flux turns new wine sour, makes crops wither, kills grafts, dries seeds in gardens, causes the fruit of trees to fall off, dims the bright surface of mirrors, dulls the edge of steel and the gleam of ivory, kills bees, rusts iron and bronze, and causes a horrible smell to fill the air. Dogs who taste the blood become mad, and their bite becomes poisonous as in cases of rabies . . . So magical is the power of women during their monthly periods that they say that hailstorms and whirlwinds can be driven away if menstrual fluid is exposed to the flashes of lightning."

RECOMMENDED READING

Browning, R. "Theodore Balsamon's Commentary on the Canons of the Council in Trullo as a Source on Everyday Life in 12th C Byzantium." In *He Kathemerine Zoe Sto Byzantio*, 421–7. Athens: Kentro Byzantinon ereunon, 1989.

Clark, E. A. *Women in the Early Church*. Wilmington, DE: M. Glazier, 1983.

Gallagher, C. "Gratian and Theodore Balsamon: Two 12th Century Canonistic Methods Compared." In *Byzantium in the 12th Century: Canon Law, State & Society*, edited by A. N. Oikonomides, 61–89. E. Greek Text. Athens: Etareia Byzantinon kai Metabyzantinon Meleton, 1991.

Church Law and Church Order in Rome and Byzantium: A Comparative Study. Aldershot: Ashgate, 2002.

Hartmann, W. and K. Pennington, eds. *The History of Byzantine and Eastern Canon Law to 1500*. Washington, DC: Catholic University of America Press, 2012. See especially pages 170–214.

Laporte, J. *The Role of Women in Early Christianity*. Lewiston, NY: Edwin Mellen Press, 1982.

McGuckin, J. A. "The Issue of Human Rights in Byzantium and the Orthodox Tradition." In *Christianity and Human Rights: An Introduction*, edited by J. Witte, Jr. and F. S. Alexander, 173–90. Cambridge: Cambridge University Press, 2010.

The Ascent of Christian Law: Patristic and Byzantine Formulations of a New Civilization. New York: St. Vladimir's Seminary Press, 2012.

Meehan, A. "Theodore Balsamon." *The Catholic Encyclopedia*. New York: Appleton, 1907.

Miller, E. "Lettres de Théodore Balsamon." *Annuaire de l'Association pour l'Encouragement des Études Grecques en France* (1884): 8–19.

Rodopoulos, P. *An Overview of Orthodox Canon Law*. Rollinsford, NH: Orthodox Research Institute, 2007.

Stevens, G. P. *De Theodoro Balsamone*. Rome: Pontificia Università Lateranense, 1969.

Stolte, B. "Justice: (Byzantine) Legal Literature." In *The Oxford Handbook of Byzantine Studies*, edited by E. Jeffreys, 691–8. Oxford: Oxford University Press, 2008.

Viscuso, P. D. "A Late Byzantine Theology of Canon Law." *Greek Orthodox Theological Review* 34 (1980): 203–19.

"Marital Relations in the Theology of the Byzantine Canonist Theodore Balsamon." *Ostkirchliche Studien* 39 (1990): 281–8.

"Theodore Balsamon's Canonical Images of Women." *Greek, Roman and Byzantine Studies* 45 (2005): 317–26.

Guide for a Church under Islam. The 66 Canonical Questions Attributed to Theodore Balsamon. Brookline, MA: Holy Cross Orthodox Press, 2014.

8

Gratian

Anders Winroth

BIOGRAPHICAL INTRODUCTION

Gratian taught canon law at Bologna around 1140 CE. He was the first such teacher anywhere and thus put together his own textbook, which he called *Concordia discordantium canonum* (*Concord of Discordant Canons*). The work soon became more conveniently known as the *Decretum*. The original title signaled a program. Councils, popes, emperors, and church fathers had issued myriads of authoritative legal statements (canons) during the first millennium of Christian history. Often these canons contradicted each other. Gratian set out to harmonize such discord, using the newly developed methods of early scholasticism to arrive at a reasoned statement of what the law of the Roman Catholic Church should be. He produced an oddly organized work that quoted some 1,860 canons and discussed and harmonized them in almost 1,000 discursive comments (*dicta*) in his own voice. His work is preserved in a handful of manuscripts, and he is conventionally referred to as Gratian 1.

Gratian appears still to have been active in Bologna in 1143, but he probably soon thereafter stopped teaching to take up a position as bishop of Chiusi in Tuscany. He died in that position on 10 August in an unknown year, perhaps as early as 1144. Gratian 1 worked out almost every aspect of family law found in the *Decretum*, which in its second, much-spread recension still bears the unmistakable imprint of the solutions and opinions of its first author. Gratian 1's successor or successors as teachers at the burgeoning law school in Bologna were dissatisfied with the *Decretum*, which they felt was incomplete. They thus added, in the 1140s, some two thousand further canons, but they were more sparing with commentary, so a reader is often uncertain how to fit the new texts into the interpretative framework constructed by Gratian 1. The second recension mostly preserves the judgments and conclusions

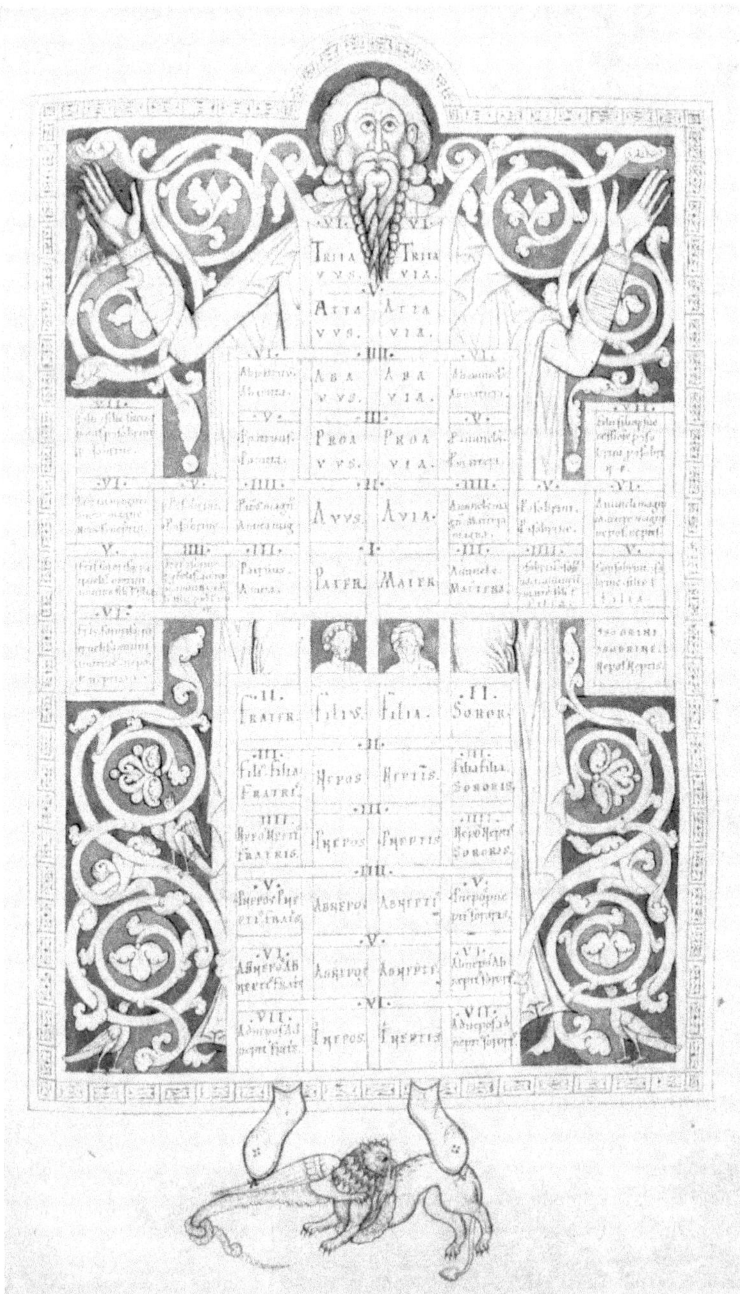

FIGURE 8.1. Gratian, a table illustrating the prohibited degrees of consanguinity (Salzburg?, ca. 1160). Bayerische Staatsbibliothek München, Clm 13004, fol. 309r. *Reproduced with permission.*

of its predecessor. These later editors of the *Decretum*, whose work is preserved in some six hundred manuscripts as well as numerous printed editions, are conventionally referred to as Gratian 2. In the field of family law, little differs between Gratian 1 and Gratian 2; except where stated otherwise, what follows summarizes that law as found in both recensions.

Gratian 2's recension of the *Decretum* became fundamental for the development of European law as the oldest part of the *Corpus iuris canonici*, which was in continuous use within the Catholic Church until 1917. Law teachers who commented on Gratian's work – their comments are preserved as marginal glosses as well as in separate works – laid the foundation for the rapid development of canon law in the late twelfth and early thirteenth centuries, over time rendering some individual sections of the *Decretum* more or less obsolete.[1]

FAMILY LAW

Gratian devoted a substantial part of his work to marriage law, while he touched on other fields of family law only in passing. He thus provided an impetus for the commentary tradition and later legislation to deal with family law in more detail. Gratian 1, for example, discussed at some length clerics who were "greedy for filthy lucre," in the process quoting a canon from the Council of Chalcedon (451) that noted that clerics were allowed to serve as guardians or curators, but only when such duties devolved on them unavoidably. Elsewhere in the *Decretum*, while discussing whether monks might be given duties outside their monasteries, Gratian 1 cited an imperial Roman law that excluded clerics from the duties of guardianship. The two statements contradict each other, but they were drawn from Gratian's sources in passing while Gratian discussed tangentially related matters; thus neither Gratian 1 nor Gratian 2 addressed the contradiction. This is typical of their methods, but the presence of these statements in the *Decretum* meant that later canonists resolved the contradiction, thus developing the law of guardianship.[2]

[1] Gratian's biography and the compositional history of his *Decretum* are controversial among scholars; see Winroth, *The Making of Gratian's* Decretum; Winroth, "Recent Work on the Making of Gratian's *Decretum*," 1–29; and Winroth, "Where Gratian Slept," 105–28. For a contrasting view, see Pennington, "The Biography of Gratian, the Father of Canon Law," 679–706.

[2] D. 86 c. 26 and C. 16 q. 1 c. 40. Roumy, "Family Law."

MARRIAGE LAW

Since the eleventh century, the church had claimed exclusive jurisdiction over the law of marriage, the details of which remained intensely debated both at princely courts and in canonistic and theological circles.[3] Gratian 1 set out to bring some order to this legal field, devoting a substantial section of his *Decretum* – causae 27–36 – to various aspects of marriage law. This section is known as the *Treatise on Marriage*, although the term postdates Gratian.

To organize his discussion, Gratian told ten narrative vignettes, or "cases," one for each causa, from which he derived forty-two questions (two to ten per causa), which provided the structure of the text. Most of these questions address aspects of marriage formation in particular; for example: "Is marriage possible between those entering religion?" (C. 27 q. 1); "Should an unwilling daughter be given in marriage?" (C. 31 q. 1); or, "If a husband after long captivity returns to his wife, who thought he was dead and therefore had remarried, may he reclaim her as his wife?" Gratian felt free to digress. Causa 33, for example, basically addresses a man whom magic had made impotent and thus unable to consummate his marriage; his wife instead took up relations with another man. This was a sin, which she confessed in her heart to God, but not to a priest. Gratian took the opportunity to discuss, at great length, in C. 33 q. 3, whether Christians must confess their sins to a priest in order to be absolved in the eyes of God, an issue of at best tangential significance for marriage law. Gratian's treatment of the law of penance in the midst of his discussion of marriage law is typical of the organization of the *Decretum*, which many commentators, from soon after its publication, criticized for deficient systematization. It seems clear, however, that rather than aiming to present a system of canon law desired by his critics, Gratian instead strove to present to his students in an attractive and memorable manner important issues in church law, teaching how to make sense of contradictory statements in the law accumulated during the first millennium of the church. In so doing, he shows himself flexible in letting the discussion in his classroom stray from any strict system.

Marriage Formation. Of fundamental importance for Gratian's *Treatise on Marriage* was the question of how a marriage comes about. Which acts constitute a marriage, and which acts make that relationship indissoluble? Some of Gratian's near contemporaries, notably French theologians

[3] Brundage, *Law, Sex, and Christian Society in Medieval Europe*, 229–55; McDougall, "Marriage: Law and Practice."

including Peter Abelard and Hugh of St. Victor, took their cue from Roman law and emphasized that consent made marriage. Others focused on sexual intercourse as bringing about the marriage. Both views cited old traditions and venerable authorities in support. It fell to Gratian to work out, in accordance with the program of his *Concordia*, a functioning legal system on the basis of these contradictory lines of thought. The outline of his system continues to define marriage law into modern times, although later law modified some details, notably in Pope Alexander III's acceptance into canon law of theologian Peter Lombard's theory of marriage formation.[4]

Gratian worked out his basic definitions of how marriage comes about in causa 27. The introductory narrative asks us to imagine a man who, despite having made a vow of chastity, nevertheless consents to marry a woman. The man keeps to his vow, so the marriage is never consummated, and the woman instead marries another man. This is when her erstwhile fiancé shows up and wants to reclaim her as his spouse. From the story, Gratian derived two questions. First, he asked whether persons entering religious orders may get married (they may not, but a vow of chastity does not dissolve an existing, consummated marriage). The second question asked whether the woman, who has given her consent to marrying the first man but has not had sex with him, is in fact married to him. This question went directly to the heart of the contemporary debate, asking whether consent alone without intercourse suffices to create an indissoluble marriage. Gratian worked out his own understanding by confronting sequences of disagreeing authorities. He did not explicitly reference the debate current in his day; instead, he cited only ancient authorities such as the Bible, the church fathers, or long-dead popes.

Gratian was notably well read in the Bible and in the canonical and theological traditions of the first millennium, which he mostly accessed through recent compilations rather than at first hand. He began his discussion of marriage formation by quoting in C. 27 q. 2 d.a.c.1 two definitions of marriage, which derive from Roman law, although Gratian did not tell us so. The first is the classic formulation from Justinian's *Institutes* 1.9.1: "Wedlock or marriage is the union of man and woman entailing that they live inseparably together." Gratian mentioned no source for that definition. The second definition – "Consent, not coitus, makes marriage" – he ascribed to Isidore of Seville (d. 636); in fact it comes from Justinian's *Digest* 50.17.30. This error as well as the lack of attribution for the first formulation may suggest that Gratian was not aware of the pedigree of

[4] See Chapter 10 by Charles Donahue, Jr. herein.

his definitions. Or, if he was aware, he preferred to pass over it in silence; Gratian 1's relationship to Roman law was also otherwise complicated.[5]

If Gratian 1 had found the two definitions in theological treatises from the early twelfth century, this would explain his ignorance; at least one such treatise quotes these two texts in close proximity without mentioning Justinian, while it mentions Isidore in such a way that a reader might think that he stood behind both definitions.[6]

After thus defining marriage, Gratian used his familiarity with theological and legal texts to line up a long row of authorities that discuss couples who are either betrothed or married to each other as well as some of the legal consequences of their relationships. His reading of these texts demonstrates that the definitions Gratian had quoted were not sufficiently clear, so he set about working out a more exact understanding of marriage. Analyzing the exact wordings and the context of each authoritative text, Gratian distinguished betrothals (consent alone) from full-blown marriages (consent and intercourse). In so doing, he imposed a logical consistency that did not necessarily exist in his sources. Gratian concluded, for example, that when Pope Siricius (in a letter that Gratian quoted as C. 27 q. 2 c. 50) allowed conjugal separation, he was in fact discussing a couple only betrothed to each other, not married. Similarly, although Augustine claimed (C. 27 q. 2 c. 9) that a woman is called "wife" from the moment of betrothal (which to Gratian meant when she gave her consent to marriage), even though she has not known intercourse, Gratian argued that this usage must not be interpreted too literally; Augustine did not imply that her marriage was as yet perfected. As Gratian pointed out, some writers, including Augustine, use the word "wife" (*coniunx*) when they talk about fiancées (*sponse*) in expectation of the future and in accordance with usage in the Bible.

Gratian borrowed vocabulary from Ambrose and Jerome (quoted in C. 27 q. 2 c. 35–37) to create a distinction (not extant in his sources) between "initiated marriage" and "perfected marriage," which allowed him to interpret his sources so that they do not contradict each other. Consent initiates marriage, while intercourse perfects it. Gratian understood the different authorities "according to this distinction" (C. 27 q. 2 d.p.c. 39): authorities stating that marriages cannot be dissolved are, Gratian claimed, talking about perfected marriages, while those allowing marriages to be dissolved are referring to

[5] Vetulani, "Gratien et le droit romain"; Winroth, "Roman Law in Gratian and the *Panormia*," 183–90.

[6] Winroth, "Neither Slave nor Free," 101.

initiated marriages. The course of Gratian's argument in this question is typical for how he also otherwise applied the methods of early scholasticism. He claimed that apparently contradictory statements in fact are in harmony because they employ the same words in different senses. Sometimes the word "wife" means fiancée, sometimes the word "marriage" means perfected marriage, and sometimes it means initiated marriage, i.e., betrothal. The original writers might have been surprised by Gratian's interpretations of their words.

Gratian thus came up with a new definition of how marriages are formed. For a marriage to be perfected and thus indissoluble, both consent and intercourse are required. Neither is sufficient without the other. Consent without intercourse produced only an initiated marriage, or a betrothal, and such a union could be dissolved, at least in certain circumstances. Intercourse without consent to get married was simple fornication, concubinage, or rape, depending on the circumstances. Only with both consent and intercourse did the marriage become perfected, a sacrament, and thus indissoluble.

The underlying stimulus for Gratian to frame his discussion with a story about an unconsummated marriage is clearly the theological problem of the relationship between Christ's earthly parents, Mary and Joseph. Many scholars from the second century CE onward have inferred from the New Testament that Mary maintained her virginity throughout her life, even while she was married to Joseph. Augustine added (quoted in C. 27 q. 2 c. 3), as Gratian understood him (d.p.c. 39), that Mary and Joseph were joined in a perfected marriage. Despite all his efforts, Gratian still had to apply special pleading to explain this relationship, which does not fit his model of perfected marriages: Mary's and Joseph's marriage was perfected despite the lack of intercourse, because of their faith, the birth of offspring, and as a sacrament. Gratian's understanding of the relationship of Christ's parents annoyed later commentators, who criticized him severely and in response worked out a different theory of marriage formation to replace Gratian's.

When Gratian in C. 27 analyzed the definition of marriage, he brought up further problematic cases beyond that of Mary and Joseph that helped him define more clearly the exact limits of marriage. Several of these would receive separate fuller treatments later in the *Decretum*. As parallels to the man vowing chastity, Gratian, for example, discussed an impotent man and a man castrated by his enemies (C. 27 q. 2 d.p.c. 28-d.p.c. 29). Neither of them is capable of intercourse, and this prevents them from marrying; but if they already are married, their misfortunes do not dissolve an already consummated marriage. While he never discussed castration again, Gratian analyzed impotence at greater length in C. 33 q. 1, noting among other things that it prevents the formation of a marriage if it means that the couple never have intercourse.

Both consent and intercourse were needed for a valid marriage, and the consent of both the man and the woman needed to be free and uncoerced. Gratian 1 emphasized that the bride must not be coerced into marriage by her father or anyone else (C. 31 q. 1). He did not spell out whether the parents needed to give their permission or consent for a marriage to be valid, although he described as normal procedure that her father would hand the bride over to the groom at the ceremony. Gratian 2 added relevant laws and concluded, more restrictively than Gratian 1, that "without the father's consent there cannot be lawful marriage" (C. 31 q. 1 d.p.c. 12).[7] For the future, Gratian's strong emphasis on the consent of bride and groom would, nevertheless, determine legal developments. Gratian may have thought that it was desirable that the families agreed and that the exchange of vows took place publicly with witnesses, but none of this was, strictly speaking, necessary; as long as there was consent and intercourse, the resulting marriage was perfectly legitimate and indissoluble.

To enter marriage was, in Gratian's view, a part of unchanging natural law, so the church recognized marriage also between non-Christian persons, although such marriages were not sacramental. The marriage continued if a non-Christian couple converted to Christianity, and even if one of the parties later abandoned Christianity. The Christian partner was allowed to separate from his or her apostate spouse, but was not allowed to remarry as long as the spouse was alive.

Not everyone was permitted to marry. Christians were not allowed to marry non-Christians. Priests, monks, nuns, and others who had solemnly promised chastity were unable to marry. Upon being widowed, the surviving spouse had, however, the right to marry again. An abductor was allowed to marry the woman he had abducted, if she and her father agreed and the spouses washed away with penance the sin they had incurred through the abduction (C. 36 q. 2).

Divorce and Separation. An unconsummated union – an initiated marriage – could be dissolved, at least if good reasons existed, such as one party wishing to enter a monastery. An unconsummated engagement between two children who had reached the age of reason (seven years) but not puberty (twelve for girls and fourteen for boys) could also be broken if either spouse wished after reaching

[7] Winroth, "Marital Consent in Gratian's *Decretum*," 111–21.

puberty. Underage spouses (younger than seven) were unable to give consent, so any such union was void.

The perfected, consummated marriage, on the other hand, was indissoluble, except in a few, not very common cases. If one party had been insane when giving consent, there could have been no consent, and the marriage was thus null. If either the bride or the groom was mistaken about the identity of the person they married, the marriage was likewise void. The same applied to marriages in which a free person did not know that his or her spouse was a slave or a serf when they married. Mistakes about wealth or chastity did not, however, constitute grounds for dissolving the union. If your husband or wife turned out to be poorer or less chaste than you thought, you still had to remain in a consummated marriage (C. 29).

Canon law from the early Middle Ages had allowed the husband to divorce an unfaithful wife. Gratian quoted a statement by "Ambrose" (in fact, it is the anonymous writer commonly known as Ambrosiaster) to that effect (C. 32 q. 7 c. 17), but he declared blankly that this statement is a forgery (d.p.c. 18). He happened to be correct, but he made his statement simply to get rid of an inconvenient authority, not because he had anticipated modern critical research about the authenticity of patristic works. Unlike most earlier writers, Gratian insisted that men and women should suffer the same punishment for adultery. When the innocent partner becomes aware of the spouse's infidelity, he or she must refuse any further marital relations until the spouse has performed penance. Neither spouse would, however, be allowed to remarry as long as the other was alive.

Marital Debt. Spouses joined in a consummated, or perfected, marriage owe each other the marital debt, i.e., sexual relations, in accordance with the admonition of the Apostle Paul (1 Corinthians 7:3–4). Both husband and wife had equal rights to demand the marital debt, another case where Gratian insisted on equality between the sexes. This right was absolute, even trumping spiritual recommendations (which Gratian reproduced) to avoid sexual relations during fast days and holidays and when the wife is menstruating, pregnant, or lactating. Supported by Augustine (C. 33 q. 4 c. 12), Gratian said that couples need observe these recommendations only if both agree. If one partner nevertheless insisted on intercourse, the other spouse must render the debt.

When a couple was bound together by marital affection without being formally married, Gratian considered the woman a concubine. He did not condemn such relationships; in fact, he said that they were licit, as long as the man was a layman content with a single concubine and not also married.

Consanguinity, Affinity, and Incest. Gratian counted relations as incestuous if the spouses were related by blood (consanguinity), by marriage (affinity), or by spiritual bonds (spiritual kinship). He maintained the prohibition against marriages with blood kin within seven degrees of consanguinity according to canonical computation, in which siblings were related in the first degree, cousins in the second, etc. (C. 35 q. 2&3). Since married spouses became one flesh, the same incest prohibitions extended to the family of the spouse. Thus, a widower could not marry his deceased wife's sister, or indeed any of her relatives within seven degrees. Children born in an incestuous relationship did not count as legitimate and thus had no right to inherit (C. 35 q. 7).

When Gratian discussed these matters, he ran into considerable difficulties, encountering many valid legal statements that disagreed on how many degrees were prohibited. Some said six degrees while others extended the prohibition to the seventh degree. Gratian posited that his sources counted degrees differently so that they in fact agreed, but he was troubled enough that he devoted an entire question to discussing how to count degrees (C. 35 q. 5), where he also provided a long overview of the different words used in Latin for different relatives. This discussion was occasioned by the confusion of the immediately preceding question (C. 35 q. 4), where Gratian explained why the prohibition extends to the seventh degree: he quoted Isidore of Seville stating that the reckoning was in harmony with the six ages of the world. Isidore obviously counted degrees differently from how Gratian counted them.

Scriptural examples of Old Testament patriarchs marrying within forbidden degrees also embarrassed Gratian, who explained, with reference to Augustine, that such marriages took place out of necessity, since no suitable marriage partners could otherwise be found (C. 35 q. 1 d.a.c. 1 and c. 1). Gratian also recognized that the church was able to issue dispensations to couples who had married unaware of their kinship, as long as they were not more closely related than the fourth degree (C. 35 q. 8). The reason why Gratian devoted so much space to these matters might have been that he intuited that it was impractical to extend the prohibited degrees as far as he did; this is an aspect of Gratian's marriage law that was substantially changed at the Fourth Lateran Council in 1215, when the prohibition was restricted to four degrees.

The incest prohibitions also extended to spiritual kin, in accordance with the idea that a kind of kinship is created at baptism between the baptized person and his or her godparents. A godparent is unable to marry the godchild. Further, a godparent may not marry the widowed natural parent of his or her godchild, a prohibition that extends also to the widowed spouse of a godparent. Similarly, the biological child of a godparent is prohibited from marrying his or her parent's godchild. Gratian 1 quoted a papal letter of Pascal II that extended that prohibition to any child born of the biological parent after the relevant baptism (C. 30 q. 4 c. 5, placed at C. 30 q. 3 c. 5 by Gratian 2), but Gratian 2 problematized that verdict by juxtaposing it with another papal letter, by Urban II, allowing such unions (C. 30 q. 3 c. 4). Gratian 2 never resolved the contradiction, leaving the matter for the glossators to work out.

The completed *Decretum* quickly became the subject of teaching and commentary at the many law schools that cropped up around Western Europe, notably in Bologna and Paris. Generations of law teachers and other jurists expounded family law on the basis of the work of the two Gratians, attempting to work out the many wrinkles left in the text. The interpretative work on the *Decretum* deeply influenced judicial decisions and legislation by the popes.

RECOMMENDED READINGS

Brundage, James A. *Law, Sex, and Christian Society in Medieval Europe*. Chicago: University of Chicago Press, 1987.

McDougall, Sara. "Marriage: Law and Practice." In *The Cambridge History of Medieval Canon Law*, edited by John Wei and Anders Winroth. Cambridge: Cambridge University Press, forthcoming.

Noonan, John T., trans. *Marriage Canons from the Decretum of Gratian and the Decretals, Sext, Clementines and Extravagantes*. Edited by Augustine Thompson, O.P., unpublished, 1993.

Reid, Charles J., Jr. *Power over the Body, Equality in the Family: Rights and Domestic Relations in Medieval Canon Law*. Grand Rapids, MI: Wm. B. Eerdmans Publishing, 2004.

Roumy, Franck. "Family Law." In *The Cambridge History of Medieval Canon Law*, edited by John Wei and Anders Winroth. Cambridge: Cambridge University Press, forthcoming.

Winroth, Anders. *The Making of Gratian's* Decretum. Cambridge: Cambridge University Press, 2000.

"Recent Work on the Making of Gratian's *Decretum*." *Bulletin of Medieval Canon Law* 26 (2004–6): 1–29.

"'Neither Slave nor Free': Theology and Law in Gratian's Thoughts on the Definition of Marriage and Unfree Persons." In *Medieval Church Law and the Origins of the Western Legal Tradition: A Tribute to Kenneth*

Pennington, edited by Wolfgang P. Müller and Mary E. Sommar, 97–109. Washington, DC: Catholic University of America Press, 2006.

"Marital Consent in Gratian's *Decretum*." In *Readers, Texts and Compilers in the Earlier Middle Ages: Studies in Medieval Canon Law in Honour of Linda Fowler-Magerl*, edited by Kathleen G. Cushing and Martin Brett, 163–80. Aldershot, UK: Ashgate, 2008.

"Roman Law in Gratian and the *Panormia*." In *Bishops, Texts, and the Use of Canon Law around 1100: Essays in Honour of Martin Brett*, edited by Kathleen G. Cushing and Bruce C. Brasington, 183–90. Aldershot, UK: Ashgate, 2008.

9

Peter Lombard

Giulio Silano

BIOGRAPHICAL INTRODUCTION

Peter Lombard, the Master of the Sentences, was a prominent participant in the twelfth-century process by which scholars and scholarship emerged to a new prominence in the Western church and society. His work testifies to the growing specialization within scholarship and the development of programs and methods of study suitable to the formation of scholars who were no longer monks, but who intended to use monastic learning to bring church and society into greater adherence to the requirements of the Gospel. To this end, Peter and his contemporaries shouldered the task of bringing out both the doctrinal coherence and the practical application of the Christian intellectual inheritance.[1]

Very little is known about Peter's life. His place of origin remains disputed, although his sobriquet makes clear that he was born in northern Italy, around the end of the eleventh century. The earliest unimpeachable reference to Peter is in a letter of St. Bernard of Clairvaux, from perhaps 1138 to 1140, in which he asks that Peter be given hospitality at the abbey of St. Victor in Paris, for what was expected to be a short stay. He ended up remaining in Paris for the rest of his life, and it was to prove a very fruitful stay. By 1144, a poet in far-off Bavaria could list him as one of the celebrated theological luminaries of the Parisian schools. Somewhat unusually for a foreign schoolmaster, Peter also became fully integrated within the Parisian clergy to the point that, in 1159, he was elected bishop of Paris. He died on 21 or 22 July 1160.[2]

[1] A brilliant review of these developments is found in the valedictory work of Southern, *Scholastic Humanism and the Unification of Europe*, v. 1: *Foundations*.

[2] The sources for Peter's life are presented and canvassed by Ignatius C. Brady, the brilliant editor of the *Sentences*, as prolegomena to his 1971 edition.

FIGURE 9.1. Portrait of Peter Lombard, Bishop of Paris: The glory of their times; or The lives of ye primitive fathers, containing their chiefest actions, workes, sentences, and deaths. / Lupton, Donald, d. 1676.
Courtesy of the Pitts Theology Library, Candler School of Theology, Emory University

On Peter's tombstone, his works were presented as consisting of the *Sentences* and glosses on the Psalms and on the letters of Paul; these are, apart from some sermons, Peter's surviving works. The composition of the *Sentences* – the work that made Peter immortal in the annals of Christian scholarship – was probably protracted and may have occupied most of Peter's teaching activity. In this work, Peter attempts "to reveal the hidden depths of theological investigations and to convey an understanding of the church's sacraments."[3] The work consists principally of excerpts from the fathers of the church. It exploits earlier efforts to collect such authoritative opinions, reflection on which is at the heart of what was coming to be called theology. In marginal glosses on these precedents, Peter often speaks in the first person. The invitation is for the reader to do the same. By mastering the tradition that Peter has so usefully presented, the reader can become a questioner and participant in the endless process of describing what the Christian tradition has been, what it is, and what it may become.

The *Sentences* are divided into four books. Book 1 treats of God as Trinity; book 2 concerns creation, the angels, the Fall, and grace; book 3 addresses the reparation of fallen humankind by the Incarnation of the Word, together with the virtues, vices, and commandments; and book 4 presents the sacraments and the last things, including a lengthy discussion of marriage.

For all the formal preeminence of the fathers in the *Sentences*, the selection of their texts does not appear to come from a full and fresh reading of their texts; that would have been eccentric. The patristic texts that Peter presents are largely those that the schoolmen had already designated as significant. Abelard's *Sic et non* and Gratian's *Decretum* are two of the great collections Lombard mined in producing his own patristic anthology. The greatest cause of its almost unique success is the work's usefulness. It presented a brief and clear summary of all of Christian doctrine, and it collected in one place most of the texts that everyone had come to regard as crucial in the development of that doctrine. It also presented a very comprehensive collection of the questions that schoolmasters had raised, discussed, and settled or failed to settle in their classrooms. A profound sense of the open-endedness of the theological enterprise characterizes the book and appears to account for its fruitful use for many generations, to the point that the basic theological course for faculties of theology almost into the 1960s would still be marked by the division of topics in the *Sentences*.

While the fundamental importance of Peter's *Sentences* in the history of Western theological reflection is undoubted, the question may still occur

[3] Prologue, § 2.

of why the work should be considered within an effort to understand the relationship of Christianity and family law. For the word "family" never occurs in Peter's work. Moreover, he is not regarded as a practitioner of jurisprudence.

The omission of the term "family" is not peculiar to Peter. Gratian, too, omits it. Insofar as family signifies household, the structuring of households for temporal purposes appears to have been a topic that ecclesiastics were satisfied to leave to their secular counterparts. But insofar as marriage is crucial for constituting and perpetuating households, and since the high medieval church successfully claimed exclusive jurisdiction over marriage, what ecclesiastics thought about marriage was of great relevance to the development of marriage law. As Charles Donahue, Jr. makes clear in his discussion of papal marriage legislation in the next chapter, popes began their thoroughgoing revision of that legislation by settling the questions that Gratian, Peter Lombard, and their students had raised in the schools. Indeed, it was by paying attention to the debates in the schools that popes learned that there were questions, and that they themselves were called to settle those questions and to do so along the lines suggested by the masters.

As for Peter not being a legal practitioner, it is probable that the distinction between theologians and canon lawyers did not become marked until several decades after Peter and Gratian. Peter appears to have been one of the most attentive readers of Gratian and, in his discussion of marriage, relies largely on Gratian's collection, which Peter appears to have been the first to use so thoroughly. It is not that we cannot distinguish somewhat different concerns and emphases in their respective treatment of marriage – indeed, these differences hint at a coming firm, clear, and sometimes much-lamented distinction between jurists and theologians in the church. But in their day it would have been difficult to say that their tasks and materials differed significantly. Both engaged in presenting a tradition more than a millennium old in a way that, by grasping some of the methods in which the tradition had developed, they might extend these coherently to the intellectual and practical problems of their own day. It is possible, too, to think of Peter's treatment of marriage in the *Sentences* as the first commentary on Gratian's extensive discussion of the topic in his *Decretum*. Peter differs, though, in not being bound to follow Gratian's device of discussing their shared authorities in terms of specific cases; Peter thus could bring out the coherence and lucidity of Gratian's own analysis of the issues. Nonetheless, as Donahue makes clear, later popes like Alexander III were as attentive to Peter's views on marriage as they were to Gratian's, and they did not appear to have regarded these two different accounts of marriage as competitive or mutually exclusive.

MARRIAGE IN THE *SENTENCES*

In the first three books of the *Sentences*, Peter introduces his readers to what the Christian tradition had to say regarding the mysteries of God's nature, the creation and fall of angels and humankind, the mystery of Christ's incarnation and the restoration of fallen man, and the virtues and precepts that the Christian ought to cultivate and observe in the attempt to imitate Christ. Book 3 closes with a reflection on the relative inadequacy of the old Law because what it commanded could not be done well or easily in the absence of grace. This same grace now abounds in the Gospel because of Christ's redeeming work (D. 40 cc.1–2). And while the sacraments of the Law were only signs, the sacraments of the church are not only the principal signs, but also instruments of that grace now freely available to Christians (D. 40 c. 3). These signs are the main subject of book 4, taking up forty-two of the fifty distinctions into which the book is divided. Of these forty-two distinctions, sixteen (distinctions 26–42) are given over to marriage.[4]

Peter's presentation of marriage specifically begins with an affirmation of its ancientness and high dignity. The other sacraments were made necessary by sin and would not have been necessary apart from sin, but the sacrament of marriage was instituted at the very creation of woman in paradise, when the man understood that he was called to union with her (D. 26 c. 1 n. 2). Marriage was again instituted "after sin, as a remedy, and outside paradise, for the sake of avoiding illicit stirrings; the first, so that nature might be multiplied, and the second so that nature might be rescued and vice curbed" (D. 26 c. 2 n. 1). Before original sin, sexual union would have happened without lust and would have been a good deed worthy of reward; after sin, this same union does not happen without lust, and so its reprehensible character must be redeemed by the pursuit of the goods of marriage (D. 26 c. 1 n. 3).

Nuptials themselves, then, are a good, despite the condemnation that some heretics heap upon them (D. 26 c. 5 n. 1). The goodness of marriage itself is evident from its divine institution in Genesis, as also from Christ's presence at the marriage at Cana in Galilee and his concomitant miracle allowing its joyful celebration (D. 26 c. 5 n. 2).

The sacred thing of which marriage is a sacred sign is "the joining of Christ and the church ... For as there is between the spouses a joining according to the consent of souls and the mixture of bodies, so the church joins herself to

[4] The presentation of marriage in the *Sentences* that follows reprises what I wrote in my Introduction to *The Sentences – Book 4: On the Doctrine of Signs*.

Christ by will and nature" (D. 26 c. 6 n. 1). The consequence of this analogy for human spouses is that they cannot regard their union as an exclusively physical one. In sacramental marriage, "the bride is joined to the bridegroom spiritually and corporally, that is, by charity and the conformity of nature" (D. 26 c. 6 n. 1). Christian marriage has two constitutive moments: the exchange of marital consent by the spouses and their sexual union. Their consent is crucial because it signifies the spiritual joining of Christ and the church, which happens through charity. The conformity of nature is signified by the sexual union of the spouses (D. 26 c. 6 n. 1).

Because this conformity to nature does not occur without sexual intercourse, some authorities refuse to call a woman married who does not experience intercourse (D. 26 c. 6 n. 2). A superficial interpretation of this opinion would lead to the impious conclusion that there was an incomplete marriage between Mary and Joseph, whereas this was a marriage "so much the more holy and complete as it was the more free of carnal work" (D. 26 c. 6 n. 3). Peter's view is that an unconsummated marriage is yet a marriage that signifies "that union of Christ and the Church which is in charity, but not the one which is in conformity with nature" (D. 26 c. 6 n. 4). This sort of marriage is somewhat lacking in its signifying power because it cannot symbolize that joining by which the members of Christ's body are united to their head by the Incarnation (D. 26 c. 6 n. 4). But an unconsummated marriage is no less holy since it remains "a sign of spiritual joining and love of souls, by which spouses are to unite themselves" (D. 26 c. 6 n. 5).

After these foundational preliminary considerations, Peter is ready to offer a definition of marriage as "the marital joining of husband and wife of lawful standing, retaining an undivided manner of life" (D. 27 c. 2). Marriage is a way of life constituted by two people who are not barred by law from establishing it; its undividedness pertains to the inability of a spouse to promise continence or even to go off to pray (i.e., abstain from conjugal sex) without the other's permission. The bond these two establish between themselves is lifelong and exclusive and requires "that each treat the other as he would himself" (D. 27 c. 2). At least, all this is true of the marriage of Christians who are not barred by law (D. 27 c. 2).

Marriage comes into being through expression by the spouses of a form of consent specific to marriage. They must express clearly, in the present tense, that they are taking each other as husband and wife (D. 27 c. 3 n. 1). If they do not will in their hearts what they express by their mouths, there is yet a marriage, so long as there was no compulsion or fraud (D. 27 c. 3 n. 1). Authorities show that this expression of consent alone constitutes the marriage, whether or not consummation follows (D. 27 c. 3 n. 2). Spouses are such, then, from their exchange of vows (D. 27 c. 4 n. 1); since Mary and Joseph exchanged such vows, they are properly called spouses (D. 27 c. 4 n. 2). Peter does not address the question whether Mary may be called Joseph's wife; any temptation to conclude that Peter regards consummation as insignificant ought to be attentive to the issue of whether and when a woman who is a spouse may also be called a wife.

Peter turns next to the question whether words of future consent also effect marriage and whether such a promise is irrevocable (D. 28 c. 1 n. 1). The student is invited to consider that "it is by far one thing to promise, and another to do" (D. 28 c. 1 n. 2). As a consequence, those who merely exchange a promise to marry cannot be called marriage partners; if they breach their first promise and marry other people, the subsequent marriages hold, but penance is to be imposed on them for their breach of promise or perjury (D. 28 c. 1 n. 2).

Custom and law prescribe certain formalities for the celebration of marriage, such as parental consent, the conferral of a dowry, the presence of a wedding party, the blessing by a priest; all these are fine and good things, which confer dignity and decency on a marriage, but they are not required for its validity (D. 28 c. 1 n. 4). Present consent alone is the substance of the sacrament (D. 28 c. 2 n. 1).

A particular difficulty is presented by the secret exchange of words of present consent. Like publicly expressed vows, such an exchange creates a marriage, but it will not be enforceable by the church. Only subsequent manifestation of the secret consent by the partners makes the marriage inviolable and subject to the church's enforcement mechanisms (D. 28 c. 2 n. 2). Whether the consent is secret or public, its object can be neither mere cohabitation nor carnal joining. Brother and sister cohabit, but they cannot be married; Mary and Joseph were married, but Mary did not consent to carnal joining, because she had always proposed to remain in virginity (D. 28 c. 3 n. 1). It seems best to say that the object of marital consent is "conjugal partnership, expressed by words of present tense, as when a man says: *I take you as mine*, not mistress, not slave-girl, but marriage partner" (D. 28 c. 3 n. 2). It was to indicate this that, at creation, woman "is not formed either from the highest part, nor from the lowest, but from the side of man, for the sake of conjugal partnership" (D. 28 c. 4 n. 1).

Consent must be free; when there is coercion, there is no consent and so no marriage (D. 29 c. 1 nn. 1–3). But if those coerced choose afterward to cohabit when they have the freedom to leave, then they are decreed to have consented (D. 29 c. 1 n. 3). Certain types of error are also taken to vitiate consent irremediably. Mistake as to person is such an error (D. 30 c. 1 n. 2).

Neither error as to a person's wealth nor error as to one's moral qualities invalidates a marriage (D. 30 c. 1 n. 5). Error of condition nullifies consent, but a fuller discussion of this error is deferred until later (D. 30 c. 1 n. 2).

The discussion of the ends or causes for the contracting of marriage is preceded by the assertion that all the ends of marriage were met in the case of Mary and Joseph (D. 30 c. 2). The principal end of marriage is the procreation of offspring, since this was the end for which God first commanded marriage (D. 30 c. 3 n. 2). A second cause is the avoidance of fornication. Marriage is also worthily contracted for "the reconciliation of enemies and the reestablishment of peace" (D. 30 c. 3 n. 2). Less worthy causes include the sort of physical beauty "which often compels spirits enflamed with love to enter into marriage so that they may fulfill their desire" (D. 30 c. 3 n. 2). Desire for riches, and many other causes that frequently lead to marriage, ought not to be discounted. Peter is not willing to doubt the validity of marriages motivated by these causes so long as present consent is expressed, and "even if it is love which has drawn them to this" (D. 30 c. 3 n. 3). There are, after all, good biblical examples even of this last cause for marriage. Nor is the intrinsic goodness of marriage contaminated by improper ends, "as when the beauty of a partner moves the spirit" (D. 30 c. 4 n. 1). It is also good to remember that the marriage of Mary and Joseph did not occur without secondary ends, such as Mary's need for support and protection (D. 30 c. 4 n. 2).

The goods of marriage, which have already been adumbrated in the discussion of the ends of marriage, excuse sexual activity that would otherwise be sinful. The three goods, identified already by St. Augustine, are faith, offspring, and sacrament. Faith denotes the exclusiveness of the marriage bond; offspring becomes a good when a child is received with love and educated religiously; the good of the sacrament entails the indissolubility of the marriage bond (D. 31 c. 1 n. 1).

That the marriage bond is indissoluble does not mean that the partners do not ever separate. There can certainly be bodily separation between them, as happens because of fornication or when partners have agreed to be continent for the sake of religion (D. 31 c. 2 n. 1). But such bodily separation cannot become sacramental; throughout their joint lives, they continue to be signs of Christ's union with the church, so neither spouse is ever free to marry another while they both live (D. 31 c. 2 nn. 1 and 2). Indeed, "the third good of marriage is called 'sacrament' not because it is the marriage itself, but because it is the sign of a sacred thing, that is, the spiritual and inseparable joining of Christ and the church" (D. 31 c. 2 n. 3).

Sometimes one or another of these three goods is not being preserved in a specific marriage union. Adultery violates the good of faith, and offspring are sometimes lacking or are received for earthly and not religious reasons. The lack of these goods, whether temporarily or permanently, cannot undo the sign value or validity of marriage, which always remains (D. 31 c. 2 n. 4). This sacramentality can inhere in a marriage even when marriage partners have entered into their marital union solely for the sake of intercourse, so long as they have not taken steps to avoid offspring (D. 31 c. 2 n. 5). As for those who take such steps in such a context, "they are not marriage partners, but fornicators" (D. 31 c. 3).

Since steps to avoid offspring can include abortion, the question arises whether the procurers of abortion are to be considered homicides (D. 31 c. 4 n. 1). If the fetus is formed, those who abort it are guilty of homicide, says Peter; if it is not yet formed, then they are subject to a fine (D. 31 c. 4 nn. 2 and 3).

When all three goods are present in a marriage, sexual activity between the spouses is free of all guilt. If sexual activity occurs without desire for offspring, then it constitutes a venial fault (D. 31 c. 5 n. 1). If these goods are entirely lacking, then sexual intercourse is criminal, and the spouses are behaving toward each other as adulterers and prostitutes (D. 31 c. 5 n. 2).

Because the apostle Paul seems to allow conjugal intercourse only by way of indulgence, Peter observes, there are those who argue that marriage itself is sin (D. 31 c. 6 n. 1). This is not at all to be granted. The apostle's permission is to be taken to refer to that marital intercourse that occurs by reason of incontinence and not for the sake of offspring; in such intercourse, there is said to be the evil of incontinence (D. 31 c. 6 nn. 2 and 3). This evil is itself in some measure redeemed by the good of marriage (D. 31 c. 7 nn. 1–3). What follows is "that marriage partners who come together only for the sake of offspring, or those who render the debt upon demand, are preserved from sin by the sanctity of marriage and the nuptial good" (D. 31 c. 7 n. 5). Had it been otherwise, after the Flood, God would not have commanded human beings to grow and multiply.

So fundamental is the right to sexual intercourse in marriage that the usual relationship of authority of the husband over the wife does not apply to the desire for sex; in this, neither partner can ever deny the other's request (D. 32 c. 1 n. 1). With regard to sex, the partners are equal, and neither may promise continence without the other's consent (D. 32 c. 1 nn. 1 and 2). And sex cannot be denied even when one's partner is moved to desire by weakness and incontinence (D. 32 c. 1 n. 2). Among other things, one partner cannot practice continence without the consent of the other, because such practice may lead the other into adultery and other immoral activities (D. 32 c. 2 nn. 1–4). But if a husband has allowed a wife to take a vow in a nunnery, he cannot afterward recall her (D. 32 c. 2 n. 5).

On his way to the presentation of the lawful impediments to marriage, Peter poses the question whether laws regarding marriage are changeable or fixed. For example, the biblical patriarchs engaged in polygamy; did they sin? The answer is that God's dispensation "appears to vary with the variety of times" (D. 33 c. 1 n. 1).

Polygamy was not the only evil allowed by the Law; divorce was another, which God allowed so that worse evils might not follow (D. 33 c. 3). But all these evils were removed with Christ's coming because, when Christ's grace was extended everywhere, the law of nuptials was reduced to its earlier and more decent institution, so that one should join with one in reflection of Christ and the church (D. 33 c. 4 n. 2).

If there can be variations in God's law itself, then it is not surprising to discover that there has been variation in time as to the lawfulness of marriage. The rules in this matter were of one sort before the Mosaic Law, of another sort after the giving of the Law, and of yet another in the time of grace; furthermore, there have been changes from the times of the primitive church (D. 34 c. 1). Moreover, according to the rules in Peter's own day, some married persons were living entirely lawful lives, some entirely unlawful, and some in the middle. Lawfulness for marriage consists in not being barred by impediments such as "the vow of continence, or a sacred order, or relationship, or disparity of cult or condition, or frigidity of nature, or whatever else" (D. 34 c. 1). The fully unlawful are those bound by these same impediments. The middle group are those afflicted by frigidity or condition; these marriages turn out to be contingent (D. 34 c. 1). Those married to the frigid or impotent may be counseled to remain in their marriages, but they cannot be compelled to do so; the party who is frigid or impotent ought not to be allowed to marry again (D. 34 c. 2 nn. 1–3). If the parties do not agree about the truth of the matter, the husband's assertion that he has had intercourse with his wife is to be believed, if the charged impotence is said to be natural (D. 34 c. 2 n. 4). The case is otherwise if the impotence is said to arise from sorcery, which seems to denote an impotence relative only to one's spouse (D. 34 c. 3 n. 1). Insanity is also a bar to marriage if it exists at the time of the marriage contract (D. 34 c. 4).

When the right of dismissal of a spouse exists, it applies equally to both spouses, so "the wife can cite the husband over his fornication, just as he can cite her" (D. 35 c. 1 n. 1). Furthermore, one spouse cannot dismiss the other for adultery if the complaining spouse is guilty of the same offense (D. 35 c. 2). If separation has occurred because an innocent spouse has established the guilt of the other, the dismissing spouse must remain continent or reunite with the dismissed spouse (D. 35 c. 3 n. 1). A statement of Ambrose that would discriminate in favor of the husband is suggested to be the result of forgery (D. 35 c. 3 n. 2). Some authorities that seem to deny the possibility of reconciliation of separated spouses are understood to regard the case in which the adulterous partner refuses to desist from adultery (D. 35 c. 3 nn. 5–8). But a man may not marry a woman with whom he has committed adultery (D. 35 c. 4 n. 1). At least, this is the case if the adulterers have not repented, or had plotted against the previous husband, or had agreed to marry after the death of the same husband (D. 35 c. 4 n. 3).

Peter agrees that the minimum age for marriage is the one set in the Roman laws, namely, fourteen for boys and twelve for girls. If they married earlier, even with their parents' consent, they may separate; if they have agreed to remain together after puberty, they can no longer separate (D. 36 c. 4 n. 1). Espousals cannot occur before the parties reach the age of seven, which is taken to be the age of reason (D. 36 c. 4 n. 2).

The various impediments Peter has outlined to this point allow for separation but do not require it. He also outlines several impediments that make marriage absolutely impossible (D. 36 c. 4 n. 3). The first is sacred order; a man who is a priest, deacon, or subdeacon is absolutely unable to enter into marriage; if he has purported to do so, a divorce must be decreed. Those in lower orders, unless they are in religion or have vowed continence, are allowed to marry (D. 37 c. 1 n. 1). Second, a man who murders his wife may not marry again (D. 37 c. 2 n. 1), though the sources establishing this second absolute impediment appear to imply that one may kill one's wife for adultery. This provides an occasion for some reflection by Peter on the nature of ecclesiastical discipline: its sole concern with regard to criminals is that they be "wounded by a spiritual wound" (D. 37 c. 2 n. 2), that is, be brought to repentance. It is a curious way to make the point. It leaves the reader with the impression that the church would not criticize a law that allowed a husband to kill his wife for adultery, when Peter seems interested in making the opposite point: if such a law exists, the church should disregard it, because adultery is to be punished by a spiritual sword (D. 37 c. 2 n. 2).

Since marriage comes into being by the exchange of vows and is barred by prior vows of continence, Peter next considers the nature of the vow, which he defines as "an attestation of a spontaneous promise, which is properly to be done to God and concerning those things which are of God" (D. 38 c. 1). This exchange of vows is to be distinguished from "the vows of fools," which are not to be observed (D. 38 c. 1). Peter then distinguishes between vows made by all

Christians, such as the baptismal vow of renouncing the devil and his pomps, and the vows made by only some Christians, such as a vow of virginity or continence (D. 38 c. 2 n. 1). The latter form of vow may be private or public; while the breach of any vow is sinful, only the breach of a public vow is a matter of scandal and subject to punishment by the church (D. 38 c. 2 n. 1). As a consequence, those who have made a secret vow of continence sin gravely if they marry, but their marriage will not be severed in the absence of proof of the vow. Those who have made a public vow of continence are subject to condemnation even for the mere wish to marry (D. 38 c. 2 nn. 2 and 3).

The most obvious effect of marriage vows is the exclusivity of the sexual relationship between the spouses; as a consequence, adultery is a most serious offense whose gravity is second only to the abandonment of God (D. 38 c. 2 n. 10). But the vow also requires respect for nature within the married sexual relationship itself; acts that are offensive when practiced on a harlot are even more offensive when inflicted on one's wife (D. 38 c. 2 n. 10).

Disparity of religious affiliation is "one of the causes by which people become unlawful for the contracting of marriage" (D. 39 c. 1 n. 1). The prohibition of marriage between Christians and gentiles (i.e., pagans) or Jews is said to be analogous to the Old Testament proscription of marriages between Jews and gentiles, lest the Jews fail to remain true to their faith (D. 39 c. 1 nn. 2 and 3). And yet the Apostle had said that a believer should be willing to remain in a marriage to an unbeliever (D. 39 c. 2 n. 1). But Paul's assertion had to do with those who had married unbelievers before they themselves had come to faith; it follows that it should not be read as allowing a believer to marry an unbeliever (D. 39 c. 2 n. 2). More interestingly, Peter reads the Pauline exhortation as proof that "there is marriage among the infidels," and it is so firm that only a divine mandate can render it void for the sake of avoiding idolatry (D. 39 c. 2 n. 3). But the Apostle's counsel is only a counsel; because the living out of the sacramental value of marriage is not possible with an unbelieving spouse, the believer is allowed to dismiss such a spouse (D. 39 c. 2 n. 3). As for the effects of such a dismissal, if the dismissed spouse had been willing to remain married, the believing spouse may not marry another; if the unbeliever has departed because of the believer's faith, then the believer may marry another (D. 39 c. 5 n. 4).

Relationship and affinity, whether natural or spiritual, are also impediments to marriage (D. 40 c. 1 n. 1). Blood relationships until the seventh degree constitute a bar to marriage (D. 40 c. 1 n. 2). A justification for counting to the seventh degree is that it renders marriage an eschatological sign; bride and groom may join after the seventh degree, "just as, after this life, which is lived in seven days, the church shall be joined to Christ" (D. 40 c. 3 n. 3). In any case, where circumstances require it, the church will not exact observance with regard to the furthest of these degrees; Gregory I allowed the English a less stringent observance until they should become solid in the faith (D. 40 c. 4 n. 2).

Affinity arises from marriage itself; because the spouses become one flesh, they become related to their spouses' kin in the same degree as their spouses (D. 41 c. 1 nn. 1 and 2). At the death of one of the spouses, the other, in remarrying, ought to observe the degrees of consanguinity toward the relatives of the deceased spouse (D. 41 c. 1 nn. 3 and 4). But some authorities would apply a lesser standard in the case of affinity than of consanguinity (D. 41 c. 2 nn. 1–4). It may be that the stricter standard represents the full rigor of the law and the other the dispensation of mercy, "since the church can dispense in the union of persons linked by affinity until the third degree, as Gregory dispensed in them for the degree of consanguinity" (D. 41 c. 2 n. 4).

The last sort of relationship that can stand in the way of marriage is spiritual relationship or proximity, which exists "between a godfather or a godmother, and between those of whom one raised the other from the baptismal font, or sponsored him in catechism or confirmation. It also exists among the carnal and spiritual children of the same man" (D. 42 c. 1 n. 3). But the fraudulent later creation of a spiritual relationship cannot dissolve a prior marriage (D. 42 c. 2 n. 3–5). Indeed, even in the absence of fraud, a prior marriage is not dissolved by the subsequent establishment of a spiritual relationship (D. 42 c. 2 n. 6). Underlying Peter's discussion of these norms appears to be the unstated opinion that the rules of spiritual relationship pursue the social good of encouraging people to look for prospective spouses beyond the circle of those to whom they are already bound. In such a perspective, the rules are useful at the moment of marriage formation, but they should not become a hindrance to married life afterward.

The final question on marriage Peter entertained is whether it is lawful to marry many times (D. 42 c. 7 n. 1). Although such marriages are fully legitimate and allowed by scripture, they are not without shame (D. 42 c. 7 n. 2). If the Apostle forbids a twice-married man from the priesthood, it is not because of any vice intrinsic to second marriages, but "because of the virtue of the sacrament, so that the woman should be one of one, just as [the church is] the one [bride] of the only one" (D. 42 c. 7 n. 4). Yet priests perhaps ought not to be present at the festivities for second and later marriages (D. 42 c. 7 n. 5), with full solemnity of celebration being preserved for the first marriage alone (D. 42 c. 7 n. 6).

With this question, Peter ends his treatment of marriage and the sacraments. His students are now well equipped to handle even the more technical marriage cases that may come before them in whatever capacity they will be called to serve the church. They will now be able to address the people for whose souls they will care as they live out their married lives in the light of the Resurrection, of the judgment, and of the life to come.

PETER AND GRATIAN

This brief overview of Peter's treatment of marriage readily makes clear that it presents us with the essential lines of marriage law as they were codified by papal legislation and received by all jurisdictions in Christendom. Its traces are still found in much of our own marriage law, despite the radical redefinition of the institution in very recent times. It is not a surprise that there is substantial concurrence between Gratian and Peter Lombard. The efforts to distinguish opinions between the two have been mighty, but in the end all one can say is that Peter is a stronger proponent of consent as the sole constituent of marriage. It is not that the two disagree regarding the importance of both consent and consummation, but the one seems readier than the other to suggest that marriage is fully and finally constituted when consent in words of present effect is uttered. But why the difference? Gratian and Peter share the goal of developing in their students a form of prudence that will enable them to be effective pastors and bearers of authority. But Peter is more frankly interested also in encouraging the formation of an intentional piety in his students and their eventual listeners.

One way to illustrate the difference is to note the different concern the two authors exhibit with regard to the marriage of Mary and Joseph. Gratian is not especially worried if it should be found that their marriage could have been annulled. He is even willing to consider that they eventually separated. This is unthinkable for Peter Lombard. He points to Mary and Joseph as exemplary for Christian spouses who seek to live pious lives in the married state, so it is important that the marriage of Mary and Joseph be perceived as complete and indissoluble, despite the lack of consummation. The cultivation of piety, although most explicit in this example, is a recurring purpose as Peter returns over and over to the sanctifying function of marriage and to the importance of its sacramentality. In effect, the sacrament of marriage is the sign to which the church looks in order to learn how to be church. It is also the sign to which celibates are to look in order to become fertile in their own state of life. These are all elements to which Gratian is not disposed to pay attention, since they are subjective and tend to complicate judgments about validity and other practical matters that arise with regard to marriage. In the end, the legislation regarding marriage might well have been much the same if Peter had not examined the issues. But the deeper reasons that gave that same legislation the long life it enjoyed may well owe more to Peter than to Gratian.

RECOMMENDED READING

Colish, Marcia L. *Peter Lombard*. 2 volumes. Leiden; New York; Cologne: E. J. Brill, 1994.

Doyle, Matthew. *Peter Lombard and His Students*. Toronto: Pontifical Institute of Mediaeval Studies, 2016.

Evans, G. R., ed. *The Medieval Theologians: An Introduction to Theology in the Medieval Period*. Oxford: Blackwell, 2001.

Evans, G. R. and Phillipp W. Rosemann, eds. *Mediaeval Commentaries on the Sentences of Peter Lombard*. 3 volumes. Leiden and Boston: E. J. Brill, 2001–15.

Lombard, Peter. *The Sentences. (4 volumes.) Book 1: The Mystery of the Trinity*. Giulio Silano, trans. Toronto: Pontifical Institute of Mediaeval Studies, 2007.

The Sentences. Book 2: On Creation. Giulio Silano, trans. Toronto: Pontifical Institute of Mediaeval Studies, 2008.

The Sentences. Book 3: On the Incarnation of the Word. Giulio Silano, trans. Toronto: Pontifical Institute of Mediaeval Studies, 2010.

The Sentences. Book 4: On the Doctrine of Signs. Giulio Silano, trans. Toronto: Pontifical Institute of Mediaeval Studies, 2010.

Monagle, Clare. *Orthodoxy and Controversy in Twelfth-Century Religious Discourse: Peter Lombard's Sentences and the Development of Theology*. Turnhout, Belgium: Brepols, 2013.

Rogers, Elizabeth Frances. *Peter Lombard and the Sacramental System*. New York: n.p., 1917; reprint edition Merrick, NY: Richwood, 1976.

Rosemann, Phillipp W. *Peter Lombard*. Oxford: Oxford University Press, 2004.

The Story of a Great Medieval Book: Peter Lombard's "Sentences." Toronto: University of Toronto Press, 2007.

10

Popes Alexander III and Innocent III

Charles Donahue, Jr.

BIOGRAPHICAL INTRODUCTION

Gratian and Peter Lombard, both writing in the twelfth century and relying on basically the same collection of authorities, disagreed on some rather fundamental points about marriage. Perhaps the most important disagreement was whether an indissoluble Christian marriage was formed simply by the exchange of present consent between the couple (Lombard) or whether consent to marry had to be followed by sexual intercourse between the couple (Gratian). Disagreements about fundamental principles of law can of course go on for years, even centuries, within a group of scholars committed to working out the law. But the question when someone is married is basic, and the answer to it affects a very large number of people, particularly when marriages are thought to be indissoluble. If there is an authority within the legal system that can resolve the debate, the pressure on that authority to do so will be considerable.

Christianity had long recognized the authority of general church councils. Western Christianity had also recognized the authority of the pope. The relationship between those two authorities was not completely clear. For most legal purposes, Gratian considered the decision of the pope to be as good as that of a council. Normally, the pope exercised his legal authority through decretal letters: the answer that the pope gave to questions that had been submitted to him either in abstract form or in the context of an actual dispute. Examples of papal decretal letters are found as early as the fourth century, and a large number of them were included in the canonical collections that circulated in the twelfth century. Hence, it is not surprising that someone should have thought that it might be appropriate to get the pope definitively to resolve the questions that had been raised about the law of marriage, not only

FIGURE 10.1. Alexander III, European School (nineteenth century) / Private Collection / © Look and Learn / Bridgeman Images.

FIGURE 10.2. Portrait of Pope Innocent III (Gavignano or Anagni, 1160-Perugia, 1216), fresco, by an unknown artist, ca. 1219, detail. Subiaco Monastery (Sacro Speco), Subiaco, Italy. / De Agostini Picture Library / G. Nimatallah / Bridgeman Images

by Gratian and Peter Lombard, but also by a rather large group of scholars around them.

What is perhaps surprising is how often questions were raised. The pontificate of Alexander III (1159–81) may have produced more decretal letters than the pontificates of all the popes prior to him, and that of Innocent III (1198–1216) probably produced more than that of Alexander III. A majority of these decretals were not about marriage, but those about marriage were a significant part of the production. One whole book of the five in Gregory IX's official collection of decretals (*Liber extra*, the *Decretals of Gregory IX* of 1234) is devoted to the law of marriage, and most of the decretals there reported are those of Alexander III or Innocent III.

The role of the papacy in creating the law of marriage that was to prevail in the West until the Reformation is part of a much wider phenomenon, what Maitland described as the "centripetal, Romipetal" force that drew disputes and abstract legal questions to the papacy.[1] That great centripetal force was itself part of an even wider phenomenon, the move of the twelfth century to law. An attempt to explain that phenomenon cannot be a part of this chapter. We must take it as a given, and turn to two men who played key roles in making it happen, and specifically to their contributions to the law of marriage.

Alexander III came from Siena and was named Orlando (Rolandus) before he became pope. His family was probably of the minor Sienese nobility, but later attempts to identify him with a particular Sienese family are unreliable. He was probably born before 1120, perhaps as early as 1110. The identification of him with the Rolandus who wrote one of the earliest commentaries on Gratian's *Concordance of Discordant Canons*, though often made, is so unlikely that we must consider it simply wrong.[2] Contemporaries do comment, however, on his learning, and there seems little reason to doubt that he had an academic background, probably in theology and perhaps in Roman and/or canon law. He was called to service in the Roman church by Pope Eugenius III, perhaps in 1148, when he was a canon of Pisa. In 1149, he became cardinal priest of St. Mark. He was chancellor of the Roman church during the pontificate of Hadrian IV (1154–9), and from that position he was elected pope upon the death of Hadrian. The election was disputed and led to a schism that lasted for most

[1] Maitland, "William of Drogheda and the Universal Ordinary," in Maitland, *Roman Canon Law in the Church of England*, 105.

[2] Noonan, "Who was Rolandus?" 21–48.

of Alexander's pontificate. At the peace of Anagni in 1176, the Holy Roman Emperor, Frederick Barbarossa, recognized Alexander as pope, and the schism collapsed. In 1179, Alexander celebrated the Third Lateran Council. He died in August 1181.

Innocent III was born Lotario de' Conti in Gavignano, near Anagni, in 1160 or 1161. His father was Count Trasimund of Segni, and both his father and mother were members of the Roman noble family of Conti. Lotario studied theology at Paris. Whether he studied law is controverted, though he may have studied it at Bologna. In the 1180s and 1190s, he worked his way up in the papal bureaucracy, becoming a cardinal in 1190. When Celestine III died in January 1198, Lotario was elected Pope Innocent III, with little controversy, although he was only thirty-seven. Many regard his pontificate as the height of medieval papal power. He launched the Fourth and the Albigensian Crusades. He reorganized the papal bureaucracy. He interfered effectively and often in temporal affairs. In 1215, he celebrated the Fourth Lateran Council. He died suddenly in July 1216.

THE CLASSICAL CANON LAW OF MARRIAGE

The approach to what follows will be to state principles of the law of marriage as Alexander III and Innocent III devised them as rules.[3] Indeed, by the time of the *Liber extra*, these rules had become "the classical canon law of marriage." It is important to remember, however, that these rules were expressed, for the most part, in decretals. Decretals can be thought of as being like modern legislation, but they are not expressed in the form of modern legislation. They are almost always expressed as answers to specific questions, usually posed by bishops, or as guidance as to how actual disputes are to be resolved. A treatise-like scheme of rules about marriage was written by the canonist Tancred at the very end of the pontificate of Innocent III, and revised by the canonist Raymond of Peñafort around 1235. Tancred's scheme is used as a guide to presenting the rules, but it is uncertain that either Alexander or Innocent had such an overall scheme in mind as they issued their decretals. It is also important to remember that the answer to a question posed by a bishop might have been different if the bishop had posed the question in a different way, or that the result in a case might have been different if the facts had been different.

[3] The following discussion is based on Charles Donahue, Jr., *Law, Marriage, and Society in the Later Middle Ages*, chapter 1, to which reference should be made for further support. The decretals on which the scheme is based are cited in the text in parentheses.

Alexander III assumed four characteristics of Christian marriage when he began issuing decretals on the topic: First, marriage was between a man and a woman and was monogamous. The first feature of this characteristic was common to the Jewish, Greek, and Roman worlds in which Christianity began. The second feature was, so far as we can tell, largely the Jewish practice in the time of Jesus, and was also the practice and, to a large extent, the law of the Greco-Roman world. Second, a Christian marriage once fully formed was indissoluble while both parties were living. This characteristic was thought, with some justification, to have been the teaching of Jesus as found in the New Testament,[4] and it received a powerful reinforcement in the West in the reform movement of the eleventh century. Third, close relatives could not validly marry. While this prohibition had its origins in both Jewish and Roman law, it had been greatly expanded in the early Middle Ages. The extent of the prohibition was a matter of debate in the eleventh and twelfth centuries, and traces of these debates and their resolution can be found in Alexander's and Innocent's decretals. Fourth, marriage between Christians, once fully formed, was a sacrament of the church. This idea was not fully articulated until Peter Lombard, or just a bit before him, but it seems to be accepted without comment in Alexander's and Innocent's decretals.

FORMATION OF MARRIAGE

In the classical canon law of marriage, a sacramental marriage is formed in either of two ways (X 4.1.15, Alexander III): (1) By present consent freely exchanged between a Christian man and a Christian woman capable of marriage. This makes a marriage that is indissoluble so long as both of them live, unless, prior to the consummation of the marriage, one of them chooses to enter the religious life. (2) By future consent exchanged between a Christian man and a Christian woman capable of marriage. This makes an absolutely indissoluble marriage so long as both of them live, if subsequent to the exchange of future consent and prior to the formation of another marriage, the couple who have exchanged future consent have sexual intercourse with each other.

The scheme of these rules, which in some ways combines the views of Gratian and of Peter Lombard, is first seen clearly in decretals of Alexander III in the context of cases in which he was called upon to determine the priority between two attempted marriages. He probably came to this resolution slowly. At various times, he seems to have thought of making present-consent

4 See discussion of New Testament teachings in Chapter 2 by Gary Hauk herein.

marriages absolutely indissoluble, at other times making them indissoluble only if they were accompanied by the usual solemnities. It would seem that decretals from the end of his pontificate are the only ones that clearly state these rules.[5] Innocent III limited the grounds for dissolution of an unconsummated present-consent marriage to entry into religion. Alexander and his immediate successors had contemplated other such grounds: supervenient affinity, supervenient impotence, supervenient leprosy, and possibly others, but Innocent III closed the door (e.g., X 4.13.6). A respectable body of canonical and theological opinion maintained that the pope had the power to dissolve any unconsummated marriage, but from Innocent III to the beginning of the fifteenth century no pope is known to have done so. When the popes began to dissolve such marriages in the fifteenth century, they did not publicize the fact. That they were doing so does not seem to have been generally known until the sixteenth century.

Pope Gregory IX (1227–41) changed the statement of the second rule. For Gregory (as it had been for many of the canonists), engaging in sexual intercourse after the exchange of future consent created a presumption that the parties had presently consented.[6] This was, at least in the public forum of the courts, a *de iure* presumption; no evidence could be introduced to rebut it (X 4.1.30). Hence, after Gregory IX, all marriages were formed by present consent, either actual or presumed. The rules as stated previously, however, seem to be the way in which practicing lawyers thought about them.

An exchange of future consent, if not followed by sexual intercourse, did not form a marriage. The parties could be relieved of any obligations that they had thereby incurred for cause, perhaps even by mutual consent. It was debatable whether the obligations of future consent were enforceable when one of the parties was willing and the other was not. It was clear that a contract of marriage would not be specifically enforced against someone who had married another by either of the two methods described earlier.

Hence, in the absence of subsequent sexual intercourse (and, in the forum of the courts, "provable subsequent sexual intercourse"), it made a large difference whether the consent was characterized as present or future. On the basis of the decretals, there seem to have been relatively well-defined formulae for expressing each kind of consent, at least for those speaking

[5] See Donahue Jr., "The Dating of Alexander the Third's Marriage Decretals," 70–124.

[6] In Donahue Jr., *Law, Marriage, and Society*, at n. 7, this development is attributed to Innocent III, without reference. The doctrine can be derived from Innocent's decretal *Per tuas*, X 4.5.6, but its first clear statement does not come until Gregory IX.

in Latin, but there were many ambiguous possibilities outside of those formulae. The problem became even more complicated, as few ordinary people in medieval Europe expressed themselves in Latin, and there was a large amount of litigation on the topic in the later Middle Ages.[7]

What of nonsacramental marriages? By the beginning of the thirteenth century, it was clear that a marriage between Christians was sacramental, if it was a marriage at all. It was also clear that there could be no marriage between a Christian and a non-Christian. Marriages between non-Christians were recognized as marriages, but they were not sacramental. Nonsacramental marriages and the related issue of what happens if one of the non-Christians in a nonsacramental marriage becomes a Christian were discussed by canonists and theologians, but in a Europe in which the vast majority of the population was Christian and those who were not (principally Jews) were endogamous and handled marriage matters in their own courts, such marriages did not give rise to many practical questions.

IMPEDIMENTS TO MARRIAGE

By the beginning of the thirteenth century, the impediments to marriage were neatly divided into two kinds, diriment and impedient. The former invalidated any attempted marriage; the latter did not invalidate the marriage but rendered it unlawful. Those who married in the face of an impedient impediment could be penalized, but their marriage was valid and could not be dissolved. By the beginning of the thirteenth century, it was also clear that for an impediment to be diriment, it had to have existed at the time that the marriage was contracted. The one possible exception to this rule, supervenient entry into religion following an unconsummated present-consent marriage, is probably better thought of as a voluntary dissolution of a marriage that exists but is not yet absolutely indissoluble.

The canonists and popes of the twelfth and early thirteenth centuries made considerable progress in trimming the luxurious growth of impediments that was their heritage from the past. They also made considerable progress in rationalizing and classifying the impediments. They had not yet achieved a complete rationalization and classification, so the following outline reorganizes the impediments.

7 See the discussion in Raymond of Peñafort (Raimundus de Pennaforte), *Summa de poenitentia et matrimonio cum glossis Johannis de Friburgo*, 4.2, p. 511 (gloss); and Helmholz, *Marriage Litigation in Medieval England*, 34–40, with references.

Vices of Consent

Insanity. Those who are insane are incapable of consent. This impediment was recognized by Innocent III (X 4.1.24) and by all the canonists, but little is said about it. It is also not prominent in the cases.

Impotence and Frigidity. Physical incapacity for sexual intercourse removed both primary causes of marriages as then construed: the procreation of offspring and the avoidance of fornication. It was, however, only after some hesitancy that the classical canon law recognized impotence or frigidity as a ground for dissolving a present-consent marriage, and it did so only if the condition existed at the time of present consent, and only if the party who was capable of intercourse did not know of the other's inability (X 4.15.6, Innocent III).

Nonage. Nonage combined notions of mental and physical incapacity. In classical canon law, the espousals of those below the age of seven were null. Persons that young lacked the mental capacity to consent. Espousals of persons between the age of seven and puberty (notionally fixed at twelve for girls and fourteen for boys) were binding in the same way that future consent was binding: they could become indissoluble marriages if the parties had intercourse or exchanged present consent after reaching the age of puberty, but before either of those events happened, they created an obligation but no marriage. The obligation could be dissolved for cause, and it would not prevail over a subsequent marriage entered into after the parties had reached the age of puberty. If one of the parties was over the age of puberty and the other under, the party above the age of puberty was held to the contract while the other party was below the age of puberty. When the latter party reached the age of puberty, he or she had the option to rescind (X 4.2.8, 7, Alexander III).

Force or Fear. Since the canon law based its notion of marriage on the free consent of the parties, one would expect that it would be open to the argument that consent that was forced or prompted by fear impeded the marriage. The law was open to this argument, but authoritative statements on this topic are quite cautious. Alexander III issued four decretals on the topic (X 4.1.6, X 1.40.1, X 4.1.14, X 4.1.15). While all four decretals recognize that marriage (or entry into religion) is not binding if it is forced, they seem to reflect a change in attitude toward the impediment. The first two decretals state that even if the consent is forced, it may subsequently be ratified. The latter two do not. The first decretal distinguishes between types of force, and the second (admittedly in a somewhat different context) seems to suggest that only mortal fear will vitiate the consent. The third decretal suggests no standard, but offers a strong statement that forced marriages are a bad idea, and the fourth, while it adopts an objective standard, adopts one considerably more relaxed than the second: "the fear that would turn a constant man."

Error. If marriages were to be based on consent, one would expect that that consent could be vitiated by mistake, just as contractual consent may be vitiated by mistake. Classical canon law resisted this conclusion, ultimately holding that only mistake of person (I marry Joan thinking that I am marrying Alice) and mistake of status (I marry a slave thinking that I am marrying a free woman) would vitiate the consent. The assumption of this latter doctrine is that a marriage between a free person and one of servile condition could be a valid marriage. This assumption was in marked contrast to Roman law, where slaves could not validly marry each other or a free person. A remarkable decretal of Hadrian IV (X 4.9.1, 1151 X 1159, perhaps written by Alexander; he was chancellor at the time) held that such was not the case in canon law.

Condition. In classical canon law, the impediment of condition referred to two quite different types of conditions. The first is the type involved in the previous paragraph, where one of the parties married in ignorance of the other's servile condition. The second is the situation where the parties made their consent conditional on the happening of some event: "I take thee to wife if my parents consent," or "I take thee to wife if your father will give me so much in dowry." Classical canon law ultimately came to the conclusion that such conditions did serve to suspend the binding effect of the marriage. If the condition was fulfilled, the parties were married automatically. They also were married automatically if they subsequently exchanged the words of present consent unconditionally or if they had intercourse (X 4.5.6, Innocent III). Further complexities were introduced if the condition was contrary to the nature of marriage, or if it was shameful or disgraceful. The former type of condition voided the marriage; the latter did not void the marriage, but was simply ignored (X 4.5.7, Gregory IX).

In the practical realm of decretals, particularly decretals in real cases, conditions were not of great importance. For example, Alexander's one decretal on conditional marriages involves a quite normal condition and one that was regarded as honest: "I will take you to wife if you give me so much as dowry." Alexander's resolution of the problem anticipates, if it does not quite completely cover, the solution that the later law was to reach (X 4.5.3).

Religious Impediments

Disparity of Cult. The impediments of disparity of cult, orders, and vow all had as their focus the maintenance of marriage as a secular relationship between Christians. As noted previously, classical canon law held firmly that a Christian could not marry a non-Christian. On marriage to heretics there was some hesitancy, but the ultimate resolution was that such marriages were valid, though illegitimate.

Orders. Priests and deacons were not permitted to marry, but if they did, they had to dismiss their wives (who were not their wives, but concubines), do penance, and return to their clerical service. So far as subdeacons were concerned, there was some hesitancy. Alexander III says in one decretal that they may not marry (X 4.6.1). In another, he praises the bishop of Le Mans for having made a subdeacon abjure his wife, and says that if the subdeacon enters the religious life and behaves himself, he may be promoted to higher orders. If he does not wish to enter religion, he cannot function as a subdeacon or be promoted to higher orders, but he may function in minor orders (X 4.6.2). In other decretals, Alexander is more qualified about subdeacons. The classical law suppressed Alexander's hesitancy about whether the order of the subdiaconate was a diriment impediment to marriage. It was, and the only issue was how to punish those subdeacons who did marry. In this regard, the second decretal described earlier became the model, just as the first was taken for the statement of the basic rules.

Vows. From the time of Gratian, classical canon law distinguished between simple vows and solemn vows. Only the latter were a diriment impediment to marriage. The converse of the proposition that one who has taken a solemn vow of chastity cannot marry is that one who is married cannot take a solemn vow of chastity, at least not without the consent of his or her spouse. This much was clear by the time that Alexander III wrote, but precisely what was to happen if one spouse, with the consent of the other, wished to embrace the religious life was not clear. Alexander clarified it (X 3.32.8). If one member of the couple wishes to espouse religion with the consent of the other, the other must take a vow to live chastely. If that person can be trusted to keep the vow while living in the world, he or she may; if not, he or she must also live in a religious house.

Crime. The classical canon law recognized that crime was a diriment impediment to marriage in two situations: (1) Where a couple had committed adultery, and one or both of them then conspired in the death or participated in the killing of the spouse(s) of either or both of them, they could not marry after the death of the spouse(s). (2) Where a couple had committed adultery and had pledged faith to each other that they would marry, they could not marry after the death of the spouse or spouses of either or both of them. This latter impediment also applied to those who went through a form of marriage while the spouses of one or both of them were alive, since such a form of marriage would involve a pledge of faith.

To these basic rules, Alexander III added an important qualification, which was received in the classical law (X 4.7.1). Where one of the parties to the adulterous second marriage was unaware of the adultery, only that party could ask for a divorce after the first spouse was dead. Otherwise, the second marriage was validated as soon as it became possible to do so.

The Problem of Incest

Medieval canon law on the topic of incest was extensive. It applied to those who were related by blood (consanguinity), by marriage (affinity), and by spiritual bonds, usually arising out of baptism (spiritual affinity). The tendency of the preclassical canon law was to expand the number of persons who were forbidden to marry because of one kind of relationship or another. Prior to Alexander III, the twelfth-century canonists had largely engaged in collecting the sources and trying to determine precisely the rules reflected in the mainstream sources. This process did result in pruning from the authoritative materials some of the more extreme statements of the rules and in fixing a limit on their expansion. The prohibition was limited to the sixth or seventh degree of consanguinity and the same degree for those who married into a consanguineous line (affinity). The computation of the degrees was by the canonic method, i.e., by tracing the number of acts of generation back to a common ancestor (where the number of generations was unequal, the larger number was used for purposes of determining the prohibition). Hence, the seventh-degree limit was reached with sixth cousins (fifth cousins once removed, fourth cousins twice removed, etc.).

Consanguinity. Alexander III's decretals on the topic of consanguinity began the trend to cut back on the reach of the impediment. These decretals may be laid out on a series of spectra: whether and how long the marriage has existed, how remote the degrees are, and how reliable the evidence of the consanguinity is. The longer the marriage has gone unchallenged, the more remote the degrees, or the less reliable the evidence, the more Alexander was likely to sustain the marriage. Innocent III continued Alexander's practice.

The problem with this approach from a juridical point of view is that it makes decisions unpredictable. All depends on the facts of the particular case. In the Fourth Lateran Council, Innocent III took a different approach. He reduced the prohibited degrees of consanguinity and affinity from six or seven to four, but insisted on strict observance of the rules as modified.[8]

This ruling made obsolete whatever had previously been said about consanguinity or affinity in the fifth degree and beyond. It also made obsolete Alexander's (and to some extent Innocent's) carefully constructed spectrum of the length in which the marriage had gone unchallenged. It did not make obsolete what Alexander had said about separating couples who had married in defiance of an interdict. Nor did it affect what he had said about dispensing with the *ordo* in cases of notoriety – although notoriety, he said, could hardly be had in cases not of the first or second degrees. These are the only decretals of Alexander's on the topic of consanguinity that appear in the *Liber extra* (X 4.16.3, X 4.19.3). Alexander's rulings in this area were more influential than their survival rate would suggest, however. The principle that Alexander established – that the prohibition of intermarriage in the more remote degrees of consanguinity was a matter of human, not divine, law – meant that parties could be dispensed to marry within those degrees. Popes continued to employ the dispensing power in the more remote degrees of consanguinity (fourth and third). Alexander had been the first to do so extensively. Alexander's cautions about accepting the evidence of those who had an opportunity to object at the time a marriage was entered into and did not do so also found resonance in the later law, though on this topic it was a decretal of Innocent's that appeared in the *Liber extra* (X 4.18.6). Finally, another decree of the Fourth Lateran Council set firm rules (which both Alexander and Innocent had anticipated) about who could be witnesses in cases of consanguinity and affinity and how they were to testify. The effect of this decree was to make proof in such cases more certain, but also more difficult.[9]

Affinity. After the Fourth Lateran Council, the impediment of affinity applied only to those related within the fourth degree of consanguinity to the spouse of the affine. It also only applied to the person who had sexual relations outside of marriage with someone within the consanguineous line. The baroque variations of affinity that went under the names of affinity of the second type and affinity of the third type were abolished by the council.

[8] 4 Lateran (1215), c.50, in Tanner, *Decrees of the Ecumenical Councils*, 1:257–8.

[9] 4 Lateran (1215), c.52, in Tanner, *Decrees of the Ecumenical Councils*, 1:259.

Alexander III faced early and often the problem that would later be called *affinitas per copulam illicitam* – when a man and a woman have illicit sexual relations, and then either or both of them later seek to marry a blood relative of the person with whom they have had sexual relations. The case was made more difficult if the subsequent marriage had already taken place, or if the illicit intercourse occurred after the marriage had taken place.

Alexander clearly struggled with these cases, and he came up with a number of distinctions that suggest that he had doubts about whether an affinity by illicit intercourse really impeded the marriage, or at least whether it did so by divine law. If this was the path that Alexander's decretals on *affinitas per copulam illicitam* was taking, then the canonists suppressed it. None of Alexander's decretals on the topic appears in the *Liber extra*. The Fourth Lateran Council drew no distinction between *affinitas per copulam illicitam* and affinity arising out of a lawful marriage.

Spiritual Affinity. The problem of spiritual relationship had spawned a law whose prominence was out of proportion to its practical import. The problem was that the past had left a singularly obscure set of canons, and the popes were continually asked to resolve issues related to these canons. Although there was debate about what gave rise to a spiritual relationship, the first two "species" of prohibition were clear enough: a spiritual parent (godfather, godmother) could not marry his or her spiritual child ("spiritual paternity"), and a spiritual parent could not marry the natural parent of his or her spiritual child ("copaternity"). Beyond that, the law was unclear, whether, for example, one could marry one's father's or mother's godchild, though the canonists tried to make it clearer.

Public Honesty. Affinity could not impede a marriage unless one of the potential marriage partners had had sexual intercourse (lawfully or unlawfully) with a blood relative of the other. But if one of the parties had contracted to marry a relative of the other, either as adults or before they had reached the age of puberty, the classical canon law recognized an impediment to their marrying each other, even though no true marriage had ever existed with the relative, and even if there had never been sexual intercourse between them. It was thought scandalous, for example, for a man to marry the mother of his former fiancée. And because of this focus on scandal, the impediment was called that of public honesty.

The impediment of public honestly was somewhat modified by the Fourth Lateran Council, in that the degrees of the prohibition were reduced to four. The impediment remained throughout the classical period and beyond, however, although the degrees were radically reduced by the Council of Trent in 1563.[10]

IMPEDIENT IMPEDIMENTS: THE PROBLEM OF CLANDESTINITY AND SOLEMNITY

The only impedient impediment that regularly came before the ecclesiastical courts was lack of solemnity, which the canonists treated as a branch of the impedient impediment of marriage against the interdict of the church. Only two contemporary decretals appear in the *Liber extra* under the title "Concerning clandestine espousals."

The first is a reply of Alexander III to the bishop of Beauvais concerning whether "we [i.e., the pope] ought to issue a dispensation concerning clandestine marriages" (X 4.3.2). Alexander replies that no dispensation is necessary. If the parties to an occult (unprovable) marriage do not publish it, there is nothing that the church can do about it. The church does not judge about things that are hidden. Further, if the parties do publish the marriage (and no impediment appears), the marriage is valid *nunc pro tunc*. Alexander then spells out the obvious implications of this ruling for the legitimacy of the children of the marriage – that they are legitimate.

The second decretal, a canon of the Fourth Lateran Council, takes a considerably less relaxed attitude toward clandestine marriages.[11] The proper way to get married, the council declared, is publicly after the proclamation of banns. Any priest who participates in a marriage where banns have not been proclaimed is to be suspended from office. The council did not prescribe the "suitable penance" for the parties to such a marriage (other than the loss of the benefits of putative marriage,[12] not technically a penance), nor did it invalidate such marriages. They were illegitimate, but they were still marriages. The importance of this last qualification for our understanding of the classical canon law of marriage cannot be overstated. Marriages are made by the consent of the parties or, in the case of future consent, their consent plus intercourse. The church could, and did, strongly

[10] See discussion of this Council in Chapter 15 by Rafael Domingo on Thomas Sanchez and in Chapter 20 by Russell Hittinger on Pope Leo XIII.

[11] 4 Lateran (1215), c.51, in Tanner, *Decrees of the Ecumenical Councils*, 1:258.

[12] An invalid marriage nonetheless produced legitimate children if the couple married publicly and were unaware of the invalidity. See Donahue Jr., *Law, Marriage, and Society*, chapter 1 at n. 113.

encourage parties to publicize their marriages in advance of the event. This way the church could ensure that the parties were truly capable of marriage, and difficult problems of proof might be avoided. But neither Alexander nor his successors until the Council of Trent took the step of invalidating such marriages.

It was left to the local churches to deal with the problem of clandestinity. There was considerable variation in what the local churches did.[13]

DIVORCE AND REMARRIAGE

As already intimated in part, classical canon law allowed divorce of a consummated marriage with permission to remarry only when there was a diriment impediment to the marriage. This divorce corresponded to what today we call annulment. Divorce without permission to remarry so long as both partners were alive, what we today call separation, was allowed in the case of the adultery of one of the parties and, perhaps, in other cases as well. At the beginning of the thirteenth century, the law was not clear about what might be other grounds for separation.[14] The case of the unconsummated present-consent marriage was more complicated, as noted previously, but the classical law allowed its dissolution, at least officially, only in the case where one of the parties entered the religious life. The basic principles of indissolubility and separation in the case of adultery were well established by the beginning of the thirteenth century, as was the proposition that no divorce of either type could take place without the judgment of the church. This meant, at a minimum, in the case of a marriage that was public, that the public forum of the church had to be invoked.

Remarriage of widows and widowers was not forbidden, but was regarded as problematical in the Eastern church and by some authorities in the Western church. Neither church allowed such marriages to be blessed, making them second-class marriages. Alexander III has little to say on the topic, except that second marriages should not be blessed. He ordered that a chaplain who had done so be suspended from office and sent to the apostolic see, presumably for absolution (X 4.21.1). Innocent III in one notable decretal resoundingly confirms the validity of such marriages, citing, appropriately, 1 Corinthians 7:8–9 and refusing to brand with infamy even those widows who remarried within

[13] A discussion of those in England and France may be found in my "Thoughts on Diocesan Statutes," 253–71.

[14] The later developments are outlined in Donahue Jr., *Law, Marriage, and Society*, chapter 10, at n. 11–20.ddß

the traditional mourning period (X 4.21.5). There the classical canon law remained, though it increasingly insisted on clear proof of the death of the former spouse.[15]

CONCLUSION

It is by no means clear that Alexander III intended to create a coherent system of marriage law based on decretals when he began issuing decretals about marriage, most of which seem to date from the second half of his pontificate. It is more likely that Innocent III had that idea from the very beginning. Whatever the case, by the end of Innocent's pontificate, a coherent and comprehensive system of marriage law could be created mostly out of relatively recent decretals, particularly those of these two men, and that is what the canonists did. The system proved long lasting. No major changes were made in it until the last session of the Council of Trent in 1563. The system was not only the one in effect in church courts but was also, for the most part and at least so far as the formation and dissolution of marriage was concerned, the system in effect in the secular law of Western Europe, because the secular law deferred to the church's law on those issues.

So far as the individual contributions of the two men are concerned, those of Alexander regarding the formation of marriage were probably the most important. The striking thing is not so much what Alexander requires, but what he does not require. According to the rules that emerged at the end of his pontificate, no solemnity or ceremony was required to form a valid and absolutely indissoluble marriage. The decree of the Fourth Lateran Council on the promulgation of banns introduced a solemnity requirement, but this requirement affected only the legitimacy of the marriage, not its validity. Litigation about informal marriages was a staple of the business of the church courts throughout the later Middle Ages. Alexander's rules about marriage formation also do not require the consent of anyone other than the couple themselves to form a valid marriage. In this regard, his rules are strikingly different from Roman law, which required the consent of the fathers of the couple (if the fathers were still living). Alexander's rules can be argued to have had the effect of giving young people more say about whom they would marry. Perhaps Alexander even intended that effect.

[15] See Witte Jr., *The Western Case for Monogamy over Polygamy*, 182–6, for further elaboration with extensive references.

Innocent's contribution to marriage law is harder to summarize. He emphasized the role of present consent perhaps more than did Alexander. He saw, perhaps more clearly than Alexander, the difficulties to which informal marriages could give rise, but ultimately he was unwilling to take the step taken by the Council of Trent, to invalidate them. Perhaps his most important contribution was to cut back on the range of the incest prohibition, but then to insist that the reduced prohibition be strictly followed, except where a papal dispensation had been obtained.

RECOMMENDED READING

Boso's Life of Alexander III. Edited and translated by Gerard M. Ellis. Totowa, NJ: Rowman and Littlefield, 1973.

Brundage, James A. *Law, Sex, and Christian Society in Medieval Europe*. Chicago: University of Chicago Press, 1987.

D'Avray, D. L. *Medieval Marriage: Symbolism and Society*. Oxford: Oxford University Press, 2005.

Decrees of the Ecumenical Councils. Edited and translated by Norman P. Tanner. 2 vols. London: Sheed and Ward, 1990.

Donahue, Charles, Jr. "The Dating of Alexander the Third's Marriage Decretals," *Zeitschrift der Savigny-Stiftung für Rechtsgeschichte: Kanonistische Abteilung* 68 (1982): 70–124.

Law, Marriage, and Society in the Later Middle Ages. Cambridge: Cambridge University Press, 2007.

Gesta Innocentii III: The Deeds of Pope Innocent III. Translated by James M. Powell. Washington, DC: Catholic University of America Press, 2004.

Hartmann, Wilfried and Kenneth Pennington, eds. *The History of Medieval Canon Law in the Classical Period, 1140–1234: From Gratian to the Decretals of Pope Gregory IX*. Washington, DC: Catholic University of America Press, 2008.

Helmholz, R. H. *Marriage Litigation in Medieval England*. Cambridge: Cambridge University Press, 1974.

Jasper, Detlev and Horst Furhrmann. *Papal Letters in the Early Middle Ages*. Washington, DC: Catholic University of America Press, 2001.

Moore, John C. *Pope Innocent III (1160/61–1216): To Root up and to Plant*. Leiden: Brill, 2003.

Noonan, John T. "Who Was Rolandus?" In *Law, Church, and Society. Essays in Honor of Stephan Kuttner*. Edited by Kenneth Pennington and Robert Somerville, 21–48. Philadelphia: University of Pennsylvania Press, 1977.

Raymond of Peñafort (Raimundus de Pennaforte). *Summa de poenitentia et matrimonio cum glossis Johannis de Friburgo*. Rome, 1603; reprinted

Farnborough: Gregg Press, 1967. Partly translated as *Summa on Marriage*. Translated and edited by Pierre Payer. Toronto: University of Toronto Press, 2005.

Sayers, Jane E. *Innocent III: Leader of Europe, 1198–1216*. London: Longmans, 1994.

Tancred of Bologna (*Tancredus bononiensis*). *Summa de Matrimonio*. Edited by Agathon Wunderlich. Göttingen: Apud Vandenhocke et Ruprecht, 1841.

X (followed by book, title, and chapter numbers) = *Decretales Gregorii Noni [liber Extra]*. *Corpus Iuris Canonici*. Edited by Emil Friedberg. Vol. 2. Leipzig: ex officina Bernhardi Tauchnitz, 1879; reprinted Graz: Akad. Druck- und Verl.-Anst., 1959.

11

St. Thomas Aquinas

Philip L. Reynolds

BIOGRAPHICAL INTRODUCTION

Legal historians speak of family law during the central and late Middle Ages in two senses, one pertaining to marriage itself and the other to its legal and economic consequences. Church law regulated marriage, defining its validity or invalidity, mutual obligations, and divorce.[1] Secular law regulated the consequences of marriage pertaining to kinship, dowries, property, and inheritance. Thomas Aquinas contributed to family law only in the first sense. He assumed that stable, patriarchal families were fundamental to the political and ecclesiastical community, and he knew of no other way to ensure that stability than by regulating marriage and sexual behaviour. The law of marriage in the central Middle Ages was extremely intrusive and constraining by modern standards, whereas family life and the raising of children were virtually unregulated – the converse of what prevails today.

As a Dominican friar and a theologian, Thomas was professionally interested in marriage chiefly as one of the sacraments, but this sacrament, in his view, presupposed a secular "material contract," much as baptism presupposed water (*IV Sent.* 27.1.2, qu[a] 1 [83]).[2] The underlying contract established a natural and civic partnership, on which classical philosophers such as Aristotle and Cicero had shed light. Moreover, like all medieval churchmen, but especially as a member of a religious order dedicated to preaching and sacramental

[1] For a summary of this regimen, see Donahue Jr., *Law, Marriage, and Society in the Later Middle Ages*, 14–45, as well as Prof. Donahue's Chapter 10 in this volume.

[2] Editions of chief works of Thomas cited here, with abbreviations. *Scriptum super libros Sententiarum* [*Sent.*]: *Opera Omnia* (Paris: Apud Ludovicum Vivès, 1871–2), vol. 11, for *IV Sent.* 23 ff.; otherwise, the incomplete edition by Pierre Mandonnet (vols. 1–2) and Maria F. Moos (vols. 3–4) (Paris: Sumptibus P. Lethielleux, 1929 and 1933–47). *Summa contra Gentiles*, or *Liber de veritate catholicae fidei contra errores infideliumi* [SCG], ed. C. Pera, P. Marc, and P. Caramello, 3 vols. (Turin and Rome: Marietti, 1961, 1967). *Summa theologiae* [ST], 5 vols. (Ottawa: Institute of Medieval Studies, 1941–5).

FIGURE 11.1. Thomas Aquinas (b/w photo) / © SZ Photo / Scherl / Bridgeman Images

confession, Thomas was keenly interested in sexual ethics. Marriage and sexual intercourse were naturally and teleologically tied to the begetting and raising of children, in his view, and this tie entailed moral constraints on sexual activities. These constraints pertained to the innate natural law, "written on the hearts" of humanity, and more generally to compliance with the order of nature.

Thomas set out his position on sex, marriage, and family in two major theological syntheses: his early commentary on Peter Lombard's *Sentences* (known as the *Scriptum*) and the *Summa contra Gentiles*. His most extensive treatment of the theory of laws is in his unfinished *Summa theologiae*. These works emerged successively in different phases of his short but intensely productive career.

Thomas was born in Aquino, Italy, and joined the Order of Preachers (the Dominicans) in April 1244, when he was about nineteen years old and studying liberal arts in Naples.[3] By the autumn of 1245, he was studying in Paris, notably with Albertus Magnus (d. 1280), who had come to Paris in 1243 or 1244 to lecture on Peter Lombard's *Sentences*, by then the standard textbook of theology.[4] When the Dominican Order sent Albert to establish a school for Dominicans in Cologne in 1248, Thomas accompanied him as his assistant. In Cologne, Thomas heard Albert lecture on Aristotle's *Nicomachean Ethics* in the new Latin translation by Robert Grosseteste.

Thomas returned to Paris in 1252 as a bachelor (teaching assistant) lecturing on the *Sentences*. He became Dominican regent master (professor) of theology in Paris in 1256, editing the *Scriptum* for publication and lecturing on scripture before returning to Italy in 1259.

Having begun his *Summa contra Gentiles* in Paris in 1258, Thomas completed it in 1265, when he was master of studies at the minor Dominican priory of Orvieto. Setting aside the scholastic technique of *quaestiones* (plausible contradictions) and solutions, Thomas tried in the *Summa contra Gentiles* to expose the rational structure of the Christian faith in continuous prose, constructing doctrines step by step, and citing proof texts from scripture only for confirmation or as a last resort.

From 1265 through 1268, Thomas was regent master of a new school for Dominican friars in Rome, where he began work on the *Summa theologiae*, his attempt to provide an adequate intellectual framework for the friars' work in preaching and sacramental confession.[5] Thomas was Dominican regent

3 On Thomas's life and work, see Torrell, *Saint Thomas Aquinas*.

4 See Chapter 9 herein by Giulio Silano.

5 Boyle, "The Setting of the *Summa theologiae* of St. Thomas – Revisited," 1–16.

master again at the University of Paris from 1268 through 1272, where he continued work on the *Summa* and on much else besides.

In 1273, having reached the third part of the *Summa theologiae*, which would have covered the incarnation of Jesus Christ, the seven sacraments, and the Last Things, Thomas began teaching in Naples. Here his career as an author ended abruptly after an ecstatic experience or breakdown in December of that year. He died in March 1274. He had reached the sacrament of penance in his *Summa*, but that section was unfinished, and he had not touched the remaining sacraments – extreme unction, holy orders, and marriage – or the Last Things. To complete the *Summa*, Thomas's secretary, Reginald of Piperno, took material verbatim from the early *Scriptum* and rearranged it to fit the *Summa*'s plan. This posthumous addition to the *Summa theologiae* is known as the *Supplement*.

Thomas discusses marriage extensively only in the *Scriptum* (book IV, distinctions 26–42), as the last of the seven sacraments. This treatment also includes most of what Thomas says in the *Scriptum* about natural law and the natural order. But there is no general exposition of law in the commentary, and Thomas's theory of laws and especially of the natural law at this early stage was still inchoate and exploratory. It remains little studied and poorly understood today.

After writing on marriage in the *Scriptum*, Thomas briefly developed some of his ideas about marriage and sexuality in his *Summa contra Gentiles*. This work contains no general exposition of law, however, and Thomas rarely mentions natural law. Instead, Thomas posits a human "instinct of nature" and emphasizes compliance with the order of nature.

Thomas's *Summa theologiae* includes an extensive exposition of the theory of laws (ST I-II.90–108), which includes a definitive and influential account of the natural law. Sadly, however, Thomas stopped writing before he reached the sacrament of marriage, although the material on this topic from the early *Scriptum* was included (anachronistically) in the *Supplement*.

NATURAL LAW AND THE FAMILY

As understood in the medieval schools, the natural law was the innate, unchangeable, and universal basis of morality and positive law, rooted in human nature and "written on their hearts" (Romans 2:15). Whereas the binding force of positive law came from the will of prudent legislators and rulers (for in Thomas's view only a just law was truly law), the binding force of natural law was inherent in nature (*III Sent.* 37.un.3, ad 2 [Moos 3:1245]).[6] Divine law, divided

6 On Aquinas's view of positive law, see Finnis, "The Truth in Legal Positivism," 195–214.

into the Old Law and the New Law, guided believers to final union with God; it not only corrected and completed but also surpassed positive human law.

When Thomas began teaching and writing, speculation about natural law was well developed yet still exploratory and controversial. Medieval scholars were familiar with two ways of construing natural law: as an animal instinct that humans shared not as humans, but as animals; and as the first, self-evident principles of practical reasoning, such as the positive and negative versions of the Golden Rule (Matthew 7:12, Tobias 14:16) and perhaps the Ten Commandments.[7] One way to resolve the distinction between these two understandings of natural law was to recognize both by treating the term "natural law" as equivocal. William of Auxerre (d. 1231), whose writings Thomas knew well, adopted this approach while arguing that natural law in the proper sense resulted from divine illumination of the mind.[8] Thomas's teacher, Albertus Magnus, rejected the former aspect of this view, arguing that both the animal and the human aspects of natural law presented themselves to the human mind as innate, self-evident principles of practical reasoning.[9]

Moreover, to explain marriage, Albert developed a broader discourse about the natural order alongside invocations of the innate natural law. For example, in his commentary on distinction 33 of book IV of the *Sentences*, on Old Testament polygamy, Albert devoted three articles respectively to whether marriage, polygyny, and polyandry were natural.[10] The notion of innate natural law appears only incidentally in this discussion. Instead, Albert writes as a naturalist, situating human beings as one species among the animals and noting comparisons, contrasts, and correlations. He observes that members of species in which the father's help is needed in raising the young are more inclined to form stable breeding pairs. For example, birds form breeding pairs because one partner has to look for food while the other incubates, and they remain together until the fledglings leave the nest.[11] Like all animals, humans raise their offspring to full maturity, but human maturity is intellectual and moral as well as corporeal, and it takes a long time.[12]

Thomas refined Albert's position, albeit without explaining how the natural principles of animal life communicated themselves to the mind as self-evident

7 Greene, "Instinct of Nature: Natural Law, Synderesis, and the Moral Sense," 173–98.

8 William of Auxerre, *Summa aurea* III, tr. 18, c. 1 & c. 4 [hereafter SB] 18A, and *Summa aurea* IV, tr. 17, c. 3, qq. 2–3, in SB 19 (1985), 394 9.

9 Albertus Magnus, *De bono*, tr. 5, q. 1, art. 2, *Opera omnia*, 28:268–71.

10 Albertus Magnus, *IV Sent.* 33.1–3, *Opera omnia*, Borgnet edition, 30:289–96.

11 *IV Sent.* 33.1, arg. 3c (289b); ad 1 (290); ad 4 (290b).

12 *IV Sent.* 33.1, resp. (290); arg. 5c (289b–290a). Albert quotes at length from Aspasius's commentary on Aristotle's NE VIII to make this point, but in fact this part of the fragmentary commentary was supplied by the translator, Robert Grosseteste.

rational principles. Thomas was less of a naturalist than Albert, but he adopted features of Albert's treatment of the natural order in his own discussion of marriage. Like Albert, Thomas predicated three kinds of arguments on what was natural. First, to show that something is natural, one may show that it meets basic natural needs in a manner congruent with human nature. Second, inasmuch as fulfilling such needs is a thing's purpose, one may argue that it is wrong to thwart that purpose by using the thing for some other, incompatible end. Third, one may argue that certain actions, regardless of their consequences, do not befit human nature or the human species. The first consideration, from need, is most akin to innate natural law, since it posits goods that fulfill natural inclinations. In the field of sexual ethics, it is difficult to derive prohibitions from innate natural law or need, but easy to derive them from function and fittingness.

Scriptum super libros Sententiarum

Thomas used his inquiry into marriage in book IV of his commentary on Peter Lombard's *Sentences* as an opportunity to develop his understanding of how morality and law are rooted in human nature. First, to explain how the basis of human action is natural, Thomas pointed out that natural agents are inclined to act toward their ends from necessity and always in the same way. For example, fire always heats and always moves upward; earthy bodies always gravitate downward. Rational agents have free will and thus are not bound to act naturally in that sense, but their actions are founded on innate inclinations. Even voluntary action, while non-necessary by definition, cannot be non-necessary "all the way down."[13] Basic natural inclinations persist in human action, therefore, but by the mediation of free choice (*IV Sent.* 26.1.1, resp. [67b]).

Second, the basic inclinations of all agents, rational and irrational, arise from their natures, or forms. And since the form of anything has both generic and specific aspects, some of any agent's inclinations pertain to its genus and others to its species. For example, a magnet gravitates downward by virtue of its genus as an earthy body, but attracts iron by virtue of its species (*IV Sent.* 33.1.1, resp. [140b]). The same distinction is found in human agents and in the natural law.

Third, human action is rooted not in a single form, but in a pair of corresponding innate forms, one in the intellect and the other in the will. Thus, a cognitive conception of an end gives rise to a corresponding will to achieve it and guides the agent toward the end. The natural law consists of

[13] *De veritate* 22.5, resp., Leonine edition, vol. 22.3, 623–4. See also ST I–II.1.7, resp., and ST I–II.1.5, resp.

these basic conceptions (*IV Sent.* 33.1.1, resp. [140–1]). The most basic, known as primary precepts, are absolute, whereas the derived secondary precepts are defeasible.

Following Albert, Thomas proposed an argument from natural needs to show that marriage is natural (*IV Sent.* 26.1.1, resp. [67–8]). Marriage satisfies two basic human needs: first, the begetting and raising of offspring to full maturity; second, the mutual service of male and female in household matters, or their "sharing of the tasks necessary for life," for each gender has its own special virtues and talents. Thomas maintained that these two needs, or ends, are respectively primary and secondary. He noted that they correspond to the two benefits of marriage that Aristotle posited in book VIII of the *Nicomachean Ethics* (1162a16–29), where Aristotle construed marriage as a mode of friendship and argued that human beings are naturally even more conjugal than they are political. For these reasons, Thomas argued, nature inclines human beings to marriage, and natural reason endorses marriage. Thomas pointed out that Christian marriage has a third end, in addition to procreation and complementarity, for as a sacrament, it signifies the union between Christ and the church, as indicated in Ephesians 5:32 (*IV Sent.* 33.1.1, resp. [141a]).

The second of the two ends exemplifies the principle that human beings are naturally social and political animals, who collaborate to achieve self-sufficiency.[14] Thomas was familiar with this theme from its brief appearance in the *Nicomachean Ethics* (X, 1169b16–22). Aristotle developed it much more fully in the *Politics*, where he tried to show both that the human being is related to the political community as part to whole, and that this relationship is teleological and manifest in an appetite for communal living.[15] But the *Politics* was not available in Latin until around 1260. Nor did Thomas have access to it via Muslim philosophy, for there was apparently no Arabic translation. Albert and Thomas were familiar, however, with Avicenna's comparable argument that to achieve self-sufficiency, humans, unlike other animals, must form communities so that they can specialize and divide their tasks.[16]

Even the primary end of marriage, procreation, Thomas argues, is qualified by the social and political dimension of human nature. The natural law does not require that all human beings should marry and procreate, because division of labor makes communal self-sufficiency possible. Just as some must specialize in farming and others in building, so some must specialize

[14] Scully, "The Place of the State in Society According to Thomas Aquinas," 407–9.

[15] F. Miller, *Nature, Justice, and Rights in Aristotle's Politics*, 27–66.

[16] *De anima* V.1, in Avicenna Latinus, *Liber De anima seu Sextus de naturalibus IV–V*, 69–75.

in raising children and others in contemplation, for nothing is more inimical to a life of contemplation than marriage and the family (*IV Sent.* 26.1.2, resp. [68–9]).

Thomas subsumed under complementarity – i.e., collaboration to achieve the "necessities of life" – the remedial avoidance of fornication, from 1 Corinthians 7:2, which theologians usually construed as an end of marriage in its own right. The partners help each other by fulfilling the conjugal debt, so that marriage constrains unruly sexual desire (*IV Sent.* 33.2.1, ad 4 [148b]). Moreover, the secondary end is implicit in the primary end, for the chief vocation of parents is to "lay up treasure" for their children (2 Corinthians 12:14). Thus, all the parents' mutual service and sharing is ultimately directed to the begetting and raising of offspring (*IV Sent.*, 31.1.2, ad 1 [122b]; *IV Sent.* 33.2.1, resp. [148]).

Thomas did not fully explain the primary/secondary distinction, but he seems to assume that the secondary end presupposes the first, which alone is sine qua non. Both are apparently distinct from the countless accidental reasons that individuals may have for marrying (on which see *IV Sent.* 30.1.3, resp. [111b]). By way of illustration, Thomas noted that nutrition is the primary end of a meal, whereas establishing a context conducive to negotiations over business matters is an appropriate secondary end (*IV Sent.* 33.1.1, resp. [140b]). This distinction between the primary and secondary ends of marriage, founded respectively on procreation and complementarity, does not appear explicitly in any of Thomas's subsequent works.

To solve the problem of Old Testament polygamy, Thomas proposed an argument from instrumental function. Like all agents, Aquinas argued, human beings have "proper actions," which manifest their generic and specific nature. The corresponding conceptions in the intellect, which constitute the natural law, not only endorse those actions, but also guide them to the fitting achievement of their proper ends. Moreover, the action in question may either *prevent* achievement of an end or only *impede* it, by making it less effective or less fitting. Construing marriage as a proper action, Thomas inquires how well polygyny achieves the primary and secondary ends of marriage: procreating and rearing children, and sharing the necessities of life. Thomas argues that only what prevents achieving the primary end is absolutely prohibited, whereas what impedes a primary end or either prevents or impedes a secondary end is prohibited only conditionally. Such weaker prohibitions, if they have been posited, may still have the force of law due to the legislator or ruler, but the prohibition can be dispensed with in view of circumstances. To reach that conclusion Thomas made an intermediate claim: that preventing a primary end transgresses a primary precept of the natural law, whereas only impeding the primary end or preventing or impeding a secondary end transgresses only secondary precepts. Now, whereas primary precepts cannot be made void, secondary precepts can. (This step in the argument is surely circular.) Polygyny does not prevent begetting and raising children, Thomas claimed. Nor does it *prevent* the secondary end (complementarity), but it does *impede* it, since one man cannot equally satisfy the needs of several wives. The law of monogamy, therefore, is conditional and dispensable. God dispensed the Patriarchs from monogamy because of the special circumstances of the Israelites at that time (*IV Sent.* 33.1.1, resp.; ad 1 [140–1]).

Thomas focused on the primary, procreative end of marriage. He identified this end with the *bonum prolis* ("good of offspring"), which Augustine had posited as one of the three goods, or benefits, by virtue of which marriage is an honorable estate (*IV Sent.* 33.2.1, ad 4 [148b]).[17] The primary, procreative end is generic, for this is the aspect of marriage that "nature has taught to all animals." The secondary end is specifically human and social. Nevertheless, although all animals pursue the procreative end, they do not all do so in the same way. For example, the extent to which the male of a species bonds with the female depends on the extent to which the father's care is required in raising the offspring. Among humans, the father's help is required for a long time, and male and female bond more closely and enduringly than in most other species (*IV Sent.* 26.1.1, ad 1 [68a]). The good of offspring is best achieved through an enduring, monogamous partnership between a man and a determinate woman, so that the man will know which woman is the mother of his children and thus recognize his own children. That sense of consanguinity motivates him to care for, instruct, and discipline them (*IV Sent.* 26.1.1, ad 1 [67b]).

Fornication and concubinage are unnatural and transgress the natural law, Thomas argued, because even if the man intends to beget children, he does not intend adequately to care for them until they reach maturity. That requires a stable, even permanent partnership. The root of the transgression is that the agent does not direct the relevant action, sexual intercourse, to its "due end," but instead pursues it merely for pleasure. God added carnal pleasure to sexual intercourse in all animals not for its own sake, but so that they would perpetuate their species. As rational beings, therefore, humans ought to refer coitus to its due end and ultimately to God, although there is nothing wrong with carnal pleasure per se. An error of a different sort arises when, in pursuit of pleasure, the man performs sexual acts that cannot be "fittingly ordered" to their end (*IV Sent.* 33.1.3, qu[a] 1, resp. [145b–146a]). This

[17] Peter Lombard devotes *Sent.* IV, dist. 31 to Augustine's three goods of marriage: faith (*fides*), offspring (*proles*), and sacrament (*sacramentum*), i.e., indissolubility.

error includes not only sexual acts that are essentially non-procreative, such as sodomy or anal sex, but also heterosexual vaginal intercourse performed in unseemly positions.[18]

Thomas maintained that the procreative end of marriage requires the spouses to remain together not only for a long time, but even as long as they are alive. Nature intends them to do so, and the natural law requires it. To this extent, "the inseparability of marriage belongs to the law of nature" (*IV Sent.* 33.2.1, resp. [148a]). It is true that in many cases, the exigency of inseparability will not arise because the need for childrearing is absent (e.g., when the woman is infertile), but Thomas pointed out that the natural law pertains to the human species and not to individuals (ibid., ad 4 [148b]). He conceded, however, that divorce and remarriage are more opposed to the sacramental signification of marriage than they are to the good of children alone, for marriage signifies Christ's indissoluble union with the church. Moreover, in restoring marriage to its pristine condition and perfecting it by condemning divorce, Jesus Christ raised it to a level of obligation that neither human (i.e., secular) nor Mosaic law could achieve (ibid., ad 1; ad 2 [148a]).

Finally, again following Albert, Thomas separated marriage into several strata, each defined not only by its own end and rationale, but also by a different branch of law. For example, Thomas claimed that marriage is decreed by the law of nature inasmuch as it fulfills an office of nature, by civil law inasmuch as it fulfills an office of the political community, and by divine law inasmuch as it is a sacrament (*IV Sent.*, 34.1.1, ad 4 [164b]). An office is a task, role, or obligation consequent upon a specific status. This aspect of Thomas's theory of marriage remained undeveloped in the *Scriptum*, but he took it further in the *Summa contra Gentiles*.

Summa contra Gentiles

In book III of the *Summa contra Gentiles*, Thomas discussed the moral constraints and imperatives pertaining to the good of offspring. To show that simple fornication is a sin, Thomas begins with the premise that the proper (i.e., natural) instrumental purpose of sexual intercourse is to beget children and to raise them to bodily, moral, and spiritual maturity. To ejaculate without intending to achieve that end is bad, therefore, and to do so deliberately, by seeking pleasure alone, is a sin. Contrariwise, a stable, permanent marriage is generally necessary to achieve that primary end fully. Marriage, therefore, is natural.

[18] On inappropriate coital positions, see Albertus Magnus, *IV Sent.* 31.24, in *Opera omnia*, Borgnet edition (Paris, 1890–9), 30:262–3.

Thomas rehearsed the arguments that he used in the *Scriptum* regarding both procreative pair bonding in diverse species and the need for man and woman to collaborate in achieving the necessities of life (SCG III.122). It is true that a single woman of sufficient means might provide for herself and her children, but "natural rectitude" pertains not to what belongs accidentally to individuals, but rather to what belongs essentially to the species (SCG III.122 §2953).

Similar arguments prove that marriage is naturally indivisible. Divorce is contrary to the well-being of offspring; it is unfair to wives, who need their husbands' protection rather than being dismissed when their good looks and fertility fade; and it is contrary to the nature of marriage as the "greatest friendship" (another allusion to Aristotle, *NE* VIII, 1162a16–29). Thomas assumed that men would be doing the divorcing in question, since in his view it would be obviously unnatural for women to take the upper hand by divorcing their husbands (SCG III.123 §2960–4).

Thomas posited a natural instinct for monogamy that pertains more to fairness and domestic harmony than to procreating and raising children. Observation of irrational animals shows that males defend exclusive access to their females partly to secure sexual pleasure and partly to know which offspring are their own. Both aims are inconsistent with polyandry, which for that reason is not permitted by the laws or customs of any community. But polygyny does not prevent the father from knowing who his children are, and this is "the principal good that is sought from marriage." Nevertheless, polygyny is intrinsically unjust because it reduces wives to the level of handmaids, is inconsistent with friendship, and is a source of domestic strife (SCG III.124 §2969–74). This is essentially the position that Thomas expounded in the *Scriptum* by positing primary and secondary ends of marriage.

Thomas assumed that the exigencies and implications of the good of children communicated themselves to the rational agent as natural instincts. Parents, especially fathers, have a natural instinct to want to know who their biological children are, and whatever prevents that certitude, such as a woman's freedom to have children by another male, is "contrary to the natural instinct of the human species" (SCG III.123 §2963). Although Thomas did not construe these instincts as laws, he did argue that they are the basis of both divine and human laws. Just as discoveries in the speculative sciences are based on naturally known first principles, so positive human law is based on natural instincts (SCG III.123 §2965).

The begetting of children is the only "natural act" that preserves the species rather than the individual, whereas nutrition and excretion preserve the individual alone. Consequently, procreation is the only natural act that is ordered to the common good rather than to the private good.

And since law by definition is meant to preserve and enhance the common good, it is appropriate that there should be both human and divine laws regulating procreation. Divine law also makes up for the deficiencies and limitations of human law, just as revelation surpasses the capacity of natural human reason, for human beings do not desire the beatific vision instinctively but only when it is revealed to them in faith. It follows that the legal regulation of marriage is twofold, Thomas argued. First, because there is a natural instinct in the human species toward indivisible monogamy, it is necessary that positive human law should enforce monogamy. Second, divine law adds a "certain supernatural reason" to those exigencies, for marriage is especially apt to signify the union between Christ and the church, inasmuch as it too is indissoluble and monogamous (SCG III.123 §2965).

Thomas expounded the threefold ordering of marriage and procreation more fully in book IV of the *Summa contra Gentiles*. Here, he argues that procreation is ordered to three collective ends: the perpetuity of the species, which is a good of nature; the perpetuity of a certain political community, which is a political good; and the perpetuity of the church, or the community of all the faithful. To each of these ends corresponds a specific "directing principle," which controls and regulates marriages so that they contribute to the well-being of the collective. In the first respect, marriage is an office of nature. It is directed by nature inasmuch as nature inclines to the perpetuity of the species. In the second respect, marriage preserves the political community and is "subject to the ordination of civil law." In the third respect, marriage as one of the sacraments is ordered to the good of the church, for it preserves the ecclesiastical community. Thus, as a sacrament it is subject to ecclesiastical governance and protected and celebrated by the ministry of the clergy (SCG IV.78 §4120).

Summa theologiae

Thomas's theory of laws in the third part of the *Summa theologiae* is based on the principle that the individual is related to the community as a part to the whole, for the whole is more perfect than the part. More precisely, the whole *is* the perfection of the part:

> Since one human being is a part of the multitude, any human being with all that he is and has belongs to the community, just as any part with all that it is belongs to the whole. Hence, too, nature inflicts a loss on the part in order to preserve the whole.
>
> (ST I-II.96.4)

In the *Scriptum*, Thomas had cited Aristotle as saying that the "common good is better and more divine than the good of an individual."[19] To prove that it is natural to love God more than all created things, Thomas argued that created things are related to God as parts to the whole, for everything good is contained and unified in the Creator. Just as one uses an arm to fend off injury to one's head, on which the existence of the whole depends, and just as individuals will sacrifice themselves in war to save their community, so one loves one's good in God more than one loves it in oneself.[20]

A law is a "rule and measure" of practical reason that guides agents and actions to their proper ends. More precisely, law is the overarching, ultimate rule and measure in any given domain of action. The goal of laws that guide human actions is "the ultimate end of human life," namely, their perfect well-being. Law must pertain to the good of the community, therefore (*ST* I–II.90.1–2; 94.3, ad 1). In short, law is "an ordinance of reason for the common good" that has been made and promulgated by whoever has responsibility for the community as a whole (I–II.90.4, resp.).

Although this is a political definition, Thomas assumed that it could be extended by analogy to the other relevant domains. The eternal law is God, inasmuch as God is the divine providence or governance that guides the cosmos. God promulgates this law partly by giving things their forms, or natures. This promulgation is especially law-like in rational agents, for it presents itself to the intellect as a set of guiding rational principles, known as the natural law. Human legislators, who care for political communities, extrapolate natural law through deduction and determination (specification) and posit human law. Divine law both makes up for the deficiencies of human reason and volition and guides human beings to their ultimate end, which is union with God (I–II.91.1–4).

Reversing the position he had proposed in the *Scriptum*, Thomas now argues that inclinations in the will are prior to the conceptions in the intellect that comprise the natural law. The natural law consists of the first, self-evident principles of practical reasoning. These are naturally known because *reason naturally apprehends whatever the human being is naturally inclined toward as good* (I–II.94.2, resp.; 94.4, resp.). Equally, reason naturally regards whatever is contrary to the natural inclinations as something to be shunned. Human beings naturally pursue the good and shun evil, and the

[19] *III Sent.*, 32.1.5, qu[a] 4, arg. 2 (Moos 3:1011). *IV Sent.* 2.1.3, arg. 3 (Moos 4:86). Cf. Aristotle, *NE* I, 1094b7–11. See Eschmann, "*Bonum commune melius est quam bonum unius,*" 62–120.

[20] *III Sent.* 29.un.3, resp. (Moos 3:929). D. M. Gallagher, "Thomas Aquinas on Self-Love as the Basis of Love of Others," 23–44.

good ramifies inasmuch as the human being is an existing substance, an animal, and a rational being. Every substance is naturally inclined to preserve its own existence; thus, the natural law requires each human being to do what is necessary to preserve life and to ward off dangers. As animals, humans are inclined to preserve goods that they share with all animals, such as the preservation of their species and sexual intercourse. As rational beings, they are inclined to be social and to pursue truth. At each level, the intellect's conceptions of the end and its immediate requirements enable the agent to pursue and realize the inclinations (I–II.94.2, resp.).

By virtue of inclinations at the animal level, "the things which nature has taught to all animals, such as sexual intercourse, the raising of children, and things of that sort, are said to belong to the natural law" (I–II.94.2, resp.). Thomas's list of inclinations and corresponding rational principles is imprecise and haphazard, and he does not show how the principles amount to precepts. In what sense does sexual intercourse belong to the natural law? It is surely an instrument, not a good, and one that by his own account is as easily abused as used. Thomas assumed that the implied precept not only prescribes sexual intercourse between male and female (albeit not in celibates), but also precludes sexual intercourse between males. Sodomy, Thomas claimed, is against nature not only in the general sense that it contrary to virtue (for human beings are naturally inclined to be virtuous), but also in the specific sense that it is "contrary to the intercourse between male and female, which belongs naturally to all animals" (I–II.94.3, ad 2).

Thomas presents a detailed analysis of *luxuria*, which is the pursuit of sexual activity for pleasure alone, without due regard for begetting and raising children. *Luxuria* comes in two varieties, according to whether the act is open to procreation or not. Sins of fornication, adultery, rape, incest, and seduction belong to the first class. Masturbation, sodomy, and bestiality belong to the second class and are traditionally known as unnatural vices (ST II–II.153.3, resp.).

In general, *luxuria* is the sin of exceeding the "order and mode of reason" in sexual acts, for the sinner seeks carnal pleasure in them in a manner that is not in accordance with right reason (II–II.154.1, resp.). The notion of excess here is not quantitative, but rather pertains to the relationship between an action and its due end. The sins of *luxuria* are especially grievous because "the more necessary something is, the more one must preserve the order of nature regarding it, and consequently the more the act is sinful when the order of nature is abandoned." In this case, the ordering at stake is especially necessary because it pertains to the common good, the basis of all law (II–II.153.3, resp.).

All sins of *luxuria* are disordered in that they oppose the order of right reason regarding attainment of the appropriate end. But some conspicuously perverse acts are disordered also "in another way, over and above that, by opposing the natural order of sexual acts that befits the human species, and this is called vice against nature." Even vaginal heterosexual intercourse can err in this way, for right reason guides the agent to achieve the due end *in a fitting manner* – in this case, in the missionary position. The additional defect is a lack of congruity in relation to the human species, or human nature. Thomas placed bestiality, intercourse between persons of the same sex (male or female), and masturbation in this special category of natural incongruity (II–II.154.11, resp.).

Thomas considered the vices of *luxuria* and especially the unnatural vices especially grave because in his view they contravened the order of nature in fundamental ways, for "the things that are according to nature" are the very principles of moral reasoning. Reason presupposes whatever is determined by nature, and it disposes other matters on that basis. In speculative reasoning, one begins with principles that are naturally and innately known, and errors regarding such principles are especially serious. Likewise, in practical reasoning, one begins with things "determined according to nature," and the sins against nature strike at the very root of the proper ordering of sexual activity (II–II.154.12, resp.).

Thomas refers explicitly to the innate natural *law* in relation to sexual sins in the *Summa* only when he discusses fornication as entailing a failure to take responsibility for one's offspring. Unlike sins against nature, simple fornication is "opposed to the end of the sexual act" rather than to its mode (II–II.154.1, resp.). Sound upbringing requires that a child be raised in the setting of a stable male–female partnership, so that the man has a determinate partner and knows who his children are, since fathers naturally care more for their own offspring than for those of other men. Thomas reminds the reader of the patterns found among irrational animals, where stable pair bonding is linked to the need for a father's care. Promiscuity is against the nature of humanity, and the restraints and imperatives that nature imposes on sexual activity belong to the natural law. Furthermore, because sexual intercourse is ordered to the common good of the entire human race, it follows that "this union of male and female, which is called marriage" is a matter appropriate for determinate regulation by positive law. It is true that a father might care for a child whom he has begotten through fornication, but laws are posited to regulate what happens in general, and not what happens in each particular case.

Thomas promised to say more about the laws of marriage when he discusses the sacrament in the third part of the *Summa* (II–II.154.2, resp.). This was to be a promise he could not fulfill. What would Thomas have said about the natural, human, and divine laws of marriage if he had completed the third part of his

Summa theologiae? He would probably have developed the idea of multiple legal aspects, which he had touched on briefly in both the *Scriptum* and the *Summa contra Gentiles*. He would surely have emphasized the relationship between marriage and the common good: not only that of the political community, but also that of the church. And he would surely have drawn on insights he had gained from studying and commenting on Aristotle's *Politics*. But one can only guess how he might have applied the theory of natural law that he had sketched in the *prima secundae pars* to the special case of marriage and procreation.

RECOMMENDED READING

Arnhart, Larry. "Thomistic Natural Law as Darwinian Natural Right." *Social Philosophy and Policy* 18.1 (2001): 1–33.

Aroney, Nicholas. "Subsidiarity, Federalism, and the Best Constitution: Thomas Aquinas on City, Province, and Empire." *Law and Philosophy* 26 (2007): 161–228.

Baur, Michael. "Law and Natural Law." In *The Oxford Handbook of Aquinas*, edited by B. Davies and E. Stump. Oxford: Oxford University Press, 2011.

Crowe, Michael B. *The Changing Profile of the Natural Law*. The Hague: Nijhoff, 1977.

Guevin, Benedict M. "Aquinas's Use of Ulpian and the Question of Physicalism Reconsidered." *New Blackfriars* 63 (1999): 613–28.

Jensen, Steven J. *Knowing the Natural Law: From Precepts and Inclinations to Deriving Oughts*. Washington, DC: Catholic University of America Press, 2015.

McCluskey, Colleen. "An Unequal Relationship between Equals: Thomas Aquinas on Marriage." *History of Philosophy Quarterly* 24.1 (2007): 1–18.

Reynolds, Philip L. *How Marriage Became One of the Sacraments: The Sacramental Theology of Marriage from Its Medieval Origins to the Council of Trent*. Cambridge: Cambridge University Press, 2016.

Sweeny, Eileen. "Thomas Aquinas on the Natural Law Written on Our Hearts." In *Reason, Religion, and Natural Law: From Plato to Spinoza*, edited by J. A. Jacobs, 133–54. New York: Oxford University Press, 2012.

12

Martin Luther

Steven Ozment and John Witte, Jr.

BIOGRAPHICAL INTRODUCTION

Martin Luther (1483–1546), the fiery German theologian, sparked the Protestant Reformation of church, state, and society that eventually broke into Lutheran, Calvinist, Anabaptist, and Anglican forms. Luther studied law briefly before he entered an Augustinian friary in 1505. While there, he studied theology and some canon law, first at the University of Erfurt, then at the new University of Wittenberg. After taking his doctorate in 1512 from Wittenberg, Luther stayed on as a theology professor for the rest of his life. From his lectern and accompanying Wittenberg pulpit, he began to attack the medieval Catholic Church and its theological and canon law system. In 1517, he posted his Ninety-Five Theses challenging the church's theology of sin, salvation, and the sacraments, then defended his views in several sensational debates and pamphlets. He burned the medieval canon law books in 1520 and issued a long and bitter broadside on *The Babylonian Captivity of the Church*, under the tyranny of the pope, whom Luther called the Anti-Christ.[1] For these and other scandalous actions, including the betrayal of his monastic vows, Luther was excommunicated by the pope and nearly executed by the emperor at the Diet of Worms in 1521. He escaped back to Saxony, hiding for two years in Wartburg Castle before resuming his public professorial and pastoral duties in Wittenberg.

This text is based on a short draft chapter that Steven Ozment prepared before becoming too infirm to continue the work. It draws further on Ozment, *When Fathers Ruled* and Ozment, *Ancestors*, as well as Witte Jr., *Law and Protestantism*.

[1] In *Luther's Works*, 31:394 [hereafter LW].

FIGURE 12.1. Double portrait of Martin Luther and Katherine von Bora, 1529 (oil on panel), Cranach, Lucas, the Elder (1472–1553) / Galleria degli Uffizi, Florence, Italy / Bridgeman Images

From 1515 to 1545, Luther issued a torrent of writings that fill nearly one hundred thick folio volumes.[2] These included a famous German translation of the Bible; sundry biblical commentaries and sermons; church liturgies and songs; church laws, catechisms, and confessional tracts; polemical writings and table talks; formal consilia and private letters; various pamphlets and two dozen substantial tracts on legal, political, economic, and social reforms. Included among the latter were five major tracts on marriage,[3] two on celibacy and monasticism,[4] and two more on establishing public schools for children.[5] Many of Luther's other writings also included marriage and family themes, and he worked closely with scores of other distinguished theologians and jurists to reform German family law.

Luther's early preoccupation with marital reform was driven in part by his theology. Many of the core theological issues of the Protestant Reformation were implicated by the prevailing Catholic theology and canon law of sex, marriage, and family life. The Catholic Church's jurisdiction over marriage, for example, was for Luther a particularly flagrant example of the church's usurpation of the magistrate's authority. The Catholic sacramental concept of marriage, on which the Church predicated its jurisdiction, raised deep questions of sacramental theology and biblical interpretation. The canonical prohibition on marriage of clergy and monastics stood sharply juxtaposed to Lutheran doctrines of the priesthood and Christian vocation. The thick tangle of impediments to marriage, the Church's prohibitions against complete divorce and remarriage, and its close regulations of sexuality all stood in considerable tension with Luther's views of civil and religious freedom. That a child could enter marriage without parental permission or church consecration betrayed, in his view, the basic responsibilities of family, church, and state to minor children.

This early preoccupation with family reform was also driven, in part, by Luther's social theory. Luther saw an ascending divine order of creation,

2 *D. Martin Luthers Werke* [hereafter WA]; *D. Martin Luthers Werke: Tischreden* [hereafter WA TR]; *D. Martin Luthers Werke: Briefwechsel.*

3 *A Sermon on the Estate of Marriage* (1519), in LW 44:3–14; *The Estate of Marriage* (1522), in LW 45:11–49; *On Marriage Matters* (1530), in LW 46:259–320. See also *The Persons Related by Consanguinity and Affinity Who Are Forbidden to Marry According to the Scriptures, Leviticus 18* (1522), in LW 45:3–9; and *That Parents Should Neither Compel Nor Hinder the Marriage of Their Children and That Children Should Not Become Engaged Without Their Parents' Consent* (1524), LW 45:379–93.

4 *The Judgment of Martin Luther on Monastic Vows* (1521), LW 44:243–400; *An Answer to Several Questions on Monastic Vows* (1526), LW 46:139–54.

5 *To the Councilmen of All Cities in Germany That They Establish and Maintain Christian Schools* (1524), LW 45:339–78; *A Sermon on Keeping Children in School* (1530), LW 46:207–58.

running from the family (*paterfamilias*), to the state (*paterpoliticus*), to the church (*patertheologicus*).[6] These three orders and offices (*drei Stände*) were created by God and stood equal before God and before each other. Each was called to discharge essential tasks in the earthly kingdom without interference from the others. The reform of the family, therefore, was as important as the reform of the church and the state. Indeed, marital reform was even more urgent, said Luther, for the marital household was the "oldest," "most primal," and "most essential" of the three social estates, even though it was the most deprecated and subordinated of the three in his day. The marital family is the "mother of all earthly laws," Luther wrote, the first school of justice and mercy, the incubator of religion and morality, and the first site of education, charity, and social welfare. Indeed, "marriage pervades the whole of nature," Luther wrote.[7] A total reformation of church, state, and society must thus begin with the family.

Finally, the Lutheran reformers' preoccupation with family law reform was driven by the Catholic Church courts. A number of early leaders of the Reformation faced aggressive prosecution for grave violations of the canon law of marriage and celibacy. Among the earliest Protestant leaders were ex-priests and ex-monastics who had forsaken their orders and vows and often married shortly thereafter. Indeed, one of the acts of solidarity with the new Protestant cause was to marry or divorce in open violation of the canon law and in defiance of a bishop's instructions. This was not just an instance of crime and disobedience. Catholic authorities regarded this as outright blasphemy, particularly when an ex-monk such as Brother Martin Luther married an ex-nun such as Sister Katherine von Bora in 1525, a prima facie case of double spiritual incest. As Catholic Church courts began to prosecute these canon law offenses, Protestant theologians and jurists rose to the defense of their coreligionists.

MARRIAGE VERSUS CELIBACY

Luther trained some of his initial reformist attack on the mandatory celibacy of monastics and clerics. Drawing on his own and his wife, Katherine's, bitter experiences with monastic life, Luther rejected the medieval Church's subordination of marriage to celibacy and its elevation of spiritual contemplation over corporal action. We are all sinful creatures, he argued. Lust has pervaded the conscience of everyone. Marriage is not just an option; it is a necessity for

[6] See a variation on this theory by later German theologian Emil Brunner, in Chapter 19 herein.
[7] WA TR Nos. 7, 3528; WA 30/1:152; WA 49:297ff.; WA 2:734; LW 44:81ff.

sinful humanity. For without it, a person's distorted sexuality becomes a force capable of overthrowing the most devout conscience. A person is enticed by nature to concubinage, prostitution, masturbation, voyeurism, and other sinful acts. "You cannot be without a [spouse] and remain without sin," Luther thundered from his Wittenberg pulpit. You will test your neighbor's bed unless your own marital bed is happily occupied and well used.[8]

"To spurn marriage is to act against God's calling ... and against nature's urging," Luther continued. The calling of marriage should be declined only by those who have received God's special gift of continence. "Such persons are rare, not one in a thousand [later he said one hundred thousand] for they are a special miracle of God."[9] The Apostle Paul has identified this group as the permanently impotent and eunuchs; very few others can claim such a unique gift. To require celibacy of clerics, monks, and nuns was thus beyond the authority of the Church and ultimately a source of great sin. Celibacy was a gift for God to give, not a duty for the Church to impose. It was for each individual, not for the Church, to decide whether he or she had received this gift. By demanding monastic vows of chastity and clerical vows of celibacy, the Church was seen to be intruding on Christian freedom and contradicting scripture, nature, and common sense. By institutionalizing and encouraging celibacy, the Church was seen to prey on the immature and the uncertain. By holding out food, shelter, security, and economic opportunity, the monasteries enticed poor and needy parents to oblate their minor children to a life of celibacy, regardless of whether it suited their natures. Mandatory celibacy, Luther taught, was hardly a prerequisite to true clerical service of God. Instead, it led to "great whoredom and all manner of fleshly impurity and... hearts filled with thoughts of women day and night."[10]

The same was true for cloistered women, Luther continued. "[A] woman is not created to be a virgin," but to marry, "to conceive, and to bear children." When "young, foolish, and inexperienced girls" are oblated in nunneries, they grow up to find themselves without help in the most difficult struggle of their lives, namely, the suppression of their sexual nature, something even women armed with God's true Word and special grace seldom conquer. Luther believed that only "unmerciful" parents and friends and "blind and mad" bishops and abbots would permit young women to suffer and waste away in chaste cloisters. Luther thus encouraged

[8] LW 54:31. [9] LW 28:912, 27–31; LW 45:18–22. [10] LW 12:98.

and praised the "rescue" of nuns, by family and friends who would raid the cloisters and release the "imprisoned" nuns. In a pamphlet titled *Why Nuns May Leave Cloisters with God's Blessing* (1523), Luther compared these rescues to Moses's deliverance of the children of Israel from Egyptian bondage.[11] Several times, he helped publish (and sometimes prefaced) the letters and testimonies of former nuns, monks, and priests who had forsaken their vows and escaped their cloistered lives.[12] Unlike some other Protestant reformers, however, Luther did not countenance violence against nuns and monks who wished to stay, and he urged the authorities to keep the monasteries open until their last survivors had passed away.[13]

While he thought chaste monasticism should be allowed to die a natural death, Luther also thought that the celibate clergy should be replaced with married priests and bishops. Luther concurred with the Apostle Paul that a celibate person "may better be able to preach and care for God's word." But, he immediately added, "It is God's word and the preaching which makes celibacy – such as that of Christ and of Paul – better than the estate of marriage. In itself, however, the celibate life is far inferior."[14]

Not only is celibacy no better than marriage for clergy, but clergy are no better than laity. Luther rejected traditional teachings that the clergy were higher beings with readier access to God and God's mysteries. He rejected the notion that clergy mediated the channel of grace between the laity and God through the sacraments, preaching, and prayer. Sounding his famous doctrine of the priesthood of all believers, Luther argued that clergy and laity were fundamentally equal and that all persons had direct access to God through conscience, prayer, and worship.

Luther's doctrine at once "laicized" the clergy and "clericized" the laity. He treated the traditional clerical office of priest, deacon, or bishop as just one vocation alongside many others that a conscientious Christian could pursue. He treated all traditional lay offices as forms of divine calling and priestly vocation, each providing unique opportunities for Christian service. Preachers and teachers in the church must carry their share of civic duties just like everyone else. And they should participate in earthly activities such as marriage and family life just like everyone else. Indeed, church ministers were to be exemplars of marriage and family life. The minister's household was to be a source and model for the right order and government of the local church, state, and broader community.

[11] Luther, *Ursach und anttwort das iunkfrawen kloster gottlich verlassen mugen*, A3b–A4b.

[12] See examples in Ozment, *When Fathers Ruled*, 9–25; Witte Jr., *Law and Protestantism*, 59–64.

[13] LW 45:169–72, 341. [14] LW 45:47.

THE GOODS AND GIFTS OF MARRIAGE AND FAMILY LIFE

Luther was utterly conventional in teaching that marriage was created by God as a "two-in-one-flesh" union between a man and a woman with the freedom, fitness, and capacity to marry each other. Marriage was designed for the mutual love and support of husband and wife, the mutual protection of both parties from sexual sin, and the mutual nurture and care of their children.[15] Virtually all adults, clerical and lay alike, are called to marriage, Luther argued, because this institution offers two of the most sublime gifts that God has accorded to humanity – the gift of marital love and the gift of children.

Luther wrote exuberantly about this first gift. "Over and above all [other loves] is marital love," he wrote. Marital love drives husband and wife to say to each other, "'It is you whom I want, not what is yours. I want neither your silver nor your gold . . . I want only you. I want you in your entirety, or nor at all.' All other kinds of love seek something other than the loved one: this kind wants only to have the beloved's own self completely."[16] Luther wrote, "There's more to [marriage] than a union of the flesh. There must [also] be harmony with respect to patterns of life and ways of thinking."[17]

> The chief virtue of marriage [is] that spouses can rely upon each other and with confidence entrust everything they have on earth to each other, so that it is as safe with one's spouse as with oneself.
>
> . . . God's Word is actually inscribed on one's spouse. When a man looks at his wife as if she were the only woman on earth, and when a woman looks at her husband [as] if he were the only man on earth; yes, if no king or queen, not even the sun itself sparkles any more brightly and lights up your eyes more than your own husband or wife, then right there you are face to face with God speaking.[18]

Luther did not press these warm sentiments to the point of denying the traditional leadership of the paterfamilias within the marital household. Luther had no modern egalitarian theory of marriage. But Luther also did not betray these warm sentiments to the point of becoming the grim prophet of patriarchy, paternalism, and procreation that some modern critics make him out to be. For Luther, love was a necessary and sufficient good of marriage. He supported marriages between loving couples, even those between younger men and older women beyond childbearing years, or between couples who knew that they could have no children.[19] He stressed repeatedly that husband

15 See detailed sources in Witte Jr., *From Sacrament to Contract*, 119–35.

16 WA 2:167; see also WA 13:11; WA 17/2:350ff.

17 WA TR No. 5524; LW 54:444.

18 Quoted in Hendrix, "Luther on Marriage," 335–50. See also LW 31:351ff.

19 See, e.g., WA TR Nos. 4, 5212; LW 2:301ff.

and wife were spiritual, intellectual, and emotional partners, each to have regard and respect for the strengths of the other. He called his own wife, Katherine, respectfully, "Mr. Kathy," and said more than once of her, "I am an inferior lord, she the superior; I am Aaron, she is my Moses." He repeatedly told husbands and wives alike to tend to each other's spiritual, emotional, and sexual needs and to share in all aspects of childrearing and household maintenance – from changing their children's diapers to helping their children establish their own new homes when they had grown up.[20] And he encouraged wives to pursue their own careers within and beyond the home with the support of their husbands. Luther's wife, Katherine, succeeded at several careers of her own alongside raising their six children. She expanded their home, a former cloister, into a boarding house, profitably extended its vegetable gardens, and repaired and operated the cloister brewery, producing beer good enough to be served at the Saxon elector's court.

In addition to the divine gift of love, marriage also sometimes bestowed the divine gift of children. Luther thought of procreation as an act of co-creation and co-redemption with God. He wished for all marital couples the joy of having children, not only for their own sakes, but for the sake of God as well. Childrearing, he wrote, "is the noblest and most precious work, because to God there can be nothing dearer than the salvation of souls . . . Most certainly, father and mother are apostles, bishops, [and] priests to their children, for it is they who make them acquainted with the Gospel."[21]

This last image – of parents serving as priests to their children – was a new and further application of the Protestant doctrine of the priesthood of all believers. It further softened the hard medieval distinction between a superior clergy and a lower laity. The care and education of children fell not only to the natural parents, however. Luther and his fellow reformers called on priests (as *patrestheologici*) in local churches to catechize children as they prepared for a full life of communion, and the reformers produced a welter of catechisms and confessional books to facilitate this instruction. They also called on magistrates (as *patrespolitici*) to create state-run schools for the religious and civic education of all children, boys and girls alike. For the reformers, each child was called to a unique Christian vocation, and it was the responsibility of the parent, priest, and prince alike to ensure that each child was given the chance to discern his or her special gifts and prepare for the particular vocation that best suited those gifts. This teaching drove the creation of public schools in Protestant lands, now under the authority of the state rather than the church. Luther's close Wittenberg colleague, Philip Melanchthon, the

[20] WA TR Nos. 4910, 5041, 5189. [21] LW 45:46.

so-called teacher of Germany, developed educational materials and laws and called the public school a "civic seminary" that allowed families, churches, and states to cooperate in imbuing civic learning and spiritual piety in children.[22]

While Luther instructed children to love, honor, and obey their parents, as the Bible required, he railed against parents (and guardians) who abused their children or neglected parental duties. He devoted a special tract to counseling parents and grown-up children who were ready for marriage. Luther insisted that valid marriages required parents to consent to their children's budding unions. But he condemned the outrageous injustice of parents arbitrarily withholding their consent or bullying their children into unwanted marriage. Children should appeal to secular authority for justice if their parents thwarted their heart's desire. Here Luther stood on traditional ground, since throughout the Middle Ages boys and girls of canonical age (fourteen and twelve) had the right, however infrequently exercised, to dissent formally from unwanted arranged marriages. If a formal appeal to secular authority did not bring a positive result, then Luther advised unhappy children to do as Christians in the past had done when tyrannized – pack up, flee to another land, and there marry at will. Luther believed that parents had a basic duty to provide good marriages for all their children; each father was "duty bound to get his child a good mate who will be just right for him, or who seems to be just right for him." If parents ignored this responsibility, or forced on their children unwanted spouses, then children could, in good conscience, take matters into their own hands. In matters of marriage, as in matters of faith, Luther opposed bullying the heart and conscience.[23]

MARRIAGE IS NOT A SACRAMENT, BUT A SOCIAL ESTATE

While marriage was a creation and gift of God for the couple and their children, it remained a social institution of the earthly kingdom, not a sacrament of the heavenly kingdom. Marriage was, in Luther's words, "a natural order," "an earthly institution," "a secular and outward thing."[24] "No one can deny that marriage is an external, worldly matter, like clothing and food, house and property, subject to temporal authority, as the many imperial laws enacted on the subject prove."[25]

To be sure, Luther agreed, marriage can symbolize the mysterious union of Christ and the church, as St. Paul wrote in Ephesians 5:32. The sacrifices

[22] See Witte Jr., *Law and Protestantism*, 257–92. [23] LW 45:338–92; WA TR Nos. 185, 5541.
[24] LW 21:93. [25] LW 46:265.

husband and wife make for each other and for their children can express the sacrificial love of Christ on the cross. A "blessed marriage and home," can be "a true church, a chosen cloister, yes, a paradise" on earth. But these analogies and metaphors do not make marriage a sacrament on the order of baptism and the Eucharist. Sacraments are God's gifts and signs of grace ensuring Christians of the promise of redemption, which is available only to those who have faith. Marriage carries no such promise and demands no such faith. "[N]owhere in Scripture," writes Luther, "do we read that anyone would receive the grace of God by getting married; nor does the rite of matrimony contain any hint that the ceremony is of divine institution." Scripture teaches that only baptism and the Eucharist (and perhaps penance, the early Luther allowed) confer this promise of grace. All other so-called sacraments are "mere human artifices" that the church has created to augment its legal powers and to fill its coffers with court fees and fines.[26]

The Catholic Church, Luther continued, has based its entire sacramental theology and canon law of marriage on a misunderstanding of Ephesians 5:32, which reads: "This is a great mystery, and I am applying it to Christ and the church." The Greek term *mysterion* in this passage means "mystery," not "sacrament," said Luther. St. Jerome had just gotten it wrong a millennium before, when he translated the Greek word *mysterion* as the Latin word *sacramentum* in the first Latin translation of the Bible, the Vulgate. The Catholic Church has gotten it wrong ever since. In this passage, St. Paul is simply describing the loving and sacrificial union of a Christian husband and wife as a reflection, an echo, a foretaste of the perfect mysterious union of Christ and his church. But that analogy does not make marriage a sacrament that confers sanctifying grace. The Bible is filled with analogies and parables designed to provide striking images to drive home lessons: "Faith is like a mustard seed": it grows even if tiny. "The kingdom of heaven is like yeast": it leavens even if you can't see it. Or "the Son of man will come like a thief in the night": so be ready at all times for his return. The marriage analogy is similar: "Marital love is like the union of Christ and the church": so be faithful and sacrificial to your spouse. Ephesians 5 is not divining a new sacrament, Luther insisted, but driving home a lesson about marital love.[27]

Moreover, Luther argued, it made no sense for the Catholic Church to call marriage a sacrament without giving the clergy a role in this sacrament or providing a mandatory liturgy of preparation and celebration. Neither the husband nor the wife can be a cleric if they seek marriage in the Catholic Church. Yet, regardless of what they know or intend, canon law says that these

[26] LW 36:11, 92–8; 44:85. [27] LW 36:97ff.

two laypersons perform a sacrament just by making a present promise to marry, or making a future promise to marry and then having sex. And that purported sacramental act binds them for life. This just piles fiction upon self-serving fiction, Luther concluded. The Catholic Church forbids its clergy to marry because marriage is a natural association beneath them in dignity. Yet the Church pretends that marriage is a sacrament even if the clergy do not participate in its formation or if the marriage does not take place in the Church. "This is an insult to the sacraments," Luther charged. The Church's real goal, he said, is jurisdictional, not theological in declaring marriage to be a canonical sacrament. There is no valid biblical or theological basis for this claim.[28]

Denying the sacramental quality of marriage had dramatic implications for how a marriage should be formed, maintained, and dissolved. First, the Lutheran reformers argued, there should be no formal religious or baptismal tests for marriage. Medieval canon law required that marriages be contracted only between baptized Christians in good standing with the Church. Luther rejected this. Parties would certainly do well to marry within the faith for the sake of themselves and their children. But this is not an absolute condition. Religious differences should not be viewed as an impediment to a valid marriage or a possible path to annulment, but a challenge to be more faithful within marriage and to induce proper faith in each other.

> [M]arriage is an outward, bodily thing, like any other worldly undertaking. Just as I may eat, drink, sleep, walk, ride with, buy from, speak to, and deal with a heathen, Jew, Turk, or heretic, so I may also marry and continue in wedlock with him. Pay no attention to the precepts of those fools who forbid it. You will find plenty of Christians – and indeed the greater part of them – who are worse in their secret unbelief than any Jew, heathen, Turk, or heretic. A heathen is just as much a person – God's good creation – as St. Peter, St. Paul, and St. Lucy, not to speak of slack or spurious Christians.[29]

Second, because marriage was not a sacrament, divorce and remarriage were licit, and sometimes even necessary. To be sure, the Lutheran reformers, like their Catholic brethren, insisted that marriages should be stable and presumptively indissoluble. But this presumption could be overcome if one of the essential marital goods were chronically betrayed or frustrated. If there were a fundamental breach of marital love by one of the parties – by reason of adultery, desertion, or cruelty – the marriage was broken. The innocent spouse who could not forgive this breach could sue for divorce and remarry. If there

[28] Ibid. [29] LW 45:25.

were a failure of procreation – by reason of sterility, incapacity, or disease discovered shortly after the wedding – the marriage was also broken. Those spouses who could not reconcile themselves to this condition could end the marriage, and at least the healthy spouse could marry another. And if there were a failure of protection from sin – by reason of frigidity, separation, desertion, cruelty, or crime – the marriage was again broken. If the parties could not be reconciled, they could divorce and seek another marriage.[30] In each instance, divorce was painful, sinful, and sad, and it was a step to be taken only after ample forethought and counsel. But it was a licit and sometimes an essential step to take. Divorce and remarriage were strictly prohibited in Catholic circles; they became options for broken marriages among Lutherans and other Protestants.

Third, because marriage was not a sacrament, it also did not belong primarily within the jurisdiction of the Church. Medieval canon law and Church courts governed most aspects of marital formation, maintenance, and dissolution. Luther and his colleagues pushed much of the regulation to the secular law and state courts. Luther underscored this several times in his sermons and instructions to fellow pastors:

> First, we [pastors] have enough work to do in our proper office. Second, marriage is outside the church, is a civil matter, and therefore should belong to the government. Third, these cases [of marital dispute] have no limits, extend to the height, the breadth, and the depth, and produce many offences that bring disgrace to the gospel . . . [W]e prefer to leave this business to civil officials. The responsibility rests on them. Only in cases of conscience should pastors give counsel to godly people. Controversies and court cases [respecting marriage and family life] we leave to the lawyers.[31]

This did not mean that marriage was beyond the pale of God's authority and law, nor that it should be beyond the influence and concern of the church. "It is sheer folly," Luther opined, to treat marriage as "nothing more than a purely human and secular state, with which God has nothing to do."[32] Marriage and family remain important public concerns, in which church officials and members must still play a key role. Luther and other reformers took seriously the duty of pastoral counseling in marriage disputes that raised matters of conscience. As pastors themselves, Luther and other reformers issued scores of private letters to parishioners who came to them for counsel. Moreover, as theologians, they taught and preached God's law and will for marriage and the

30 WA Br 3:288–290; WA 15:558ff.

31 WA TR No. 4716; LW 54:363–4. See also WA TR No. 3267; LW 54:194.

32 LW 21:95.

family, and pressed for reforms when prevailing family laws violated God's law. Furthermore, to aid church members in their instruction and care, and to give notice to all members of society of a couple's marriage, the local parish church clerk was to develop a publicly available marriage registry that all married couples would be required to sign. The pastors and teachers of the local church were to instruct and discipline the marriages of its members by pronouncing the public banns of betrothal, by blessing and instructing the couple at their public church wedding ceremony, and by punishing sexual turpitude or egregious violations of marriage law with public reprimands, bans, or, in serious cases, excommunication. Finally, it was incumbent upon all members of the church to participate in the spiritual upbringing and counsel of all new children, as their collective baptismal vows required.

THE LUTHERAN REFORMATION OF FAMILY LAW

While the church still had a role to play in the guidance and governance of marriage and family life, chief legal authority now lay with the Christian magistrate, Luther insisted. The civil magistrate holds authority from God. The magistrate is to reflect God's will and God's law, while ruling in ways that respect God's creation ordinances and institutions. The magistrate's civil calling is no less spiritual than that of the church. Marriage is thus still completely subject to godly law, but this law is now to be administered by the state, not the church.

This new Lutheran marital theology logically and inexorably led to the creation of a new state law of the family in Lutheran lands. Just as the act of marriage came to signal a person's conversion to Protestantism, so the marriage act promulgated by a local city or territory came to symbolize a community's acceptance of Protestantism. Hundreds of new state marriage acts or ordinances emerged in Lutheran Germany and Scandinavia in the first decades of the Reformation.[33] The secular authorities were assisted in this policy by Luther's view that secular princes were "emergency bishops" responsible for religious reform. Luther called upon magistrates to establish civil statutes and civil courts to adjudicate family conflicts. It took more than a century for Lutheran lands in Germany and

[33] Most of these laws are collected in Sehling, *Die evangelischen Kirchenordnungen des 16. Jahrhunderts*, vols. 1–5, continued under the same title, Sprenger-Ruppenthal, vols. 6–25. For overviews, see Dieterich, *Das protestantische Eherecht in Deutschland bis zur Mitte des 17. Jahrhunderts*; Ozment, *When Fathers Ruled*, 25–99; Witte Jr., *From Sacrament to Contract*, 136–54.

Scandinavia to transition fully to a state-run family law. But the state and its civil law, not the church and its canon law, were the new legal rulers of marriage and family life.

The new Protestant state laws, however, took over a number of basic principles and rules of marriage and family life inherited from medieval canon law, classical Roman law, and ancient Mosaic law. A typical sixteenth-century state law in a Lutheran city or territory still treated marital formation as a two-step process, first of engagement, then of marriage. A valid engagement and marriage contract required the mutual consent of a man and a woman who had the age, fitness, and capacity to marry each other. Marriage was a presumptively permanent union that triggered mutual obligations of care and support for the spouses, their children, and their dependents. Marriage often involved complex exchanges of betrothal gifts and dowry and triggered presumptive rights of dower and inheritance for widow(er)s and legitimate children. Marriages could be annulled on the discovery of various impediments and upon litigation before a proper tribunal; in the event of dissolution, both parents remained responsible for the maintenance and welfare of their children, and the guilty party bore heavy financial obligations to the innocent spouse and children alike. All these assumptions remained common both to the new Protestant civil laws and to the traditional Catholic canon laws and Roman civil laws of marriage.

But the Lutheran Reformation also made crucial legal changes – beyond the critical shift of marital jurisdiction from the church to the state. Because the reformers rejected the subordination of marriage to celibacy, they rejected laws that forbade clerical and monastic marriage, that denied remarriage to those who had married a cleric or monastic, and that permitted vows of chastity to annul vows of engagement and marriage. Because they rejected the sacramental nature of marriage, the reformers rejected impediments of crime and heresy and prohibitions against divorce in the modern sense. Marriage was for them the community of the couple in the present, not their sacramental union in the life to come. Where that community was broken by one of the parties, the innocent spouse could sue for divorce. Because persons by their lustful natures were in need of God's remedy of marriage, the reformers removed numerous legal, spiritual, and consanguineous impediments to marriage not countenanced by scripture. Because of their emphasis on the godly responsibility of the prince, the pedagogical role of the church and the family, and the priestly calling of all believers, the reformers insisted that both marriage and divorce be public. The validity of marriage promises depended on parental consent, witnesses, church consecration and registration, and priestly instruction. Couples who wanted to divorce had to announce their intentions in the church and community and petition a civil judge to dissolve the bond. In the process of marriage formation and dissolution, therefore, the couple was subject to God's law, as appropriated in the civil law, and to God's will, as revealed in the admonitions of parents, peers, princes, and pastors.

Luther was deeply involved in crafting and advocating these legal reforms in the first two decades of the Reformation. He eventually attracted a whole coterie of other theologians, moralists, and jurists to teach these reforms in the universities, and to implement them – city by city, territory by territory – in the more than two hundred polities of the Holy Roman Empire that converted to the Lutheran cause as well as the Nordic lands that eventually established Lutheranism. Because of all these changes, marriages in Lutheran lands were easier to enter and exit. Family life was more public and participatory. Wives and children were afforded greater rights and protections. Abused spouses were given a way out of miserable homes. Divorcees and widow(er)s were given a second chance to start life anew. Ministers were married, rather than single, and called to exemplify and implement the ideals of Christian marriage and sexual morality in their own parsonages. Many of the legal reforms of marriage introduced by the Lutheran reformers would remain at the heart of the German and broader Western legal tradition until the twentieth century.

But not all was sweetness and light in the Lutheran Reformation of domestic life. Yes, Luther did regard marriage as an essential remedy for lust and a singular pathway for procreation of children. But these sentiments led him and his fellow reformers several times to countenance polygamy for spouses caught in loveless or sexless marriages or incapable of having children. In our day, these early Protestant precedents have provided important platforms for the modern case for the pluralization of marriage.[34] Yes, the Protestant reformers did outlaw monasteries and cloisters. But these reforms also ended the vocations of many single women and men, placing a new premium on the vocation of marriage. Ever since, adult Protestant singles have chafed in a sort of pastoral and theological limbo, objects of curiosity and pity, even suspicion and contempt. These are stigmata adult singles still feel today in more conservative Protestant churches, despite new singles ministries to help them. Yes, the Protestant reformers did remove clerics as mediators between God and the laity, in expression of St. Peter's teaching of the priesthood of all believers. But they ultimately interposed husbands between God and their wives, in

[34] See Witte Jr., *The Western Case for Monogamy over Polygamy*, 205–18.

expression of St. Paul's teaching of male headship within the home. Ever since, Protestant married women have been locked in a bitter struggle to gain fundamental equality both within the marital household and without – a struggle that has still not ended in more conservative Protestant communities today.[35]

RECOMMENDED READING

Dieterich, Hartwig. *Das protestantische Eherecht in Deutschland bis zur Mitte des 17. Jahrhunderts*. Munich: Claudius Verlag, 1970.

Frassek, Ralf. *Eherecht und Ehegerichtsbarkeit in der Reformationszeit*. Tübingen: Mohr Siebeck, 2005.

Harrington, Joel F. *Reordering Marriage and Society in Reformation Germany*. Cambridge: Cambridge University Press, 1995.

Hendrix, Scott. "Masculinity and Patriarchy in Reformation Germany." *Journal of the History of Ideas* 56 (1995): 177–93.

"Luther on Marriage." *Lutheran Quarterly* 14/3 (2000): 335–50.

Lazareth, William. *Luther on the Christian Home*. Philadelphia, PA: Muhlenberg Press, 1960.

Lindberg, Carter. "The Future of a Tradition: Luther and the Family." In *All Theology Is Christology: Essays in Honor of David P. Scaer*. Edited by Dean O. Wenthe, et al. Fort Wayne, IN: Concordia Theological Seminary Press, 2000.

Luther, Martin. *Luther's Works*. Edited by Jaroslav Pelikan and Helmut T. Lehmann. 55 vols. St Louis, MO: Concordia, 1955–68.

Ozment, Steven. *When Fathers Ruled: Family Life in Reformation Europe*. Cambridge, MA: Harvard University Press, 1983.

Ancestors: The Loving Family in Old Europe. Cambridge, MA: Harvard University Press, 2001.

Stjerna, Kirsi Irmeli. *Women and the Reformation*. Malden, MA: Blackwell Publishers, 2009.

Witte, John, Jr. *Law and Protestantism: The Legal Teachings of the Lutheran Reformation*. Cambridge: Cambridge University Press, 2002.

Wunder, Heide. *He Is the Sun, She Is the Moon: Women in Early Modern Germany*. Translated by Thomas Dunlap. Cambridge, MA: Harvard University Press, 1998.

35 See Ozment, *When Fathers Ruled*, 50–79.

13

John Calvin

Barbara Pitkin

BIOGRAPHICAL INTRODUCTION

John Calvin (1509–64) was the French humanistically trained lawyer and later Protestant theologian and minister who spearheaded the religious reformation of the Swiss city of Geneva between 1536 and 1564 (apart from an interlude in Strasbourg from 1538 to 1541). A brilliant writer of theological treatises encapsulating and defending Protestant doctrine, he was also a prolific commentator, lecturer, and preacher on the Bible and the principal architect of the newly reformed church in Geneva. In addition, he served as a frequent legal adviser to the town's civic authorities, who worked to create and enforce laws and policies for this newly independent city. Calvin's ideas and writings and the forms of worship, church organization, and social structures they inspired spread to other parts of Europe, where they were taken up, adapted, and later carried overseas by missionaries and immigrants consciously embracing and promoting a Calvinist (or Reformed) version of Protestant Christianity.

Reflecting the heightened expectations for reform of church and society in late medieval and early modern Europe, Calvin held an expansive vision that was at once doctrinal, ecclesiastical, and moral. His views on family matters – such as the nature and purpose of marriage, the place of children in church and society, and the regulation of sexual morality and behaviour – were not the starting point of his reforming agenda, nor were his ideas about many of these issues very much out of step with ideals that had existed for centuries. Even the novel aspects of his program, such as the abolition of required clerical celibacy, the elevation of marriage as the ideal state for all men and women fit for it, and the allowance for divorce and remarriage under certain conditions,

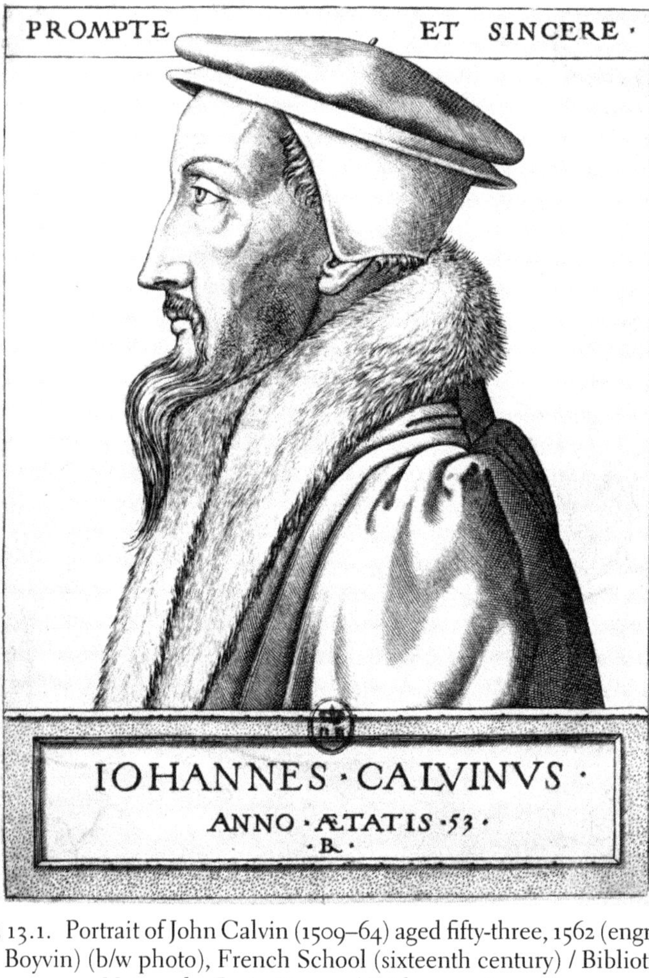

FIGURE 13.1. Portrait of John Calvin (1509–64) aged fifty-three, 1562 (engraving by René Boyvin) (b/w photo), French School (sixteenth century) / Bibliotheque Nationale, Paris, France / Bridgeman Images

were not unique. Rather, these new policies reflected broader changes common to many mainstream and radical Protestant reformers. Nevertheless, efforts to reform the family in Calvin's Geneva had a decisive impact on Genevan society at all levels and provided a highly successful model for church and state cooperation in supporting and regulating family affairs. Moreover, the ideas concerning family matters promulgated in Geneva and the mechanisms introduced to implement them inspired other communities in the Calvinist world and beyond.

Calvin's contribution to the organization of family life in Geneva can be broadly construed as twofold. First, he promoted a theology of marriage, sex, children, and family in theological treatises, sermons, commentaries, letters, and civil and ecclesiastical advice and ordinances. Second, he helped establish a paternalistic institutional framework for improving stability in family matters, principally through his organization of the church offices and in procedures he designed for cooperation between ecclesiastical and civil authorities in regulating moral and criminal matters.

Calvin contributed to the reform of the family as one who was a family man himself. However, for someone who wrote so much and devoted such effort to trying to improve domestic relations in Geneva, Calvin was quite reticent about himself, and little is known about his own family life. He married Idelette de Bure, a widow with two children from her previous union, in Strasbourg in August 1540. After moving to Geneva, the couple had at least one son, James, and possibly other children, though none of them survived infancy. Nevertheless, their domestic situation must have been far from simple. The Calvins lived in a large house provided by the city near the main city church of St. Pierre, which they shared with the growing family of John's brother Antoine, household servants, other employees working for Antoine's business, and perhaps an occasional student or long-term visitor. When Idelette died in 1549, Calvin was devastated and assumed responsibility for raising his stepchildren. It is likely that his sister-in-law, Anne Le Fert, assumed the role as household manager, but it also seems clear that relations within this large and prominent home were not completely harmonious. In 1557, Anne was convicted (on slim evidence) of adultery in a trial in which Calvin supported her husband (his brother). She was banished from Geneva and divorced from Antoine, who retained custody of their children in the Calvin home. Both parties later remarried, though allowing a convicted adulterer to remarry was unusual, even among Protestants.[1]

[1] This case is discussed in Kingdon, *Adultery and Divorce in Calvin's Geneva*, 71–97.

Though such a prominent household can hardly be representative of normal domestic conditions in Geneva, these considerations of life in Calvin's own home point to four topics that guide the following discussion of his theological and institutional reform of the family in Geneva: (1) marriage; (2) children; (3) broader kinship and household relationships; and (4) sexual misconduct. In each of these areas, we can consider both the ideas and themes articulated by Calvin and some of the responses in Genevan society to the policies that they inspired.

MARRIAGE

The reorganization of the church and civil life occasioned by Geneva's newly won independence and adoption of Reformed religion resulted in the development of policies toward marriage starting in the 1540s. As they developed these policies and laws, Calvin, his pastoral colleagues, and the magistrates assumed many earlier attitudes toward marriage and understood their task to be to ensure the proper formation and continuation of solid domestic relationships. Although they rejected traditional theological understandings of marriage as a sacrament and clerical celibacy, they kept much of canon law concerning marriage and created institutions like the Consistory to support a more effective cooperation between church and civic authorities to achieve the inherited goals for successful conjugal unions. As in all times, marriage had an important economic dimension; any agreement to marry involved a property contract outlining how the goods each party brought into the marriage were to be managed. Here, too, the Genevan authorities preserved many of the pre-Reformation laws and customs. Only after Calvin's death was a new marital property law entered into the civil code in Geneva. But it included only minor changes involving the rights of widows.[2]

Despite these continuities with tradition, the new religious orientation of the city and Calvin's leadership challenged and reshaped in key ways the theology and law concerning marriage. This can be seen first of all in the new institutional oversight regulating marital affairs. The articulation and implementation of new marriage policies and laws took surprisingly long, reflecting the fact that the precise relationship and respective jurisdictions of the civic and new ecclesiastical authorities was subject to ongoing negotiation. Prior to the Reformation, the bishop's court had handled marriage matters, including disputes over marital property. Afterward, many of these issues came under the purview of the magistrates, but with Calvin's guidance, the

[2] Witte Jr. and Kingdon, *Sex, Marriage and Family Life in John Calvin's Geneva*, 395–6.

church and civic authorities collaborated in this task. The *Ecclesiastical Ordinances* Calvin drew up for the organization of the church in 1541 called for, among other things, the creation of a new marriage ordinance and the establishment of the Consistory – an all-male ecclesiastical body made up of the city's pastors and lay officers (elders) chosen from Geneva's several elected city councils. The Consistory aimed to guide Genevans' behaviour and enforce morality, meeting weekly to hear cases on a wide range of suspected or alleged moral infractions and functioning as "a hearings court, as a compulsory counseling service, and as an educational institution."[3] The Consistory dealt with matrimonial issues in part by providing pastoral advice on personal relations and referring legal matters (including marital property and inheritance disputes) and criminal cases to the Council. A marriage liturgy appeared in 1542 (modified slightly in 1545), and a draft of the marriage ordinance was presented to the Council in 1545, subsequently revised and expanded in 1546, but formally adopted only in 1561.

A second shift can be seen in the heightened emphasis Calvin gave to marriage as a covenant, affirming the sacred character of the institution but in a way consistent with Protestant theology. In his early rejection of the medieval theology of marriage as a sacrament and his critique of the church's oversight of the parties, timing, and conditions of marriage, Calvin argued, like Luther and other Protestant reformers, that marriage had no bearing on one's spiritual status or salvation. Though instituted by God, marriage was a matter of the earthly kingdom and therefore subject to the jurisdiction of the civic authorities. However, especially in his commentaries, lectures, and sermons on the Bible, as well as in letters and other documents advising authorities about particular cases, Calvin also elaborated a covenantal image of marriage. Here he built on the medieval notion that marriage was a sacred contract, freely and mutually chosen by a man and a woman legitimately able to enter into such an arrangement, constituted and sealed by promises made to one another. For example, in a sermon on 2 Timothy 5, he ventured, "God reigns in a little household, even one in dire poverty, when the husband and the wife dedicate themselves to their duties to each other. Here there is holiness greater and nearer the kingdom of God than there is even in a cloister."[4] While the covenant was mutual, it was not egalitarian; Calvin held that wives' subordination to their husbands was ordained in creation

[3] Kingdon, *Adultery and Divorce in Calvin's Geneva*, 4.

[4] Quoted in Witte Jr., *From Sacrament to Contract*, 110.

and worsened by the Fall into sin. Yet he also thought husbands should love their wives and that men and women "ought to be connected together by mutual benevolence, for the one cannot do without the other."[5] Thus marriage in Geneva continued to be a serious business with a definite spiritual dimension, technically a civil affair but one supported and regulated by the religious authorities.

A final element in the reform of marriage in Calvin's Geneva can be seen in the creation and implementation of formalized policies governing the formation, maintenance, and dissolution of conjugal unions.[6] These new policies, such as the Marriage Ordinance, covered in detail matters pertaining to the formation of marriages, and the Consistory dealt repeatedly with situations relating to courtship, betrothals, and weddings. To minimize the prospect of marital agreements resulting from physical or psychological coercion, outside pressure, deception, drunkenness, or some other impairment, Calvin and his colleagues mandated a number of practices that the medieval church had recommended but not required, most of which aimed to make the process more transparent and public. They insisted that engagement promises be made in the presence of at least two reputable witnesses, and that fathers (or mothers, if the fathers were absent) consent to the union of underage parties. Once a couple became engaged, the upcoming marriage was announced by the publication of banns for three consecutive Sundays. These declarations – signed by magistrates and announced by ministers at church services – allowed opportunity for anyone to contest the union, if, for example, one of the parties was already betrothed or married to someone else or otherwise not free to marry. The exchange of marriage vows was likewise to be public, celebrated in a regular church service three to six weeks after engagement.

Calvin and his colleagues did not want to leave too much time between engagement and wedding, because they took a strict line on both the seriousness of betrothal promises and the prohibition of cohabitation or sexual activity before the church ceremony. Some couples, however, viewed their engagement as a license for sexual relations, and the Consistory dealt repeatedly with engaged couples accused of premarital fornication. Those found guilty were admonished and sometimes subject to spiritual sanctions (e.g., temporary suspension from the Lord's Supper) or sent to the magistrates for

[5] This from his commentary on 1 Corinthians 11:11. Calvin, *Commentary on the Epistles of Paul to the Corinthians*, 1:359–60.

[6] Details concerning these policies and excerpts from Consistory cases and Calvin's writings that deal with these matters can be found in Witte Jr. and Kingdon, *Sex, Marriage, and Family in John Calvin's Geneva*.

criminal punishment (e.g., three days in jail on bread and water). Most often, however, they were ordered to get married as quickly as possible and abstain from sex in the meantime, so as not to run the risk of producing an illegitimate child.

Another indication of the high regard for betrothals can be seen in the authorities' reluctance to dissolve them except for legitimate reasons, such as unfitness for marriage, coercion, lack of parental consent, or a previously contracted marriage by one party. This was a departure from the traditional practice of allowing engagements to be called off for any reason by mutual consent. Genevan officials would not allow properly engaged couples to break off their agreement simply because they changed their minds or because of conditions (such as failure to provide a promised gift) that were not seen as undermining free, mutual consent to the union. The time between engagement and wedding ceremony was not a cooling-off period, but an opportunity for bringing to light any legal reasons why the marriage should not go forward. The Consistory routinely heard disputes over whether a couple had been properly betrothed or (in the case of weddings conducted outside Geneva) married, and whether the conditions specified for getting married were valid. Where the Consistory found that free consent had been compromised or discovered evidence invalidating the union, they would allow the engagement to be annulled. But if couples merely had second thoughts, the Consistory would order them to marry. This was a sign of how seriously Calvin and his colleagues viewed promises of betrothal as part of the marriage covenant; for them, courtship was the time for getting to know one another and the stage when a relationship could be ended. Properly concluded engagements, however, signaled a firm commitment, and meant that couples should be married in a public church ceremony presided over by a minister within six weeks.

Weddings in Geneva took place right after the sermon at a regular church service on a weekday or a Sunday, as long as the Lord's Supper was not being celebrated. The setting in public worship signaled the congregation's assent to the union and was a departure from previous custom. Couples who had been married in Catholic ceremonies outside of Geneva or in secret were also supposed to have their marriages recognized in this way. The bride and groom were allowed to mark the occasion as long as decorum was observed – policies and laws specified that couples could not have "drummers or fiddlers" accompany the wedding party to church, and that post-ceremony festivities should forgo excessive dancing, drinking, or feasting. Even attire was regulated.

Once sealed in a wedding, marriage in Geneva was intended to be permanent. Couples were expected to cohabit, and failure to do so could raise suspicions of adultery or other sexual crime (or abandonment of familial obligations). Consistent with his view of marriage as a mutual covenant, Calvin insisted that wives as well as husbands had conjugal rights and were to share the responsibilities of parenting. He and his colleagues discouraged and tried to mitigate marital discord and spousal abuse. However, their insistence on reconciling spouses in the interest of preserving and strengthening the marriage bond meant that occasionally spouses who had been repeatedly beaten had no legal means to escape their situation and could only hope that the offending party, once punished by the civil authorities, would change his ways. That said, Witte Jr. and Kingdon also note that the criminal sanctions for mistreatment of spouses "became increasingly severe in the later years [of Calvin's career] as the Consistory and Council sought to clamp down on domestic abuse."[7]

Despite the overwhelming preference of Calvin and the Consistory and Council for reconciling spouses, they recognized that sometimes attempts at peaceful resolution of differences failed. New policies and laws thus also addressed situations when a union might be dissolved through annulment or divorce. As in the formation and maintenance of marriages, the dissolution of marriages was a public and communal process involving hearings conducted in the Consistory and, if the case advanced, before the Council.

In Reformation Geneva, the traditional practice of separation while remaining legally (and sacramentally) married was not an option; relationships had to be formally dissolved through annulment or divorce so that people could have the opportunity to remarry – ideally entering into the kind of mutually satisfying covenantal relationship that Calvin envisioned or, at the very least, avoiding fornication. Once confirmed and consummated, a marriage could be annulled only because one of the parties was found to be underage, was already engaged or married to someone else, or had not consented to the union; or upon discovery that the relationship was incestuous, that one of the parties had a contagious disease or physical deformity that prevented sexual relations, or that presumed virginity was lacking.[8] In most of these cases, both parties were free to marry someone else.

The emergence of Protestant communities like Geneva raised the complicated question of the validity of marriages between Catholics and Protestants. Over time this became less of an issue in Geneva, since its inhabitants were supposed to be members of the Reformed church, and eventually most met this

[7] Ibid., 45. [8] Ibid., 46.

expectation or moved away. But for Genevans with family members in Catholic areas, or for Reformed Protestants living elsewhere, Calvin did not hold "that religious differences between Protestants and Catholics constituted grounds for divorce unless persecution presented an immediate threat to their safety."[9] Such unions were discouraged, however, and the Consistory intervened in several such cases.[10]

In Calvin's Geneva, divorce was granted only on the grounds of proven adultery or willful desertion. Calvin considered adultery the most serious violation of the marriage covenant, and even thought the unwarranted separation of spouses to be a form of adultery. Either spouse could sue for divorce, and remarriage was permitted – even encouraged – particularly for the wronged spouse. But overall the law and policies were very conservative, and divorces were rarely granted – according to Kingdon, only twenty-six times for adultery between 1541 and 1564.[11] On the whole, the Marriage Ordinance and the activities of the Consistory aimed toward the peaceful resolution of discord and the reconciliation of spouses or betrothed parties.

CHILDREN

Although Calvin had no biological children of his own who survived infancy, he was intensely interested in children and childrearing. With the Jewish and Christian traditions, he affirmed that a primary goal of marriage was procreation and held that strong marriages provided the best environment for the nurture of offspring, whom he viewed, following Psalm 127, as a "heritage of the Lord."[12] He was quite involved, often personally, in implementing public policies that had important and sometimes controversial implications for families and children. His reform of the church included writing catechisms for the spiritual education of young and old. He significantly revised the rationale for infant baptism, expressing his conviction that the elect are from birth full inheritors of God's covenant and members of God's church. As with his views on marriage, Calvin's understanding of children and their place in family, church, and society preserved many of the attitudes permeating the Western tradition. At the same time, his theological orientation and concern to enhance moral order in Geneva challenged some traditional practices and signaled a shift in children's place in the community.

9 Hendrix, "The Reform of Marriage in Calvin's Geneva," 120.

10 Witte Jr. and Kingdon, *Sex, Marriage, and Family in John Calvin's Geneva*, 354–82.

11 Kingdon, *Adultery and Divorce in Calvin's Geneva*, 176.

12 The following discussion draws on Pitkin, "The Heritage of the Lord," 160–93.

A first shift can be seen in the way Calvin's view of the nature, spiritual needs and capacities, and broader obligations of children was shaped by his biblical, theocentric theology of grace. With the dominant theological traditions of the Augustinian West, Calvin held that even infants were not innocent, but rather tainted with original sin and in need of God's forgiveness and grace. Despite this, he did not dwell on evidences of corruption in children, nor did he use their sinfulness from birth to justify harsh treatment of them. Importantly, he did not view children as more sinful than anyone else; indeed, he spoke of their spiritual capacities as rivaling those of their elders. For example, in an unusual interpretation of Psalm 8:2, Calvin went against the prevailing tradition that understood "babes and infants" as older children capable of speech or as a symbol of the disciples. Rather, he argued, even infants at the breast and young children can proclaim God's glory in their own ways. Calvin also imbued the obligations of children and parents with a spiritual dimension, drawing on biblical references to parent–child relations. For example, in his commentary on Psalm 127, he encouraged parents to view their children as gifts of divine providence and saw parents' primary obligation to be to teach godliness. In his commentary on the Ten Commandments, he underscored the duty of children to submit to their parents; given his abhorrence of anarchy and chaos, he worried more about subordinates violating the authority of superiors than about superiors exploiting those below them.

A second distinctive turn is Calvin's rationale for preserving the practice of infant baptism and his implementation of new policies governing the practice. Like other magisterial Protestants, Calvin kept infant baptism and designated it a sacrament, but he also transformed its meaning. His primary justification for infant baptism was not the sinfulness of children, nor even their need for faith or perhaps latent possession of it, but the fact that God commanded it, because elect children, for Calvin, are already members of God's covenant. He insisted that children of believing parents had a right to baptism because they already possessed the promise or covenant from God that baptism signified, thus overturning the traditional understanding of this sacrament as a washing away of original sin and essential for salvation. Since Calvin also held that only God knew who was elect, the expectation was that all children in Reformed Geneva would be baptized. The Consistory repeatedly allowed baptism of illegitimate children, even when paternity was not yet determined, at least partly in recognition of the divine mandate and what was owed the child.

Like marriage, however, baptism in Geneva was significant not just for the individual, but also for family and community; it marked not just a child's relationship to God, but also his or her entrance into the wider social network.[13] For Calvin, baptism nourished both parental and communal faith and therefore needed to take place in the context of public worship. The rite confirmed the promise to believing parents that God will be God to them and to their descendants (Genesis 17:7); in baptism, parents can "see with their very eyes the covenant of the Lord engraved on the bodies of their children."[14] In another departure from tradition, Calvin insisted that fathers (rather than godparents) present their children for baptism; he also would have liked mothers to be present, but they would often be at home recovering from the birth. In practice, however, the Genevan custom usually prevailed in which godparents presented infants for baptism and promised to raise them in the Reformed faith (though the responsibility for this in fact fell mostly to the parents). Through its witness, the congregation affirmed the child's incorporation in the religious and social community and committed itself to spiritual and material care of its newest member by supporting the vows of the sponsors and parents.

A final area in which Calvin shaped ideas and practices surrounding children and childrearing can be seen in policies and practices he helped develop for raising children and supporting and regulating family life. Calvin wrote a catechism as a basis for spiritual education and implemented weekly catechetical church services that focused on the tenets of the Reformed faith. He actively organized schooling in Geneva, supported the town's reorganization of social welfare, and frequently encountered situations concerned with children and responsibilities toward them. The Consistory routinely heard cases pertaining to children and their upbringing or care.[15] In cases of illegitimate or abandoned children, Calvin and his colleagues sought to determine parentage and financial responsibility. They also dealt with questions of whether a child had been legitimately baptized, regulated who could serve as baptismal sponsors, and convinced the civic authorities to promulgate a list of approved, godly names for children. They investigated when people misbehaved at baptisms by leaving early, not showing up at all, or otherwise disrupting the proceedings.

At times these efforts met with resistance. Riots broke out in the late 1540s over efforts to regulate names given at baptism, revealing tensions between the ministers and some native Genevans over ecclesiastical power and parents' rights. Long-standing social customs surrounding fathers' roles in organizing post-baptismal festivities conflicted with the new expectation that they attend

[13] Spierling, *Infant Baptism in Reformation Geneva*, 2.

[14] Calvin, *Institutes of the Christian Religion*, book 4, chapter 16, paragraph 9.

[15] Watt, "Childhood and Youth in the Geneva Consistory Minutes," 43–64.

the church services in which their babies were presented for baptism.[16] And sometimes the ministers' judgment about who was and who was not a suitable godparent and the responsibilities entailed in the position ran counter to some townspeople's ideas about these important bonds of spiritual (and sometimes material) kinship.

Though Calvin and his colleagues showed flexibility in continuing the nonbiblical tradition of godparents, they insisted that godparents be members of the Reformed church in good standing. Calvin himself served as a godparent for nearly fifty children between 1550 and 1563.[17] Yet the Consistory sometimes overlooked the choice of a non-Reformed or otherwise unsuitable godparent and did not disenfranchise "any godparents once the baptism had occurred." Moreover, they did not require those who had stood as baptismal sponsors in Catholic baptisms outside of Geneva to reject the promises they had made as sponsors.[18] While those who committed these infractions would be reprimanded and might be sent to the Council for punishment or required to repent publicly of their misdeeds, the Consistory's main goal seems to have been – as was the case with engaged couples convicted of fornication – to improve the faith and morality of the guilty so that they could live in a more godly fashion.

BROADER KINSHIP AND HOUSEHOLD RELATIONSHIPS

As we have seen, Calvin himself was part of broader social networks in which quasi-familial obligations extended to those related by spiritual kinship (such as godparents) and households with non-biological members (servants, apprentices, and boarders) living under the same roof. The reform of the family in Geneva also affected these kinds of relationships and individuals, and these important connections were transformed by the religious changes of the city and their social impact.

While Calvin and his colleagues permitted the continuation of the traditional role of baptismal sponsors or godparents, they sought to reform this institution in ways that created different kinds of bonds between children and their biological parents and godparents. This effort brought change to the traditional ideas of family and kin. In the late medieval church, the spiritual kinship that baptism created between child and godparent was so close that marriage was not permitted between godparents and godchildren, between godparents of the same child, or between biological parents and the godparents of their children, since such unions were regarded as

[16] Spierling, *Infant Baptism in Reformation Geneva*, 91–3. [17] Ibid., 115. [18] Ibid., 126.

incestuous.[19] Thus for many, the choice of a godparent or godparents represented a way to expand a child's spiritual and social safety net by literally extending the immediate family circle.

The Consistory could at times tolerate godparent arrangements that were less than ideal from its perspective; however, as Spierling has shown, reforming efforts in Geneva sought to transform these relationships in three key ways.[20] First, new policies and procedures concentrated on a sponsor's responsibilities for spiritual education more than the spiritual or social connections or possible material obligations. That said, it was nearly always the parents, and not godparents, who were called before the Consistory for failing to send their children to catechism or otherwise ensure their religious upbringing. Second, whenever possible, the ministers and elders sought to prevent unsuitable godparents from presenting children for baptism. For instance, Genevans banned from the Lord's Supper for immoral or ungodly behaviour or insufficient grasp of Reformed faith were also prohibited from standing as godparents. For many Genevans, as for the Reformed ministers, baptism was both a spiritual and a social, community ritual. But sometimes they had different ideas about the social network into which the child was being incorporated: was this the whole congregation and the wider Reformed church in Geneva, or was this a more traditional extended family circle of biological and godparent kin? Those prevented from serving as sponsors who held the latter view frequently chafed at this restriction and sometimes sought to get around it. Finally, the Genevan baptismal records almost exclusively mention only godfathers.

This patriarchal and paternalistic orientation is also evident in efforts to establish and support godly households that included members beyond the biological or blended family. As in Calvin's own situation, households in Geneva often included servants, apprentices, other employees, and students. Many of these household members were from outside Geneva, sometimes from Catholic areas. With the new religious orientation of the city, these domestic arrangements thus often played a crucial role in efforts to foster the city's new religious identity and to monitor and uphold godliness.

While living in the homes of their masters, mistresses, or hosts, these individuals were expected to conform to the city's religious and behavioural expectations. Employers, in turn, "were officially responsible for servants' well-being, discipline, and religious education, including attendance at catechism services."[21] The Council also arranged for early morning Sunday worship services to accommodate some servants' schedules. Here again – as with

19 Ibid., 110. 20 This discussion draws on chapter 4 of Spierling's study.

21 Spierling, "Putting 'God's Honor First,'" 88.

marriage and childrearing – there is both continuity with traditional ideals and transformation that reflects religious changes. The idea that heads of household were responsible for the behaviour of their domestic employees was not new.[22] Nevertheless, the closer monitoring of domestics' religious beliefs and activities, and the expectation that they would receive the same Reformed religious instruction and be involved in the same communal rituals as the rest of the inhabitants of Geneva, was novel. Ideally, even servants and others living under the same roof would be bonded with the householders by explicitly religious ties in a godly home.

SEXUAL MISCONDUCT

One final area in which Calvin contributed to the shaping of the theological and legal traditions of marriage, sex, and family lies in the increased efforts he supported to regulate illicit or criminal sexual behaviours, such as adultery, fornication, rape, incest, polygamy, prostitution, sodomy, and bestiality. Witte notes that Calvin tended to view all such conduct, and even sexually suggestive behaviour, as forbidden by the seventh commandment.[23] Though Protestant reformers like Calvin emphasized the goodness and necessity of modest, marital sex, they were convinced they needed to regulate the sexual activities of average people for their own good, for the good of society, and for the protection of the vulnerable. The flip side of the policies and institutions designed to strengthen the new views of marriage, children and childrearing, and domestic and kin relationships can be seen in the reform, prosecution, and punishment of sexual misdemeanors and crimes as offenses to God and dangers to social order. Here again reforming efforts provide another window into the negotiated process of reform in Geneva, as policies and the jurisdictional authority for implementing them took time to develop. A new ordinance on fornication and adultery failed to pass in 1556; when it finally succeeded ten years later (two years after Calvin's death), public protests broke out.[24]

In their desire to root out and punish sexual immorality, Calvin and his colleagues were not necessarily any different than most societies throughout much of history, but the heightened expectations for godly living and the new institutional oversight in Reformation Geneva meant that more illicit activity came to the attention of the authorities. Usually it was the Consistory that first inquired into these affairs, trying to find out if there was any truth behind the suspicions or accusations of sexual misconduct. If the evidence pointed to more

[22] Ibid., 92. [23] Witte Jr., "Marriage and Family Life," 461.
[24] Monter, "Women in Calvinist Geneva," 190.

serious sexual crimes, the case would be referred to the Council for further investigation, prosecution, and punishment, while more modest sexual infractions remained within the Consistory, which admonished those involved for giving appearance of sexual impropriety and told them to shape up. According to William Monter, between 1564 and 1569, the Consistory punished more than 250 people for various forms of sexual misconduct by suspending them from the Lord's Supper. Each year about a dozen of these cases involved premarital sex by engaged couples or relations between masters and servants.[25]

Geneva's strenuous efforts to regulate sexual behaviour aimed to preserve female chastity in a world that prioritized inheritance, paternity, male honor, and patriarchal control.[26] The authorities further aimed to make marital formation more transparent, public, and swift in part to provide the proper context for sexual relations and procreation. Illegitimate pregnancies were not only seen as the fruit of ungodly sexual relations, but also presented enormous economic complexities of paternal financial responsibility and inheritance issues. Calvin drew on biblical examples of fornication, adultery, prostitution, and incest to preach against all of these behaviours, not hesitating to criticize harshly as sinful the sexual immoralities of the biblical faithful. He may have had very strict standards when it came to what he understood as adultery, but he was not alone in his concern to promote sexual activity that he held was legal and proper. Many of the cases that came before the Consistory were reported by concerned family members or neighbors. Servants and other members of an extended household often served as key (if also at times conflicted) witnesses in cases involving such intimate doings.[27]

Sleeping arrangements in cramped Genevan households could involve several people of possibly different sexes sharing a room or even a bed, heightening the opportunities for impropriety or at least the appearance of it. Moreover, a certain level of suggestive sexual innuendo and activity and even sexual harassment appears to have been an accepted part of daily life in Geneva, as can be surmised both from the ongoing efforts of the ministers and the Consistory to instruct and hold people to the new standards and from resistance by those who resented some of these policies. Illicit sexual activity also often occurred in connection with other behaviours that the church authorities viewed as undesirable, such as drinking, dancing, other "frivolous" activities, and blasphemous speech, which further complicated official inquiries.

25 Ibid., 191.

26 The authorities were also very concerned about sexual activity they deemed unnatural (e.g., sodomy, bestiality, group sex), but in the interests of space this topic will not be treated here. See Naphy, *Sex Crimes*, 87–177.

27 Spierling, "Putting 'God's Honor First,'" 89.

For some – especially women routinely subject to male sexual advances – the increased oversight and moral stringency of Calvin and his colleagues might have been welcome. Indeed, William Monter has suggested that the court system's handling of sexual misconduct cases only "*seemed strict* to Genevan public (i.e., male) opinion because it prosecuted men as vigorously as it did women."[28] Moreover, these enhanced processes also offered a modicum of protection for the accused by authorizing forms of investigation, prosecution, and punishment that followed steps that had been carefully delineated and collectively implemented.

State-imposed punishment of sexual immorality in Geneva at the time of Calvin varied according to the circumstances and the crime. Betrothed couples who engaged in premarital sex could be thrown in jail on bread and water by the Council, but then would be ordered to marry without delay. Moreover, their sin would be announced in the banns and at their wedding, and any child they conceived prior to the church ceremony would be designated a bastard in the public baptismal registry.[29] The penalties for adultery between two parties married to other spouses or a married individual and an unmarried partner depended on gender, marital status, and social class, and included imprisonment, whipping, and banishment, as in the case of Anne Le Fert (Calvin's sister-in-law). There was also broad support in Geneva for the death penalty in especially serious cases: for repeat offenders, particularly scandalous public incidents, and complicated situations in which adultery was part of a series of other offenses.[30] This policy was based on biblical prescriptions and Roman legal precedents and was implemented a number of times in the early 1560s before becoming formal law in the ordinance of 1566. Although a definite double standard allowed for harsher punishment of female adulterers, the law was often not applied in a strict way. As Naphy notes, "Geneva took a much less severe view of adultery than their laws implied and, in particular, on a case-by-case basis they made decisions which often seem impossible to understand or explain. The result, though, was often leniency for women."[31]

CONCLUSION: IMPACT AND LEGACIES

Calvin's reform of the family was part of a broader effort to mold Geneva into a godly society in which all were instructed in and embraced the tenets of the

28 Monter, "Women in Calvinist Geneva," 192; my emphasis.

29 Witte Jr. and Kingdon, *Sex, Marriage, and Family in John Calvin's Geneva*, 423.

30 See the discussion of several cases in Kingdon, *Adultery and Divorce in Calvin's Geneva*, 116–42.

31 Naphy, *Sex Crimes*, 45–8.

Reformed faith and ordered their lives accordingly. In spearheading this aspect of his reformation, Calvin drew on many traditional Christian theological and legal traditions concerning marriage, children, family, and sex, transforming them to fit his theocentric Protestant theology of grace. He stressed the covenantal nature of marriage as an institution with private and public dimensions, the godliness of childrearing and a new vision of children's place in the religious community, the blessing of an orderly domestic sphere, and the importance of honorable sexual relations between duly married spouses. For Calvin, these were all part of the earthly kingdom and thus not conditions for salvation or even unequivocal signs of election, but he nevertheless saw the promotion and inculcation of morality in the domestic sphere as a divine mandate and a necessary component of a godly society. It was a task to which he personally devoted much time and energy – in sermons, in regular leadership of the Consistory, in advising the civic authorities, and presumably even in his own home.

Regardless of religious confession, many of Calvin's early modern contemporaries shared his ideal of family as a spiritual community centered on the marriage covenant and sought to emulate the same kind of patriarchal framework through which he aimed to create godly households. Calvin's main contribution to Christian theology and law concerning marriage, children, family, and sex was thus a comprehensive synthesis of existing traditions, Reformed theological ideals, and institutional implementation in Genevan society – "a top-to-bottom *reformulation* of ideas and institutions, theology and law, learning and living."[32]

The system developed in Geneva influenced Reformed communities elsewhere, especially in France, the Netherlands, Scotland, and England. In many of these places, Reformed Christians lived as minority communities, so there was no possibility of the kind of cooperation with the magisterial powers that was the case in the city-state of Geneva. Nevertheless, church leaders and consistories elsewhere took a strong interest in regulating domestic life, implementing many of the same reforms that Calvin had introduced in Geneva.

RECOMMENDED READING

Calvin, John. *Institutes of the Christian Religion* [1559]. Edited by J. T. McNeill. Translated by F. L. Battles. 1960; rpt. Louisville, KY: Westminster John Knox, 2006.

Commentary on the Epistles of Paul to the Corinthians. 2 vols. In vol. 20 of Calvin's Commentaries, 1: 359–60. Rpt. Grand Rapids, MI: Baker Book House, 1989.

[32] Witte Jr., "Marriage and Family Life," 456 (my emphasis).

Hendrix, Scott. "The Reform of Marriage in Calvin's Geneva." In *Caritas et Reformatio: Essays on Church and Society in Honor of Carter Lindberg*, edited by David M. Whitford, 113–32. St. Louis, MO: Concordia Publishing House, 2002.

Kingdon, Robert M. *Adultery and Divorce in Calvin's Geneva*. Cambridge, MA: Harvard University Press, 1995.

Mentzer, Raymond A. "Morals and Moral Regulation in Protestant France." *Journal of Interdisciplinary History*, 31/1 (2000): 1–20.

Monter, E. William. "Women in Calvinist Geneva, 1550–1800." *Signs* 6/2 (Winter 1980): 189–209.

Naphy, William G. "Calvin and Geneva." In *The Reformation World*, edited by Andrew Pettegree, 309–22. New York: Routledge, 2000.

Sex Crimes: From Renaissance to Enlightenment. Charleston, SC: Tempus Publishing, Inc., 2002.

Pitkin, Barbara. "The Heritage of the Lord: Children in the Theology of John Calvin." In *The Child in Christian Thought*, edited by Marcia J. Bunge, 160–93. Grand Rapids, MI: Eerdmans, 2001.

"Children and the Church in Calvin's Geneva." In *Calvin and the Church*, edited by David L. Foxgrover, 144–64. Grand Rapids, MI: CDC Product Services for the Calvin Studies Society, 2002.

Spierling, Karen E., *Infant Baptism in Reformation Geneva: The Shaping of a Community, 1536–1564*. Aldershot, Hants, England: Ashgate, 2005; rpt. Louisville, KY: Westminster John Knox, 2009.

"Putting 'God's Honor First': Truth, Lies, and Servants in Reformation Geneva." *Church History and Religious Culture* 92 (2012): 85–103.

"Women, Marriage, and Family." In *T&T Clark Companion to Reformation Theology*, edited by David M. Whitford, 178–96. London: T&T Clark, 2012.

Watt, Jeffrey R. "Childhood and Youth in the Geneva Consistory Minutes." In *Calvinus Praeceptor Ecclesiae: Papers of the Eighth International Congress for Calvin Research*, edited by Herman J. Selderhuis, 43–64. Geneva: Librairie Droz, 2004.

Witte, John, Jr. *From Sacrament to Contract: Marriage, Religion, and Law in the Western Tradition*. Louisville, KY: Westminster John Knox, 1997, 2nd ed., 2012.

"Marriage and Family Life." In *The Calvin Handbook*, edited by Herman J. Selderhuis, 455–65. Grand Rapids, MI: Eerdmans, 2009.

Witte, John, Jr. and Robert M. Kingdon. *Sex, Marriage and Family Life in John Calvin's Geneva*. Vol. 1: *Courtship, Engagement, and Marriage*. Grand Rapids, MI: Eerdmans, 2005.

14

King Henry VIII

Henry Ansgar Kelly

BIOGRAPHICAL INTRODUCTION

Henry Tudor, the second son of King Henry VII of England, had strong religious views all his life, but also strong emotions, which sometimes influenced the directions and nuances of his attitudes toward religion. He was born in 1491, five years younger than his brother, Arthur. When Arthur died in 1502, Henry became heir to the throne. He also inherited Arthur's widow, Catherine of Aragon, marrying her provisionally in 1504 at the age of thirteen and for good in 1509, two months after becoming king.

He showed his interest in theology early, attacking Martin Luther on the subject of Luther's discounting of most of the sacraments, including the sacrament of matrimony. Henry's Latin treatise *Assertio septem sacramentorum adversus Martinum Lutherum*, largely written by theologian John Fisher, the bishop of Rochester, and learned humanist Thomas More, was published in 1523. For that the pope declared Henry, and his royal successors to this day, "*Defensor Fidei*," Defender of the Faith.

For much of the next decade, Henry's main interests in religion were connected with his efforts to get free of his marriage to Catherine, centering especially on certain biblical texts and the jurisdiction of the pope over marital law and England. Though Henry was introduced to various Lutheran ideas, especially through Anne Boleyn, his second queen, he was generally unsympathetic to them. He was willing enough, after having himself declared Supreme Head of the Church in England in 1534, to dissolve religious houses and confiscate their lands and goods. But he did not favor marriage of clergy or some other favorite Protestant reforms, as was clear in the Act of Six Articles of 1539, which upheld transubstantiation and prescribed penalties for religious

FIGURE 14.1. Portrait of Henry VIII (1491–1547) aged forty-nine, 1540 (oil on panel), Hans Holbein the Younger (1497/8–1543) / Palazzo Barberini, Rome, Italy / Bridgeman Images

dissenters.[1] On the question of making the Bible available to all in English, at first he sided with bishops who opposed the idea, but by 1541 he was won over, and parishes were to be fined if they failed to have an English Bible available to the parishioners.

HENRY VIII AND THE IMPEDIMENTS OF KINSHIP AND AFFINITY

Matrimony had been designated as the seventh sacrament in the twelfth century; unlike the other sacraments, however, it had not been instituted by Christ during his ministry on earth, but rather by God in the Garden of Eden.[2] Therefore the laws laid down in the Old Testament regarding who could and could not marry were thought to remain in force. Further laws about marriage were added locally during the early Middle Ages.

A particularly influential text, found in Gratian's *Decretum* (ca. 1140),[3] was the canon *Quaedam lex*, which was compiled as part of the life of Gregory the Great (d. 604) written by John the Deacon of Rome (ca. 880).[4] It consisted first of all of the opening of Gregory's authentic response to Augustine of Canterbury on prohibited marriage. The pontiff stated that Roman law allowed first-cousin marriage, but experience showed that there was danger to the offspring of such unions. Therefore, Christian unions were limited to second cousins and beyond – except that John changed it to third cousins and beyond.[5] Then John added a passage from another letter of Gregory's, this time a forged one, the work of "Isidorus Mercator" (ca. 840).[6] Here, Gregory is

1 Kelly, "Mixing Canon and Common Law in Religious Prosecutions under Henry VIII and Edward VI," 927–55.

2 See Chapter 9 herein on Peter Lombard.

3 Gratian, *Decretum*, ed. Emil Friedberg, *Corpus iuris canonici*, 2 vols. (Leipzig: ex officina Bernhardi Tauchnitz, 1879–81; repr. ed., Graz: Akad. Druck- und Verl.-Anst., 1959), 1:1268–9: Cause 35, questions 2–3, chapter 20, *Quaedam lex*. The canon can be found in an earlier edition of Gratian in J.-P. Migne et al., *Patrologia Latina* (PL), 221 vols. (1841–1902), 187:1672–3. See Chapter 8 herein on Gratian.

4 John the Deacon, *Sancti Gregorii Magni vita* 2.37, PL 75:101–2.

5 Gregory the Great, *Liber responsionum* = epistle 11.56a, 2:332–42, at p. 335. The opening part of the answer to the question on prohibited marriage is cited from the earlier edition in PL 77:1183–1200 (year 11, letter 64), col. 1189, by Joyce, *Christian Marriage*, 2nd ed., 514. Recent opinion accepts the whole letter as authentic: see Elliot, "Boniface, Incest, and the Earliest Extant Version of Pope Gregory I's *Libellus responsionum* (JE 1843)," 62–111.

6 PL 130:1134: Pseudo-Gregory I answering Pseudo-Felix, Bishop of Messina (letter invented by the pseudonymous Isidorus Mercator, misleadingly called "Pseudo-Isidore"). See Joyce, *Christian Marriage*, 518–19. Brundage, *Law, Sex, and Christian Society in Medieval Europe*, 141, mistakenly cites Gregory's response to Augustine as including the Isidorian extension to the seventh degree.

made to say that he allowed the English to marry within the fourth degree only temporarily, by way of dispensation, while insisting that the binding law for all Christians forbade marriage to consanguines and affines through the seventh generation (sixth cousins).

This supposed pronouncement by the most revered of all popes, after St. Peter himself, together with other canons of similar import collected by Gratian, guaranteed that this was the law, and it remained so until the thirteenth century. That is, it was thought impossible to marry anyone closer than one's seventh cousin or one's spouse's seventh cousin.

The Fourth Lateran Council in 1215 reduced the barrier to third cousins, meaning that now fourth cousins were suitable for marriage.[7] But the papacy assumed the authority to grant dispensations to marry closer relatives up through first cousins. Closer than that, one encountered the Levitical degrees, which were considered restrictions imposed by God. Even this, however, did not mean that the pope could not suspend them for good reasons.

On the practical level, popes had been giving such dispensations since at least the early fifteenth century. The earliest known recipient was the great-great-grandmother of Henry VIII, Margaret Holland. She was first married to John Beaufort, brother of Henry IV, and, when he died, she was dispensed by the Pisan Pope John XXIII in 1411 to marry Beaufort's nephew Thomas, brother of Henry V,[8] in spite of Leviticus 18:14, addressed to all nephews and nephews-in-law: "Thou shalt not show the filth of the brother of thy father, neither shalt thou nigh to his wife, which is joined to thee by affinity"; and Leviticus 20:20: "He that doth fleshly knowing with the wife of his father's brother, or of his mother's brother, and showeth the filth of his kin, both shall bear their sin; they shall die without children."[9]

At the end of the century, in 1495, a nephew of Ferdinand of Aragon was allowed to marry not his aunt-in-law, but his actual aunt; and then, in 1500, one of Ferdinand's daughters, Maria, was allowed to marry her brother-in-law, her sister Isabella's widower.[10] In 1504, a third sister, Catherine of Aragon, was to be allowed to marry her brother-in-law, young Henry Tudor, in spite of

[7] See Chapter 10 herein on Innocent III.

[8] Kelly, "Canonical Implications of Richard III's Plan to Marry His Niece," 284–9. See further Chapter 1 herein on these Mosaic laws of marriage and sexual relations.

[9] Before Tyndale's translation of the Pentateuch was printed in 1530, the only English versions available were the Early Version and Later Version of the Middle English Bible (tendentiously called "the Wycliffite Bible"), produced at the end of the fourteenth century. I use the Later Version. See Kelly, *The Middle English Bible*.

[10] Kelly, *The Matrimonial Trials of Henry VIII*, 14.

Leviticus 18:16: "Thou shalt not show the filth of the wife of thy brother, for it is the filth of thy brother."

Years later, after Catherine had failed to produce a son for Henry (and after Henry had fallen in love with Anne Boleyn), Henry was even more impressed with the version of the prohibition in Leviticus 20:21: "He that weddeth [*duxerit*, literally 'taketh'] the wife of his brother doth an unlawful thing; he showeth the filth of his brother; he shall be without children." The trouble was that another verse of scripture, Deuteronomy 25:5, commanded a man to marry his brother's widow if there had been no children: "When brethren dwell together, and one of them is dead without children, the wife of the dead brother shall not be wedded to another man, but his brother shall take her, and shall raise seed of his brother." This was called the law of levirate, and it was familiar from the New Testament (Matthew 22:24, Mark 12:19, Luke 20:28).[11]

But however much Henry believed that his failure to beget a son by Catherine was caused by his violating divine law, the question whether the pope could make an exception to the law was not of immediate concern; for even the king must have realized that he had no hope of obtaining a papal annulment by calling a papal dispensation into question. It would be necessary to concentrate instead on faulting the dispensation on technical legal grounds. But it is worth mentioning that Henry's chancellor, Cardinal Thomas Wolsey, Archbishop of York and legate *a latere* of the Apostolic See, so readily assumed the pope's power of dispensation that he considered trying to obtain a dispensation from the pope to allow Henry's daughter Mary to marry her half-brother Henry Fitzroy, Henry's illegitimate son by Elizabeth Blount.[12] It was acknowledged by everyone, of course, that there was nothing intrinsically wrong or unnatural about brother–sister marriage, since it had been necessary at the beginning of the human race, with the offspring of Adam and Eve.

The canon law of marriage was complicated. The basic kinship impediments were consanguinity and affinity. Consanguinity meant a blood relationship between the man and the woman, like being first cousins. Affinity was

11 For a modern discussion of the Levitical and Deuteronomical laws, see Kilchör, "Levirate Marriage in Deuteronomy 25:5–10 and Its Precursors in Leviticus and Numbers," 429–40. He concludes that if the Deuteronomy passage is older, which is the usual assumption, then the Leviticus law abolishes it; but if the reverse is true, then Deuteronomy makes an exception in the law (p. 439). One possibility, mentioned on p. 437, is that the Levitical command applies when the married brother is still alive. Cf. John the Baptist's objection to Herod Antipas: "It is not lawful for thee to have thy brother's wife" (Mark 6:18). Cardinal Cajetan wrote to Henry VIII in 1534 with this interpretation (Kelly, *The Matrimonial Trials of Henry VIII*, 230).

12 Kelly, "Kinship, Incest, and the Dictates of Law," 73.

originally taken to mean the relationship between one spouse and his or her in-laws: for example, between a husband and his wife's cousin. By Henry's time, affinity had long been interpreted as stemming not from marriage, but from sexual intercourse, so not only between a man and the relatives of his wife (if their marriage had been consummated), but also between him and any woman related to any other woman he had had sex with. Henry was thus related by first-degree affinity to Anne Boleyn, because her sister, Mary, had previously been his mistress.

Formerly there had been an affinity that came just from having a spouse, even before the marriage was consummated. That circumstance was now called "the justice of public honesty." When affinity was in the first degree – for instance, between a man and his wife's sister – public honesty was an important barrier to remarriage, but no one doubted that the pope had power to dispense with it.

According to Catherine, Arthur had never consummated their marriage, and therefore she was not related to Henry by affinity but only by public honesty. One of the tactics of the king's men was to impugn the dispensation granted by Julius II for Henry to marry Catherine, in that it was for the wrong impediment – affinity rather than public honesty. This tactic met with no success.[13]

Thus, by papal law as it was then practiced, there had been an easily dispensable barrier (public honesty) between Henry and Catherine, and a divinely ordained barrier (affinity) between him and Anne. He clearly believed the opposite, and he was reinforced in his belief by Thomas Cranmer, who wrote a treatise meant for Henry's eyes alone, *Twelve Articles*,[14] establishing that it was marriage and not intercourse that gave rise to affinity, a common-sense view that eventually won out universally. Meanwhile, however, a major effort of the public campaign for the annulment was to prove in court the likelihood, at the legatine trial in 1529, that the marriage of Arthur and Catherine had indeed been consummated.

When Henry finally took the matter into his own hands in 1533, after Cranmer's appointment as the archbishop of Canterbury had been confirmed by the pope, it was the indispensability of the Levitical degrees that came to the fore as the basis for annulling Henry's marriage, in a trial held at Dunstable. But for good measure it was also asserted that the marriage between Arthur and

[13] See Kelly, *The Matrimonial Trials of Henry VIII*, Index, s.v. "public honesty"; see also d'Avray, *Papacy, Monarchy, and Marriage, 860–1600*, 174–7.

[14] Kelly, *The Matrimonial Trials of Henry VIII*, chapter 13: "Cranmer and the King's Conscience," 222–38.

Catherine had been consummated. In the Act of Succession passed by Parliament in 1534, all marriages made within the Levitical degrees were declared invalid. As normally understood, this would include Henry's marriage to Anne, because of his previous sexual relations with her sister, Mary. In another act of 1534, Henry was recognized as Supreme Head of the Church in England, opening the way for more innovations in the laws of marriage.

HENRY VIII AND THE IMPEDIMENT OF PRECONTRACT (BIGAMY)

Another important aspect of marriage law for Henry was the nature of the marriage "contract," a term that referred not to financial arrangements, but to the very essence of marriage, the present-tense consent between the man and woman to become husband and wife. It was this alone that constituted a marriage, and once made, with or without witnesses, in or out of church, whether consummated by sexual intercourse or not, the bond was absolutely indissoluble, with no possibility of divorce (in the modern sense of legally breaking up a valid marriage).[15] The pope's powers to dissolve unconsummated marriages were even more strongly contested than his powers over the Levitical degrees: some canon lawyers said he could dissolve them, whereas other canonists, along with almost all theologians, denied such power; no examples of actual dissolutions before Henry's time have been found.

Henry obviously feared that Anne Boleyn had been secretly married in just such a way, for in 1527 he had obtained from Pope Clement VII an extraordinary dispensation allowing him (once freed of his marriage to Catherine) to marry any woman whomsoever, even though she was already married, as long as the union had not been consummated.[16]

When Cranmer wrote his treatise for Henry, probably early in 1533, he clearly did not know about Anne's previous marriage, since he argued that there was no way that such a marriage could be dissolved. Therefore, when he came to preside at the trial in 1536 impugning Henry's marriage to Anne, his conviction stood him in good stead for declaring the union invalid.

Since Anne was to be found guilty of treason and executed the next day, why, one might ask, did Henry insist on annulling the marriage before

15 There were actually a half dozen ways of dissolving a valid marriage, detailed by Noonan Jr., *Power to Dissolve*, notably, by one spouse entering a religious order within two months of contracting marriage and before consummation. Henry's ministers toyed with the idea that it would help toward annulment if Catherine were to retire to a nunnery, even though she had been married for twenty years and had produced children.

16 Kelly, *The Matrimonial Trials of Henry VIII*, pp. 51–3.

dissolving it by her death? The answer is that the annulment made the offspring of the union – their daughter, Elizabeth – illegitimate, just as Henry's first annulment had rendered his daughter Mary illegitimate.

Henry next married, with no delay and with no impediment in the way, Jane Seymour, who produced the long-desired male heir, a son they named Edward. Jane died in childbirth.

Henry's fourth marriage was a negotiated one, to the German noblewoman Anne, daughter of the Duke of Cleves. The wedding took place at the beginning of 1540, but Henry was immediately disappointed in his bride and sought a way out to marry his new inamorata, Catherine Howard, Anne's Boleyn's first cousin. Matters came to a head in July that year. On 5 July 1540, Parliament passed an extraordinary bill reducing marriage impediments. There was, of course, no need to eliminate the barrier of second-degree affinity between Henry and Catherine, since an earlier Parliament had limited all kinship impediments to the Levitical degrees. The most important provision of the new law concerned "precontract," that is, a previous and still existing marriage on the part of either the man or the woman intending to marry and woman intending to marry. (Historians frequently misunderstand precontract to mean "preliminary contract of some sort" rather than "previous marriage.") Canon law had always recognized that an *intended* marriage, that is, a betrothal, would be dissolved by an actual present-tense marriage to someone else. Now Parliament went further and declared that an *actual* marriage, if never consummated by sexual intercourse, would automatically be dissolved by a new marriage, if and when the new marriage was consummated. This is the way that Henry's 1527 dispensation was to have worked, except that there had been no provision about the new marriage needing to be consummated.

It is assumed that the real purpose of Parliament's provision on precontract was to clear away any previous marriage that Catherine might have had. Of course, Henry could have used it to end his marriage to Anne of Cleves, for he had evidence that she was already married to Francis of Lorraine. But he chose a different method. In a trial of his fourth marriage before a double convocation of the clergy, completed on 9 July, it was declared that the union was invalid because he had entered it with insufficient consent, being constrained by "force and fear" – that is, having been bullied into the match by his chief minister, Thomas Cromwell.

However, the parliamentary statute did serve as a back-up and ensured that Henry's marriage to Anne of Cleves would be disposed of, in case the annulment announced by convocation was called into question. But the main justification given in the bill itself was to remedy an abuse of papal law, whereby it had been possible to break up an openly contracted and solemnized marriage of long duration, to which children had been born, by finding a precontract, that is, an earlier marriage of one of the partners to someone else, and proving it by two witnesses, even though no such objection had been raised at the time of the subsequent marriage – in other words, the basis that had been used to annul the marriage of Henry VIII to Anne Boleyn!

THE PROBLEM OF CLANDESTINE MARRIAGES

Even apart from the machinations caused by Henry VIII's personal situations, there was a real need to reform marriage law. The chief business of the ecclesiastical courts was marriage entanglements arising from the policy of recognizing the validity of clandestine marriages.[17] It was incredibly easy to get married. All that was necessary was for an eligible man (or boy over the age of thirteen) and eligible woman (or girl over the age of eleven) to agree between themselves to get married, and they were immediately married, with no possibility of being unmarried until one of them died. Moreover, if they agreed only to get married sometime in the future, this would constitute a betrothal, *sponsalia de futuro*, and if they subsequently had sex, their union would suddenly convert into a real marriage, *sponsalia de praesenti*, and they would be bound to each other forever.[18]

Such secret marriages were illegal and sinful, punishable both by one's confessor in private and by the bishop's or archdeacon's court in public, and subject to penance and punishment; nevertheless, they were valid and inescapable. This quirk of law led to the most tangled cases of conscience and practical dilemmas. Let us say that a man and woman, John and Joan, entered into such a marriage secretly, and for some reason they did not proceed to public acknowledgment and wedding in church (solemnization). John then proceeded to marry another woman, Marjorie, publicly in another village; after children were born to this second marriage, Joan discovered what John had done and petitioned in the archdeacon's court that John be declared her husband. If John denied the original marriage, the archdeacon could only leave him and Joan to their consciences. Joan, knowing that she was married, could never marry again during John's lifetime. As for John, if he confessed to his parish priest that he had already been married when he married Marjorie, the priest would tell him that in the eyes of God he was married to Joan, but in the eyes of the church he was married to Marjorie and must continue living with her. However, he must never initiate sexual relations with Marjorie,

[17] Kelly, *Love and Marriage in the Age of Chaucer*, 168–76.
[18] See the origins of these medieval canon law rules in Chapter 10 herein.

though if she made the overture he must comply. He also had to agree to perform whatever penance the priest assigned him.

If, however, Joan was able to prove that John had married her, say, by the testimony of her sisters who actually overheard their declaration, or if John admitted it under oath, the archdeacon would declare the second marriage null and void and order John to take up residence with Joan, leaving Marjorie and her children bereft. If John admitted that he had said the words of marriage to Joan but did not mean them, intending only to seduce her, the verdict would be the same: in the eyes of God there was no marriage, but in the eyes of the church there was, and he was bound to it.

The solution attempted under Henry VIII to this messy situation was, as noted earlier, to declare an unconsummated marriage dissolved when one of the spouses entered into another marriage and consummated it. This, however, went against Archbishop Cranmer's theology, and in 1548, a year after Henry died, Parliament under Edward VI repealed the provision of making precontract automatically voidable. The excuse given for the reversion was that the new law had encouraged breach of contract.

The result was that English men who had gone along with the new religious legislation were back where they started, the same place that papal loyalists had been all along. The whole country was ordered back to papal law under Mary, Henry VIII's daughter by Catherine of Aragon, when, having previously been rehabilitated from her illegitimacy, she became queen in 1553. All was reversed again when Mary died in 1558 and her half-sister, Elizabeth, took over the realm. It was seemingly not noticed that Elizabeth was still officially illegitimate, since Mary had avoided repealing the part of the Act of Succession of 1536 that declared her so. And since the Levitical degrees were in full force, with divine affinity understood as induced by sexual intercourse, Elizabeth would be illegitimate not only because of her mother's bigamous marriage (caused by her precontract), but also by the fact that Anne was related to Henry VIII by first-degree affinity because of Henry's liaison with Mary Boleyn.

Shortly into Elizabeth's reign, at the end of 1563, the Catholic Council of Trent solved the problem of clandestine marriages by declaring them not only illicit (as they always had been), but also invalid from the beginning. To cite the text of the decretal *Tametsi*:

> This holy Synod sees that those prohibitions have not succeeded because of men's disobedience, and perceives the grave sins that have their origin from such clandestine marriages, especially in the case of those who live in a state of damnation from having left their first wives with whom they secretly

> contracted marriage and then openly contracted with other women and now live with them in perpetual adultery. Therefore, since the Church does not judge hidden matters, it can only address these evils by applying an efficacious remedy.[19]

"Living in perpetual adultery": that reminds us of Henry VIII's fears, which started this whole saga. Being married to his wife's brother could not precisely be called adultery, since his brother was dead, but it was almost as if he were alive, because of the Levitical law. But his scruples did not extend to Anne, even though she was by canon law his sister-in-law by sexual affinity. Nor did the fact that she was already married bother him, for, as we have seen, he obtained a papal dispensation to marry again in spite of precontract, once declared free of his marriage to Catherine. But even without papal dispensation, in his conscience Henry was already free of that marriage.

Once married to Anne, and having tired of her, he doubtless easily convinced himself that this marriage had not been valid after Cromwell assured him that Anne had consummated her precontract. Just so, presumably, he would believe that he had not really married Anne of Cleves because his heart was not in his consent to the union, having acted under political and moral pressure from Cromwell and the others who had arranged it. (Cromwell paid for it with his head shortly afterward.)

The marriage legislation passed in England did not reflect the sort of moral qualms manifested by Henry VIII and the Council of Trent. Even though Henry maintained Catholic belief concerning the Eucharist, he does not seem to have resisted the reformist abolition of the sacrament of confession; this in turn would have eliminated the need to make formal examinations of conscience. The act of 1548 on precontract did not go into questions like whether such unions were indissoluble (as Cranmer had professed before), nor was any legislation devoted to the question whether divinely prohibited affinity came only from marrying (Cranmer's original view) or from copula, as declared by the Act of Succession of 1536 (passed after the execution of Anne Boleyn, still in force), or from both marriage and copula, which was what the 1534 Act of Succession said.

We do know that Cranmer wished to make some radical changes to marriage law, as part of the general reform of canon law that was drawn up at this time, including the possibility of divorce (breaking up of a valid marriage) when one of the spouses commits adultery, and the allowance of remarriage for the innocent spouse. But the project never came to fruition.

19 For the Latin original, see *Enchiridion symbolorum*, 418, no. 1814.

LATER DEVELOPMENTS

Catholics who remained faithful to Rome would, of course, still observe the traditional canon law on marriage. By a technical quirk, the Trent decree *Tametsi* did not go into force until it was openly promulgated in each country or political entity, and as a result it did not apply in England. Therefore, the old laws on clandestine marriage and precontract were still in force among English Catholics as well as among adherents of the English Church.[20]

Earlier in 1563, the year of *Tametsi*, Matthew Parker, Archbishop of Canterbury, issued a table of forbidden degrees, making clear that blood relationship in the first degree (brother-sister) and first degree once removed (uncles/aunts, nephews/nieces) were divinely prohibited, as were the same relations of one's spouse after the spouse's death. So no marriage was allowed with sister-in-law, brother-in-law, uncle-in-law, aunt-in-law, niece-in-law, or nephew-in-law. And since affinity was said to be contracted either by unlawful intercourse or by lawful marriage, many other persons were also declared out of bounds by divine law: for instance, just as a man could not marry his wife's sister, so he could not marry the sister of a girl he had slept with once (thus, Henry VIII could not marry Anne Boleyn, because her sister Mary had been his mistress). Presumably God's law also prohibited breaking off an engagement to a woman and thereafter marrying her sister. Of course all affinal relationships in the direct line were also forbidden, notably father-in-law/daughter-in-law, mother-in-law/son-in-law.

On the other hand, a member of the new Church of England could marry any kind of cousin, even first cousins. This was an unheard-of freedom among Christians, although Jewish law had long allowed it.[21] In the old dispensation, and still true for loyal Catholics, for all practical purposes, you could not marry any cousin. Only fourth cousins or beyond were permitted, and who was likely to know any fourth cousins? Just as today, so then, even third cousins would hardly be recognizable. Still, under unusual circumstances, third and second cousins, and even first cousins, could be permitted to marry. Under still more unusual circumstances, some of the relationships mentioned in the book of Leviticus could be dispensed: so reaffirmed the Council of Trent.

The new codification of canon law produced in 1917[22] reduced the forbidden relations of consanguinity to the third degree; only second and first

[20] See Helmholz, *Roman Canon Law in Reformation England*, 69–73.

[21] See Chapter 1 herein.

[22] *Codex iuris canonici*; I use the edition of Rome, 1922, with preface by the chief compiler of the code, Cardinal Pietro Gasparri, and analytic index.

cousins needed dispensations (can. 1076). As already was the practice, first-cousin dispensations were granted only for serious reasons, one of which was the advanced age of the woman – which canonists set at twenty-four![23] Affinity now arose only from marriage, whether consummated or not (can. 97); therefore the impediment of affinity from illicit sexual relationship was eliminated. Affinity in the direct line (for instance, daughter-in-law, stepdaughter) invalidated all marriage, as always. Collateral affinity was reduced to the second degree, which meant that one could marry one's deceased wife's second cousin without obtaining a dispensation (can. 1077). The impediment of public honesty now arose from an invalid marriage or from public or notorious concubinage, which invalidated marriage in the direct line – for instance, to the daughter or mother of a putative wife or mistress (can. 1078).

However, dispensations from all closer degrees were obviously possible, except the direct line of consanguinity (parent-child, grandparent-grandchild) and first degree collateral (brother-sister): "Marriage is never to be permitted if there should exist any doubt that the parties are related by blood in any degree of the direct line or in the first degree of the collateral line" (can. 1076.3). This was not to say, however, that dispensations were actually impossible in these degrees in exigent circumstances. Cardinal Gasparri gives an example of a brother–sister marriage in Chile that was allowed to stand in 1916 when the couple became Catholic.[24]

Roman Catholic canon law was further revised in 1983.[25] The ban on consanguinity was reduced still further: henceforward, only first cousins and uncles and aunts and nieces and nephews needed dispensations (can. 1091).

Only direct affinity now impeded marriage (can. 1092); brothers-in-law and sisters-in-law were now allowed to marry. Understood, of course, is the death of the first spouse. Public honesty remained the same, being like direct affinity, except for invalid marriages (can. 1093). Thus, if a man's marriage were annulled, he could not marry his wife's mother or daughter, even though he could marry her sister. Furthermore, adopted brothers and sisters may not marry, nor may a man marry his adopted daughter (can. 1094).

As for the Church of England and English law,[26] Archbishop Parker's table of prohibited relationships was incorporated into the Book of Common Prayer, where it remained to modern times. Unlike traditional canon law, however, a marriage within these degrees was not void from

[23] Gasparri, *Tractatus canonicus de matrimonio*, 3rd ed., 1:241, no. 357.

[24] Gasparri, *Tractatus canonicus de matrimonio*, editio nova ad mentem, 1:133, 432–3; Kelly, "Kinship, Incest, and the Dictates of Law," 75.

[25] *Codex iuris canonici auctoritate Ioannis Pauli Pp. II promulgatus.*

[26] For what follows, see Kelly, *The Matrimonial Trials of Henry VIII*, 283–5.

the beginning, but only voidable, when brought to court. But an act of 1835 made them void from the start. In 1861, an act did away with any affinity except that caused by a legal marriage. No longer, then, was it divinely prohibited to enter into wedlock with a relative of someone you had an affair with. In 1907, the Deceased Wife's Sister's Marriage Act responded to what Gilbert and Sullivan sang about in *Iolanthe*, "He shall prick that annual blister, Marriage with deceased wife's sister." The grounds for the exception were in the text of Leviticus itself: "Neither shalt thou take a wife to her sister, to vex her, to uncover her nakedness besides the other, in her lifetime" (KJV, Leviticus 18:18). In 1921, the Deceased Brother's Widow's Marriage Act allowed the sort of marriage that Henry VIII had with Catherine of Aragon, in spite of Henry's conviction that it was against divine law, thereby giving more force to the Deuteronomical command than to the Levitical ban. An act of 1931 subtracted more degrees from the proscribed list, namely, nieces and aunts of a man's deceased wife, and uncles and nephews of a widow's deceased husband.

The Marriage Act of 1949 removed still more degrees, and left only the following relationships off-bounds, listed according to traditional canonical computing, with modifications made in the Marriage (Prohibited Degrees of Relationship) Act of 1986:

A. Direct consanguinity:
   1st degree: parent/child
   2nd degree: grandparent/grandchild
B. Collateral consanguinity:
   1st and 1st degree: brother/sister
   1st and 2nd degree: uncle/niece, aunt/nephew
C. Direct affinity:
   1st degree:
      (a) parent-in-law/child-in-law (1986: OK if both widowed; 2007: OK even if only divorced)
      (b) stepparent/stepchild (1986: OK if both twenty-one)
   2nd degree:
      (a) grandparent-in-law/grandchild-in-law
      (b) step-grandparent/step-grandchild (1986: OK if both twenty-one)
D. Collateral affinity (while first spouse is alive):
   1st and 1st degree: brother-in-law/sister-in-law
   1st and 2nd degree: uncle-in-law/niece-in-law, aunt-in-law/nephew-in-law

Let us look at part C, direct affinity, first degree, section (a), in-laws. After 1986, John Doe may marry his son's wife after John's wife died and after his son died. After 2007, by virtue of the Marriage Act of 1949 (remedial) Order 2007,

John may marry his daughter-in-law even if she is only divorced from his son and even if John is only divorced from his wife. Similarly, after 1986, John may marry his widowed mother-in-law after his wife died; now, after 2007, John may marry his mother-in-law while his father-in-law is still alive and while their daughter (John's ex-wife) is still alive. But John still may not marry his granddaughter-in-law or his grandmother-in-law under any circumstance, as far as stated law is concerned.

As for part C, first-degree direct affinity, section (b), step-relations: after 1986, John Doe may now marry his stepmother, that is, a widowed or divorced wife of his father. This is the relationship that so shocked St. Paul in writing to the Corinthians (1 Corinthians 5:1). But both have to be over twenty-one, and she cannot have been living with John as his stepmother before he turned eighteen. Similarly, John may marry his stepdaughter (his ex-wife's daughter by another man) as long as both are twenty-one, and as long as she was not living with John as his stepdaughter before the age of eighteen. The same rules hold for step-grandparents and step-grandchildren.

When it comes to collateral affinity (part D), it is still on the books that a man may not marry his uncle's wife until his uncle is dead. This is what Thomas of Lancaster (brother of Henry V) did, after his uncle John Beaufort died, when in 1412 Thomas married Beaufort's widow, Margaret Holland, acting on the first recorded dispensation in the Levitical degrees, granted by the recognized pope of the time. (Beaufort and Holland were the great-great-grandparents of Henry VIII.)

It is also still the law that brothers-in-law and sisters-in-law may not marry until their spouses die. That is exactly what young Prince Henry Tudor did after his brother Arthur died and left Catherine of Aragon a widow without children, after being dispensed by Pope Julius II. That is what Deuteronomy commanded a brother in his circumstances to do, but Leviticus, as then interpreted, forbade it.

As with many aspects of religion, morals, and life, so with the laws of incest: progress is seen sometimes in addition, sometimes in subtraction. For instance, in the realm of liturgy, it is common to expand services out of laudable motives to the point of making them burdensome; then a reform movement will reduce them to proper size or eliminate them altogether. Just so, motives of decency and familial integrity were at work in stipulating forbidden relationships. Whatever the motivations for the great expansion of forbidden degrees in the early Middle Ages, ever since that time there has been constant pressure to reduce them. There has been surprisingly little concern over dangers of interbreeding, after the topic was first introduced by Gregory the Great. But doubtless this genetic danger, and not the sort of religious scruple that troubled Henry VIII, is the main reason why the majority of states in the United States still prohibit first-cousin marriage.

RECOMMENDED READING

Brundage, James A. *Law, Sex, and Christian Society in Medieval Europe*. Chicago: University of Chicago Press, 1987.

D'Avray, David L. *Dissolving Royal Marriages: A Documentary History, 860–1600*. Cambridge: Cambridge University Press, 2014.

Papacy, Monarchy, and Marriage, 860–1600. Cambridge: Cambridge University Press, 2015.

Donahue, Charles, Jr. *Law, Marriage, and Society in the Later Middle Ages: Arguments about Marriage in Five Courts*. Cambridge: Cambridge University Press, 2007.

Helmholz, R. H. *Marriage Litigation in Medieval England*. Cambridge: Cambridge University Press, 1974.

Roman Canon Law in Reformation England. Cambridge: Cambridge University Press, 1990.

Ingram, Martin. *Church Courts, Sex, and Marriage in England, 1570–1640*. Cambridge: Cambridge University Press, 1987.

Joyce, George Hayward. *Christian Marriage: An Historical and Doctrinal Study*. 2nd edition. London: Sheed and Ward, 1948.

Kelly, Henry Ansgar. "Canonical Implications of Richard III's Plan to Marry His Niece." *Traditio* 23 (1967): 269–311.

"Kinship, Incest, and the Dictates of Law." *American Journal of Jurisprudence* 14 (1969): 69–78.

Love and Marriage in the Age of Chaucer. Ithaca, NY: Cornell University Press, 1975; reprint, Eugene, OR: Wipf and Stock, 2004.

The Matrimonial Trials of Henry VIII. Stanford, CA, 1976; reprinted with new foreword, Eugene, OR: Wipf and Stock, 2004.

Noonan, John T., Jr. *Power to Dissolve: Lawyers and Marriages in the Courts of the Roman Curia*. Cambridge MA: Harvard University Press, 1972.

Phillips, Roderick. *Putting Asunder: A History of Divorce in Western Society*. Cambridge: Cambridge University Press, 1988.

Scarisbrick, J. J. *Henry VIII*. London: Folio Society, 1968; reprinted with new foreword, New Haven, CT: Yale University Press, 1997.

Sheehan, Michael M. *Marriage, Family, and Law in Medieval Europe: Collected Studies*. Edited by James K. Farge. Toronto: University of Toronto Press, 1996.

15

Thomas Sanchez

Rafael Domingo

BIOGRAPHICAL INTRODUCTION

Jesuit Thomas Sanchez (Tomás Sánchez de Ávila) was a luminary of the Spanish Golden Age most noted for his contributions to the moral theology and canon law of marriage. Master of moral casuistry, man of erudition, meticulous writer, pious priest, and prudent spiritual guide and confessor, Sanchez was the primary post-Tridentine Catholic authority on marriage-related issues. His encyclopedic *Treatise on Marriage* (*De sancto matrimonii sacramento disputationum tomi tres*)[1] laid the foundations of the Catholic Church's moral theology and canon law of marriage until the promulgation of the first Code of Canon Law in 1917. Indeed, Sanchez's *Treatise on Marriage* is to the canon law of marriage what Blackstone's *Commentaries* is to Anglo-American law, or Robert-Joseph Pothier's *Treatise* is to French civil law. He did for canon law what Joseph Story did for U.S. law and Emer de Vattel did for international law.

Despite living far from the center of the scholastic academic world, Thomas Sanchez attained the intellectual reputation of his Spanish Jesuit colleagues Diego Laínez, Saint Francis Borgia, Francisco Suárez, Luis de Molina, Gabriel Vásquez, and Alfonso Salmerón. A man of great modesty, humble detachment, hard asceticism, and deep spirituality, Thomas Sanchez (probably unwittingly) determined the direction of the Catholic understanding of marriage for centuries. But the task was not easy. He struggled left and right. His *Treatise* was highly praised by both Pope Clement VIII and the Roman Curia, but his doctrine on mental reservation (a qualification tacitly added in

[1] I will use the following edition: R. Patris Thomae Sanchez Cordubensis e Societate Jesu, *De sancto matrimonii sacramento disputationum tomi tres* (Paris: Sumptibus Philippi Borde, Laurentii Arnaud & Claudii Rigaud, 1654). A digital version of this edition is now available on the Internet at the Biblioteca Digital Hispanica of the Biblioteca Nacional de España: http://bdh-rd.bne.es/viewer.vm?id=0000168941&page=1.

TOMVS TERTIVS
DISPVTATIONVM
DE SANCTO MATRI-
MONII SACRAMENTO.
AVTHORE THOMA SANCHEZ
Cordubensi è Societate IESV.

In hoc tertio tomo continentur liber octauus, qui est de Dispensationibus; & nonus, qui de Debito coniugali: ac demum decimus, qui de Diuortio agit, cum indice Rerum locupletissimo.

Anno 1623.

CVM PRIVILEGIO.

Madriti, Apud Ludouicum Sanchez, Regium Typographum.

FIGURE 15.1. Thomas Sanchez. Used by permission of the University of Navarra Library.
Old Collection FA 136.800-III

making a statement) was implicitly condemned by Pope Innocent XI. Sanchez's contribution was duly recognized by some canonists (e.g., Adhémar Esmein) but undermined by others (e.g., Friedrich von Schulte). His writings were considered highly profitable by some confessors and moralists (e.g., Alphonsus Maria de Liguori) but morbid, nasty, and almost pornographic by the most rigorist Jansenists. Sanchez's casuistry and probabilism were explicitly criticized by Blaise Pascal in his *Provincial Letters*.[2] Montesquieu, too, must have been referring to Sanchez when he mercilessly attacked the casuists in his *Persian Letters*: "Here are the casuists, who open the secrets of the night up to the light of day. Their imagination gives shape to all the monsters that the demon of love can produce, and putting them together and comparing them in all different ways, they make such monsters the object of all of their thoughts."[3]

Sanchez's works were both praised and criticized by his Jesuit colleagues. Because of his approach to some controversial moral issues, especially regarding the conditions for the moral justification of seeking sexual pleasure, the general superior of the Jesuits, Claudio Acquaviva, wrote to Sanchez (in November 1608, December 1608, and March 1609) asking for general moderation and modifications, to protect the Society of Jesus against Protestant attacks. Sanchez accepted the corrections.[4] After his death, Sanchez's works were censored by the Superiors of the Society of Jesus. Despite it all, Sanchez became popular for his wisdom, asceticism, and holiness. Students joked of Sanchez that he knew marriage better than the devil, and that, paradoxically, he was an expert on all the intricacies of the marriage bed without ever having married.

We do not have much information about Thomas Sanchez's life. What we do know suggests that his was the ordinary and relatively quiet life of a full-time casuist focused on writing, teaching, preaching, and spiritual guidance in the south of Spain. The most interesting account of his life that we have is an obituary written by Jesuit Luis Ponce, then rector of the College of Granada, on Wednesday, 19 May 1610, just hours after the fifty-nine-year-old Sanchez had died of pneumonia.[5]

Sanchez was born in the Andalusian city of Cordoba (Spain) in 1550, probably in October, to a wealthy and educated family. In 1567, he entered the Society of Jesus, just eleven years after its founder, Ignatius of Loyola, had died. Sanchez's admission into the Society was at first refused because of his

[2] Pascal, *The Provincial Letters*, 47–8. [3] See Montesquieu, *Persian Letters*, 200.

[4] Extracts of the letter can be read in Lozano Navarro, *Tomás Sánchez*, 81.

[5] The letter was published by Bajén Español, *Pensamiento de Tomás Sánchez, S.J. sobre moral sexual*, 356–64. See Hartmann and Pennington, eds., *The History of Courts and Procedure in Medieval Canon Law*.

strong stammer. But after praying for a cure to the Virgin Mary at the shrine of Our Lady of the Holy Fountain (Nuestra Señora de la Fuensanta), highly venerated in Cordoba, Sanchez was miraculously healed, and his application was granted. (According to some contemporaneous accounts, however, he did always retain a slight stammer.)

Sanchez moved to Granada in 1568, the same year that the second Morisco[6] rebellion started, the so-called Rebellion of the Alpujarras. He spent the rest of his life in the Jesuit College of Saint Paul, founded in 1554. Around 1575 or 1576, Sanchez was ordained as a priest, and on 8 February 1587, in accordance with the Jesuit Constitutions, he and fellow Jesuit Martín de Guzmán professed a fourth vow of obedience to the pope, in the Church of Saint Catalina in Cordoba. It is possible that this delay in his profession was the result of some troubles Sanchez had had with the Inquisition and the superiors after a witness declared at the Inquisition that Sanchez had advised him not to make any declaration as a witness.

In Granada, Sanchez was deeply engaged in evangelizing the Moriscos; in shepherding his brothers as master of novices, spiritual director, and confessor; and in advising the rector of the College of Granada as well as Archbishop Pedro de Castro y Quiñones, to whom Sanchez dedicated his *Treatise* on marriage. Still, Sanchez spent the better part of his time on his scholarly work – sometimes as much as twelve hours a day.

Sanchez's spirit of penance, firm austerity, and gift for resolving problems of conscience were legendary. He based his spirituality on contemplation of the love of Christ in the Eucharist and the patience of Jesus crucified, as well as sincere devotion to the Virgin Mary. He would suffer hardship in silence and never make excuses. According to his spiritual director, Sanchez never lost his baptismal innocence. He was buried in the church of the College of Saint Paul in Granada (currently the parish of the martyrs Justus and Pastor). Following several transfers, his mortal remains have come to rest since 1921 in the cemetery of the Society of Jesus on the campus of La Cartuja at the university in Granada.

A posthumous and anonymous portrait of Sanchez hangs at the Faculty of Theology of the University of Granada. Sanchez is seated at his desk writing in

6 The Moriscos (Spanish for "Moor-like") were Muslims in Spain and Portugal who were forced to convert to Christianity at the beginning of the sixteenth century. Many Moriscos continued to practice Islam, most in secret, but some did so openly. A decree issued by King Philip II of Spain in 1567 (Pragmatic Sanction of 1567) obliged the Moriscos to adopt Spanish language, dress, and customs. A number of unsuccessful rebellions by the Moriscos led to their relocation from Granada to other parts of Spain, particularly Castile. At the beginning of the seventeenth century, the Moriscos were expelled from Spain to North Africa.

the presence of Diego Granado, another famous Jesuit of the college. His gaze is sweet and deep, and his face serene; his baldness is prominent, and his beard slightly worn. We know that the portrait was painted (or finished) after 1634, because it includes Sanchez's posthumous book *Consilia* (1634).

TREATISE ON MARRIAGE AND OTHER WORKS

Sanchez's most important work is his monumental *De sancto matrimonii sacramento disputationum tomi tres.* Its first volume came out in Genoa in 1602, and the remaining two volumes were published in Madrid in 1605. It is a leading work not just for theologians, but also for canon and civil lawyers.[7] Sanchez's approach was deeply influenced by the doctrines of Thomas Aquinas, whom he called "Prince of Theologians,"[8] as well as by contemporary legal authors such as Martín de Azplicueta (Doctor Navarrus) and Diego de Covarrubias y Leiva. The *Treatise* shows an extraordinary knowledge of Spanish civil law (*The Partidas, The Laws of Toro, The New Recompilation*) and canon law (*Corpus Iuris Canonici*), as well as of biblical and theological sources.

The three volumes are divided into ten books, which fall into one of two broad categories: the formation of a marriage (*matrimonium in fieri*), and marital life itself (*matrimonium in facto esse*). Following the Decretals of Gregory IX (book IV title I), Sanchez opens book 1 of his treatise by dealing with betrothal. In book 2, he deals with the essence of marriage and of marital consent. Here is probably where the reader can find Sanchez's most important contributions on marriage. The fifty-four *disputationes* of book 3, on clandestine consent, are focused specifically on the (then recently promulgated) Tridentine requirement that marital consent be exchanged before a parish priest and two witnesses. Book 4, on coerced consent, is quite original; here Sanchez defends a new doctrine on duress that was generally accepted by canonists and is still reflected in the 1983 Code of Canon Law. Sanchez also firmly defends the validity of marriage without parental consent, in accordance with Tridentine legislation. In book 5, on conditional consent, he emphasizes the idea of freedom of contract. Sanchez affirms the possibility of conditional consent even after the Council of Trent imposed a requirement of formal solemnization. Book 6, on donations between spouses, was certainly interesting for contemporary lawyers but is now entirely obsolete. Book 7, on impediments, incorporated the new Tridentine adjustments to the law concerning affinity and consanguinity. The most developed part of book 7 treats

7 See *De matrimonio, proemio*, fol. I.
8 *De matrimonio, proemio*, fol. I. See Chapter 11 herein on Thomas Aquinas.

the natural impediment of impotence (disputations 92–114). That Sanchez dedicates the whole of book 8 to dispensations (in general and in the realm of marriage) shows their growing importance to modern canon law and the deepening connection between canon law and pastoral care.[9] Book 9, on conjugal debt, was the most controversial because of Sanchez's approach to sexual pleasure. The book constitutes a general treatise on sexual morality and the capital sin of lust. Finally, book 10 deals with the reasons that can justify separation from the marriage bed and from cohabitation, specifically in cases of adultery, apostasy and heresy, inducement to sin, and illness.

During Sanchez's lifetime, two new editions of his work were published (Venice, 1606, and Antwerp, 1607). Its multiple editions (Antwerp, Lyon, Venice, Madrid, Paris, among others), especially after his death, show that the *Treatise* was broadly available in Europe. The *Treatise* was also the object of various epitomes, digests, briefs, and compendia (E. L. Soares in 1648, J. A. Cadeus in 1656, and F. Noel in 1732, among others). Even a book compiling all the aphorisms contained in the *Treatise* was published in Frankfurt in 1712.[10] Parts of book 9, on conjugal debt, were censured and criticized for their retail realism. In a defense, Sanchez himself acknowledged "that writing on goofy things is indeed shameful and indecent. However, doing so by necessity and public utility, and maintaining composure in style and manner of saying is not indecent but very fitting and fair to do, and even mandatory for those who shall hold the office of teachers."[11]

In 1613, soon after Sanchez's death, a second work appeared in Madrid titled *Explicatio Mandatorum Decalogi* (*Explanation on the Ten Commandments*). The work is best known, however, by the title of later editions: *Opus morale in præcepta Decalogi*.[12] Its first volume was prepared by Sanchez, but the second was compiled based on manuscript notes. These works also went through several editions. Something similar happened with his third work on legal and

[9] It was an omission in *disputatio* 7 no. 4 of this book that led to the listing of the whole third volume of a posthumous edition of the treatise (Venice, 1614) on the *Index of Prohibited Books* from 1627 to 1900. The reason was that the new edition of Sanchez's *Treatise* omitted a mention of the right of the pope to legitimate children without the permission of the civil authority. The omission was interpreted as a restriction of papal sovereignty. The prohibition was maintained in the constitution *Officiorum ac munerum* (25 January 1897) of Pope Leo XIII, but it was lifted in 1900.

[10] *Aphorismi R. P. Thomae Sanchez*. A digital version of the book is available at the Bayerische StaatsBibliothek Digital: http://reader.digitale-sammlungen.de/de/fs1/object/display/bsb10597238_00005.html. This summary was first published by decree of the Sacred Congregation of the Index in 1627.

[11] See part of Sanchez's self-defense published by Lozano Navarro, *Tomás Sánchez*, 114.

[12] A reprint of this work: *Opus morale in praecepta Decalogi*.

moral opinions, *Consilia seu opuscula moralia* (Lyon, 1634). Sanchez could not finish his *Consilia*, and it was published based on his notes and manuscripts. It is not easy to know exactly what belongs strictly to Sanchez and what was added or deleted by the editors. A short instruction for confessors, probably written by Sanchez on the occasion of the pastoral visit of Archbishop Pedro de Castro to the diocese of Granada in 1591, was published in 1982.[13]

HISTORICAL CONTEXT

Sanchez lived at the beginning of the convulsive period of the Catholic Revival or Counter Reformation, which started with the Council of Trent (1545–63) and ended with the Peace of Westphalia (1648). The Protestant Reformation not only brought a breach in the unity of faith of the Christian world; it also gave rise in many areas, specifically in marriage, to new ecclesiastical practices or disciplines. A great variety of core theological and moral issues of the Protestant Reformation were affected by the canon law of marriage. Unlike Catholics, the Reformers rejected the sacramental nature of marriage, the monopolization of marriage by ecclesiastical law, the prohibition against divorce (including remarriage), and the inherent superiority of celibacy to marriage. According to the Reformers, civil law and not canon law should regulate and govern marriage. As a consequence, the Reformers reconceptualized the institution of marriage by developing a new civil law of marriage. They promoted the creation of marriage courts to replace ecclesiastical courts; they removed many impediments not countenanced by scripture; they allowed clerical and monastic marriage and remarriage; and they advocated for the public character of both marriage and divorce.[14]

For these reasons, it is understandable that in the doctrinal and disciplinary agenda of the Council of Trent, marriage occupied a central place. In the seventh session (3 March 1547), the council approved the decree On Sacraments, whose first canon reproduced the list of the seven sacraments adopted at the Council of Florence (1439), which included marriage.[15] The issue of marriage was specifically discussed in 1547 and 1552, but, owing to political circumstances, it was not until 1563 that

[13] See *Práctica sobre los mandamientos de la ley de Dios y de la Iglesia*, 215–333. On the different editions of the works of Thomas Sanchez, see Olivares, "Ediciones de la Obra de Tomas Sanchez," 53–119.

[14] For a general overview on the Protestant Reformation on marriage, see Witte Jr., *Law and Protestantism*, esp. 199–255. See further Chapters 12–14 herein on Martin Luther, John Calvin, and Henry VIII.

[15] See Schroeder, *Canons and Decrees of the Council of Trent*, 51.

marriage was definitively debated and embodied in the famous decree *Tametsi*, adopted in the forty-fourth session of the Council of Trent, on 11 November 1563.[16]

Tametsi prohibited clandestine marriages, thenceforth recognizing as valid only those unions that were contracted in the presence of a pastor and two or three witnesses. So the Church's practice would depend not just on the doctrines on consent and impediments, but also on the requirement of canonical form for marital validity. Without this canonical form, the weddings of Catholics would be considered invalid. *Tametsi* also declared that the bond of marriage was contracted by the will of the spouses and that parental consent was not necessary for validity. Finally, *Tametsi* declared, against the Protestant Reformers, particularly Martin Luther, that adultery did not dissolve the marriage bond and therefore was not an acceptable basis for remarriage. Although *Tametsi* was not binding where the laws of Trent were not promulgated, *Tametsi* transformed as a matter of fact both Catholic discipline and Catholic doctrine on marriage.

From an intellectual-historical point of view, Sanchez lived at the height of the Second Scholasticism and, more specifically, at the beginning of the so-called Jesuit scholasticism. The latter's main features were a reinforcement of the link between law and moral theology, and a burgeoning of casuistry. Jesuitical literature emphasized the idea that patristic and scholastic philosophy and Roman and canon law should converge in the systematization of Catholic moral doctrine in manuals and treatises. The Jesuits' commitment to casuistry was a natural development of their own spirituality and organization, very much focused on problems of personal choice and discernment and on involvement in human activities rather than withdrawal. Casuistry tried to bolster confidence in moral principles, though it really only promised moral probability rather than moral certainty. Indeed, the doctrine of moral probabilism was at the heart of high casuistry.[17] Based on the work of thinkers like Domingo de Soto and Thomas Cajetan, Spanish theologian Bartolomé de Medina defended the thesis that if an opinion is probable, it is licit to follow it, even if the opposite opinion is more probable. With different nuances and arguments, probabilism was supported by many Jesuits such as Gabriel Vásquez, Luis Molina, Francisco Suárez, and Thomas Sanchez himself.

16 For an English translation of *Tametsi*, see ibid., 183–90.

17 For an overview on moral casuistry, see Jonsen and Toulmin, *The Abuse of Casuistry*, esp. 164–75.

SANCHEZ'S CONTRIBUTION TO THE CANON LAW OF MARRIAGE

An architect of the post-Tridentine system of canon law on marriage, Sanchez fit together all the pieces of a complex puzzle of the law of marriage. He was more encyclopedic than original, but even so, he made important contributions to the canon law of marriage by providing good reasons and arguments as well as a solid structure to the institution as a whole. He developed a coherent contractual doctrine on marriage while supporting its sacramental character. He built a useful bridge between marital contract and the sacrament of marriage, between theology and law, civil law and canon law, and law and morality. In doing so, he also made some contributions to sexual morality.

Sanchez (*De matrimonio* 2.1.2) identified seven elements for the existence of a marriage, namely: (1) internal consent (*consensus*); (2) external contract (*contractus*); (3) mutual transfer of power over the body (*traditio*) as an immediate contractual effect; (4) a permanent bond (*vinculum*) that arises from the contract; (5) mutual obligation of the conjugal debt (*debitum conjugale*); (6) a right of each spouse over the other (*ius*); and finally (7) the consummation of the marriage (*consummatio*). Sanchez holds that the essence of marriage is neither in the internal consent nor in the external contract. These constitute efficient causes of marriage, but not its essence as such, since they are operative only in its formation. Neither does he locate the essence of marriage in consummation (2.1.3). As a matter of fact, Sanchez argues, the marriage between the Virgin Mary and Saint Joseph was a true marriage despite never being consummated. Nor is the essence of marriage, for Sanchez, found in the marital debt, or in the right to each spouse over the other. In case of adultery, for instance, the obligation of giving the conjugal debt ceases, but the marital bond remains. So the essence of marriage lies in the unique and permanent conjugal bond (*conjunctio*) by which spouses are formally united as a consequence of mutual self-giving (2.1.6 and 8). The external contract is only an expression of this mutual self-giving.

Sanchez explained with new nuances and implications the essence of marriage as both a natural and a sacramental institution. Marriage is a natural institution created by God when the divine Creator blessed man and woman with the words, "Be fruitful and multiply" (Genesis 1:28). In addition to the natural contract of marriage, Christian marriage is also the sacrament of the covenant of Christ and the church, Sanchez insisted. Since marriage signifies and communicates grace, marriage between baptized persons is a true sacrament of the New Covenant. The presence of Jesus at the wedding in Cana symbolizes his approval of marriage (2.4.4), but the most powerful Gospel support for the elevation of marriage to the category of a sacrament can be found in Matthew 19:6: "So they are no longer two but one." Following Robert Bellarmine, Sanchez also found good support for the sacramentality of marriage in the letter of Saint Paul to the Ephesians 5:22–3: "Wives, submit yourselves to your own husbands as you do to the Lord. For the husband is the head of the wife as Christ is the head of the church, his body, of which he is the Savior."

For baptized people, contractual (natural) marriage and sacramental marriage are not identical but are inseparable. The sacramentality is not a super-addition or supplement to the natural marriage nor a new marriage instituted by Christ, but an emanation of natural marriage itself by the fact that the spouses are united to Christ through baptism. For that reason, if one of the baptized parties intentionally rejects the sacramental aspect of the marriage, no natural contractual marriage can arise either. Moreover, Sanchez's view that the baptism of (previously wedded) spouses makes their marriage sacramental without any active renewal of consent is today accepted (over Bellarmine's contrary view) by canonists.

For Sanchez, procreation (including the subsequent education of children) is the intrinsic and primary end of marriage and cannot be negated by the parties. In addition to this end, there are other, subjective and *external* ends of marriage that depend on the spouses rather than the nature of marriage itself, such as mutual support and the so-called remedy against concupiscence, that is, protection against sexual sin. These ends do not constitute the essence of marriage and are subordinated to the first and primary end, which, for Sanchez, is procreation.

Sanchez's approach to sexual morality is based on the principle of the radical equality and complementarity of the spouses (9.2.1) and on the goodness of sexual intercourse within marriage when it is ordered to its natural end. Sanchez distinguishes between the obligation to accept the good of procreation (*proles*) and the obligation to copulate. Sexual intercourse is a meritorious and good act within marriage provided that the spouses are in the grace of God. Therefore, there is no sin when spouses copulate together. They have the right to do so, directly derived from the marital contract. However, the exercise of this right is not a mandatory obligation for fulfilling the ends of marriage. On the other hand, it is immoral to try to exercise the right in pursuit of pleasure alone (9.11). Pleasure cannot be treated as an end in itself, since it is just the consequence of an act. Moreover, it is mortally sinful to seek sexual pleasure beyond marriage. Additionally, sperm is always ordered to generation, so a man may not ejaculate voluntarily outside of proper marital intercourse (9.17.15).

Indissolubility as an essential property of marriage lies neither in the contract nor in the sacrament of marriage. It is based on the union between Christ and the church by the mystery of incarnation. For this reason, only a consummated sacramental marriage is absolutely and radically indissoluble. The indissolubility of an unconsummated sacramental marriage is merely relative and is based on mutual love, rather like the union between Christ and the soul in the state of grace, or between the members of the church and Christ; for mortal sin can break the personal union with God but not the indissoluble union between God and the church as such. The indissolubility of a consummated natural marriage is based on divine positive law (2.13.2). Natural marriage between unbaptized people is indissoluble because the law of Christ compels all human beings, but exception can be made to dissolve natural marriage for the good of the faith. This possibility of dissolution shows that the indissolubility of natural consummated marriage is not based on natural law, since the latter is universal and permanent and cannot allow exceptions (2.13.7).

According to Sanchez, when baptized Christians intend to exclude the sacramental good, their marriage is null and void from the beginning, since that exclusion affects the essence of marriage, the permanent bond. This happens, for instance, when the partners intend to contract a temporary marriage or a non-exclusive union. However, when one or both of the spouses intentionally exclude fidelity or procreation, that does not make a marriage null from the beginning but just voidable; it does not affect the permanent essential character of the bond, merely the fulfillment of the contract (2.29.11). For that reason, an intention contrary to the goods of fidelity or procreation makes a marriage null and void from the beginning only when it is expressly formalized in the contract. In this case, the invalidity of marriage derives not from the internal consent (intention) of either or both of the parties who exclude fidelity or procreation, but from the very existence of such an excluding stipulation in the contract of marriage. A contrary approach, still with some traces of Sanchez's doctrine, can be found in the current canon 1001 §1 1983 CIC.

Sanchez became an expert at differentiating marriage from other contracts when necessary to protect the essence of marriage, especially regarding defects in consent. His doctrine on marital duress was relevant and very influential, especially among the Jesuits. According to Roman law and classical canon law, based on the Aristotelian tradition, contracts effected by duress were not invalid and null automatically but just voidable at the petition of the coerced party. "Although under compulsion, I consented," wrote the late classic Roman jurist Paulus.[18] Sanchez himself insisted on the validity and subsequent voidability of a contract effected by coercion,[19] but he recognized that this general rule could not be applied to sacramental marriage, which demanded a higher degree of

[18] See Paulus, D. 4.2.21.5, in *Justiniani Digesta. Corpus Iuris Civilis* I (ed. Theodor Mommsen, Paul Krüger), available at: http://droitromain.upmf-grenoble.fr/Corpus/d-04.htm#2.

[19] See *De matrimonio* 4.8.4 and 4.15.6.

freedom and purification of the will. The effect of duress on sacramental marital consent was the complete nullity of marriage *ab initio*. However, since the non-baptized are not subject to the laws of the Catholic Church, a marriage contracted by them under duress will be valid but voidable (4.14.4).

Sanchez opened the doors to secular law by giving reasonable scope to the newborn nation-state. Unlike Basilio de Ponce de León,[20] among others, Sanchez defended the idea that secular princes could establish marital impediments for their Catholic subjects, unless this power was reserved by the pope (2.3.2; see also 7.3.2).[21] He also argued that a custom could derogate a diriment impediment.[22] In doing so, Sanchez tried to build a bridge between canon law and the law of nation-states. According to Sanchez, the sacramental character of marriage does not preclude it from the ordination of the civil law. As long as marriage is a civil contract, it should be submitted to civil law. However, the church can limit the power of Christian princes in order to protect the spiritual goods of marriage. Non-Christian princes have the right to regulate marital contracts for non-Christians in accordance with natural law. Civil law can add or increase penalties when an act is forbidden and contrary to canon law, but it cannot punish what is permissible in canon law (for instance, civil law cannot punish daughters who marry without paternal consent by authorizing their disinheritance).[23]

Sanchez's *Treatise* was an important source of inspiration for the first Code of Canon Law by the Catholic Church in 1917, as well as of hundreds of judicial decisions of the Apostolic Tribunal of the Roman Rota on marital issues. The Roman Rota quoted Sanchez 464 times between 1918 and 1947 in judicial decisions regarding marriage annulments based on defect of consent, coerced consent, and the impediment of impotence.[24] But Sanchez's legacy remains even today. Some canons of the 1983 Code of Canon Law of the Catholic Church were based on Sanchez's arguments. Canon §1142 captures Sanchez's teaching on the power of the Roman pontiff to dissolve, for just cause, an unconsummated marriage even between baptized persons. Canon 1159 captures

20 Ponce de León, *De sacramento matrimonii tractatus*, book 6, chapter 2, no 2.

21 See a contrary regulation in canon 1075§2 of the 1983 Code of Canon Law: "Only the supreme [head of the Catholic Church] has the right to establish other impediments for the baptized."

22 Canon 1076 of 1983 Code of Canon law prohibits it: "A custom which introduces a new impediment or is contrary to the existent impediments is reprobated." On diriment impediments, see further Chapter 10 herein on Popes Alexander III and Innocent III.

23 On the relation between canon law and civil law in Sanchez, see Donahue Jr., "The Role of the Humanists and the Second Scholastics in the Development of European Marriage Law from the Sixteenth to the Nineteenth Centuries," 50–1.

24 For the grounds on which Roman Rota decisions are based, see Ulrich Mosiek, *Die "probati auctores" in den Ehenichtigkeitsprozessen der S. R. Rota seit Inkrafttreten des Codex Iuris Canonici.*

his doctrine on the possibility of convalidating a marriage with a defect of consent if the spouse who did not consent now consents. Examples abound.

CONCLUSION

Thomas Sanchez's work on marriage is probably the most important attempt of the post-Tridentine period to synthesize the canon law of marriage. It was the standard guide for confessors, spiritual directors, canonists, and theologians for centuries. It is a product of his time, but in many ways it also transcends his time by being based on good reasons and argumentation as well as historical tradition and encyclopedic erudition. Influenced by moral probabilism and legal consensualism, Sanchez categorized, systematized, and clarified the Tridentine doctrine of marriage in light of classical canon law. Indeed, at no point does it break with the latter tradition. Following the standards and inspiration of the Second Scholastics, Sanchez first presented the historical solution offered by the European *ius commune*, even where the Council of Trent had made substantial modifications. Systematic, voluminous, and technical, like other legal treatises written by the Jesuits of his day, Sanchez's *Treatise on Marriage* masterfully intertwines the moral, legal, and theological dimensions of the marital institution. Sanchez goes into deep detail on moral issues, like a doctor interrogating his or her patients, but the book is not morbid, for it is written by an ascetic and humble person with the 'sole intention of helping confessors, moral theologians, and canonists.

Sanchez emphasized the relation between the canon law of marriage and the general doctrine of contract law. In his approach to marriage as a contract, Sanchez overestimated the legal dimension of marriage, imposing on marriage some rules of contract law that cannot be applied to an intimate communion of love that affects the spouses to their core. Marriage cannot be treated as a contract, because no contract can give rise to a personal commitment of love so radical as the one that arises from the conjugal bond. In this context, the pastoral constitution *Gaudium et Spes* of the Second Vatican Council and subsequent documents of the Catholic Church have preferred the words *covenant*, *communion*, *union*, and *bond* to *contract*.[25] Even so, as Catholic marriage is today in a process of

[25] See, for instance, the pastoral constitution *Gaudium et Spes* (1965) no 48.1; canon 776 of The Code of Canons of the Eastern Churches (1990), Catechism of the Catholic Church (1992) nos. 1601–66, the Compendium of the Catechism of the Catholic Church (2005) nos. 337–50. The 1983 code, however, did not dispense with the idea of marriage contract (see, for instance, the foundational canon 1055§2). It mentions marriage as a covenant in just three canons (c. 1055§1, 1057§2, and 1063 no 4).

decontractualizing – going, in some ways, in the opposite direction from the one Sanchez proposed – his work may now merit more attention than ever.

RECOMMENDED READING

Alfieri, Fernanda. *Nella camera degli sposi. Tomas Sanchez, il matrimonio, la sessualita (secoli XVI–XVII)*. Bologna: Società editrice il Mulino, 2010.

Bajén Español, Melchor. *Pensamiento de Tomás Sánchez SJ sobre moral sexual*. Granada: Universidad de Granada, 1976.

Brundage, James A. *Law, Sex, and Christian Society in the Medieval Europe*. Chicago: University of Chicago Press, 1990.

Carrodeguas Nieto, Celestino, *La sacramentalidad del matrimonio. Doctrina de Tomás Sánchez*. Madrid: Universidad Pontificia de Comillas, 2003.

Decock, Wim. *Theologians and Contract Law. The Moral Transformation of the ius commune (ca. 1500–1650)*. Leiden; Boston: Martinus Nijhoff Publishers, 2013.

Donahue, Charles, Jr. "The Role of the Humanists and the Second Scholastic in the Development of European Marriage Law from the Sixteenth to the Nineteenth Centuries." In *Law and Religion. The Legal Teaching of the Protestant and Catholic Reformations*, edited by Wim Decock, Jordan J. Ballor, Michael Germann, and Laurent Waelkens, 45–62. Göttingen: Vandenhoeck & Ruprecht, 2014.

Fantappiè, Carlo. *Chiesa romana e modernità giuridica*. Vol. I. *L'edificazione del sistema canonistico (1563–1903)*. Milan: Giuffrè, 2008.

Johnsen, Albert R. and Stephen Toulmin. *The Abuse of Casuistry: A History of Moral Reasoning*. Berkeley; Los Angeles: University of California Press, 1990.

Lozano Navarro, Juan José. *Tomás Sánchez*. Granada: Comares, 2000.

Mäkinen, Virpi and Petter Korkman, eds. *Transformations in Medieval and Early-Modern Rights Discourse*. Dordrecht: Springer, 2006.

Naz, Raoul. "Sanchez, Thomas." In *Dictionnaire de droit canonique*, 7: 864–70. Paris: Letouzey et Ané, 1965.

Olivares, Estanislao. "Más datos para una biografía de Tomás Sánchez." In *Archivo Teológico Granadino* 60 (1997): 25–50.

Viejo-Ximénez, José Miguel. "Tomás Sánchez." In *Diccionario General de Derecho Canónico* VII, edited by Javier Otaduy, Joaquín Sedano, and Antonio Viana, 144–6. Cizur Menor: Aranzadi, 2013.

Witte, John, Jr. *Law and Protestantism: The Legal Teaching of the Lutheran Reformation*. Cambridge; New York: Cambridge University Press, 2002.

16

John Selden

Jason P. Rosenblatt

BIOGRAPHICAL INTRODUCTION

John Selden (1584–1654) was acknowledged by his contemporaries and by posterity to be the most learned person of seventeenth-century England.[1] Edward Hyde, First Earl of Clarendon, further emphasized Selden's strong commitment to decorum:

> Selden . . . was of so Stupendous Learning in all Kinds, and in all Languages . . . that a Man would have thought He had been entirely conversant among Books, and had never spent an Hour but in Reading and Writing; yet his Humanity, Courtesy, and Affability was such, that He would have been thought to have been bred in the best Courts, but that his Good Nature, Charity, and Delight in doing good, and in communicating all He knew, exceeded that Breeding.[2]

Selden's career justifies Clarendon's emphasis on his scholarship, nobility of character, and charity. Respecting decorum to a remarkable degree, Selden defended the liberty of the subject in a number of venues, always adjusting his arguments to his audience: on the floor of the Westminster Assembly of Divines in the 1640s, where he was a minority lay member at odds with the majority of Presbyterian ministers, whose attempts to gain civil power he opposed; in the House of Commons, where he was one of the few survivors

[1] While he may not have equaled Newton, Hobbes, or Milton in creative genius, his erudition was unmatched. For example, he had a reading knowledge of twenty languages: English, Latin, Greek, Hebrew, Arabic, Aramaic, French, German, Spanish, Italian, Welsh, Old English, Anglo-Norman, Turkish, Syriac, Armenian, Samaritan, Persian, Slavonic, and Ethiopic. Selden quotes all his sources in their original languages, but this chapter does not, lest the various fonts create problems for the press.

[2] Hyde, *The Life of Edward Earl of Clarendon*, 1:29.

FIGURE 16.1. Portrait of John Selden (1584–1654) from "Lodge's British Portraits," 1823 (litho), English School, (nineteenth century) / Private Collection / Ken Welsh / Bridgeman Images

to continue in the Long Parliament of the 1640s his opposition, begun in the 1620s, to the abuse of royal prerogative; at table while living in a *ménage à trois* with the Earl and Countess of Kent, where his candid, unpretentious, transcribed conversation found its way into the literary canon as *Table Talk*; and in his immense scholarly works on various topics, especially Jewish law, not least the Jewish law of sex, marriage, and family life, and his three-volume *De Synedriis*, a history of the Great Synedrion as a continuous civil rather than ecclesiastical institution.

Clarendon was right to connect Selden's charity with his desire to communicate all he knew. His generous heart must be taken into account when considering the remarkably well-documented examples of philanthropy by a commoner from the middle class. His correspondence documents his direct relief of impecunious scholars. While a generous spirit cannot be legislated, Selden's view of scholarship participated in a tradition dating back at least to Pythagoras, who was the first to have said, "Friends hold all things in common."[3] Selden exhibited a broad spectrum of sharing, with his scholarly contributions at one end and individual acts of charity at the other.

Selden's *De Jure Naturali et Gentium, Iuxta Disciplinam Ebraeorum* (*On Natural Law and the Law of Nations According to the Teaching of the Jews*) (1640) conceives of the moral imperatives of natural law in terms of the rabbinic Noachide laws or *praecepta Noachidarum*, divine universal laws of perpetual obligation. These were the pre-Mosaic commandments against idolatry, blasphemy, shedding blood, sexual sins, theft, and eating part of a living animal, along with the positive injunction to establish a legal system. Selden believed that these shared moral rules provide a basis for relationships among all human beings. Like his precursor Hugo Grotius, he was a pioneer in the field of international law.

Selden put into practice his commitment to pluralism and to a greater understanding and cooperation among adherents of diverse religious traditions. He pleaded, unsuccessfully, in the House of Commons in behalf of toleration for Roman Catholics as "believers in Jesus Christ" and learnedly discoursed on the distinction between idolatry and prayers for the saints. He collected rare and even unique Arabic manuscripts and praised the learning of Muslim philosophers. He was the patron of the great Arabist Edward Pococke. Selden's own publication in 1642 of a long extract from the work of Eutychius is notable as the first full Arabic text (as distinct from quotations)

[3] According to Timaeus of Locri, as recorded by Diogenes Laertius.

in movable type printed in England. Between 1631 and his death in 1654, Selden devoted most of his scholarship to Jewish studies. His library contained more than seven hundred Hebrew and Aramaic books and manuscripts, and Maimonides was the guide on whom he most relied.

SELDEN ON MARRIAGE AND UNIVERSAL LAW

A few generalizations about Selden's thought might set the context for what follows. As G. J. Toomer has pointed out, attempts to understand Selden's conception of the purpose of scholarship within the framework of some large philosophical or religious theory are probably misconceived.[4] His scholarly approach is to document a culture's laws and customs. He was the greatest legal historian of his day,[5] and his mastery of English, Roman, and canon law in addition to Jewish law allowed him to point out important interconnections among them, while recognizing each of them as a self-contained system with its own central text and jurisprudence. Selden's Torah was law, and, at a time and place where Jews were often demonized, he admired Judaism as a religion founded on law. In fact, he rejected the Bible's Decalogue as intended only for the children of Israel and accepted instead the rabbinic Noachide laws as the most ancient of divine moral imperatives incumbent upon all of humankind. Selden doubted the existence of an innate universal law. For him, the law of nature is founded not on natural reason – he is a post-Aristotelian skeptic – but rather on a divine command. He states this most directly in *Table Talk*:

> I cannot fancy to myself what the law of nature means, but the law of God. How should I know I ought not to steal, I ought not to commit adultery, unless somebody told me so? Surely 'tis because I have been told so. 'Tis not because I think I ought not to do them, nor because you think I ought not; if so, our minds might change: whence then comes the restraint? From a higher power; nothing else can bind. I cannot bind myself, for I may untie myself again; nor an equal cannot bind me, for we may untie one another. It must be a superior, even God Almighty.[6]

4 Toomer, *John Selden*, 2:817. This is a magnificent work by a polymath whose comprehensive and deep knowledge puts all subsequent Selden scholars in his debt.

5 To honor him, the learned society devoted to the study of English legal history and to the publication of historical records of English law, which F. W. Maitland founded in 1887, is named the Selden Society.

6 "Law of Nature," in *Table Talk*, 101. All page references to *Table Talk* are to this edition.

Selden was unique among seventeenth-century Christian Hebraists not only in the degree of his admiration for the rabbis and the absence of a conversionary motive in his scholarship, but also in the extent to which he saw the Talmud as a complex legal system. He refers to it frequently as the Jewish "Pandects," a word applied to the Roman *Digest* assembled by Emperor Justinian from centuries of early Roman juridical opinions.[7] The title *De Jure Naturali et Gentium*, with its distinction between natural law and the law of nations, reflects the same commonplace distinction in Roman law as well as the important role of *ius naturale* in medieval Catholic canon law. Selden discusses the legal aspect of the *beth din shel ma'alah* (the heavenly tribunal). He regards *beth* (literally, "house of") in the references to *beth Hillel* and *beth Shammai*, usually translated as "school of," as instead the courts of Hillel and Shammai. And he bestows on the sages of the Talmud titles that also apply to himself, "Magistri" and "Jurisconsulti" (scholars of the law).[8]

In *De Jure*, Selden accepts the rabbinic identification of natural law with the Adamic and Noachide laws, considered by rabbinic tradition as the minimal moral duties incumbent on all of humankind. Besides citing Maimonides's code, the *Mishnah Torah*, he quotes in its entirety the *locus classicus* in the Talmudic tractate *Sanhedrin* (58 a–b), which enumerates the seven Noachide laws.[9] Selden's synthesizing imagination and comprehensive understanding of other legal systems enable him to find their compatibility with these laws. In a rare assertion of his unique contribution to scholarship, he announces: "While the subject of this book is in fact 'the law of nature and of nations,' there is more to it than that: it is subtitled 'according to the teaching of the Hebrews,' and here it breaks new ground."[10] He believes that the oral rabbinic law inscribed in the Talmud is more ancient than any other and therefore more authoritative than the speculations of "the moralists, political writers, jurists, and theologians" who have debated questions of obligation and permission. The first quote on the first page of *De Jure* is the ancient adage "*Nec Natura potest Justo secernere iniquum*" ("Nature cannot tell justice from iniquity").

[7] A point made by Toomer in *John Selden*, 2:442.

[8] Indeed, at least one contemporary rabbi, Leon Modena (1571–1648) repays the compliment. Selden is identified on the title page of the definitive edition of his *Opera Omnia* as "Joannis Seldeni Jurisconsulti."

[9] Unless otherwise noted, all page references to Talmudic tractates are to the Babylonian Talmud.

[10] *De Jure Naturali et Gentium* (1640), Preface, Sig. A3. Parenthetic book, chapter, and page references are to this first edition. Heartfelt thanks to Michael Wyetzner for sharing the typescript of his important forthcoming edition and translation of this work.

Selden's most extensive discussions of family law occur in book 5 of *De Jure*, on the Noachide prohibition of illicit sexual intercourse, and throughout his *Uxor Ebraica* (*The Hebrew Wife*), a documented study of the laws of incest, illicit intercourse, marriage, and divorce as they apply to Jews. In both works, Selden displays a remarkable synthesizing imagination, providing comparisons from many other legal systems, including but not limited to Roman, Christian, and Islamic law.

Regarding the degrees of incest according to natural law, Selden accepts as authoritative the rabbinic four modes of differentiation for the law's six prohibitions, as enunciated by Maimonides: the difference between species, which prohibits bestiality; between the sexes, which prohibits male homosexual relations; between what is one's own and what belongs to another, which prohibits adultery; and between oneself and one's close relations, which prohibits sex with one's mother, stepmother, and birth sister (5.2:541, 5.11:597–8).

Selden navigates the vast sea of the Talmud with Maimonides as his guide. Since Maimonides himself cites no sources, Selden relies on intermediate commentaries on the *Mishneh Torah* to find the approximate textual neighborhood of the Talmudic discussion of a subject: the *Maggid Mishneh* of Vidal of Tolosa, the *Kesef Mishneh* of Joseph Karo, and the folio references provided by Samuel Archevolti of the *Sefer H'Aruch* of Nathan b. Jehiel. But as Toomer points out, "even with these aids, the task was not trivial."[11]

Selden quotes the biblical verse cited in the Talmud to prohibit a variety of sexual unions: "a man shall leave his father and mother and cleave to his wife, and they shall be one flesh" (Genesis 2:24). He recognizes that this is counterintuitive: "[The rabbis] cite this verse as though the law had arisen at the moment the sexes were created; and they think it has to do not with the bond of marriage, which is the context in which the Gospels quote this passage [Matthew 19:5; Mark 10:7], but with those unlawful relations, or *revealings of disgrace*, that were forbidden even before the law of Moses" (5.2:541). The first clause of the verse forbids a man to have intercourse not only with his mother, but also with his father's wife and with another man's wife, while the second clause excludes intercourse with animals.[12] At the same time, Selden, a natural skeptic, agrees with Maimonides that this is an example of an *asmachta*, an exception in Talmudic hermeneutics, since it does not actually base the law on this verse but only uses it as a hint for a law

[11] Toomer, *John Selden*, 2:443. [12] Ibid., 2:534.

the sages had created themselves. For Maimonides and some others, the verse functions mainly as a mnemonic.

The biblical verse that institutes marriage for Selden is Genesis 1:28, pronounced by God immediately after the creation of our first parents, then repeated after the flood to Noah and his sons (Genesis 9:1), both given to the entire human population responsible for fulfilling it. He cites authorities who connect *fruitful* in "be fruitful and multiply" with the marriage bed, as though it were called *the place of bearing fruit* (5.3:545). Selden cites numerous sources to demonstrate the emphasis on marriage under purely natural law as dependent entirely on sexual intercourse. Both Hebrew and Latin have words that designate at once marriage and sexual intercourse – e.g., *ba'al* and *bo'el* (Hebrew) and *maritare* (Latin, to have sex, to take a wife). He even quotes Varro on the subject of dogs in heat, who communicate by smell that they are ready to *maritare* (have sex): "And this is also why Pliny and Columella refer to trees which are covered by vines and other kinds of flexible winding shrubs as *arbores maritae*. So the source of this expression is obviously the conjugal embrace itself" (5.4:552). Selden contrasts this with Roman law, where consent rather than intercourse is the essence of marriage.[13]

Following Maimonides's interpretation of the Talmud, Selden regards marriage under natural law as a completely unfettered relationship. Before the restrictions imposed by Mosaic law, marriage consisted of mutual consent and entrance into the bridal chamber to engage in sexual relations (5.4:551). The union was dissolved according to the will of one of the partners and without a bill of divorce. In fact, drawing on the story of Judah and Tamar (Genesis 38), the rabbis inferred that natural, pre-Mosaic law even permitted prostitution, provided that neither of the partners was married: "If a woman had control and ownership of her own person – that is, she was not bound by consent or consummation to a marriage – she could . . . sell herself and in this way hand herself over to a sexual relationship without agreeing to share her life . . . And certainly in the East the law itself often allowed women to grant these sorts of indecent liberties" (5.4:553).

It is tempting to conclude that these minimalist universal laws of family relations according to the rabbis fit with Selden's own personality as revealed in *Table Talk*: "Of all actions of a man's life, his marriage does least concern other people; yet of all actions of our life, 'tis most meddled with by other people."[14] Selden's open union with the Countess

[13] "Nuptias non concubitus sed consensus facit" (5.4:553).

[14] "Marriage," in *Table Talk*, 109.

of Kent created a scandal in some circles,[15] although their mutual devotion was evident.[16]

The Noachide law that appealed most strongly to lawyer Selden can impose significant limits on the natural law concerning sexual relations. The only positive law among the seven is "*dinim, judiciorum*," the commandment to set up courts of law: "courts or a judicial system, including those obligations which we usually call 'civil'" (Sig. A4r). It is important to note that Selden's position on this law is a rare instance of inconsistency in his scholarship. In the earlier chapters of *De Jure*, he scrupulously records the view of Maimonides and most other rabbinic interpreters, who see the courts as merely enforcing the other six laws. But in the later sections, including the chapters devoted explicitly to this law, Selden emphasizes the court's power under natural law to create additional laws. Surely, this view of the court's expanded jurisdictional authority underscores its importance to Selden as a civil lawyer and member of Parliament:

> The rabbis use the general term *dinim*, judgments, to include any sanctions, decrees, and customs which were legally added to the existing civil law, as well as any procedures, lawsuits, and court sentences used to punish violations of law and custom. That is why the term *beth din*, or house of judgment, referred sometimes to a tribunal or court which judged or settled actions at law and disputes according to the laws in effect at the time; and sometimes to a place or gathering where new laws were framed and enacted to be used from then on. (7.4:801)[17]

15 See, e.g., Aubrey, *Brief Lives*, 1:400: Selden was "Sollicitor [rather, legal advisor] to the Earle of Kent, whose Countess being an ingeniose woman, and loving men, did let him lye with her, and her husband knew it." Aubrey adds: "I remember my Sadler (who wrought many yeares to that family, told me, that Mr Selden had got more by his Prick, then ever he had donne by his practise" (1:406), alluding to the Countess's will, which left him her immense fortune and all of her private property, including the house at Whitefriars. But Aubrey is not the only one who relished tales of their alleged sexual conduct. Algernon Sidney, Sir Robert Southwell, and Jean-Baptiste Lantin noted that the couple, fearing that they might tire of one another, settled on a solution: Selden procured young men for the countess, and she reciprocated by providing three or four young ladies with whom he "amused and refreshed himself." See Bennett's comprehensive account in her notes on Aubrey (2:1325–6).

16 When the Countess of Kent died, Selden wrote that she was "so universally bewailed as I think never was or shalbe any other. Really she was a most incomparable person." Junius, *Correspondence*, no. 178 (824). Cited by Toomer, *John Selden*, 1:314.

17 "Generali nomine *dinim* seu *Judiciorum* continentur quidem apud Talmudicos tam Sanctiones, Constitutiones & mores qualescunque ritè superinducti, quàm actiones, Litium decisiones ac sententiae forenses quae in legum seu morum violationis vindicta versantur. Unde & *beth din, domus Judicii* nunc pro Tribunali aut foro, quà lites atque actiones, juxta jus jam antè obtinens, id cognoscit dirimitque, sumitur; nunc pro loco aut coetu quo sanciuntur constituunturque novae leges quae in posterum adhibendae."

As Selden points out, every nation is free to establish its own civil laws, and these could include laws of divorce:

> In fact, when the Hebrews said that Noachides, that is gentiles, *could not have a bill of divorce*, they obviously meant that while they themselves were bound to do this according to biblical law, there was no essential reason why gentiles should require such a bill, since they were living according to the natural law to which they were bound. They could apply this practice as they liked, which in fact they did, by means of civil legislation, which they added to their natural law. (5.7:569)

He adds: "That is how both the Greeks and the Romans came to use bills of divorce" (569).

Selden insists on the capital importance of this Noachide precept to set up courts of law: "It is this provision of which the other six are so to speak the product and substance; and isn't it obvious that there would be no point in legislating commandments and prohibitions unless we also equipped them with the judgments that could deter transgression and exact punishment?" (7.4:801).

SELDEN'S *UXOR EBRAICA*: ON THE CIVIL FAMILY LAW OF THE JEWS

For Selden, the Bible as it is interpreted in the Talmud constitutes the civil law of the Jews: the only set of civil laws to be promulgated by God. In his magnificent Hebrew and Aramaic scholarship, Selden respects, to an extent remarkable for the times, the self-understanding of Judaic exegesis. It is worth remembering that for Augustine, the Jews are living letters of the law, who are to be preserved, although doomed to wander the earth in a degraded state that is proof of the truth of Christianity. But beginning in the thirteenth century and extending into the seventeenth, the Augustinian paradigm was replaced by a more pernicious one. Among other influences, Ramón Martí in his *Pugio Fidei* and Nicolas Donin in the Disputation of Paris (1240) charged that the Talmud has replaced the Old Testament, which eliminates the Augustinian rationale for allowing the Jews to survive.

Selden goes further than perhaps any other early modern Christian Hebraist to demonstrate that far from corrupting the Hebrew Bible, the rabbis offer humane interpretations of its harshest laws. He knows that in the Talmud "an eye for an eye" becomes monetary compensation. And there are many examples in *Uxor Ebraica* (1646). For example, he begins its third book by examining Deuteronomy 22:13–14, 20–1, on a husband's claim that his bride had not been a virgin, if she had been so represented: if the charge proved true, the woman was to be stoned to death. Selden demonstrates that the rabbis of the Talmud interpreted this law very narrowly. They pointed out that the Bible's word to designate the bride, *naarah*, applies only to a girl between the ages of twelve and twelve and a half. A girl below the age of twelve is a *qetanah* (a child), and above twelve and a half she is a *bogeret*, one who has attained full puberty. Moreover, even within the narrow limit of six months, the law does not apply to a girl who was raped or seduced, nor to one of non-Israelite origin, nor to a virgin who was deflowered before betrothal. "In other words," concludes Selden, "unless she was deflowered between betrothal and consummation, the complaint had no standing."[18] He adds that a reduction in the size of the dowry paid at the end of the marriage, either through divorce or death, was the penalty for a woman outside of those narrow limits who represented herself as a virgin but was not. Regarding the *ta'anat betulim*, "signs of virginity" (Deuteronomy 22:20), Selden notes that neither Philo nor Josephus mentions producing a bloody bed linen as proof, and he refers to "modern medical writers, jurists, and theologians for doubts about the reality of the hymen and the possibility of determining virginity" (*Uxor*, 3:322–5).

Selden's extraordinary comprehension of rabbinic thought extends beyond laws to what other Christian Hebraists would dismiss as absurd rabbinical fables. He quotes from tractate *Sanhedrin* 22a Rabbi Judah's dream that forty days before an embryo is formed, "a *Bath-kol* or heavenly oracle announces to whom the foetus will be married." Far from ridiculing the story, he places it in its context, where it is part of a lengthy discussion, complete with biblical proof-texts, on the precious nature of marriage to one's first wife, "the wife of one's youth" (*Uxor*, 3.21:461–2). He recognizes it as *lashon havai*, deliberate rhetorical exaggeration, in this case to indicate that one's first wife is somehow preordained and should not be divorced "without serious reason." The dream follows immediately Rabbi Samuel bar Nachman's statement that nothing is irreplaceable – every loss can be retrieved – except the wife of one's youth (*Sanhedrin* 22a; *Uxor*, 461). The *locus classicus* for this rhetorical figure is tractate *Tamid* 29a, which provides examples of this intentional use of hyperbole from the Pentateuch, the prophets, and the rabbinic sages.

Uxor Ebraica approaches the topic of family relations in ways that are characteristic of all of Selden's mature scholarship: an intense, even primal appetite for learning; a synthesizing imagination that allows him to see

[18] Selden, *Uxor Ebraica*, 3.1:317–20. Parenthetical book, chapter, and page references are to this first edition. I have also relied on the translation in Jonathan Ziskind's *John Selden on Jewish Marriage Law: The Uxor Ebraica*.

connections among a vast range of texts, especially in Roman, Christian, and Jewish law, although not limited to them; a special emphasis on Christianity as "a kind of reform Judaism, from which it was born" (*Uxor*, 2:24:235); an Erastian position of state supremacy in ecclesiastical affairs; an agenda expressed through scholarship rather than polemic, with documented evidence so vast and compelling that the argument seems to turn of its own weight, without being pushed; and a tour de force of interpretation. In this brief introduction to Selden's work, one or two examples of each will have to suffice.

The *Uxor* begins with an example of learning for its own sake as the *summum bonum*: four chapters on the extreme rigorist interpretation of the Bible's incest laws by the Karaites, a Jewish sect that recognizes only the *Tanakh* and not the Talmud as the supreme legal authority. Selden also supplies his Christian readers with common Jewish formulas from uncommon sources (e.g., the *ketubah*, or marriage contract, from *Le-Khal Hefetz* [Venice, 1552], Eliezer of Melli's collection of thirty-eight documents for various occasions) and uncommon formulas from common sources (e.g., a daughter's formal renunciation of a betrothal arranged by her father when she was a minor, from Selden's principal source, Maimonides's *Mishneh Torah* [*Gerushin*, 11.11]). One of the most interesting and surprising documents he offers readers is an extraordinarily effusive blessing, with images from Proverbs and Canticles, found in a Spanish prayer book (*Seder Tephiloth Iudeor. Hispanien*, page 351). Selden provides both the original Hebrew and his Latin translation, which swerves from its familiar opening formula. It reads in part: "Blessed art thou, O Lord our God, king of the universe, who has placed a nut and lilies of the valley in Eden or paradise. No stranger possessed the sealed well" (3.1:326). It is clearly a prayer of thanksgiving for a bride's virginity but with no indication of who recites it: the bridegroom, the father of the bride, or the congregation.

Selden's synthesizing imagination leads him to emphasize the parallels in paganism and Christianity with Jewish rites and practices of marriage and divorce. He finds them inherently interesting, even when a historical connection is dubious. As in *De Jure*, regarding natural law, he regards the bride's entering the bridal chamber for the purpose of intercourse as the act that constitutes marriage (Talmudic tractate *Qiddushin* 5a). He compares this to the "Donatio propter Nuptias" (2.9:159) in Roman law and connects both with the parable of the wise and foolish virgins: "and those women who were prepared entered with him to the wedding, and the door was closed" (Matthew 25:10; *Uxor* 2.13:187). The marriage rite is described at some length in the apocryphal Book of Tobit (7:9–8:21), where Raguel gives his daughter Sarah in marriage to Tobias and calls to his wife, "Sister, prepare the other room and lead her into it." Selden also quotes from a unique copy of a 1516 Constantinople edition, where "'the inner chamber' was . . . obviously the *khuppah* or nuptial chamber into which the bride was led at the marriage and the marriage was consummated" (185). He rehearses at length the rabbinic argument that leading the betrothed woman into the bower, rather than matrimonial blessing, effects matrimony.[19] Poet John Milton revered Selden, whom he praised as "the chief of learned men reputed in this land." Indeed, Adam recounts in *Paradise Lost* (8.510–11), "To the Nuptial Bow'r/ I led her blushing like the Morn," and perhaps this silent act solemnized his marriage to Eve, his blushing bride.

Selden discusses the three types of marriage among the Romans: *coemtio*, involving a symbolic purchase, which he compares with the Jewish betrothal with a coin; *usus*, cohabitation for a year, similar to marriage by intercourse (*biah*) in the Talmud; and *confarreatio*, a religious ritual performed with certain words and in the presence of ten witnesses (2.21:244), which Selden compares to the seven blessings (*sheva brachot*) at Jewish weddings. Later in the *Uxor*, he discusses *diffarreatio*, whereby, according to Sextus Pompeius and others, "the breakup of a man and his wife was accomplished," by a formula reversing that of the *confarreatio* (3.27:546). Regarding the great frequency of divorce in the paganism of later ages, Selden cites numerous authorities, including Tertullian, who said, "Divorce is now promised as if it were the fruit of marriage" (3.27:550).

Selden brings together his double mastery of early English law and of ancient and medieval rabbinic law in his discussion of the dower, which he treats not as the gift or money that the bride gives the groom, but rather as the portion of a deceased husband's estate that the law allows to his widow for her lifetime.[20] He discusses the medieval English practice of settling the bride's dower at the church door before the ceremony (2.27:279–85). He even quotes Chaucer on the Wife of Bath: "Housbandes at chirche dore she hadde fyve." He also refers to "Ranulph de Glanville, Henry de Bracton, and the author of the *Fleta*," as well as to Fitzherbert and others, to prove that the widow had a legal right to part of her deceased husband's estate (281). He notes that "leading jurists of our day" have misread Bracton, as if he held that no part of the

[19] *Uxor*, 2.12:182 ff: "Non benedicto sponsorum facit seu perficit nuptias, sed deductio in thalamum."

[20] Selden's mastery of English legal history is evident from his notes on Sir John Fortescue's *De Laudibus Legum Angliae*, his editions of the *Summa Magna* and *Summa Parva* attributed to Ralph de Hengham, his essays *Original of Testaments* and *Intestate Goods*, and his unsurpassed edition of the *Dissertatio ad Fletam*. His knowledge of English law is also evident in his *Titles of Honor*, *Historie of Tithes*, *Eadmer*, and *Mare Clausum*.

husband's movable goods belonged to the wife or children except for what was specifically left to them. His marginal note refers to the great Edward Coke's *Institutiones Juris Anglicani* (282). Of primary interest to Selden is the Jewish marriage contract or *ketubah*, which itemizes the amount of money due to the widow or to the divorced wife.

Selden prefaces his chapters on the wedding rites and marriage practices among Christians by insisting that Christianity, being a kind of reformed Judaism, retained many things from that religion, and that those who neglect this connection are either deceived or deceivers.[21] Alternative speculations that disregard the retention of Judaic ritual and law in early Christianity are "the insane foundations of cloud cuckoo land that have arisen" (3.27:544). Toomer points out that Selden, who gives no examples of such misunderstanding of the historical origins of Christianity, has in mind "contemporary attempts by some Presbyterians to set up theocratic rule, allegedly based on New Testament precedents."[22]

Selden's tour de force of interpretation in the *Uxor* is related to his agenda. A section of the *Uxor* of capital importance (3.18–3.23:428–500) is the Talmudic account of the schools (or courts) of Hillel and Shammai, which Selden compares with the Proculian and Sabinian schools of Roman law as well as with the Gospel pronunciations on divorce. Most interpreters of the New Testament hold that Jesus dissociated himself directly from a regulation of the Torah on one occasion only: when, in defiance of Pharisaic interrogation (Matthew 5:31–2, 19:3–9), he rejected explicitly and categorically the deuteronomic right to divorce. But in the *Uxor* Selden interprets Jesus's words as consistent with that right as interpreted in the Talmud. The Mosaic law authorizes a husband to write a bill of divorce if, through "some shameful thing" (or "unseemliness"), his wife should fail to find favor in his eyes (Deuteronomy 24:1). Jesus, while speaking to the Pharisees, who are baiting him, appears to reject this law and to grant divorce only for "fornication" (Matthew 5:31–2). The extraordinarily learned, comprehensive, and ingenious rabbinic context that Selden provides widens the meaning of both the key Hebrew and Greek terms in this passage (*ervath davar* and *porneia*, respectively), so that they include any kind of obnoxious behaviour.

The school (or court) of Shammai, emphasizing *ervah* (unseemliness), permitted divorce only when some shameful behavior, including but not

[21] *Uxor*, 2.4:235; Toomer, *John Selden*, 2:663.

[22] Toomer, *John Selden*, 2:684. "Cloud cuckoo land" is the fictional city for the birds in the clouds, *nephelococcygia*, in *The Birds* by Aristophanes. It may also allude to the act of finding shapes in the clouds.

limited to adultery, made the continuation of marriage impossible. The followers of Hillel, like Jesus's interrogators, argued that divorce should be granted for any *thing* (*davar*) – that is, for any sort of cause. Selden, who reads the Gospel passages on divorce in the light of Talmudic tractate *Gittin* (lit., "divorce") 90a and its commentaries, demonstrates the consistency of Jesus's position with that of the school of Shammai. Jesus's reproof and rejection extend not only to the school of Hillel and Rabbi Akiba (who would permit divorce even if one sees a woman who might please him more than his wife), but also to the permissive view of mere separation as divorce according to the Noachide or natural law.

Selden's command of Aramaic and rabbinical Hebrew, which allows him to reconstruct the exact language of the exchange in Matthew, is matched by his learned distinction between the Gospel terms *moichatai* (committing adultery) and *porneia*, which is usually translated as "adultery." The two terms are used in the same verse as if to enumerate different things, and Selden demonstrates, with numerous texts from the Hebrew Bible and its Greek translation, that *porneia*, like *ervah*, denotes not only adultery, but "sin and baseness of any kind," including whoring after strange gods as well as whoring after magic and soothsayers (*Uxor*, 3.23:489–90).

To bury the lede is a journalistic sin, but it may be a scholarly virtue. As already noted, Selden eschews polemic in favor of scholarship for its own sake, so his agenda must be inferred by his astute readers. Since he cites no sources after the sixteenth century, one would never know from the text of the *Uxor Ebraica* that passionate arguments about divorce were circulating in England in the 1640s. As a member of Parliament as well as the Westminster Assembly of Divines, Selden was very much aware of these debates. The last chapter of Milton's revised and expanded *Doctrine and Discipline of Divorce* (1644) is devoted to Selden's *De Jure*, "that noble volume written by our learned *Selden*, *Of the law of nature & of Nations*, a work ... useful and ... worthy to be perus'd, whosoever studies to be a great man in wisdom, equity, and justice."[23] But Selden owned two of Milton's tracts arguing for divorce on grounds of incompatibility, *Tetrachordon* and *Colasterion*, "twin-born progeny," published in 1645.[24] Selden and Milton reached the same conclusion: that Jesus's pronouncements on divorce were directed only to the Jews governed by Mosaic law

23 Milton, *Doctrine and Discipline of Divorce*, 2:350.

24 Bodleian Library ms. Selden supra 111, the catalog of Selden's books made shortly after his death while they were still on the shelves in his house at Whitefriars. "Twin-born progeny" (Milton's Sonnet XII) alludes to these treatises.

and do not apply to Christians. This leaves every human government free to legislate on marriage and divorce as it sees fit. It is possible that in this instance the poet, a creative genius and skilled polemicist, may have influenced the scholarly genius. By writing in Latin and remaining above the fray, and by having his readers draw the conclusions that he has scrupulously prepared for them, Selden avoided attacks on his position.

Milton, writing clearly and with great polemic force in English, was wounded by the negative reception to his most passionate prose, as revealed in the introduction to the second edition of *Doctrine and Discipline of Divorce* as well as in his Sonnets XI and XII, which both bear the heading "On the detraction which followed upon my writing certain treatises."

In the *Uxor*, Selden provides overwhelming evidence that the rigors of canon law on divorce contradict the more liberal laws among pagans, Jews, and early Christians. Finally, on the very last page, he concludes in a sentence fragment, parenthetically:

> Indeed, among our British people (who by act of Parliament enacted more than a century ago relaxed the degrees of affinity and consanguinity established by the pontificial law, retaining only what is in Scripture, but nevertheless kept in its entirety the pontificial teaching on divorce after the Reformation) ... a provincial synod of clerics [declared] ... that no court may make a judgment on deprivation of bed and board unless in addition neither spouse be permitted a remarriage. (3.23:620–1)

Even this, his most definitive statement on contemporary domestic law, leaves it up to the reader to infer inevitably the need to reform the laws of divorce, especially in light of England's great divorce from Rome.

More than ninety years ago, David Ogg described Selden accurately as one who stands out alone in a century of greatness, "seeking not fame but truth in an erudition more vast than was ever garnered by any other human mind."[25] And even Ogg, concentrating on Selden as a historian of the laws and constitutional institutions of England, has not a word to say about the six rabbinical works that constitute his most mature scholarship on many matters, including notably sex, marriage, and family life. One can only add that if readers of Selden in the twenty-first century can learn from him to remove the overlay of anti-Semitic prejudice that still begrimes not only the words *synagogue* and *Sanhedrin* but also *Pharisee* (whose negative connotations Selden, a partisan of the oral law, did much to expunge), then his cultural influence will not have ended.

25 Selden, *Ad Fletam Dissertatio*, lxvi.

RECOMMENDED READING

Barbour, Reid. *John Selden: Measures of the Holy Commonwealth in Seventeenth-Century England*. Toronto: University of Toronto Press, 2003.

Berkowitz, David Sandler. *John Selden's Formative Years: Politics and Society in Early Seventeenth-Century England*. Washington, DC: Folger Shakespeare Library, 1988.

Christianson, Paul. *Discourse on History, Law, and Governance in the Public Career of John Selden, 1610–1635*. Toronto: University of Toronto Press, 1996.

"John Selden." In the *Oxford Dictionary of National Biography*. Oxford and New York: Oxford University Press, 2004.

Herzog, Isaac. "John Selden and Jewish Law." In *Judaism: Law and Ethics*, edited by Chaim Herzog. London: Soncino, 1974.

Rosenblatt, Jason P. *Torah and Law in Paradise Lost*. Princeton, NJ: Princeton University Press, 1994.

Renaissance England's Chief Rabbi: John Selden. Oxford: Oxford University Press, 2006; revised paperback edition, 2008.

Sommerville, Johann P. "John Selden, the Law of Nature, and the Origins of Government." *Historical Journal* 27 (1984): 437–47.

"Hobbes, Selden, Erastianism, and the History of the Jews." In *Hobbes and History*, edited by G. A. John Rogers and Tom Sorell, 160–88. London and New York: Routledge, 2000.

"Selden, Grotius, and the Seventeenth-Century Intellectual Revolution in Moral and Political Theory." In *Rhetoric and Law in Early Modern Europe*, edited by Victoria Kahn and Lorna Hutson. New Haven, CT, and London: Yale University Press, 2001.

Toomer, Gerald J. *Eastern Wisedome and Learning: The Study of Arabic in Seventeenth-Century England*. Oxford: Oxford University Press, 1996.

John Selden: A Life in Scholarship. 2 vols. Oxford: Oxford University Press, 2009.

Tuck, Richard. *Natural Rights Theories: Their Origin and Development*. Cambridge: Cambridge University Press, 1979.

"'The Ancient Law of Freedom': John Selden and the Civil War." In *Reactions to the English Civil War 1642–1649*, edited by John Morrill. London: Macmillan, 1982.

"Grotius and Selden." In *The Cambridge History of Political Thought, 1450–1700*, edited by J. H. Burns and Mark Goldie. Cambridge: Cambridge University Press, 1991.

Philosophy and Government 1572–1651. Cambridge: Cambridge University Press, 1993.

Ziskind, Jonathan. *John Selden on Jewish Marriage Law: The* Uxor Ebraica. Leiden: E. J. Brill, 1991.

17

Mary Wollstonecraft

Eileen Hunt Botting

BIOGRAPHICAL INTRODUCTION

Born into a troubled, middle-class, Anglican family in the garment district of London, Mary Wollstonecraft (1759–97) learned early that she would have to support not only herself, but also others through her intellect and work ethic. Largely self-educated, she sought the tutelage of better-off friends, ministers, and neighbors in pursuing her youthful interest in theology, philosophy, and literature. She financially sustained her extended family through work as a lady's companion, schoolmistress, governess, and, finally, professional writer. She charted an unconventional path in love, marriage, and motherhood, which made her a controversial public symbol of the opportunities and pitfalls of female independence. Wollstonecraft overcame these life challenges to become the internationally renowned leading women's rights advocate of the European Enlightenment. She was also the first philosopher to pen a book-length defense of women's rights as a kind of human rights in the wake of the democratic debates of the French Revolution.[1]

This landmark book of 1792 – *A Vindication of the Rights of Woman*[2] – was well known in the British Isles, continental Europe, and the United States during the 1790s. It has continued to influence women's rights discourse and activism around the world. Nineteenth-century novelists, journalists, abolitionists, chartists, labor organizers, suffragists, socialists, anarchists, missionaries, and a variety of feminists found in the text a rich

[1] Gordon, *Vindication*; Botting, "Editor's Introduction: Reading Wollstonecraft's *A Vindication of the Rights of Woman*, 1792–2014," in Wollstonecraft, *A Vindication of the Rights of Woman*, 1–15 (hereafter cited as *Rights of Woman*).

[2] London: Joseph Johnson, 1792.

FIGURE 17.1. Portrait of Mary Wollstonecraft Godwin (1759–97) Author of A *Vindication of the Rights of Woman*, engraved by W. T. Annis, pub. 1802 (engraving) (b/w photo), Opie, John (1761–1807) (after) / Private Collection / Bridgeman Images

resource for their arguments and activism concerning the promotion of social justice for women.

The young Wollstonecraft was privately tutored and mentored by several Protestant intellectuals: John Arden, a dissenter and scientific lecturer whose daughter Jane befriended Wollstonecraft in Yorkshire in their mid-teens; Mr. Clare, a clergyman who served as her informal teacher in north London in her late teens; and the Calvinist-turned-Unitarian Reverend James Burgh and his wife, Hannah Harding, who assisted her in establishing a coeducational day school on Newington Green in north London in her mid-twenties. Around 1784, Wollstonecraft met the Reverend Price, a rational dissenter and abolitionist preaching at the Newington Green Church. Although she continued to attend Anglican services, she soon theorized the foundation of human rights similarly to this dissenting minister. Given that she was raised Anglican, found her teachers among Protestant ministers, and wrote extensively on theology as an adult, it is not surprising that Wollstonecraft took a broadly Protestant Christian approach to laying a foundation for women's human rights.[3]

WOLLSTONECRAFT'S CHRISTIAN METAPHYSICAL AND ETHICAL FOUNDATION FOR WOMEN'S HUMAN RIGHTS

Given their male biases and general sidelining of women, Christian sources for natural rights theories were as problematic as Enlightenment-era social contract theory for Wollstonecraft's philosophical purposes. Just as she rejected the conceptual divide between the state of nature and the social contract, so she also rejected scriptural accounts of an original state, such as the story of Adam and Eve, as productive for ethics or politics. Such origin stories were empirically unverifiable and thus prone to distorting the facts of the human condition. This was especially true in trying to understand the relationship between the sexes, as the story of Adam and Eve had been repeatedly used to defend women's subordination to men, even by great minds such as poet John Milton. According to Wollstonecraft's feminist biblical hermeneutics, "Man, from the remotest antiquity, found it convenient to exert his strength to subjugate his companion" through

[3] Botting, *Family Feuds*, 158; Botting, *Wollstonecraft, Mill, and Women's Human Rights*, chapter 1.

"inventions" such as "Moses' poetical story" about Eve being made from Adam's rib.[4]

Rather than rely on scriptural accounts or conjectural stories about the origins and progress of humanity, Wollstonecraft established a few "first principles" by which humans and their rights might be rationally understood from a metaphysical/ethical perspective. In the opening chapters of the *Rights of Woman*, Wollstonecraft defined rights as "the privilege of moral beings." Moral beings are human beings, designed by God to achieve "pre-eminence over the brute creation" through the exercise of "reason" to acquire "virtue" and "knowledge." She argued that women might "procure" rights through the "exercise of reason." By using reason to gauge moral action toward others, women would "obtain the sober pleasures that arise from equality." She insisted that such "sober pleasures" were secondary to the primary reason for women's understanding of themselves as rights-bearing subjects: women's "first duty is to themselves as rational creatures." The rights of women were therefore derivative of their duties, especially the duty to develop their moral and intellectual potential as rational creatures of God.[5]

Responding to the deficiencies of Christian and social-contract theories of natural rights for securing freedom and well-being for women, Wollstonecraft thus developed an alternative theological and philosophical foundation for the full inclusion of women in the rights of humanity. In crafting a universalistic and egalitarian understanding of human rights, she drew on a variety of schools of thought within the rational Christian dissenter tradition. Dissenting Christians were the non-Anglican Protestants in England who had gained the right to practice their alternative forms of Christianity under the Toleration Act of 1689.

Wollstonecraft's intellectual exposure to rational Christian dissent of the sort Price espoused took place between 1784 and 1786, when she heard his sermons at the Newington Green Church. Her first publications on issues such as female education, marriage, and family – *Thoughts on the Education of Daughters* (1787), *Mary, a Fiction* (1788), and *Original Stories from Real Life* (1788) – show the deep Augustinian influence of Anglican Christianity on her early political thought. Yet these major writings before the French Revolution also indicate her growing engagement with the alternative school of religious and political thought represented by rational Christian dissenters such as Burgh and Price. It was Wollstonecraft's two political treatises, *A Vindication of the*

[4] Wollstonecraft, *Rights of Woman*, 52. [5] Ibid., 37, 71, 82, 175.

Rights of Men (1790) and *Rights of Woman*, which reflected her full adoption of the Pricean approach to grounding human rights on a rational theological foundation.[6]

Price was the son of a Presbyterian minister. His Newington Green Church was founded as a Presbyterian church in 1708. In the late eighteenth century, this church became more strongly associated with the broader dissenting Christian movement from Trinitarian to Unitarian theology. Price's own theological views on the Trinity moved in this direction. He considered himself an Arian: he did not view Jesus as co-substantial with God, but rather as a creature made by God before Jesus's physical incarnation. For this reason, he thought Jesus should not be worshipped, for worship ought to be reserved for God.[7]

Wollstonecraft, by the time she wrote the *Rights of Men*, seems to have pushed beyond Price's Arianism toward a Socinian, or Unitarian, view of God. Rebuffing Edmund Burke's hypocritical combination of elitism and Christianity, she implied that the Irish statesman respected Jesus for his regal "lineage" from David, whereas her devotion to "the carpenter's son" depended only on his appointment by "Divine authority." Like other late eighteenth-century Socinians, such as Joseph Priestley, Wollstonecraft revered Jesus as a mortal man (a "carpenter's son") who was chosen by the one God to serve as the greatest moral exemplar for humanity. Her anti-Trinitarian theology did not make her any less devoutly Christian, however. In the *Rights of Men*, she proclaimed a deep personal and emotional bond with the one God of the Old and New Testaments, alongside a piety toward the moral example of Jesus, in a way that revealed the resilience of orthodox elements of her Protestant faith.[8]

On matters of moral theology, Price and Wollstonecraft argued against voluntarism and empiricism in favor of rationalism. Voluntarists, such as William of Ockham, had argued that the moral law was an expression of God's will. Empiricists, such as Thomas Hobbes, had argued that there was no stable enforcement of the laws of nature (beyond the constant right to practice self-defense) until government and positive law were established by the will of the absolute sovereign. Both schools presumed

[6] Botting, *Family Feuds*, 136–55; B. Taylor, *Mary Wollstonecraft and the Feminist Imagination*, 103–8; Hutton, "The Ethical Background of the Rights of Women," 27–40.

[7] Botting, *Family Feuds*, 158–9.

[8] Wollstonecraft's view of God as unitary remains stable, even as she moves toward her own creative formulation of a Romantic deism in her *Letters Written during a Short Residence in Sweden, Norway, and Denmark* (1796). See Botting, *Family Feuds*, 179. Wollstonecraft, *Rights of Men*, in Wollstonecraft, *The Works of Mary Wollstonecraft*, 5:61 (hereafter cited as *Works*).

that morality was an expression of the will of a sovereign ruler, divine or mortal. Both Price and Wollstonecraft rejected these schools of thought on the grounds that they made morality arbitrary. Wollstonecraft critically read Burke's defense of political institutions as sources of moral authority along these lines: "nature and Reason, according to your system, are all to give place to authority; and the gods, as Shakespeare makes a frantic wretch exclaim, seem to kill us for their sport, as men do flies." If moral rules were merely expressions of divine or personal will, then morality could be reduced to the volitional whims of the Creator or human rulers.[9]

Instead, Price and Wollstonecraft took a rationalistic approach to conceptualizing God and humanity's relationships to the moral law. For both of them, the moral law is objective, because it is rational and has this ontological property independently of God's will. If the moral law was merely an expression of God's will, then morality could be reduced to the whims of an all-powerful sovereign Creator who failed to subject Himself to the rules of reason. To avoid this pitfall of theological voluntarism, Price and Wollstonecraft set forth a two-part rationalistic account of the basis of morality that pertained to both God and humankind: (1) the moral law exists independently of God's will but as part of divine nature as the supreme rational being, and (2) the moral law is universal in its application to all humans, who may grasp it via reason because they are made in the image of God. As Wollstonecraft explained in theological terms in the *Rights of Men*, "I FEAR God! I bend with awful reverence when I inquire on what my fear is built – I fear that sublime power, whose motive for creating me must have been wise and good; and I submit to the moral laws which my reason deduces from this view of my dependence on him. – It is not his power that I fear – it is not to an arbitrary will, but to an unerring reason I submit. – Submit – yes ... to the law that regulates his just resolves." Price and Wollstonecraft's theological and metaphysical definition of the moral law as part of God's essence, but independent of God's will, had roots in Thomas Aquinas. It also had Enlightenment Protestant expressions among rights theorists such as Locke.[10]

This conception of the moral law as grounded on reason, independently of any being's will, gave the idea of human rights the possibility of an objective and universal foundation. Following Price, Wollstonecraft in her *Rights of Men* posited a theological and metaphysical account of the

[9] Wollstonecraft, *Rights of Men*, in *Works*, 5:61. [10] Ibid., 35.

grounding of "sacred rights" on the "eternal foundation of right." This foundation was evident in "the immutable attributes of God": first and foremost, the reason that God and God's human creatures shared. In his 1767 theological *Dissertations*, Price had defended a conception of God as rational, providential, and caring: "a God without a Providence is undoubtedly a contradiction. Nothing is plainer than that a Being of perfect reason will in every instance take such care of the universe as perfect reason requires." Wollstonecraft likewise opened her *Rights of Woman* with a similar theodicy: "Firmly persuaded that no evil exists in the world that God did not design to take place, I build my belief on the perfection of God." For Wollstonecraft as well as Price, the realization of the sacred rights of humanity was part of God's rational and benevolent providential plan for the development of human potential within creation.[11]

For Price and Wollstonecraft, human beings had moral rights and moral duties – in short, ethical relationships with one another – because they had access, via reason, to understanding the universal principles of morality. These principles were part of God's nature as the supreme rational being, but they were principles to which God voluntarily subjected the divine will. Humans, too, had a choice: a choice to direct their freedom of will and rationality to the understanding and application of these principles in their interactions with each other. As Wollstonecraft argued in the *Rights of Men*, "the more man discovers the nature of his mind and body, the more clearly he is convinced, that to act according to the dictates of reason is to conform to the law of God." The human subject's freedom of will, combined with her rationality, empowered her to enact the moral duties derived from the objective and universal law of God, and the rights derived from such duties.[12]

Both Price and Wollstonecraft thus reserved a robust place for freedom of the will in their accounts of moral theology, ethics, and human rights. Rational Christian dissenters typically emphasized the legitimate expression of the freedom of the will in the civil and political rights to freedom of conscience and religious toleration. This English nonconformist tradition grew in power after the Toleration Acts of 1689, which had permitted non-Anglican Protestants to establish churches such as the one on Newington Green.[13]

11 Wollstonecraft, *Rights of Men*, 60; Price, *Four Dissertations*, 6; Wollstonecraft, *Rights of Woman*, 40, 111.

12 Wollstonecraft, *Rights of Men*, 52.

13 Taylor, *Mary Wollstonecraft and the Feminist Imagination*, 105.

Price had developed a strong human rights theory while preaching in various capacities at Newington Green since 1758. He supported the abolition of chattel slavery and backed the American and French Revolutions. In 1776, he argued that among the "inalienable rights of human nature" was the right to exercise free will through participating in the social compact; through such willful popular participation, governments would finally be rendered legitimate in their powers. Furthermore, the practice of moral, religious, and civil liberties raised human beings above the level of "a poor and abject animal." He defined moral liberty as the exercise of free will and reason in order to put God's moral law into action. Moral liberty, for Price as for Wollstonecraft, was the rational self-governance of individual human beings according to universal principles of morality. This concept of moral liberty undergirded their ideal conceptions of citizenship as participation in a self-governing republic with a popular legislative assembly. Although they thought that moral liberty was an important component of civil and political liberty, it was not a precondition for one's entitlement to civil and political rights. The case of chattel slavery illustrated this point: the slave was not allowed to be either physically or morally free, but still deserved to be granted her liberty so that she could learn to be free physically, morally, civilly, and politically.[14]

Wollstonecraft's rational theological approach to universal human rights built on Price but extended the argument explicitly and systematically to women. While Price repeatedly referenced the inalienable rights of humanity in his sermons and political writings, he never seems to have made a public, recorded plea for women's human rights. His abolitionist arguments against human slavery only implied women's human right to be free from slavery. Wollstonecraft, on the other hand, began to argue specifically and systematically for women's human rights alongside the abolition of slavery in her earliest political treatise, the 1790 *Rights of Men*.

Before penning the *Rights of Men*, Wollstonecraft did not often use the language of rights in the sense of subjective, or individually held and exercised, rights. The influence of Price at Newington Green seems to have triggered a shift in Wollstonecraft's conception of rights. As a student, teacher, and theorist, she long had an interest in the issue of female education – but she had not previously framed it as a right of each and every human individual. In her early publications, she conceptualized education as a moral duty of adults to be performed in relation

[14] Price, "Observations on the Nature of Civil Liberty," in id., *Political Writings*, 21–3, 33.

to their children; on the obverse side, it was a moral duty of children to follow their parents' instruction to ensure their own development toward consistent practice of God's moral law. By the time she composed the *Rights of Men*, Wollstonecraft had begun to theorize an egalitarian view of universal human rights – beginning with education and leading to republican political participation. Her view followed Price in its grounding in the theology of rational dissent. However, her specific application of the concept of subjective rights to women was a philosophical milestone in the realization of the concept's universalistic and egalitarian potential.

IMPLICATIONS FOR FAMILY LAW

Wollstonecraft's theory of women's human rights, as grounded on her Christian metaphysics and ethics, has strong implications for the egalitarian reform of family law. She advanced arguments for the egalitarian reform of patriarchal familial institutions in Western European cultures and legal systems (male headship in the family; primogeniture; coverture; domestic violence against women; divorce; child custody; children's rights), as well as non-Western cultures and legal systems (polygamy as practiced by North African and Turkish Muslim peoples). Her own advocacy for such legal and cultural reform inspired later women's rights advocates from around the world to build on her arguments to shape social movements directed toward the advancement of women's human rights in the family, civil society, and the state.[15]

We have seen how Wollstonecraft rejected the traditional Christian justification of male headship in the family by debunking the use of the Genesis story of Adam and Eve to defend man's supposed God-given authority and superiority over woman. In her *Rights of Woman*, she also criticized Jean-Jacques Rousseau's helpmeet ideal of marriage along similar lines. Contra Rousseau's *Emile* (1762), she contended that women do not by nature need a patriarch's guidance. Like Rousseau, Wollstonecraft acknowledged that men are physically stronger than women. Unlike Rousseau, she did not accept that this physical dominance legitimated any kind of moral, social, or political authority of men over women. To Rousseau's claim that women need the rational guidance of their fathers and husbands, she retorted, "Husbands – as well as their helpmates – are often only overgrown children." Cleverly drawing the argument of Rousseau's *Second Discourse on Method* (1755) to its logical conclusion, she concluded that wives *and* husbands are equally incapable of

[15] Botting, "The Personal Is Political," 270–8.

genuine moral autonomy under the present trappings of European civilization. Even Rousseau's radical reformulation of education in *Emile* was not enough to remedy the situation, since it preserved the patriarchal structure of the family. Extending the reach of Enlightenment-era egalitarianism from the state to the family, Wollstonecraft argued that the "the *divine right* of husbands" must be demystified and deconstructed just as the divine right of kings has been debunked. Only then will men and women enjoy an equal chance to practice the moral and civic virtues in the realms of family, civil society, and the state and, most importantly, prepare their souls for God's scrutiny in the next life.[16]

In her rebuttal of Edmund Burke's defense of hereditary property in his *Reflections on the Revolution in France* (1790), Wollstonecraft applied this Christian feminist critique of the patriarchal family to the problems generated by the legal practice of primogeniture – which placed most, if not all, of family estate in the hands of the eldest son with little left for younger sons, daughters, or illegitimate children to inherit. The *Rights of Men* extensively detailed how the institution of primogeniture caused the moral corruption of the family. By sacrificing the interests of the younger children for the sake of the eldest son, primogeniture perverted the natural parental affection that should be expressed unconditionally and equally to each child. Primogeniture forced elder daughters into the legal prostitution of arranged marriage and drove younger daughters into convents and younger sons into exile. The fear of losing their family inheritance incited children to lie in order to avoid a father's angry curse. Primogeniture encouraged late, loveless, and adulterous marriages, turned husbands into gallants and wives into coquettes who neglected their marriages for the sake of adulterous affairs, and permitted parents to wield *lettres de cachet* to imprison children who refused to marry the persons chosen for them. Tragically, primogeniture split the family apart for the sake of preserving the family estate.

So that the legal privileging of the eldest son would no longer corrupt the natural affections of the family, Wollstonecraft demanded the abolition of aristocracy, aristocratic estates, and primogeniture. In counterpoint to Burke's defense of these familial hierarchies, Wollstonecraft envisioned the egalitarian transformation of the family and society at large after the abolition of these inegalitarian institutions. Once they reached the age of reason, children would no longer be subject to the rule of their parents, and no longer would they be subject to forced marriages. Men would give up gaming for virtuous ambitions; women would give up coquetry to be rational women and good

[16] Wollstonecraft, *Rights of Woman*, 48, 67.

mothers who suckle their own children and fulfill their part in the social contract; and love would take the place of gallantry. Natural parental affection would be restored once all children were loved equally and favored only insofar as their merit deserved. The vulgarity of the rich and the poor would fade away, for the virtues of individual merit and industry would supersede the effeminizing and animalizing vices of luxury and poverty. Aristocratic estates filled with superficial, superfluous objects of architectural luxury would be replaced with pastoral farms that were more pleasing and useful to the people. In this future enlightened age, there would be bliss and harmony in the family, the school, the playing fields, the church, and the state, which Wollstonecraft, in her early years, thought would be experienced only in heaven.

In the *Rights of Woman*, Wollstonecraft trained her eye on the moral and political problems generated by the English common-law idea of coverture – the notion that a wife's life, property, identity, and name were covered under and represented by her husband's legal identity, making married women a legal "cypher" in her time. Under this rule, married women lost all rights to private property and, tragically, child custody in cases of separation or divorce. The aristocratic practices of primogeniture and entail (keeping the family estate in one piece) exacerbated the overall economic inequality of women. Regardless of class, women had incentives to marry and stay married for status and wealth rather than for love or respect of their mates.[17]

By contrast, she argued that women "must have a civil existence in the state, married or single." Few women chose the latter – what the unmarried author of the *Rights of Woman* poignantly called "a single life with dignity" – because of the difficulty of making an independent living as a woman. They rather fell into it, as spinsters and widows, or through lowly women's work as ladies' companions, wet nurses, governesses, teachers, and "the next class" of "milliners and mantua-makers." Unveiled in chapters 9 through 12 of her *Rights of Woman*, her solution to this systematic oppression was fourfold: (1) the egalitarian transformation of the family through abolition of coverture and other patriarchal legal and cultural practices surrounding marriage, inheritance, and childrearing; (2) the expansion of economic opportunities for women, so that they might have the chance for independent careers, not just ill-paying jobs or unequal marriages; (3) the extension of equal civil and political rights to women; and (4) long-term social reform of gender and class norms through free public coeducation.[18]

Wollstonecraft's novels *Mary, a Fiction* (1788) and *Maria, or the Wrongs of Woman* (1798), respectively, confront the need for women's property rights in

[17] Ibid., 74. [18] Ibid., 58, 178.

marriage and women's rights to divorce and custody of their children. She partly based the plot of her first novel, *Mary*, on her journey to Portugal in 1785. The twenty-six-year-old Wollstonecraft sailed for Lisbon to care for her recently married, pregnant best friend, Fanny Blood, who tragically died as a result of childbirth soon after Wollstonecraft's arrival. The "Heroine of this Fiction," the eponymous Mary, is a composite of the author Wollstonecraft, her sister Bess (who was recently separated from her husband), and Fanny. Wollstonecraft was unmarried at the time she wrote the novel, yet she imagined her namesake Mary struggling to realize independence within the conventions of patriarchal marriage as she strives to aid her dying friend Ann. Just prior to her trip to Lisbon, Wollstonecraft had assisted her sister Bess in leaving a loveless and possibly sexually exploitative marriage. The struggle of her "Heroine" Mary to avoid a similar marriage trap, in which she would be forced to give her body to a man she loathed, is the dominant narrative thread of the novel.[19]

Although the protagonist Mary is married when she arrives in Lisbon, she "never had any particular attachment" to her husband. Tellingly, she contracted with him to live apart for a year prior to their living together as husband and wife. The unstated implication is that the marriage was unconsummated. Mary's feelings of "disgust" for her husband suggest that she would prefer to avoid this inevitability as long as possible. Mary's father arranged the loveless marriage for the sake of preserving the family estate. As the third-person narrator dryly observes, "While this important matter was settling, Mary was otherwise employed." The "heroine" is caring for her ailing friend Ann and her impoverished family when her father brokers the marital deal that will cost her her youthful freedom.[20]

Despite the heroine's deft navigation of her personal tragedies and charting of "strange conduct" in friendship and love, the novel ultimately forces the reader to confront the grim realities of eighteenth-century patriarchal marriage. Social pressure compels Mary to reunite with her husband, yet her disgust at seeing him again is so strong that she faints. She negotiates another year's hiatus from cohabitation, but the time abroad flies by, and soon they are living together: "she gave him her hand – the struggle was almost more than she could endure." Mary sacrifices her sense of bodily integrity to enter into a marriage that disgusts her. Without the motive of love of a living human being, Mary loses her wily will to evade the marriage she hates. While the laws of entail and coverture set into motion her tragic, forced choice, the devastation of her loss of friendship propels it. Mary can only waste away her last years on

[19] Wollstonecraft, *Mary, a Fiction*, in *Works*, 1:7. [20] Ibid., 18, 25.

earth imagining she was "hastening to that world *where there is neither marrying*, nor giving in marriage."[21]

The radical theological message of *Mary, a Fiction* was the same as its feminist message: marriage, as practiced in the eighteenth century, was a profoundly bad deal for women. Even the most heroic and resourceful of them could not escape its insidious effects on personal health, well-being, and, most importantly, freedom. Looking forward to a heaven without sex or marriage thus emerged as the only complete exit option available to women of the time.

Wollstonecraft partly based *Maria* on her sister Bess's dramatic exit from what was likely an abusive marriage in 1784. Wollstonecraft and her sister Everina orchestrated Bess's escape because their recently married sibling had fallen into a terrible depression. The price of flight was leaving behind her baby, over whom she had no parental rights under the rules of coverture. The child died of illness soon afterward, making the sisters' decision to liberate Bess even more morally complex in unanticipated consequences.

Both novels drew a visionary connection between the patriarchal structure of marriage and the problem of sexual violence against women and related issues such as abortion. The heroines Mary and Maria each resist forced sex in marriage (marital rape). In *Maria*, the eponymous heroine describes "personal intimacy without affection" as "the most painful state" for any woman. Even more powerful is the novel's tale of the destitute young servant Jemima's desperate use of "the potion that was to procure abortion" after her expulsion from the home of the master who raped her. In section I of chapter 5 of the *Rights of Woman*, Wollstonecraft critiqued Rousseau's dangerous conflation of sex and rape with an evocative metaphor: if Rousseau is right that women are designed by nature to fulfill men's desire for forced sex, then women are chained to an "iron bed of fate." In contrast to this patriarchal view of women's total sexual subordination to men, Wollstonecraft consistently argued throughout her oeuvre that women ought to be free from all forms of sexual coercion, both inside and outside the institution of marriage.[22]

Also consistent across her writings was Wollstonecraft's development of a theory of the human rights of children that had no philosophical precedent. It was original not only in the content and scope of rights she imagined for children, but also in the justification she provided for understanding children as rights-bearing subjects alongside adults. As for the content and scope of

[21] Ibid., 72–3.

[22] Wollstonecraft, *Maria, or the Wrongs of Woman*, in *Works*, 1:112, 139; Wollstonecraft, *Rights of Woman*, 106.

children's rights, she theorized children's possession of the same rights as adult humans, minus the right to full citizenship. While full citizenship (including equal access to public goods such as property, careers, voting, and office holding) would only be granted at the age of majority to either sex, the state's provision of the right to free primary and secondary education would enable girls' and boys' development into full citizens capable of participation in a modern representative republic. Public education would then function as a kind of school for citizenship. Her extended proposal for universal primary education (as well as more class-inflected forms of secondary education) is set forth over the course of chapter 12 of the *Rights of Woman*.

In a radical move that distanced Wollstonecraft from even the most progressive theorists of family life in the seventeenth and eighteenth centuries, in chapters 10 and 11 of the *Rights of Woman*, she also specified the fundamental right of children to be free from physical or psychological abuse by their parents or elders, which derived from the perfect, universal, and fundamental obligation of adults not to abuse minors. The experience of such abuse, on her account, nullified the perfect, yet special duty of adult children to care for their parents in their old age. If they were given care and a rational education at home rather than abuse, children might also experience the family as a school for citizenship like the local schools they attended during the day. In addition, they would freely and reciprocally care for their parents in their old age. If the state failed to guarantee their right to be free from domestic abuse, children could still find at school an expansive space for the free and full development of their capabilities as human beings through the exercise of their rights to physical, moral, and intellectual education. If both the state and the family failed them, adult children at least had the right to extricate themselves from any further obligation toward their abusive parents.

In addition to her advocacy of egalitarian reform of the legal and cultural institutions of Western European family life, Wollstonecraft advanced moral views on polygamy as practiced by Muslim peoples in North Africa and Turkey. When she wrote for the *Analytical Review* in London from 1788 to 1792, she acquired a taste for travel memoirs. She researched works by German explorer Johann Reinhold Forster and English theologian James Cookson, who discussed the practice of polygamy in Africa. Following Montesquieu, the French Enlightenment philosopher, Forster even made theoretical claims about why polygamy seemed more prevalent in warm climates. In her *Rights of Woman*, Wollstonecraft philosophically challenged Forster's argument that the natural environment determined polygamy. By rejecting the natural necessity of polygamy, she sought to discredit the patriarchal view that woman "must be inferior to man, and made for him" and his sexual pleasure. This critique of polygamy supported her general moral argument in favor of monogamous marriages in which women were respected as ends in themselves, not merely used as means to other ends.[23]

In her *Rights of Woman*, she set forth an extended moral justification of marriage as primarily a relationship between equal moral beings, and secondarily a relationship that concerned natural functions such as sexual reproduction. She defended marital pairs over multiple spouses for the reason that marriage is ideally a dyadic, perfectionistic (or virtue-oriented) friendship. Polygamy or polyandry might be permissible if marriage were meant to be like a business or corporate contract, in which maximum productivity for the group is the goal. In a perfectionistic friendship, however, the goal is the mirroring and mutual inspiration of the higher virtues in one another.[24]

Like Aristotle, Wollstonecraft upheld the dyadic form to be the best, or virtue-oriented, friendship, but she explicitly and unequivocally extended this idea of higher friendship in an egalitarian way to male–female marital relationships. Beyond the practical consideration that such lofty virtue might prove more difficult to achieve in plural marriages, Wollstonecraft's defense of the smaller dyadic form belied her normative assumption that the process of sexual reproduction itself produced supplemental reasons for the moral practice of monogamy. The best evidence of this assumption is found in her 1797 *Lessons*, which envisioned and even idealized the active roles of biological parents in joint childcare of their toddler. More broadly, her metaphysical perspective allowed for Cookson's view that divine providence mandated monogamy as a beneficial moral ideal for humanity. She disagreed, however, with Forster's culturally biased and morally relativistic claim that God ordained monogamy for Europe, while nature dictated polygamy for Africa.[25]

CONCLUSION

The study of Wollstonecraft's moral and political philosophy and its Christian metaphysical foundations remains productive for scholars of family law today. Wollstonecraft's theologically grounded theory of the egalitarian family – characterized by equality of spouses and equality of siblings, and the benevolent provision of basic rights to children by dutiful and caring parents – resonates strongly with the predominant twenty-first-century Western legal conception of what the structure and function of the family ought to be. Her dissenting Christian theological commitments led

[23] Wollstonecraft, *Rights of Woman*, 98. [24] Abbey, "Back to the Future," 78–95.
[25] N. Taylor, *The Rights of Woman as Chimera*, 180.

Wollstonecraft to defend a ground-breaking conception of universal human rights, which is broadly compatible with the secular values of modern democratic states.

RECOMMENDED READING

Abbey, Ruth. "Back to the Future: Marriage as Friendship in the Thought of Mary Wollstonecraft." *Hypatia* 14:3 (1999), 78–95.

Botting, Eileen Hunt. *Family Feuds: Wollstonecraft, Burke, and Rousseau on the Transformation of the Family*. Albany: State University of New York Press, 2006.

"Editor's Introduction: Reading Wollstonecraft's *A Vindication of the Rights of Woman*, 1792–2014." In Mary Wollstonecraft, *A Vindication of the Rights of Woman*, 1–15. Edited by Eileen Hunt Botting. New Haven, CT: Yale University Press, 2014.

Wollstonecraft, Mill, and Women's Human Rights. New Haven, CT: Yale University Press, 2016.

Gordon, Lyndall. *Vindication: A Life of Mary Wollstonecraft*. New York: HarperCollins, 2005.

Hutton, Sarah. "The Ethical Background of the Rights of Women." In *Philosophical Theory and the Universal Declaration of Human Rights*, edited by William Sweet, 27–40. Ottawa: University of Ottawa Press, 2003.

Price, Richard. *Four Dissertations*. London: T. Cadell, [1767] 1777.

"Observations on the Nature of Civil Liberty." In id., *Political Writings*. Edited by D. O. Thomas, 20–75. Cambridge: Cambridge University Press, 1991.

Taylor, Barbara. *Mary Wollstonecraft and the Feminist Imagination*. Cambridge: Cambridge University Press, 2003.

Taylor, Natalie. *The Rights of Woman as Chimera: The Political Philosophy of Mary Wollstonecraft*. New York: Routledge, 2007.

Wollstonecraft, Mary. *The Works of Mary Wollstonecraft*. Edited by Janet Todd and Marilyn Butler. 7 vols. New York: New York University Press, 1989.

A Vindication of the Rights of Woman. Edited by Eileen Hunt Botting. New Haven, CT: Yale University Press, 2014.

18

Abraham Kuyper

James D. Bratt

BIOGRAPHICAL INTRODUCTION

Abraham Kuyper (1837–1920) was the founder of the neo-Calvinist movement that arose in the Netherlands in the late nineteenth century. He aimed to recover Calvinism's historic public role and to reassert it amid the characteristically modern circumstances that fully arrived in the Netherlands in his generation: an industrial economy, urban society, democratic politics, secularizing academy, and the separation of church and state. Outside of the urbanism, these were foreign to the conditions in which the Dutch Reformed Church had once enjoyed a privileged status. Yet, Kuyper argued, since that status had significantly compromised the cause of true faith, the new situation represented a rich opportunity to realize Christianity afresh. He hoped to sift through the Reformed tradition and rescue its more promising parts, even if substantial alterations occurred in the process. Kuyper's project used progressive means toward conservative ends.[1]

He began with the rehabilitation of Calvinist thought, first in theology and then in political theory and social ethics; much of Kuyper's titanic energy went into a remarkable publishing program across all those disciplines and more. He also knew that words would avail little without concerted action and that, to be sustained over the long run, action needed to be based in institutions. He founded a complete array of these, each the first of its type in the nation, each meant to be distinctively Calvinist in program: a daily newspaper and Sunday magazine to create, educate, and inspire a mass following; a modern political party, the Antirevolutionary Party, to advocate a Calvinist line for national policy and promote democratization in its own right; a private university, the Free University of Amsterdam, to fill the ranks of leadership, along with a network of Christian day schools to nurture the rank and file; and a purified

[1] The standard English-language biography is Bratt, *Abraham Kuyper* [hereafter Bratt, *AK*].

FIGURE 18.1. Political speeches by Abraham Kuyper and others (1889).
Collection PJ / Alamy Stock Photo

Reformed church freed of what, to Kuyper's mind, were the diluted theology and bureaucratic lethargy that constituted the worst legacy of ecclesiastical establishment.

Against long odds, against fierce opposition from both within and without the ranks of the Reformed, amid constant personal contention and stress – not to mention the huge ambition – that brought him to periodic personal collapses, Kuyper sustained this program over a fifty-year career, from his first pastorate in 1863 to his death in 1920. Whether he intended it or not, one legacy of his work was the pattern of a "pillarized" society that prevailed in the Netherlands into the 1960s. Another was the inspiration that many people in the Dutch immigrant diaspora in North America, South Africa, and Indonesia drew from his example, and the models they adapted from his enterprise. Lately, these have won attention beyond that ethno-confessional network as a distinctive and compelling entry on the short list of options for how to relate religion to public life under the conditions of postmodern pluralism.[2]

The family loomed large at every key point in Kuyper's initiatives. The step with which he began, the reassertion of historic Reformed orthodoxy, served to resurrect all the old quandaries about the doctrine of divine election. To resolve them, he deployed the doctrine of the covenant, which he understood primarily in terms of family connections; in the process, he reaffirmed a historic, household-centered Reformed model of spiritual formation. His political enterprise took off from controversies over public education in the 1870s; here Kuyper opposed the emerging uniform, state-dictated system in the name of parental rights over child nurture. This resistance not only made his movement viable and energetic, but also grew into a comprehensive political program, grounded in creative reflection on the norms and practices of modern society and issuing in concrete policy proposals. Two later emerging challenges – the industrial economy and political feminism – drew opposite responses from him according to his perception of their impact on the home. In sum, thinking about the family took Kuyper from grassroots action to the far reaches of theoretical reflection, galvanized the programmatic responses that defined his legacy, and defined some key tensions in his project.

[2] See, for instance, the Abraham Kuyper Center for Public Theology at Princeton Theological Seminary. Likewise, Fuller Theological Seminary has established a collaborative doctoral program with the Vrije Universiteit Amsterdam focused on the neo-Calvinist tradition. Lexham Press is producing critical English translations of Kuyper's major works in public theology.

COVENANT THEOLOGY

Kuyper embarked on his career in the mid-1860s, sharing his generation's widespread yearning for a revitalized nation. In his view, that required first of all a revitalized church, and a revitalized church required the rehabilitation of classic Reformed theology, starting with its most controversial tenet of predestination. Thus the Sunday after he was installed in his pulpit in Amsterdam, he preached on "The Comfort of Divine Election," the first time in a century, he gibed, that the topic had been broached in the national capital. He would devote one of the first of his many long series of theological commentary in his church magazine to the same subject.[3] It is important to register that, if Kuyper belongs in a volume on Christianity and family law because of his distinctive sociopolitical thought and policy prescriptions, these were grounded in theological conviction and their attendant religious practices.

For Kuyper, the doctrine of election was crucial for the good Calvinistic purpose of reaffirming divine sovereignty as the controlling principle of all Christian theology, and all of Christian life. On the outside, God's ordinances made a cosmos out of an otherwise chaotic run of elements both in the moral and in the natural world. On the inside, only God's sovereignty could secure the salvation of the sinner amid human weakness and vacillation. Moreover, the classic objections to the doctrine, Kuyper insisted, could be readily answered. Divine election ought not lead to human pride since, by all biblical evidence, God chose the weak and worthless of the world for his purposes, not the high and mighty. Politically, election implied democracy, not hierarchy, since all people are equal in God's sight, demolishing human pretensions and differentiations. Nor did the doctrine, rightly understood, lead to passivity or fatalism, since divine election always entailed a calling to a purpose. That purpose, being grounded on the firmest of foundations, could go forward with confidence and energy, whatever odds or obstacles might appear to the human eye.

Still, Kuyper admitted, intellectual and especially psychological barriers to belief remained on this point. From the human side, "there is a contradiction" between human damnation and God's gracious will; "that we *must* acknowledge."[4] Viewed abstractly, God's choices might seem arbitrary and invite charges that God is the author of sin. And Kuyper's soteriology *was* inclined

3 The Amsterdam sermon is "De Troost der Ewige Verkiezing," in *Predicatiën in de jaren 1867 tot 1873*. *Dat de Genade Particulier Is* ran in Kuyper's Sunday magazine *De Heraut* from April 1879 to June 1880 before being published in book form in Amsterdam in 1884. I cite the English translation by Marvin Kamps, *Particular Grace*.

4 Kuyper, *Particular Grace*, 240. Kuyper's rendition of the *ordo salutis* (the process of personal redemption) summarized in the rest of this paragraph is given in detail in his *The Work of the Holy Spirit*, trans. Henri DeVries, 203–447.

to the abstract. In his view, divine election took place before all creation. Since everything, including persons, first exists as a thought in the divine mind, God implanted in the elect long before they were born a new person rooted in Christ. Over the course of life, the elect experience the presence and rising salience of this new, regenerate self. They also engage their calling to become agents toward God's ultimate purpose, namely, the regeneration of the entire cosmos from its fallen state, with the elect at the end of time being a new human race occupying a redeemed and fulfilled creation. Hence the activism of Kuyper's model of the Christian life, intertwined with the most robust reassertion of the first principle of divine sovereignty. But hence, too, renewed complaints about theology as abstract speculation.

To solve that problem, Kuyper immediately turned to the equally Calvinist tradition of covenantal theology. In fact, the covenant of grace was the flip side of divine election; it is "the glorious channel through which the water of life flows to us from the depth of *election*." What was glorious in the picture was not some pristine majesty of a distant God, but the persistence of divine love as it advances its purposes through the murky imponderables of human life. From the operations of the covenant, it is clear that God does not treat us like "sticks and blocks," but as real people in ordinary time, enwrapped in "transitional, mixed, and unconscious circumstances." As a "brook," the covenant bears the waters of salvation down from the mountaintops of election "through all the bumps and twists of our earthly life," bearing us safe and sure to our destined end. The covenant also forges a new community spanning space and time. By it believers are endowed with the task assigned them in God's mighty plan. The covenant places people who are already aware of their redemption as a saving witness amid "the broad circle of people who do not know it yet." It establishes a bond between the present generation with both their forebears and their progeny in the faith. In short, the covenant provides the anchors, the evangelists, and the succession of God's grace for long-term Christian living, translating election into palpable human terms.[5]

But what did covenant have to do with family? Pretty much everything. First, as Kuyper put it, family lineage was "the normal means" by which one was brought under God's covenant promises. A Dutch-American pastor put it more forcefully: "God does not save people at random . . . but follows a certain order, and perpetuates his covenant from generation to generation through the families

[5] Kuyper presented his covenantal theology in *De Heraut* immediately after the series on election, September 1880–October 1881. The series was published as *De Leer der Verbonden*; quotations 319, 303, 323, 324–5, 303.

of believers."[6] If that seemed to promise little for evangelism, it was deemed especially important in the United States to ward off the attractions of revivalism that were so endemic to the national scene. More than ethnic solidarity (or, in the Netherlands, contentment within the Calvinist pillar) was at stake. Covenant theology assumed a model of spiritual development by means of communal nurture that would proceed slowly, steadily, and deeply through the ordinary course of family life. This model was intentionally opposed to the sensationalism of evangelical marketing, on the one hand, and the austere rationalist reflection prescribed on the other, both of which were premised on autonomous individuals making detached decisions. By contrast, covenant immersed people with others – with family first of all.

Entry into this process started with the baptism of infants – as early in life as possible, Kuyper taught, even if the mother, still recuperating from childbirth, was not able to be present; her role was covered by her husband as covenantal head of the family. Not that the little ones or their parents thereby received a free pass. As the baptismal formulary put it: "we are by God, through baptism, admonished of and obliged unto new obedience, namely, that we cleave unto this one God . . . that we trust in Him and love Him with all our heart, with all our mind, and with all our strength; that we forsake the world, crucify our old nature, and walk in a godly life." The church was to do its part through regular catechesis. But the parents promised more: to instruct their child in Christian doctrine "and cause him to be instructed therein, to the utmost of their power."[7] Obviously, that entailed daily gathering around "the family altar" in Bible reading and prayer. But once day schooling became mandatory as a matter of national policy, "utmost" might come to entail more. Kuyper insisted that it did, and from the consequences of that insistence built a national political movement.

THE POLITICS OF EDUCATION

Six years into his pastoral ministry, Kuyper entered the lists of national politics on the issue of public education. This initiative was consistent with his dawning sense that the renewal of the church alone would not be adequate to the real need of the day. The problems of modern life were many, to be sure, but in his thinking what mattered most were society's controlling ideas and values. Here the rising danger was a philosophical materialism that, riding on

6 Ibid., 335; Hendriksen, *The Covenant of Grace*, 65.

7 "Form for the Baptism of Infants." The formulary follows closely the traditional Dutch Reformed liturgy that Kuyper would have used.

the back of scientific and technological progress, threatened to reduce daily life to a remorseless competition and turn people's ultimate concern to a scramble for riches. Given that diagnosis, the battlefront ran through the institutions of culture formation, the school as much as the church. The issue was particularly pressing because the dominant liberal party in Dutch politics, having supervised a generation of improvements to the nation's physical infrastructure so as to integrate it into the emerging global economy, now sought an upgrade in human capital to make the Netherlands competitive in that economy. They proposed radical improvements in the quality of Dutch education, including a program of thorough secularization to eliminate the putative superstitions of religion that still hung on in the era of science and progress. A bill to that effect came to the floor of Parliament in 1878 and galvanized Kuyper into creating the first mass political party in Dutch history. To that effort he brought a creative conceptual innovation that he had been working on for a decade.[8]

The Dutch Constitution of 1848 mandated that public schools train children in all the "Christian and social virtues" but without offending the conscience of any pupil or parent. Traditional Calvinists, gathered in the Union for Christian National Education, increasingly divided over how to walk that fine line. Those who wanted to maintain something of a sacred canopy over public space assented to diluting the religious content of instruction. The more theologically rigorous objected that the resulting moralism was too weak to satisfy parents with strong commitments while still functioning as an established religion that marginalized dissenters. Kuyper's political mentor, Guillaume Groen van Prinsterer, suggested that two separate school systems be organized, one for Protestants and one for Catholics, but that suggestion distressed those who yearned to retain whatever could be salvaged of national Reformed hegemony. Kuyper's keynote address at the Union's 1869 convention, in answering that objection, outlined the program he would follow for the next fifty years.[9]

His talk established three principles. First of all, authority over education lay with the family, not the state. The government could properly stipulate certain competencies, quality facilities, teachers' salaries, and so on, but decisions about pedagogy and the curriculum's philosophical framework belonged to the parents. To impose objectionable convictions on them, as the secularization initiative would for traditionalist Christians, was to violate freedom of

8 This context is laid out in Bratt, *AK*, 64–70.

9 On Dutch educational history, see ibid., 67–70. For more detail, see Kossmann, *The Low Countries, 1780–1940*, 206–13, 297–305. Kuyper's 1869 speech is *Het Beroep op de Volksgeweten*.

conscience. At the same time, imposing religious principles on secular families, or Protestant ones on Catholics or Jews, was an equal violation. The only solution, Kuyper concluded, was a formal and equitable pluralization of public education. This second tenet – principled (that is, not just prudential) public pluralism – would have ramifications for his entire political program. So would a third. The Progressive Liberals' program, Kuyper pointed out, would fall most heavily on poor Christian families who were bound by their baptismal vows to raise their children in the faith, but could not afford the double costs the new school law entailed: higher taxes for upgraded secular schools and additional tuition for the Christian school. His solution – an equitable sharing of public education revenues on a student per capita basis – was therefore a matter of social justice as well as of respect for private conscience.

Kuyper combined these principles with a genius for organization in a campaign against the proposed school law of 1878. His nationwide "People's Petition" not only garnered more than 300,000 signatures from Protestant circles (Catholic leaders gathered 165,000 more), but also created a network of local leaders around which he could found the independent Antirevolutionary Party the next year. Education remained its foremost issue for forty years until, in the "pacification of 1917" negotiated by a national unity government under wartime exigencies, the Antirevolutionary and Catholic Parties won full public funding for religious schools in exchange for supporting universal suffrage in civil elections. So salient was this agenda item in the eyes of opponents and loyalists alike that Kuyper had to insist repeatedly that his was not a one-issue party, but had a comprehensive program for all national affairs, growing out of a comprehensive vision. Family matters laid the foundation there, too.[10]

FAMILY AND SOCIAL THEORY

For Kuyper, the family was the seedbed and school of society. In both the biblical account and the thinking of the German historical school on which he drew heavily, it was the first institution to appear in human history. It was the decisive site where nature and nurture met – and, hopefully, meshed. There, people first learned the vital lessons of social functioning, particularly how to balance personal autonomy with mutual interdependence and

[10] On the "People's Petition," see Bratt, *AK*, 115–17. The relevant political history on this issue is detailed in Kossmann, *Low Countries*, 297–302.

responsibility. All this meant that family well-being constituted a prime goal of public policy and a prime measure of its effectiveness. At the same time, it was no discrete and isolate node, but deeply integrated into broader society; it was a "little commonwealth," not just a "haven in a heartless world." The family's authority was the source of, model for, and limit on the state, as the dramatic encounter over public education showed. In its ideal form, it exhibited church-like qualities in being crowned with love and becoming a school for morals. But as a microcosm of society, it was inevitably shaped by larger forces too, so that broad social trends and exterior public policy could become matters of "family values." In short, the family was integral to Kuyper's whole social philosophy and political program.[11]

That philosophy is most widely known as "sphere sovereignty," first labeled as such by the title of a speech with which Kuyper inaugurated the Free University of Amsterdam in 1880.[12] It was a theory of social ontology rooted in creation. That is, God had endowed the human race with any number of latent powers along with a commission to unfold these over the course of history (Genesis 1:28). Human nature thus bears innate political and economic functions, artistic and scientific capacities, and instincts for communication and learning. Over time, as these powers developed, they became housed in discrete institutions with their own rules and procedures. The Fall into sin had twisted these powers and perverted their expression; not least, they acquired a passion to imperialize on each other's territory. Yet their core purpose remained intact, and no small part of Christian witness was to work in these spheres aright. More broadly, a good society was one in which each domain was given maximum freedom to develop its own potential, following its own norms. That much of this work might go well, even among the unregenerate and despite the pervasive effects of the Fall, Kuyper explained in another of his distinctive teachings, that of common grace. For public policy, the guiding mandate was to restrict or roll back sphere imperialism. The worst offender in the past, Kuyper said, had been the church in (nearly) monopolizing education and art and in restricting science. But the rising threat was the centralized state with its public universities and intrusive economic regulations. The fight Kuyper had waged over the proposed school law thus also served as a memorable laboratory experiment in applied social theory.

[11] Bratt, *AK*, 142–5. Kuyper, *Our Program*, 190–2, 199–201. Kuyper's most extensive treatment of the family comes in *Pro Rege*, II, 347–541.

[12] Kuyper, "Sphere Sovereignty," 461–90.

From this basis Kuyper developed the central, consociational strand of his political theory. There were others: a celebration, looking backward, of the Calvinist revolutionary tradition of constitutional resistance to tyranny, centered on the "lesser magistrates"; and a defense, looking forward, of the necessity of charismatic leadership in democratic politics. These dwelt uneasily with his party's Antirevolutionary label and fears of concentrated power, however, so he settled – especially in his years of active power – on a theory emphasizing the division of powers in a decentralized system. The theory strongly resembled that of Johannes Althusius (1557–1638), a syndic in the city of Emden when that "Geneva of the North" served as a beacon and refuge for the struggling Dutch republic. Althusius's great treatise, *Politica Methodice Digesta* (1603), had set forth a Calvinist, antiroyalist answer to the French Catholic Jean Bodin's theory of unitary sovereignty. One can see it as a picture of the family extrapolated to its broadest degree.[13] For Althusius, human nature was indelibly associational, making communities the building blocks of society. So also began Kuyper's social ontology: "Our human life ... is so structured that the individual exists only in groups, and only in such groups can the whole become manifest."[14] Each human association, Althusius continued, was empowered by its original purpose, but was also bound by the inherent limits therein so as not to intrude on others in its own or adjoining domains. Certain powers were delegated upward to the next level by decision of smaller units. The household was the most basic; individuals were first of all members of families. The heads of families – typically fathers – delegated some of their *political* power to town councilors, who in turn appointed mayors and syndics. For economic purposes, citizens joined guilds; for religious purposes, churches; for recreation, clubs. Successive intermediate levels of association then conveyed authority up the scale to more general gatherings: towns constituted a province, provinces a nation, nations an empire.

Human society was thus a pyramid of associations where power remained as close to the base as possible, and in which different functions of human life developed freely according to the purposes of that function and not at the call of another. No one at any level ruled without the consent of the governed, and

[13] Bratt, *AK*, 77–82, 132–5, 351–3. The three relevant primary texts are "Sphere Sovereignty," echoing Althusius; "Calvinism: Source and Stronghold of Our Constitutional Liberties" [1874], in *Abraham Kuyper: A Centennial Reader* [herein after *AKCR*], 279–322, evoking the Calvinist revolutionary tradition; and "Our Instinctive Life" [1908], ibid., 255–78, on charismatic leadership.

[14] Kuyper, "Sphere Sovereignty," 467.

decision-making remained closest to those most competent to make and implement them. Moreover, authorities at every level were constrained by the laws divine and natural that set norms for that domain. Thus, individuals within a consociation – the father in the home, guild A in the town economy, province X in the nation – could be disciplined by their fellows or their superiors for violating their trust. As Kuyper put it, the state was simultaneously a sphere *among* spheres and a power that properly "rises high *above* them" to regulate their mutual interaction and to step in whenever individual rights were abused or the weak exploited by the strong. A principal calling for Christians in politics, therefore, was to so strengthen spontaneous resistance to abuse and exploitation that governmental intrusion would not be necessary. As Kuyper observed late in life after watching the course of Dutch industrialization, businesses and banks were called to restrain themselves in their quest for power and wealth; having failed therein, they had only themselves to blame when the state imposed regulations to redress grievances and secure more just arrangements going forward.[15]

THE CHALLENGE OF THE MODERN

The latter note showed Kuyper's readiness to adapt to changing conditions; yet he could also reject such a move as a compromise of principle. This ambivalence became particularly evident in his response to two epochal social changes that unfolded in the second half of his career: the class conflict catalyzed by industrialization, and the rise of feminism in conjunction with democratization. Both challenged his ideal of the home but offered different possibilities for redress. He thought that the "social question" about rich and poor could be answered in a way commensurate with that model; the gender challenge could not, because it challenged the home as a site of sexual control.

Kuyper's model of the family can be summarized as nuclear, heteronormative, strictly monogamous, and benevolently patriarchal. Its social policy implications were clear. Kuyper's program called for concerted state action against infractions of "public decency," such as prostitution and drunkenness, and he could always count on a warm response from readers when he editorialized against public displays of sexuality, whether on the street, on the stage, or in art. He envisioned a disciplined citizenry with an energetic work ethic but without greed; self-reliant but compassionate; taking care of

[15] Quotation, ibid., 468. On corporate failure of self-regulation and his new higher regard for the state, see Kuyper, *Pro Rege*, III, 239–49.

their shops and homes and neighborhoods so that the authorities did not have to. This picture assumed the availability of reliable, dignified work; it also assumed – as did Alexis de Tocqueville in *Democracy in America* – that public discontents were bred at home. Unlike Tocqueville, Kuyper had no room for sexual double standards for men, nor did he surrender to licensing avarice as the price to be paid for constraining lust. Hence his willingness – eagerness – to discipline the industrial machine but his deep anxiety at the specter of feminism.[16]

The harsh course of Dutch industrialization in the last third of the nineteenth century qualifies as a second test case of Kuyperian theory, equal to the earlier one of public education. After some fitful beginnings in the 1870s, the industrial sector followed the larger agricultural economy into a profound depression in the 1880s, bringing the Netherlands to a destitution unseen for fifty years. Kuyper responded with a series on manual labor in his daily newspaper and, simultaneously with Pope Leo XIII's encyclical *Rerum Novarum* in 1891, convened the Christian Social Congress in Amsterdam, where he delivered a blistering critique of the spirit and practices of laissez-faire capitalism, "The Social Question and the Christian Religion." Kuyper did not endorse socialist solutions for the contemporary crisis, but he did assert that socialists were correct to insist on a structural critique of the existing economy and that Christians who did not like the socialist blueprint needed to issue one of their own.[17]

Kuyper's main policy proposals on this front can be briefly enumerated. On the one hand, workers' rights, responsibilities, and grievances ought to be integrated into the formal legal system by the creation of a complete code of labor like those for commercial, civil, and criminal matters. At the same time, workers ought to be empowered through the extension of voting rights to all adult males in civil elections and through the creation of a pyramid of labor councils in the halls of industry, from the grassroots up, where fair arrangements with management could be hammered out. As with politics, Kuyper thought that an equalization of power on the shop floor would make for relative justice without outside intrusion. Theologically, any answer to the era's social question had first to honor the image of God in every person and not reduce laborers to a "factor of production"; second, reject any targeting of a particular class of people, be it labor or capital; because, third, solidarity was

16 Kuyper, *Our Program*, chapter 15. Cf. Tocqueville, *Democracy in America*, 335–40, 698–708.

17 For context, see Kossmann, *Low Countries*, 412–18; and Bratt, *AK*, 221–8. The translation of Kuyper's 1891 address is *The Problem of Poverty*. His newspaper series (*Handenarbeid* [Amsterdam: J. A. Wormser, 1889]) is available in English translation as "Manual Labor," in *AKCR*, 231–54.

both the biblical ideal for human society and the pragmatic grounds of its true flourishing. From the family up, God created human beings to live relationally under the canopy of transcendent norms. Thus, any economic theory that started with the autonomous individual fell short of Christian standards. Kuyper's economics, like his politics, was first of all a communal theory with a communal ethic.

But what did the economy hold for the home in the parlous conditions of industrialism? Here again Kuyper began with cultural formation: "Because we are conscious beings, almost everything depends on the standard of values which our consciousness constructs." The cultivation of Christian patience in adversity was on this list, but not by itself, lest it amount to more opiate for the masses. The spirit of compassion and an insistence on justice and equity were there too. These values needed to be inculcated by the agencies competent for and commissioned to this effort: families, churches, schools, and organs of public opinion. But values had to be translated into structural realities, and here Kuyper was quite willing to go past his old strictures against big government. If the state could regulate morals, it could also pass legislation to promote public health, prescribe minimum housing standards, limit the exploitation of women's and children's labor, impose tariffs to protect home manufacture, guarantee the right to belong to unions and to strike, and provide insurance against accidents on the job. All these policies Kuyper endorsed. In fact, he thought the Progressive Liberals' support for industrial workers' health insurance too restrictive; it ought to be made mandatory for *everyone*, with a public option. Put more generally, private enterprise was essential, but so was some basic security if one would see and seize life's chances. Free markets were good, but never free from the wiles of concentrated power. Morality was fine for churches to preach, but covetousness, corporate theft, and the grinding of the weak were sins, too, and sphere sovereignty gave the state plenty of warrant to redress – better yet, to prevent – them.[18]

All such principles and measures would make for happy homes in the industrial world, but another rising tide threatened to swamp them. So Kuyper deemed political feminism. Some distinctions need to be drawn here. Women's enterprise in the domain of culture formation he exalted; one of his most memorable encounters on his tour of the United States in 1898 involved upper-middle-class women in Northern cities who hosted his lectures, helped build libraries and music associations, led the way in health care and moral crusades, and demonstrated a remarkable acquaintance with

18 Bratt, *AK*, 223–8, 298–301, 304–5; quotation, Kuyper, *Problem of Poverty*, 73.

current affairs at home and abroad. Kuyper added quickly – and inaccurately, as it turned out – that these cultural activists were content without political enfranchisement. In fact, they would be near the front of the line in the coming battle for women's suffrage.[19]

That was the issue that precipitated his pronouncements on the women's question in the 1910s. Doubtless his own exile to the sidelines of power by this time aggravated his ire; the younger generation that had supplanted him in party leadership included some who favored women's suffrage as part of a great compromise that would put an end to decades of wrangling over education and the franchise in Dutch politics. Kuyper had long championed universal *household* suffrage as a way to achieve democracy without ceding to the individualistic atomization that critics feared in that system. Household suffrage gave everyone in society political representation through the head of the home, their primary community. That head would normally be the husband/father, devolving to the wife/mother in his absence. This would maintain society's vital organic bonds instead of the mechanistic individualism espoused by the opposition.[20]

Kuyper's further excursions on gender roles betrayed an anxiety that went beyond political theory, however. It involved sex appeal. Man might initiate the mating dance, but woman exercised "an irresistible magnetic power" that bent him to her will. Perhaps in fear of that, too many men on the current scene were avoiding marriage, availing themselves of paid sex and leaving too many women frustrated at not being able to attain their natural desire for matrimony and motherhood. This was the "chief cause of feminism," Kuyper fumed. No wonder that feminists turned toward grasping power that belonged by nature to men. Their cause was "nothing but an attempt to retard, falsify, and bastardize . . . a fixed ordinance of God," and nothing but trouble would ensue from it. The explosive power of sex reverberated well beyond the individuals involved; its restriction to the marital bed was the foundation of social health. Feminism resulted from and furthered dysfunction; votes for women were its crucial sign.[21]

In his calmer moods, Kuyper modulated his tone and his content. He never stopped preaching that the assertion of proper authority was the key to social order, and that proper authority was patriarchal. Yet his Calvinism always recalled that power brought with it great temptation

19 Kuyper, *Varia Americana*, 39–41.

20 Bratt, *AK*, 345–9, 360–3; Kuyper, *Heilige Orde*, 18–22; quotations, ibid., 18, 19.

21 Kuyper, *Pro Rege*, II, 401–22; quotations, 405–6, 413, 420–2.

and greater responsibilities, and so was mindful that authority be exercised with a gentle touch. This was most crucial for the family as the first sphere in the order of creation. A *Christian* family, in Kuyper's view, could be distinguished by the redemption wrought upon its myriad interrelationships by God's re-creation of all things in Christ, and the burden of proof fell entirely on those in power. Household staff ought to have cause to give thanks for the respect and gratitude they received for their work. The first duty of the father toward children was not to abuse his power; the second was to provide for their holistic formation. Here the wise father shared authority with his wife; in fact, she had a sovereignty of her own in the mixed sphere of the household. Under Kuyper's Victorian, separate-spheres ideology, the mother had the better and more powerful part on this front. But homemaking in the broader sense – of forming children's character and socializing willful husbands – also had some public carryover that Kuyper acknowledged. If the home is the seedbed of society, then society at large could use a woman's touch; hence his support for their power in culture formation and in the paid professions – teaching, philanthropy, and female specialties in medicine – commensurate with women's nature.[22]

Kuyper's anxieties about the rise of feminism were published at the threshold of World War I, which dealt a deep blow to his confidence in the technological and moral progress of the West. In its aftermath, his movement solidified into one of the pillars of Dutch society, coherent, detached, and closely monitored within for orthodoxy. This provided one of the strongest bastions of resistance to the Nazi takeover of the Netherlands in World War II, but lost much of the dynamic interplay with contemporary developments in European society that had marked Kuyper's own work. When the sense of stasis and claustrophobia proved too much in the 1960s, all the pillars started to break up, the neo-Calvinist one too. In that breakup, family and gender relations once again constituted a key frontier, both in theoretical reflection and in everyday behaviour. In that sense, too, Kuyper was a prophet.[23]

RECOMMENDED READING

Bratt, James D. *Abraham Kuyper: Modern Calvinist, Christian Democrat.* Grand Rapids, MI: Eerdmans, 2013.

ed. *Abraham Kuyper: A Centennial Reader.* Grand Rapids, MI: Eerdmans, 1998.

[22] Ibid., 347–68, 422–55; quotations, 441. See also his *De Eerepositie der Vrouw.*

[23] For an overview of these dynamics, see Blom and Lamberts, eds., *History of the Low Countries,* 429–70.

De Bruijn, Jan. *Abraham Kuyper: A Pictorial Biography*. Grand Rapids, MI: Eerdmans, 2014.
Kossmann, Ernst Heinrich. *The Low Countries, 1780–1940*. Oxford: Clarendon Press, 1978.
Kuyper, Abraham. *Our Program: A Christian Political Manifesto*. Bellingham, WA: Lexham Press, [1879] 2015.
The Problem of Poverty. Translation of *Het sociale vraagstuk en de christelijke religie* [1891]. Edited and translated by James W. Skillen. Grand Rapids, MI: Baker, 1991.
Lectures on Calvinism. Grand Rapids, MI: Eerdmans, [1899] 1931.
Lugo, Luis E., ed. *Religion, Pluralism, and Public Life: Abraham Kuyper's Legacy for the Twenty-First Century*. Grand Rapids, MI: Eerdmans, 2000.
Mouw, Richard. *Abraham Kuyper: A Short and Personal Introduction*. Grand Rapids, MI: Eerdmans, 2011.
Van der Kooi, Cornelis, and Jan de Bruijn, eds. *Kuyper Reconsidered: Aspects of His Life and Work*. Amsterdam: VU Uitgeverij, 1999.
Wintle, Michael. *Pillars of Piety: Religion in the Netherlands, 1813–1901*. Hull: Hull University Press, 1987.
An Economic and Social History of the Netherlands, 1800–1920. Cambridge: Cambridge University Press, 2000.

19

Emil Brunner

Don S. Browning† and John Witte, Jr.

BIOGRAPHICAL INTRODUCTION

Emil Brunner (1899–1966) was one of the great European Protestant minds of the twentieth century. He was educated in Switzerland, served in the Swiss military, and then was a pastor in Zurich before embarking on a distinguished career as a professor of theology at the University of Zurich. He was an active participant in the World Council of Churches and the global Moral Re-armament Movement and stood at distinguished lecterns throughout the world.

Brunner drew deeply on the writings of his Protestant forebears Martin Luther and John Calvin, and he was strongly influenced by the teachings of Danish theologian Søren Kierkegaard and German philosopher Edmund Husserl, among others. A staunch defender of biblical Christianity, Brunner resisted theological liberals like Paul Tillich, who saw God as "the ground of being" and understood revelation to be necessarily a mere symbol that points beyond itself. Yet Brunner was also a staunch defender of natural law, natural theology, and natural reason, which he defended against many other Protestants, notably his famous Swiss contemporary Karl Barth, who declared his famous "Nein!" against him. Brunner believed in salvation by faith in Christ, but he also insisted that Christians – and all others – could understand God's will for their personal and collective lives through the natural law that

† Don S. Browning passed away in 2010. This text is drawn in part from an unpublished manuscript on "Christian Marriage and Modern Marriage Law" that the two authors were working on at his death, and it is used with permission of the Browning family and estate. Browning also touched on Emil Brunner's work in his *From Culture Wars* 242–3; and in *Marriage and Modernization* (Grand Rapids, MI: Wm. B. Eerdmans, 2003), 140–2.

FIGURE 19.1. Emil Brunner and Karl Barth, Courtesy of the Center for Barth Studies, Princeton Theological Seminary on behalf of the Karl Barth Stiftung of Basel, Switzerland

God had "written on their hearts" and through the natural order that God had created, even though it was corrupted by human sin.

Brunner was a prolific scholar, whose writings circulated widely in Europe, North America, Japan, and South Korea. In his three-volume *Dogmatics*,[1] he laid out the doctrinal fundamentals of Christian theology with a strong emphasis on the "I–Thou" relationship between God and humanity, whereby God equips and calls each person to respond to God and divine law. In his *Divine Imperative*,[2] he examined how God's commands for human living, set out in scripture, conscience, reason, and nature, provide the foundation for the flourishing of human personhood and social institutions. *Man in Revolt*[3] probed the causes and consequences of defiance of these divine imperatives, and *The Mediator*[4] analyzed the pathway to salvation through and in Christ. Brunner wrote biblical commentaries and other technical works on religion. He also left several important books on social ethics, not least his *Justice and the Social Order*,[5] *Eros and Agape*,[6] and his Gifford Lectures, titled *Christianity and Civilization*.[7]

THE NATURAL-RATIONAL FOUNDATION OF THE MARITAL FAMILY

In a number of these works, Brunner addressed themes of sex, marriage, and family. He started by distinguishing three kinds of human interests stemming from what he called the "psychophysical nature" of human beings. These interests are the human need for (1) sex, intimacy, and offspring; (2) labor, acquisition, and economic well-being; and (3) safety, security, and control over the contingencies of life. In Brunner's view, these basic human interests are fostered and fulfilled by different spheres of society: (1) sex and procreation by marriage and the family; (2) acquisition and economic well-being by labor and the market; and (3) safety and control by the state and its laws. This was a deliberate variation on the famous "three estates theory" (*Drei-Stände-Lehre*)

1 Brunner, *Dogmatik*. See also his *Wahrheit als Begegnung*, translated by A. W. Loos as *The Divine-Human Encounter*.

2 Brunner, *Das Gebot und die Ordnungen*, translated by Olive Wyon as *The Divine Imperative: A Study in Christian Ethics*.

3 Brunner, *Der Mensch im Widerspruch*, translated by Olive Wyon as *Man in Revolt*.

4 Brunner, *Der Mittler*, translated by Olive Wyon as *The Mediator: A Study of the Central Doctrine of the Christian Faith*.

5 Brunner, *Gerechtigkeit: eine Lehre von den Grundgesetzen der Gesellschaftsordnung*, translated by Mary Hottinger as *Justice and the Social Order*.

6 Brunner, *Eros und Liebe*. 7 (London: Nisbet, 1948).

of Luther and other early Protestants, who had postulated the family, state, and church as the founding institutions of the created natural order.[8] Brunner treated the church as a distinct voluntary (not a natural) estate, as we shall see, and he insisted that the economy was its own separate sphere rooted in the natural order.

Brunner believed that these three basic psychophysical interests and the accompanying social spheres of family, economy, and state can be known and analyzed by human reason. The goods toward which these interests are oriented, and the inner logic or rationality that identifies them, have their roots in natural law and the created natural order. "These forms of community . . . are all independent of faith, and of the love which flows from faith," Brunner wrote. "This does not mean that their significance and their true nature can be rightly known outside the sphere of faith." But it does mean that all human beings, of whatever faith or nonfaith, have some basic understanding of these natural interests and human impulses toward the different spheres of communal life. These spheres both reveal and "conceal within themselves the Divine orders of creation," which comprise God's original design and intention for the fulfillment and flourishing of all humans, said Brunner. Virtually every human civilization, therefore, develops these three institutions, however variant in form and function.[9]

The orders of creation can be seen in the primeval commands described in the creation story of Genesis 1 and 2, Brunner argued. There we read that "male and female" are separated by God yet called to join together as "two in one flesh," in order to "be fruitful and multiply" (the order of the family). Humans are called to work and to "fill the earth and subdue it" (the order of the economy). And humans are commanded to "have dominion over the earth" and rule over all creation, but also to "dress and keep it" (the order of the state). Furthermore, Brunner contended, these natural forms of community – the family, the economy, and the state – constitute something like divine training schools for higher and more fulfilling forms of life that God wills in creation. He believed that, from the perspective of human reason, these spheres function to articulate and meet basic human needs. But from the perspective of faith, they are gifts of God even though they are changed and broken by sin.[10]

Brunner offers a good example of a natural law theory rooted in what some moral philosophers and theologians call the "premoral goods" of marriage and

[8] See Chapter 12 herein on Martin Luther.

[9] *Divine Imperative*, 333–6; *Dogmatics* 2:26–31. [10] *Divine Imperative*, 336–7.

family life.[11] In this view, premoral goods are to be distinguished from morality. For instance, if someone says, "This water is good," she is not saying it is morally good. She is making a premoral or nonmoral judgment; she is saying it is clean, has a nice, refreshing taste, and is likely healthy to drink. If she is a mother interested in her children's health and then claims that the mayor and the commissioner of sanitation *should* provide clean water for her offspring, she is making a moral judgment. And if she says that these authorities should provide clean water *equally* for everyone – not just the elite or the wealthy, and not even just for her own family – she is making a moral statement about justice or fairness. But notice, although water is not itself a moral good, it is a premoral good, one without moral valence in itself. Water does not have a will and cannot act – either morally or immorally. We never say, "Water is moral." But we do say, "Mary is moral; she is a good person; she does the right thing."

The distinction between premoral and fully moral judgments runs throughout our everyday moral and legal discourse, whether we are talking about water or talking about Brunner's psychophysical goods of sex and procreation, economic well-being, or security and order. Brunner's three sets of interests or goods are not moral goods because it is entirely possible to pursue and attain them in totally ruthless and immoral ways. In fact, in the covenant theology that Brunner developed on the strength of biblical teachings, it was precisely the purpose of the covenantal organization of the spheres of family, market, and state to bring moral order to the pursuit of these premoral interests or goods. Arriving at an analysis of the reality and centrality of these goods and interests was, according to Brunner, the function of natural law. It was the task of covenant and its overall narrative about the purposes of life and divine ends of life to give moral organization to these interests, both internally to specific persons and externally in relation to the spheres of society.

JUSTICE AND LOVE IN THE FAMILY

In laying out his theory of the morality or moral goods of marriage and family life, Brunner recited with appreciation the three goods of marriage identified by St. Augustine and the medieval scholastics: children (*proles*), fidelity (*fides*),

[11] See the views of premoral goods in neo-Thomistic moral theologian Louis Janssens and the nearly identical concept of the nonmoral good in American moral philosopher William Frankena in Browning, *Christian Ethics and the Moral Psychologies*, 190–220.

and sacramental stability (*sacramentum*).[12] He also echoed Isidore of Seville's formula, repeated by the Protestant reformers, that marriage served the mutual love and support of husband and wife, the mutual procreation and nurture of children, and the mutual protection of both spouses from sexual sin.[13] But Brunner ultimately developed his own formula of the goods or ends of marriage in terms of love and justice, and he insisted that children be viewed not just as a product or end of marriage, but as an integral part of a marital family.

"Marriage and the family are communities . . . in which justice lies most open to the influence of love," Brunner wrote. "In true marriage and the family, a synthesis of three highly heterogeneous principles becomes possible – natural love (*eros*), justice, and Christian love (*agape*)." When marriage is viewed only as a natural institution, the focus is on the sexual body, erotic love, and contractual commitments, and when those die, the marriage often ends by separation or divorce. Here justice sounds in the cold calculus of the courts, with battles over divorce, child custody, marital property, and more. Such minimal justice of the family is critical to maintain and inevitably needed in our broken world, for people of faith and no faith alike. Christian husbands and wives, parents and children need to respect this natural order of justice in the state at minimum and use its institutions when spiritual expedients no longer avail them.[14]

But a Christian marriage is ideally also a divine union of covenantal fidelity founded and focused on the enduring and sacrificial form of love called agape. "Only where husband and wife recognize absolute equality of worth in each other, and strive to express that equality" in all they do for and with each other is "the law of justice fulfilled" in a Christian marriage. Yes, St. Paul says: "The husband has a *right* to his wife, the wife has a *right* to her husband," which indicates their mutual rights to sex, nurture, protection, forgiveness, support, and fidelity. But in a Christian marriage built on agape, such rights and duties, fidelity and sacrifice will emerge "spontaneously, without the imperative of justice," without the guidance and governance of church or state, and without tribunals that calculate these rights and duties and the costs of their breach. Love and justice gradually grow and come together in a Christian marriage voluntarily, in as perfect a harmony as is possible in a world still marred by sin. Brunner maintained the traditional

12 See Chapter 4 herein on St. Augustine of Hippo.

13 See Witte Jr., "The Goods and Goals of Marriage."

14 *Justice*, 142–3; *Divine Imperative*, 350–5.

biblical teaching that the husband is the head of the wife within the home, though not necessarily in society. But he insisted that this was not "a degradation of the woman" but a protection of her "true dignity." And this was not an invitation for a man to dominate his wife and children, but an injunction to practice enduring fidelity and sacrifice for his wife and family, much as Christ did for the church and its members.[15]

Men and women are created with different sexual bodies, in no small part in order to come together as "two in one flesh" and to "be fruitful and multiply." This does not mean that every sexual act has to have a procreative intent or end. Brunner rejected what he thought to be the "unrealistic demands" of procreative perfectionism taught by parts of the Christian tradition.[16] "Sexual intercourse is intended by the Creator not only as a means of procreation, but also as a means of expressing the love of married people for each other." Sexual intimacy of itself is a perennial and "permanent need," a "characteristic of human life" for almost all adult human beings, save those unique few who are called to celibacy. Sex is there for marital couples to embrace and enjoy with each other, even if and when they cannot have children. Nonetheless, children are an essential natural and spiritual good of the marital family, said Brunner, and a blessing if they are produced by the sexual union. "The religious view tallies with that of biology: the sexual apparatus [of human bodies] 'serves' procreation." Children are endemic to the institution of marriage, Brunner insisted, even if they are not part of every marriage, let alone every act of sexual intimacy between married couples. As such, "procreation, the root of all human life, is withdrawn from private judgment. All capricious, self-serving prevention of procreation in marriage is a destruction of the divine order."[17]

Brunner seemed concerned here primarily with abortion; he said later that a "child has a right to be born" – both a natural and a divine right. "The dignity of the child is equal to the dignity of the parent; the primal right of the child as a person is equal to theirs. The child has a sacred right against its parents which in some cases must be protected by the community" – not only in cases of abortion or infanticide, but in instances of chronic need, neglect, deprivation, or abuse. Here, the state must sometimes intervene, with coercion if needed. Indeed, Brunner wrote, the legal protection of children's rights by the modern state "is the fruit of Christianity."[18]

15 *Justice*, 14–145; *Eros und Liebe*, 12–14; *Divine Imperative*, 356–9, 373–83.

16 See discussion herein of this sexual perfectionist theme in Chapter 4 on Augustine by David Hunter and Chapter 21 on Pope Paul VI by Stephen Pope.

17 Ibid., 366–7; *Dogmatics*, 2:63–5; *Man in Revolt*, 348–52.

18 *Justice*, 145–7; *Divine Imperative*, 367–71.

Trinitarian Family Recognition. Brunner described the father–mother–child relationship within a Christian family in Trinitarian terms. "All members belong to each other – the father to the child, the child to the father, the mother to the child, the child to the mother, just as the husband belongs to the wife, and the wife to each other." Each member of the family has his or her own office and function in the marital family. But there is also a fundamental unity in this diversity of domestic persons and offices. And when this unity is fully expressed and respected, "a real family is the perfect example of the cooperation of love and justice."[19]

This Trinitarian family relationship is not only a faint reflection of the Trinitarian Godhead, but also a direct expression of the "natural recognition" of father, mother, and child. Historical natural law theorists and modern anthropologists, Brunner wrote, both agree that the mother's recognition that a child is hers comes more easily than the father's, given the lengthy pregnancy, arduous childbearing, and infant nursing undertaken by the mother. The father's recognition of a child is more contingent and situational, and males have a stronger tendency toward infidelity, divorce, and polygamy. But scientists also agree that most human males recognize and care for their offspring more often than other mammalian males do, which says much about what is unique about the human species and its reproductive strategy. For Brunner, this human distinction reflected the order of nature for human families created by God, and it is expressed more fully in the covenantal bonds of enduring and exclusive love that become the Christian family.[20]

Brunner added something that is often forgotten – the importance of the child's recognition that a given woman and a given man are responsible for its existence. The "trinity of recognitions" implied in this bio-existential reality throws mother, father, and child together in irrevocable ways, Brunner argued. "Since I, the father, as well as the mother and the child, know irrevocably that this fact is irrevocable, then we three persons are bound together in a way in which no other three persons have ever been bound together, in an unparalleled and indissoluble relation ... This trinity of being we call the human structure of existence." This structure of existence is uniquely human not only because it is a biological reality, but also because it is recognized to be so by all three members of the one-flesh union brought together in love. Even separation or divorce does not destroy the reality of this bio-existential one-flesh

19 *Justice*, 147; *Eros und Liebe*, 33, 38–43; see also *Dogmatics*, 1:205–40 on the doctrine of the Trinity.

20 *Divine Imperative*, 356–69; *Man in Revolt*, 352–61. On the roots of this view in Thomas Aquinas, see Browning, *From Culture Wars*, 113–24.

union of mother, father, and child. "We cannot 'break' love, but we can break faith."[21]

Brunner believed that nature itself, at the human level, both anticipates and is completed by God's intention that husband, wife, and child are united in the marital family and remain one flesh together. Jesus himself, in his commentary on Genesis 2:24, advanced the idea that this one-flesh union should be lifelong: "So they are no longer two, but one flesh. Therefore what God has joined together, let no one separate" (Matthew 19:6). In this passage, Brunner argued, Jesus underscored that a Christian marriage should be exclusive and enduring. Adding another spouse through polygamy not only insults the dignity and equality of husband and wife, but also severs the essential natural tie between at least one of the parents and some of the children, producing inevitable discord and rivalry within the home. "The sexual union must be strictly monogamous . . . primarily for the child's sake." Similarly, divorcing a spouse and taking another when a minor child is still present, though sometimes sadly necessary, "is a catastrophe for children," for it again severs an essential biological tie between one parent in the home and the child and destroys the "trinity of recognition" that uniquely becomes a Christian household.[22] Brunner left unexplored related questions about adoption of unrelated minor children and of remarriage by a widowed parent with minor children. Following Protestant convention, he likely would have found these acceptable alternatives to the ideal form of natural family ties, if not sublime expressions of Christian charity.

THE CHURCH AND THE FAMILY IN SOCIETY

Brunner recognized a fourth social sphere besides the family, market, and state – the sphere of religion, which for him is mainly exemplified by the church in both its empirical and ideal forms. The sphere of the church is not directly derived from a human psychophysical interest or involuntary natural condition. A person is born without choice into a family, participates automatically in the economy, and comes inevitably under the jurisdiction of a state as a subject or citizen. By contrast, membership in a church or religious community is voluntary in modern society, said Brunner, although infant baptism blurs that distinction.[23]

Brunner described the church in conventional Protestant terms as "a community of believers, in fellowship with God, and founded on the Word of

[21] *Divine Imperative*, 346, 360; *Eros und Liebe*, 38–43. [22] *Justice*, 145–7.

[23] *Divine Imperative*, 552–4; *Dogmatics*, 3:27–37.

God." Regardless of whether the church is congregational or hierarchical, free or established, a single community or a global denomination, Brunner argued, its fundamental task is to preach the Word, administer the sacraments, catechize the young, care for the poor and needy, and prophesy against injustice. Brunner encouraged the church to maintain internal order and moral discipline, but he warned against "false legalism" and Pharisaism in the form of an elaborate canon law system or hierarchical church court structure, which he thought too reminiscent of medieval Catholicism and too redolent of the structure of the modern state. He also warned against the church becoming beholden to the state or too involved in state politics.[24]

From Brunner's Protestant theological perspective, each of the spheres of family, economy, state, and church deserves a high degree of autonomy from the other spheres in pursuing its unique functions, developing its internal logic and ethic, and refining its specific strategies. Brunner echoed Dutch theologian and statesman Abraham Kuyper in arguing that the social spheres should respect each other's special functions and resist interfering in and undermining other spheres, yet also support the other spheres in accomplishing their unique goals. Each social sphere has its own sovereignty, Kuyper put it. For instance, the market should help the family supply its economic needs, but should not disturb or distort the family's intimacy or its goals of procreation and nurture. The state should not own or completely control family, market, or church, even though it should assist each to fulfill its special tasks. The church should not directly control family, market, or government, although it should remind them of their higher moral, social, and covenantal obligations.[25]

Catholic subsidiarity theory, exemplified in this volume by Popes Leo XIII and John Paul II,[26] had a different way of talking about a similar vision of society that we find in Protestant covenantal thinkers like Kuyper and Brunner. The Catholic Church advanced this theory at the turn of the twentieth century, when the legal and social control of society by the church had been long gone but was threatened with replacement by either the socialist state or the capitalist market. Catholic subsidiarity theory, informed as it was by Aristotelian and Thomistic theories of the importance of the goods of the natural family and kin altruism, was designed to keep both government and market from controlling and thereby undermining the integrity of the increasingly embattled domestic sphere. The doctrine of subsidiarity insisted

[24] *Divine Imperative*, 539–54.

[25] Ibid., 554. See further Chapter 18 herein on Abraham Kuyper.

[26] See Chapters 20 and 22 herein on Popes Leo XIII and John Paul II.

that neither the market, through excessive work demands and commercialization, nor the state, through its paternalism and control, should undermine the marriage-based family or undercut the church's special protection and nurture of this institution. In both Protestant and Catholic formulations, the state and market had specialized functions, but they had to constrain themselves and cooperate in preserving and enhancing a pluralistic society. Much of this Brunner absorbed and distilled in his understanding of the place of the family in church, state, market, and society.

What the church offered the family was a support structure at critical stages in a family's life, Brunner argued. The church was the site of weddings, and it was critically responsible to prepare a couple for their budding union, instruct them in God's will for marriage and family life, and help them achieve the goods of family life through pastoral care, visitation, and support. The church was the site of baptisms, where parents and godparents, families and congregations together pledged to love and support and nurture the faith and life of this newly baptized Christian. The church was the site of catechesis and preaching, where those young in faith learned the ways of God and prepared themselves for the full embrace of God and the church in public confirmation or profession of faith. The church was sometimes the site of primary education, done in coordination with other social institutions, usually including the state. The church was the site of diaconal care, which provided widows and orphans, the poor and needy, the stranger and sojourner with food, shelter, medical care, and emergency relief, again alongside the state and other voluntary associations. And the church was the site of funerals, which were critical moments of pastoral care and support as the family mourned its losses and rearranged the responsibilities and tended to the needs of those family members who were left.[27]

The church was also responsible to provide "salt and light" to society at large, to exemplify the meaning of love and justice in its own community, and to speak prophetically against injustice and oppression. This was especially true in the area of sex, marriage, and family life, Brunner argued, which in his day had been rent asunder by world wars as well as by modernization and liberalism. Brunner's remarks about the "crisis of marriage and the family" offered shortly after World War II prove keenly prescient of the place and plight of the marital family in the twenty-first century:

> The causes of this crisis are many and varied, internal and external: the destruction of the economic unity of the family by industrial life and the

[27] *Dogmatics*, 3:53–71, 111–21; *Divine Imperative*, 504–16; 552–61.

> increase in the means of communication, the housing problem of our great cities, the economic, social, legal, political, and intellectual emancipation of women, the numerical surplus of women [after the war], the invention of contraceptives, and, above all, profound spiritual changes which can only be suggested by recalling the use of slogans emphasizing the claims of the individual, such as the "rights of personality," or "the freeing of the individual personality from the tutelage of collective groups." Christian society, the Church, and Christian theology would be well advised to take the problem of marriage more seriously than they have done hitherto ... [T]he crisis in marriage presents the Christian ethic with the most serious and the most difficult problem with which a Christian ethic has to deal ... We [are] dealing with the very foundations of human existence.[28]

Such insights have helped to motivate later Protestants in North America, Europe, and, increasingly, the global south to make marriage and family a more central part of their ministry and mission. Indeed, as Chapter 25 herein on Jean Bethke Elshtain illustrates, modern Protestants (including the two authors of this chapter) have joined with each other and with Catholics, Jews, and other people of faith and good will in a modern "marriage movement." That movement calls church, state, and society to shore up this vital institution of the marital family, even while emphasizing the rights and dignity of women, children, singles, and same-sex parties in a way that Brunner would not have countenanced.[29]

SUMMARY AND CONCLUSIONS: BARTH V. BRUNNER

As earlier chapters in this volume have made clear, Christianity has long had a double language to address issues of sex, marriage, and family life: (1) a philosophical language rooted in reason, nature, custom, and experience that is understandable by all, and (2) a theological language rooted in the Bible and revelation that sometimes has analogies in other traditions of faith, thought, and belief, including those of secular legal theory.

Emil Brunner offers a good example of a modern Protestant theologian using this double philosophical and theological language to analyze the complex institution of the marital family. Brunner maintained that reason could discern the human interests motivating the spheres or orders of creation, including the order of the marital family. But he also believed that human reason alone could not normatively define and properly actualize these

[28] Ibid., 340–1.

[29] See, e.g., *Man in Revolt*, 347–8, describing homosexuality as "that unnatural, demonic deformation of sexuality." On children's rights, however, see *Justice*, 146–7.

interests fully without revelation. As a Christian theologian, Brunner was not a philosophical foundationalist in asserting that reason can grasp knowledge of these interests and spheres. That is, he was not first emptying his mind of the witness of the Christian tradition and then using reason to build up, from some empirical or rational ground floor, the normative role of marital monogamy in a one-flesh union of father, mother, and child. Rather, he was using reason to gain a certain degree of "distance," in contrast to pure objectivity, from the normative tradition that shaped the Christian witness. It is through this "distanciation," as Paul Ricoeur put it, that reason becomes capable of discerning some of the rhythms of our natural human sexuality and other natural needs that then anticipate and incline us toward covenanted lifelong monogamy. Furthermore, these forms of distanciated social-scientific reason and empirical observation may help us see the beneficial consequences – the goods – that flow from this covenantal relation.[30]

Thus, for Brunner, the theologian, marriage and the family together constituted one of the many spheres of society that Christians should order on the basis of God's commands in creation. The male-female differentiation of Genesis 1:27, the declaration that it is "not good for the man to be alone" (Genesis 2:17), and the command that a man leaves "his father and mother and clings to his wife, and they become one flesh" (Genesis 2:24) were features of God's order of creation for marriage and family. All this for Brunner was the marital ideal as seen by the eyes of faith. But he did not stop with this. Brunner believed that the fundamental social spheres of life – marriage, government, and market – evolved out of basic human interests that could be known and analyzed by reason and reflections on natural experience. From the perspective of human reason, these spheres function to articulate and meet the needs of all human beings, even though, from the perspective of faith, they could be understood to be gifts of God in the order of creation.

By taking this step, however, Brunner also came into conflict with the teachings of his immensely influential contemporary and fellow Swiss Reformed theologian Karl Barth. In fact, their disagreements led to a famous debate between them about natural law, natural theology, and natural rights. Barth thought that Brunner had sold out to an inadequate Roman Catholic theory of natural law. He called Brunner's idea of orders of creation a "horizontal" ethic that had lost contact with the transcendent, particularly the Christocentric way of the cross. He once wrote of Brunner: "But we cannot help feeling that at the root of his conception of 'order' there lies something

[30] Ricoeur, *Hermeneutics and the Human Sciences*, 59–62.

akin to the familiar notion of *lex naturae* which is immanent in reality and inscribed upon the heart of man, so that it is directly known to him."[31]

Unlike Brunner and the Lutheran sources on which he called, Barth did not speak directly of estates of nature, let alone the order and ordinances of creation. Barth acknowledged occasionally that there were differentiated spheres of life such as family, government, and business. He also believed that God's commands addressed these different spheres or orders. But Barth denied that these divine commands contained norms, laws, or orders that could be abstracted from God's command and gain a life of their own as independent principles of natural or rational governance. For such views wrongly bestow norms to marriage and family independently of the direct will of God. Marriage and family, Barth taught, receive their normative meaning through the direct command of God as revealed in the history of creation, reconciliation, and, most definitively, the redemptive activity of Jesus Christ.[32]

Barth's ethic of marriage and the family is riddled with the language of divine command. We are commanded to be male or female, but not necessarily to marry. As male and female, we are commanded to be in co-partnership with one another. God's command means that we can only be man in relation to woman and only woman in relation to man.[33] This command of God extends to both male–female differentiation and male–female relationship: "We have to say both that man is necessarily and totally man or woman, and that as such and in consequence he is equally necessarily and totally man *and* woman."[34] Of course, for Barth the language of command is more indicative than imperative; it announces our definition and status before God more than it imposes an external moral demand. It is, as Ricoeur put it, more gift than arbitrary divine edict.[35] Commands for Barth are intended to free human beings more than to restrict and control them. Nonetheless, a command for Barth makes Christian ethics (even in the sphere of sex, marriage, and the family) a matter of direct encounter with the Word of God and quite independent of the regularities of reason and nature – and of anything approaching a theory of natural law.

Barth, in our view, is wrong in his interpretation of Brunner. Brunner says that reason can discern the human interests embedded in the spheres of creation, including the order of family and marriage, and can work to improve

[31] Barth, *Church Dogmatics*, III/4: 20; see also Brunner and Barth, *Natural Theology*.
[32] Barth, *Church Dogmatics* III/4: 18–23. [33] Ibid., 117. [34] Ibid., 118.
[35] Ricoeur, "The Logic of Jesus, the Logic of God."

them so far as possible. Christians, therefore, could and should fully engage the whole community on fundamental questions of sex, marriage, and family life, and should be involved in the thinking, teaching, and policy making of the state, economy, media, academy, and other institutions besides the church that affect the marital family. This is not to deny but to affirm that the fuller normative teaching about sex, marriage, and family life is revealed in the Bible and in the ongoing testimony of the Spirit of God that helps the church and each of its members uncover biblical truth, Brunner believed. Reason helps us understand the substructures of the spheres of life. It helps us discern the premoral goods that must be properly ordered in human life. It gives us hints about their fulfillment. But the ideals and goals of the family and other spheres, according to Brunner, are themselves revealed more fully in scripture and are ideally exemplified in the church and the lives of its members. And it is just because of this that church members must reach out, humbly but insistently, to offer salt and light, examples and arguments, prophecy and pastoral care for the marital family, the most fundamental of human spheres, "the mother of all earthly ordinances," as Luther had put it.[36]

Barth has none of this kind of thinking in his theology and ethics. For this reason, Barth did not enter into dialogue with other perspectives and disciplines on aspects of human life such as marriage and the family in the way in which Brunner could and did. Barth could only confess what he presumed to be the command of God witnessed to in scripture and apprehended by faith in the moment. That hermeneutic could work for the church or for a principally Christian society that accepts scripture and tradition as the foundation for family, economy, state, and church alike. But it is harder to make this work in the pluralistic, let alone post-Christian, society emerging in the mid-twentieth century. By claiming too much for the Word of God and the cross of Christ, Barth marginalized Christianity from modern discourse about the family and, finally, even marginalized his point of view from ongoing deliberations about the family within the contemporary church. He inadvertently made some strands of Protestant theology increasingly irrelevant to the contemporary church, state, and social debates about the meaning of sex, marriage, and the family. Brunner offered a rather different and ultimately a more constructive way of engagement. Modern Protestants and many others in a post-Christian culture might do well to reread him.

[36] See Witte Jr., *Law and Protestantism*, 199–256.

RECOMMENDED READING

Barth, Karl. *Church Dogmatics*, 5 vols. Edited by G. W. Bromiley and T. F. Torrance. Edinburgh: T. & T. Clark, 1961.

Browning, Don S. "A Natural Law Theory of Marriage." *Zygon* 46 (September 2011): 733–60.

Browning, Don S., et al. *From Culture Wars to Common Ground*. 2nd ed. Louisville, KY: Westminster John Knox Press, 2000.

Brunner, Emil. *Eros und Liebe*. Berlin: Furche-Verlag, 1937.

Justice and the Social Order. Translated by Mary Hottinger. New York: Harper & Bros., 1945.

The Divine Imperative: A Study in Christian Ethics. 7th imprint. Translated by Olive Wyon. London: Lutterworth Press, 1961.

Dogmatics. 3 vols. Translated by Olive Wyon. Philadelphia, PA: Westminster Press, 1980.

Brunner, Emil and Karl Barth. *Natural Theology: Comprising "Nature and Grace" by Emil Brunner and the Reply "No" by Karl Barth*. Translated by Peter Fränkel. Reprint edition. Eugene, OR: Wipf and Stock Publishers, 2002.

McGrath, Alister E. *Emil Brunner: A Reappraisal*. Malden, MA: Wiley-Blackwell, 2014.

Witte, John, Jr. *Church, State, and Family: Reconciling Traditional Teachings and Modern Liberties*. Cambridge: Cambridge University Press, 2018.

20

Popes Leo XIII and Pius XI

Russell Hittinger

BIOGRAPHICAL INTRODUCTION

Gioacchino Vincenzo Pecci was born on 2 March 1810 at Carpineto in the Latium region of Italy. For a millennium this area was part of the Papal States. When Pecci was five years old, the Congress of Vienna (1815) restored Latium, then under the sway of Napoleon, to papal governance. Yet he would become the first pope since the eighth century to inherit no papal temporalities in Italy. Ordained a priest in 1837, Pecci spent forty years as an administrator, diplomat, priest, and then bishop in the papal dominions. Made nuncio to Brussels in 1843, he saw firsthand the Industrial Revolution in northern Europe, and perhaps pondered the work of a rather gentle liberal constitution in a predominately Catholic country.

Consecrated archbishop of Perugia in 1846, he spent the next thirty-two years as a reformer in Umbria, notably in the field of education. Elected pope in 1878, Leo launched the most intense and sustained period of papal teaching in the history of that institution. He rehabilitated the literary mode of the papal encyclical to teach synthetically on a wide range of subjects, including marriage. Scholars speak of a Leonine era, which ended not on Leo's death in 1903, but on the death of Pope Pius XII in 1958. The body of teachings over these decades, while complicated, had the appearance of a "great coherency."[1]

A vital contributor to the Leonine project was Pope Pius XI, born in 1857 as Ambrogio Damiano Achille Ratti. Ordained a priest in 1879, only a few

[1] See Schuck, *That They Be One*, 45; Hittinger, "Introduction," 1–38, and "Leo XIII," 39–105.

FIGURE 20.1. Pope Leo XIII (litho), German School (nineteenth century) / Private Collection / © Look and Learn / Elgar Collection / Bridgeman Images

FIGURE 20.2. Pope Pius XI on the throne, 1927 (b/w photo) © SZ Photo / Scherl / Bridgeman Images

months after Leo's election, he procured three doctorates – in canon law, theology, and philosophy – before being elected pope in 1922. In almost every respect a student of Leo, Pius XI reprised not only Leo's encyclical on Christian marriage, *Arcanum Divinae*, but also *Rerum Novarum* and *Aeterni Patris*. By way of clarification and complication, he treated Leo's legacy as a living tradition.

During the Leonine era, the teachings of the Council of Trent on matrimony were reworked in three important magisterial documents: Leo's *Arcanum Divinae* (1880), the first systematic teaching on marriage in some three hundred years since Trent; the *Code of Canon Law* (1917), which produced more than one hundred canons consolidating juridical aspects of marriage; and Pius XI's *Casti Connubii* (1930), a reprise of Leo's encyclical on its fiftieth anniversary, issued under the same subtitle, *De Matrimonio Christiano*. The reforms of the Vatican Council II period notwithstanding, the Leonine and Pian encyclicals remain the *only* papal encyclicals devoted exclusively to expounding and vindicating matrimony as a whole.

TRIDENTINE CENTURIES

The matrimonial doctrine and canons of the Council of Trent (1563) had a long shelf life in the Catholic world. The next council, three centuries later, Vatican Council I (1870), did not treat matrimony. On that topic Trent outlasted its own era of Reformation and Counter-Reformation.

Trent brought the doctrinal essentials into view by way of a brief doctrinal statement, twelve canons that anathematize erroneous views, and twelve additional disciplinary canons dealing with canonical form, impediments, and other circumstances of matrimony.[2] Except for the first disciplinary canon, called *Tametsi*, which over subsequent centuries caused juridical and pastoral perplexities, the council produced a tidy piece of work. Relying chiefly on scripture, the council states that the perpetual and indissoluble bond of matrimony was instituted by God in the beginning. Adam's canticle to Eve – "This at last is bone of my bones, flesh of my flesh; she shall be called Woman, because she was taken out of Man" (Genesis 2:23) – bespeaks a primeval recognition and consent to the bond of "one flesh," which is confirmed by the words of Christ regarding the origin, unity, and perpetuity of marriage (Matthew 19:6). The council emphasized that the natural love and perpetuity of conjugal life are perfected and raised to be a sign of the unity of

[2] Council of Trent, XXIV session (Nov. 1563), in Tanner, *Decrees of the Ecumenical Councils*, 3–759 (hereafter Tanner).

Christ and the Church (Ephesians 5). Therefore, marriage is numbered among the seven sacraments of the New Law. Bishops at Trent were especially eager to disclaim any idea that the church institutes or causes matrimony, much less that the church intrudes upon Christ's institution of the sacrament. Thus, the first canon anathematizes the opinion that the sacrament "has been devised by men in the Church and does not confer grace."[3]

The work of Trent also lived for many centuries in the minds and hearts of Catholics because of the Roman Catechism (1566). First prepared for pastors, over some three centuries, it was translated into vernacular languages and adapted to institutions of Christian formation at different levels. The catechism on marriage consists of thirty-four topics (*quaestiones*), covering much more theological territory than did the council. At the same time, it managed to be very concise, especially in comparison to the magisterial and conciliar documents of the twentieth century. Although the first English translator complained of its "severe, scholastic form," which might prove "uninviting to those who seek to be amused," the work has didactic rather than dialectical form.[4] Indeed, the remarkable success of the Roman Catechism is owing to its familiar language, an important requirement for anyone who would explain a sacrament that so affects the ordinary life of the laity. The Catechism is also well balanced. The essential properties of the conjugal union (unity and indissolubility) and its goods or ends (children, fidelity, protection against sin, and sacrament) are integrated without any atmosphere of a "theory." Indissolubility is a predicate of the natural order with regard to both married love and its ordination to children and family, but the Catechism insisted that indissolubility is chiefly owing to the sacrament.[5] While the language of contract was not ignored, the juridical features were embedded in the notion of consent to a union that is ontologically unique: a permanent and exclusive one-flesh union that is a source of grace in addition to what is given by baptism. Considerable attention therefore was given to cooperation with grace on the part of Christians who consent to marriage.[6]

The evolution of matrimonial doctrine and practice immediately after Trent was marked by slow accretions rather than by response to a galvanizing event like the Protestant Reformation. The peculiar nature of national governance after the Peace of Westphalia (1648) – namely, a geographically and confessionally segmented Christendom – gave rise to quandaries over

[3] Tanner, Doct. can. 1, 754.

[4] Donovan, *The Catechism of the Council of Trent*, 10; *Catechismus Ex Decreto Concilii Tridentini* (hereafter Rom. Cat.).

[5] Rom. Cat., Pars II, Cap. VIII, qu. xi. [6] Ibid., qu. xxiii–xxxiv.

promulgation, enforcement, and more generally the jurisdiction over marriages between Christians. For instance, France accepted Trent's doctrinal statement on marriage, but refused to receive officially the reform or disciplinary canons, particularly *Tametsi*, which required marriages to be formed by the publication of banns, exchange of vows in the presence of a priest and two other witnesses, and the priest's pronouncement of the blessing in the name of the Trinity.[7] Further complicating the issue, *Tametsi* was not universally promulgated. In the zones where it was not promulgated, Protestants and Catholics alike were not under the Tridentine canon regulating validity of marriage. Perhaps worse, they were not sure whether Trent or medieval decretals, which allowed clandestine marriage, applied to their situation. These problems, and many more besides, are of interest to anyone studying the history of canon law and church–state relations.[8]

One issue, however, would not be ironed out through the slow shop-work of juridical decrees. It simmered during the centuries after Trent before erupting on the eve of the French Revolution. Let us call it the "separation thesis." Trent insisted that the church does not institute either the natural or sacramentally capacitated bond of marriage. God alone institutes marriage, the Christian couple alone mutually consents to it in the manner of an efficient cause, and the external canonical form suffices to validate it. Ecclesiastical jurisdiction in matrimonial cases among the faithful, therefore, depends not on purely juridical powers, but rather on the twofold sacrality of the institution (by creation and sacrament) and the dignity of the *christifideles* (Christ's faithful). Provided that there are no impediments, and that no essential property or native good(s) of conjugal union are excluded, consent to marriage for the faithful is a sacrament, albeit pending proper canonical form. Yet for untutored common sense, whatever validates or invalidates the matrimonial union seems to exercise causal power over the institution as such. It was perhaps inevitable that reform-minded sovereigns such as Holy Roman Emperor Joseph II (1765–90) would declare the civil and the religious contract "separable." As his minister Johann von Cobenzl explained, marriage is "a matter which is first and foremost civil . . . in which the religious element is only accessory."[9]

Importantly, this was not merely a contest between church and state over which positive law validates a marital contract. It reached more deeply to the

7 Tanner, Reform can. 1, 755.

8 See this history traced by Joyce, *Christian Marriage*; Killeen, *What Brings a Marriage into Existence*.

9 Imperial Patent on Marriage (1783). Citation of Cobenzl in Joyce, *Christian Marriage*, 256.

form and definition of marriage. Separation implied that for Christians and non-Christians alike, marriage is a civil contract, to which the sacrament may be added without prejudice to the primary definition of the institution. The sacrament was something private, or subjective. In the case of the Josephite reforms in Austrian lands, the full meaning and impact of the separation thesis was initially somewhat muted. Catholics were able to go to the priest in a church wedding and observe the nuptial ritual for the sacrament. Cases that arose regarding the accessory status of church weddings could be adjudicated by ecclesiastical authorities, but only by the local bishops loyal to Austrian law. For Joseph and his bureaucracy, the church's authority over the definition of marriage was "borrowed" and ought to be returned.

The first authoritative response from Rome complained about the derogation from Trent regarding ecclesiastical power in the matter of diriment impediments and judgments in matrimonial cases more generally.[10] Soon enough, it became clear that the separation thesis had to be theologically addressed on its own terms. In the Syllabus of Errors (1864), Pius IX listed ten erroneous propositions about Christian marriage, including the separation thesis: "In force of a merely civil contract there may exist between Christians a real marriage, and it is false to say either that the marriage contract between Christians is always a sacrament, or that there is no contract if the sacrament be excluded."[11] But the Syllabus listed rather than refuted erroneous propositions. Leo and his successors inherited the burden of explaining the theology latent in Trent as it applies to the separation thesis.

THE LEONINE ERA: FROM REFORMATION TO REVOLUTION AND BEYOND

After the French Revolution (1789), the Tridentine teachings needed to be freshly articulated, adjusted, and applied to an era of revolution and liberal social reform based on the spirit of the Enlightenment. In France, the Catholic culture of vows was swiftly turned upside down: new state decrees prohibited monastic vows and required a clerical oath to the Civil Constitution of the Church (1790); marriage was made only a civil contract,

10 Pius VI, *Auctorem Fidei* (28 August 1794), enumerating eighty-five erroneous propositions at the Synod of Pistoia (1786). The diocesan synod took place under the care of Joseph's brother Leopold, Grand Duke of Tuscany. See Denzinger. *Enchiridion Symbolorum* 2658–60 (new numbering).

11 Pius IX, *Quanta Cura*, Syllabus §§65–74, the separation thesis at §73. ASS 3 (1867–8), 168–76.

and celibacy for the secular clergy was relaxed (1791); decrees regulating divorce and abolishing the monarchy (1792) spelled the demise of the great vows of the laity. These reforms were echoed in many European nations that accepted Napoleon's legal reforms. In his encyclical on marriage, Leo XIII called the French Revolution the "great conflagration."[12] Henceforth, the magisterial Protestant teachings of the sixteenth century, to which Trent had reacted so forcefully, made only cameo appearances in papal encyclicals.

Leo's *Arcanum* was occasioned by reform bills for civil marriage and divorce in Italy and France. During French occupation, much of Italy had come under the law of civil marriage and divorce in the Napoleonic Code (1801). Victor Emmanuel II abolished divorce in the Piedmont (1852), for reasons moral and civil rather than sacramental, and soon thereafter indissolubility of marriage was entrenched in the code of the new Italian state (1865). But liberal reform was back on the legislative agenda in the Piedmont in 1879.[13] With typical élan, France managed to go through three civil marriage and divorce regimes in one generation: from the laws of the Revolution, to the somewhat more restrained law of the Napoleonic Code, to an indissolubilist regime after the Restoration (1816). In the very year of Leo's election, the legislative tide in the Third Republic had turned toward a liberal law of divorce. Indeed, the reform bill succeeded only a year after *Arcanum*, and was passed by the Senate in 1884.[14]

Fifty years later, at the beginning of his encyclical *Casti Connubii*, Pius XI likened his magisterium to a "watch tower" from which he espied new developments affecting marriage and family. In addition to the ever-familiar tensions between church and state over liberal reforms of family law, he worried about the emergence of eugenics in the courts of public policy. This relatively new issue was brought to a head by the Fascist ideologies in Italy and Germany, but also by Soviet totalitarianism, which reduced marriage and

[12] *Arcaum divinae* (10 February 1880), §28. Acta Leonis vol. II, 29. English translations collected by Carlen, *The Papal Encyclicals* and posted now on the Vatican website contain section numbering that was not in the originals, at least not until the early 1960s. Hereafter, we cite the interpolated section and the page from the relevant *Acta*.

[13] Leo sent an admonitory letter to the bishops of the Piedmont, complaining that the pending reform would create "a marital morality all its own, purely human in character, under forms and guarantees that are merely legal; and then with all its power goes on forcibly to impose this morality on the consciences of its subjects, substituting it for the religious and sacramental morality." Ci siamo (1 June 1879), *Acta* I, 240. As it turned out, the bill was not enacted.

[14] Thus standing with Belgium (1830), Hungary (1868), Germany (1875), and soon Portugal, which went from a stringent indissolubilist regime to putting in place the most liberal divorce law in Western Europe (1910). See Phillips, *Putting Asunder*, 403–73.

family to their material elements and thus rendered them amenable to state mobilization. Although the pope made a discreet allusion to the Report of the Lambeth Conference allowing the use of contraceptives (June 1930), it is not quite true that changes in Anglican moral theology precipitated *Casti*. Along with several other moral issues – abortion, eugenics, and adultery – contraception was addressed in a long excursus criticizing dominion over the human body, whether contraception is sanctioned by private choice or public law.

During the Leonine era, the contest between church and state on issues of marriage was never quiet. Defeats in the political forum often followed successes, and initial successes were sometimes obtained at steep cost, and even then to little if any avail.

We will treat the encyclicals *Arcanum* and *Casti* under three headings, each of which affords a different portal into the teachings: first, as part of social doctrine; second, as part of sacramental theology, including the definition of matrimony, its institutional origin, and the specific nature of the conjugal union; and third, as part of the magisterial response to the Enlightenment.

MATRIMONY AND SOCIAL DOCTRINE

A new development since Trent was the Catholic social teaching movement, which crystallized during Leo's pontificate and was carefully cultivated by Pius XI as a "doctrine." Popes of the Leonine era had a broad understanding of which issues belong to this evolving *traditio*. Leo himself insisted that the social question is not "merely an economic one," but rather is above all "a moral and religious matter."[15] Esteemed church historian Roger Aubert has called the school issue "the classic battleground," for education, parents, and marriage were almost always addressed in proximity.[16] Leo and Pius pulled these together on a wide map of social order according to the notion of three "great" or "necessary" societies.

Leo begins *Arcanum* by pointing out that the state and the church have a mutual interest in preserving whatever helps persons to live "well and happily," which is to say, societies necessary for human flourishing[17] (*Arcanum* §4, 12). Pius XI states: "Now there are three necessary societies, distinct from one another and yet harmoniously combined by God, into which man is born: two, namely the family and civil society, belong to the natural order; the third, the

15 *Graves de Communi* (18 January 1901), §1, *Acta* vol. XXI, 10.

16 Aubert et al., *The Church in the Industrial Age*. 209.

17 Pius XI's discourse on the necessary societies, *Divini Illius* (31 December 1929), §§12–14, AAS 21 (1929), 52–3.

Church, to the supernatural order" (*Casti* §11, 52). Leo's division puts marriage first, because while people are not born into marriage, matrimony is the "principle and foundation" of domestic society (*Arcanum* §5, 12). To paraphrase and revise the Aristotelian dictum, the human person is a matrimonial-familial animal, a political animal, and an ecclesial animal. Human persons will live well and happily if there is concord among family, polity, and church.

So framed, this scheme of necessary societies puts the weight of authority on the side of the church. Two of the three societies, marriage and the church, are rooted in sacramental order either in the sacraments of the New Law (marriage) or in the "ordinary" sanctifying powers of the church. Either way, there is a supernatural bond, and therefore the higher and lower necessary societies support traditional arguments for the jurisdictional primacy of the church – albeit, refurbished to address polities that are quite different than the consecrated regimes of earlier centuries. Moreover, Leo and Pius raised the ante by arguing that sacrality is a primeval predicate of marriage and family. Leo says that a marriage "established for reciprocal affection and for the interchange of duties" (*Arcanum* §14, 19), even among non-Christians, is "sacred by its own power, in its own nature, and of itself," and therefore does not belong to the "*imperio* of civil rulers."[18] Pius cites in the same vein the dictum of the Roman jurist Modestinus: "Marriages are the union of male and female, a sharing of life and the communication of divine and human rights" (*Casti* §84, 571–2). Given parents' obligations to educate and religiously form their children, Pius insists that "the family is more sacred than the State and that men are begotten not for the earth and for time, but for Heaven and eternity" (*Casti* §69, 565).

Leo best summarized this leitmotif of social doctrine: "let us take as a starting-point a well-known truth admitted by all men of good sense and loudly proclaimed by the history of all peoples; namely, that religion, and religion only, can create the social bond."[19] Although commentators of a later generation tended to isolate particular moral, theological, and canonical pronouncements of *Arcanum* and *Casti*, the popes wove these things together in a much richer vision of a Christian restoration or renewal of society.

[18] Leo says *fideles et infideles*. His language is very strong: *sua vi, sua natura, sua sponte sacrum*. Id. §19, 23. He refers here to a "memory of origins" still present in human conscience, as well as to the Christian theology of the union between the first spouses as an *adumbratio* of Christ's incarnation.

[19] *Au milieu des sollicitudes* (16 February 1892), §5, *Acta* XII, 21.

DEFINITION OF MARRIAGE AND ITS ENDS

Reminiscent of Trent and its catechism, Leo begins *Arcanum* with the origin of the institution of matrimony. In Genesis, the six days of creation are completed by the union of man and woman. Leo follows the pedagogical custom of synthesizing Genesis 1:27–8 and Genesis 2:22–4 because Jesus does so when teaching on indissolubility (Matthew 19:4–6) (*Arcanum* §5, 12).[20] The doctrine of one-flesh unity contains two notions: human persons as bearers of God's image helping to complete creation by their fertility, and human persons as moving by love to a nuptial completion. Thus, by creation, the union of man and woman in matrimony was "deeply sealed" by the properties of "unity and perpetuity." These properties constitute what Leo calls the "form of marriage." By "form," he means simply the very thing to which spouses give consent (*Arcanum* §6, 13). His case is ontological rather than juridical.

With respect to the "foundations of nature" (*Arcanum* §125, 27), Leo's reference to an insculpted law is taken from a familiar scholastic rubric for a law that moves its subject by communicating an inherent form. The Roman Catechism, for example, speaks of the human person moved from within to rationally desire the social union of one flesh.[21] The Evangelical Law imparts a new *habilitas* to the soul, now moved inwardly by grace. The properties of conjugal union from the beginning are not changed so much as confirmed, elevated, and made firm by the sacrament, which is a new form (*Arcanum* §2, 10).[22] A certain firmness is divinely engrafted into the essential properties of unity and indissolubility, confirming and perfecting natural love not only by the consent to the union, but also by ongoing sanctification (*Casti* §38, 554).

We are brought back to the eighteenth-century nemesis, the separation thesis. All other conditions having been met regarding canonical form and impediments, the Christian faithful are automatically married in the sacrament by consenting to marriage itself, Catholic doctrine teaches (*Casti* §39, 554). To be sure, the full perfection of the spouses requires their cooperation with grace, and in this sense, the sacrament can be a blessing or good to be achieved. But as for consent to the union itself, Leo writes, "certain it is that in Christian marriage the contract is inseparable from the sacrament, and that, for this reason, the contract cannot be true and legitimate without being a sacrament as well. For Christ our Lord added to marriage the dignity of a

20 On the two accounts of Genesis, see Burke, *The Theology of Marriage*: 61.

21 Rom. Cat. qu. xiii.

22 In *Casti* §5: "strengthen and confirm and elevate [*communitum, confirmatum, elevatum*]."

sacrament; but marriage is the contract itself, whenever that contract is lawfully concluded." He continues, "Among Christians, every true marriage is, in itself and by itself, a sacrament; and . . . nothing can be further from the truth than to say that the sacrament is a certain added ornament, or outward endowment" (*Arcanum* §§23–4, 25–6). The "bond is nothing other than marriage itself," he adds, and therefore there cannot be two different contracts. For Christians, a pact to exclude the natural properties of marriage is no sacrament, and to exclude the sacrament is no marriage. While Leo followed Trent and its sequels by using the word "Christians" or "faithful," Pius followed the Code of Canon Law (1917), which used the term "baptized."[23]

In fact, Pius's effort to blend recent canonical dicta with the theological accounts of marriage from Trent to *Arcanum* sowed the seeds of a problem even before the next council. What is the relationship between the essential properties of the conjugal union and its blessing or ends? What is marriage *for*? The simple answer is that on the basis of sacred scripture, there are three goods: procreation, mutual assistance, and quieting of concupiscence. Just how they are ranked, and how the sacrament shapes their pursuit, is more complicated.

Let us take procreation. With typical brevity, Trent refers only to the Genesis 2:24 report of "one-flesh" unity. Given its doctrinal focus on unity, indissolubility, and sacrament, Trent does not bother with sorting or ranking the three ends or goods of marriage. The Catechism fills in the rest of the picture. Beginning with the Catechism and continuing through the magisterial documents of the Leonine period, the good of procreation is invariably stated with a very explicit qualification: that for Christians, the sacrament enlarges the telos of procreation, from family and ordinary domestic order to the education of children as members of a "people" in the cult of the true God.[24] In *Arcanum*, Leo follows suit: "By the command of Christ, it not only looks to the propagation of the human race, but to the bringing forth of children for the Church, fellow citizens with the saints, and the domestics of God" (*Arcanum* §10, 7). Pius repeats the obligation of the baptized to educate children in the worship of the true God (*Casti* §13, 544). Interestingly, he also contends that by the ordinance of creation, the end of procreation extends to education in the cult of God; therefore, formation in the virtue of religion, the font of the social virtues, is a duty of marriage as such. His reason is human dignity, the inclination of our rational nature to know the truth about God

[23] *Inter baptizatos*, *Casti* §39, 554, citing *The 1917 or Pio-Benedictine Code of Canon Law*, trans. Edward N. Peters can. 1012 (hereafter CIC–1917).

[24] Rom. Cat., qu. xiv.

(*Casti* §13, 544). Indeed, as the church moved into the twentieth century, this argument that procreation is ordered to the whole good of the child became all the more insistent, owing in part to the "school question," referred to in no fewer than eleven sections of *Casti*. Also, in the face of nationalism, it was not enough to say merely that married people procreate, lest the state claim that the matrimonial duty having been accomplished, the children must be handed over to the civil community.

As for protection from sexual sin, once again Trent was silent, but not the Catechism. Although it quotes Paul's admonition that marriage is a *medicine* to licentious desires (1 Corinthians 7:2), it is also clear that the spouses are habitually able "to repose in one another's affections" by virtue of the sacrament conferring grace.[25] The quieting of concupiscence is not treated as a separate secondary end so much as an effect of mutual love perfected by grace. In *Arcanum*, Leo does not explicitly mention the *remedium*. Instead, he writes that spouses are bound "to have such feelings for one another as to cherish always very great mutual love, to be ever faithful to their marriage vow, and to give one another an unfailing and unselfish help" (*Arcanum* §11, 17f). Relying on the recently promulgated Code of Canon Law (can. 1013 §1), which is the first official ranking of the secondary ends of marriage, Pius speaks of the medicine as a secondary end ranked in two directions: secondary with respect to the primary end of procreation and along with fidelity as the 'second' of two secondary ends (*Casti* §59, 561). Elsewhere in the encyclical, however, he puts the medicinal efficacy in the context of the graces of the sacrament: spouses subject to God by divine grace will be able to subject passions and concupiscence to themselves (*Casti* §97, 577).[26]

A certain pattern emerges in these magisterial documents. The blessings or ends of matrimony were integrally related to conjugal union. Considered in the light of the sacrament, procreation includes Christian education, suggesting that domestic society is an *ecclesiola*, or little church, while the quieting of concupiscence falls within the context of grace reforming the souls of spouses in their nuptial practice.[27]

What about the good of mutual assistance (fidelity)? The Roman Catechism treated mutual assistance according to the traditional model of a lifelong domestic helpmate. The first reason is the blessing that flows from the union: "under the vicissitudes of life and the infirmities of old age, this union

25 Ibid., qq. xiv and xvii. At qu. xxiii the goods are enumerated "for the faithful" as *proles, fides, sacramentum*. The medicine is assimilated to the perfection of grace interior to spousal fidelity.

26 Still more pointedly at §101, 579.

27 The best short treatment of the *remedium* is Burke, *Theology of Marriage*, 181–242.

is a source of mutual assistance and support."[28] Concurring motives for choosing a spouse – beauty, congeniality of disposition, and illustrious descent – are taken as common sense, provided that they are consistent with the holiness of marriage.[29] A lengthy excursus on the love of Christ for the church culminates in the teaching that the grace "perfects natural love," enabling spouses to "repose in each other's affections." The Catechism, therefore, depicts mutual assistance as something deeper than domestic assistance, for it points not only to the good of the family, but also to the perfection of the spouses having a distinct valence not reducible to their domestic labors. Leo follows suit: "Not only, in strict truth, was marriage instituted for the propagation of the human race, but also that the lives of husbands and wives might be made better and happier" (*Arcanum* §26, 26).

An important adjustment of the picture was undertaken by Pius XI. Whereas Trent included but did not rank the ends of marriage, and Leo seemed to have simplified the scheme by suggesting two rather than three ends, Pius inherited the new Code of Canon Law, which tersely stated: "The primary end of marriage is the procreation and education of children: the second [end] is mutual support and a remedy for concupiscence."[30] The Code provided no adequate definition of marriage and its ends, though in fairness it laid down juridical canons rather than a treatise on love. Pius decided to give due weight to the Code and to the evolving doctrine since Trent by distinguishing two different ways that matrimonial ends can be counted and prioritized.

In a restricted sense, children are the first good, Pius writes (*Casti* §17, 59). For such is indicated in the matrimonial contract by which the spouses, by words or other signs, mutually transfer to one another power over the body. According to the Code: "each party gives and accepts perpetual and exclusive rights to the body (*ius in corpus*), for those actions that are of themselves suitable for the generation of children."[31] Interestingly, Pius does not mention the phrase *ius in corpus*, but rather *ius proprium*, suggesting an exchange of all that is proper to matrimony itself (*Casti* §6, 541). The children "hold the first place" (*Casti* §11, 543)[32] because procreative acts constitute a natural

[28] Rom. Cat., qu. xiii. It says *prima igitur*, the mutual assistance and common life flowing from the union, and speaks of procreation afterwards, *altera est* ... Churchmen have always liked lists. This, however, is an inclusive list, not a ranking.

[29] Ibid., qu. XIV. [30] CIC–1917 can 1013 §1.

[31] CIC–1917, Can. 1081. See Rom. Cat., qu. vi. Note, however, the faulty translation of *potestas* as *dominium*. The exchange pertains to *usus matrimonii*, the use of matrimony, which is usufructory. Power over one's own body is within moral law, as is the specifically nuptial exchange, provided it be for just the matrimonial purposes. See *Casti* §71, 54.

[32] Ibid. §11, 543.

specification of what is unique to the one-flesh union, and because every social union aims at a good beyond itself.[33]

In a broader sense, mutual perfection of the spouses is the first good.

> This mutual molding of husband and wife, this determined effort to perfect each other, can in a very real sense, as the Roman Catechism teaches, be said to be the chief reason and purpose of matrimony, provided matrimony be looked at not in the restricted sense as instituted for the proper conception and education of the child, but more widely as the blending of life as a whole and the mutual interchange and sharing thereof.
>
> (*Casti* §24, 549)[34]

The "love of husband and wife which pervades all the duties of married life," he writes, "holds pride of place in Christian marriage" (*Casti* §23, 547). While God institutes the ends, laws, and goods of marriage, the human act depends on a "generous surrender" of one's own person to another "for the whole span of life" (*Casti* §9, 543).

This was a temporary solution, perhaps the best that could be done in 1930. Without the hierarchical ranking of canon 1013 §2, would he have devised a simpler solution, perhaps the one already suggested by Leo? Of course we do not know. Soon enough, theologians noticed that the encyclical teachings on marriage did not mesh neatly with the new canons and the jurisprudence that arose from them. Proponents of the primacy of the spousal good, who then were styled personalists, were rather stiffly resisted by Pius XII.[35] In the Vatican II era, the primary–secondary distinction was dropped altogether, in favor of two ends: first, procreation and education, and second, what now is called the conjugal good, *bonum coniugum*. But this is yet another story.[36]

NATURALISM, CONTRACT, AND CONSTRUCTIVISM

It remains for us to consider two deeper philosophical challenges that focused magisterial attention in the encyclicals on marriage: naturalism and liberal contractarianism. Leo and Pius polemically spliced these two "isms" together to represent the following position: the voice of nature speaks about the reproductive function of sexual intercourse, but it remains silent about the

[33] According to a scholastic distinction between the intrinsic common good that marks the shared form of common action (of a marriage or polity) and the extrinsic common good consisting of the goods or ends being pursued. See Hittinger, "Coherence," 83–5.

[34] Citing Rom. Cat., qu. xiii, with its formula *prima igitur*.

[35] See Killeen, *What Brings a Marriage into Existence*, 199–214.

[36] See Burke, *The Theology of Marriage*, 50–102.

social forms, including matrimony; thus, fixed social forms arise from legislation or private contract. We need to put this argument into context because it affords an important and mostly forgotten perspective on the treatment of matrimony during the Leonine era.

As we have noted, both popes appealed to ancient Roman sources to adorn their case that the "voice of nature" and the "testimony of conscience" affirm the sacrality of marriage. It is noteworthy, especially in view of their Thomistic training, that neither mentions the first authority – namely, the jurist Ulpian, whose dictum on marriage appears at the outset of the *Institutes*: "The *ius naturale* is what nature has taught all animals. It is not merely for humankind, but for all animals of the sky, earth, and sea. From it spring the intercourse between male and female, which we call marriage, as well as the bearing and rearing of children. We see that other animals acknowledge its force."[37]

Appearing at the outset of the *Institutes* and the *Digest*, Ulpian's dictum had enormous authority for the medieval mind.[38] Thomas Aquinas famously included the formula "what nature has taught all animals" in his outline of the first precepts of the natural law.[39] Yet Christian jurists could not fail to see problems. In the first place, scripture taught that humankind was not created in a natural succession with other animals. The divine command to procreate and the command to exert dominion over the beasts are subsequent to the special creation of humankind in the divine image. Second, thinkers well enough understood that nature does not necessarily teach monogamy, at least not for the animals. This incongruity was enough for Thomas Aquinas's teacher, Albert the Great, to dismiss Ulpian's formula for purposes of natural science. Third, they understood that the rubric "all animals" prescinds from specifically human difference. Indeed, elsewhere in the *Digest*, Ulpian's student Modestinus defines marriage as "the union of male and female, a sharing of life and the communication of divine and human rights."[40] This dictum, rather than the one from Ulpian, was quoted by Pius in *Casti Connubii* (*Casti* §84, 571f). It throws light on his insistence that marriage is a "union of souls" that makes it entirely different from the "union of animals" (*Casti* §7, 542).

37 *Justinian Institutes*), I, 1.2.

38 On the Roman law on marital formation, see Chapters 3 and 6 herein on Constantine and Justinian, and further Reynolds, Marriage in the Western Church.

39 Aquinas, *Summa Theologiae*, I–II, 94.2. The troubled medieval appropriation of Ulpian is treated extensively by Crowe, *The Changing Profile of the Natural Law*.

40 *The Digest of Justinian*, 23.2.1,.

The notion that humans, in their zoological fundamentals, are animals "taught by nature" became something more than an incongruous metaphor during the Enlightenment, when the voice and laws of nature became a commonplace for philosophers, jurists, explorers, and naturalists. The ancient distinction between what exists by nature and what comes into existence by virtue of human artifice was used effectively by Enlightenment thinkers to critique their own culture en route to major reforms of social and legal conventions. For example, the drafters of the proposed Civil Code in France (1801) opined: "marriage as it existed before the establishment of Christianity, which preceded all positive law, and which derived from the very constitution of our being, is neither a civil nor a religious act, but a natural one."[41] Just as some Enlightenment *philosophes* went in search of natural religion, so too others speculated in the fashion of Rousseau about the natural consort of man and woman. Diderot, for example, hypothesized that nature's true voice covers only sexual function, a pact for reproduction, all else being artifice.[42]

The first important Catholic thinker to use the term *naturalisme* in connection with "enlightened" theories of marriage was Louis de Bonald, who in 1801 argued in considerable detail that the naturalists affirmed only propinquity of organs, leaving the forms of social relations between men and women, parents and children, totally to the will or the whim of the state and certain commercial interests. Bonald furnished a compendium of arguments that look rather similar to those appearing later in the century, though there is no documentary evidence that he was read or even paraphrased by magisterial authorities.

The term *naturalismus* drifted into magisterial statements as early as 1832,[43] and thereafter appeared as a formulaic tag for a range of ideas that were never adequately specified. The Syllabus of Errors included naturalism along with pantheism and absolute rationalism (§§1–7), presumably to note errors touching on rejection of the supernatural, religious doctrine and provident divine causality. Condemned at Vatican I as a political and social ideology seeking to establish the "reign of reason or nature," naturalism was said to undermine not only religion, but "the rational nature itself."[44] Leo associated it with the

[41] Material from the *Projet du code civil* included in Louis de Bonald, *On Divorce*, 34ff.

[42] Rex, "Contrariety in The Supplément," at 162.

[43] Leo XII, Ubi Primum (5 May 1824). Bullarium Romanum, continuatio, vol. VIII, 45–9. §13, 47.

[44] Vatican I session 3, 24 April 1870. Dei Filius, Tanner 803. Schuck, *That They be One*, makes the best attempt to note the various meanings on the basis such things as the Index of Forbidden Books.

doctrine of the Freemasons. By the early twentieth century, commentators sometimes referred to theories of social evolution from the primitive to the civilized, which is more or less the original meaning in the eighteenth century.[45]

We do not need to sort out these pieces of Enlightenment thought that were semi-digested by the Catholic magisterium. For we know reasonably well what Leo and Pius were arguing against in defense of matrimony against naturalism. Spliced together, the thesis that nature leaves the conjugal form indeterminate and its companion thesis about the efficacy of private contracts put in place a more powerful version of the separation thesis. For as the popes understood it, this is not about a separation of civil and sacramental marriage, but a separation of the natural and the institutional grounds of marriage.

Leo inveighed against naturalists who teach that sacrality and indissolubility are completely extrinsic to the matrimonial bond, adding, "they worship above all things the divinity of the State" (*Arcanum* §19, 22). God and created nature aside, the decisive word of the state makes matrimony. Four years later, Leo put his opponents' position slightly differently: "domestic life in the teaching of the naturalists is almost all contained in the following declarations: that marriage belongs to the genus of commercial contracts, which can rightly be revoked by the will of those who made them, and that the civil rulers of the State have power over the matrimonial bond."[46] The absence of a doctrine of sacrality leaves conjugal form to be determined either by the state or, more likely, by private contract with state sanctions.

Fifty years later, Pius inferred that, from the premise of an indeterminate matrimonial form, there must follow plural forms under private contract. He framed the basic principle as follows:

> Some confidently assert that they have found no evidence of the existence of matrimony in nature or in her laws, but regard it merely as the means of producing life and of gratifying in one way or another a vehement impulse; on the other hand, others recognize that certain beginnings or, as it were, seeds of true wedlock are found in the nature of man since, unless men were bound together by some form of permanent tie, the dignity of husband and wife or the natural end of propagating and rearing the offspring would not receive satisfactory provision. At the same time they maintain that in all

[45] On the 1911 *Encyclopedia Britannica's* entry on marriage and social evolution of primitive societies, see Joyce, *Christian Marriage*, 31–6.

[46] *Humanum Genus* (20 April 1884), *Acta* vol. IV, 43–70. §21, 57.

> beyond this germinal idea matrimony, through various concurrent causes, is invented solely by the mind of man, established solely by his will.
>
> (*Casti* §49, 558)

Most importantly, Pius attributes to his opponents the position "that the generative power which is grounded in nature itself is more sacred and has a wider range than matrimony" (*Casti* §50, 558). Hence, what the state cares about is reproduction, from which follow its rightful political and legal interests in eugenics, demographics, and the like. The rest, including the form and ends beyond reproduction, can be left to private contract (*Casti* §86, 573). "Armed with these principles, some men go so far as to concoct new species of unions, suited, as they say, to the present temper of men and the times, which various new forms of matrimony they presume to label 'temporary,' 'experimental,' and 'companionate'" (*Casti* §51, 559). It may be supreme irony that these popes countered a position that was a caricature of the Catholic understanding of the "natural" primacy of procreation.

While the tradition taught that "man naturally has no dominion over man," the modern, natural model puts marriage on the same plane as Adam's dominion over the beasts. On this view, the natural turns out to be a source of despotism over the body, over the woman, and over the child. Leo argues that God "so decreed that man should exercise a sort of royal dominion over beasts and cattle and fish and fowl, but never that men should exercise a like dominion over their fellow men."[47] The human agent does not stand either to his own body or to the body of another as master to instrument. Once dominion is transferred to the human body, the human person encounters the human world as Adam did the animals.[48] Leo was convinced that the principle of equality as a natural right cannot be recovered from this model (*Arcanum* §7, 13).[49]

CONCLUSION

The Leonine era left many important issues on the table of moral and sacramental theologians, not to say the canonists. Pius XII did not issue an encyclical teaching on marriage, preferring instead to treat different facets of matrimony, morals, and science in various allocutions and audiences.[50] The tangle of questions about the essentials and ends of matrimony would later be

[47] *In plurimus* (1888), *Acta* VIII, 171f. [48] *Sapientia christianae*, §12, *Acta* X, 18.

[49] See also *Casti* §7, 542.

[50] See Ford and Kelly, *Contemporary Moral Theology, Vol. II Marriage Questions.*

sorted out by Vatican II and the revised Code of Canon Law (1983).[51] Even so, fifty years after that council, questions about matrimony and sacramental life remain at the forefront of ecclesiastical discussion. Canonical, theological, and pastoral approaches to matrimony continue to evince frayed edges, which has ever been the case. Pius XI's discussion of plural forms, private contracts, and state sanctions can be read as though it had been written yesterday. Leo and Pius treated naturalism as an ideology or a pseudoscience. Many new problems have emerged with respect to biological and social sciences, calling attention once again to the problem of dominion over the human body.

That magisterial teachings on matrimony were not only clarified and deepened, but also tested against practices and theories that had been almost unimaginable at the Council of Trent represents in some important measure the success of the Leonine era. It did not, however, produce a fully orbed teaching on the family. To be sure, quite a lot was said about parental obligations and rights with regard to rapid changes in the domestic economy. *Rerum Novarum* discussed the natural right to the fruits of human labor in the context of preserving and perfecting domestic society as a true and irreplaceable theater of human flourishing. But when Pius XI asserted that "the family is more sacred than the state," his attention was focused chiefly by the issue of education and schools.[52] If the Reformation and Counter-Reformation launched a new era of religious education for clergy and laity, the Leonine era witnessed the rise of schools.

Leo XIII approved the decrees of the Third Plenary Council of Baltimore (1884), which launched the largest parochial school system in the history of the Catholic Church. The practice of formally soliciting a promise by the non-Catholic spouse in a mixed marriage to cooperate in the religious education of children was affirmed and strengthened by the Code of Canon Law, which required not only a promise, but also moral certitude on the part of the priest regarding its implementation. Schooling was a preoccupation not just of Catholics, but of the culture at large, for families were immersed in and enveloped by formal education. Arguably, no institution more deeply affected family life in modern times. In the Catholic world, the rise of formal education left a very deep mark on vowed religious life as well.

[51] See Chapters 21 and 22 herein on Paul VI and John Paul II.

[52] A good summary of Leo's thought on the school question is provided by Elsbernd, "Papal Statements on Rights," 305–9. See also her very nuanced summary of *Casti* at Ibid., 643ff. Her word studies show very plainly how family issues were centered on education. Pius XI, for example, refers fourteen times to the rights of the family and parents, in every case regarding education.

Although seeds were sown for the doctrine of the family as an *ecclesiola* (little church), its theological development during the Leonine era fell well short of the work of Vatican II and the magisterial documents of John Paul II – *Familiaris Consortio* (1991) and *Gratissimum Sane* (1994).[53] Given that the revised Code of Canon Law (1983) mentions *familia* in the substantive only three times, much work is still be done on the ecclesiastical status of the family.[54]

RECOMMENDED READING

Aubert, Roger, et al. *The Church in the Industrial Age. History of the Church.* Edited by Hubert Jedin, et al. New York: Crossroad, 1981.

Brundage, James A. *Law, Sex, and Christian Society in Medieval Europe.* Chicago, IL: University of Chicago Press, 1987.

Burke, Cormac. *The Theology of Marriage: Personalism, Doctrine, and Canon Law.* Washington, DC: The Catholic University of American Press, 2015.

Carlen, Claudia, ed. *The Papal Encyclicals.* 5 vols. Wilmington, NC: McGrath Publishing Co., 1981. Accessible at www.vatican.va.

Crowe, Michael B. *The Changing Profile of the Natural Law.* The Hague: Martinus Nijhoff, 1977.

de Bonald, Louis. *On Divorce.* Translated by Nicholas Davidson. New Brunswick, NJ: Transaction Publishers, 1992.

Donovan, Jeremy. *The Catechism of the Council of Trent.* Chorley, Lancashire, UK: Christian Books Today, 2009.

Elsbernd, Mary. "*Papal Statements on Rights: A Historical Contextual Study of Encyclical Teaching from Pius VI–Pius XI (1791–1939).*" Dissertation: Catholic University of Louvain, Belgium, 1985.

Ford, John C., S.J., and Gerald Kelly, S.J. *Contemporary Moral Theology. Vol. II Marriage Questions.* Westminster, MD: The Newman Press, 1963.

Gerosa, Libero. *Canon Law. London*, Continuum International Pub., 1996.

Hittinger, F. Russell. Introduction and Chapter on Leo XIII. In *The Teachings of Modern Roman Catholicism: On Law, Politics, & Human Nature,* edited by John Witte, Jr. and Frank S. Alexander, 3–74. New York: Columbia University Press, 2007.

"The Coherence of the Four Basic Principles of Catholic Social Doctrine: An Interpretation." In *Pursuing the Common Good: How Solidarity and Subsidiarity Can Work Together*, edited by Margaret S. Archer and Pierpaolo Donati, 75–123. Vatican City: Pontifical Academy of Social Sciences, 2008.

53 On these, see Chapter 22 herein on John Paul II.

54 Gerosa, *Canon Law*, 192.

Joyce, George Hayward, S.J. *Christian Marriage: An Historical and Doctrinal Study*. London & New York: Sheed and Ward, 1933.
Killeen, Brendan. *What Brings a Marriage into Existence: An Historical Re-examination of the Canon Law of the Latin Church*. Scranton, PA: University of Scranton Press, 2010.
Lawler, Michael G. "Faith, Contract, and Sacrament in Christian Marriage: A Theological Approach." *Theological Studies* 52 (1991): 712–31.
Peters, Edward N., ed. *The 1917 or Pio-Benedictine Code of Canon Law*. San Francisco, CA: Ignatius Press, 2001.
Phillips, Roderick. *Putting Asunder: A History of Divorce in Western Society*. Cambridge: Cambridge University Press, 1988.
Reynolds, Philip Lyndon. *Marriage in the Western Church*. Boston/Leiden: Brill Academic Publishers, 2001.
Schuck Michael J. *That They Be One: The Social Teaching of the Papal Encyclicals 1740–1989*. Washington, DC: Georgetown University Press, 1991.
Tanner, Norman P., ed. *Decrees of the Ecumenical Councils*, 2 vols. London: Sheed & Ward, 1990.

21

Pope Paul VI

Stephen J. Pope

BIOGRAPHICAL INTRODUCTION

Giovanni Battista Montini (26 September 1897–6 August 1978) was elected pope on 21 June 1963. His major accomplishment was overseeing the completion of the work of the Second Vatican Council (1962–5), begun by his predecessor, Pope John XXIII. Montini was born in Concesio in Lombardy. His father, Giorgio Montini, was a lawyer, a member of the Italian parliament, and the director of Catholic Action, an organization that encouraged Catholic laity to be involved in the social order. His mother, Giudetta Alghisi, came from rural nobility. Montini entered seminary in 1916 and was ordained on 29 May 1920, receiving a doctorate in canon law that same year in Milan and pursuing further studies in Rome.

At age twenty-five, Montini was recruited to work for the Vatican Secretariat of State, where he spent the bulk of his career. He became one of the main assistants to Vatican Secretary of State Cardinal Eugenio Pacelli, who was elected Pope Pius XII in 1939. During World War II, Montini had the task of responding to thousands of letters to the pope from people in serious need. Drawing on considerable organizational skills, he created an office that provided important information about millions of refugees and prisoners of war. Along with other Vatican officials, Montini established the Pontifical Commission for Assistance to provide aid to refugees throughout Italy.

On 12 December 1954, Pius XII appointed Montini the archbishop of Milan, one of the largest and most prestigious archdioceses in Italy. As archbishop, he was known for creative pastoral efforts, interest in labor rights, hospitality to Anglicans and other non-Catholics, and promotion of the lay apostolate. Two months after Angelo Roncalli was elected Pope

FIGURE 21.1. Paul VI / Photo © Patrick Morin / Bridgeman Images

John XXIII, he made Montini a cardinal. The pope surprised the world when he announced his decision to open an ecumenical council to discuss ways of improving the church's relationship to the modern world. Cardinal Montini was placed in a variety of Vatican offices, traveled widely, and maintained a close relationship with the pope. After Pope John XXIII died of stomach cancer, the council was suspended while cardinals met to elect a new pope. Montini was elected on 21 June 1963. He was perceived as ideologically neutral enough to get elected by a contentious body split among cardinals who were either progressive (the majority), conservative (the aggressive minority, whose leaders were in the curia), or some combination thereof. He chose the name Paul, the apostle to the gentiles, to signal his commitment to evangelization.

Paul VI's pontificate began in a spirit of openness to modern culture, strong support for human rights, and awareness of the church's need for reform. He had a reputation for being approachable, sophisticated, and well read. Though conscientious and cautious to the point of indecision, he was not afraid to initiate change. He moved quickly to reduce the regal trappings of the papacy, support ecumenical outreach to Anglican and Orthodox Christians, advocate a strong commitment to justice and peace, and promote fraternal relationship with Jews (his 1964 visit to Israel was the first by any pope).

Shortly after his election, Paul VI announced the reopening of the Vatican Council. The greatest achievement of his papacy took place on 8 December 1965, when he guided the council to a successful conclusion. After three years, the largest and most diverse group of bishops ever assembled in one place produced sixteen major documents that would determine the character of the church for centuries. These documents charted a course for the church's understanding of itself as a communion, a sacrament, and the "People of God," rather than primarily as an institution governed by laws and bureaucrats. One of its key documents, *Gaudium et Spes* (*Joy and Hope*), "The Pastoral Constitution on the Church in the Modern World," offered a fresh way of understanding marriage and the family.

After the Vatican Council, Paul VI's innovations included establishing the Synod of Bishops, streamlining the Roman Curia, setting retirement ages for bishops (seventy-five) and an age limit for cardinals voting in papal elections (eighty), revising the liturgy (including use of vernacular languages), and creating what became the Pontifical Council for Interreligious Dialogue. He was the first pope to name women, Saint Teresa of Avila and Saint Catherine of Siena, as doctors of the church. His pontificate seemed perfectly suited to promoting the council's commitment to *aggiornamento*, updating the church, and establishing a new, more dialogic and fraternal relationship with the wider world.

Gaudium et Spes

Paul VI promulgated *Gaudium et Spes* on 7 December 1965. Though he did not write it, he issued it with his full authority, and it is a key resource for any assessment of his vision of the family. The introduction to the document observes, "the Church has always had the duty of scrutinizing the signs of the times and of interpreting them in the light of the Gospel."[1] One of the key domains of the times is marriage and the family, addressed in the second half of the document as one of five "problems of special urgency."[2] This part of *Gaudium et Spes*, titled "Fostering the nobility [or dignity] of marriage and the family," begins by noting that families are challenged by divorce, polygamy, sexual promiscuity, the rise of overt hedonism, and "illicit practices against human generation."[3] The health of society depends on the health of families, and the health of families depends on the health of marriages, but both marriage and family are threatened by unjust and degrading economic, social, and political conditions.

Gaudium et Spes paints a beautiful picture of marriage as a divinely established "intimate partnership of married life and love" rooted in a "covenant of irrevocable personal consent."[4] Marriage is described in language that is personal, social, and biblical more than juridical and neoscholastic. As an intimate union of husband and wife into one flesh, marriage is fundamentally a matter of love, which, "merging the human with the divine, leads the spouses to a free and mutual gift of themselves, a gift providing itself by gentle affection and by deed[;] such love pervades the whole of their lives: indeed by its busy generosity it grows better and grows greater."[5] Such love would and should "never be profaned by adultery or divorce."[6]

This attractive vision of marriage was accepted despite the initial resistance of a number of bishops, who during the document's drafting objected that the stress on marital love hits an emotional note that would weaken acknowledgment of the irrevocable (indissoluble) character of the sacrament. In response, defenders of the wording pointed out that the language of covenant

[1] *Gaudium et Spes*, no. 4. In O'Brien and Shannon, *Catholic Social Thought:*, 167 (hereafter GS).

[2] Ibid., 195. The other areas are the proper development of culture, economics, political community, and war and peace.

[3] No. 47, ibid., 196. [4] No. 48, ibid., 198. [5] No. 49, 196. [6] Ibid.

envisions a couple's mutual and irrevocable consent to bind themselves to one another "till death do us part." More broadly, the document's biblical and personalist approach to marriage represents a shift from a conception of marriage primarily as oriented to procreation to one primarily rooted in mutual self-giving love. *Casti Connubii* had recognized both goods but treated procreation as primary.[7] *Gaudium et Spes* elevated the significance of the unitive end of sexual intercourse while continuing to acknowledge its procreative purpose. It described children as the fruit of the "intimate sharing of life and love,"[8] but not as its justification.

Gaudium et Spes describes the family as a "kind of school of deeper humanity."[9] It regards children as the "supreme gift" of matrimony.[10] Married couples are called to serve one another and their children with self-giving love, and spousal love has a deeply sacramental meaning: "Authentic married love is caught up into divine love and is governed and enriched by Christ's redeeming power and the saving activity of the Church, so that this love may lead the spouses to God with powerful effect and may aid and strengthen them in sublime office of being a father or a mother."[11] Parents have a duty to safeguard life, to welcome children into their family, and to give priority to their rearing and education, especially as Christians and members of the church.

Parents who raise their children with love and wisdom are cooperating with and concretely interpreting the love of God to them. Motherhood and fatherhood are sacred roles through which men and women promote the sanctification of their children, themselves, and their wider communities. Goodness does not just flow from parents to children: "As living members of the family, children contribute in their own way to making their parents holy. For they will respond to the kindness of their parents with sentiments of gratitude, with love and trust. They will stand by them as children should when hardships overtake their parents and old age brings its loneliness."[12]

Christian marriages and families have a role to play in the renewal of culture. Strong Christian families witness to the reality of Christian values. They also should promote the value of marriage and family in the public sphere. Given the importance of the family as a social institution, governments have a duty to support whatever conditions can contribute to their well-being.

[7] Contrast *Casti Connubii* no. 11, with GS no. 49. *Casti Connubii* at https://w2.vatican.va/content/pius-xi/en/encyclicals/documents/hf_p-xi_enc_19301231_casti-connubii.html.

[8] No. 48, in O'Brien and Shannon, *Catholic Social Thought*, 196. [9] No. 52, ibid., 200.

[10] No. 50, ibid., 198. [11] No. 48, ibid., 197. [12] Ibid.

PAUL VI'S SOCIAL TEACHINGS

Paul VI issued eight encyclicals and many other influential documents. His three most influential documents were: (1) *Populorum Progressio* ("On the Development of Peoples," 26 March 1967), his encyclical on human development; (2) *Octogesima Adveniens* (14 May 1971), an apostolic letter to Maurice Cardinal Roy on the church's engagement in social issues; and (3) *Evangelli Nuntiandi* (8 December 1975), his apostolic exhortation on evangelization. Two other important documents deserve mention: those issued by the Latin American bishops in 1968 in Medellín, Colombia, and the 1971 Roman Synod document "Justice in the World." All of these documents treat the family as a fundamental component of the common good.

Populorum Progressio constituted a major achievement in Catholic social teaching, particularly regarding the centrality of human development to the mission of the church. For Paul VI, "integral" development included not only expanding political freedom and economic opportunity, but also progress in cultural, social, moral, and spiritual domains. The church is concerned not only to promote humanity's spiritual well-being, but also to resist situations that violate human dignity – for example, lack of food, inadequate access to health care, discrimination, and unemployment. Integral human development includes the health of the family, the most basic social structure. Special attention must be given to families threatened by discrimination and crushing poverty. Overpopulation can harm the common good, but governments cannot reduce it by employing immoral means: "When the inalienable right of marriage and of procreation is taken away, so is human dignity."[13]

The primary responsibility for transforming the world lies with the laity, who "should take up as their own proper task the renewal of the temporal order." They are called to take their own initiative and "infuse a Christian spirit into the mentality, customs, laws, and structures of the community in which they live."[14] Families play an important social role in raising and educating children, so that as adults they can play their part in civic affairs.

Paul VI appreciated the global scope of the church's moral responsibility and encouraged bishops around the world to commit themselves to giving greater attention to their social mission. In this spirit, the bishops of Latin America came together in Medellín, Colombia, from 24 August to 6 September 1968 to discuss what the Gospel asks Christians to do in their troubled lands. The pope flew to Medellín to open the conference and was warmly accompanied by prophetic archbishop Dom Helder Camara. The

[13] No. 37, ibid., 249. [14] No. 81, ibid., 259.

bishops endorsed the "preferential option for the poor" and issued a strong message of solidarity with the suffering poor of their continent. If the church wants to support integral human development, then in Latin America, it must first work for the liberation of oppressed peoples so that they can become agents of their own lives.

Paul VI wrote *Octogesima Adveniens* to Cardinal Maurice Roy, president of the Pontifical Council for Justice and Peace, to mark the eightieth anniversary of Leo XIII's encyclical *Rerum Novarum*. He pointed out that while the church is called to enunciate general guidelines and key ethical norms relevant to social problems, it is not capable of providing concrete solutions for every problematic situation. Local leaders, and particularly the laity, must discern what should be done in their contexts. Paul VI did, though, focus on one particular problem that had emerged as a major source of human suffering: urbanization. Mass migration from rural areas to cities in search of a sustainable livelihood, he said, had led to the weakening of communities and families once built around an agricultural way of life. "Within industrial society urbanization upsets both the ways of life and the habitual structures of existence: the family, the neighborhood, and the very framework of the Christian community."[15] Life in cities, moreover, involves a host of social ills, from dehumanizing living conditions and juvenile delinquency to drug addiction and violent crime. Communities must make it an urgent priority to repair the torn social fabric that is damaging families. This includes reaching out to youth, protecting workers' rights, defending those on the fringes, and respecting the equal right of women to participate in cultural, economic, social, and political life without at the same time undermining their "proper role . . . at the heart of the family."[16]

The clearest (if not the most authoritative) expression of the social mission of the church during Paul VI's pontificate was the 1971 Roman Synod document "Justice in the World." The synod fathers taught, "Action on behalf of justice and participation in the transformation of the world fully appear to us as a constitutive dimension of the preaching of the Gospel, or, in other words, of the Church's mission for the redemption of the human race and its liberation from every oppressive situation."[17] All Christians have the right and duty to promote the common good in all the spheres in which they act, including in their family lives.[18] We act as members of the church in our own families and therefore must always practice justice in them. The family is thus not a private

15 *Octogesima Adveniens*, "A Call to Action," no. 10, in O'Brien and Shannon, *Catholic Social Thought*, 268.

16 No. 13, ibid., 270. 17 "Justice in the World," in ibid., 289. 18 Ibid., 296

sphere walled off from the world, but rather a school for justice, because it is where children are taught to respect the dignity of every person.[19]

Paul VI's apostolic exhortation *Evangelii Nuntiandi*, "Evangelization in the Modern World," provided an important account of the relation of the Gospel to liberation. The Gospel proclaims salvation as liberation from personal sin, but also offers hope to masses of poor people caught in oppressive conditions. The pope explicitly addresses the church's message to families whose members are diminished because of unjust social structures.[20] As a place of evangelization, the family has been called "the domestic church."[21] Especially significant here is a theological recognition that the church itself is formed *by* the family as well as formative *of* the family. The family itself has a mission of preaching the good news: "The parents not only communicate the Gospel to their children, but from their children they can themselves receive the same Gospel as deeply lived by them."[22] Families inspired by the Gospel become evangelizers of other families, their neighborhoods, and their wider communities. Parents and their children have a genuine apostolate, a form of Christian service, both in the home and to the wider world.[23]

Humanae Vitae

On 25 July 1968, Paul VI promulgated the encyclical *Humanae Vitae*, "Of Human Life: On the Regulation of Birth."[24] His predecessor had formed a secret commission to study the question; Paul VI made its existence public and expanded its size. Some bishops wanted the topic discussed during the Vatican Council, but the pope asked them to refrain because the commission was already subjecting this delicate topic to a thorough analysis. Yet to the wider Catholic world, that such a discussion was even taking place suggested that the Vatican might be open to modifying the teaching. The commission's five years in operation raised expectations for change, not only among laypeople, but also among priests and bishops.

Pius XI's earlier condemnation of artificial birth control must be seen in the context of a variety of efforts in Europe and North America to promote

[19] Ibid. [20] *Evangelii Nuntiandi*, no. 29, in ibid., 313. [21] No. 71, in ibid., 333.

[22] Ibid; see also *Lumen Gentium* 11. On this topic, see Bourg, *Where Two or Three Are Gathered*.

[23] See also Decree of the Apostolate of Lay People, *Apostolicam Actuositatem*, in Flannery, *Vatican Council II*, 403–42.

[24] English translation of *Humanae Vitae* from http://w2.vatican.va/content/paul-vi/en/encyclicals/documents/hf_p-vi_enc_25071968_humanae-vitae.html (hereafter HV).

population control, including the use of sterilization for eugenic purposes, Margaret Sanger's "American Birth Control League," and laws allowing compulsory sterilization of people with intellectual or other disabilities or who were just deemed "undesirables." *Casti Connubii*,[25] Pius XI's unequivocal condemnation of artificial birth control, was rendered soon after Anglican leaders, gathered at Lambeth Hall in August 1930, declared that, under certain conditions, Christians may use artificial contraception. Pius XI adamantly rejected artificial contraception as contravening the natural good of the "marital act" as well as violating its divinely revealed meaning. Pius XII followed suit in 1951 in his "Message to Catholic Midwives," and John XXIII did the same in his 1961 encyclical *Mater et Magistra*.[26] These statements, in turn, depended on an ancient tradition stretching back to St. Augustine's interpretation of the story of Onan in Genesis 38:8–10.[27]

The nearly four decades between *Casti Connubii* and *Humanae Vitae* brought dramatic changes to public conceptions of gender roles, gender equality in the workplace and at home, sexual mores, marriage and divorce, and family structures. The emergence of strong advocacy for individual rights in the public sphere accompanied a loosening of bonds of solidarity within families and communities.

Paul VI's use of *Humanae Vitae* to reaffirm his predecessors' prohibition of all forms of artificial birth control disappointed, even shocked, many Catholics. Matters were aggravated when it became known that the pope's decision contradicted the recommendations of the majority report of the papal commission. The encyclical triggered an unprecedented storm of protest, polemic, and general consternation throughout the church. It had a greater impact on Catholic conversations about sex, marriage, and family than any other Christian document written in the twentieth century. We will first look at the encyclical itself and then discuss its reception.

Humanae Vitae is divided into three parts: the first introduces the question of birth control and the competence of the magisterium, the second provides doctrinal principles, and the third issues pastoral directives.

Paul VI, the first pope to write his own encyclicals, wanted to respond to a variety of new developments. The newly available anti-ovulant form of birth

[25] Ibid., Nos. 53–9.

[26] Mater et Magistra, no. 193, in O'Brien and Shannon, *Catholic Social Thought*, 115–16.

[27] "Then Judah said to Onan, 'Go in to your brother's wife and perform the duty of a brother-in-law to her; raise up offspring for your brother.' But since Onan knew that the offspring would not be his, he spilled his semen on the ground whenever he went in to his brother's wife, so that he would not give offspring to his brother. What he did was displeasing in the sight of the LORD, and he put him to death also." See Valsecchi, *Controversy*, 1–8.

control known as "the pill" seemed to avoid *Casti Connubii*'s objection to disruptive or intrusive forms of birth control (rubber condoms had become available in the 1850s). The pope opened the encyclical by acknowledging a variety of new conditions, particularly global population pressures and the hardships often incurred by large families, the danger that states might attempt population control through draconian measures, the increased respect for the dignity of women and the equal rights of men and women within the work world, and the enhanced appreciation for the significance of conjugal love for strong and faithful marriages. Yet most important of all, the pope insisted, was the slow and steady extension of the modern attitude of domination over nature to humanity itself, "even over laws that regulate the transmission of life."[28] These "signs of the times" had led people to ask whether the old norms remained relevant. Some theologians had proposed that the principle of totality suggested that the openness to procreation ought to characterize a marital relationship as a whole, but not necessarily each act of marital intercourse. The pope acknowledged that human development might have reached a point where it seemed proper for human beings to make their own conscientious decisions about the size of their families.

After extensive deliberations, a majority of the papal commission had advised a loosening of the prohibition on artificial birth control. They maintained that the norm is neither revealed, nor ancient, nor rationally persuasive as a matter of natural law. Paul VI deliberated over the commission report for more than two years and vacillated until several conservative advisers persuaded him to hold the line. In the end, he was persuaded by the argument that changing the teaching would undermine papal authority.[29] The document noted that the commission had not agreed unanimously and that some members advocated positions at variance with "the moral doctrine on marriage constantly taught by the magisterium of the church." Because the commission's position could not be taken as "definitive and absolutely certain,"[30] the pope reasoned, he had to exercise his own judgment.

28 HV, No. 2.

29 Moral theologian John Ford advised against changing the doctrine on the grounds that it would undermine papal authority. See Hebblethwaite, *Paul VI*, 469.

30 HV, No. 6. The majority report of the commission, written by distinguished moral theologian Josef Fuchs, S.J., and supported by fourteen of its nineteen moral theologians, held that married couples ought to exercise their conscience to determine whether to use birth control in their circumstances. The majority of bishops voted to approve the report, which concluded that the Catholic position "could not be sustained by reasoned argument" (cited in Hebblethwaite, *Paul VI*, 469). Listening to married couples during the commission hearings led Fuchs to change from his earlier rejection of artificial birth control. "We have to educate people to assume responsibility and not just to follow the law." Cited in Keenan, *A History of*

The second part of *Humanae Vitae* issues doctrinal principles governing use of artificial contraception. It begins by recalling that married love participates in the twofold end of the human person, the temporal and the eternal. Marriage is not a human invention, but is divinely instituted in order to enable couples to grow into an exclusive, lifelong loving union that would provide the best context for raising children. Marriage, moreover, is "invested with the dignity of a sacramental sign of grace,"[31] because it represents the union of Christ and the church. Showing the influence of the philosophical movement known as personalism, Paul VI speaks of marriage primarily as an interpersonal and social rather than juridical and contractual reality. Instead of speaking of the "conjugal rights" built into the marital contract, for example, he speaks of marriage as an expression of reciprocal self-giving love that brings mutual enrichment and "profound and enduring happiness."[32] Because it seeks to go beyond itself, marital love receives its natural expression in the fruitfulness of procreation. Children are the visible symbols of the loving union of their parents and the "supreme gift" of marriage.

This theological vision sets the context for the most controversial section of the encyclical. The pope argues that while married couples must exercise "responsible parenthood," even when it comes to the size of their families, the means they employ must conform to the demands of the "objective moral order which was established by God."[33] Responsible parenthood, properly interpreted, means respect for the "proper functions" of the "biological laws that apply to the human person, and of which a right conscience is the true interpreter."[34] God's will is inscribed in the biological functions of sexual intercourse, and, specifically, in its procreative end. This leads to the key line of the encyclical: "each and every marital act must of necessity retain its intrinsic relationship to the procreation of human life."[35] Contrary to what some Christians were suggesting, the pope insisted, God has established the *inseparable* moral connection of the unitive and the procreative meanings of sexual intercourse. On the basis of both faith and reason, every Christian can understand that procreation is "the result of laws written into the actual nature of man and woman."[36] To interfere with this natural design is to contradict the will of God. Any and all uses of artificial contraception

Catholic Moral Theology, 121. Chapter 6 provides a helpful review of the reception of *Humane vitae*.

31 HV, No. 8. 32 Ibid., No. 9. 33 Ibid., No. 10. 34 Ibid. 35 Ibid., No. 11.

36 Ibid., No. 12.

are "intrinsically wrong" and can never be justified even for laudable intentions.[37] This prohibition pertains not only to the use of artificial birth control but also, a fortiori, to direct sterilization and abortion. The pope did, however, condone the deliberate restriction of marital intercourse to infertile times in the wife's menstrual cycle. He maintained that taking advantage of the biological cycles to avoid conception is morally different from using artificial means to directly prevent conception, because in the former case, couples do not obstruct the "use of the faculty provided them by nature."[38]

Paul VI's discussion of doctrinal principles concludes first by registering a variety of negative consequences that would come from using artificial contraception and then by reminding readers that Christians cannot be faithful to Christ while assuming the right to do whatever they want with their bodies. He points out that artificial contraceptives facilitate fornication by the unmarried and adultery by the married. Eliminating the major consequence of sex, they also make it easier for men to treat women as sexual objects. Finally, the pope warns governments not to endorse, let alone mandate, artificial contraception as a way of dealing with social disorders associated with population expansion. Responsible parenthood properly belongs to married couples, not public authorities.

The final section of *Humanae Vitae* offers pastoral directives to help people live up to the sometimes very difficult requirements of the moral law in this domain. The pope reminds readers to cultivate self-discipline, and particularly the virtue of chastity, in a world that is becoming more and more self-indulgent.[39] He maintains that respecting the law of God in the transmission of life will promote the kind of self-mastery and self-sacrifice that contribute to healthy family life. This position also has implications for social ethics: the pope urges public authorities to recognize the family as "the primary unit in the state" that must be respected for the sake of the common good. Governments can address their population challenges, he writes, "by enacting laws which will assist families and by educating the people wisely so that the moral law and the freedom of citizens are both safeguarded."[40] Rising populations are leading to human misery, but the cause of this misery is greed, structural injustice, and widespread complacency. Instead of relying on a technological fix, governments need to promote structural reforms that would give everyone an opportunity to earn a living wage. This final section of the encyclical closes with exhortations to various groups to respect and promote the moral law in the

[37] Ibid., No. 14. [38] Ibid., No. 16. [39] Ibid., No. 21. [40] Ibid., No. 23.

particular ways open to them: scientists, Christian couples, doctors and nurses, priests, and bishops.

RECEPTION OF *HUMANE VITAE*

Humanae Vitae has been described as the "Vietnam" of the Catholic Church.[41] *Gaudium et Spes* condemned previously prohibited forms of birth control (i.e., surgical sterilization and condoms), but left open the question whether some new, less-intrusive forms of birth control might be permissible.[42] *Humanae Vitae* slammed the door on that possibility. It was issued during a time of global social upheaval and massive challenges to authority of all kinds. Mass communications spread the headline "POPE BANS PILL" around the world almost instantly.[43] News of the pope's prohibition was met by a large outcry. As months passed, surveys in a number of countries indicated that ordinary Catholics refused to accept the prohibition.[44] The pope was surprised and dismayed by the intense public reaction. The Dutch, Belgian, Canadian, and many other episcopal conferences attempted to provide pastorally useful and, in some cases, highly qualified interpretations of *Humanae Vitae*.[45]

Many theologians felt that the encyclical represented a reversal of the pope's earlier attitude of openness to contemporary culture, commitment to dialog, and personalism.[46] British moral theologian Kevin Kelly later wrote that Paul VI's letter focused "on the nature of the sexual act itself rather than on the nature of the human person."[47] *Humanae Vitae* was also perceived as an attempt to redraw the sharp pre-Vatican II line dividing the active magisterium as the teaching church and a passive laity as the learning church.

Critics challenged the encyclical's moral reasoning. Medical ethicist Richard McCormick, S.J., wrote: "many theologians will agree that there are serious methodological problems, even deficiencies, in the analysis used to support the conclusion [of *Humanae Vitae*]," and that its

41 Among others, Steinfels, *A People Adrift*, 257, and Gleason, *Keeping the Faith*, 192.

42 See GS, No. 51. See O'Malley, *What Happened at Vatican II*, 284–5.

43 Hebblethwaite, *Paul VI*, 517.

44 A Gallup "Values and Beliefs" survey conducted in May 2014 found that 86 percent of Catholics asked said that birth control is "morally acceptable." Rebecca Riffkin, "New Record Highs in Moral Acceptability," *Gallup*, 30 May 2014, available at .www.gallup.com/poll/170789/new-record-highs-moral-acceptability.aspx.

45 See Horgan, *Humanae Vitae and the Bishops*.

46 See Callahan, *The Catholic Case for Contraception*; Curran, et al., *The Responsibility of Dissent*.

47 Kelly, *New Directions in Sexual Ethics*, 105.

conclusions remain "a teaching subject to solid and positive doubt."[48] Moral theologian Charles Curran of the Catholic University of America organized a public statement signed by more than six hundred theologians who agreed that, in some circumstances, Catholic spouses could in good conscience use artificial birth control; widespread dissatisfaction was also registered in a dissenting statement issued by a large number of European theologians.

Critics complained that *Humanae Vitae* put conformity to a biologically fixed natural order over the practical needs and responsibilities of married couples who, for good reasons, might want to limit the size of their families. The church itself acknowledged the duty of responsible parenthood, but then took away a major innovation to exercise that responsibility, even though it was already used by millions of presumably conscientious people.

The top-down manner of exercising magisterial authority led critics to wonder what had happened to the respect for the conscience of the believer enunciated by *Gaudium et Spes*: "Deep within their conscience individuals discover a law that they do not make for themselves but that they are bound to obey, whose voice, ever summoning them to love and to do what is good and avoid what is evil rings in their hearts."[49] *Humanae Vitae* suggested that the consciences of every married couple using artificial birth control, even for the good of their own children, was leading them to engage in "intrinsically evil" acts.

The traditionalist and authoritative style of *Humanae Vitae* seemed to undercut the Second Vatican Council's move not only toward the primacy of the conscience, but also toward greater collaboration, collegiality, and co-responsibility in the church.[50] The encyclical undermined the credibility of the magisterium. Toward the end of the encyclical, Paul VI urged priests to obey the norms of *Humanae Vitae*, "not only because of the reasons adduced, but rather because of the light of the Holy Spirit, which is given in a particular way to the pastors of the church."[51] While not the pope's intention, this statement was read by critics as appealing to the Holy Spirit in place of less-than-convincing logic. In any case, as Peter Steinfels pointed out, *Humanae Vitae* stirred questioning among

48 McCormick, "Notes on Moral Theology," 731, 737.

49 GS, No. 16, as well as the strong endorsement of conscience in *Dignitatis Humanae*, the Declaration on Religious Freedom.

50 See Mahoney, *The Making of Moral Theology*, chapter 7.

51 HV, No. 28.

clergy and laity alike about the church's competence in matters of sexuality.[52]

Humanae Vitae triggered an explosion of publications by moral theologians over methodological questions. These included the role of human experience in moral formation, the function of conscience and personal responsibility in the Christian life, the relation of theologians to the magisterium, the intelligibility of natural law ethics within contemporary intellectual culture, the relation of natural law norms to scripture, and the status of absolute norms and the category of so-called intrinsically evil acts.

Questions of authority were paramount. *Humanae Vitae* led to debates over how to interpret and assign authority to church documents, particularly with regard to non-infallible doctrines. It also provoked discussions about the status of doctrines that, over the long haul, show little indication of being effectively confirmed ("received") by the laity. These concerns led to questions about the place of the "sense of the faithful" in the interpretation of Catholic doctrine and, more importantly, in what sense Catholic doctrine can be said to need better formulation or development over time as the church gains experience, better information, and deeper insight.[53]

Debates that began with *Humanae Vitae* contributed to an unprecedented degree of polarization within the church that intensified during the vitriolic "culture wars" during the pontificates of Pope John Paul II and Pope Benedict XVI.[54]

Catholic conservatives have tended to argue that protecting the family begins with protecting the unborn. Some argue that permitting artificial birth control puts society on a slippery slope to abortion and euthanasia. They argue that the "culture of death" is rooted in a conception of human freedom detached from obedience to God and willing to exercise power over life and death itself. They point to countries that have practiced eugenics, forced sterilization, and coerced abortions.

The recently emergent new natural law theorists defend the teachings of *Humanae Vitae* by employing a philosophically retooled conception of natural law that avoids the encyclical's "physicalism" (the illegitimate attempt to derive moral norms from the physical structures of our sexual faculties). The new natural law theory slightly predated *Humanae Vitae*, but

[52] Steinfels, *A People Adrift*, 257.

[53] According to the Council's Decree on Ecumenism, no. 6: "Therefore, if the influence of events or of the times has led to deficiencies in conduct, in Church discipline, or even in the formulation of doctrine (which must be carefully distinguished from the deposit of faith itself), these should be appropriately rectified at the proper moment."

[54] See Chapter 22 on Pope John Paul II herein.

picked up a full head of steam in the moral controversies it unleashed.[55] New natural lawyers see the spiritual, moral, and biological union of a married couple as a basic human good that is actualized in the act of sexual intercourse.[56] Engaging in sexual acts that do not actualize the one-flesh union, they argue, violates the good of marriage and effectively treats sexual activity as nothing more than a means to individual gratification. Married couples who violate the good of marriage act selfishly and sow the seeds for the destruction of their own families. New natural lawyers insist on philosophical grounds that relations within marriage and family are inherently undermined by artificial birth control. They criticize contemporary society for communicating a misleading and destructive understanding of the nature of marriage and the family, not as goods in their own right, but as instrumental to the desires and preferences of autonomous individuals. Since any rational person, and not just Christians, ought to value the good of marriage and the family, they reason that law and public policy ought to support heterosexual married couples and promote social and economic conditions that facilitate childrearing.

The revisionist alternative in moral theology accords with nearly all of Paul VI's personalist and Christian vision of marriage, sex, and family, with the exception of the claim that each act of sexual intercourse must be open to procreation. Spouses who are psychologically or economically strained may want to limit the size of their families for the sake of their children and their marriage. In such cases, revisionists argue, procreation presents an obstacle to the unitive purpose of sex. Natural family planning also seems artificial in its own way and in any case is far from reliable.

Whereas *Humanae Vitae* argued from precedent and a neoscholastic account of the natural finality of the marital act, and the new natural lawyers argued deductively from their philosophical theory of the marital good, revisionist moral theologians tend to argue in terms of the concrete experience of married couples. Lisa Sowle Cahill, for example, writes: "I am confident that most Catholic couples would be incredulous at the proposition that the use of artificial birth control necessarily makes their sexual intimacy selfish, dishonest, and unfaithful."[57] Revisionists like Cahill maintain that marriage as a whole, not each act of intercourse, holds together the unitive and procreative meanings of sex.

55 Grisez, "The First Principle of Practical Reason."

56 See Grisez, *The Way of The Lord Jesus Christ, Volume 2: Living a Christian Life*; Finnis, "Is Natural Law Theory Compatible with Limited Government?"

57 Cahill, "Abortion, Sex, and Gender."

CONCLUSION

Paul VI unleashed a massive debate on the meaning of marriage, sex, and the family. John Paul II's more self-assured style did not convince married Catholics in the developed world to obey *Humane Vitae*. To many theologians, the church made a huge mistake in opposing the use of condoms (even, strangely, when they had nothing to do with preventing conception) in an age of HIV/AIDS. Many young people are attracted by the church's advocacy of human dignity, social justice, and human rights, but pay no attention to its pronouncements about sex, marriage, and family. This is an enormous loss for the formation of young people and their participation in the life of the church. To be sure, widespread mistrust in institutions over the past half-century is owing to a complex variety of social, economic, and cultural factors. It would be foolish to blame *Humanae Vitae* for Catholic indifference to the magisterium, but that document did help to create a rift that has yet to be healed. The loss of trust was exacerbated by John Paul II's absolute intolerance of any theologian or bishop who wanted to revisit the question of artificial birth control.

The underlying issue that emerged in the debate over the encyclical concerns the nature and authority of the church, an issue still unresolved after the Second Vatican Council. Since *Humanae Vitae*, an impressive array of theologians and philosophers has raised pressing questions about the equality of women and men, the sexual division of labor within families, and the full participation of women in the life of the church as well as the wider society. Christian families in many places are undergoing a major transformation, but the structures and culture of the Catholic Church are not.

On the positive side, however, Paul VI presented an attractive vision of marriage and family in affective, biblical, and relational terms. The pope offered a beautiful depiction of marriage as a lifelong bond of mutual, self-giving love and moved the church away from a hierarchical understanding of the relation of husband and wife. Rather than presenting marriage as a second-best avenue for people not called to ordained celibacy or vowed religious life, the pope upheld marriage as a path to personal holiness and a form of apostolic service. From the 1960s and 1970s, the church ceased speaking about procreation as the primary end of marriage while continuing to underscore the nature of marriage as an indissoluble and exclusive union of a heterosexual couple. It has understood Christian families as grounded in the marriage covenant and exhibiting, in a sacramental way, Christ's love for the church.

Paul VI took for granted the tradition of a breadwinner father and a homemaker mother. He concurred with his predecessors' understanding that the well-being of the family depended on economic and social justice. Where fathers are not paid a living or family wage, wives must take up paid work and leave their children to the care of others.[58] Single mothers are even worse off when they are left to raise children on earnings insufficient for a decent livelihood.

Paul VI reminded public authorities of their responsibility to protect permanent, monogamous marriage as a critically important institution of any just and healthy society. He recognized the global danger of overpopulation and acknowledged that large families present a special obstacle to the well-being of women, couples, and families caught in poverty. Yet the solution he proposed was woefully inadequate.

His controversial encyclical *Humanae Vitae* reflected a core Catholic conviction about the intimate connection of sex, love, and procreation. It resisted any attempt to treat them as separable realities whose meaning is determined solely by the choices of autonomous agents. He also upheld a vision of marriage as much more than a private contract, and a view of children as more than one lifestyle option among others. The family is an expression of embodied love that typically blends different lines of biological kinship. It is also a properly social and legal institution that recognizes the duties of parents, even at serious personal cost to themselves, to provide their children with a healthy upbringing, supportive care, and education. The well-being of families is not merely the private concern of their own members, but is rather a matter of the common good and, therefore, a matter of public, political responsibility.

RECOMMENDED READING

Hebblethwaite, Peter. *Paul VI: The First Modern Pope*. Mahwah, NJ: Paulist Press, 1993.

Komonchak, Joseph. "*Humanae Vitae* and Its Reception: Ecclesiological Reflections." *Theological Studies* 39 (1978): 221–57.

Noonan, John T., Jr. *Contraception: A History of Its Treatment by Catholic Theologians and Canonists*. Cambridge, MA: Harvard University Press, 1965.

Pope, Stephen J. *Human Evolution and Christian Ethics*. Cambridge: Cambridge University Press, 2007.

58 Leo XIII, Rerum Novarum, "The Condition of Labor," nos. 16–17, in O'Brien and Shannon, *Catholic Social Thought*, 21–2.

Rahner, Karl, S.J. "On the Encyclical *Humanae Vitae*, a 25-Year Retrospective." *Theological Investigations* vol. 9. New York: Herder, 1974.

Smith, Janet E. *Humanae Vitae: A Generation Later*. Washington, DC: Catholic University of America Press, 1991.

Smith, Janet E., ed. *Why Humanae Vitae Was Right: A Reader*. San Francisco, CA: Ignatius Press, 1993.

Tentler, Leslie Woodcock. *Catholics and Contraception: An American History*. Ithaca, NY: Cornell University Press, 2004.

Valsecchi, Ambrogio. *Controversy: The Birth Control Debate 1958–1968*. Introduction by Gregory Baum. Translated by Dorothy White. Washington, DC: Corpus Books, 1968.

22

Pope John Paul II

Robert P. George and Gerard V. Bradley

BIOGRAPHICAL INTRODUCTION

Born into a middle-class Polish family on 18 May 1920, the man who would become Pope John Paul II came of age during the German occupation of Poland during World War II. Karol Wojtyla's intellectual gifts manifested themselves early in his life, as did his aptitudes for acting and vigorous physical exercise. After a secondary education in state schools, he entered Krakow's Jagiellonian University in 1938 – just before the Nazis closed it. Because they threatened to deport anyone without a work card, Wojtyla performed manual labor throughout the war, chiefly as a quarryman for the Solvay Chemical Company.[1]

Wojtyla entered a clandestine seminary in the autumn of 1942 and was ordained on 1 November 1946. Father Wojtyla pursued graduate studies in Rome, where he earned a doctorate at Angelicum University; his dissertation was *The Problems of Faith in the Works of St. John of the Cross*. During nearly a quarter of a century as a professor of ethics at Lublin Catholic University and at the Krakow seminary, Wojtyla immersed himself in Continental philosophy, especially that of Kant, Husserl, and Scheler (the principal subject of his second dissertation, at Lublin Catholic). Although Wojtyla was not a specialist in either classical or Thomistic studies, distinguished American political philosopher James Schall, S.J., wrote that his collected philosophical papers

[1] The indispensable reference for all aspects of Wojtyla's life in Poland – and much more – is George Weigel's *Witness to Hope: The Biography of John Paul II*. The authors thank Marcy Kreimier, University of St. Thomas Law School Class of 2017, for her invaluable research assistance, to which she brought an impressive knowledge of Pope John Paul II.

FIGURE 22.1. Pope John Paul II, Gdansk, 1987. Pope John Paul II's third pilgrimage to Poland / Forum / Bridgeman Images

were as "good a review and as clear a representation of the essentials of classic ethics [of Aquinas and Aristotle] as any I have ever seen."[2]

Pope Benedict XVI said in 2006 that even as a young priest Karol Wojtyla "had the idea of 'teaching how to love,'" and that he saw the need for a "systematic study" of the subject.[3] In fact, Professor Wojtyla carried on an active pastoral ministry especially geared to young people preparing to marry. He later said that his first book, *Love and Responsibility* (1960), was born of "pastoral necessity," specifically the need of young couples to be instructed in their vocations to marriage and sexual love.[4] Wojtyla's play, *The Jeweler's Shop*, also published in 1960, told the story of three marriages. In it, he explored the truth that conjugal love depends on transcending emotional attraction and must be grounded in the genuine self-giving of each spouse to the other.

Love and Responsibility presented a powerful though implicit challenge to the Communist dictatorship under which its author lived, precisely by its resolute insistence on the primacy and integrity of the family, a social unit that must be free of state control and that invariably inhibits the totalitarian impulse. Wojtyla's second book, *The Acting Person* (1969), argued (in part) that Marxism's fundamental mistake was not about history or the economy, but anthropology. Wojtyla maintained that "its economic and social failures derived from a misunderstanding of human nature."[5]

Wojtyla's intelligence, character, and charm would have made him a significant figure in postwar Europe regardless of his profession. French theologian Yves Congar noted in his diary during the Second Vatican Council that Wojtyla "made a very great impression. His personality is imposing. A power radiates from it, an attraction, a certain force that is very calm, but incontestable."[6] Pope Pius XII named Wojtyla an auxiliary bishop in 1957. Pope Paul VI named him archbishop of Krakow on 13 January 1964 and cardinal on 26 June 1967.

[2] Review of Karol Wojtyla, *Person and Community-Selected Essays* (translated by T. Sandok), in *The American Journal of Jurisprudence* 39 (1994): 499.

[3] "Address of His Holiness Benedict XVI to Members of the Pontifical John Paul II Institute for Studies on Marriage and Family on the XXVth Anniversary of Its Foundation" on 11 May 2006, sections 6 and 7, available at: https://w2.vatican.va/content/benedict-xvi/en/speeches/2006/may/documents/hf_ben-xvi_spe_20060511_istituto-gp-ii.html (last visited 17 February 2016).

[4] See Weigel, *Witness*, 140, quoting John Paul II, *Curriculum Philosophicum*.

[5] Luxmoore and Babiuch, "Did Karol Wojtyla See and Rescue the Good in Marxism?".

[6] Quoted in Lawler et al., *The Church in the Modern World*, 714 (citing Congar's *My Journal* (2014)).

Cardinal Wojtyla was elected Pope John Paul II (hereafter, John Paul) on 16 October 1978, the first non-Italian pontiff in more than four centuries.

In 1983, John Paul promulgated a new Code of Canon Law, which he later said was "imbued with the Council's thought, particularly in what concerns the personalistic understanding of marriage."[7] He brought out in 1997 a new universal *Catechism of the Catholic Church* (the first since Trent in 1566).[8] John Paul played a critical role in the collapse of the Soviet empire in Eastern Europe. He was by the year 2000 the most recognizable person in the world. "The sheer drama" of Wojtyla's life, wrote biographer George Weigel, "would defy the imagination of the most fanciful screenwriter."[9]

John Paul's voluminous papal writings include significant works on social justice (the leading encyclical on this subject is *Centesimus Annus*, 1991), morality (most importantly, *Veritatis Splendor*, 1993), and the moral foundations and obligations of civil law (see especially *Evangelium Vitae*, 1995). All of them included significant references to the family. And all supplied foundations for John Paul's more pointed treatments of family, civil society, and law. Of those works, the most important are his apostolic exhortation *Familiaris Consortio* (1981; hereafter FC), published in the wake of the church's 1980 Synod on the Family, and his "Letter to Families" (1994; LF), in celebration of that "Year of the Family."

John Paul also published some books unrelated to the authority of his office. These include *Crossing the Threshold of Hope* (1994), which ranged widely over the human condition and discussed the leading issues facing humankind at the dawn of the millennium. *Gift and Mystery* (1996), a concise autobiography, appeared fifty years after his priestly ordination. *Memory and Identity: Personal Reflections* was published shortly before his death in 2005. It is a profound meditation on suffering, powerfully informed by his own protracted debilitating illness, one effect of which was finally to render him incapable of speech.

John Paul died on 2 April 2005 and was canonized as Saint John Paul II on 27 April 2014.

[7] "Address Of The Holy Father John Paul II to the Tribunal Of The Roman Rota" on 28 January 1991, section 7, available at: http://w2.vatican.va/content/john-paul-ii/en/speeches/1991/january/documents/hf_jp-ii_spe_19910128_roman-rota.html (last visited 17 February 2016).

[8] On the Tridentine catechism and its teachings on marriage, see Chapter 15 herein on Thomas Sanchez and Chapter 20 herein on Popes Leo XIII and Pius XI.

[9] Weigel, *Witness*, 2.

MAIN CURRENTS

John Paul did not create or even significantly develop the core of what he consistently taught, preached, and wrote about the family. In his academic and papal writings and across a lifetime of speeches and pastoral work, he defended perennial Christian teaching. His aim (as he described it in a 1991 speech to the Roman Rota, the church's matrimonial court) was "that people of today are offered the entirety of the gospel message about marriage."[10] His objective could be described accurately, too, in these words from the Second Vatican Council's *Constitution on the Church in the Modern World* (*Gaudium et Spes*; hereafter GS): "to present certain key points of the church's teaching in a clearer light," and "to guide and encourage Christians and all others who are trying to preserve and to foster the dignity and supremely sacred value of the married state" (GS 47). John Paul endeavored to be, in other words, a servant of the truth.

For John Paul, according to his understanding of natural law, the Gospel, and Christian tradition, the "family" was not synonymous with "marriage." But it was nearly so: although the childless married couple constituted a family, children perfected the couple's union; marriage is intrinsically oriented to procreation, and not fully intelligible save by understanding the married couple as in a relationship of the type naturally oriented to procreation and the rearing of children. This is true even of a man and woman who marry in their eighties. John Paul said that children "crown" the parents' "love for each other" (LF 9), "consolidate" the covenant between them, and "enrich and deepen" their "conjugal union" (LF 7). Marriage is the essential foundation of the family; other (non-marital) uses of the term "family" are extensions of the focal meaning or are analogous, attenuated, or metaphorical.

John Paul rejected any dichotomy between nature and grace, as if there were two marriages, one profane and another sacred. "[A]longside natural marriage, one cannot describe another model of Christian marriage with specific supernatural requisites."[11] Jesus elevated natural marriage to a sacrament, thus making it a sign of his own unconditional loving commitment to his church. "What marriage is in nature becomes, by the will of Christ, a true sacrament of the new covenant, sealed by the blood of Christ the Redeemer" (LF 18).

Notwithstanding the Old Testament patriarchs' domestic arrangements, John Paul held that monogamy was the *natural* (not just the revealed) truth

[10] *Supra* note 6.

[11] "Address of John Paul II to the Prelate Auditors, Officials and Advocates of the Tribunal of the Roman Rota" on 28 January 2003, section 8, available at: http://w2.vatican.va/content/john-paul-ii/en/speeches/2003/january/documents/hf_jp-ii_spe_20030130_roman-rota.html (last visited 17 February 2016).

about marriage. (He welcomed the decline of polygamy, not only because polygamy was false, but also because it subordinated women.)[12] John Paul affirmed, too, the *natural* indissolubility of a valid, consummated marriage, and the *natural* moral law behind the norm excluding contraception. This unity of truth about marriage not only established contact with Saint Paul's declaration in Romans 2:14–15 about the law written on the hearts of Gentiles. It is also one foundation of John Paul's repeated declarations about the civil authorities' strict obligations to protect and to promote the family.

John Paul fully embraced the Second Vatican Council's clarification of the relationship between the ends of marriage – procreation, spousal friendship, remedy for concupiscence – and its essence. The council addressed the problematic inherited view that these ends (chiefly procreation) were extrinsic to marriage, so that marriage itself appeared to be only an instrumental good. In GS, sections 47–52, the Vatican fathers developed an integrated view of marriage that synthesized without denying anything essential in what had previously been taught. The council taught that marriage just *is* "an intimate community of conjugal life and love" (GS 48), which is uniquely actualized and expressed through the marital act (GS 49). Children fulfill the communion of spouses, for by "their own natural character, the institution of marriage and conjugal love are directed to the procreation and raising of children" (GS 50). According to Germain Grisez, this "formulation avoids the suggestion that marriage and conjugal love are means to the end of having offspring, and points instead to the view that" children "normally belong to the full unfolding of the marriage."[13]

John Paul defended this complex but unified view of marriage throughout his papacy. "Personalism" is the most common label for what is distinctive in John Paul's thought about marriage and family life (and indeed his account of human flourishing altogether). It is a form of Christian humanism characterized by at least three thoughts. First, moral norms guide persons' free choices in line with the ideal of the integral good of human beings – themselves and others who are affected by their choices and to whom they have responsibilities; norms are not rules to which one must conform for the sake of some extrinsic end (such as gaining heaven and avoiding hell). Second, God's commandments give expression to these moral truths, which bind persons not by dint of superior will, but by their being *true*; that is, because they order our choices in line with

[12] "Address of the Holy Father John Paul II to the Tribunal of the Roman Rota" on 28 January 1991, section 5.

[13] Grisez, *Living A Christian Life*, 565. Grisez's treatment of the Second Vatican Council's clarification of marriage (at pages 561–7) is succinct, insightful, and sound.

integral human well-being and fulfillment. Personalism (and Christian humanism) thus excludes legalism and voluntarism. Third, persons can fulfill themselves only through their free choices. In no technical or recondite sense of the terms, people must be the authors of their own lives. And so, in one of countless similar personalistic appreciations of marriage, John Paul wrote approvingly that "there is a more lively awareness of personal freedom and attention to the quality of interpersonal relationships in marriage, to promoting the dignity of women, to responsible procreation, to the education of children" (FC 6).

John Paul sharply contrasted personalism with individualism. Already before his papacy, he wrote that "[i]ndividualism sees in the individual the supreme and fundamental good, to which all interests of the community or the society have to be subordinated."[14] In a later speech to the Rota, in 1999, Pope John Paul wrote that this individualism tends toward self-centeredness in outlook and subjectivism in morality. And individualism is surely not the implication or corollary of a proper emphasis on each person's freedom, which instead truly "consists in the human being's possibility of conforming responsibly, that is by personal choice, to the divine will expressed in the law, and in this way to become more and more like his Creator."[15]

John Paul maintained throughout his pontificate that public authorities' responsibility for the common good included scrupulous care for the family. Marriage and family are not matters of merely private satisfaction or aspects of some persons' identities. John Paul held and taught that the flourishing of marriage and family was part of the political common good, in two distinct ways. One way looks inward, to the role of marriage and family in each person's flourishing, and depends on the common good as maintenance of conditions in which persons can more or less easily pursue genuine goods for the fulfillment of themselves and others (here John Paul's understanding is squarely in line with the Vatican Council's teachings). In turn, public authority is obliged, for example, to enforce policies protecting parents' moral authority over children and their education; support a cultural milieu in which children can be brought up to embrace the virtues of chastity, honesty, constancy, and the like; and be sure not to put any counterfeits of marriage (such as non-marital sexual cohabitation) on a moral par with the real thing. The second way looks outward, from the family to the greater society built on the family. Already in 1960, John Paul asserted that "the family is a small

[14] Wojtyla, *The Acting Person*, 273.

[15] "Address of John Paul II to the Tribunal of the Roman Rota" on 21 January 1999, section 6, available at: http://w2.vatican.va/content/john-paul-ii/en/speeches/1999/january/documents/hf_jp-ii_spe_19990121_rota-romana.html (last visited 17 February 2016).

society, and the existence of all large societies – nations, state, Church – depends on it."[16] He never strayed from this commitment.

Finally, the frank urgency of John Paul's teachings about the family owes much to his reading of the "signs of the times." At the beginning of his pontificate, he judged that the family was under cultural and, to a lesser extent, legal assault. In 1981, he wrote that "the family is the object of numerous forces that seek to destroy it or in some way to deform it" (FC 3). The corrosive and distorting forces were many. Individualism promoted hedonism and selfishness. The ambient meaning of love "confused a vague feeling or even a strong psychophysical attraction with real love for another person," which consists in a "sincere desire for his or her welfare."[17] (John Paul held that one antonym of love was lust.) Toward the end of his life, he judged that the family was facing an epochal crisis. Perhaps the key warning sign was by that time the *legal* war on the family, in which non-marital (and thus immoral) sexual acts and non-marital cohabitation were not only tolerated, but valorized and even facilitated and promoted by public authorities. The epitome of this assault was the equation of homosexual partnerships with genuine marriage.

John Paul's most notable contribution to the subject matter of this volume surely was that, for two decades, he was the world's most visible proponent of the truth (as he found it in Christian tradition) about family. But he also contributed creative developments of that tradition, and the balance of this chapter considers three of them. The first is John Paul's "Theology of the Body," a sophisticated theological apologetic for the church's teachings about marriage and sexual morality, especially the moral norm excluding contraception in all cases. He articulated this rich vision in more than one hundred Wednesday Audiences (public discourses) during the first five years of his pontificate. The second is John Paul's extended treatment of the dignity and vocation of women, particularly in his apostolic letter *Mulieris Dignitatem*. Published on 15 August 1988 (the Feast of the Assumption of Mary into Heaven), *Mulieris Dignitatem* is in large part a biblically based argument for the essential equality of women and men. The third is John Paul's sustained but more episodic teachings about the relationship between moral truths, including those pertaining to sexual activity and marriage, and the civil law. At the heart of these interventions is John Paul's unequivocal rejection of contemporary claims in favor of a distinctive public reason in contrast to a cabined private morality that even a public official might affirm to be true, albeit inoperative when acting in his or her official capacity. He maintained instead (most perspicuously in *Veritatis Splendor*, 1993) that public authorities are bound,

[16] Wojtyla, *Love and Responsibility*, 217. [17] *Supra* note 15, at section 3.

and civil law and public policy must be guided, by the same basic moral norms as everyone else. There are no special exceptions, and no prerogative of dispensation, even for the master of millions.

"THEOLOGY OF THE BODY"

Two decades before John Paul II, in 1963, Pope John XXIII had created a pontifical commission to prepare for the Vatican's participation in a United Nations conference on population growth. Pope Paul VI expanded the commission's membership and assignment in 1964 to consider, not the church's firm and constant teaching against contraception, but whether the anovulent birth control pill fell within it. For the pill seemed to some to be an improbable contraceptive; it was removed in time and space from the sexual act and usually out of mind too. Because it had no apparent effect on the sexual behaviour of the married couple, some Catholic moralists (who inclined to a physicalist understanding of human acts, and who thus tended to identify the wrongness of contraception with the visible distortions of the sexual act typical of condoms or withdrawal) thought that, perhaps, the use of the pill did not properly fall under the church's historic condemnation of contraception.[18]

But there were additional reasons to study anew the church's teaching, reasons that brought into question the norm against contraception as such. Among these reasons was the emerging valorization of the unitive significance of the marital act, which seemed morally worthy apart from procreative possibility. The emerging social and marital equality of women changed many persons' thinking about responsible parenthood (basically, how many children to have). As jobs and the professions opened up to them, fewer women understood themselves to be called to a single-minded life of child-rearing. Contraceptives advertised as nearly 100 percent effective would evidently serve the modern woman better than any version of the rhythm method of regulating conception. Besides, medical progress meant that almost all children conceived would survive infancy and grow to adulthood, just as the effort and expense of raising them all to adult competency in modern societies increased dramatically. Concerns for overpopulation, however exaggerated and almost comically apocalyptic, played a role too.

A majority of what came to be called the Pope's Birth Control Commission eventually (in 1966) concluded that each couple's marriage must be open to the transmission of new life. But they also concluded that not every marital act

[18] See details in Chapter 21 herein on Pope Paul VI.

need be. The proper referent of the norm (of openness to life) was the couple's whole married life, viewed in total. Thus contraception (by whatever non-abortifacient method) could, they suggested, be morally approved as a means of spacing children or even delaying them indefinitely.

The commission's contentious proceedings were punctuated by the Vatican Council's not-quite-unmistakably-clear assertion of the immorality of contraception in 1965 (see GS 51.) But Pope Paul VI rejected the majority's suggestion. In the encyclical letter *Humanae Vitae* (hereafter HV), promulgated on 25 July 1968, he affirmed that contraception – that is, deliberately sterilizing a sex act by any means with the aim of preventing conception – was absolutely excluded by both natural moral law and Christian revelation. Paul VI never used the term "contraception." *Humanae Vitae* morally excluded "any act which – when marital intercourse is anticipated, being engaged in, or leading to its natural consequences – is intended (either as end or as means) to impede procreation" (HV 14).[19] The gravamen of the condemned act was the willingness to deprive sexual congress of the generative effect it might otherwise have (or was thought or expected to have).

Archbishop Wojtyla influenced the composition of HV, if not directly (he was a member of the commission, but the Polish government forbade his attendance at its meetings), then through a separate study commission in Krakow that sent its conclusions, "The Foundations of the Church's Doctrine on the Principles of Conjugal Life," to Paul VI in February 1968. These conclusions reflected the moral analysis of *Love and Responsibility*, and HV reflects much of its thinking about the conjugal act and responsible parenthood. George Weigel opines that the Krakow document "offered a more compelling explanation of why this position was better fitted to the dignity of the human person, and particularly to the dignity of women."[20]

Pope John Paul II's lectures on the "Theology of the Body" (ToB) are in significant part an apologetic for HV. The 129 public speeches that make up ToB began on 5 September 1979 and concluded on 28 November 1984.[21] In the last discourse, John Paul said that the whole work could be summed up in the title, "'Human love in the divine plan,' or more precisely, 'The redemption of the body and the sacramentality of

[19] All quotations from HV are taken from the translation prepared by John Finnis and published by the Catholic Truth Society in 2008.

[20] Weigel, *Witness*, 209.

[21] All of these addresses can be accessed (in chronological order) at: www.ewtn.com/library/PAPALDOC/JP2TBIND.htm (last visited 17 February 2016). All citations to these talks are to the translations provided at this website, and hereafter just the date of the address and the particular section of it are supplied in the footnote.

marriage.'"[22] A few months earlier he described it as "a specific, evangelical Christian pedagogy of the body," derived from the "character of the Bible, and especially of the Gospel."[23]

The vast bulk of ToB analyzed Christ's words about marriage "in the beginning" (and thus about indissolubility); adultery in the heart (considering the Sermon on the Mount); the resurrection of the body; and the marriage sacrament, based on Ephesians 5:21–33.[24]

The heart of ToB is John Paul's abiding commitment to a non-dualistic metaphysics of the person: we *are* our bodies and do not merely inhabit them as if we were ghosts in machines. He stated that his reflections were based on the "*language of the body reread in truth*."[25] As he explained that pivotal term, "The human body is not merely an organism of sexual relations."[26] It is at the same time "the means of expressing the entire man, the person, which reveals itself by the language of the body." This language has important meaning, "especially in reciprocal relationships between man and woman," because "the language of the body should *express* ... the *truth of the sacrament*."[27]

On 11 July 1984, John Paul turned specifically to HV as a "concrete application" of the preceding reflections on "human love in the divine plan." He declared that this step would "take us to the conclusion of our now long journey."[28] It did, sixteen lectures later. The agenda for these lectures comprised four questions. First, why not contracept? What is the reasoning behind the norm affirmed in HV? Second, how should couples think about responsible parenthood? What number of children should they have? Third, how is the prudent use of infertile periods to avoid pregnancy morally different from contraception? Fourth, why should couples make the sometimes prodigious effort to live in accord with HV, that is, to practice marital chastity with its periodic continence?

John Paul's answers to these questions overlap somewhat and are mutually reinforcing. As to the *first*: besides a philosophical explanation of the indispensable twin powers of the sexual act (unitive and procreative), John Paul's answer was an invitation for couples to elevate their vision and thus to endow their lovemaking with sublime meaning:

22 28 November 1984, section 1. 23 8 August 1984, section 5.

24 This breakdown of topics tracks the summary that John Paul provided in his final ToB address, 28 November 1984.

25 11 July 1984, section 4 (emphasis in original). 26 22 August 1984, section 2.

27 Ibid. (emphasis in original). 28 11 July 1984, section 1.

> As ministers of the sacrament which is constituted by consent and perfected by conjugal union, man and woman are called to *express* that mysterious *language of their bodies, in all the truth which is proper to it.* By means of gestures and reactions of the whole dynamism, reciprocally conditioned, of tension and enjoyment – whose direct source is the body in its masculinity and femininity, the body in its action and interaction – by means of all this, man, the person, "speaks."[29]

As to the *second* question: the motivation for limiting marital acts to infertile times is usually the same as the motivation for using contraception – to avoid pregnancy. But the *means* are decisively different. Motivations do not settle the nature of anyone's action, much less the morality of it. A couple practicing what has come to be called natural family planning performs no act that divides the unitive from the procreative. They harbor no intention and thus bear no willingness to stymie the potentially procreative effect of what they do.

As to the *third* question: recourse to infertile times is often *morally* required by the second great moral norm expressed in HV and, in turn, explicated by John Paul in his ToB audiences: responsible parenthood. Although John Paul referred couples to the "objective moral order" (and even spoke of a "morally correct number of children"[30]), he made abundantly clear that it is a matter of discernment for each couple: "It is the married couple themselves who must in the last analysis arrive at these judgments before God."[31] The married couple's decision whether to try to conceive a child involves "common reflection and effort" and a candid consideration of "their own good and the good of their children, already born or yet to be born."[32] But John Paul most emphatically rejected any suggestion that a couple should leave family size to chance, as if they should make love any time and suppose that the consequences were somehow beyond their responsibility.

The good of the couple to be considered includes not only each spouse's physical and psychological well-being, but also the household's capacity to support additional dependents. It also includes the whole set of vocational responsibilities of each spouse. Thus a considered decision by the couple that each spouse should work outside the home could be reached with the appropriate "sense of human and Christian responsibility" and "docile respect for God," even if it entailed avoiding conception for the foreseeable future.[33]

The good of children to be considered includes the couple's capacity to educate them for *their* specific vocation, which obviously requires more

[29] 22 August 1984, section 4 (emphasis in original). [30] 5 September 1984, section 3.
[31] 1 August 1984, section 2. [32] Ibid. (quoting GS 50). [33] Ibid. (quoting GS 50).

resources and parental effort than it did in simpler times. The couple must also consider additional goods, including those of the "society to which they belong," and indeed the good of all humankind.[34]

Last: John Paul explained in his ToB talks that practicing continence would empower couples. For only by acquiring or perfecting the ability to master one's physical nature could one "express the entire man, the person, which reveals itself by means of the language of the body."[35] "Continence is not only – and not even principally – *the ability to abstain*, that is, mastery over the multiple reactions that are interwoven in the mutual influence of masculinity and femininity." Positively, it is "*the ability to direct* the respective *reactions*, both as to their content and their character."[36] This self-mastery *permits* the spouses to give themselves totally to each other, to make of their conjugal love a gift of each to the other.[37]

MALE AND FEMALE HE CREATED THEM

John Paul in 1988 promulgated the apostolic letter on the "Dignity and Vocation of Women" – *Mulieris Dignitatem* (MD).[38] Much of MD is devoted to what its author called a meditation on women's "essential equality." The meditation is theological, for the central ground of the equality of the sexes in MD is the undifferentiated way in which men and women figure in the economy of salvation. John Paul wrote, for example, that "*[m]an is a person, man and woman equally so*, since both were created in the image and likeness of the personal God" (MD 6; emphasis in original). Man and woman are "equally capable" of understanding and receiving the Christian faith, "of receiving the outpouring of divine truth and love in the Holy Spirit. Both receive his salvific and sanctifying 'visits'" (MD 20). "[T]he evangelical idea is addressed to human beings without any distinction of sex" (MD 25).

Mulieris Dignitatem is remarkable among post–Second Vatican Council papal teachings for its scant references to theological writers, the church's philosophical tradition, or other papal writings. John Paul's sources are predominantly scriptural. The letter is really a profound *biblical* meditation on the dignity and vocation of women. At several points John Paul shows that biblical texts that appear to sanction (or even to command) women's subordination to men do not do so when properly contextualized and interpreted. John Paul II interprets Saint Paul's assertion that the husband is head of the family, for

34 5 September 1984, section 3. 35 22 August 1984, section 2.

36 31 October 1984, section 5.

37 This topic is treated at length in the prior chapter on Paul VI.

38 Available at: http://w2.vatican.va/content/john-paul-ii/en/apost_letters/1988/documents/hf_jp-ii_apl_19880815_mulieris-dignitatem.html (last visited 17 February 2016).

instance, as a call (or command), not for wives' subordination to their mates, but to *mutual* self-sacrifice, each spouse to the other. It is a matter of "*mutual subjection out of reverence for Christ*" (MD 29; emphasis in original).

The heart of this biblical exploration is the example of Jesus. "In all of Jesus's teaching, as well as in his behaviour, one can find nothing which reflects the discrimination against women prevalent in his day" (MD 16). Christ opposed the "tradition which discriminated against women," a tradition "in which the male 'dominated' without having proper regard for woman and her dignity"; Christ's "whole attitude towards women" was "extraordinary, if seen against the background of his time." "It is universally admitted – even by people with a critical attitude toward the Christian message – that *in the eyes of his contemporaries Christ became a promoter of women's true dignity* and of the *vocation* corresponding to this dignity" (MD 15; emphasis in original).

In MD, John Paul sought to bring all these theological reflections into fruitful contact with then still-new anti-sex discrimination legal norms and with emergent cultural transformations concerning the social status and opportunities of women. He welcomed "the hour" – his time – "when the vocation of woman is being acknowledged in its fullness, the hour in which women acquire in the world an influence, an effect and a power never hitherto achieved." Now the "human race is undergoing so deep a transformation" in its understanding of woman's contributions to the improvement of humanity's condition (MD 1).

John Paul referred several times to traditions of "unjust discrimination" and to "situations in which the woman remains disadvantaged or discriminated against by the fact of being a woman." He did not further describe these situations and said little about how to correct them. MD makes almost no contact with the church's own social doctrines, including those pertaining to the rights of workers. It was obviously John Paul's strategy in MD to avoid policy prescriptions and to steer clear of concrete political debates. This judgment is debatable; having referred pointedly to certain unjust situations calling for correction, John Paul might usefully have developed the thought *without* invading the proper province of the laity to bring Gospel principles into the temporal order. But this strategic misstep (if that is what it was) does not detract from his extraordinary testimony to the essential equality of women and men.

"MASTER OF THE WORLD"

Reason, even unaided by revelation, includes the judgment that among the moral principles and norms that are valid for all persons, at all times and in all places, are some exceptionless negative moral norms, such as that torture and slavery are never permissible. It is thus reasonable to affirm and unreasonable to deny the position asserted by John Paul in his 1993 encyclical on moral philosophy, *Veritatis Splendor*: "*When it is a matter of the moral norms prohibiting intrinsic evil, there are no privileges or exceptions for anyone*. It makes no difference whether one is the master of the world or the 'poorest of the poor' on the face of the earth. Before the demands of morality we are all absolutely equal" (VS 96; emphasis in original). This is the cornerstone of all Catholic social doctrine, as it is of John Paul's teachings about how public authority should treat the family.

This *unicity* of morality means that there is no tenable distinction such as some recent liberal political philosophers have attempted to draw between so-called public reason(s) and private or nonpublic reason(s). The concept of public reason(s) is supposedly required by justice when addressing political matters in a pluralist society. It is part of an apparatus meant to banish from the public realm what are most often referred to in this body of thought as comprehensive doctrines about human good or well-being. The exceptionless negative moral norms bind public authorities along with everyone else. And they are linchpins of any truly just social order. In a Doctrinal Note that he approved and directed to be published, John Paul declared that "[d]emocracy must be based upon the true and solid foundation of non-negotiable ethical principles, which are the underpinning of life in society."[39] John Paul emphasized repeatedly throughout his writings after around 1995 that moral relativism, which many thought to be a corollary of democracy, would instead prove to be democracy's undoing.

John Paul taught that public authorities are morally obliged to consider the whole truth about human sexuality, marriage, and the family *when* they come to consider actions, laws, and policies that affect the family. To consider the whole truth is not by any means to suggest that the coercive power of law should be brought to bear on the *whole* realm of marriage and family life. Far from it. John Paul held what the Christian tradition has always held, namely, that the "scope of the civil law is certainly more limited than that of the moral law."[40] Many intra-familial moral duties – of parents to children, of children to parents, of siblings to each other – are beyond the

[39] "Doctrinal Note on Some Questions Regarding the Participation of Catholics in Political Life" promulgated on 24 November 2002, section 3, available at: http://www.vatican.va/roman_curia/congregations/cfaith/documents/rc_con_cfaith_doc_20021124_politica_en.html (last visited 17 February 2016).

[40] "Considerations Regarding Proposals to Give Legal Recognition to Unions Between Homosexual Persons" published 3 June 2003 with the approval of John Paul II, section 6, available at: http://

morally legitimate reach of the civil law. Parents have the right to decide about their children's religious education (and education generally) without state interference. Even here, however, public officials would have to understand the whole truth about human well-being – especially as it pertains to family matters – to know *that* they should not interfere, and to understand *why not*. In a well-ordered polity, public funds might (in fact, prima facie, *should*) be made available to parents desiring a religious elementary education for their children. But, again, a conscientious decision by public authority to do so should be informed by the whole truth about familial well-being. So too a conscientious decision *not* to make funds available in light of poor educational performance by recipient schools or owing to putative constitutional restraints.

Perhaps the most important relevant implication of the unicity of morality is that the "civil law cannot contradict right reason without losing its binding force on conscience."[41] This is *not* to say that "an unjust law is no law at all" (the truth of which slogan is limited to the important proposition that the ordinary moral obligation to obey a civil law is inoperative or attenuated in the case of unjust enactments, replaced by a duty to conform to the requirements of the law insofar as the common good calls for it). It is rather to say that public authority should never presuppose, imply, or attribute moral value to an act or relationship that, in truth, has none.

We have already considered an example of this requirement in action: a married couple's contracepted sexual intercourse. Prudence and a concern for values that may be placed at risk by too intrusive a state may well dictate that public authority should not prohibit these private acts. But the ground for steering clear of them is not, and should not be advertised as, any favorable moral judgment of contraception. The reason for leaving these couples alone is that the likely harmful effects on true goods – including marital harmony and privacy – metaphorically outweigh any good that could come by attempts to ban contraception.

With regard to the very many rights and benefits to which everyone is entitled regardless of their living situation, cohabiting partners – including those of the same sex – should "make use of the provisions of law – like all citizens from the standpoint of their private autonomy – to protect their right

www.vatican.va/roman_curia/congregations/cfaith/documents/rc_con_cfaith_doc_20030731_homosexual-unions_en.html (last visited 17 February 2016).

41 Ibid.

in matters of common interest."[42] But it would be gravely unjust to secure these just entitlements by means predicated upon legal recognition of an immoral sexual relationship, much worse by means that elevated same-sex relationships to the status of marriage. For this would move beyond treating homosexual behaviour as a private phenomenon and instead recognize it as a "relationship in society, foreseen and approved by law, to the point where it becomes one of the institutions in the legal structure."[43] Legal recognition of same-sex unions as marriages or as tantamount to marriage "would obscure also certain basic moral values which belong to the common inheritance of humanity."[44] Catholic politicians are obliged to oppose any such legal recognition, because of the moral obligations they share with others, but also "in a particular way, in keeping with their responsibility" precisely as persons exercising public authority.[45]

CONCLUSION

In 1994, John Paul summarized the burden of his pontificate, insofar as marriage and family were concerned: "I speak with the power of this truth to all people of our day, so that they will appreciate the grandeur of the goods of marriage, family and life; so that they will come to appreciate the great danger which follows when these realities are not respected, or when the supreme values which lie at the foundation of the family and of human dignity are disregarded" (LF 23).

This was, he firmly believed, no less (and perhaps no more) than his duty as a pastor of souls. For he understood pastoral concern as "the search for the *true* good of man, a promotion of the values engraved in his person by God." It is "directed to the ever clearer discovery of God's plan for human love, in the certitude that the *only true* good of the human person consists in fulfilling this divine plan."[46]

RECOMMENDED READING

Allen, Sr. Prudence. "Mulieris Dignitatem Twenty Years Later." *Ave Maria Law Review* 8 (2009): 13–47.

Bransfield, Brian. *The Human Person According to John Paul II*. Boston, MA: Pauline Books and Media, 2010.

Coughlin, John. "Natural Law, Marriage, and the Thought of Karol Wojtyla." *Fordham Urban Law Journal* 28 (2000): 1771–86.

[42] Ibid., section 9. [43] Ibid., section 6. [44] Ibid., section 11. [45] Ibid., section 10.

[46] ToB, 25 July 1984, section 6 (emphasis in original).

Dauphinais, Michael and Matthew Levering. *John Paul II and St. Thomas Aquinas*. Ann Arbor, MI: Sapienta Press, 2006.

Dziwisz, Stanislas and Gian Franco Svidercoschi. *A Life with Karol: My Forty Year Friendship with the Man Who Became Pope*. New York: Doubleday, 2008.

John Paul II and Michael Waldstein. *Man and Woman He Created Them: A Theology of the Body*. Boston, MA: Pauline Books and Media, 2011.

Martin, Ralph. *John Paul II and the New Evangelization: How Can You Bring the Good News to Others*. San Francisco, CA: Ignatius Press, 2006.

Schreck, Alan. *The Legacy of John Paul II: The Central Teaching of His 14 Encyclical Letters*. Steubenville, OH: Emmaus Road, 2012.

Weigel, George. *Witness to Hope: A Biography of Pope John Paul II*. New York: Cliff Street Books, 2005.

The End and the Beginning, Pope John Paul: The Struggle for Freedom, the Last Years, the Legacy. New York: Doubleday, 2011.

Wojtyla, Karol. *Sources of Renewal: The Implementation of the Second Vatican Council*. San Francisco, CA: Harper & Row, 1980.

23

Paul Evdokimov

Michael Plekon

BIOGRAPHICAL INTRODUCTION

Paul Evdokimov (1900–69) was one of the most articulate theologians of the émigré Russians who settled in France after the Russian Revolution. He graduated from the Sorbonne and was in the first class to graduate from St. Sergius Orthodox Theological Institute in Paris, the first Orthodox theological school established in the West, with significant support coming from the American YMCA. Described by his friend and colleague Olivier Clément as a bridge builder, Evdokimov was, like other émigré intellectuals of the "Paris school," a veritable Renaissance figure. He was a specialist in ancient and modern philosophy and theology, able to write about the desert monastics, church fathers, and medieval thinkers as well as his contemporaries Sartre, Camus, Jung, and Bonhoeffer. He was an ecumenical go-between, connecting his Orthodox church with both the Catholic and the Reformation churches. This he did through historical studies of liturgy, iconography, the spiritual life, and scriptural exegesis. As if this were not enough, he was an internationally recognized expert on Russian literature, Dostoevsky in particular. In a memoir, he names philosopher Nicholas Berdyaev and theologian Fr. Sergius Bulgakov as his principal teachers; their influence is evident throughout his own writing. But he was also shaped by colleagues such as theologians Nicholas Afanasiev, Lev Zander, his close friends Elisabeth Behr-Sigel and Fr. Lev Gillet, and historians Anton Kartashev and George Fedotov, to mention just a few. Antoine Arjakovsky has given us an exhaustive look at this amazing assembly of lively, critical, and creative intellectuals in Paris between the wars and thereafter in his masterful study.[1]

[1] Arjakovsky, *The Way*.

FIGURE 23.1. Paul Evdokimov. *Courtesy of Tomoko Faerber-Evdokimoff*

Among these many intellectuals gathered around Evdokimov, Berdyaev is best known for his championing of freedom in the church and of engagement in the world. It is clear that he followed another teacher, Fedotov, who created a new hagiography or way of studying the lives of holy people. Bulgakov was one of the most creative theologians in the modern era. He revisited the basic Christian dogmas, seeking to reflect on them in the language and thinking of his time. Along with the others named earlier, he was passionately committed to the ecumenical movement, as a founding member of the Anglican-Orthodox Fellowship of St. Alban and St. Sergius and what we know after 1948 as the World Council of Churches. Afanasiev rediscovered the "Eucharistic ecclesiology" of the early church as well as its ethos of love, not law. He influenced the Second Vatican Council's documents on the church and contemporary ecclesiology with his vision. Kartashev looked back to the way the church resolved divisions in earlier centuries. Lev Gillet tried to bridge the churches of the East and West not only in what they shared from before division, but also in what they needed to share of their own distinctive traditions afterward.

Evdokimov and other Paris school thinkers were struck by the hospitality and generosity of their Western Christian hosts, saw in them sisters and brothers in Christ, and thus deliberately tried to build bridges between the Eastern and Western churches in their writings and ecumenical work. On their own, they realized the alienation of Russian intellectuals and artists from the faith and so strove to "church" society and culture, that is, to reestablish ties among them. They were convinced that the Gospel was to be lived out in all the complexity of everyday life. They saw the relationship of church and society as essential, indeed transformative. They welcomed the challenges of modernity rather than being terrified by them. They were open to rather than condemning of the modern Western world around them. Some of them, in youthful revolutionary and reformist idealism, had abandoned the church, only to return with a new understanding of the church and a profound commitment to life in the world with those outside their own ethnic and church communities. Like those in the *nouvelle theologie* or "return to the sources" movement – with some of whom they studied and talked – these émigré thinkers saw the world as made and redeemed by God. They were educated not only in literature and philosophy, but also in the arts. They embraced the culture of the twentieth century while recognizing the demonic forces at work among the Bolsheviks, the Nazis, and other fascists. As epitomized by now-canonized Mother Maria Skobtsova, they demonstrated intense dedication to those displaced by revolution and impoverished by the Great Depression, and later those hunted down by the Nazis. As Arjakovsky's panoramic examination makes clear, these émigré thinkers were themselves shaped by the Moscow council of 1917–18. A veritable Vatican II of the Orthodox world, this council wrought an amazing reconciliation of many perspectives and produced a blueprint for sweeping reforms of the church and church life at every level. Hyacinthe Destivelle's study makes the scope and significance of this council's work clear.[2] These reforms could not be implemented in Russia, but were put to work in the Russian Orthodox Exarchate in Paris and Western Europe under the remarkable Metropolitan Evlogy (Georgievsky).

EVDOKIMOV'S VISION: THE UNIVERSAL VOCATION TO LOVE AND SERVICE

Paul Evdokimov was a product of this Paris school and one of its finest teachers and writers. His writings are shaped both by the openness of the Paris school to society and culture and by commitment to careful historical research. He looked to the lives of believers in the modern world as the location for the living out of the faith they treasured. He surely returned to the sources of scripture, liturgy, and the church fathers, but he also felt that the lived experience of modern people needed to be consulted, both nonbelievers and believers. Thus one hears in him the voices of Jung, Claudel, Solovyov, and Bukharev, but also Sartre, DeBeauvoir, Barth, and Bulgakov, among others.[3]

The core of Evdokimov's thinking about marriage, love, and vocation is to be found in *The Sacrament of Love*, although other works address related issues, such as gender roles and identities. His late spouse told me that before his death, he had been preparing a substantial revision of what appeared in *Woman and the Salvation of the World*, so I will not consider that text here. Writing on marriage in the 1950s and early 1960s, Evdokimov offered few explicit considerations of, much less solutions to, issues that are controversial today, such as same-sex marriage or couples living together before marrying. While he does not examine factors in society related to the breakup of marriages, he resembles Pope Francis in understanding the church's teaching as compassionate, therapeutic, and forgiving. And he makes a valuable contribution by offering a way of thinking about marriage as well as monasticism

[2] Permiakov and Plekon, eds., *The Moscow Council*.

[3] His thinking on holiness in our time has been a focus of my own work. Thus I have listened to a number of persons of faith in such volumes as Plekon, *Living Icons*; id., *Hidden Holiness*; id., *Saints as They Really Are*; id., *Uncommon Prayer*; id., *The World as Sacrament*.

as a vocation. On the basis of his careful study of the history of marriage in the church, he was critical about the way the shape and details of twentieth-century marriage were held up as ideal, overlooking the evolution of marriage from the ancient world, from Judaism, and from Greco-Roman and other traditions, and then the emerging thought and practices of the early church.

MARRIAGE, LOVE, AND HOLINESS: ANTHROPOLOGY AND THEOLOGY

Evdokimov looks carefully at both secular history and church tradition. His examination extends to images of marriage and sexuality, purity and corruption from classical antiquity, as well as from the Hebrew Bible, the New Testament, and later Christian sources. Evdokimov perceives over time a distortion of the scriptural vision of women and men, sexual union, and love. From the original beauty and goodness of creation, the effects of the Fall from sin came to distort everything about the body, sexuality, and relationships. There were classical roots for this in Hellenic and Gnostic repulsion from the body's temporal, fallible, corruptible nature, but also later in Christian ascetical perspectives. These came to view anything having to do with the body as contrary to holiness, as dirty and corrupting. Even within marriage, the sexual expression of spouses was seen as a necessary evil for what became the primary purpose of marriage, procreation.

Central to all of Evdokimov's thinking is the Christian anthropology he employs, one rooted in the Russian legacy of "the humanity of God," developed by Solovyov and Bulgakov.[4] God became human so that human beings could become, again, in the image and likeness of God. All of salvation history, the divine plan of God's self-pouring-out, or *kenosis*, the redemption through the incarnation, life, death, and resurrection of Christ, was for this end – the reconciliation of God and humankind.[5] Marriage is a profoundly beautiful human relationship, a gift of God of immense worth in itself. Marriage is connected by the Hebrew prophets to God's covenant with God's people. Thus the intense human eroticism of the Song of Songs

4 Valliere, *Modern Russian Theology*.

5 See his teacher Sergius Bulgakov's great theological trilogy: *The Lamb of God, The Comforter and The Bride of the Lamb*.

celebrates the erotic union of lovers while at the same time imaging the love of the Lord for Israel. One of the most beautiful passages containing his anthropology comes from *The Sacrament of Love*. The human person is a child of God, created in God's image and, *par excellence*, a "liturgical being."

> A saint is not a superman, but one who discovers and lives his truth as a liturgical being. The best definition of a person comes from the liturgy: the human being is the one of the *Trisagion* and of the *Sanctus* ("I will sing to the Lord as long as I live") ... It is not enough to say prayers; one must become, *be* prayer, prayer incarnate. It is not enough to have moments of praise. All of life, each act, every gesture, even the smile of the human face, must become a hymn of adoration, an offering, a prayer. One should offer not what one has, but what one is. This is a favored subject in iconography. It translates the message of the Gospel: *chairé*, "rejoice and be glad," "let everything that has breath praise the Lord." This is the astonishing lightening of the weight of the world, when man's own heaviness vanishes. "The King of Kings, Christ is coming," and this is the "one thing needful." The doxology of the Lord's Prayer ("the kingdom, and the power and the glory") is the heart of the liturgy. It is to respond to his vocation as a liturgical being that man is charismatic, the one who bears the gifts of the Holy Spirit and the Holy Spirit Himself: "You have been sealed with the Holy Spirit ... you whom God has taken for His own, *to make His glory praised*" (Eph. 1:14) ... The best evangelization of the world, the most effective witness to the Christian faith, is this full liturgical hymn, the doxology which rises from the depths of the earth, in which moves the powerful breath of the Paraclete who alone converts and heals.[6]

Evdokimov, really a theological poet like Gregory of Nyssa, is not given to abstraction. He writes from and about the lived experience of prayer – of each of us becoming prayer, becoming what we pray. Incarnation happens again in our being, in our relationships, our lovingkindness to our neighbors, our work. All that Evdokimov has to say about marriage is rooted in vocation. All baptized persons are called to enact the Gospel, to do the work of the Lord wherever life places or takes them. The call of holiness is for all the baptized, a perspective shared with the Vatican II reappropriation of the church as the people of God, as well as with the return-to-the-sources theologians who paved the way for that council.

An important Eastern church framer of this sense of vocation was Evdokimov's colleague and friend Nicholas Afanasiev, who emphasized the priesthood of all the baptized in his rediscovery of Eucharistic ecclesiology.[7]

6 Evdokimov, *The Sacrament of Love*, 83–4.
7 Afanasiev, *The Church of the Holy Spirit*.

Another friend and colleague with similar views was Olivier Clément.[8] Many other spiritual writers of our time held this vision, including Dorothy Day and Thomas Merton. Evdokimov captures this vision in the image of the Crucified Lord's arms outstretched, open to all, drawing all to himself.

> It appears that a new spirituality is dawning. It aspires not to leave the world to evil, but to let the spiritual element in the creature come forth. A person who loves and is totally detached, naked to the touch of the eternal, escapes the contrived conflict between the spiritual and the material. His love of God is humanized and becomes love for all creatures in God. "Everything is grace," Bernanos wrote, because God has descended into the human and carried it away to the abyss of the Trinity. The types of traditional holiness are characterized by the heroic style of the desert, the monastery. By taking a certain distance from the world, this holiness is stretched toward heaven, vertically, like the spire of a cathedral. Nowadays, the axis of holiness has moved, drawing nearer to the world. In all its appearances, its type is less striking, its achievement is hidden from the eyes of the world, but it is the result of a struggle that is no less real. Being faithful to the call of the Lord, in the conditions of this world, makes grace penetrate to its very root, where human life is lived.[9]

This is a more horizontal, worldly sense of vocation; as Mother Maria Skobtsova would put it, the love of God and love of neighbor are inseparable. Like his Western church colleagues who returned to the sources of the scriptures, liturgy, and the fathers for renewal, Evdokimov views holiness as a universal vocation, not the distinctive heroism of the few officially recognized or canonized, not trumped by monasticism or the ordained ministries. In baptism, all are consecrated as priests, kings and queens, and prophets. Marriage and monastic life both enable the baptized to become signs of the kingdom, offering themselves to God in obedience, purity of heart, and poverty of spirit.

Contrary to strong currents in both the Eastern and Western churches, Evdokimov refuses to see monasticism as a higher calling than marriage. Both vocations are equally authentic ways of living out the Gospel.[10] Both involve chastity – not only sexual restraint, but purity of heart and honesty, the deeper meanings of chastity. Both demand witness/martyrdom and self-sacrifice, the emptying of oneself in caring for the other.[11] Crucial here, and developed in other texts, is Evdokimov's view of monasticism's New Testament roots in the call to follow the Lord as disciples. Discipleship is a radical transformation or

[8] Clément, *On Human Being*. [9] Evdokimov, *The Sacrament of Love*, 92. [10] Ibid., 67.
[11] Ibid., 70–1.

metanoia – the call of Christ at the very start of the Gospels and his ministry. Monastic life is maximal, yet this does not make it superior to marriage, parenthood, or single life.[12] The desert mothers and fathers aimed to make a sacrifice of all they had and of all they were.[13] Their exertion or asceticism was not to annihilate themselves, but to become one with God, with their neighbors, and with all creatures in love. Isaac the Syrian, a great ascetic writer, spoke of prayer and love for everything – our neighbors, the animals, even demons.[14]

MARRIAGE: THE SACRAMENT OF LOVE AND IMAGE OF HEAVEN

The title of his book Evdokimov takes from John Chrysostom, who called marriage the sacrament of love. He understood that both married and celibate Christians were called to the same Gospel command to be perfect as the heavenly father, to commit themselves to prayer, to love their neighbors by engaging in the works of mercy. There is no ranking of monasticism above the vocation of marriage. This mistaken priority grew out of later sources – Hellenic disgust with the body, sex, and a similar monastic disdain for them. In the sixteenth-century Reformation and later in Vatican II, this distorted view would be corrected. One cannot find it in the scriptures, the liturgy, or the writings of church teachers. There is to be love of God and the neighbor, whatever one's state in life, gender, age, or position in society.[15] The initiation rites/sacraments are the ground of the universal call to holiness and the vocation of love and service for every Christian. For Evdokimov, what most importantly links marriage and monasticism – in fact, what is the basis of every vocation – is the priesthood of all believers conferred in baptism and chrismation, and confirmed throughout life in the Eucharist.[16]

With Afanasiev, Evdokimov recognizes the functions and role of those called and ordained to serve the rest of the church – bishops, presbyters, and deacons – but notes that their calling is one of service, not rule over the laity. The notion that clergy have superior authority has caused and still causes great damage in the church. Those set apart and ordained for ministerial service must be first baptized and consecrated/anointed to the universal priesthood before any further calling and ordaining is even possible. In the early church, those ordained to be servants of all were called from within the community of each local church.[17] Their authority was the power of love, always grounded in their responsibility to the rest of the community. Their selection by the

[12] Ibid., 74–6. [13] Ibid., 77. [14] Ibid., 80–2. [15] Ibid., 83–4. [16] Ibid., 85–6.
[17] Evdokimov, *The Church of the Holy Spirit*, 136–47.

community was a witness of the Spirit, of their gifts and abilities to serve and, therefore, to lead, teach, and preside at the Eucharistic assembly. *The Church of the Holy Spirit*, Afanasiev's principal work, marvelously parallels Evdokimov's *The Sacrament of Love*. Both offer a thorough historical argument as well as a theological case for the grounding of all vocations in the ecclesial community created by baptism and constantly affirmed in the Eucharist.

So for Evdokimov (and here he is expressing the somewhat historically different perspective of the Eastern church), marriage is the vocation to holiness. At the core is the relationship of love between the spouses. Marriage is personal but also ecclesial, since marriage is an image of the relationship of Christ to the church and of each soul with God. Evdokimov is not interested only in the historical path of marriage in Christian teaching, though. He connects all vocations, as the previous block quote makes clear, to the appearance of and the need for new forms of holiness in our time, new ways of living out the Gospel. These offer a "drawing nearer to the world. In all its appearances, its type is less striking, its achievement is hidden from the eyes of the world, but it is the result of a struggle that is no less real."[18]

The world and outlook of Christendom, Constantinian or otherwise, is for him gone. Yet some still yearn for this alliance of church and state, and in some places, like Russia, the vision of *Russkiy mir*, or "the Russian world," attempts to recreate the symbiosis of state, church, and people. Like his colleagues in the Paris school, Evdokimov does not see our world as a secular wasteland, a godless jungle of promiscuity and corruption. He does not just see evil afoot in our world, but rather calls attention to the new and diverse ways of holiness with which the Spirit blesses us today. Evdokimov could not have foreseen the "pope of mercy," Francis, but he knew and loved another, the "pope of love," John XXIII. The church is no longer constrained by the social, political, and economic forces of the past. Rather, these persons of faith are still in communion with the Holy Trinity, and the world needs, yes, depends for its salvation on the cosmic love of saints.[19]

> The forms of social life undergo rapid and unforeseen changes; by contrast, the religious action of every believer possesses a great stability. One can become attentive to the designs of God in the prodigious progress of science and technology ... bring together those who are lonely and create living communities of witnesses ... kindle the spirit of adoration and make a

[18] Evdokimov, *The Sacrament of Love*, 92. [19] Ibid., 94.

prayer out of every work even in the cement and concrete heart of the most modern city.[20]

Evdokimov echoes John Chrysostom. Marriage is an icon of God, an "image of heaven."[21] He takes us on an intellectual history of marriage. There in Genesis are the first spouses, Adam and Eve. Blessed they are, but also they fall and are burdened – as are all of us, their children – with pride and greed, resistance to God, and the rest of the human condition. The Eastern church emphasizes original blessing, image and likeness to God, rather than original sin. The creature takes leave, distances her/himself from God, putting Paradise elsewhere. Whatever social, economic, political, and cultural roles marriage has in human history, the Incarnation means that marriage is always an image of the covenant, the intimacy, the love and forgiveness between God and humankind. Quite rightly does Chrysostom call marriage the sacrament of love. And love as the very heart of God's nature, love as the outpouring or emptying of God in creation, must also be the core of marriage. The image of this is the symmetry of the Trinity of love to the trinity formed by the spouses united in God, the third person in their marriage.[22] Love transforms. Loves makes the two one. For Chrysostom, marriage sets up a "domestic church." Clement of Alexandria calls marriage the "micro kingdom." The church is the body of Christ, a communion with God and communion of communions or communities. With Christ as the head, the communion of marriages as well as monastic and parish communities build up and comprise Christ's body.[23]

A number of scholars believe that Evdokimov and Afanasiev both shaped Vatican II teaching, both on the church itself and on the relationship of the church to the world. While Afanasiev's name was mentioned in a preconciliar study document, both of them attended the council as ecumenical observers. One can conclude that both contributed to the return to the sources evident in both Vatican II documents that touch on marriage and family life, *Lumen Gentium* and *Gaudium et Spes*. While presenting the Eastern church's view, Evdokimov anticipated a new vision of marriage at Vatican II. Contrary to much Western church thinking over the centuries, particularly about marriage as a remedy for desire and a means of procreation, Evdokimov puts forward the Eastern church's view, strongly stated by Chrysostom, that the purpose of marriage is the union of the spouses in love.[24] For Chrysostom, as

20 Evdokimov, *The Sacrament of Love*, 101. 21 Ibid., 101–2. 22 Ibid., 115–17.

23 Evdokimov, *The Sacrament of Love*, 118.

24 Ibid., 120. See Chapter 5 herein on Chrysostom.

for Evdokimov, marriage is "a mysterious icon of the church."[25] Marriage is where one sees the "ongoing/permanent Pentecost," as Bulgakov called the Spirit's work in the world. The Spirit gives light and life, fire and healing, opens the kingdom to the world and the world to the kingdom.[26] Marriage surely brings forth life, not just through the physical birth of children, but also in the union of the spouses and in the household of their children and other relatives.

There are tendencies and turns in the history of the church's understanding of marriage that are indeed difficult. The complexity, some would say negativity, of Paul and the Gnostic, Hellenic, and later monastic revulsion for sexuality, women, marriage, and childbearing must be encountered and engaged.[27] Evdokimov does this with a remarkable balance or sense of economy as well as compassion.[28] I mean this both in theological and pastoral terms. Since the world- and body-rejecting streams are not supported by the scriptures themselves and need discernment, it is not legitimate to allow selfish and destructive tendencies of human beings simply to renounce our bodies and sexuality or to relegate women to a secondary, suspect role. The Hebrew scriptures do not support such spiritualist, anti-body views, and the Incarnation and the humanity of God only highlight the negativity of these views. John Chrysostom was himself an ascetic and a celibate, but he never felt that spouses were inferior to monastics. Evdokimov agreed. Spouses and parents have vocations for love and care that are their paths to holiness.[29]

So much is said about the media, entertainment, and popular culture in our time with respect to sexuality and marriage. Here again, one will not find extreme points of view or solutions to our conflicts from Evdokimov. He does have opinions about everything from contemporary art to literature, from music to the pace of work, and even about the addiction to work, the temptation to work rather than live. He is discerning, and one will try in vain to pull him over to one or another extreme side in the modern culture wars. He is quite critical of the devaluation of sex but careful about disembodied glorification. Not just promiscuity but hyper anti-sexual Puritanism are both dehumanizing, in his view. As out of sync as his sense of the complementarity of women to men is – again, a perspective in revision at his sudden death – he nevertheless leaves a humane, sensitive attitude. After all, he is shaped by Dostoevsky, on whom he did his dissertation, but also by

25 Evdokimov, *The Sacrament of Love*, 123. 26 Ibid., 125.
27 See Chapter 2 herein on Jesus and St. Paul.
28 Evdokimov, *The Sacrament of Love*, 161–4. 29 Ibid., 162–4.

de Beauvoir and Jung and Freud, as well as Simone Weil and Bonhoeffer. In my view, he aims at discerning what is destructive from what is good and beautiful and human when it comes to love and sexuality and marriage. Manipulation, abuse of a person as sexual object or commodity – here is where he becomes critical and prophetic. Whether celibate or married, female or male, old or young, affluent or of low income, we are all called to love God and the neighbor. Evdokimov was an enemy of social and economic inequality.

PASTORAL COMPASSION

Finally, we see compassion and discernment as he touches, even if briefly, on matters such as contraception and divorce. The Eastern church has tended not to make sweeping, absolute rules, and Evdokimov did not either. Contraception is a matter of freedom – that of the spouses and their spiritual father, their circumstances, their abilities. Divorce is a way marriage ends in the Hebrew Bible, under careful conditions. The Christian tradition has found it more difficult to accept divorce, even though the church too must recognize the ending of marriages, their failures. Always tragic, divorce is not simply "allowed" by the Eastern church, as some evangelicals and Catholics believe. Rather, the leading principle is to work for the good of the individual, of each of the spouses, when a marriage has ended.[30]

Evdokimov recognizes the power and the hope, as well as the mystery, of the relationship entered and then put into practice in a marriage. He notes that only over time are incompatibilities revealed, the ability but also the inability of persons to be transformed, to contribute authentically to the relationship and household. There are always cases of neglect and betrayal, but also those where all the effort and good will still cannot bear fruit. Spouses can be "misloved" as well as not-loved, abused, betrayed, and abandoned. Canonical or sacramental indissolubility cannot have primacy over the good of the spouses, over love. The Eastern church does not simply allow divorce. It does realize, however, that spouses can end a marriage and then want to live, to start over again. The tragedy and sin of destruction needs to be recognized for what it is. The process of divorce and transformation must be serious, as serious as the marriage entered and ended. In the view of the kingdom of heaven, there is a radical inversion of social and cultural norms – the last become first, the poor are fed and the mighty cast down, the tax collectors and prostitutes are first into

30 Evdokimov, *The Sacrament of Love*, 186–90.

the kingdom. Forgiveness and *metanoia*/transformation are always possible, because grace abounds, as does mercy. How contrary to human standards of justice and retribution this is.

CONCLUSIONS

Paul Evdokimov does not provide comprehensive, satisfying solutions or even assessments of issues that are currently real and controversial, that divide us today regarding marriage, sex, and love. There has been much discussion and some conflict in recent years about how marriage should be understood in our society, and about what the church teaches about it from scripture and tradition. Some of this discussion and conflict has been occasioned by efforts to afford the same legal status to all, by recognizing same-sex marriage as the law does heterosexual marriage. It has seemed necessary, by some, to defend marriage from such efforts, yet this is hardly the only sense in which marriage has been in crisis. Consider the high rates of divorce; the choice by many not to marry though sharing a life in every respect; and spousal abandonment and abuse.

In the churches, some think there is little to debate, discuss, or examine. Contemporary expectations and patterns of marriage are seen as timeless, with little attention given to historical and cultural diversity. For some, the scriptures and church tradition appear to define marriage as between men and women who are in love with each other, who will have only one spouse in their lives, and who marry for the purpose of bearing and raising children. Others feel the need for reconsideration, for a more generous, inclusive reading. On more careful inspection, it is clear that in the Hebrew Bible and Christian New Testament, these models of romance-based monogamy and the nuclear family are not the only ones. We find polygamy, larger tribal extended families, and many rules for whom one can marry as well as rules for the ending of marriage. Provisions are made, too, in the case of a spouse's death for inheritance of property and further support of a parent and children. In the New Testament, there is the understanding that some members of the Christian community will be married to individuals outside of it. And while marriage in the New Testament is highly valued, its failure and dissolution are also envisioned.

Evdokimov confirms much of this biblical witness about sexuality, marriage, and family, but there were many issues, most all those most controversial today, that Evdokimov simply does not discuss. That said, he does develop both an anthropology and a theology of vocation, love, and marriage. He takes the Bible seriously and as primary. He consults the tradition with great discernment, using celibates to praise and support marriage while viewing monasticism as having its own distinctive charism and place. He is careful not to privilege any state or vocation, recognizing the potential in every human life for holiness. He is never a moralist, owing both to the Eastern church's nonlegalistic approach to ethics and to the personalism he learned from Berdyaev and many other contemporaries.

We hear a lot of things in Evdokimov. His is a voice of restraint as well as of discernment and compassion. Rather than rage against polemicizing atheists like Richard Dawkins and Christopher Hitchens, Evdokimov wanted to listen carefully to atheists and agnostics, doubters and critics. He wrote about the understandable boredom thinking people experienced with archaic, unintelligible services and meaningless texts, their revulsion for fanatics (both traditionalist and progressive) as well as for the joy-killing men in black.[31] Evdokimov took serious atheism seriously, treating it at length and even suggesting that divinity schools set up an endowed chair for it.[32]

First and foremost always, in the Eastern church, is the person, a child and icon of God. As for God – God is, as Lev Gillet ("the monk of the Eastern church," his pen-name) put it, "love without limits."[33] God is the "mercy within mercy within mercy" that Thomas Merton recognized.[34] This God, as Evdokimov said in another, well-known essay, is love to the point of absurdity, a "foolish love."

One notices right away the lightness and humanity of Evdokimov, his genuine pastoral sensitivity in reflections on marriage, integral and broken, on the suffering of divorce, and the difficulties of parents. The ease with which church pronouncements are absolutized, turned into law, a defiant line in the sand – this will always be alien to his understanding of the relationship of the individual to the church and to Christ. His approach is not, as a cynical ranking hierarch put it, admirable perspectives appropriate to the post–World War II years but no longer useful today. To the contrary – though writing decades ago, Evdokimov offers a vision of a truly living tradition, a perspective "worthy of God" and faithful to the Gospel.

In the immense cathedral that is the universe, the human person who is priest, whether worker or scholar, makes of everything an offering, a hymn, a doxology. According to Merleau-Ponty, "humanity is condemned to meaning," each person is invited to live out the faith, to see what is not seen, to contemplate the wisdom of God in the apparent absurdity of history, and to

31 Evdokimov, *Ages of the Spiritual Life*, 17.

32 Ibid., 21–48; *In the World, of the Church*, 59.

33 Gillet, *In Thy Presence*, 1977.

34 Merton, *The Sign of Jonas*, 362.

become light, revelation, and prophecy. Marveling thus at the existence of God, "the world is full of the Trinity," a layperson is also slightly mad with the foolishness of which St. Paul speaks, with the paradoxical humor of the "fools of Christ," alone capable of shattering the overly serious, heaviness of the doctrinaires. A layperson is one freed by his faith from the "great fear" of the twentieth century, fear of the bomb, of cancer, of communism, of death; such a person's faith is always a way of loving the world, a way of following his Lord even into hell. This is certainly not a part of a theological system, but perhaps it is only from the depths of hell that a dazzling and joyous hope can be born and assert itself. Christianity in the grandeur of its confessors and martyrs, in the dignity of every believer, is messianic, revolutionary, explosive. In the domain of Caesar, we are ordered to seek and therefore to find what is not found there – the Kingdom of God. This order signifies that we must transform the world, change it into the icon of the Kingdom. To change the world means to pass from what the world does not yet possess – for this reason it is still this world – to that in which it is transfigured, thus becoming something else – the Kingdom.[35]

RECOMMENDED READING

Arjakovsky, Antoine, *The Way: Religious Thinkers of the Russian Emigration in Paris and Their Journal*, trans. Jerry Ryan, eds., John A. Jillions and Michael Plekon (Notre Dame, IN: University of Notre Dame Press, 2013).

Behr-Sigel, Elisabeth. *The Ministry of Women in the Church*. Crestwood, NY: St. Vladimir's Seminary Press, 1990.

Evdokimov, Paul. *The Sacrament of Love*. Translated by Anthony P. Gythiel and Victoria Steadman. Crestwood, NY: St. Vladimir's Seminary Press, 1995.

Ages of the Spiritual Life. Revised translation by Michael Plekon and Alexis Vinogradov. Crestwood, NY: St. Vladimir's Seminary Press, 1998.

On Human Being. Hyde Park, NY: New City Press, 2000.

In the World, of the Church: A Paul Evdokimov Reader. Translated and edited by Michael Plekon and Alexis Vinogradov. Crestwood, NY: St. Vladimir's Seminary Press, 2001.

Nicholas Afanasiev The Church of the Holy Spirit. Translated by Vitaly Permiakov; edited by Michael Plekon. Notre Dame, IN: University of Notre Dame Press, 2007.

[35] Evdokimov, *Ages*, 224–5.

Orthodoxy. Translated by Jeremy Hummerstone. Hyde Park, NY: New City Press, 2011.

Meyendorff, John. *Marriage: An Orthodox Perspective*. Crestwood, NY: St. Vladimir's Seminary Press, 1975.

Plekon, Michael. *Living Icons: Persons of Faith in the Eastern Church*. Notre Dame, IN: University of Notre Dame Press, 2002.

Hidden Holiness. Notre Dame, IN: University of Notre Dame Press, 2009.

Saints as They Really Are: Voices of Holiness in our Time. Notre Dame, IN: University of Notre Dame Press, 2012.

Uncommon Prayer: The Experience of Prayer in Everyday Life. Notre Dame, IN: University of Notre Dame Press, 2016.

The World as Sacrament: An Ecumenical Path Toward a Worldly Spirituality. Collegeville, MN: Liturgical Press, 2017.

Schmemann, Alexander. *For the Life of the World*. Crestwood, NY: St. Vladimir's Seminary Press, 1973.

Valliere, Paul. *Modern Russian Theology*. Grand Rapids, MI: Wm. B. Eerdmans Publishing, 2000.

24

Derrick Sherwin Bailey

Mark D. Jordan

BIOGRAPHICAL INTRODUCTION

D. S. or Sherwin Bailey (1910–84) was an Anglican theologian and church historian. Though he wanted chiefly to provide an adequate theology for contemporary Christian marriage, he contributed importantly to debates over the criminal regulation of sex and the pertinence of psychological science to the renewal of religious traditions. His influential work illustrates both the prospects and the limits of "progressive" Christian thinking about human sexuality at the middle of the twentieth century.

Bailey began his theological studies in 1940 after some years of business employment.[1] While preparing for priestly ministry, he pursued a long-standing interest in theological accounts of married love (as in the essay "Love and Marriage").[2] Appointed chaplain to Anglican students at the University of Edinburgh in 1944, he undertook doctoral study in church history. His dissertation treated an early English reformer who dealt "at inordinate length with compulsory celibacy and the abuses and immorality it was held to have occasioned among clergy, monks and nuns."[3] In 1951, Bailey was offered a position as traveling lecturer on sex and marriage by the Church of England's Moral Welfare Council. Deciding to accept the post, Bailey reasoned to himself that he would bring to it not only psychological

[1] Details of Bailey's biography can be found in various standard sources, such as the entry by Matthew Grimley in *Oxford Dictionary of National Biography*, accessed online. For characterizations of Bailey's motives, I rely on his unpublished memoir. I am extremely grateful to his family for allowing me to read portions of it.

[2] I treat here only Bailey's works on Christian theology of sex and marriage, omitting a number of his historical studies on other topics.

[3] Bailey, *Thomas Becon and the Reformation of the Church of England*, 111.

FIGURE 24.1. Derrick S. Bailey. Used by permission of family

interest, but also historical expertise. The combination would characterize his writing on sexual ethics, including a book he was just then finishing, *The Mystery of Love and Marriage* (1952).

Bailey's work for the council quickly placed him at the center of public debates about the churches' role in policing sexual morality. In April 1952, he proposed an Anglican study group on homosexuality; in 1954 the group offered a preliminary report, *The Problem of Homosexuality*. The report advocated decriminalizing private same-sex activity between consenting adults on grounds of justice and new psychological knowledge. In the next year, Bailey offered his own monograph, *Homosexuality and the Western Christian Tradition* (1955). The book proposed to show how church history both animated and confused contemporary attitudes about same-sex desire, especially between men. Because Bailey held that Christian tradition had settled the question by the end of the Middle Ages, he concentrated on Christian scriptures and earlier theological or legal texts. Still, his conclusion was pointedly contemporary. The errors and deficiencies of traditional condemnations of male–male love stripped current criminal law on homosexuality of its supposedly divine justification.

Bailey's historical arguments would go on to influence church deliberations, political campaigns, and university-based scholarship. He had more immediate uses for them. Acting as a private scholar, he submitted his historical monograph to the "Wolfenden committee," that is, the British government Committee on Homosexual Offences and Prostitution. Bailey also edited the Moral Welfare Council's final submission to that committee and oversaw its publication in 1956 (*Sexual Offenders*). In 1957, the Wolfenden committee endorsed decriminalization. Ten years later, the British Parliament passed a Sexual Offences Act that accepted the Wolfenden committee's main recommendations and so endorsed much of Bailey's reasoning.

Bailey had already returned to his old concerns with the development of Christian accounts of marriage. In 1959, he published *The Man–Woman Relation in Christian Thought*. A few years later, he produced a shorter and simpler version of his historical narratives and ethical proposals (*Common Sense about Sexual Ethics*, 1962). His ministry had in the meantime taken another direction. In 1959, Bailey left the Moral Welfare Council to become rector of a village parish. Three years later, he was appointed canon residentiary at Wells Cathedral. He devoted most of his writing in later years to the history of that cathedral. Bailey died of natural causes in 1984.

THE THEOLOGY OF MARRIAGE AS "ONE FLESH"

Bailey completed his first constructive work on Christian marriage as he was about to leave his chaplaincy at Edinburgh for the lectureship at the Moral Welfare Council. *The Mystery of Love and Marriage* recalls Bailey's earlier insights. One of his decisive intellectual experiences in theological college had been a lecture on romantic love by Charles Williams, prominent writer and friend of C. S. Lewis. Williams and Lewis shaped Bailey's sense of the problem of marriage in Christian theology. They guided his search for neglected sources, especially in literature.

Bailey begins with the judgment that Christian thinkers never developed an adequate theology of what is distinctive about marriage. Marriage should be characterized by the special unity (in Greek, *henosis*) brought about between husband and wife in loving sexual intercourse. *Henosis* is the "one flesh" explained in the story of Adam's recognizing Eve (Genesis 2:24) and recalled by Jesus in some of his sayings on divorce (Mark 10:7, Matthew 19:5). Though *henosis* is plainly named in the scriptures, it was not developed as a theology of sexual relation by early Christian thinkers. According to Bailey, they were prevented from understanding it for various reasons, including distrust of sexual bodies and misogynistic insistence on women's social inferiority. To conceive marriage truly as one flesh would require a new conception of married love. The conception arrived only in the eleventh century, in literary and mystical writing about courtly passions. Such romantic love is now widely assumed as the obvious basis for marriage, but C. S. Lewis described its appearance in the Middle Ages as a "revolution."[4] Even then, Christian theologians were slow to appreciate it. Other historical changes were required, including the recognition of married clergy and the social enfranchisement of women. Only in the twentieth century, Bailey suggests, is theology prepared at last to convert the new understanding of love into an adequate account of marriage.

Bailey's own account sees in marriage a unique union of love through which man and woman appear to each other as persons rather than objects. The union is mysterious and "metaphysical."[5] Bailey explains it so far as he can by relying both on Charles Williams's reading of Dante and on Martin Buber's exploration of the I–Thou encounter. Loving relation in marriage is intensified by sexual intercourse, which conveys meaning beyond language.

4 Bailey, *The Mystery of Love and Marriage*, 4. (I am citing the American edition.)

5 Ibid., 22, 39, 67.

Sexual love makes possible the emergence of a "new biune organism," a woman and a man united in a way that fulfills their mutual dependence.[6] The marital relation is thus a suitable analogy for the relations within the Trinity, the union of divine and human in the incarnation, and the relation of Christ to the church.

Bailey's new theology of marriage leaves many elements of Christian moral teaching intact. It insists, for example, that sexual acts are morally permissible only within marriage. It reaffirms that marriage must be sexually exclusive and that every effort must be made to preserve it until the death of one of the partners. Other parts of Bailey's teaching are anti-traditional. Sometimes, he corrects what he regards as technical exaggerations in received theologies, such as the emphasis on consent rather than physical consummation. At other times, Bailey appeals to principles that threaten to unsettle traditional teaching more generally. For Bailey, the ground or basis of the one-flesh bond is the revelatory love that establishes the personal relation. If the love disappears, the marriage bond is broken. Without love, the bond has lost its real or ontological ground, whatever its institutional status.[7] Bailey tries to limit the destabilizing consequences of his view by arguing that the presence of love cannot be used by church and state to mark the beginning of a marriage or its end. True love cannot be discerned by those who stand outside its bond. Still, Bailey's sharp distinction between the ontological and institutional aspects of marriage, together with his emphasis on the ontological as the only true basis for one flesh, may unsettle established opinions and regulations. It might also suggest to some readers that they should reject the institutional altogether in favor of the ontological – and so adopt an ethics based exclusively on what is real in one flesh rather than what is social or contractual.

Bailey explicitly criticizes some traditional claims about marriage, including the emphasis on procreation. He finds only weak scriptural evidence for the primacy of procreation in marriage. If the Hebrew Bible occasionally returns to the divine command, "be fruitful and multiply" (Genesis 1:28), that can be explained as a nomadic group's best strategy for survival. The New Testament, by contrast, does not emphasize procreation at all. For Christians, the principal end of marriage ought to be the union between husband and wife, not the provision of offspring. Bailey draws particular consequences from this claim. He argues, for example, that while a marriage must be open to the possibility of procreation, a couple may properly decide to avoid conception in some particular sexual acts. The argument hints at the rapid change already

6 Ibid., 31. 7 Ibid., 45–7.

taking place in Christian teachings on contraceptive intent and the means it might be permitted to use.

Equally important for future debates is Bailey's example in assessing Christian traditions. Bailey is a learned historian. He qualifies judgments and reminds his readers how much he must omit when compiling coherent narratives. Still, Bailey does not hesitate to diagnose an important failure in Christian theological traditions about marriage. He detects in some authoritative texts unhappy attitudes to sex, including ignorance, fear, and hatred. He concludes that certain scriptural passages – such as Jesus on divorce and remarriage – are so enigmatic as to be indecipherable. He turns to medieval literature or contemporary philosophy to supply what theology lacks. In these and other ways, Bailey begins a thorough reworking of Christian traditions about sex and marriage. He writes in the preface: "I believe that the grave sexual disorder of our time demands, in certain respects, a reorientation of the Church's attitude to sex and marriage, and in particular the development of a theology of sexual love."[8] Introducing a student's bibliography published in the next year, Bailey declares more expansively that "there are important questions relating to sex and marriage which demand careful study by the theologian and historian – and . . .some of these questions are now under discussion virtually for the first time."[9]

The consequences of such declarations might be more difficult to predict or to constrain than Bailey anticipates. If Christian churches have all along lacked a theology of sexual love, if they have not in two millennia discussed important questions about marriage, then some readers might conclude that Christian teaching is not merely incomplete, but misguided. While Bailey certainly does not mean to encourage such skepticism, his judgment on tradition might suggest it to some nonetheless. The suggestion is only strengthened when Bailey takes up more scandalous sexual topics.

THE "PROBLEM" OF HOMOSEXUALITY

Bailey regularly recalled the complicated Christian history behind contemporary debates over sex. Nowhere was this reminder more pertinent than in regard to homosexuality. Defenders of criminal sanctions against same-sex acts would often justify the statutes by appealing to what they claimed was an unbroken tradition of Christian condemnation reaching back to Genesis.

[8] Ibid., ix. [9] Bailey, *The Theology of Sex and Marriage*, 8.

Bailey knew better. He found the uneven accumulation of Jewish and Christian teaching about homosexuality mistaken and deficient in ways that undercut its helpfulness for contemporary debate.

Bailey was called to address the topic of homosexuality soon after his appointment to the Moral Welfare Council. In January 1951, a reader wrote to the Anglican monthly review, *Theology*, complaining about churches' silence in the face of increasing public debate. In the next month, the same journal published a short reply by Bailey. Over the next five years, Bailey would write or edit several hundred pages on homosexuality in political and theological contexts. This chapter treats these writings topically rather than chronologically and focuses on Bailey rather than on the larger social, legal, or ecclesiastical movements.[10]

Faced with claims for continuous and unanimous tradition, Bailey begins by contesting the most familiar scriptural warrant for condemning (male) homosexuality. The story of the divine destruction of Sodom (Genesis 18–19) authorizes the stigmatizing term "sodomy," which was later written into so many laws, both civil and ecclesiastical. The story was taken as an unambiguous and universal condemnation of male–male desire in all times and places. Its terms were also treated as fully equivalent to modern notions about sexual dispositions or practices. Whatever the scriptures said in condemnation of Sodom could thus be applied to current cases in the criminal courts or the tabloids. Bailey insists to the contrary that the story of Sodom was definitely *not* the Bible's word on same-sex relations, much less on contemporary forms of homosexuality. The exclusively homosexual meaning was added to Genesis 18–19 only much later, under the influence of eccentric, nonbiblical notions.[11] The misreading was adopted by early Christian writers and then passed into moral and legal codes. We should now regard these as "unfortunate consequences [that] have attended the reinterpretation of an ancient story in the interests of propaganda."[12]

From his first article in 1951, Bailey also argues that there has been an important conceptual break between Christian scriptures or traditions and contemporary understandings of sexuality. Adopting the terminology of the late nineteenth-century sexologists, Bailey distinguishes the same-sex acts or desires of a *pervert* from those of an *invert*. A pervert is a heterosexual who engages in such practices for one reason or another. An invert is a person who

[10] For a more inclusive history, see Jones, *Sexual Politics in the Church of England, 1857–1957*, esp. chapter 7.

[11] Bailey, *Homosexuality and the Western Christian Tradition*, 1–28. [12] Ibid., 155.

has a deep-seated and in some sense natural disposition toward same-sex desire and love, "the homosexual who cannot help, and did not choose, his condition."[13] For Bailey, the scientifically established fact that there are inverts troubles any direct appeal to the Christian past. Neither the scriptures nor the older theological traditions recognize the condition of inversion. Whatever the story of Sodom is about, according to Bailey, it does not treat "genuine inversion, or take into account the psychological and pathological aspects of homosexuality, as we are now aware of them."[14]

Here, as in his earlier writing on one flesh, Bailey shows himself willing to criticize errors in Christian teachings. He also judges them "defective" so far as they did not recognize the distinction between inversion and perversion. Because it confuses the two, Christian tradition has "but an indirect and dubious relevance" to contemporary debates over homosexuality. Indeed, the inherited teaching about homosexuality "can no longer be regarded as an adequate guide by the theologian, the legislator, the sociologist, and the magistrate."[15] It fails not only as theology, but also as a justification for human laws.

This decisive judgment on tradition does not end the theologian's work. With homosexuality, as with marriage, Bailey wants to preserve the most salient moral teachings even as he displays the inadequacy of traditional arguments for them. Bailey's critique of direct invocations of tradition does *not* lead him to radically different moral conclusions about same-sex love. He writes that inversion is a "mysterious and unfortunate condition," an "abnormality" and "peculiar handicap" due at least in some cases to childhood maladjustments.[16] These maladjustments are not only or principally personal failings. They are symptoms of societal failures, especially in the relations of husbands and wives. Instead of punishing inverts with criminal penalties, society ought to admit its responsibility for the conditions that bring them into existence; it ought to improve marriage and family life in order to reduce inversion. "Society . . . has a heavy responsibility towards the inverts whom it creates by its relational failures and its wars." So even if private acts among consenting adults are decriminalized, inversion itself will remain a social problem and perhaps an index of the prior decay of marriage and family life.[17]

After this critique of tradition and contemporary social failures, what remains of the moral judgment on same-sex acts? Bailey distinguishes, crucially, between the condition of inversion and any acts that might issue from it. "The condition is in itself morally neutral."[18] The evaluation of this distinction

[13] Bailey, "The Problem of Sexual Inversion," 47–52. [14] Ibid., 51.
[15] Bailey, *Homosexuality*, 169, 173. [16] Ibid., 167, 176. [17] Ibid., 166, 168. [18] Ibid., 168.

between condition and acts is one of Bailey's most significant contributions to later debates. Less influential, but no less remarkable, is Bailey's careful refusal to pronounce on the morality of same-sex acts performed by someone who suffers the morally neutral condition of inversion. Bailey calls it "one of the most perplexing ethical problems of our time." After recapitulating the claim by male inverts that same-sex acts are natural *for them*, Bailey adds only this: "Faced with the novel and delicate responsibility of making an assessment of the invert's behaviour which does justice both to his abnormal condition and the personal problems which it creates, and to the claims of morality, we find that our tradition gives us no assistance."[19] If the tradition cannot help, then there is evidently an urgent task for theology in the present.

Bailey's writing on homosexuality made it possible for theologians to take up that task. He influenced British debates about the decriminalization of homosexuality. He advanced discussion of sexual issues more generally in the Church of England and other English-speaking denominations. His historical scholarship prepared for a line of later academic works that would greatly increase historical knowledge about sexuality in Christian traditions and societies. Bailey would be engaged directly, for example, in John Boswell's *Christianity, Social Tolerance, Homosexuality* (1980), the book usually credited with securing academic credibility for historical studies of homosexuality in the United States.

Equally important is the budget of problems that Bailey's writing on homosexuality bequeaths to later theology. This includes his refusal to settle the morality of same-sex acts performed by a person he would call an invert. There is more. Bailey attributes the relative neglect of female–female relations and the obsession with male–male ones to the larger gender imbalance in society. Christendom has been preoccupied with male homosexuality because Christendom has been androcentric and patriarchal (or, as Bailey says, "patrist"). Bailey urges his readers to recognize that traditions of Christian sexual morality are traditions of gender politics. He also makes one further suggestion without pursuing it: there may be, he says, "a significant connection between traditional Western views of homosexuality and homosexual practices on the one hand, and of women and marriage on the other."[20] In retrospect, the suggestion must seem prescient. It also suggests that Bailey did not understand his work on homosexuality as a distraction from his long-standing concerns with marriage.

[19] Ibid., 169. [20] Ibid., 161.

RELIGIOUS MORALITY AND CRIMINAL LAW

Bailey's careful refusal to pass judgment on the ethics of an invert's acts was not practiced by others – including some of his colleagues. The preliminary report of the Moral Welfare Council's working group on homosexuality was quite clear about the immorality of such acts. "Homosexual acts are sins against God, whether or not they are also crimes against the State."[21] With the committee, if not on its terms, Bailey found himself in the odd position of arguing that the state should *not* use the criminal law to punish something that was in fact – or at least might well be – a serious sin.

There are several pieces in Bailey's argument for legal reform. Over the years, Bailey points to the inconsistencies and cruelties of the actual operation of the British criminal system with regard to homosexuality. He insists as well on the futility of criminalizing same-sex desire. In his first article on the topic, he concludes, "It is, without doubt, a Christian duty to press for the removal of this anomalous and shameful injustice, which has done untold harm and has achieved no good whatever."[22] The committee pamphlet adds detail without changing the argument. It insists on the state's obligation to protect the young, but notes that the current criminal statutes may actually endanger them by driving adults away from settled relationships with peers. There is a list of legal anomalies in the criminalization of male–male relations and "subsidiary considerations" of its consequences, which include suicide, blackmail, social isolation, moral deterioration, restricted diagnosis or therapy, and police brutality or complicity.[23] Bailey repeats these and other arguments in summary form in his own voice.[24]

Making these various arguments, Bailey assumes a distinction between religiously instructed morality and criminal law. The distinction was both influential and controversial. The Wolfenden committee adopted it roughly in Bailey's terms. It argued that "there must remain a realm of private morality and immorality which is, in brief and crude terms, not the law's business."[25] Advancing this argument, the report provided the occasion for a notable dispute in English-speaking jurisprudence, the so-called Devlin-Hart debate. An experienced judge of the Queen's Bench, Patrick Devlin originally read "with complete approval [the Wolfenden report's] formulation of the functions of the criminal law in matters of

[21] Church of England, Moral Welfare Council, *The Problem of Homosexuality*, 15.

[22] Bailey, "Sexual Inversion," 49. [23] *Problem*, 21–3. [24] Bailey, *Homosexuality*, 174–5.

[25] *Report of the Committee on Homosexual Offences and Prostitution*, paragraph 61, p. 24.

morality."[26] Asked to deliver a lecture in jurisprudence at Oxford, Devlin began to explore the grounds of his approval. He was led by study to reverse it. His new claims about morals and the criminal law were answered in turn by H. L. A. Hart.[27] The Devlin–Hart debate was one sequel to Bailey's work on homosexuality, but it did not exhaust the questions raised by distinguishing crime from sin. To delimit a "realm of private morality and immorality" does not answer the political question: what provisions should the law make for human transactions or relationships assigned to that realm? To say that more simply: once same-sex relations are decriminalized, what becomes of them within civil law?

Bailey does not pursue this question in his writings. He is quick to deny that decriminalizing same-sex acts should imply recognition of same-sex marriage.[28] In his first essay on the topic, he insists that same-sex love can never be equivalent to real marriage: "While gladly recognizing that a genuine homosexual love may have elements of beauty and altruism, there seems no reason to believe that homosexual intercourse has any quality which makes it strictly comparable to the intercourse of husband and wife."[29] The council's pamphlet is more direct. Since inverts should not risk failure in marrying partners of the other sex, and since approving same-sex marriage would undermine society, those who suffer the condition should follow the example of (heterosexual) women who cannot find a husband: they should "*accept their condition, and by seeking to sublimate their sexual lives in various socially useful ways achieve personal fulfillment*" (italics in original).[30]

The issue could not be left there – any more than the urgent question about the morality of an invert's acts could be left with Bailey's careful silence. For an increasingly secular society, what does it mean to permit a group of enduring adult relationships that look very much like marriages without making any legal or social provision for them? The theological version of this question is more acute: if the union of one flesh is an ordinary means of sanctification, how can the churches concede that there is a group of adults who, through no apparent fault of their own, are unable to enter into that relationship?

26 Devlin, *The Enforcement of Morals*, vi. 27 Hart, *Law, Liberty, and Morality*.

28 Bailey here replies to the sort of suggestion made by one of his sources: Northcote, *Christianity and Sexual Problems*, 294–5.

29 Bailey, "Sexual Inversion," 50. 30 *Problem*, 14.

THE MUTUAL DEPENDENCE OF FEMALE AND MALE

Having completed his increasingly elaborate inquiries into homosexuality, Bailey turned to a larger account of the history of Christian teaching on sex. His next book appeared in Great Britain as *The Man–Woman Relation in Christian Thought*, and in the United States as *Sexual Relation in Christian Thought* (both 1959). The British title is more exact, because the book is centrally concerned with the mutual dependence of the two sexes.

Bailey spends most of his pages on a historical narrative of Christian theologies for sexual relations. He repeats a number of his earlier judgments, but now illustrates or supports them with a larger body of evidence in which the emphasis remains admittedly Anglican. Only in the final chapter does Bailey offer constructive remarks "towards a theology of sex." Since he still understands sex as the making of one flesh, and since one flesh can be achieved properly only within marriage, a theology of sex is principally a theology of marriage. Indeed, it is important to see how fully the two projects overlap. Bailey wants to insist – against the institutional preoccupations of the Western churches – that a theology of marriage cannot be a subfield of the law of contracts. It must deal with sexual relations, since those relations distinguish marriage from other forms of human union. At the same time, a theology of sex is almost entirely a theology of marriage – since sexual relation is meant to express the permanent and exclusive love that marriage is.

The particular metaphysics of the one flesh can be achieved only in the union of man and woman. On Bailey's reading of the two creation stories in Genesis (1:26–31, 2:7–24), God made sexual difference "a divisive factor separating humanity into two radically different yet mutually complementary elements – male and female; in the individual, it is an informing principle which permeates his being to its depths, and conditions every facet of his personality and his life." The language of division may mislead. For Bailey, the human being mirrors the image of God (*imago Dei*) to other humans "primarily by virtue of his [or her] essential structure as a bi-personal male-female unity." Bailey gives full weight to the terms "bi-personal" and "unity." Human beings are made to be together as male and female in all settings and contexts. "Each needs the other's help, not merely for procreative and domestic purposes, but in all the manifold concerns and enterprises of human life."[31] So Bailey is suspicious of single-sex institutions,

[31] Bailey, *The Man–Woman Relation in Christian Thought*, 269, 271, 282. (I am citing the American edition.)

and he reminds those called to celibacy that they too must learn from the complementary sex what it is to be human.[32]

Bailey is adamant about not identifying male and female with any particular social constructs of masculinity and femininity. He cites Margaret Mead on the variety of gender systems in New Guinea.[33] He criticizes some contemporary portrayals of gender roles as dangerously misleading and rebuffs efforts to formulate expectations for one gender without thinking always of its relation to the other. Yet Bailey also criticizes Simone de Beauvoir for her famous formulation, "one is not born, but rather becomes a woman."[34] Bailey responds that she "clearly fails to appreciate that to be human one must be either male or female; in her anxiety to repudiate false notions of sexuality, she falls into the error of repudiating sex itself."[35] The error is fundamental – not only for sexual ethics, but also for human life. Indeed, the differentiation of man and woman "is a metaphysical as well as a physical and cultural distinction, and cannot be abolished without destroying Man's [i.e., humankind's] intrinsic nature."[36] In a footnote, Bailey sets aside the prospect of an individual's changing sex as an irrelevant rarity.[37] He also spends time distinguishing his teaching from any myth or theory of androgyny. Man and woman are not produced by the fission of some prior human creature that contained both sexes. They were created from the beginning as distinct but mutually dependent complements. "Metaphysically speaking, man is always purely masculine and woman is always purely feminine – a statement which would be truistic, were it not that the contrary opinion is so commonly assumed and maintained."[38]

Bailey's claim is clear – emphatically so. His basis for it is not. Bailey cites as evidence the Genesis creation stories and other scriptural passages. He sees them partly confirmed by suggestions in Karl Barth, Emil Brunner, and Martin Buber. Elsewhere he repeatedly attributes them to Charles Williams and C. S. Lewis. Still this roster of authorities does not explain the metaphysical certainty with which Bailey sets forth his claims. The source for that certainty seems to be in some self-validating experience. For Bailey, the sexual structure of the human creature is not definable or even discoverable in

[32] The critique of sex-segregated institutions is one point of contact between Bailey's text and the discussion of "man and woman" in Karl Barth's *Church Dogmatics*, III.4 §54 no. 1. But Bailey's relation to Barth is ambivalent. In his bibliography of works on sex and marriage, for example, Bailey cites the *Dogmatics* without praising it. He chooses instead to list critical discussions of it, including his own (*Theology*, 11, item 29).

[33] Bailey, *Sexual Relation*, 246, 278. [34] Ibid., 277, citing de Beauvoir, *The Second Sex*, 273.

[35] Bailey, *Sexual Relation*, 277. [36] Ibid., 288. [37] Ibid., 276, note 2. [38] Ibid., 291.

abstraction: "it is an interior awareness of the meaning of manhood or womanhood which is experienced *only* in the immediacy of sexual encounter, and disappears with the termination of meeting" (italics added).[39] Again, real knowledge of one's own sex or sexual difference "is always existential and dependent upon a capacity for sincere and responsible relational ventures; it can never be derived at second-hand from social stereotypes or conventional ideas of what is manly or womanly."[40]

In retrospect, it is tempting to identify this fundamental conviction in Bailey with the rise since the 1960s of theologies of sexual complementarity, whether Roman Catholic or Evangelical, and so to type him as "conservative" rather than "liberal." Certainly Bailey agrees with those theologies of complementarity in rejecting cultural attempts to blur gender or reduce it to a social construction. But Bailey also differs from the later theologies in his emphasis on the mystery of sexual difference and its availability only during direct experience. In the same way that Bailey rejects natural law arguments against contraception as too presumptuous in their claims about the functions of human sexual organs, so too he seems to reject any attempt to capture the male–female relation in principles or systems. He wants to emphasize the metaphysical excess of the fundamental distinction of the two sexes. One of the striking things about Bailey's theology is thus how badly it fits within later distinctions between "conservative" and "liberal" platforms, whether theological or political.

SEXUAL ETHICS BEFORE ITS FUTURE

Bailey's last book on sexual ethics appeared in 1962. He finished it after he had left the Moral Welfare Council for a village parish. The book circulated in the United States as a mass-market paperback under the title *Sexual Ethics: A Christian View*. The cover shows a college campus with five students – at a time when male students wore ties and "coeds" wore skirts cut below the knees. Certainly the publisher hoped for a wide readership faced toward the future. In fact, the book repeats Bailey's old lessons as it regards a future that it views with a mix of hope and worry.

Bailey defines sexual ethics as "the moral principles which should govern the mutual relations of men and women."[41] He immediately excludes a

[39] Ibid., 282. [40] Ibid., 281.

[41] Bailey, *Common Sense about Sexual Ethics*, 7. (I am citing the American edition.)

number of topics. He is not going to talk about the morality of "various techniques and procedures" that belong to "the field of sexology." The book will not be a sex manual with moral notations. Bailey also sets aside "such topics as artificial insemination, sterilization, abortion, and homosexuality, since they belong rather to the field of morality and the law." It is unclear whether other sexual topics, such as paraphilias or fetishes, would be excluded as sexology or as criminal law. What remains is a book confined to male–female marriage and just three "problems" arising in it: chastity, contraception, and divorce followed by remarriage.

Within this restricted scope, Bailey repeats arguments from his earlier books. He is forced to expand or sharpen them because of changing cultural circumstances. It is not enough any longer simply to assert traditional views about restricting coition to marriage. The rise of the new morality means that Bailey must now argue against premarital sexual relations during an engagement. Again, his treatment of contraception must now recognize the possibility that new, pharmaceutical means are about to become available. He is writing, after all, on the eve of the introduction of the pill.

The interest of the book does not lie in these small adjustments. It is found rather in Bailey's decision to reiterate and sharpen his views within his narrowed scope of marital topics. Bailey will not yield his original convictions about the central place of the metaphysics of male–female relation. He will not be moved by social accounts of gender any more than he was moved by the churches' long preoccupation with details of the marriage contract. So perhaps it is not surprising that Bailey also does not provide in this book a fuller moral judgment on the morality of same-sex acts. There is no room in his account of the one flesh for male–male or female–female unions. They do not possess the right gender complementarity. So Bailey writes no more about them in his final account of sexual ethics. It might also be that he considered himself ill-suited or ill-placed to speak about them truthfully.[42]

At the beginning of this last book, Bailey says that the church of the twentieth century is "called to undertake a radical reconsideration of God's will for man and woman."[43] A year later, in a summary essay for an anthology, he writes more grandly that Christian ethics is "being remoulded in the twentieth century as it was in the seventeenth and the thirteenth centuries, in order that the will of God for contemporary men and woman may be more

[42] The mentions of same-sex acts in this book are few and brief. For example, Bailey speaks of "homosexualism" and prostitution as signs of Roman decadence (ibid., 17). He also mentions "homosexualism" as one object of church legislation (ibid., 30–1).

[43] Ibid., 8.

clearly known and more faithfully followed."[44] The formulation of these aspirations shows at once the acuteness of Bailey's moral sensibility, the clarity of his historical discernment, and the limits on his understanding of one flesh.

RECOMMENDED READING

Bailey, Derrick Sherwin. "Love and Marriage." *Theology* 44 (April 1942): 202–10 and 44 (May 1942): 275–82.

The Mystery of Love and Marriage: A Study in the Theology of Sexual Relation. London: SCM Press; New York: Harper and Brothers, 1952.

Thomas Becon and the Reformation of the Church of England. Edinburgh and London: Oliver and Boyd, 1952.

The Theology of Sex and Marriage: A Short Guide for Readers and Students. Westminster: Moral Welfare Council / Church Information Board, 1953.

Homosexuality and the Western Christian Tradition. London, New York, and Toronto: Longmans, Green, 1955.

The Man–Woman Relation in Christian Thought. London: Longmans, 1959. American edition: *The Sexual Relation in Christian Thought*. New York: Harper, 1959.

Common Sense about Sexual Ethics: A Christian View. London: Victor Gollancz, 1962. American edition: *Sexual Ethics: A Christian View*. New York: Macmillan 1963.

"Sexual Ethics in Christian Tradition." In *Sexual Ethics and Christian Responsibility*. Edited by John C. Wynn, 139–56. New York: Association Press, 1970.

(comp., ed.). *Sexual Offenders and Social Punishment. Being the Evidence Submitted on Behalf of the Church of England Moral Welfare Council to the Department Committee on Homosexual Offences and Prostitution, with Other Material Relating Thereto*. Westminster: Church Information Board, 1956.

Carey, Jonathan Sinclair. "D. S. Bailey and 'the Name Forbidden among Christians.'" *Anglican Theological Review* 70/2 (1988): 152–73.

Jones, Timothy Willem. *Sexual Politics in the Church of England, 1857–1957*. Oxford: Oxford University Press, 2013.

Willett, Graham. "The Church of England and the Origins of Homosexual Law Reform." *Journal of Religious History* 33/4 (2009): 418–34.

[44] D. S. Bailey, "Sexual Ethics in Christian Tradition," in *Sexual Ethics and Christian Responsibility*, ed. John C. Wynn (New York: Association Press, 1970), 139–56, at 156.

25

Jean Bethke Elshtain

M. Christian Green

BIOGRAPHICAL INTRODUCTION

Jean Bethke Elshtain (1941–2013) was neither a lawyer nor a scholar of law, but rather a singularly fluid and adept scholar of political theory and religious ethics. Her professional and scholarly career at Brandeis, Vanderbilt, and the University of Chicago began with the topics of feminism and the family and eventually expanded to include Christian just war theory, Augustinian political theology, theories of sovereignty of states and selves, and more. In essay upon essay – the genre in which her erudition and expressive powers shone especially brightly – she covered a comprehensive range of concerns at the intersection of politics, religion, ethics, and law on matters of domestic, national, and international importance. Her personal religious journey led this granddaughter of Russian-German immigrants to America from her original Lutheranism to reception into the Roman Catholic Church in the years before her death in 2013.

As her scholarly career, accompanied by motherhood to four children, took off in the 1960s and 1970s, Elshtain was an observer of, and by some accounts a sympathetic participant in, the cultural revolutions of that time, including feminism and various movements for social justice. But in the background of these commitments lurked a sense that feminism and liberal politics were leaving families, children, and women themselves behind. This concern was one that she addressed early in essays on what might be called her "Androgyny or Antigone" question.[1] Against the sameness and strict equivalency of the sexes that could lead to a sort of androgyny, a position many feminists and liberals at the time seemed to advocate, Elshtain argued,

[1] See Green, "Androgyny or Antigone."

FIGURE 25.1. Jean Bethke Elshtain. *Photo by Matthew Gilson / University of Chicago*

"[S]omething happened to androgyny on its way to becoming feminist dogma. Human bodies disappeared – they were dismantled, dismembered or, at least, dis-remembered. Androgyny was dusted off, stripped of its deeply sensual and sexed roots and its previous mythic meaning. In place of the body, contemporary androgynists put 'free will' or 'flexible sex roles' or the 'union of positively valued traits.'"[2]

The androgynous perspective contrasted deeply with Elshtain's sense of the embodied dimension of human sexuality, marriage, and family. Her emphasis on embodiment put Elshtain squarely in line with the deeply Christian trope of the church as the body of Christ. It also showed an affinity with a natural law theology that was largely scorned in her Lutheran religion of origin, but that is deeply rooted in the Catholic moral tradition to which she was drawn as an avid student and eventual convert.

Particularly troubling for Elshtain in the new liberal feminist calls for equality and rights in the family was the prospect of a reliance on the liberal state as the guarantor of status and rights. Indeed, Elshtain argued with characteristically robust rhetoric, "For feminists to discover in the state the new 'Mr. Right,' and to wed themselves thereby, for better or for worse, to a public identity inseparable from the exigencies of state power and policy would be a mistake."[3] In the face of this then-dominant androgynous and statist version of feminism, Elshtain declared her project to "reclaim for women a social identity that locates them very much in and of the wider world but positions them against overweening state power and public identity defined in its terms." In other words, as she put it, "My aim is to define and to defend a female identity and a feminist perspective that enables contemporary women to see themselves as the daughters of Antigone."[4] For Elshtain, the story of Antigone provided an entrée into examining the relationships among men, women, families, and the state in her landmark first book, *Public Man, Private Woman*.

[2] Jean Bethke Elshtain, "Against Androgyny," *Telos* 47 (1981): 6, reprinted in Elshtain, *Real Politics*, chapter 13.

[3] Elshtain, "Antigone's Daughters." This essay was reprinted in numerous anthologies on women and politics and indicates Elshtain's early origins and reception in feminist scholarly circles. A revised version of the article was published as "Antigone's Daughters Reconsidered: Continuing Reflections of Women, Politics and Power," in *Life-World and Politics*, 222–36.

[4] Ibid., 46–7.

PUBLIC MAN, PRIVATE WOMAN: CREATING A SPACE FOR FAMILY

Public Man, Private Woman: Women in Social and Political Thought (1981) marked the beginning of Elshtain's engagement with feminism and family issues, as well as the beginning of her ultimate departure, or serious detour, from the feminist fold. Drawing on a quote from Ludwig Wittgenstein about the "nastiness" of intellectual inquiry, Elshtain began her preface by observing, "*Public Man, Private Woman* is a nasty book. It is intended to be. In the pages that follow I have attempted to think 'really honestly' from the vantage point of a political theorist who has been influenced, for over fifteen years, by her involvement with the feminist movement."[5] Evincing the religious dimension of her argument at a time when she was still firmly ensconced within the field of political theory, she observed:

> Within the Christian tradition in which I was raised this process is called "bearing witness." One who bears witness voices the discontents of society's silenced, ignored, abused, or invisible members. The witness proffers reasons for that suffering in order that the silenced may find a voice, cry out for justice, demand to be seen. The witness is a disturber of the peace just as political discourse, if critique is its aim, must disturbingly shatter the artificial calm of official know-nothingness.[6]

Though nominally a book about the status of women in Western political thought, it also makes clear from the outset Elshtain's concern for the family as a venue for the moral agency of women and men alike. Against the grand historical panoply of theorizing about the division of public and private realms, Elshtain maintained, "My aim is more modest. I shall tease out of the tapestry of past and present the meaning of that division as it appears in accounts of the relationship that pertains between that aspect of the public world deemed political and that contrasting dimension of social life called private, most often in the household or family."[7]

What follows is a long journey of hermeneutical retrieval of Western understanding of men, women, and family, beginning with Aristotle's rejection of his teacher Plato's recommendation that a system of communal childrearing would ensure both women's equality and social harmony. Aristotle recommended instead something closer to the modern notion of a nuclear family, a sexual and sociobiological family in which men and women fulfill clearly

[5] Elshtain, *Public Man, Private Woman*, xi. [6] Ibid., xii. [7] Ibid., 4.

different and biologically defined roles. Plato's egalitarian vision of women has had a better reception among feminists than Aristotle's apparent subjection of women, Elshtain noted, but she preferred Aristotle's understanding of the nature of the family. She noted that Aristotle's largely teleological, material, and functionalist understanding of the family appears to "allow for some diversity within unity."[8] This is an Antigone-like point that challenges hegemonic public understandings of the family, particularly by the state, that do not afford private space in which difference, including differences between the sexes, rather than androgyny, can be understood and embraced. Indeed, while cognizant of the ways in which Aristotle seems to trap women in the private sphere of the family, Elshtain noted the ways in which he fosters new participation and cooperation between men and women in the private realm of the family and between families and state in the public realm of the *civitas* or *polis*. As Elshtain observed, when it comes to matters of gender and family, "There is no small dose of irony in the fact that a thinker who resolutely buttressed a politics of exclusion has become a symbol of a politics of participation . . . This leaves the door open for feminist thinkers to turn Aristotle to their own purposes and to take up and insist on a concept of citizenship as the touchstone of collective and individual public identities."[9]

These Aristotelian possibilities were, however, lost on one of Elshtain's other career-long interlocutors in the Western tradition, Protestant reformer Martin Luther. Elshtain noted that Luther read Aristotle and "detested" him, determining his *Ethics* to be the "worst book ever written."[10] Reflecting his theological convictions concerning the frailty of human nature and the fallibility of human institutions, by this account, Luther seems to have attempted something of a Platonic move against Aristotle. But instead of placing humans and families under the order of the state, Luther did the inverse, by retreating into the private world of the family against the corruption of both the church and the state, thereby collapsing the family in upon itself as a "haven in a heartless world."[11] As Elshtain described it, "Responding to the social dislocation around him, a chaos refracted in the interstices of his soul, Luther

8 Ibid., 42.

9 Ibid. 53. Indeed this melding of private family values and public political participation would be a recurring theme of some of Elshtain's later work extending from analysis of the mothers of the Plaza de Mayo in Argentina to the social reform work of Jane Addams at Hull House. See especially Elshtain, *Jane Addams*.

10 Elshtain, *Public Man, Private Woman*, 80.

11 The allusion here is to Lasch, *Haven in a Heartless World*, which appeared four years before *Public Man, Private Woman*. Elshtain greatly admired Lasch, and upon his death she wrote, "Christopher Lasch was a man of grace who found much of late modernity graceless; a man of wit who found much of our politics witless; a man of purpose who lamented our culture's

responded by constructing a tiny redeemed point of order amidst the turbulence and change. He would not build an external community."[12] She later remarked, "The era of the Reformation represents an ebb tide in the normative import of public institutions and the social locus they provided."[13] Thus, Elshtain concluded, "It is not surprising, then, that for Luther the political sphere was little more than a realm of coercion and unfreedom ... The true epicenter of his existence is a pietistic, ever-scrutinized *vie intérieur*."[14]

But this pietistic depiction of Luther may not be the whole story. Elshtain's writing on these points predated important understandings that would emerge on the legal history of the Protestant Reformation and the work Luther had initiated to reform the law of marriage and remove it from Roman Catholic sacramental and canon law authority. Elshtain would become familiar with this literature and the more public projects of Luther as a legal reformer, especially of marriage and family.[15] Further, one significant point that Elshtain seemed to have borrowed from Luther in ways that informed her theory of family was what she called Luther's "redemption of the everyday."[16] From reports of his changing his children's diapers to his proclivity for profane language, Luther delivered a robust account of the embodied and material world of family life. In Elshtain's words, "Luther transformed the possibilities of meaningful public and private discourse by demonstrating that serious attention should be paid to important and vital questions through the vehicle of the vernacular, the down-to-earth language of the ordinary person."[17] This could not help being reflected in his family law reforms, which rejected sacramental control and admitted new practices, such as permission for divorce and clerical marriage. These reforms were grounded in the real lives of actual couples, often in the bliss but sometimes in the trenches of marriage and family arrangements that proved unworkable and maybe even an inducement to greater sin.

frenetic purposelessness; a man of hope who saw in boundless optimism a deep despair." Elshtain, "Eulogy for Christopher Lasch."

12 Elshtain, *Public Man, Private Woman*, 81. 13 Ibid., 82. 14 Ibid., 83.

15 See Elshtain, "There Oughta Be a Law,'" 74, n. 15, citing Witte Jr., *Law and Protestantism*; Witte Jr. and Kingdon, *Sex, Marriage, and Family Life in John Calvin's Geneva*; Witte Jr., *The Reformation of Rights*. See also Witte Jr., *From Sacrament to Contract*.

16 Indeed, Elshtain acknowledges this theme explicitly in the afterword to the second edition; see Elshtain, *Public Man, Private Woman*, 355.

17 Ibid., 86. See further Chapter 12 herein on Martin Luther.

The rise of political liberalism in the early modern period ushered in "contractarian, constitutional, and voluntarist theories of politics" that came to apply to the family, Elshtain continued. Liberal theorists "recast distinctions between public and private in order to take the family out of the politics and politics out of the family."[18] For women, "the effect of these splits was to further privatize the private world and to reduce the language of women to that of cloying sentiment as the private world was cut off even further from public discourse."[19] Even though there was risk in this sort of hyper-privatization of the family, public solutions, in Elshtain's view, are not always a panacea. "Public grants of parity to women have gone hand in glove within liberalism ... with extraordinary disparity in the distribution of goods and services and in the concrete allocation of economic and social power."[20] Particularly troubling for Elshtain in the social contractarian theories of Hobbes, Locke, and other early liberal theorists was the hypertrophy of the contractual ideal, especially in the family. As Elshtain memorably queried, "Where does the family belong in a liberal contractual society? Do human beings enter the world as unfree subjects within the family? Or do they come into life with a contract in one hand and a pen in the other, stipulating contractual duties, rights, and responsibilities?"[21] Such an overly contractual view of the family and family law were at odds with Elshtain's Christian moral anthropology and understanding of human nature.

More palatable than the strong contractualism of Hobbes, with its elements of patriarchalism and authoritarianism, was what might be called the softer and more mutual contractarianism of Locke. In Locke's understanding of the family, Elshtain noted, "As parents are obligated to raise their children, children are obligated to honor their parents. Although conjugal society is a freely contracted one, voluntary and shared, it does not serve as the model for a freely contracted political state."[22] The private family and the public state are deeply intertwined, but they need to be kept separate, too. As Elshtain put it, "To infuse the public language of liberalism into the private world is to replace older patriarchal perspectives ... with another distortion, one that decrees that *all* social obligations are derived from the rationally conceived obligations of individuals whose motivations are seen as narrowly egoistic."[23] In this

18 Ibid., 106. 19 Ibid., 119. 20 Ibid., 122. 21 Ibid.

22 Ibid., 123. Not discussed here, because of space, is Elshtain's analysis of the thought of Jean-Jacques Rousseau, a thinker with whom Elshtain is even more congenial, especially in Rousseau's retrieval of the natural dimensions of the family and his critique of Locke's understanding of the social contract. See ibid., 147.

23 Ibid., 126. The "elimination of *all* distinctions" between private and public becomes Elshtain's major argument against Karl Marx's theory of the family, which otherwise receives sympathetic treatment in her analysis for being premised on a "social theory of human nature." Ibid., 190, 196, 189.

new public language of "contract and exchange," Elshtain argued, "women held the line against allowing market language to dominate private meaning," but they did so at the risk of being marginalized as merely speaking the "language of sentiment, a language increasingly cloying as it lost part of the force of the Christian ethic of caring and responsibility."[24]

Elshtain's treatment of the family in *Public Man, Private Woman* reflected her early commitment to a Christian natural-law moral anthropology: "The victory of liberalism and the rejection of all modes of 'naturalism' was carried out systematically on the level of abstract theory and constitution-making, but was only a partial success if one looks to the resistance of the family to the rationalizations of its inner life and relationship."[25] In her writings on the Argentinian mothers of the Plaza de Mayo, on the social work of Jane Addams, and on other political activities drawing on the familial ethos of care and responsibility, Elshtain chronicled these forms of resistance to the political state.[26] But the problem is far from merely historical when it comes to family law in liberal states today. In societies across North America, Europe, and elsewhere in the advanced Western world, strong new movements of contractualism are again at the fore, raising important questions about whether marriage and family are natural or spiritual, covenantal or contractual, private or public.[27] These matters are far from resolved – and they were grasped powerfully and presciently in *Public Man, Private Woman*.

By the end of the book, it is apparent how central the understanding of family is to Elshtain's analysis of feminism, public and private, and the state of contemporary society. "To talk of an ideal of the private world within the context of contemporary American society is to talk about the family," Elshtain maintains.[28] Indeed, she prefaces her analysis of public, private, and the family in the book's concluding sections by stating:

> I begin with a reaffirmation: familial ties and modes of childrearing are essential to establish the minimal foundation of human social existence. What we call human capacities could not exist outside of a familial mode; for human beings to flourish a particular ideal of the family is necessary ...

[24] Ibid., 127. [25] Ibid., 128.

[26] See Elshtain, "The Passion of the 'Mothers of the Disappeared' in Argentina"; Elshtain, "Making Peace with Justice"; Elshtain, *Jane Addams*.

[27] See Witte Jr., *Church, State, and Family*. [28] Elshtain, *Public Man, Private Woman*, 322.

> [T]he family's status as a moral imperative derives from its universal, pan-cultural existence in all known past and present societies. We are not dealing with a tangential, episodic form but a transhistorical one.[29]

As in so many places in Elshtain's analysis of the family, the needs of children, apart from the desires of adults, play a prominent role. She argues:

> Children will incur an assault to their humanness, an affront they will know in the tissue of their bio-psychic beings, if they suffer from the diseases of neglect and nonattachment. A being without a presumptive need for attachments of a special kind – concrete, particular, and continuing – *would not suffer distortion and damage if such relations were absent* . . . [S]o the knowl edge we now have of what happens to children *in the absence of strong, early attachments to specific adult others*, allows us to assert that we are dealing with a categorical imperative of human existence.[30]

The failure of various schools of contemporary feminist thought to grasp adequately this central function of the family in the moral formation of children, analyzed extensively in the book's second half, through the witness of her Christian moral anthropology, is what prompts Elshtain's critical break from most of those forms of feminist thought. Indeed, against various institutional, communal, and individual forms of family proposed by various schools of feminist thought, Elshtain argues:

> To call some abstract structure, or loose collection of like-minded, unrelated peers "families" is to treat our most basic human relationships frivolously as mere historic accidents, or as the excreta of oppressive relations having no deep inner logic, meaning, or purpose of their own . . . The feminist political thinker must similarly ask at what price she would gain the world for herself or other women, utterly rejecting those victories that come at the cost of the bodies and spirits of human infants. Unless this reflexivity is ongoing and central, feminism is in peril of losing its soul.[31]

In the afterword to the second edition of *Public Man, Private Woman*, thinking what she would do differently if writing it all over again, Elshtain maintained: "In my discussion of the Christian moral revolution, I would deepen and extend the 'redemption of everyday life' in Christian doctrine against gnostic disparagers, past and present."[32] This "redemption of the everyday" certainly

[29] Ibid., 326–7.

[30] Ibid., 328. Elshtain later asserts, "The feminist concerned with a reconstructive ideal of the private sphere must begin by affirming the essential needs of children for basic, long-term ties with specific others." Ibid., 331.

[31] Ibid., 331. [32] Ibid., 355.

includes the family in both its public and private dimensions, and its natural and covenantal purposes, both to its members and to the wider society. In defending against gnosticism, Elshtain also defends a deeply Christian understanding of the natural, material, and relational understanding of the family. She does so seemingly in solidarity with Aristotle, whose theory of the private family *oikos* she finds congenial, as it is received into the Christian tradition alongside, but sometimes in tension with, the public world of the state and *polis*.

REBUILDING MARRIAGE AND RENEWING FAMILIES

Elshtain's theoretical work on the family in the 1980s positioned her well to participate in the public debates over family life that exploded on the American political scene in the 1990s.[33] Much of that debate would center on the Personal Responsibility and Work Opportunity Act, otherwise known as Welfare Reform, passed with no small amount of controversy during the administration of President Bill Clinton in 1996. But this major piece of legislation, which would greatly impact American families, particularly those headed by single mothers, was preceded by such cultural phenomena as Marilyn Quayle's ode to women's "natural" role in the families at the 1992 Republican National Convention and later Vice President Dan Quayle's criticism of the television program *Murphy Brown* and its main character's choice of single motherhood. That cultural debate prompted the publication by social historian Barbara Dafoe Whitehead, a frequent Elshtain collaborator, of the influential and widely read *Atlantic* article "Dan Quayle Was Right."[34] Whitehead followed this article with the equally widely read and influential book *The Divorce Culture*, which chronicled the rise of what might be called the liberal, voluntary, and contractual family in the rising incidence of divorce, which began in the 1960s with the legislative move toward "no-fault" divorce and culminated in the high divorce statistics in the 1980s – all of which would have tremendous and mostly negative implications for women, children, and families.[35] Whitehead, Elshtain, and other leading family scholars and public intellectuals would coalesce into what became known as the marriage movement. That movement located many of the ills of contemporary society in the dissolution of families through divorce and the emerging

33 For the best analysis of these debates in religious circles, see Browning, et al., *From Culture Wars*.

34 Whitehead, "Dan Quayle Was Right."

35 Whitehead, *The Divorce Culture*.

culture in which sexual partners formed relationships and conceived children without marrying at all.[36]

The marriage movement gave rise to volumes of analysis of contemporary marriage trends. It would lead to international invitations for Elshtain to address organizations like the World Congress of Families, which lifted up the Christian dimensions of what was becoming a global marriage movement.[37] Yet, interestingly, many of the most public contours of the global debate were couched in terms not so much theological as scientific, as social science data were emerging on the effects of new family forms. Elshtain's address to the WCF in 1999, for example, made ample use of social statistics with nary a reference to religion or Christianity. But religious and sometimes even secular discussions of marriage and family in this period drew on biblical and religious notions of nature, covenant, and other metaphors that gave the movement its religious flavor.

This was an interesting time for religious discourse on the family, as it seemed that the discussion in the United States, and by extension the global discussion, was attempting something like a perfect Rawlsian political liberalism of discourse couched in a religiously neutral language of social science rather than the moral language of religious traditions. It is as if the leaders of the marriage movement wanted to win the marriage debate on the merits of science rather than theology. But as the movement toward same-sex marriage took off in the 2000s, with the legalization of same-sex marriage first in Massachusetts and then in other states, the issue of same-sex marriage largely overtook other marriage issues, culminating in nationwide legalization via the U.S. Supreme Court's *Obergefell v. Hodges* decision in the summer of 2015, two years after Elshtain's death.

Elshtain wrote and spoke against same-sex marriage and seemed to espouse a natural law theory of marriage that did not appear to countenance its same-sex forms.[38] At the same time, in private conversations, Elshtain often seemed deeply sympathetic to the claims of gay and lesbian couples to basic human rights of love and recognition, and even to their desires and capacities to raise children and to raise them well. Some of Elshtain's colleagues in the marriage movement later recanted their opposition to same-sex marriage, finding ways to include same-sex couples in renewing and rebuilding social covenants and commitments to strong marriages and families.[39] When

36 See, e.g., Blankenhorn, Bayme, and Elshtain, *Rebuilding the Nest*; Popenoe, Elshtain, and Blankenhorn, *Promises to Keep*.

37 Elshtain, "What's at Stake in the Family Debate?"

38 See, e.g., Elshtain, "Foreword," in George and Elshtain, *The Meaning of Marriage*.

39 See Blankenhorn, *The Future of Marriage*.

Elshtain left this world, these matters were very much in a state of legal, political, and cultural flux – thus we shall never know how she would have resolved them. Some clues may be gleaned, however, from Elshtain's writings on the law as a source of political and cultural change, the topic to which we now turn.

CHASTENED LAW AND IRONIC LIBERALISM

What emerges from Elshtain's writing on the law itself is that she had a chastened view of law. *Skeptical* seems too strong a term, but *chastened*, a term Elshtain liked,[40] seems to get it right – and *realist*, another term she claimed, seems right, too. In a notable article on law and the moral life, Elshtain defended her statement to a radio show caller's accusation that she advocated "legislating morality" – "We do it all the time," she said.[41] But what does legislating morality mean? Elshtain wrote:

> This involves the conviction that there are truths to be discerned, to be made known and manifest, and to be honored insofar as frail human beings can live up to certain standards. These truths help to constitute norms that may themselves be overridden or violated under certain conditions. The moral realist recognized that truth embodied in human institutions – and the law is one such institution – can never achieve perfection. Such perfection will always elude us, given the way that we come to know the truth and try to write it into law is bound to be epistemically flawed, as our minds are imperfect instruments. The implication of this latter recognition is that laws are not writ in stone but alterable over time as new recognitions dawn that either deepen prior normative commitments or put pressure upon them.[42]

This cautionary plea for epistemic humility of the law can be read in both conservative and liberal directions, as suggested in Elshtain's acknowledgment that law understood in this way can confirm or challenge extant normative commitments. But it also reflects an understanding of the law as an all-too-human institution, along with a sense of the way in which law both reflects and constructs human relations and affairs.

This understanding has particular implications for law in its dealing with that most human of human relations, the family. There is an affinity between Elshtain's moral realist perspective on law and life and an important observation made by Carl Schneider and Margaret Brinig, the editors of a widely used family law casebook:

40 See Green, "Sovereignty and Chastened Liberalism."
41 Elshtain, "Law and the Moral Life." 42 Ibid., 384–5.

> [Family law] deals with one of the happiest parts of human existence – the rewards of life among the people who love us most, and whom we love most. Yet law, much more than economics, the dismal science, deals with people in some of the most degraded parts of human existence – the failures, disappointments, and corruptions of family life.[43]

This observation seems likely to have resonated with Elshtain, particularly in the emphasis on the redemption of the everyday lives of families so evident in her work. Elshtain also sought to defend and redeem the law itself as something that Schneider and Brinig refer to as an institution that "concerns people in their concreteness."[44] Elshtain's view of law is not irredeemably pessimistic – law is the bearer of moral description and is in many cases tasked with the adjudication and restraint of human corruption, but it also carries and shapes our higher aspirations.

In other writings, Elshtain does want to rescue law from the "perils of legal moralism" and the knee-jerk inclination to sue in cultures as litigious as the United States. In some places, Elshtain traces her concern for some of the excesses of law and legal moralism back to the theology of Martin Luther and the idea that "Christian freedom meant taking risks and embracing the capacity of people to seek salvation, through grace, in a manner free from excessive tutelage."[45] For as much as law may carry our aspirations, it also has a tendency toward overreach that must be chastened:

> Chastening legal overreach that turns law into a tyranny over human beings requires that law acknowledge that it cannot eliminate or prohibit every human action ... Law helps to habituate human beings to virtue. But, again, there are limits. Not every sin is a crime and not every sin can or should be punished by the civil law.[46]

In a notable public debate with the Right Honourable Beverley McLachlin, the Chief Justice of the Supreme Court of Canada, over the "dialectic of normative commitments" between law and religion, Elshtain emphasized the need for this to be a "dialectic of citizens" in a "culture of democratic argument," and that "resort to the courts should be just that – a last resort – not the first move made in this dialectic."[47] The law might be a place where definitions and disputes over marriage and family are worked out in real life – but it is far from an ideal venue.

[43] Schneider and Brinig, *An Invitation to Family Law*, ix. [44] Ibid., 409–11.

[45] Elshtain, "The Perils of Legal Moralism," 552.

[46] Elshtain, "'There Oughta Be a Law,'" 72.

[47] Elshtain, "A Response to Chief Justice McLaughlin," 39.

CONCLUSION: LAW, RELIGION, AND THE FAMILY – FROM PRIVATE TO PUBLIC AND BACK AGAIN

At the outset of her scholarship on the family, Elshtain was concerned to carve out a space for the private family – its virtues and values – against the pressure of a variety of overbearing public ideologies. These included the totalitarian excesses of communist and authoritarian regimes, overly androgynous versions of feminism, and a general turn toward the state to determine the status and contours of family life in ways that seemed to threaten the autonomy and self-determination of the families themselves. Her writings on the family demonstrate an abiding concern both for the redemption of everyday life that she found in Luther and for the principles of subsidiarity and the common good that she found in Thomas Aquinas. Even as a witness to what she saw in the excesses of some political movements, particularly the feminism with which she had initial sympathy, she had an abiding concern for the status of women as citizens and moral agents and the needs of children as developing moral agents in their own right. Elshtain also challenged patriarchy without challenging patriarchs – men had important roles to play as fathers and citizens in her view. And the family itself had an important role in shaping the virtue and character of its members and in serving the wider common good. The nuclear family was not an isolated and solipsistic entity in her understanding.

Particularly in her original conception of families as private and public, Elshtain anticipated, but did not live to witness fully, some of the crucial questions emerging around the family today – particularly around the question of what some have described as a trend toward "private ordering."[48] This is the idea that the availability of traditional marriage, non-marriage, non-marital cohabitation, same-sex marriage, and other family forms and configurations gives everyone freedom to craft and construct their families in any way they choose This pluralism of family forms has not been an easy or uncontroversial achievement. The U.S. Supreme Court's legalization of same sex-marriage in the summer of 2015 was welcomed by many as the hallmark of a society committed to dignity and equality for all. But it prompted others to defy the law by refusing to issue marriage licenses at all, whether to same-sex or opposite-sex couples. Whether this refusal constituted dereliction of duty or exercise of Christian freedom, it stands as an example of a larger threatened abdication of marriage by both law and

[48] See Bix, "Private Ordering and Family Law"; id., "The Private and Public Ordering of Marriage"; Browning, *Reviving Christian Humanism*, 136ff.; Swennen, *Contractualisation and Family Law: A Global Perspective*.

religion. Both legal and ecclesiastical circles have voiced a desire to "get out of the marriage business" – leaving only the private contracts of couples as the arbiters of marriage, that bedrock of family. This is the ultimate privatization of the family. It takes no stretch of the imagination to think that Jean Bethke Elshtain would see such abdication as just as tyrannical as the overreach of law into domestic life.

Ultimately, it was to tyrannies both public and private that Elshtain served as an Antigonean witness. Straddling political theory and religious ethics, a pilgrim between the Protestant and Catholic traditions, Elshtain provided a cautionary and chastening guide for those who would subject the family to either extreme. Elshtain's theories of family and law, which had their beginnings in a "nasty book," culminate in a spirit of humanity and humility, forgiveness and vulnerability,[49] that witnesses to the possibilities of a "reconstructive ideal of the private sphere" and a "revitalized, ironic liberalism" in the public sphere around matters of family and civic life.[50]

RECOMMENDED READING

Blankenhorn, David, Steven Bayme, and Jean Bethke Elshtain, eds. *Rebuilding the Nest: A New Commitment to the American Family*. Milwaukee, WI: Family Service America, 1990.

Elshtain, Jean Bethke. *Public Man, Private Woman: Women in Social and Political Thought.* Princeton, NJ: Princeton University Press, 1981.

Power Trips and Other Journeys: Essays in Feminism as Civic Discourse. Madison: University of Wisconsin Press, 1990.

Real Politics: Politics at the Center of Everyday Life. Baltimore, MD: The Johns Hopkins University Press, 2000. See especially the essays in part III, "Children, Bodies, Families, and Feminism."

"The Heart of the Matter: The Family as a Site of Fundamental Ethical Struggle." In Steven M. Tipton and John Witte, Jr., eds. *Family Transformed: Religion, Values, and Society in American Life.* Washington, DC: Georgetown University Press, 2005.

ed. *The Family in Political Thought.* Amherst: University of Massachusetts, 1982.

George, Robert P. and Jean Bethke Elshtain, eds. *The Meaning of Marriage: Family, State, Markets, and Morals.* Dallas, TX: Spence Publishing, 2006.

[49] These two themes are mentioned in her afterword to the second edition. See Elshtain, *Public Man, Private Woman*, 356, 365.

[50] Ibid., 331, 365.

Green, M. Christian. “Androgyny or Antigone: Jean Bethke Elshtain’s Feminism.” *Capital Commentary*. Washington, DC: Center for Public Justice, 2013.

Popenoe, David, Jean Bethke Elshtain, and David Blankenhorn. *Promises to Keep: Decline and Renewal of Marriage in America*. Lanham, MD: Rowman and Littlefield Publishers, 1996.

Bibliography

Abbey, Ruth. "Back to the Future: Marriage as Friendship in the Thought of Mary Wollstonecraft." *Hypatia* 14:3 (1999): 78–95.

Afanasiev, Nicholas. *The Church of the Holy Spirit.* Translated by Vitaly Permiakov; edited by Michael Plekon. Notre Dame, IN: University of Notre Dame Press, 2007.

Alfieri, Fernanda. *Nella camera degli sposi. Tomas Sanchez, il matrimonio, la sessualità (secoli XVI-XVII).* Bologna: Società editrice il Mulino, 2010.

Allen, Sr. Prudence. "Mulieris Dignitatem Twenty Years Later." *Ave Maria Law Review* 8 (2009): 13–47.

Anné, Lucien. *Les rites des fiançailles et la donation pour cause de mariage sous le Bas-Empire.* Louvain: Desclée, de Brouwer, 1941.

Arjakovsky, Antoine, *The Way: Religious Thinkers of the Russian Emigration in Paris and Their Journal*, trans. Jerry Ryan, eds., John A. Jillions and Michael Plekon (Notre Dame, IN: University of Notre Dame Press, 2013).

Arnhart, Larry. "Thomistic Natural Law as Darwinian Natural Right." *Social Philosophy and Policy* 18.1 (2001): 1–33.

Aroney, Nicholas. "Subsidiarity, Federalism, and the Best Constitution: Thomas Aquinas on City, Province, and Empire." *Law and Philosophy* 26 (2007): 161–228.

Astolfi, Riccardo. *La lex Julia et Papia.* 3d ed. Padua: CEDAM, 1995.

Aubert, Roger, et al. *The Church in the Industrial Age. History of the Church.* Edited by Hubert Jedin, et al. New York: Crossroad, 1981.

Aubrey, John. *Brief Lives* [1680]. Edited by Kate Bennett. 2 vols. Oxford: Oxford University Press, 2015.

Avicenna. *Liber De anima seu Sextus de naturalibus IV–V.* Edited by G. Verbeke. Louvain and Leiden: Brill, 1968

Bagnall, Roger S. "Church, State and Divorce in Late Roman Egypt" in *Florilegium Columbianum: Essays in Honor of Paul Oskar Kristeller.* Edited by R.E. Somerville and L.-L. Selig, 41–61. New York: Italica Press, 1987.

Bailey, Derrick Sherwin. *Common Sense about Sexual Ethics: A Christian View.* London: Victor Gollancz, 1962. American edition: *Sexual Ethics: A Christian View.* New York: Macmillan, 1963.

Homosexuality and the Western Christian Tradition. London, New York, and Toronto: Longmans, Green, 1955.

"Love and Marriage." *Theology* 44 (April 1942): 202–10 and 44 (May 1942): 275–82.

The Man-Woman Relation in Christian Thought. London: Longmans, 1959. American edition: *The Sexual Relation in Christian Thought*. New York: Harper, 1959.

The Mystery of Love and Marriage: A Study in the Theology of Sexual Relation. London: SCM Press, 1952. New York: Harper and Brothers, 1952.

"The Problem of Inversion," *Theology* 55 (1952): 47

"Sexual Ethics in Christian Tradition." In *Sexual Ethics and Christian Responsibility*. Edited by John C. Wynn, 139–56. New York: Association Press, 1970.

compiler and editor. *Sexual Offenders and Social Punishment. Being the Evidence Submitted on Behalf of the Church of England Moral Welfare Council to the Department Committee on Homosexual Offences and Prostitution, with Other Material Relating Thereto*. Westminster: Church Information Board, 1956.

The Theology of Sex and Marriage: A Short Guide for Readers and Students. Westminster: Moral Welfare Council / Church Information Board, 1953.

Thomas Becon and the Reformation of the Church of England. Edinburgh and London: Oliver and Boyd, 1952.

Bajén Español, Melchor. Pensamiento de Tomás Sánchez SJ sobre moral sexual. Granada: Universidad de Granada, 1976.

Banaji, Jairus. *Agrarian Change in Late Antiquity*. 2d edition. Oxford; New York: Oxford University Press, 2007.

Barbour, Reid. *John Selden: Measures of the Holy Commonwealth in Seventeenth-Century England*. Toronto: University of Toronto Press, 2003.

Barnes, Timothy D. *Constantine and Eusebius*. Cambridge, MA: Harvard University Press, 1981.

Constantine: Dynasty, Religion and Power in the Later Roman Empire. Chichester, UK: Wiley-Blackwell, 2011.

"Lactantius and Constantine," *Journal of Roman Studies* 63 (1973): 29–46.

Barth, Karl. *Church Dogmatics*. 5 vols. Edited by G. W. Bromiley and T. F. Torrance, 238–54. Edinburgh: T. & T. Clark, 1961.

Baur, Michael. "Law and Natural Law." In *The Oxford Handbook of Aquinas*. Edited by B. Davies and E. Stump. Oxford: Oxford University Press, 2011.

Benedict XVI, Pope. *Address of His Holiness Benedict XVI to Members of the Pontifical John Paul II Institute for Studies on Marriage and Family on the XXVth Anniversary of its Foundation*. May 11, 2006. Vatican City, Italy: Libreria Editrice Vaticana, 2006. Available at: https://w2.vatican.va/content/benedict-xvi/en/speeches/2006/may/documents/hf_ben-xvi_spe_20060511_istituto-gp-ii.html.

Beauvoir, Simone de. *The Second Sex*. Translated by H. M. Parshley. New York: Knopf, 1953.

Behr-Sigel, Elisabeth. *The Ministry of Women in the Church*. Crestwood NY: St. Vladimir's Seminary Press, 1990.

Berkowitz, David Sandler. *John Selden's Formative Years: Politics and Society in Early Seventeenth-Century England*. Washington, DC: Folger Shakespeare Library, 1988.

Biale, David. *Eros and the Jews: From Biblical Israel to Contemporary America*. New York: Basic Books, 1992.

Biale, Rachel. *Women and Jewish Law: An Exploration of Women's Issues in Halkhic Sources*. New York: Schocken, 1984.

Bix, Brian H. "Private Ordering and Family Law," *Journal of the American Academy of Matrimonial Lawyers*, 23 (2010): 249–85.

"The Private and Public Ordering of Marriage," *University of Chicago Legal Forum*, Vol. 2004: Issue 1, Article 9.

Bjornlie, M. Shane. *Politics and Tradition Between Rome, Ravenna and Constantinople: A Study of Cassiodorus and the Variae*. Cambridge and New York: Cambridge University Press, 2013.

Blankenhorn, David. *The Future of Marriage*. New York: Encounter Books, 2009.

Blankenhorn, David, Steven Bayme, and Jean Bethke Elshtain, eds. *Rebuilding the Nest: A New Commitment to the American Family*. Milwaukee, WI: Family Service America, 1990.

Blom, J. C. H., and E. Lamberts, eds. *History of the Low Countries*. Translated by James C. Kennedy. New York: Berghahn Books, 2006.

Bonald, Louis de. *On Divorce*. Translated by Nicholas Davidson. New Brunswick, NJ: Transaction Publishers, 1992.

Boswell, John. *Christianity, Social Tolerance, and Homosexuality: Gay People in Western Europe from the Beginning of the Christian Era to the Fourteenth Century*. Chicago: University of Chicago Press, 1981.

Botting, Eileen Hunt. "Editor's Introduction: Reading Wollstonecraft's *A Vindication of the Rights of Woman*, 1792–2014." In Mary Wollstonecraft, A Vindication of the Rights of Woman, 1–18. Edited by Eileen Hunt Botting. New Haven, CT: Yale University Press, 2014.

Family Feuds: Wollstonecraft, Burke, and Rousseau on the Transformation of the Family. Albany, NY: The State University of New York Press, 2006.

"The Personal is Political: Wollstonecraft's Witty, First Person, Feminist Voice." In Mary Wollstonecraft, *A Vindication of the Rights of Woman*. Edited by Eileen Hunt Botting, 262–79. New Haven, CT: Yale University Press, 2014.

Wollstonecraft, Mill, and Women's Human Rights. New Haven, CT: Yale University Press, 2016.

Boulding, Maria. *The Confessions*. Hyde Park, New York: New City Press, 1997.

Bourg, Florence Caffrey. *Where Two or Three are Gathered: Christian Families as Domestic Churches*. Notre Dame, IN: University of Notre Dame Press, 2004.

Boyle, Leonard. "The Setting of the Summa Theologiae of St. Thomas—Revisited." In *The Ethics of Aquinas*. Edited by in Stephen Pope. Washington, DC: Georgetown University Press, 2002.

Brady, Ignatius C. *Sententiae in IV libris distinctae*. 3d rev. ed. Grottaferrata: Editiones Collegii S. Bonaventurae ad Claras Aquas, 1971.

Bransfield, Brian. *The Human Person According to John Paul II*. Boston: Pauline Books and Media, 2010.

Bratt, James D. *Abraham Kuyper: Modern Calvinist, Christian Democrat*. Grand Rapids, MI: Eerdmans, 2013.

Bratt, James D., ed. *Abraham Kuyper: A Centennial Reader*. Grand Rapids, MI: Eerdmans, 1998.

Brown, Peter. *The Body and Society*. New York: Columbia University Press, 1988.

Browning, Don S. "A Natural Law Theory of Marriage." *Zygon* 46 (September, 2011): 733–60.

Christian Ethics and the Moral Psychologies. Grand Rapids, MI: Wm. B. Eerdmans Publishing, 2006.

Marriage and Modernization. Grand Rapids, MI: Wm. B. Eerdmans, 2003.

Reviving Christian Humanism: The New Conversation in Spirituality, Theology, and Psychology. Minneapolis, MN: Fortress Press, 2010.

Browning, Don S., et al. *From Culture Wars to Common Ground*. 2d ed. Louisville, KY: Westminster John Knox Press, 2000.

Browning, R. "Theodore Balsamon's Commentary on the Canons of the Council in Trullo as a Source on Everyday Life in 12th C Byzantium." In *He Kathemerine Zoe Sto Byzantio*. Edited by Christina G Angelidē, et al., 421–27. Athens: Kentro Byzantinon Ereunon, 1989.

Bruijn, Jan de. *Abraham Kuyper: A Pictorial Biography*. Grand Rapids, MI: Wm. B. Eerdmans, 2014.

Brundage, James A. *Law, Sex, and Christian Society in Medieval Europe*. Chicago: University of Chicago Press, 1987.

Brunner, Emil. *Dogmatik*. 3 vols. Zurich: Zwingli-Verlag, 1946. 4th ed. Translated by Olive Wyon, et al., as *Dogmatics*, 3 vols. Philadelphia: Westminster Press, 1980.

Das Gebot und die Ordnungen. Tübingen: J.C.B. Mohr, 1932. Translated by Olive Wyon as *The Divine Imperative: A Study in Christian Ethics*. 7th impr. London: Lutterworth Press, 1961.

Der Mensch im Widerspruch. Berlin: Furche-Verlag, 1937. Translated by Olive Wyon as *Man in Revolt*. 6th impr. London: Lutterworth Press, 1962.

Der Mittler. Tübingen: J.C.B. Mohr, 1932. Translated by Olive Wyon as *The Mediator: A Study of the Central Doctrine of the Christian Faith*. Philadelphia: Westminster Press, 1947.

Eros und Liebe. Berlin: Furche-Verlag, 1937.

Gerechtigkeit: eine Lehre von den Grundgesetzen der Gesellschaftsordnung. Zurich: Zwingli-Verlag, 1943. Translated by Mary Hottinger as *Justice and the Social Order*. New York: Harper & Bros., 1945.

Justice and the Social Order. Translated by Mary Hottinger. New York: Harper & Bros., 1945.

The Divine Imperative: A Study in Christian Ethics. 7th imprint. Translated by Olive Wyon. London: Lutterworth Press, 1961.

Wahrheit als Begegnung. Berlin: Furche-Verlag, 1938. Translated by A.W. Loos as *The Divine-Human Encounter*. Philadelphia: Westminster Press, 1943.

Brunner, Emil, and Karl Barth. *Natural Theology: Comprising "Nature and Grace" by Emil Brunner and the Reply "No" by Karl Barth*. Translated by Peter Fränkel. Reprint edition. Eugene, OR: Wipf and Stock Publishers, 2002.

Bulgakov, Sergius. *The Lamb of God, The Comforter and The Bride of the Lamb*. Translated by Boris Jakim. Grand Rapids, MI: Wm. B. Eerdmans Publishing, 2002–8.

Burke, Cormac. *The Theology of Marriage: Personalism, Doctrine, and Canon Law*. Washington, DC: The Catholic University of American Press, 2015.

Burns, J. Patout. "Marital Fidelity as *remedium concupiscentiae*: An Augustinian Proposal." *Augustinian Studies* 44 (2013): 1–35.

Cahill, Lisa Sowle. "Abortion, Sex, and Gender: The Church's Public Voice," *America Magazine* (May 5, 1993): 6–11.

Callahan, Daniel, ed. *The Catholic Case for Contraception*. London: Macmillan, 1969.

Calvin, John. *Commentary on the Epistles of Paul to the Corinthians*. 2 vols. In vol. 20 of *Calvin's Commentaries*, 1: 359–60. Reprint. Grand Rapids, MI: Baker Book House, 1989.

Institutes of the Christian Religion [1559]. Translated by F. L. Battles; edited by J. T. McNeill. Reprint, 1960. Louisville, KY: Westminster John Knox, 2006.

Carey, Jonathan Sinclair. "D. S. Bailey and 'the Name Forbidden among Christians,'" *Anglican Theological Review* 70/2 (1988): 152–73.

Carlen, Claudia, ed. *The Papal Encyclicals*. 5 vols. Wilmington, NC: McGrath Publishing Co., 1981. Available at: www.vatican.va

Carrodeguas Nieto, Celestino. *La sacramentalidad del matrimonio. Doctrina de Tomás Sánchez*. Madrid: Universidad Pontificia de Comillas, 2003.

Castello, C. "Assenza d'ispirazione cristiana in CTh 3.16.1" In *Religion, société et politique. Mélanges en hommage à Jacques Ellul*, 203–12. Paris: Presses universitaires de France, 1983.

Catechismus Ex Decreto Concilii Tridentini, Editio Sterrotypa Undecima. Lisiae: Ex Officina Bernhardi Tauchnitz, 1893.

Cavadini, John C. "Feeling Right: Augustine on the Passions and Sexual Desire," *Augustinian Studies* 36 (2005): 195–217.

Christianson, Paul. *Discourse on History, Law, and Governance in the Public Career of John Selden, 1610–1635*. Toronto: University of Toronto Press, 1996.

"John Selden." In the *Oxford Dictionary of National Biography*. Oxford and New York: Oxford University Press, 2004.

Chrysostom, John. *An Address on Vainglory and the Right Way for Parents to Bring Up Their Children*. Reprinted as appendix in M. L. W. Laistner. *Christianity and Pagan Culture in the Later Roman Empire*. Ithaca, NY: Cornell University Press, 1967.

A Comparison between a King and Monk/Against the Opponents of the Monastic Life. Translated and with an introduction by David G. Hunter. Lewiston, NY: Edward Mellen Press, 1988.

On Marriage and Family Life. Translated by Catherine P. Roth and David Anderson. Crestwood, NY: St. Vladimir's Seminary Press, 1986.

On Virginity and Against Remarriage. Translated by Sally Rieger Shore. Introduction by Elizabeth Clark. Lewiston, NY: Edwin Mellen Press, 1983.

St. John Chrysostom: Eight Sermons on the Book of Genesis. Translated by Robert Charles Hill. Brookline, MA: Holy Cross Orthodox Press, 2004.

Works of John Chrysostom. In *A Select Library of the Nicene and Post-Nicene Fathers of the Christian Church*. Vols. 9–13. Grand Rapids, MI: Wm. B. Eerdmans, 1989.

Church of England. Moral Welfare Council. *The Problem of Homosexuality: An Interim Report*. London: Church Information Board, 1954.

Clark, Elizabeth A. "'Adam's Only Companion': Augustine and the Early Christian Debate on Marriage." *Recherches Augustiniennes* 21 (1986): 139–162.

Ascetic Piety and Women's Faith. Lewiston, NY: Edwin Mellen Press, 1986.
Jerome, Chrysostom, and Friends. New York: Edwin Mellen Press, 1979.
St. Augustine on Marriage and Sexuality. Washington, DC: The Catholic University of America Press, 1996.
Women in Late Antiquity. Oxford: Clarendon Press; New York: Oxford University Press, 1993.
Women in the Early Church. Wilmington, DE: M. Glazier, 1983.
Clemént, Olivier. *On Human Being*. Hyde Park, NY: New City Press, 2000.
Codex iuris canonici auctoritate Ioannis Pauli Pp. II promulgatus/Code of Canon Law, Latin–English Edition. Washington, DC: Canon Law Society of America, 1983.
Cohen, Abraham. *Everyman's Talmud*. New York: E. P. Dutton and Company, 1949.
Cohen, Martin, ed. *The Observant Life: The Wisdom of Conservative Judaism for Contemporary Jews*. New York: Rabbinical Assembly, 2012.
Colish, Marcia L. *Peter Lombard*. 2 volumes. Leiden; New York; Cologne: E. J. Brill, 1994.
Corcoran, Simon. *The Empire of the Tetrarchs: Imperial Pronouncements and Government AD 284–324*. Rev. ed. Oxford: Clarendon Press; New York: Oxford University Press, 2000.
Corpus Iuris Canonici. Edited by Emil Friedberg. Leipzig: ex officina Bernhardi Tauchnitz, 1879; reprinted Graz: Akad. Druck- und Verl.-Anst., 1959.
Coughlin, John. "Natural Law, Marriage, and the Thought of Karol Wojtyla." Fordham Urban Law Journal 28 (2000): 1771–86.
Crouzel, H. *L'Église primitive face au divorce du Iière au Vième siècle*. Paris: Beauchesne, 1971.
Crowe, Michael B. *The Changing Profile of the Natural Law*. The Hague: Martinus Nijhoff, 1977.
Cummings, E.T.D. *Pedalion*. Chicago: Orthodox Christian Educational Society, 1957; reprint, 1983.
Curran, Charles, et al. *The Responsibility of Dissent: The Church and Academic Freedom*. New York: Sheed and Ward, 1969.
D'Avray, D. L. *Dissolving Royal Marriages: A Documentary History, 860–1600*. Cambridge: Cambridge University Press, 2014.
Medieval Marriage: Symbolism and Society. Oxford: Oxford University Press, 2005.
Papacy, Monarchy, and Marriage, 860–1600. Cambridge: Cambridge University Press, 2015.
Dauphinais, Michael, and Matthew Levering. *John Paul II and St. Thomas Aquinas*. Ann Arbor, MI: Sapienta Press, 2006.
Decock, Wim. *Theologians and Contract Law. The Moral Transformation of the ius commune (ca. 1500–1650)*. Leiden and Boston: Martinus Nijhoff Publishers, 2013.
Deferrari, Roy J., ed., and Charles T. Wilcox, trans. *St. Augustine: Treatises on Marriage and Other Subjects*. Washington, DC: Catholic University of America Press, 1969.
Denziger, Heinrich, ed. *Enchiridion symbolorum, definitionum, et declarationum de rebus fidei et morum*. Revised edition by Adolf Schönmetzer. Barcelona: Herder, 1963.

Denzinger, Heinrich. *Enchiridion Symbolorum Definitionem et Declarationum De Rebus Fidei et Morum. Symboles et Définitions De La Foi Cathoilique*. Edited by Peter Hünermann. L'édition française Joseph Hoffmann. Paris: Les Éditions Du Cerf, 1997.

Devlin, Patrick. *The Enforcement of Morals*. London and New York: Oxford University Press, 1965.

Dieterich, Hartwig. *Das protestantische Eherecht in Deutschland bis zur Mitte des 17. Jahrhunderts*. Munich: Claudius Verlag, 1970.

The Digest of Justinian. Edited by Theodor Mommsen and Paul Krueger. Translated by Alan Watson. 4 vols. Philadelphia: University of Pennsylvania Press, 1985.

Dillon, John Noël. *The Justice of Constantine: Law, Communication, and Control*. Ann Arbor, MI: University of Michigan Press, 2012.

Donahue, Charles. *Law, Marriage, and Society in the Later Middle Ages*. Cambridge: Cambridge University Press, 2007.

"The Dating of Alexander the Third's Marriage Decretals." *Zeitschrift der Savigny-Stiftung für Rechtsgeschichte: Kanonistische Abteilung* 68 (1982): 70–124.

"The Role of the Humanists and the Second Scholastic in the Development of European Marriage Law from the Sixteenth to the Nineteenth Centuries." In *Law and Religion. The Legal Teaching of the Protestant and Catholic Reformations*. Edited by Wim Decock, Jordan J. Ballor, Michael Germann, and Laurent Waelkens, 45–62. Göttingen: Vandenhoeck & Ruprecht, 2014.

"Thoughts on Diocesan Statutes: England and France, 1200–1500." In *Canon Law, Religion, and Politics: Liber Amicorum Robert Somerville*. Edited by Uta-Renate Blumenthal, Anders Winroth and Peter Landau, 253–71. Washington, DC: Catholic University of America Press, 2012.

Donovan, Jeremy. *The Catechism of the Council of Trent*. Chorley, Lancashire, UK: Christian Books Today, 2009.

Dorff, Elliot N. *Love Your Neighbor and Yourself: A Jewish Approach to Modern Personal Ethics*. Philadelphia: Jewish Publication Society, 2003.

The Way Into Tikkun Olam (Repairing the World). Woodstock, VT: Jewish Lights, 2005.

Dorff, Elliot N., and Arthur Rosett. *A Living Tree: The Roots and Growth of Jewish Law*. Albany, NY: State University of New York Press, 1988.

Doyle, Matthew. *Peter Lombard and His Students*. Toronto: Pontifical Institute of Mediaeval Studies, 2016.

Du Plessis, P. *Borkowski's Textbook on Roman Law*. Oxford and New York: Oxford University Press, 2010.

Dziwisz, Stanislas, and Gian Franco Svidercoschi. *A Life with Karol: My Forty Year Friendship with the Man Who Became Pope*. New York: Doubleday, 2008.

Elliot, Michael D. "Boniface, Incest, and the Earliest Extant Version of Pope Gregory I's Libellus responsionum (JE 1843)." *Zeitschrift der Savigny-Stiftung für Rechtsgeschichte*: Kanonistische Abteilung 100 (2014): 62–111.

Ellis, Gerard M., ed. and trans. *Boso's Life of Alexander III*. Totowa, NJ: Rowman and Littlefield, 1973.

Elsbernd, Mary. *Papal Statements on Rights: A Historical Contextual Study of Encyclical Teaching From Pius VI – Pius XI (1791–1939)*. Dissertation: Catholic University of Louvain, Belgium, 1985.

Elshtain, Jean Bethke. "Against Androgyny." *Telos* 47 (1981): 5–21.

"A Response to Chief Justice McLaughlin." In *Recognizing Religion in a Secular Society: Essays in Pluralism, Religion, and Public Policy*. Edited by Douglas Farrow, 35–41. Montreal: McGill-Queen's University Press, 2004.

"Antigone's Daughters: Reflections on Female Identity and the State." *Democracy* 2 (April 1982): 46.

"Eulogy for Christopher Lasch." *New Oxford Review* (May 1994): 25–27.

Jane Addams and the Dream of American Democracy: A Life. New York: Basic Books, 2002.

"Law and the Moral Life." *Yale Journal of Law & the Humanities* 11 (1999): 383–413.

"Making Peace with Justice: The Story of Las Madres de la Plaza de Mayo." *International Revue of Sociology* 3(1) (1992): 51–94.

Power Trips and Other Journeys: Essays in Feminism as Civic Discourse. Madison, WI: University of Wisconsin Press, 1990.

Public Man, Private Woman: Women in Social and Political Thought Princeton, NJ: Princeton University Press, 1981.

Real Politics: Politics at the Center of Everyday Life. Baltimore, MD: The Johns Hopkins University Press, 2000.

"The Heart of the Matter: The Family as a Site of Fundamental Ethical Struggle." In *Family Transformed: Religion, Values, and Society in American Life*. Edited by Steven M. Tipton and John Witte Jr., 211–24. Washington, DC: Georgetown University Press, 2005.

"The Passion of the 'Mothers of the Disappeared' in Argentina." *New Oxford Review* (January–February 1992).

"The Perils of Legal Moralism." *Journal of Law & Politics* 20 (2004): 549–75.

"There Oughta Be a Law'—Not Necessarily." *Emory Law Journal* 58 (2008–2009): 71–86.

"What's at Stake in the Family Debate? Family Autonomy and the Civil Good." Address to the World Congress of Families II. Geneva, Switzerland, 1999. Available at: http://worldcongress.org/wcf2_spkrs/wcf2_elshtain.htm

Elshtain, Jean Bethke, ed. *The Family in Political Thought*. Amherst, MA: University of Massachusetts, 1982.

Eschmann, I. T. "Bonum commune melius est quam bonum unius. Eine Studie ueber den Wertvorrang des Personalen bei Thomas von Aquin." *Mediaeval Studies* 6 (1944): 62–120.

Evans Grubbs, Judith. "Abduction Marriage in Antiquity: A Law of Constantine (CTh IX.24.1) and its Social Context." *Journal of Roman Studies* 79 (1989): 59–83.

"Constantine and Imperial Legislation on the Family." In *The Theodosian Code*. Edited by Jill Harries and Ian Wood, 120–42. London: Duckworth, 1993; reprinted with a new preface by Bristol Classical Press, 2010.

"Church, State, and Children: Christian and Imperial Attitudes Toward Infant Exposure in Late Antiquity." In *The Power of Religion in Late Antiquity*. Edited by A. Cain and N. Lenski, 119–32. Burlington, VT: Ashgate, 2009.

"Hidden in Plain Sight: *Expositi* in the Community." In *Children, Memory, and Family Identity in Roman Culture*. Edited by V. Dasen and T. Späth, 293–310. Oxford and New York: Oxford University Press, 2010.

"Illegitimacy and Inheritance Disputes in the Late Roman Empire." In *Inheritance, Law and Religions in the Ancient and Mediaeval Worlds*. Edited by B. Caseau and S. Huebner, 25–50. Paris: ACHByz, 2014.

Law and Family in Late Antiquity: The Emperor Constantine's Marriage Legislation. Oxford: Clarendon Press, 1995.

"'Marriage More Shameful than Adultery': Slave-Mistress Relationships, 'Mixed Marriages,' and Late Roman Law." *Phoenix* 47 (1993): 125–154.

Women and the Law in the Roman Empire: A Sourcebook on Marriage, Divorce and Widowhood. London and New York: Routledge, 2002.

Evans, C. R., ed. *The Medieval Theologians: An Introduction to Theology in the Medieval Period*. Oxford: Blackwell, 2001.

Evans, G. R., and Phillipp W. Rosemann, eds. *Mediaeval Commentaries on the Sentences of Peter Lombard*. 3 volumes. Leiden and Boston: E. J. Brill, 2001–15.

Evdokimov, Paul. *Ages of the Spiritual Life*. Revised translation by Michael Plekon and Alexis Vinogradov. Crestwood, NY: St. Vladimir's Seminary Press, 1998.

In the World, of the Church: A Paul Evdokimov Reader. Translated and edited by Michael Plekon and Alexis Vinogradov. Crestwood, NY: St. Vladimir's Seminary Press, 2001.

Orthodoxy. Translated by Jeremy Hummerstone. Hyde Park, NY: New City Press, 2011.

The Sacrament of Love. Translated by Anthony P. Gythiel and Victoria Steadman. Crestwood, NY: St. Vladimir's Seminary Press, 1995.

The Way: Religious Thinkers of the Russian Emigration in Paris and Their Journal. Translated by Jerry Ryan; edited by John A. Jillions and Michael Plekon. Notre Dame, IN: University of Notre Dame Press, 2013.

Faillier, A. *Revue des Études Byzantines* (32/1974): 211–23.

Fantappiè, Carlo. *Chiesa romana e modernità giuridica*. Vol. I. *L'edificazione del sistema canonistico (1563–1903)*. Milan: Giuffrè, 2008.

Finnis, John. "Is Natural Law Theory Compatible With Limited Government?" In *Natural Law, Liberalism, and Morality*. Edited by Robert P. George, 1–26. Oxford: Oxford University Press, 1997.

"The Truth in Legal Positivism." in *The Autonomy of Law*. Edited by Robert P. George, 195–214. Oxford: Oxford University Press, 1966.

Fishbane, Michael. *Biblical Interpretation in Ancient Israel*. New York: Oxford University Press, 1985.

Flannery, Austin, O.P., ed. *Vatican Council II: Constitutions, Decrees, and Declarations*. Northport, NY: Costello Publishing Company, 1996

Ford, David, C. *Women and Men in the Church: The Full View of St. John Chrysostom*. South Canaan, PA: St. Tikhon's Seminary Press, 1996.

Ford, John C., S.J., and Gerald Kelly, S.J. *Contemporary Moral Theology. Vol. II Marriage Questions*. Westminster, MD: The Newman Press, 1963.

Frassek, Ralf. *Eherecht und Ehegerichtsbarkeit in der Reformationszeit*. Tübingen: Mohr Siebeck, 2005.

Frost, Carrie Frederick. *A Theology of Motherhood*. PhD diss., University of Virginia, 2015.

Furnish, Victor Paul. *The Moral Teaching of Paul: Selected Issues*. 2d ed., revised. Nashville, TN: Abingdon Press, 1985.

Gallagher, Clarence. *Church Law and Church Order in Rome and Byzantium: A Comparative Study*. Aldershot: Ashgate, 2002.

"Gratian and Theodore Balsamon: Two 12th Century Canonistic Methods Compared." In *Byzantium in the 12th Century: Canon Law, State & Society*. Edirted by A.N. Oikonomides, 61–89. Greek Text. Athens: Etareia Byzantinon kai Metabyzantinon Meleton, 1991.

Gallagher, David M. "Thomas Aquinas on Self-Love as the Basis of Love of Others." *Acta Philosophica* 8.1 (1999): 23–44.

Tractatus canonicus de matrimonio. 3d ed. Paris: Gabriel Beauchesne & Socii, 1904.

Gasparri, Pietro. *Tractatus canonicus de matrimonio*. Editio nova ad mentem *Codicis iuris canonici*. Vatican City: Typis Polyglottis Vaticanis, 1932.

George, Robert P., and Jean Bethke Elshtain, eds. *The Meaning of Marriage: Family, State, Markets, and Morals*. Dallas, TX: Spence Publishing, 2006.

Gerosa, Libero. *Canon Law*. London: Continuum International Pub., 1996.

Gillet, Lev. *In Thy Presence*. Crestwood, NY: St. Vladimir's Seminary Press, 1977.

Gleason, Philip. *Keeping the Faith: American Catholicism, Past and Present*. Notre Dame, IN: University of Notre Dame Press, 1987.

Gordon, Lyndall. *Vindication: A Life of Mary Wollstonecraft*. New York: HarperCollins, 2005.

Green, M. Christian. "Androgyny or Antigone: Jean Bethke Elshtain's Feminism." *Capital Commentary*. Washington, DC: Center for Public Justice, 2013.

"Sovereignty and Chastened Liberalism." In *Whose Will be Done?: Essays on Sovereignty and Religion*. Edited by John Dyck, Paul Rowe, and Jens Zimmermann, 119–36. Lanham, MD: Lexington Books, 2015.

Greene, Robert A. "Instinct of Nature: Natural Law, Synderesis, and the Moral Sense." *Journal of the History of Ideas* 58.2 (1997): 173–98.

Gregory the Great. *Gregorii I Registrum epistolarum*. 2 vols. Edited by Paul Ewald and Ludo M. Hartmann. Berlin: Apud Weidmannos, 1891–99.

Grisez, Germain. "The First Principle of Practical Reason: A Commentary on the *Summa Theologiae*, 1–2 Question 94, *Article* 2." Natural Law Forum 10 (1965): 168–201.

The Way of the Lord Jesus Christ, Volume 2: Living a Christian Life. Quincy, IL: Franciscan Press, 1993.

Guevin, Benedict M. "Aquinas's Use of Ulpian and the Question of Physicalism Reconsidered." *New Blackfriars* 63 (1999): 613–28.

Guroian, Vigen. *Ethics After Christendom: Toward an Ecclesial Ethic*. Grand Rapids, MI: Wm. B. Eerdmans, 1994.

"The Ecclesial Family: John Chrysostom on Parenthood and Children." In *The Child in Christian Thought*. Edited by Marcia J. Bunge, 61–77. Grand Rapids, MI: Wm. B. Eerdmans, 2001.

Harper, Kyle. *From Shame to Sin: The Christian Transformation of Sexual Morality in Late Antiquity*. Cambridge, MA: Harvard University Press, 2013.

Slavery in the Late Roman World AD 275–425. Cambridge: Cambridge University Press, 2011.

"The *SC Claudianum* in the *Codex Theodosianus*: Social History and Legal Texts." *Classical Quarterly* 60 (2010): 610–38.

Harries, J. "Constantine the Lawgiver." In *From the Tetrarchs to the Theodosians: Later Roman History and Culture, 284–450 CE*. Edited by S. McGill, C. Sogno, and E. Watts, 73–92. Cambridge: Cambridge University Press, 2010.

Harries, Jill. *Law and Empire in Late Antiquity*. Cambridge: Cambridge University Press, 1999.

Harries, Jill, and Ian Wood, eds. *The Theodosian Code*. London: Duckworth, 1993; reprinted with a new introduction as *The Theodosian Code: Studies in the Imperial Law of Late Antiquity*. London: Duckworth, 2010.

Harrington, Joel F. *Reordering Marriage and Society in Reformation Germany*. Cambridge: Cambridge University Press, 1995.

Hart, H. L. A. *Law, Liberty, and Morality*. London and Oxford: Oxford University Press, 1963.

Hartmann, Wilfried, and Kenneth Pennington, eds. *The History of Byzantine and Eastern Canon Law to 1500*. Washington, DC: Catholic University of America Press, 2012.

The History of Medieval Canon Law in the Classical Period, 1140–1234: From Gratian to the Decretals of Pope Gregory IX. Washington, DC: Catholic University of America Press, 2008.

Haut, Irwin H. *Divorce in Jewish Law and Life*. New York: Sepher-Hermon Press, 1983.

Hebblethwaite, Peter. *Paul VI: The First Modern Pope*. Mahwah, NJ.: Paulist Press, 1993.

Helmholz, R. H. *Marriage Litigation in Medieval England*. Cambridge: Cambridge University Press, 1974.

Roman Canon Law in Reformation England. Cambridge: Cambridge University Press, 1990.

Hendriksen, William. *The Covenant of Grace*. Grand Rapids, MI: Wm. B. Eerdmans 1932.

Hendrix, Scott. "Luther on Marriage." *Lutheran Quarterly* 14/3 (2000): 335–50.

"Masculinity and Patriarchy in Reformation Germany." *Journal of the History of Ideas* 56 (1995): 177–93.

"The Reform of Marriage in Calvin's Geneva." In *Caritas et Reformatio: Essays on Church and Society in Honor of Carter Lindberg*. Edited by David M. Whitford, 113–31. St. Louis, MO: Concordia Publishing House, 2002.

Herzog, Isaac. "John Selden and Jewish Law." In *Judaism: Law and Ethics*. Edited by Chaim Herzog, 65–79. London: Soncino, 1974.

Hittinger, F. Russell. "Introduction" and "Chapter on Leo XIII." In *The Teachings of Modern Roman Catholicism: On Law, Politics, and Human Nature*. Edited by John Witte Jr. and Frank S. Alexander, 3–74. New York: Columbia University Press, 2007.

"The Coherence of the Four Basic Principles of Catholic Social Doctrine: An Interpretation." In *Pursuing the Common Good*. Edited by Margaret S. Archer

and Pierpaolo Donati, 75–123. Vatican City: Pontifical Academy of Social Sciences, 2008.
The Holy Bible, New International Version. Grand Rapids: Zondervan Press, 1978.
Honoré, Tony. *Emperors and Lawyers*. 2d ed. Oxford: Clarendon Press; New York: Oxford University Press, 1994.
Justinian's Digest: Character and Compilation. Oxford and New York: Oxford University Press, 2010.
Tribonian. London: Duckworth, 1978.
Horgan, John, ed. *Humanae Vitae and the Bishops*. Shannon: Irish University Press, 1972.
Horrell, David G. "I Corinthians." In *The New Testament and Ethics*. Edited by Joel B. Green, 57–60. Grand Rapids, MI: Baker Academic, 2011.
Humbert, M. "Enfants à louer ou vendre: Augustin et l'autorité paternale (Ep. 10* and 24*)." In *Les lettres de Saint Augustin découvertes par Johannes Divjak*. Edited by J. Divjak, 189–203. Paris: Études augustiniennes, 1983.
Humfress, Caroline. "Civil Law and Social Life." In *The Cambridge Companion to the Age of Constantine*. Edited by N. Lenski, 205–225. Cambridge: Cambridge University Press, 2006.
"Law and Legal Practice in the Age of Justinian." In *The Cambridge Companion to the Age of Justinian*. Edited by Michael Maas, 161–184. New York: Cambridge University Press, 2005.
Hunter, David G. "Augustinian Pessimism? A New Look at Augustine's Teaching on Sex, Marriage and Celibacy." *Augustinian Studies* 25 (1994): 153–77.
"Augustine, Sermon 354A: Its Place in His Thought on Marriage and Sexuality." *Augustinian Studies* 33/1 (2002): 39–60.
"Augustine and the Making of Marriage in Roman North Africa." *Journal of Early Christian Studies* 11 (2003): 63–85.
Marriage, Celibacy, and Heresy in Ancient Christianity: The Jovinianist Controversy. Oxford and New York: Oxford University Press, 2007.
Hutton, Sarah. "The Ethical Background of the Rights of Women." In *Philosophical Theory and the Universal Declaration of Human Rights*. Edited by William Sweet, 27–40. Ottawa: University of Ottawa Press, 2003.
Hyde, Edward. *The Life of Edward Earl of Clarendon… Written by Himself*. Oxford: Clarendon Press, 1857.
Ingram, Martin. *Church Courts, Sex, and Marriage in England, 1570–1640*. Cambridge: Cambridge University Press, 1987.
Jasper, Detlev, and Horst Furhrmann. *Papal Letters in the Early Middle Ages*. Washington, DC: Catholic University of America Press, 2001.
Jensen, Steven J. *Knowing the Natural Law: From Precepts and Inclinations to Deriving Oughts*. Washington, DC: Catholic University of America Press, 2015.
John Paul II, Pope, and Michael Waldstein. *Man and Woman He Created Them: A Theology of the Body*. Boston, MA: Pauline Books and Media, 2011.
Johnson, Luke Timothy. "Divorce." In *The Oxford Encyclopedia of the Bible and Law*. Edited by Brent A. Strawn, 201. New York: Oxford University Press, 2015.
"The Complex Witness of the New Testament Concerning Marriage, Family, and Sexuality." In *Contested Issues in Christian Origins and the New Testament*, 659–78. Leiden and Boston: Brill, 2013.

Johnson, Luke Timothy, and Mark D. Jordan. "Christianity." In *Sex, Marriage, and Family in World Religions*. Edited by Don S. Browning, M. Christian Green, and John Witte Jr., 77–97. New York: Columbia University Press, 2006.

Johnston, David. *Roman Law in Context*. Cambridge, UK, and New York: Cambridge University Press, 1999.

The Roman Law of Trusts. Oxford: Clarendon Press, 1988.

Jones, Timothy Willem. *Sexual Politics in the Church of England, 1857–1957*. Oxford: Oxford University Press, 2013.

Jonsen, Albert R., and Stephen Toulmin. *The Abuse of Casuistry: A History of Moral Reasoning*. Berkeley and Los Angeles, CA: University of California Press, 1988.

Christian Marriage: An Historical and Doctrinal Study. London and New York: Sheed and Ward, 1933.

Joyce, George Hayward. *Christian Marriage: An Historical and Doctrinal Study*. 2d edition. London: Sheed and Ward, 1948.

The JPS Commentary: Exodus. Philadelphia: Jewish Publication Society, 1991.

Junius, Franciscus. *Correspondence*. Edited by Sophie von Romburgh. Leiden and Boston, 2004.

Kajanto, I. "On Divorce among the Common People of Rome." In *Mélanges Marcel Durry* (*REL* 47 bis, 1969). Edited by Marcel Durry, 99–113. Paris: Les Belles Lettres, 1970.

Keenan, James F. *A History of Catholic Moral Theology: From Confessing Sins to Liberating Consciences*. New York: Continuum, 2010.

Kelly, Kevin T. *New Directions in Sexual Ethics: Moral Theology and the Challenge of AIDS*. London and Washington: Geoffry Chapman, 1998.

Kelly, Henry Ansgar. "Canonical Implications of Richard III's Plan to Marry His Niece." *Traditio* 23 (1967): 269–311.

"Kinship, Incest, and the Dictates of Law." *American Journal of Jurisprudence* 14 (1969): 69–78.

Love and Marriage in the Age of Chaucer. Ithaca, NY: Cornell University Press, 1975; reprint, Eugene, OR: Wipf and Stock, 2004.

"Mixing Canon and Common Law in Religious Prosecutions under Henry VIII and Edward VI: Bishop Bonner, Anne Askew, and Beyond." *Sixteenth Century Journal* 46 (2015): 927–55.

The Matrimonial Trials of Henry VIII. Stanford, CA: Stanford University Press, 1976; reprinted with new foreword, Eugene, OR: Wipf and Stock, 2004.

The Middle English Bible: A Reassessment. Philadelphia: University of Pennsylvania Press, 2016.

Kilchör, Benjamin. "Levirate Marriage in Deuteronomy 25.5–10 and Its Precursors in Leviticus and Numbers: A Test Case for the Relationship Between P/H and D." *Catholic Biblical Quarterly* 77 (2015): 429–40.

Killeen, Brendan. *What Brings a Marriage into Existence: An Historical Re-examination of the Canon Law of the Latin Church*. Scranton, PA: University of Scranton Press, 2010.

Kingdon, Robert M. *Adultery and Divorce in Calvin's Geneva*. Cambridge, MA: Harvard University Press, 1995.

Komonchak, Joseph. "*Humanae Vitae* and Its Reception: Ecclesiological Reflections." *Theological Studies* 39 (1978): 221–57.

Kossmann, E. H. *The Low Countries, 1780–1940*. Oxford: Clarendon Press, 1978.

Kraemer, David, ed. *The Jewish Family: Metaphor and Memory*. New York: Oxford University Press, 1989.

Kuyper, Abraham. "Calvinism: Source and Stronghold of Our Constitutional Liberties [1874]." In *Abraham Kuyper: A Centennial Reader*. Edited by James D. Bratt, 279–322. Grand Rapids, MI: Wm. B. Eerdmans, 1998.

De Leer der Verbonden. Amsterdam: J. H. Kruyt, 1885.

De Eerepositie der Vrouw. Kampen: Kok, 1914.

Heilige Orde. Kampen: Kok, 1913.

Het Beroep op de Volksgeweten. Amsterdam: Blankenberg, 1869.

Lectures on Calvinism. Grand Rapids, MI: Wm. B. Eerdmans, 1931 [1899].

Our Program: A Christian Political Manifesto. Bellingham, WA: Lexham Press, 2015 [1879].

Particular Grace. Translated by Marvin Kamps. Grandville, MI: Reformed Free Pub. Association, 2001.

Predicatiën in de jaren 1867 tot 1873. Kampen: Kok, 1913.

Pro Rege: of, Het Koningschap van Christus. Kampen: Kok, 1911–12.

"Sphere Sovereignty." In *Abraham Kuyper: A Centennial Reader*. Edited by James D. Bratt, 461–90. Grand Rapids, MI: Wm. B. Eerdmans, 1998.

The Problem of Poverty. Translation of *Het sociale vraagstuk en de christelijke religie* [1891]. Translated by James W. Skillen. Grand Rapids, MI: Baker, 1991.

The Work of the Holy Spirit. Translated by Henri DeVries. Grand Rapids, MI: Eerdmans, 1956 [1888–89].

Varia Americana. Amsterdam: Höveker & Wormser, 1899.

Labovitz, Gail. *Marriage and Metaphor: Constructions of Gender in Rabbinic Literature*. Lanham, MD: Lexington Books, 2009.

Ladner, Gerhart B. *The Idea of Reform: Its Impact on Christian Thought and Action in the Age of the Fathers*. New York, NY: Harper and Row, 1967.

Laistner, M. L. W. *Christianity and Pagan Culture in the Later Roman Empire*. Ithaca, NY: Cornell University Press, 1951.

Lamberigts, Mathijs. "Augustine on Marriage: A Comparison of *De bono coniugali* and *De nuptiis et concupiscentia*." *Louvain Studies* 35 (2011): 32–52.

Laporte, Jean. *The Role of Women in Early Christianity*. Lewiston, NY: Edwin Mellen Press, 1982.

Lasch, Christopher. *Haven in a Heartless World: The Family Besieged*. New York: Basic Books, 1977.

Lawler, Michael G. "Faith, Contract, and Sacrament in Christian Marriage: A Theological Approach." *Theological Studies* 52 (1991): 712–31.

Lawler, Michael G., et al. *The Church in the Modern World: Gaudium et spes Then and Now*. Collegeville, MN: Liturgical Press, 2014.

Lazareth, William. *Luther on the Christian Home*. Philadelphia: Muhlenberg Press, 1960.

Lenski, Noel, ed. *The Cambridge Companion to the Age of Constantine*. Cambridge, UK and New York: Cambridge University Press, 2006.

Leo XIII. "Rerum Novarum: The Condition of Labor." In *Catholic Social Thought: The Documentary Heritage*. Edited by David J. O'Brien and Thomas A. Shannon, 14–39. Maryknoll, NY: Orbis Books, 1992.

Levine, Amy-Jill, and Marc Zvi Brettler, eds. *The Jewish Annotated New Testament*. New York: Oxford University Press, 2011.

Lindberg, Carter. "The Future of a Tradition: Luther and the Family." In *All Theology is Christology: Essays in Honor of David P. Scaer*. Edited by Dean O. Wenthe, et al, 133–51. Fort Wayne, IN: Concordia Theological Seminary Press, 2000.

Lombard, Peter. *The Sentences*. 4 volumes. Giulio Silano, translator. Toronto: Pontifical Institute of Mediaeval Studies, 2007–10.

Lozano Navarro, Juan José. *Tomás Sánchez*. Granada: Comares, 2000.

Lugo, Luis E., ed. *Religion, Pluralism, and Public Life: Abraham Kuyper's Legacy for the Twenty-First Century*. Grand Rapids, MI: Eerdmans, 2000.

Luther, Martin. *Luther's Works*. Edited by Jaroslav Pelikan and Helmut T. Lehmann. 55 vols. St Louis, MO: Concordia, 1955–68.

D. Martin Luthers Werke: Kritische Gesamtausgabe. Reprint edition. 78 vols. Weimar: H. Böhlau, 1883–1987.

D. Martin Luthers Werke: Tischreden. 6 vols. Weimar: H. Böhlau, 1912–21.

D. Martin Luthers Werke: Briefwechsel. 18 vols. Weimar: H. Böhlau Nachfolger, 1930–72.

Ursach und anttwort das iunkfrawen kloster gottlich verlassen mugen. Wittenberg: n.p., 1523.

Luxmoore, Jonathan, and Jolanta Babiuch. "Did Karol Wojtyla See and Rescue the Good in Marxism?" *National Catholic Register* (Jan. 16, 1997).

Maas, Michael, ed. *The Cambridge Companion to the Age of Justinian*. New York: Cambridge University Press, 2005.

Magnus, Albertus. *Opera omnia*. Cologne edition. Münster: Aschendorff, 1951–.

Mahoney, John. *The Making of Moral Theology: A Study of the Roman Catholic Tradition*. Oxford: Clarendon Press, 1987.

Maitland, Frederic William. *Roman Canon Law in the Church of England: Six Essays*. London: Methuen, 1898.

Mäkinen, Virpi, and Petter Korkman, eds. *Transformations in Medieval and Early-Modern Rights Discourse*. Dordrecht: Springer, 2006.

Martin, Ralph. *John Paul II and the New Evangelization: How You Can Bring the Good News to Others*. San Francisco, CA: Ignatius Press, 2006.

Matthews, John F. *Laying Down the Law: A Study of the Theodosian Code*. New Haven, CT: Yale University Press, 2000.

McCluskey, Colleen. "An Unequal Relationship between Equals: Thomas Aquinas on Marriage." *History of Philosophy Quarterly* 24.1 (2007): 1–18.

McCormick, Richard A., SJ "Notes on Moral Theology." *Theological Studies* 29 (December 1968): 275–300.

McDougall, Sara. "Marriage: Law and Practice." In *The Cambridge History of Medieval Canon Law*. Edited by John Wei and Anders Winroth. Cambridge: Cambridge University Press, forthcoming.

McGinn, Thomas A. J. *Prostitution, Sexuality and the Law in Ancient Rome*. New York and Oxford: Oxford University Press, 1998.

"The Social Policy of Emperor Constantine in Codex Theodosianus 4,6,3." *Tijdschrift voor Rechtsgeschiedenis* 67 (1999): 57–71.

McGrath, Alister E. *Emil Brunner: A Reappraisal*. Malden, MA: Wiley-Blackwell, 2014.

McGuckin, John A. *The Ascent of Christian Law: Patristic and Byzantine Formulations of a New Civilization*. New York: St. Vladimir's Seminary Press, 2012.

"The Issue of Human Rights in Byzantium and the Orthodox Tradition." In *Christianity and Human Rights: An Introduction*. Edited by John Witte Jr. and Frank S. Alexander, 173–90. Cambridge: Cambridge University Press, 2010.

St. Gregory of Nazianzus: An Intellectual Biography. New York: SVS Press, 2001.

Meehan, Andrew. "Theodore Balsamon." *The Catholic Encyclopedia*. New York: Appelton, 1907.

Mentzer, Raymond A. "Morals and Moral Regulation in Protestant France." *Journal of Interdisciplinary History*, 31/1 (2000): 1–20.

Merton, Thomas. *The Sign of Jonas*. New York: Harcourt, Brace, 1953.

Meyendorff, John. *Byzantine Theology*. New York: Fordham University Press, 1974.

Marriage: An Orthodox Perspective. Crestwood, NY: St. Vladimir's Seminary Press, 1975.

Miller, E. "Lettres de Théodore Balsamon." *Annuaire de l'Association pour l'Encouragement des Études Grecques en France* (1884): 8–19.

Miller, Fred D., Jr. *Nature, Justice, and Rights in Aristotle's Politics*. Oxford: Oxford University Press, 2004.

Milton, John. *The Complete Prose Works of John Milton*. Don M. Wolfe, general editor. 8 vols. New Haven, CT: Yale University Press, 1953–82.

Mommsen, Th., and P. Meyer, eds. *Theodosiani Libri XVI cum Constitutionibus Sirmondianis et Leges Novellae ad Theodosianum Pertinentes*. Berlin: Weidmann, 1905.

Monagle, Clare. *Orthodoxy and Controversy in Twelfth-Century Religious Discourse: Peter Lombard's Sentences and the Development of Theology*. Turnhout: Brepols, 2013.

Monter, E. William. "Women in Calvinist Geneva, 1550–1800." *Signs* 6.2 (Winter 1980): 189–209.

Montesquieu, Charles-Louis de Secondat. *Persian Letters* (1719). Translated by Raymond N. MacKenzie. Indianapolis: Hackett Publishing Company, 2014.

Moore, John C. *Pope Innocent III (1160/61–1216): To Root up and to Plant*. Leiden: Brill, 2003.

Mosiek, Ulrich. *Die 'probati auctores' in den Ehenichtigkeitsprozessen der S. R. Rota seit Inkrafttreten des Codex Iuris Canonici*. Freiburg: Herder, 1959.

Mouw, Richard. *Abraham Kuyper: A Short and Personal Introduction*. Grand Rapids, MI: Wm. B. Eerdmans, 2011.

Naphy, William G. "Calvin and Geneva." In *The Reformation World*. Edited by Andrew Pettegree, 309–22. New York: Routledge, 2000.

Sex Crimes: From Renaissance to Enlightenment. Charleston, SC: Tempus Publishing, 2002.

Naz, Raoul. "Sanchez, Thomas." In *Dictionnaire de droit canonique*, 7:864–70. Paris: Letouzey et Ané, 1965.

Noonan, John T., Jr. *Contraception: A History of Its Treatment by Catholic Theologians and Canonists*. Cambridge, MA: Harvard University Press, 1965.

Power to Dissolve: Lawyers and Marriages in the Courts of the Roman Curia. Cambridge MA: Harvard University Press, 1972.

"Who was Rolandus?" In *Law, Church, and Society: Essays in Honor of Stephan Kuttner*. Edited by Kenneth Pennington and Robert Somerville, 21–48. Philadelphia: University of Pennsylvania Press, 1977.

Noonan, John T., trans. *Marriage Canons from the Decretum of Gratian and the Decretals, Sext, Clementines and Extravagantes*. Edited by Augustine Thompson, O.P. Available at: http://faculty.cua.edu/Pennington/Canon%20Law/marriagelaw.htm.

Northcote, Hugh. *Christianity and Sexual Problems*. 2d ed. Philadelphia: F. A. Davis, 1916.

O'Brien, David J., and Thomas A. Shannon, eds. *Catholic Social Thought: The Documentary Heritage*. Maryknoll, NY: Orbis Books, 1998.

Olivares, Estanislao. "Ediciones de la Obra de Tomas Sanchez." *Archivo Teológico Granadino* 45 (1982): 53–119.

"Más datos para una biografía de Tomás Sánchez." *Archivo Teológico Granadino* 60 (1997): 25–50.

O'Malley, John W. *What Happened at Vatican II*. Cambridge, MA: Harvard University Press, 2008.

Ozment, Steven. *Ancestors: The Loving Family in Old Europe*. Cambridge, MA: Harvard University Press, 2001.

When Fathers Ruled: Family Life in Reformation Europe. Cambridge, MA: Harvard University Press, 1983.

Pascal, Blaise. *The Provincial Letters* (1656). Translated by Thomas M'Crie and William Benton. Chicago/London/Toronto: Encyclopedia Britannica, 1952.

Pennington, Kenneth. "The Biography of Gratian, the Father of Canon Law." *University of Villanova Law Review* 59 (2014): 679–706.

Permiakov, Vitaly, and Michael Plekon, eds. *The Moscow Council (1917–1918): The Creation of the Conciliar Institutions of the Russian Orthodox Church*. Translated by Jerry Ryan. Notre Dame, IN: University of Notre Dame Press, 2015.

Peters, Edward N., ed. *The 1917 or Pio-Benedictine Code of Canon Law*. San Francisco, CA: Ignatius Press, 2001.

Pharr, C., trans. *The Theodosian Code and Novels and the Sirmondian Constitutions: A Translation with Commentary, Glossary, and Bibliography*. Princeton, NJ: Princeton University Press, 1952.

Phillips, Roderick. *Putting Asunder: A History of Divorce in Western Society*. Cambridge: Cambridge University Press, 1988.

Pitkin, Barbara. "Children and the Church in Calvin's Geneva." In *Calvin and the Church*. Edited by David L. Foxgrover, 144–64. Grand Rapids, MI: CDC Product Services for the Calvin Studies Society, 2002.

Pitkin, Barbara. "The Heritage of the Lord: Children in the Theology of John Calvin." In *The Child in Christian Thought*. Edited by Marcia J. Bunge, 160–93. Grand Rapids, MI: Eerdmans, 2001.

Plekon, Michael. *Hidden Holiness*. Notre Dame, IN: University of Notre Dame Press, 2009.

Living Icons: Persons of Faith in the Eastern Church. Notre Dame, IN: University of Notre Dame Press, 2002.

Saints as They Really Are: Voices of Holiness in our Time. Notre Dame, IN: University of Notre Dame Press, 2012.

Uncommon Prayer: The Experience of Prayer in Everyday Life. Notre Dame, IN: University of Notre Dame Press, 2016.

The World as Sacrament: An Ecumenical Path Toward a Worldly Spirituality. Collegeville, MN: Liturgical Press, 2017.

Ponce de León, Basilio. *De sacramento matrimonii tractatus*. Venice: Combi, 1645.

Pope, Stephen J. *Human Evolution and Christian Ethics*. Cambridge: Cambridge University Press, 2007.

Popenoe, David, Jean Bethke Elshtain, and David Blankenhorn. *Promises to Keep: Decline and Renewal of Marriage in America*. Lanham, MD: Rowman and Littlefield Publishers, 1996.

Powell, James M. *Gesta Innocentii III: The Deeds of Pope Innocent III*. Washington, DC: Catholic University of America Press, 2004.

Price, Richard. *Four Dissertations*. London: T. Cadell, [1767] 1777.

Political Writings. Edited by D. O. Thomas. Cambridge: Cambridge University Press, 1991.

Raepset-Charlier, M.-T. "Ordre sénatorial et divorce sous le Haut Empire: un chapitre de l'histoire des mentalités." *Acta Classica Univ. Scient. Debrecen*. 17–18 (1981–2).

Rahner, Karl, S.J. "On the Encyclical *Humanae Vitae*, a 25-Year Retrospective." *Theological Investigations* vol. 9. New York: Herder, 1974.

Rapp, Claudia. *Holy Bishops in Late Antiquity*. Berkeley: University of California Press, 2007.

Summa de poenitentia et matrimonio cum glossis Johannis de Friburgo. Rome, 1603; *reprinted* Farnborough: Gregg Press, 1967.

Raymond of Peñafort (Raimundus de Pennaforte). *Summa de poenitentia et matrimonio cum glossis Johannis de Friburgo*. Rome, 1603; reprinted Farnborough: Gregg Press, 1967. Partly translated as *Summa on Marriage*. Translated and edited by Pierre Payer. Toronto: University of Toronto Press, 2005.

Reid, Charles J., Jr. *Power over the Body, Equality in the Family: Rights and Domestic Relations in Medieval Canon Law*. Grand Rapids, MI: Wm. B. Eerdmans, 2004.

Report of the Committee on Homosexual Offences and Prostitution. London: H. M. Stationery Office, 1957.

Rex, Walter E. "Contrariety in The Supplément Au Voyage De Bougainville." In *Diderot Studies* XXVII. Edited by Diana Guiragossian Carr, 149–68. Geneva: Librairie Droz, S.A. 1998.

Reynolds, Philip L. *How Marriage Became One of the Sacraments: The Sacramental Theology of Marriage from Its Medieval Origins to the Council of Trent*. Cambridge: Cambridge University Press, 2016.

Marriage in the Western Church. The Christianization of Marriage during the Patristic and Early Medieval Periods. Leiden: Brill, 1994.

Ricoeur, Paul. *Hermeneutics and the Human Sciences*. Cambridge: Cambridge University Press, 1981.

"The Logic of Jesus, the Logic of God." *Criterion* 18.2 (Summer, 1979): 4–6.

Riffkin, Rebecca. "New Record Highs in Moral Acceptability." *Gallup*, May 30, 2014. Available at: http://www.gallup.com/poll/170789/new-record-highs-moral-acceptability.aspx

Rodopoulos, Panteleimon. *An Overview of Orthodox Canon Law*. Rollinsford, NH: Orthodox Research Institute, 2007.

Rogers, Elizabeth Frances. *Peter Lombard and the Sacramental System*. New York: n.p., 1917; reprint edition Merrick, NY: Richwood, 1976.

Rosemann, Phillipp W. *Peter Lombard*. Oxford: Oxford University Press, 2004.

The Story of a Great Medieval Book: Peter Lombard's "Sentences." Toronto: University of Toronto Press, 2007.

Rosenberg, Shelley Kapnek. *Adoption and the Jewish Family: Contemporary Perspectives*. Philadelphia: Jewish Publication Society, 1998.

Rosenblatt, Jason P. *Torah and Law in Paradise Lost*. Princeton: Princeton University Press, 1994.

Renaissance England's Chief Rabbi: John Selden. Oxford: Oxford University Press, 2006; revised paperback edition, 2008.

Roumy, Franck. "Family Law." In *The Cambridge History of Medieval Canon Law*. Edited by John Wei and Anders Winroth. Cambridge: Cambridge University Press, forthcoming.

Ruden, Sarah. *Paul Among the People: The Apostle Reinterpreted and Reimagined in His Own Time*. New York: Pantheon Books, 2010.

Ruttenberg, Danya, ed. *The Passionate Torah: Sex and Judaism*. New York: New York University Press, 2009.

Sanchez, Thomas. *Aphorismi R. P. Thomae Sanchez decem eius librorum matrimonio doctrinam compendium continents*. Frankfurt: Sumpt. Johanni Georgii Muffat, 1712.

Opus morale in præcepta Decalogi; repr. ed. 2 vols. Charleston SC: Nabu Public Domain Reprint, 2012.

Práctica sobre los mandamientos de la ley de Dios y de la Iglesia. Edited by Eduardo Moore and Francisco Delgado. *Archivo Teológico Granadino* 45 (1982): 215–333.

De sancto matrimonii sacramento disputationum tomi tres. Paris: Sumptibus Philippi Borde, Laurentii Arnaud & Claudii Rigaud, 1654.

Sargenti, M. "Il diritto privato nella legislazione di Costantino." *Accademia Romanistica Costantiniana: Atti I Convegno*, 229–333. Florence, 1975.

Sarris, Peter. *Economy and Society in the Age of Justinian*. Cambridge and New York: Cambridge University Press, 2006.

Empires of Faith: The Fall of Rome to the Rise of Islam, 500–700. Oxford: Oxford University Press, 2011.

"The Justinianic Plague: Origin and Effects." *Continuity and Change* 17 (2002): 169–82.

Sayers, Jane E. *Innocent III: Leader of Europe, 1198–1216*. London: Longmans, 1994.

Scarisbrick, J. J. *Henry VIII*. London: Folio Society, 1968; reprinted with new foreword, New Haven, CT: Yale University Press, 1997.

Schmemann, Alexander. *For the Life of the World*. Crestwood, NY: St. Vladimir's Seminary Press, 1973.

Schnackenburg, Rudolf. *The Moral Teaching of the New Testament*. New York, NY: Herder and Herder, 1971.

Schneider, Carl E., and Margaret F. Brinig. *An Invitation to Family Law: Principles, Process, and Perspectives*. St. Paul, MN: West Publishing Company, 1996.

Schreck, Alan. *The Legacy of John Paul II: The Central Teaching of his 14 Encyclical Letters*. Steubenville, OH: Emmaus Road, 2012.

Schreiner, Susan E. "Eve, the Mother of History: Reaching for the Reality of History in Augustine's Later Exegesis of Genesis." In *Genesis 1–3 in the History of Exegesis: Intrigue in the Garden*. Edited by Gregory A. Robins, 135–86. Lewiston, NY: Edwin Mellen Press., 1988.

Schroeder, H. J. *Canons and Decrees of the Council of Trent*. Saint Louis, MO, and London: B. Herder Books, 1941.

Schuck, Michael J. *That They Be One: The Social Teaching of the Papal Encyclicals 1740–1989*. Washington, DC: Georgetown University Press, 1991.

Scully, Edgar. "The Place of the State in Society according to Thomas Aquinas." *The Thomist* 45.3 (1981): 407–29.

Sehling, Emil, ed. *Die evangelischen Kirchenordnungen des 16. Jahrhunderts*. Vols. 1–5. Leipzig: O.R. Reisland, 1902–13. Continued under the same title, ed. Anneliese Sprenger-Ruppenthal. Vols. 6–25. Tübingen: Mohr, 1955–.

Selden, John. *Ad Fletam Dissertatio*. Edited by David Ogg. Cambridge: Cambridge University Press, 1925.

De Jure Naturali et Gentium. London, 1640.

Joannis Seldeni, Juris Consulti. *Opera Omnia*. 3 vols. in 6 parts. Edited by David Wilkins. London: Typis Guil. Bowyer, impensis J. Walthoe, 1726.

John Selden on Jewish Marriage Law: The Uxor Ebraica. Translated by Jonathan Ziskind. Leiden: E. J. Brill, 1991.

The Table Talk of John Selden. Edited by Samuel Harvey Reynolds. Oxford: Clarendon Press, 1892.

Uxor Ebraica. London: Typis Richardi Bishopii, 1646.

Shaw, Brent. "The Family in Late Antiquity: The Experience of Augustine." *Past and Present* 115 (1987): 3–51.

Sheehan, Michael M. *Marriage, Family, and Law in Medieval Europe: Collected Studies*. Edited by James K. Farge. Toronto: University of Toronto Press, 1996.

Sirks, B. "The Colonate in Justinian's Reign." *Journal of Roman Studies* 98 (2008): 120–43.

Smith, Janet E. *Humanae Vitae: A Generation Later*. Washington, DC: Catholic University of America Press, 1991.

Smith, Janet E., ed. *Why Humanae Vitae Was Right: A Reader*. San Francisco: Ignatius Press, 1993.

Sommerville, J. P. "Hobbes, Selden, Erastianism, and the History of the Jews." In *Hobbes and History*. Edited by G. A. J. Rogers and Tom Sorell, 160–88. London and New York: Routledge, 2000.

"John Selden, the Law of Nature, and the Origins of Government." *Historical Journal* 27 (1984): 437–47.

"Selden, Grotius, and the Seventeenth-Century Intellectual Revolution in Moral and Political Theory." In *Rhetoric and Law in Early Modern Europe*. Edited by Victoria Kahn and Lorna Hutson, 318–44. New Haven and London: Yale University Press, 2001.

Southern, Richard W. *Scholastic Humanism and the Unification of Europe*. V. 1: *Foundations*. Oxford: Blackwell, 1995, and, with notes and additions by Lesley Smith and Benedicta Ward, S.L.G., V. 2, *The Heroic Age*. Oxford: Blackwell, 2001.

Spierling, Karen E. *Infant Baptism in Reformation Geneva: The Shaping of a Community*, 1536–1564. Aldershot, Hants, England: Ashgate, 2005; rpt. Louisville, KY: Westminster John Knox, 2009.

"Putting 'God's Honor First': Truth, Lies, and Servants in Reformation Geneva." *Church History and Religious Culture* 92 (2012): 85–103.

"Women, Marriage, and Family." In *T&T Clark Companion to Reformation Theology*. Edited by David M. Whitford, 178–96. London: T&T Clark, 2012.

Steinfels, Peter. *A People Adrift: The Crisis of the Roman Catholic Church in America*. New York: Simon and Schuster, 2003.

Stevens, G. P. *De Theodoro Balsamone*. Rome: Pontificia Università Lateranense, 1969.

Stjerna, Kirsi Irmeli. *Women and the Reformation*. Malden, MA: Blackwell Publishers, 2009.

Stolte, Bernard. "Justice: (Byzantine) Legal Literature." In *The Oxford Handbook of Byzantine Studies* Edited by E. Jeffreys, 691–98. Oxford: Oxford University Press, 2008.

Strawn, Brent A., ed. *The Oxford Encyclopedia of the Bible and Law*. 2 vols. New York, NY: Oxford University Press, 2015.

Sweeny, Eileen. "Thomas Aquinas on the Natural Law Written on Our Hearts." In *Reason, Religion, and Natural Law: From Plato to Spinoza* Edited by A. Jacobs, 133–54. New York: Oxford University Press, 2012.

Swennen, Frederick, ed. *Contractualisaton and Family Law: A Global Perspective*. New York: Springer, 2015.

Tancred of Bologna (*Tancredus bononiensis*). *Summa de Matrimonio*. Edited by Agathon Wunderlich. *Göttingen*: Apud Vandenhocke et Ruprecht, 1841.

Tanner, Norman P., ed. and trans. *Decrees of the Ecumenical Councils*. 2 vols. London: Sheed and Ward, 1990.

Taylor, Barbara. *Mary Wollstonecraft and the Feminist Imagination*. Cambridge: Cambridge University Press, 2003.

Taylor, John Hammond, trans. *St. Augustine: The Literal Meaning of Genesis*. New York: Newman Press, 1982.

"A Critical Evaluation of Critiques of Augustine's View of Sexuality." In Augustine and His Critics: Essays in Honour of Gerald Bonner. Edited by Robert J. Dodaro and George P. Lawless, 176–97. London: Routledge, 2000.

Taylor, Natalie. *The Rights of Woman as Chimera: The Political Philosophy of Mary Wollstonecraft*. New York: Routledge, 2007.

Tentler, Leslie Woodcock. *Catholics and Contraception: An American History*. Ithaca, NY: Cornell University Press, 2004.

Thomas, Aquinas, *Saint*. *Scriptum super libros Sententiarum: Opera Omnia*. Paris: Apud Ludovicum Vivès, 1871–72.

Summa contra Gentiles, or *Liber de veritate catholicae fidei contra errores infideliumi*. Edited by C. Pera, P. Marc, and P. Caramello. 3 vols. Turin and Rome: Marietti, 1961, 1967.

Summa theologiae. 5 vols. Ottawa: Institute of Medieval Studies, 1941–45.

Tocqueville, Alexis de. *Democracy in America*. Translated and edited by Arthur Goldhammer. New York: Library of America, 2004.

Toomer, G. J. *John Selden: A Life in Scholarship*. 2 vols. Oxford: Oxford University Press, 2009.

Eastern Wisedome and Learning: The Study of Arabic in Seventeenth-Century England. Oxford: Oxford University Press, 1996.

Torrell, Jean-Pierre. *Saint Thomas Aquinas*. Vol. 1: *The Person and His Work*. Translated by Robert Royal, rev. ed. Washington, DC: Catholic University Press of America, 2005.

Treggiari, Susan. "Divorce Roman Style: How Easy and How Frequent was It?" In *Marriage, Divorce, and Children in Ancient Rome*. Edited by B. Rawson, 31–46. Oxford: Oxford University Press, 1991.

Roman Marriage: Iusti Coniuges from the Time of Cicero to the Time of Ulpian. Oxford: Clarendon Press, 1991.

Tuck, Richard. "'The Ancient Law of Freedom': John Selden and the Civil War." *Reactions to the English Civil War 1642–1649*. Edited by John Morrill, 137–161. London: Macmillan, 1982.

"Grotius and Selden." In *The Cambridge History of Political Thought, 1450–1700*. Edited by J. H. Burns and Mark Goldie, 499–529. Cambridge: Cambridge University Press, 1991.

Natural Rights Theories: Their Origin and Development. Cambridge: Cambridge University Press, 1979.

Philosophy and Government 1572–1651. Cambridge: Cambridge University Press, 1993.

Valliere, Paul. *Modern Russian Theology*. Grand Rapids, MI: Wm. B. Eerdmans Publishing, 2000.

Valsecchi, Ambrogio. *Controversy: The Birth Control Debate* 1958–1968. Introduction by Gregory Baum. Translated by Dorothy White. Washington, DC: Corpus Books, 1968.

Van der Kooi, Cornelis, and Jan de Bruijn, ed. *Kuyper Reconsidered: Aspects of His Life and Work*. Amsterdam: VU Uitgeverij, 1999.

Vetulani, Adam. "Gratien et le droit romain." *Revue historique de droit francais et étranger* 4 (1946/1947): 11–49.

Viejo-Ximénez, José Miguel. "Tomás Sánchez." In *Diccionario General de Derecho Canónico*. Edited by Javier Otaduy, Joaquín Sedano, and Antonio Viana, VII, 144–46. Cizur Menor: Thomson Reuters Aranzadi, 2012.

Viscuso, Patrick D. "A Late Byzantine Theology of Canon Law." *Greek Orthodox Theological Review* 34 (1980): 203–19.

"Marital Relations in the Theology of the Byzantine Canonist Theodore Balsamon." *Ostkirchliche Studien* 39 (1990): 281–88.

"Menstruation: A Problem in Late Byzantine Canon Law." *Byzantine Studies* (4.1999): 116–25.

"Theodore Balsamon's Canonical Images of Women." *Greek, Roman and Byzantine Studies* 45 (2005): 317–26.

Guide for a Church Under Islam. The 66 Canonical Questions Attributed to Theodore Balsamon. Brookline, MA: Holy Cross Orthodox Press, 2014.

Viviano, Pauline A. "Covenant." In *The Oxford Encyclopedia of the Bible and Law*. Edited by Brent A. Strawn, 130–38. New York: Oxford University Press, 2015.

Volterra, E. "Intorno ad alcune costituzioni di Costantino." *Rendiconti dell'Accademia Nazionale dei Lincei*. Ser. 8, Vol. 13. Roma : Accademia Nazionale dei Lincei, 1958.

"Quelques remarques sur le style des constitutions de Constantin." *Mélanges Levy-Bruhl*, 325–34. Paris: l'Institut de droit romain de l'Université de Paris, 1959.

Watson, Alan. *The Law of Persons in the Later Roman Republic*. Oxford: Clarendon Press, 1967.

Roman Private Law around 200 BC. Edinburgh: Edinburgh University Press, 1971.

Watt, Jeffrey R. "Childhood and Youth in the Geneva Consistory Minutes." In *Calvinus Praeceptor Ecclesiae: Papers of the Eighth International Congress for Calvin Research*. Edited by Herman J. Selderhuis, 43–64. Geneva: Librairie Droz, 2004.

Weigel, George. *The End and the Beginning, Pope John Paul: The Struggle for Freedom, the Last Years, the Legacy*. New York: Doubleday, 2011.

Witness to Hope: A Biography of Pope John Paul II. New York: Cliff Street Books, 2005.

Whitehead, Barbara Dafoe. "Dan Quayle Was Right." *The Atlantic* (April 1993): 47–84.

The Divorce Culture: Rethinking Our Commitments to Marriage and Family. New York: Vintage, 1998.

Willett, Graham. "The Church of England and the Origins of Homosexual Law Reform." *Journal of Religious History* 33/4 (2009): 418–34.

William of Auxerre. *Summa aurea*. Edited by Jean Ribaillier. *Spicilegium Bonaventurianum*. Paris and Grottaferrata: Editiones Collegii S. Bonaventurae ad Claras Aquas, 1986.

Winroth, Anders. *The Making of Gratian's Decretum*. Cambridge: Cambridge University Press, 2000.

"Marital Consent in Gratian's Decretum." In *Readers, Texts and Compilers in the Earlier Middle Ages: Studies in Medieval Canon Law in Honour of Linda Fowler-Magerl*. Edited by Kathleen G. Cushing and Martin Brett, 163–80. Aldershot, UK: Ashgate, 2008.

"'Neither Slave nor Free': Theology and Law in Gratian's Thoughts on the Definition of Marriage and Unfree Persons." In *Medieval Church Law and the*

Origins of the Western Legal Tradition: A Tribute to Kenneth Pennington. Edited by Wolfgang P. Müller and Mary E. Sommar, 97–109. Washington, DC: Catholic University of America Press, 2006.

"Recent Work on the Making of Gratian's *Decretum*." *Bulletin of Medieval Canon Law* 26 (2004–06): 1–29.

"Roman Law in Gratian and the *Panormia*." In *Bishops, Texts, and the Use of Canon Law around 1100: Essays in Honour of Martin Brett*. Edited by Kathleen G. Cushing and Bruce C. Brasington, 183–90. Aldershot, UK: Ashgate, 2008.

"Where Gratian Slept: The Life and Death of the Father of Canon Law." *Zeitschrift der Savigny-Stiftung für Rechtsgeschichte: Kanonistische Abteilung* 99 (2013): 105–28.

Wintle, Michael. *An Economic and Social History of the Netherlands, 1800–1920*. Cambridge: Cambridge University Press, 2000.

Pillars of Piety: Religion in the Netherlands, 1813–1901. Hull: Hull University Press, 1987.

Witte, John, Jr. *Church, State, and Family: Reconciling Traditional Teachings and Modern Liberties*. Cambridge: Cambridge University Press, 2018.

From Sacrament to Contract: Marriage, Religion, and Law in the Western Tradition. Louisville, KY: Westminster John Knox, 1997; 2d ed., 2012.

Law and Protestantism: The Legal Teachings of the Lutheran Reformation. Cambridge: Cambridge University Press, 2002.

"Marriage and Family Life." In *The Calvin Handbook*. Edited by Herman J. Selderhuis, 455–65. Grand Rapids, MI: Eerdmans, 2009.

"The Goods and Goals of Marriage." In *Marriage, Health, and the Professions*. Edited by John Wall, Don S. Browning, William J. Doherty, and Stephen Post, 49–89. Grand Rapids, MI: Wm. B. Eerdmans, 2002.

The Reformation of Rights: Law, Religion, and Human Rights in Early Modern Calvinism. New York: Cambridge University Press, 2007.

The Western Case for Monogamy over Polygamy. New York: Cambridge University Press, 2015.

Witte, John, Jr., and Robert M. Kingdon. *Sex, Marriage and Family Life in John Calvin's Geneva*. Vol. 1: *Courtship, Engagement, and Marriage*. Grand Rapids, MI: Wm. B. Eerdmans, 2005.

Wojtyla, Karol. *The Acting Person*. Translated by Andrzej Potocki. 1969; reprint, Dordrecht; Boston: D. Reidel Pub. Co., 1979.

Love and Responsibility. Translated by H.T. Willetts. 1960; reprint, San Francisco: Ignatius Press, 1993.

Person and Community—Selected Essays. Translated by T. Sandok in *The American Journal of Jurisprudence* 39 (1994): 499.

Sources of Renewal: The Implementation of the Second Vatican Council. San Francisco, CA: Harper & Row, 1980.

Wollstonecraft, Mary. *The Works of Mary Wollstonecraft*. Edited by Janet Todd and Marilyn Butler. 7 vols. New York: New York University Press, 1989.

A Vindication of the Rights of Woman. Edited by Eileen Hunt Botting. New Haven, CT: Yale University Press, 2014.

Wunder, Heide. *He is the Sun, She is the Moon: Women in Early Modern Germany*. Translated by Thomas Dunlap. Cambridge, MA: Harvard University Press, 1998.

Zion, William Basil. *Eros and Transformation: Sexuality and Marriage: An Eastern Orthodox Perspective*. Lanham, MD: University Press of America, 1992.

Ziskind, Jonathan. *John Selden on Jewish Marriage Law: The Uxor Ebraica*. Leiden: E. J. Brill, 1991.

Index

CPSIA information can be obtained
at www.ICGtesting.com
Printed in the USA
LVHW01*2056240718
584781LV00008B/178/P

9 781108 415347